The Nostradamus Code

Originally Italian, by adoption French, and by marriage English, David Ovason did postgraduate research in the influence of hermetic thought on late-medieval literature. He is a teacher of astrology, and has been a student of Nostradamus for over forty years. This is his first book, and his second, *The Zelator: The Secret History Behind History – by a Modern Initiate of Ancient Mysteries*, is now available from Century.

THE
NOSTRADAMUS
CODE

David Ovason

ARROW

This edition published by Arrow Books Limited 1998

1 3 5 7 9 10 8 6 4 2

First pubished in the United Kingdom in 1997 as
The Secrets of Nostradamus by Century,
Random House UK Ltd,
20 Vauxhall Bridge Road, London SW1V 2SA

Arrow Books Ltd
Random House UK Ltd,
20 Vauxhall Bridge Road, London SW1V 2SA

Random House Australia (Pty) Limited
20 Alfred Street, Milsons Point, Sydney,
New South Wales 2061, Australia

Random House New Zealand Limited
18 Poland Road, Glenfield,
Auckland 10, New Zealand

Random House South Africa (Pty) Limited
Endulini, 5a Jubilee Road,
Parktown 2193, South Africa

Random House UK Limited Reg No 954009

A CIP catalogue record for this book
is available from the British Library

Papers used by Random House UK Limited are natural, recyclable
products made from wood grown in sustainable forests. The
manufacturing processes conform to the environmental regulations of the
country of origin.

ISBN 00 9968 4519

Printed and bound in the UK by
Cox & Wyman Ltd, Reading, Berks

It is not fair that you should so earnestly inquire after my secrets, when you paid so little attention to my questions.

(Goethe, *The Green Snake and the Beautiful Lily*, quoted from Rudolf Steiner's Goethe's *Standard of the Soul*, 1925, p. 87)

Contents

Author's Note

We should observe that, in the sixteenth century, the French system of accentation was not standardized. In very many cases, words which are now accented in French were often written without accents. This is especially true of book titles, which were often capitalized, and lacked accents. Generally speaking, we have given titles as they appear in the editions referred to, where accentation and orthography often differ considerably from what one might expect in modern French. Even against the standards of his day, Nostradamus was notably deficient in accentation and orthography in his quatrains. In our own versions of his verses we have attempted to reproduce as faithfully as possible the accentation and orthography which he seems to have used in those verses published during his own lifetime. This has proved necessary because, in some cases, the unconventional orthographies and accentations sometimes play an important role in the subsidiary meanings Nostradamus intended for specific words.

We should also observe that, in the days of Nostradamus, proper names were not standardized. It was not uncommon for different orthographies to be used for the names of members of the same family or clan. This explains why there are a variety of spellings for names of members of the Nostradamus family. Round about 1455, at his conversion to Catholicism, Pierre was the first to adopt *de*

Nostredame as his family name. It is recognized that our savant's chosen *Nostradamus* was merely one possible Latin version of the French *Nostredame*, which had been, in turn, a version of *Nostre Dame*, itself an amendment of *Nostra Domina* (see page 41). The savant's father had the name *Jaume de Nostredame*, yet, even so, in some records *Nostradamus* is called both *Nostradame* and *Nostredame*, with or without the *de*, which he himself repudiated in his Latinization when he adopted the nominative case. His own children were usually called *de Nostredame*, yet his brother Antoine was frequently called *de Nostradame*. The variants *Nostradam* or *Nostredam* were also common.

We point to this lack of standardization merely to account for seeming contradictions in our own text.

Foreword

I know the hazzard of Interpretation ... I will not pretend a familiarity with the Stars ... nor to unriddle all the dark Nonsense of Nostradamus; but something sure there is in all those things.

(The Fortunes of France from the Prophetical Predictions of Mr. Truswell, the Recorder of Lincoln, and Michel Nostradamus, 1678)

The purpose of this book is to reveal, for the first time, the secret methods used by Michel Nostradamus, when he penned his famous prophetic writings, published as the *Prophéties*.

The general reader may be surprised that these secrets have not been revealed before. After all, it is widely believed that the oracular verses of Nostradamus have already been translated, and that the details of his predictions are well known to scholars. However, as we shall demonstrate, this is a fiction: all translations currently available in the West are largely nonsensical, and have little or no bearing on what Nostradamus intended to say. Here we attempt to pierce through all the obfuscation and poor scholarship, to reach into the mind of this remarkable savant, who had the rare gift of unrolling the scroll of futurity.

1

The past three decades have witnessed a revolution in Nostradamus studies. A great deal of research into his life and work has been conducted by French historians (among them Robert Amadou, Robert Benazra, Michael Chomarat, Jean Dupèbe and Edgar Leroy), with the result that an entirely new light has been thrown on his biography, achievements and astrological methods, clarifying certain difficulties which arise from his predictive quatrains.[*]

Unfortunately, few of the implications of this research have reached the popular market – the publishing band-wagon of the 'sub-cultural' literature attached to Nostradamus. This deficiency is especially prevalent in the sub-cultural Nostradamian literature in English. In spite of the brilliant insights offered by the modern French school of criticism, popular writers have continued to issue 'biographies' of Nostradamus and 'commentaries' on his *Prophéties* which are replete with errors that modern research scotched long ago. One of our aims is to rectify this deficiency.

In addition to these extraordinary discoveries, material which was once so rare as to be accessible only to a handful of privileged scholars has been made available on a much wider basis by way of facsimile publication. For example, the recent facsimile reproduction of a rare *Almanach* by Nostradamus, and of a book of quatrains, published while Nostradamus was still alive, has helped enormously in clarifying some of the historical difficulties which earlier writers had no way of dealing with. Equally, the modern reprint of the extremely rare edition of the *Prophéties* of 1557 has facilitated the study of the early quatrains (*fig. 1*). We shall examine each of these developments in due course: it is sufficient here to say that the time has come not only for a reappraisal of the quatrains of Nostradamus, in

---

[*] A Nostradamus quatrain is a verse of four alternately rhyming lines, sometimes (but not always) of decasyllabic structure.

order to demolish once and for all the unscholarly writings of sub-cultural commentators, but also for a reappraisal of the life of Nostradamus, to bring the details of his biography up to date with the findings of modern scholarship.

In spite of the painstaking researches of modern French scholars, a full survey of the life and times of the savant has still to appear. In consequence, for all its importance to the development of the predictive verses, we have merely glanced at his life in the present work. Even so, we have attempted to incorporate into our findings the insights gained by scholars during the past few decades. This has helped us achieve our aim, which has been to record the arcane methods and prophetic aspirations of Nostradamus against their historical context.

The predictive verses of Nostradamus, written in the middle of the sixteenth century, dealt entirely with events which were then still in the future. It is clear from notes left by Nostradamus that the quatrains covered events beginning about one year after the publication of his first volume of verses, extending in the future for just over 800 years. This period was linked with the movements of the planets Jupiter and Saturn, which completed a special cycle in that number of years. The cycle was sometimes called the 'period of the superiors', as, in the Ptolemaic geocentric model, the two planets were believed to be in orbit above (hence, superior to) the Sun. Nostradamus' main interest lay in events in the first three centuries following his own lifetime, which means that a great number of his predictions have been fulfilled, and have revealed to those familiar with oracles the extraordinary precision of his vision. So accurate are the details and dates which Nostradamus gave in these verses that one is left with the eerie feeling that what he saw was, in some mysterious way, already a precisely determined history, rather than a nebulous vision of futurity. It is on this super-clairvoyancy that his fame and popularity rests, even if this fame has, until now, been based on a misunderstanding concerning his visions, and how he expressed them in words.

Most of the quatrains are, or were, prophetic. So far as we can see, they deal mainly with European history – especially with the history of France, Italy and England. In one or two quatrains, Nostradamus glanced at the European offshoot, the United States, and at historical events in places which were, in his day, well beyond the periphery of Europe: Turkey, Syria and the Eastern Mediterranean seaboard. Almost certainly, he is the first clairvoyant to mention America by name, at a time when the word was not even widely used to denote the newly rediscovered continents.[1]

At least 40 of his obscure quatrains appear still to relate to our own future, but remain beyond detailed interpretation. No doubt the modern reader, like Nostradamus' own contemporaries, will take up this book in the hope of insights into this coming futurity, just as all readers in the past sought in their own interpretations of Nostradamus' predictions confirmation of their hopes and fears. We shall (with some trepidation) examine the possible significance of a few of these 'future' quatrains in the following text: however we have not approached Nostradamus purely in a spirit of inquiry about what the future holds for Europe in the next few centuries. As this book will reveal, our real interest lies elsewhere.

Our concern is with the arcane method used by Nostradamus. Our conviction is that it is only by understanding the technique of oracular writing which he used that we shall be able to interpret correctly what he intended to say about what was his future, but which is now in our past.

The quatrains of the *Prophéties* – fulfilled or yet to be

fulfilled – remain the supreme example of a lost esoteric literature.* Here Nostradamus displayed mastery of an ancient language (properly speaking, of a methodology) which, sadly, is no longer used by authors, and which seems no longer to interest academic historians of literature. However, the early-twentieth-century French poet Apollinaire – no stranger to the subtlety of language – recognized one unlauded facet of the savant's genius when he observed, 'Nostradamus is a great poet.'[2]

The quatrains contain a fascinating conflict. On the one hand, there is no doubt whatsoever that Nostradamus intended to record the future, and to sketch out the main drift of European events, spanning a period of about 800 years. However, there is also no doubt that Nostradamus did not intend these carefully crafted prophecies to be understood until *after* the historical events they each predicted. He intentionally couched his prophecies in an obscure form, and he freely admitted that his aim was to render his verses impenetrable prior to their fulfilment. When, in 1558, he wrote an open letter to the French king Henry II about the quatrains, he admitted that, had he so wished, he could have unscrambled the verses to make their meanings clear. Our feeling is that had he done so, not only would no one have believed his predictions, but he would have finished up on the many pyres which burned so fiercely in sixteenth-century France to consume supposed witches and heretics. For both personal and cosmic reasons, he was wise to obscure the vision of futurity which had been vouchsafed him.

The result of this obfuscation is quite remarkable.

---

* *Esoteric* is a term used to denote a body of specialist knowledge or traditions held by an inner circle of initiates. Esoteric knowledge is a secret knowledge, a hidden stream of knowledge, access to which is restricted to the few. The Greek root, *eso*, meant simply 'within'. By contrast, exoteric knowledge is that which is available to all.

Nostradamus wrote predictions which were totally incompre-hensible prior to the events prophesied. Although Nostradamus is the most famous clairvoyant in Western occult history, we cannot think of one single example in the whole of Nostradamian literature where a commentator has accurately unscrambled the meaning of a predictive verse prior to the event it predicted.

Realizing that he intentionally obscured his verses allows us to correct a widespread misapprehension about Nostradamus. It is widely believed that the quatrains can be 'translated', as though they are couched merely in a familiar foreign language. Unfortunately – and here lies both the challenge and the beauty of Nostradamus – it is not a matter of translation. Strictly speaking, the quatrains of Nostradamus cannot be translated; few French people can make sense of what Nostradamus intended in the majority of his quatrains. This is because while Nostradamus appears to write in a crabbed sort of French, liberally scattered with Latinate or Greek constructions and termi-nations, he actually wrote in an unfamiliar arcane tongue, called in occult circles the Green Language (*fig. 2*), which is examined in detail in Chapter Four. His verses are just as troublesome to the French as they are to the English, Italians or Germans – so troublesome indeed that one influential French commentator proposed translating the crabbed French of Nostradamus into Latin, and then editing and amending this Latin in order to read meaning into the new-French verses.[3]

In view of this, we see that a genuine approach to the *Prophéties* is not by way of translation but by *interpretation*. It is simply not possible to translate Nostradamus without at the same time offering an extensive commentary, by way of explanation. While the arcane writings of Nostradamus' contemporary, François Rabelais, who wrote according to arcane sixteenth-century techniques similar to those used by our savant, have been translated into modern French on more than one occasion – even in parallel translation, Nostradamus' crabbed quatrains are so obscure as to make even such parallel translation impossible.[4] This essential fact explains the approach we have taken to the quatrains. Some attempt to set down the superficial meanings of the quatrains is necessary, if only as a preliminary to exploring their hidden depths; but while the English versions of the quatrains in this book may give the impression of being translations, we do not pretend this to be the case.

Our first task has been to establish, as accurately as possible, what Nostradamus actually wrote: this is a thankless task, for even in his own century commentators remarked upon the variety of versions of the *Prophéties* which had flooded the market. It is probably correct to say that, although the term is used widely by Nostradamus scholars, there is no *editio princeps* (or first edition) of the *Prophéties*, as the earliest printing, the Macé Bonhomme of 1555, was incomplete.[5] For a brief account, see Appendix Two.

Sensitive to these bibliographical problems, we have presented the original quatrain as near as possible to the form we assume was intended by Nostradamus, after examination of several sixteenth-century texts. In each case, this 'original' is accompanied by an English version, intended merely as a guide to those who do not read French sufficiently to make some sort of sense of the words in the quatrain. We offer this English version with some diffidence, as (we must repeat) strictly speaking, Nostradamus cannot be translated. Any real 'translation' follows in the analytical commentary – our aim being to reveal the meanings in the individual lines, and to summarize the general meaning we perceive in the quatrain as clearly as possible.

Few Western occultists have been vouchsafed his visionary power. Even fewer have had his literary gifts to set their visions down for posterity. None – save perhaps his contemporary, Rabelais – has been as talented as Nostradamus in the use of the Green Language, the secret tongue of *argot*, the speech of occultism which pervades the *Prophéties*. Even though Nostradamus lived in an age when astrology flourished in the hands of masters and scholars, few men of his time possessed his grasp of the secret methods of arcane astrology.

In his crafting of the quatrains, Nostradamus combined the Green Language with a near-lost esoteric astrology.* The main purpose of this present book is to explore these two arcane techniques, and offer a method by which the *Prophéties* of Nostradamus may be interpreted accurately for the first time.

We must not overlook the fact that Nostradamus was writing in the hope that his books would sell to a sixteenth-century readership. Not unnaturally, he tended to dilate upon matters he foresaw occurring later in that century, with the result that a large proportion of the quatrains seem to deal with that period. However, it is clear from a survey of the bulk of his prophecies that he was also deeply concerned with events which were to occur towards the end of the eighteenth century. He had not been alone in this prevision. As we shall see, the events attending what we now call the French Revolution had been recognized by one or two other clairvoyants, long before Nostradamus penned his quatrains.

---

* Esoteric astrology is that astrology which investigates the hidden principles behind the workings of Man and Cosmos. Unlike the personal astrology which is so much in vogue today, it seeks to understand the hidden rhythms and principles by which the spiritual beings govern the solar system. Usually, it takes into account the issues of spiritual hierarchies, reincarnation, as well as prenatal and post-mortem experiences.

This concern which Nostradamus shows for events to come in his own century, and during the long-awaited French Revolution (which he and other prophets saw as a pivotal fulcrum in history) is understandable. However, his interest did not blind him to the unfolding of events in other centuries. For example, while the predictions relating to the nineteenth-century quarrels between the nation-states of Europe are not as extensive as the modern French commentators would have us believe, Nostradamus did sketch out the main events of the nineteenth century. He was particularly interested in the continuation of the spiritual impulse in the French Revolution, in the expansion and contraction of the French nation during the Napoleonic Wars and Empire, in the subsequent fall of the French royal family the Bourbons, and in the Italian unification under the *Garibaldini*.

The twentieth century also occupied Nostradamus considerably, if only because of the great changes which he perceived would take place in that period. Indeed, so deeply interested was he in the twentieth century that he elected to define it uniquely, using an arcane astrological dating technique in two quatrains which bracket the first and last years of the century very precisely (see page 384 ff). No doubt his intention was to indicate just how different it would be from preceding centuries. For this century, he noted developments in Germany, Italy, England and Spain, and (as usual) concentrated on France: with such interests, it is inevitable that he should have predicted and dated with incredible accuracy the major European conflicts. He seems to have been particularly concerned with the two great wars which would convulse Europe in the twentieth century, yet, curiously, he seems to have evinced little interest in its major scientific discoveries. Details which emerge in his writings do suggest that he was aware of such horrors as aerial warfare, yet the main thrust of his interest lay in historically important future events.

When Nostradamus wrote, it was widely believed that the twentieth century would see the Last Days, the incarnation of the Antichrist and great tribulations: the following century would mark the beginning of a new age. Nostradamus seems to have gone along with this view only to some extent, and, in our opinion, not wholeheartedly. The predictions he made about the years which are still in our own futurity seem to have been made for a sixteenth-century audience, and appear to be well in accord with the popular – one might even say, official – expectations about the spiritual outcome forecast in the Biblical exegesis, which tended to read the end of the world in terms of numerical computations.

The period most favoured by prophets was that of a thousand years – the root of what is often called millennarianism. Sometimes, periods of half the magical thousand were used as the basis for cycles. Hippolytus* used this period in his great work, *Peri Antichristou*, when he foresaw the coming of the Antichrist in AD 500. In some cases, prophets preferred shorter cycles, and the half-period of 500 was truncated to 50. For example, Jean-Aimé de Chavigny, who was among the earliest serious students of Nostradamus in the first decade of the seventeenth century, had used among his predictive cycles a 50-year span, which he calls *Iubilez* (probably a version of Jubilee, now meaning a cycle of 50 years). By means of this magical round number, he determined that 1734 would mark the coming of the Antichrist. By a similar computation, he foresaw the end of the Catholic Church in the year 2500.

In contrast, the expectations behind the influential

---

* A third-century writer and presbyter of the church of Rome. The writings associated with him in the days of Nostradamus were spurious, yet his prophecies were widely known.

exegeses of St John's *Apocalypse* did not concern themselves with round figures or divisors of the magical 1,000. Indeed, there was little rationality behind their numerology, yet a great deal of magical lore. As a consequence, the opening of the seven seals which would mark the end of Time, and of the World, was an everpresent threat for those interested in prophetic literature. In the late medieval period, the most influential 'end-of-world' prophecies were those derived from the followers of the twelfth-century monk, Joachim di Fiore, whose numerology was rooted in sevens, with sub-numerologies of twos and threes (from which seven can be adduced). The followers of Joachim had predicted the end of the world for 1260, using arcane numerology based on Biblical exegesis. When the world passed this date unscathed, a Bamberg monk, using much the same method, promised an end for 1400.

A century later, with the coming of the mystical three times 500, a large number of prophecies were issued. The flood prophecies of John Lichtenberger, the astrologer of Frederick III, the Elector Palatine of the Rhine, were issued about 1488 with an eye on the dreaded 1500. Lichtenberger's prophecies were not original (prophecies rarely are), for he had borrowed them from Paul of Middleburg's* *Prognosticatio*, which had been stolen from such prophets as Hippolytus, Cyrillus and the Erythraean Sibyl. Middleburg's overriding hope (which brings us nearer to Nostradamus) was that Frederick III, whom he saw as the second Charlemagne, would vanquish the Turk.

Middleburg's prophecies unsettled his European readers,

---

* Paul of Middleburg was a fine astrologer who, as bishop of Fossombrone, had stopped issuing prognostications to spend his time in 'better studies'. However, in 1523, to counter certain predictions which he felt were both wrong and dangerous, he issued his *Prognosticum* denying (rightly, as it turned out) that a world flood would occur in 1524. Many of his prophecies are found in earlier manuscripts, however.

but did not come true. However, his subjects and archetypes are very similar to those in Nostradamus' verses. He
issued the usual promise of the recovery of Jerusalem from
the Moors, the savage onslaught of an 'eastern army', which
was reasonably interpreted as the cohorts of the Turks, the
spiritual renewal of the Church, the appearance of an
Angelic Pope and a super-hero King. His images for these
spiritual and temporal powers were the Lily and the Eagle,
imagery which would be borrowed first by the Swiss
occultist Paracelsus, the most influential hermetic writer,
alchemist and unorthodox medical doctor of the sixteenth
century, then by Nostradamus. But – and here we relapse
into the usual type of prophecy – the future was to be
difficult, for it was to be an era of terrible wars, marked by
the coming of the Antichrist. After an interlude of the
Golden Age, there would be the end of the World. That the
end of the World was imminent, and perhaps even
deserved, was rarely doubted in the sixteenth century, and
it is hardly surprising that a few of the quatrains penned by
Nostradamus have carried this expectation into modern
times.

Since, to the medieval* frame of mind, it was quite
reasonable to follow the notion of Pythagoras, who had held

---

* Some historians may object to our describing the sixteenth century
throughout this book as 'late medieval'. However, in our view, the
medieval world came to an end only when the cosmic model inherited
from the classical world was dispensed with – or, to use the famous
phrase of C. S. Lewis, was 'discarded'. It was only after the death of
Nostradamus that the Ptolemaic model collapsed under its own weight,
and under the hammering of Copernicus and his friends, and the new
astronomy was born. With this discarded image went more than a theory
of planetary epicycles, but a cosmoconception of a world directed by
spiritual beings. This, more than anything else, is what separates the
world of Nostradamus from the modern. For want of a precise date, we
might be inclined to suggest that the medieval world came to an end with
the institution of the Gregorian calendar, as a replacement for the ancient
Roman calendar of Julius Caesar, in 1582.

that the sublunar* world was founded in the resonance of numbers, it was not foolish to seek a numerology by which the end of that resonance might be determined. We shall examine something of the broad sweep of important predictions later, but at this point we should observe that medieval numerology was so complex (mainly because its roots were cabbalistic) that almost any periodicity could be taken as marking the end of Time, which would be prefaced by the coming of the Antichrist.

The round number of AD 2000, which the sixteenth century regarded with such awe, and which Nostradamus almost touched with his 1999, was not merely a doubling of the magical thousand. Its importance stemmed from a widely held belief that the world had been created about 5000 BC, and would endure for a sabbath, or septenary, of millennia. As we shall see, when we study the time-frame behind the septenary prophecies of Trithemius (who influenced Nostradamus considerably), the details behind this sabbatical belief varied enormously.

That Nostradamus seems to have predicted the coming of the Antichrist for 1999 is widely believed in modern times. However, if we have learned anything from our own study of the quatrains, it is that Nostradamus rarely means what he appears to say. With Nostradamus, the appearance is usually the disguise – what in esotericism is called the occult blind – cloaking a hidden meaning. Indeed, it is precisely when the prophet seems to be uncompromisingly simple in his statements that we must become most suspicious, and seek the truth he sought to disguise. Our

---

* Sublunar is now an archaic term, widely used in medieval astrology. It is derived from the Ptolemaic planetary model, and referred to that sphere which was contiguous with the sphere of the Moon. It therefore included the spheres of the four elements, the Earth itself, and Hell. In a general usage, it referred to all earthly things, which were subject to mutation, unlike the supralunar, which was supposed to be incorruptible.

main point, however, is that in offering AD 1999 as the time of the Antichrist, Nostradamus is merely reporting other prophecies which were widely believed in the sixteenth century, and which had an epistemological basis that we now know to have been erroneous.

In this book, we hope to examine the background to such predictions in a fresh light, and by so doing, attempt a new assessment of what Nostradamus envisaged for our own future. Naturally, this approach requires that we interpret the relevant verses accurately. As each of the quatrains has been structured according to arcane principles, to arrive at an understanding of them, we must examine the secret techniques used by Nostradamus as he wrote (constructed, is a better word) his prophetic oracles. All his methods involve techniques which border on what is now called the occult, but which in Nostradamus' day pertained to mystery wisdom, or esotericism, and were an integral part of standard occult methodology. As we have intimated, these methods include an esoteric use of astrology, an arcane sytem of dating and a symbolic use of linguistic devices derived from the Green Language, the secret language of esotericists. There are other arcane devices used in the quatrains – some derived from the symbolism of alchemy, which in his day was still a living science – but these need not concern us in this inquiry.

In the following chapters, we shall examine each of these arcane methods systematically. In Chapter Two, we shall examine Nostradamus' arcane use of astrology, followed by a study of his arcane system of dating – the Secundadeian system – that pertains to a pre-Christian angelology and planetary theory. In Chapters Four and Five, we shall examine the nature of the Green Language, and its relevance to the *Prophéties*. A brief glossary of essential Green Language techniques constitutes Appendix Five.

In the later chapters we shall glance at certain of the

more important predictions made by Nostradamus, before turning our attention to a few remaining quatrains that deal with our own future. Naturally, this progression of chapters will involve us in a detailed examination of a number of his fulfilled predictions which relate to the past, and which, from our standpoint at least, offer us a standard by which the accuracy of his predictions may be checked.

Unfortunately, as will now be clear even to those who are anxious to rush to translation and lay bare the vision of Nostradamus, the quatrains are extremely obscure. Almost all of the thousand or so quatrains in his *Prophéties* need to be read with an informed arcane and lexicographic care. Inevitably, several of the quatrains still evade our interpretation. However, thanks largely to the various clues that Nostradamus has left regarding his two secret tools of arcane astrology and Green Language, a large number have begun to disgorge their hidden meanings.

For reasons which will be given in the following section, we have elected to quote the original Nostradamus quatrains, *Epistles* and other prophetic verse and prose from the 1668 Amsterdam edition of the *Prophéties*, at times amended by reference to the Leffen edition, and the 1557 Lyon editions. See Appendix Two for notes on the early editions of the *Prophéties*.

All references to individual verses of the *Prophéties* are noted in the established convention, whereby the **century** is given Latin numerals, the verse, or **quatrain**, modern numerals: hence X.36 refers to Century Ten, quatrain 36.

On the whole, our bibliographic notes are spelled out in full in numbered endnotes. The exceptions to this rule are those author–names which repeat with considerable frequency within the text. Although these oft-mentioned authors are not always incorporated into endnote references, their works are listed in Appendix Eight – the alphabetic bibliography. To this bibliography, we have added all other titles mentioned in the text.

Wherever possible, publications available in the English language have been listed in this bibliography, even in those cases where the seminal or original texts are in French, or in another European language. It is inevitable, however, that many of our primal sources are in Latin or French. It was in Latin that Nostradamus was inclined to conduct his correspondence, and it was in this language that the finest astrological and esoteric texts of the sixteenth century were written or translated. It is in the French language that the finest research into Nostradamus has been conducted, and it is quite impossible to give an impartial account of the genius of Nostradamus without reference to the achievements of modern French scholarship.

We must emphasize that the bibliography in Appendix Eight is by no means exhaustive of books dealing with Nostradamus. It is worth noting that the incomparable chronological bibliography of Robert Benazra, published in 1990, offers 634 closely packed pages of titles relating to Nostradamus, and is still not exhaustive.

Introduction

What indeed is all this juggling with names, these Greek words turned inside out, these anagrams which mean two things at once? Do they not rather destroy than reinforce any possible belief in the prophetic powers of this Provencal Jew who apparently knew so much yet would not take the trouble to express himself clearly?

(James Laver, *Nostradamus, or the Future Foretold*, 1942)

We have studied and researched Nostradamus for several decades, and have come to the conclusion that Nostradamus was a brilliant prophet, and that a handful of his thousand or so prophecies may still have relevance to our own future. As our studies of the *Prophéties* developed, our eyes were opened to his unique linguistic genius, and we concluded that we were dealing with the most remarkable astrological oracles published in the Western world.

Our initial interest in the savant was not linguistic, however; it developed alongside a general and practical study of astrology and esotericism. Our first review of Nostradamus began in the late 1950s, when we first encountered James Laver's work on his prophecies.[1] Since then we have read a large number of books on Nostradamus, as on the occultism of his period. Although we have

17

been forced to review our opinion of Laver as a historian, and although we recognize that he really offered little new on the subject of Nostradamus, we remain convinced that his book was, given the period in which it was written, the best available general introduction to the works of the Master in English. Laver was quite right in his documented argument that Nostradamus predicted such major world events as the French Revolution, incidents from the life and death of Louis XIV and Marie Antoinette, the Great Plague and Fire of London, the death of Charles I of England and the Restoration of Charles II, the meteoric career of Napoleon, and so on. Unfortunately, as we studied Nostradamus more deeply, it began to dawn on us that Laver was often in error in his explanation as to how these quatrains predicted the events, and in some of his factual historical details, many of which he had simply lifted ungarnished and unresearched from the nineteenth-century commentator, Charles Ward.[2]

Moreover, as our knowledge of Nostradamus deepened, we came to the conclusion that neither Laver, nor his mentor Ward, had a sufficient knowledge of astrology, or of the arcane language, to reveal in full the significance of the quatrains. As a result, both these authorities had made several wrong assessments of important quatrains. This realization merely spurred us on to deepen our own understanding of sixteenth-century astrology, and the Green Language in which Nostradamus wrote. Neither Laver nor Ward appears to have been familiar with the Green Language, sometimes called the Language of the Birds (see Chapter Four for an explanation of these terms), used by esoteric writers. They were not unique; few who have written on Nostradamus realize the extent of the obfuscations which his familiarity with the secret tongue permitted. Ignorance of the Green Language has marred others' attempts to understand Nostradamus' verses, for he wrote not merely as an arcane astrologer, but also as a master of this secret tongue. We shall make a close study of the Green Language in Chapter Four, but a short account of the language is required here, if only to make our approach to the quatrains clear. The Green Language is a compact form of literature in which words and structures are hidden within sentences that appear to be otherwise meaningful in themselves.

The *apparent* meaning in a sentence of verse is the **exoteric** meaning, while the true meaning, hidden or encoded within the exoteric, is the **esoteric**, and may be decoded only by one familiar with the complex rules of the esoteric tongue. It is a multi-layered and allusive style of writing, meant to address those initiated in a particular realm. Although the Green Language is ancient, mentioned in Greek, Roman and Teutonic mythologies, it is perhaps more familiar as an encoded language in the finest writings of the sixteenth- and seventeenth-century alchemists such as Paracelsus, whose literature remains largely unexplored simply because so few moderns have the ability to read the secret language. The purpose of the Green Language, as Nostradamus used it in his quatrains, is to disguise ideas and predictions so that they will be evident only to those familiar with the tongue, yet to offer a semblance of a meaning to those who cannot read the language.

Armed with some knowledge of the esoteric tongue, and with a fairly specialist knowledge of the literature surrounding Nostradamus, we have familiarized ourselves with his quatrains, and savoured his predictions. Although we have researched widely in related occult fields, we have, until now, kept our silence concerning what Nostradamus did or did not say about the past and future histories of our world. However, recent developments in the treatment of Nostradamus – no doubt influenced by the commercialism of the imminent millennium – have made it clear that the time has come for us to speak out.

Of late, many silly and misinformed books have been published about Nostradamus, and these (aside from making money for their authors) have done little other than to distort his message. Worse than distortion, however, some of the more misinformed books have encouraged people to fear the future. It is almost a commonplace nowadays to hear people claim that Nostradamus predicted a Third World War, the collapse of Christianity, an horrific final conflict between Christians and Muslims – even the End of the World, foretold for the final years of our own century. Nostradamus predicted no such things, and those who have interpreted his verses in such a light have merely misunderstood what he wrote, or the reasons why he constructed the quatrains. Such distortions of what Nostradamus wrote, and our appreciation of the consequent widespread fear to which mistranslations of his quatrains have given rise, have encouraged us to reveal what we know.

Nostradamus has not been well served by modern writers. Two of the most widely read translators are Henry C. Roberts[3] and Erika Cheetham,[4] both of whom translate (though in neither case is this an appropriate word) and interpret his verses in an inaccurate way. They each have insisted that the end of the twentieth century will see terrible wars, a bloody confrontation between the West and Islam, the coming of the Antichrist, and even the End of the World. In making such wide-sweeping and horrible predictions, they have misread Nostradamus, for he predicted neither such ethnic conflicts nor so dire a future. Modern writers have misread Nostradamus because they failed to understand fully his arcane methods, the parameters within which he worked, the language in which he wrote, and the historical background to his predictions.

There are many modern books reflecting this inappropriate response to Nostradamus. To stay only with recent English titles, we should list among these: *Nostradamus – Countdown to Apocalypse* by Jean-Charles de Fontbrune, 1983, with the foreword by Liz Greene; *Nostradamus and the Millennium* by John Hogue, 1987; *Nostradamus: The Final Countdown* by Liz Arkel and David Blake, 1993; *Nostradamus. The Millennium and Beyond* by Peter Lorie, with Liz Greene as consultant, 1993; *Nostradamus Prophecies Fulfilled and Predictions for the Millennium and Beyond* by Francis X. King, 1995. All these books, which are selected here almost at random, are replete with errors, and misunderstandings as to what Nostradamus wrote, and evince no understanding of his arcane knowledge of either astrology or the Green Language.

Both Roberts and Cheetham failed to represent with even fair accuracy the French-seeming verses which Nostradamus wrote; furthermore, other writers have used the 'translations' offered by Roberts and Cheetham in their own works. For example, in a recent book, Anderson Black offers a 'translation' which is almost word for word a version of Cheetham, claiming that the verse foretold the future nuclear destruction of Paris. As it happened, Cheetham had copied the first line of the French verse inaccurately, which meant that her translation (let alone her interpretation) could not be accurate.[5] Even though he does not refer to the French, Black carried Cheetham's inaccurate translation into his own English verse, ignoring the simple truth that the French of Nostradamus mentioned neither nuclear explosions nor even Paris.

Roberts, using the earliest English translation, published by Garencières in 1672, sees the same quatrain as referring to a nuclear holocaust, and a reference to Pearl Harbor and Hiroshima and Nagasaki in Japan. Roberts and the later editors who have continued his work have not succeeded in recording either the original French of Nostradamus, or reasonable translations of what the seer wrote. Roberts' reliance on Garencières is misguided: this early translation was punctuated with errors, and virtually everything that Garencières wrote concerning futurity was incorrect.

Inaccurate and misleading as these modern translations and interpretations are, they are now widely accepted by those not fortunate enough to be intimately familiar with the writings of Nostradamus. Since they provide an image of our future which is filled with woe, blood and thunder – the promise of future wars, or internecine struggles between races, and the final conflagration of civilization, if not of the Earth itself – the poverty of their analysis is all the more reprehensible.

Here are a few more examples of ill-advised predictions of calamity. According to Jean Monterey, there is to be a thermo-nuclear, aero-naval war between East and West, its conclusion being in the Mediterranean area.[6] There is no quatrain which mentions such a conflict. According to Erika Cheetham, Nostradamus predicted the end of the world for the year 2000, and (somewhat ambiguously) foresaw war both before and after this period. Needless to say, Nostradamus wrote no such prophecies. The French interpreter of Nostradamus, Jean-Charles de Fontbrune, insisted that the Savant predicted Asia will threaten the USSR with chemical warfare, and the Russians will be driven from Moscow.[7] There is no Nostradamus quatrain which claims such a thing. According to Arkel and Blake, the future offered by Nostradamus is so bleak that few will survive the cataclysmic events to come. The destruction will be followed by a new age. As a matter of fact, Nostradamus mentions neither a new age, nor the idea that humanity will be destroyed in a cataclysm.

As we shall see in this book, several of Nostradamus'

prophecies have been mistranslated before – either intentionally or unintentionally, through lack of expertise. On a few occasions, misunderstandings arising from such misconstrued quatrains have influenced certain individuals into unwise actions. Napoleon and Hitler are famous examples, for they both appear to have acted in particular ways in order to 'fulfil' prophecies which they fondly imagined related to their own times and personalities. Modern commentators such as David Pitt Francis[8] have touched upon the historical and sociological impact of such prophecy fulfilment. The fact that both Napoleon and Hitler were attempting to bring to fulfilment misinterpreted predictions is irrelevant: in each case, the consequences of their actions were disastrous for millions of people. Is it not quite possible that some future warmonger – some Fundamentalist group, some crazed Messianic – will act in a similar way in our own future, and, by attempting to enact a misread prophecy, bring chaos to society?

'In 1999, as the old century is about to expire, between November 23rd and December 21st, the climactic War of Wars shall be unleashed.'

This interpretation of Nostradamus' quatrain I.16 appeared in the 1982 edition of Roberts' *The Complete Prophecies of Nostradamus*. In fact, Nostradamus did not mention either the year 1999, or the months November and/or December in this quatrain, nor did he claim that a climactic War of Wars would begin at that time, or, indeed, at any other time. Nonetheless, the Roberts translation, originally written in 1947, has gone through no fewer than eight editions, innumerable reprintings, and has probably sold more copies of the famous *Prophéties* than any other modern rendering. How is it possible for such a widely sold and popular book to be so wrong?

The answer to this question is depressingly simple. People who do not know how to read Nostradamus, who have never specialized in his methods, and who do not understand his symbolism, find themselves impelled to try their hands at translating his quatrains. Such people do not realize that Nostradamus was speaking from a knowledge of the arcane wisdom behind an age-old tradition of prophecy – at times even quoting other prophecies – around which occult methods and secret linguistic terms had been constructed. They do not realize that the understanding of this type of prophecy requires a lifetime of study.

Of course, we do not have to look far to discover why the sub-cultural approach to Nostradamus is so popular. We live in an age of violence, when *schadenfreude* is a saleable commodity, and when books which predict grotesque and terrible futures generally sell more readily than those which offer more sedate futurities. The sub-cultural Nostradamus is a product of economics, yet it is distinctly harmful in its power over people's imaginations, and should be resisted.

It must be repeated that Nostradamus has been misunderstood by so many modern writers because he wrote in an exceedingly arcane style. Therefore our reappraisal of Nostradamus is conducted in the light of sixteenth-century arcane and astrologic knowledge and usage. Our purpose is to reveal the occult background to a number of representative quatrains, and to point out (what must be the obvious) that a real understanding of the *Prophéties* requires an understanding of the arcane methodology of Nostradamus.

While the arcane methods used by Nostradamus in the construction of his quatrains are complex, they may be conveniently reduced to three basic techniques:

- First, whenever Nostradamus wishes to denote a precise date in the future, he tends to resort to an arcane system of astrology, deeply rooted in sixteenth-century techniques.

- Second, when dealing in more general time periods, such as centuries, cycles or eras, he resorts to an occult system which was well known in the sixteenth century, but which is almost totally forgotten in modern times. This is the arcane system of historical periodicities which was reintroduced to Europe by Trithemius, the Abbot of Sponheim, perhaps the most influential occultist of the late fifteenth century, in his treatment of the *Secundadeis*, or planetary angels: this is examined in detail in Chapter Three.

- Third, Nostradamus uses a linguistic system which has been favoured by esotericists and occultists for very many centuries, and which nowadays passes under the name of the Green Language.

Since it is essential for anyone who wishes to approach the prophecies of Nostradamus to have some background knowledge of these three arcane methods, we shall deal with each – within the context of the quatrains – in the following chapters. However, before we look more closely at the predictions of Nostradamus, we should glance at the structure of the quatrains themselves.

THE NATURE OF THE *PROPHÉTIES*

The titles in the early literature attached to Nostradamus did not refer to the *Centuries*, but to the *Prophéties*. The long title of the 21st edition of the verses, published in 1588, mentions that they are divided into four 'Centuries', yet still entitles the work *Les Grandes et Merveilleuses Predictions* . . . This insistence on the word *Prophéties* may have been due to the recognition that not all the Nostradamus prophecies – many of which were constructed for his *almanachs*, or Prognostications – were issued as four-line verses in parcels of a hundred. However, in 1596, Nostradamus' disciple, Jean-Aimé de Chavigny, used the word 'Centuries' in the title of his commentaries on the verses, and no doubt this helped popularize the word.

The classical Nostradamus prophecy was written in the form of a quatrain – a four-line rhyming verse. These were arranged into *Centuries*. The title *Centuries* – from *centains* in French – is from the Latin, *centenarius*, frequently reduced in English to the ambiguous word, 'centuries'. The arrangement of verses is so called not because they deal with chronologies or with events in groups of 100 years, but because the verses were grouped by Nostradamus into sections of approximately 100. However, this generalized and ambiguous title is not absolutely accurate, since one or two of the centuries do not yield precisely 100 quatrains: Century VII contains only 44 quatrains in some editions, and 48 in others. As we shall see, the first published collection of quatrains included a fourth 'Centurie' of only 53 verses.

We write as though there is some consensus about the form and nature of the first edition of the *Prophéties*, yet this is misleading. There is much more mystery around the publication dates of the *Prophéties* than is suggested in the popular books on Nostradamus. Nominally, the *Prophéties* was printed in two parts, but as there was a considerable difference between the first two parts, it should probably be described as having come out in three distinct sections. The first, published in 1555 by Macé-Bonhomme (probably Mathieu Bonhomme, a printer in Lyons from 1542 to 1569) contained the first 3 Centuries and 53 verses of the following Century – 353 verses in all. Included in this first printing was a letter to Nostradamus' recently born son,

César. In 1557 appeared the Antoine du Rosne (Lyons) edition, which is sometimes said to be the second edition of the *Prophéties*, but which is claimed by some to be a fifth edition. In 1558, a so-called *princeps* edition (of which there is a copy in the Bibliothèque Nationale, Paris) was, according to some, printed in Lyons by Pierre Rigaud. This date has been disputed, and a posthumous date of 1566 has been suggested for the 'princeps' edition, which may be viewed as the conjoining of two separately printed fasci-cules: the whole complicated story of the early editions is told with remarkable clarity by Benazra.[9] We shall demon-strate, when examining the horoscope of Nostradamus in Appendix One, that there is almost a cosmic reason why the dates 1555 and 1558 should be regarded as being realistic, since they fit perfectly into the life-structure of events promised by the birthchart of the Master. In our view, they were recorded precisely for this reason. Our main interest lies in the predictions contained within the quatrains, and since only one or two of these antedate the year of the latest possible publication date (1558) we may safely ignore disputes about the nature of the early printings.

The history of the publications of the *Prophéties* is, then, a complex one; however, some account of previous editions is required in order to explain why the specific versions of quatrains used in this present work have been adopted for translation. In a batch of recently discovered correspond-ence, a couple of letters exchanged between Nostradamus and his printers point to difficulties which both encoun-tered. This situation was made more difficult by the fact that, in the sixteenth century, printing procedures were quite unlike those used today, and it was a common practice for printers to correct errors (or even supposed errors) on the press in the course of the printing. The anonymous English commentator on Nostradamus, D.D., lamented in 1715 that

*The like Faults of the Pen and Press, are but too obvious
in the many Editions of the Prophecies of Nostradamus,
as indeed there is hardly one single Quatrain, which has
not a different Reading in the several Editions.*[10]

A good idea of the extent of such 'different readings' may
be gleaned from the treatment of a short phrase, as it slides
in a variety of different guises from sixteenth-century
editions of the *Prophéties* into modern times.

In the 1566 Pierre Rigaud edition of quatrain IX.62
appears the three-word phrase *Chera mon agora*. This triple
was reduced by Benoist Rigaud, in 1568 to *Cheramon*; the
same phrase was represented by Jaubert in his 1603
treatment of the quatrains as *Cheramonagora*, which he
translated (without adequate explanation) as *Le Marché des
Poitiers* (Poitiers market).[11] In the 1668 edition published by
Jean Jansson of Amsterdam, the phrase read: *chera ausi de
mont agora*.

It is hardly surprising that the modern versions of the
word are perplexing and varied. In a nineteenth-century
book on Nostradamus the same phrase was represented as
Chera, aussi le mons Agora.[12] In 1982, Roberts also recorded
it as *Cheramonagora*, a word he did not explain: he had
taken the word from the 1672 edition of Garencières, who
had (in this case) borrowed it from Jaubert. The modern
Italian writer on Nostradamus, Carlo Patrian, gave it as
Chera Monagora, and explained it as a means of manual
transport. Bardo Kodogo gave the variant, *Cheramon agora*,
which seems to be adopted directly from the Cheetham
version, but which Kodogo interpreted as relating to the
Common Market, the precursor of the European Union. In
turn, Cheetham informed her readers that *Cheramon-agora*
was the name of a town in Asia Minor, believed to be
present-day Uşak in Turkey: perhaps she had in mind

Cherronesus, which is the Thracian peninsula at the west of the Hellespont.

As such variants and distortions are all too common, it is essential to establish a consensus, based as nearly as possible on precisely what Nostradamus *did* write. Appendix Two is a brief bibliographical survey of the early editions of the *Prophéties*, in so far as these are relevant to our own treatment of the quatrains.

THE LANGUAGE OF PROPHECY

If the occultists are right, when Nostradamus previsioned events, he was watching the unscrolling of what are now called the Akashic Chronicles. Akashic is a name derived from Sanskrit, meaning 'luminous'. It was introduced into Western occultism by the Theosophists towards the end of the nineteenth century. It is the secret fifth element, which binds together the four traditional elements; it is thus the same as the quintessence of the ancients, and the 'Luminous Waters' of the alchemists. According to occult lore, all memories of events on earth are stored in the Akashic belt around the spiritual body of the earth. Specially trained occultists and initiates may read this memory band, which is sometimes called the Akashic Chronicle. Access to the Chronicles requires a particularly arduous occult training, and even those with higher vision can easily make mistakes. A famous example is the error made by Madame Blavatsky in misreading the events surrounding the life of Jesu ben Pandira, and confusing these with Jesus of Nazareth. Prior to the Theosophistic injection of such oriental terms into Western occultism, the Akashic Records were recognized under a variety of different names, among which the Paracelsian term *Aniadus* seems to have been used in arcane alchemical circles.

In the cabbalistic tradition, the angels who recorded the

scrolling of the records were the Recording Angels, though they are now called by most esotericists the *Lipika*.* These beings were – and indeed, *are* – responsible for recording, in what has sometimes been called the *Anima Mundi*, or World Soul, all spiritual events – such as human thoughts, deeds and words – which occur upon the earth. For historical reasons, connected with the fact that the early Roman Church adopted for its own administrative and political purposes the Roman Imperium, the Judaeo–Christian emphasis has for many centuries been fixated on the past, and on traditional forms, rather than upon innovation and futurity. One consequence of this has been an emphasis on rites for the dying, or for the dead, at the expense of proper liturgy for prenatal experience and for birth. On an esoteric level, this has meant that the teachings of reincarnation carried within the esoteric lore of the ancient mystery wisdom were ignored by the early Church, and only half the story of pre-Christian mystery wisdom regarding reincarnation was continued in the Christian mysteries. This explains why the Christian mysteries are concerned essentially with a future spiritual life, with liturgies and prayers for the dead in a post-mortem existence, at the expense of those much-needed liturgies and prayers for the return of the soul into incarnation, or birth.

This reflection may seem to have little or no relevance to Nostradamus, but in fact it has great relevance to all prophets, as it partly explains the animosity within the Church for prophetic literature; the Christian tradition has tended to emphasize the past, at the expense of the future. This explains why the Church has tended to frown upon exegeses relating to Biblical and other Christian apocalyptic

---

* Lipika is a term derived from the Sanskrit root meaning 'to read'. It is used to designate the spiritual *lip*, beings charged with recording (that is, 'reading' then 'writing down') in the Akashic the thoughts, feelings and deeds of humans.

literature, and even on the astrological method: it explains also why the prophetic literature of Christianity is so often regarded by ecclesiastical authorities as being heretical, or otherwise questionable. For whatever reasons, the Christian view of the Recording Angels has limited their scrolling of records to the past: however, in the arcane tradition these angelic beings were equally concerned with scrolling the future.

Nostradamus was not the first to set down his Akashic vision – all *genuine* prophets read from the Akashic record. Nor was he even the first to set down his vision in such obscure terms as to make the depiction largely incomprehensible prior to the unfolding of the predicted event. He was, however, the first to reveal a whole history of Europe, albeit centred on France, extending over a period of about 800 years. What is special about Nostradamus is not merely that he chose to concentrate upon the development of one particular culture, but that he created an entire literature and literary style in order to do this. There had been many prophets before Nostradamus, and (as will be demonstrated later) some of these influenced his vision and writings, but there had never been anyone so proficient in arcane literature as Nostradamus before or since.

Nostradamus, then, worked with the Akashic. He was an initiate, and had therefore earned the ability to do this. Among the large numbers of people who nowadays claim to have access to the Akashic are many who are deluding themselves – they deal with what the early Theosophists rightly termed the Realm of Glamour on the Astral Plane.*

---

* Theosophists are the members of the Theosophical Society established by Madame Blavatsky and others in New York in 1875. The word was used of certain alchemists and rosicrucians in the sixteenth to the eighteenth century. Sometimes, the Alexandrian neo-Platonists were also called theosophists. The word is from the Greek, meaning 'lovers of God'.

This point must be made because unless the distinction is drawn, the true genius of Nostradamus will not be recognized. Already, there are individuals who are reworking or interpreting Nostradamus according to what they claim as Akashic vision. Some even claim to be taking dictation through the spirit of Nostradamus – thereby revealing their total ignorance of the cosmic laws behind reincarnation, which have been set down by such specialist occultists as the German anthroposophist Guenther Wachsmuth.*

In the past few years, we have come across several examples of the so-called 'channelling' and regression techniques, applied to the name of Nostradamus. The former technique is nothing other than the old clairvoyance in a new dress, and is equally dangerous. Among examples of such material which we have received, through the mail, are the batches of 'Nostradamian' prophecies issued under the name of Dolores Cannon.[13] The material offered is the usual hotchpotch of sub-cultural dire predictions, brought up to date, yet still treated as 'interpretation' of Nostradamus: the predictions are entirely of the inventive sub-cultural type, and include the spread of AIDS, the Antichrist, economic disaster in America and the assassination of Pope John-Paul in 1992.

Nostradamus appears never to have offered explanations for his quatrains, other than to admit that they all deal with the

Certain Blavatskian Theosophists described a division of the Astral Plane (a spiritual plane higher than the material plane, invisible to ordinary sight) as the Realm of Glamour. One of its effects was to delude those clairvoyants who sought to penetrate the veil of spirit without adequate preparation. Sometimes, those under the influence of drugs (who make often illegal entry into the Astral Plane) are hypnotized by the Realm of Glamour, and take this to be the whole extent of the spiritual world.
* For a brief survey of these, see F. Gettings, *Encyclopaedia of the Occult*, 1986, page 181.

future. While he left certain indications (meant only for the eyes of those versed in arcane methods) as to which occult systems he favoured, he offered no commentaries of his own. This is an important point, for it means that all published commentaries on the *Prophéties* are a result of personal detective work, guess-work and (in some striking modern examples) incompetent plagiarism.

If there were in the ancient grimoires* a dark angel charged with the maldirection of prophecy, its name would be Nationalism. The greatest formative force in the interpretation of the quatrains has been nationalism, fed by the erroneous belief that Nostradamus was concerned only with the contemporaneity of the interpreter. Few nineteenth-century French commentators doubted that the Great City (*Grand Citée*) mentioned by Nostradamus was Paris, even though there was little internal evidence to support this view. Just so, the English commentator 'D.D.' had no doubt that the *Anglia* to which Nostradamus referred was 'the Land of the Habitation of Angels', and therefore a reference to his own England.[14]

There are few things more depressing than to wade through the thickets of 'interpretations' – usually of French origin – which seem to relate almost every quatrain to the major events during the Third Republic, and the First and Second World Wars, as though these lacunae had been the main interest behind the Master's sixteenth-century pen. At least two French writers spent a good part of their lives attempting to show that some of the quatrains were dedicated to predicting the restoration of the Bourbon dynasty to the throne of France, at a time when it was clear to the less myopic that their time was gone for ever.[15] One

---

* The grimoires are the black-books of the late medieval period, in which the rules for conjuring demons by name, sigil and ritual were set out, along with descriptions of the individual guises which the demons adopt when called into visibility.

wonders whether the French commentator Rochetaillée was right in presuming that Nostradamus was deeply concerned with the fall of the French President Maurice de Mac Mahon in 1879, the election of Jules Grévy to the Presidency of the Republic in 1879, the electoral triumph of General Boulanger in 1889, and so on. As Laver remarked when considering this French self-obsession, it is hard to believe that the death of the Prince Imperial in Zululand merits eleven quatrains, or that eight or nine should be devoted to the Dreyfus Affair.[16]

One purpose of this book is to remedy such defects in scholarship. We offer a groundwork for a new approach to Nostradamus by revealing how he used arcane astrology in his quatrains, along with a brief account of the related Trithemian planetary angels, and a more detailed survey of the Green Language terminologies which are found with such profusion in his writing. A knowledge of these arcane techniques and languages is absolutely vital in the approach to Nostradamus. This is so, because the major keywords, dates and historical references in the quatrains are usually expressed in an arcane terminology which lies outside the familiar terminologies of the European family of languages.

However, before we explain the intellectual and creative techniques of the *Prophéties* literature, we should take some stock of Nostradamus the man. We should glance, albeit briefly, at the background to his life, and at the cultural and spiritual milieu which formed the backdrop to this remarkable achievement in arcane literature.

Part One

The Life, Times and Techniques
of Nostradamus

Chapter 1

Nostradamus and His Times

In the same way, also, many have become learned men, who, having attained a suitable sidereal body, have sedulously exercised themselves in their native influence. Hence it happens that they at last draw down upon themselves the influence of their native constellation, just as rays from the sun. So an admirable science, doctrine, and wisdom are discovered ... taken from the stars alone. Heaven being thus constituted, and producing for itself a sidereal body, there arise many great minds, many writers, doctors, interpreters of Scriptures, and philosophers, according as each is formed from its constellation. Their writings and doctrines are not to be considered sacred, although they have a certain singular authority, given by the constellation and influence, by the spirits of Nature, not of God. Operations of this kind sometimes proceed from the mind of man in a stupendous manner, when men, changing their heart and soul, would make themselves like to the saints, being made such by a drunken star: whereas wine changes man, so also these are changed. It is, therefore, worth while to understand this sort of astronomy.

(Paracelsus, *The Hermetic and Alchemical Writings*, 1894, edited by A. E. Waite, Vol. II, 'Hermetic Medicine and Hermetic Philosophy', p. 302)

In the year 1555, Michel Nostradamus published the first part of his *Prophéties*, an arcane collection of predictions which was, in later times, to become the most famous French book of the sixteenth century. Who was this remarkable savant, and what was the background to his life in the middle of that century, in France?

According to his son, César (whose writings have proved to be somewhat unreliable), Nostradamus was born in southern France at Saint-Rémy-de-Provence, a small market town in the modern Département of Bouches-du-Rhône, about 15 miles north-east of Arles, on the old-style date,* 14 December 1503. We shall study the horoscope for this birth in Appendix One. It is a remarkably powerful chart, with the three superior planets (Mars, Jupiter and Saturn) conjuncted over the two fixed stars, Castor and Pollux (*fig. 3*).

If it is true, as we suspect, that Nostradamus was born a few minutes after midday, then the horoscope is hyper-charged, since the conflict engendered by the opposition between the Sun and the three superiors (that is, Mars, Jupiter and Saturn) would demand a special discipline to control creative energies. From the figure, and from the remarkable aspect which it displays, and which Nostradamus later turned into a sort of talisman for his personal seal, we may be sure that he was born with a more than unusual sense of mission. In it was all the promise contained in Paracelsus' description of the true seer, set out in the header quotation above. To fulfil this promise,

---

* 'Old Style' is the name given to the calendrical system still in use in the time of Nostradamus. It had been introduced by Julius Caesar in 46 BC, on which account it was sometimes called the Julian system. It was already under review in the mid-sixteenth century, and by 1582 it was modified by Pope Gregory XIII. Since that time it has been known both as the Gregorian, and as the 'New Style'. It was not adopted in the majority of Protestant countries for many years. Britain accepted it only in 1752, and Russia in 1918.

Nostradamus would have needed the instruction of an initiate teacher to help find expression for these powerful energies, for they would have proved destructive in any person who did not receive special instruction. His life and work is evidence that he did succeed in harnessing this power (for Nostradamus as an initiate, see Appendix Three), and it is clear that he remained, in the words of Paracelsus, a man touched by a drunken star, a *stella dilutior*, a man just a little inebriated by the influx of spirit. Who the initiate teacher of this star-struck man was remains a mystery. Indeed, considering his fame, even during his own lifetime, and even taking into account the vast amount of erudition spent by scholars searching for details of his life, the achievements of Nostradamus remain essentially an enigma.

The popular story of Nostradamus one finds in the multitude of sub-cultural books is little more than a benign fabrication – at best entertaining fables, at worst tissues of lies. A thorough and reliable account of his life would involve a tiresome destruction of fables and legends – even of the serious histories offered by such scholars as Charles Ward or le Pelletier: this is not our purpose here. Our aim is merely to present a summary of the little which is known about Nostradamus with any degree of certainty. Fortunately modern French research criticism has effected a revolution in the study of Nostradamus.

The indefatigable researches of Edgar Leroy[1] have resulted in a series of genealogical tables which have amended much that was previously supposed to have been known about the background of Nostradamus, derived mainly from Jehan de Nostredame (the savant's brother),[2] César de Nostradame (his son)[3] and Jean-Aimé de Chavigny (his friend and disciple).[4] Unfortunately, Leroy's reliable conclusion is that one knows nothing for sure about the early years of Nostradamus. Nonetheless, out of the obscurity emerge a few facts. Nostradamus' father was Jacques de Nostredame (sometimes called Jaume), who had been born in Avignon, and who, while he earned his living as a merchant, later practised as a notary. His mother was Reynière de Saint-Rémy (sometimes called Renée). One may still inspect the crumbling exterior of the house in Rue Hoche where, it is said, Nostradamus was born. Nearby, in the ancient street now called Rue de Nostradamus, one may see, above the fountain of two fishes and leonine water-spouts, a fine bust of the savant (*fig. 4*).

However, it is not in Saint-Rémy that one is likely to find the true spirit of Nostradamus – in its concern for words, etymologies and arcanities – but in an area about a mile to the south of the town. The French commentator, Jean-Paul Clébert, whose interpretation of certain quatrains is among the most perspicacious of modern times, noted the influence of a landscape very near to Saint-Rémy on the mind of the young Nostradamus.[5] He reminded us of what all visitors to Saint-Rémy cannot help but observe – that the strange word *Mansol*, which is found in six of the quatrains, is a reference to a spot less than a mile to the south of Saint-Rémy.[6] This was the old priory, the *Manseolo* of the thirteenth century, the Saint-Paul-de-Mausole of modern times, where the cloisters painted by Van Gogh still remain, alongside the mental hospital which now bears the artist's name.*

The church and cloisters of Saint-Paul-de-Mausole are the *Pol Mansol* which opens quatrain X.29. Even the so-called 'pyramid', which stands in the lavender fields in

---

* Documents contemporaneous with Nostradamus call it Saint-Paul-de-Mausole, while an earlier Latinate thirteenth-century version was Manseolo. In various quatrains, Nostradamus refers to it as Pol Mansol, Mausole or Mansole. In modern times church and hospital are called Sainct Pol de Manseole and Saint-Paul-de-Mausole, but guide-books offer variations even on these.

front of the caved walls below this same church, is mentioned by Nostradamus, as are the goat-caves excavated into these cliffs and marketed in modern times for tourists as 'ancient Roman slave enclosures'.[7] As we shall see, the possible predictive implication of the six *Mansol* quatrains can be worked out with more certainty, once their connection with Saint-Rémy, and with the adjacent Greek and Roman antiquities, has been recognized (see page 210). However, entirely typical of Nostradamus' style, this 'local' reading may prove to be nothing more than an occult blind to the deeper meaning of the quatrain.

Although the child was baptized a Christian, it is very likely that his not-too-distant ancestors were converted Jews, from Italy. Dr Edgar Leroy is specific in tracing their background to Jewish merchants who came to Carpentras and Avignon in the second half of the fifteenth century. It was the stigma attached to being Jewish in a country where the Jews had been expelled which led Nostradamus' disciple, Chavigny, to deny his Jewish origins. Nostradamus' son, César, also glossed over them. Research has confirmed beyond any doubt that his roots were Jewish.

So far as can be determined from the records examined with such care by Dr Edgar Leroy and E. Lhez, the conversion from Jewry was made by Pierre de Nostredame before 1455. Leroy records that in the registry of a document dated 12 May 1455, witnessed by the notary Jacques Giraud of Avignon, there is a marginal note:

Pro Petro de Nostra Domina Olim cum judeus esset vocato Vidono Gassonet obligatio

Obligation for Pierre de Nostredame who was called Guy Gassonet, from the time he was Jewish

It is possible, from a later witnessed document, that the

changed name was wrongly recorded, but with good reason: Pierre had married the daughter of one Jesse Gassonet of Monteux. Her father, who also had converted to Christianity, had taken the name of Richaud. However, his daughter refused to convert. Pierre, already a Christian, was therefore obliged to repudiate the marriage, at Orange. In brief, it seems from Leroy's documentation that the Pierre, or Guy Gassonet, ancestry could be traced back with certainty through three generations; through Arnaud de Velorgues, one Vital (who married Astrugie Massip), and to Astruge of Carcassonne. This would take us well back into the fourteenth century, out of surviving documentation and into richer legends. Unfortunately, the few facts about Nostradamus' simple background were well disguised by his son César in his account of the family lineage: he proclaimed that his father was descended from a line of learned doctors, well versed in languages. One need only visit an upper room in the town hall of Salon, the town in which father and son lived, to understand the urgency with which César felt he should improve his family line. On the walls of this splendid room hang two sixteenth-century portraits, facing each other across time and space. Both are reputed to have been painted by César himself. If so, he was an amateur of considerable talent. One is the picture of his father, made famous by a thousand reproductions.

The other painting (if it is by César) is a self-portrait, revealing him as a fashionable and successful man of social distinction, a musical instrument (perhaps it is a lute) at his feet. In this picture, he is far more debonair than the engraved portrait of the worried man, nearing 60, which appears as frontispiece to his own history book.[8] In modern times, we might be tempted to call César 'upwardly mobile': it was imperative that he should not show his roots to have been too deeply embedded in peasant clay: he was keen to give the impression that, if he were not exactly from noble stock, then he was at least from a line of respectable scholars.

The date of César's birth is uncertain, but, from the dedicatory Preface to the *Prophéties*, we know that it must have been round about 1554. He died round about 1630. Thanks to his considerable inheritance from his father, he seems to have been able to lead the life of a dilettante writer and artist, with an interest in local government. In microscopic characters on the portrait of his father in the Bibliothèque de la Méjanes, in Aix-en-Provence, César has written two couplets in Latin.

> *Caesaris est satis patris haec Michaelis imago*
> *Edit hic hunc genitor, prodit hic ille patrem*
> *Sic pater est natus nati, pater est quoque patris*
> *Natus et hinc rebus numina rident.*[*]

This we translate as:

This image of Michel, the father, is by César, the son.
The former engendered the latter: he has produced his father.
If the father is born of the son, then the son is also the father of the father.
The gods smile at this birth and at this curious design.

In literature at least, César seems to have been a plagiarist, to judge from his *l'Histoire et Chronique de Provence*. The final impression one has is of a gentleman of leisure, a social climber who was rather ashamed of his background, who sadly failed to develop his considerable talent as an artist.

[*] From Mouan, *Aperçus littéraires sur César Nostradamus et ses lettres inédites a Peiresc*, Mémoires de l'Academie d'Aix, vol. X, 1873. The couplets are also quoted by Leroy, pp. 114–15.

All members of the Nostradamus family seem to have received excellent educations, at a time when those who were privileged to be educated had the opportunity to drink in knowledge still imbued with esoteric lore. It is usually claimed that the youthful Nostradamus learned astrology and the rudiments of herbalism and medicine from his grandfather. It has also been suggested that it was these early interests which persuaded Nostradamus to study medicine at Montpellier University. In his own book on cosmetics, Nostradamus tells us that he spent from 1521 to 1529 working on astrology, in connection with its medical associations – in fact, 'to learn the source and origin of the planets' – in his search for healing principles. It is significant that such information is derived from a text which quite openly deals with disguise, or as he puts it, from a book designed to help women 'deceive the eyes of onlookers'. Afterwards, he is supposed to have worked in medicine at Narbonne, Carcassonne, Toulouse and Bordeaux, and, within a short time, to have established a deserved reputation in Provence as having the power to heal those sick of the plague, during the frequent outbreaks which the insanitary conditions of the time encouraged. He seems to have returned to Montpellier before 1533, for it was in this year that he completed his Doctor's degree.

Most of these 'facts' have been called into question by modern research, especially by Leroy, who questions whether Nostradamus did stay in such cities as Carcassonne and Bordeaux, during the periods so often given in history books. Research has also shown that it is unlikely that Nostradamus was ordered to appear before the inquisitors at Toulouse, round about 1534, as the majority of biographers have claimed.

Documentation for these years is sparse. However, the records for his entry into the Faculty of Medicine at Montpellier University are still preserved, for 23 October

1529. He was in Agen by 1533, but why he went there, and what he did once there, is uncertain, though most historians have followed Jean-Aimé de Chavigny in reading into his visit his friendship with Scaliger,* who by then was living in Agen.

The imaginative biographies of later years insist that he built his reputation as a doctor curing people of the plague. We do not know what the truth of this is. The later commentators mention a mysterious powder which he used to protect himself in these dangerous plague venues. He is supposed to have left the secret formula in his treatise on cosmetics.[9] Raoul Busquet describes a powder 'made by Nostradamus' which arrested the plague at Aix in 1546.[10] Of course, similar stories are told of other occultist-doctors of the period, including Paracelsus and Agrippa. The former occultist, Paracelsus, is often portrayed with this mysterious powder, the *Azoth* or *Zoth*, secreted in the pommel of his sword (*fig. 5*). In one of his arcane verses, Nostradamus actually used the word *Asotus*, which may relate to this secret, but which was taken by later chemists, unfamiliar with the arcane tradition, as a name for nitrogen. The powder was a specific against the plague, for in the hermetic literature it is the alchemical 'ripe Mercury' which, according to Paracelsus, will 'cure all diseases in the three kingdoms of Nature'.[11] Unfortunately, with typical spagyric† caution (for it was unwise of alchemists to reveal their secrets), Paracelsus fails to offer the recipe for this

---

* Julius Caesar Scaliger (1484–1558), Italian scholar and soldier. In 1525 he accompanied de la Rovere to Agen, as his physician. He had an encyclopaedic knowledge, and seems to have been at the forefront of scientific speculation in his day.
† The word *spagyric* is almost an equivalent of 'alchemy', and was one of several words invented by Paracelsus. There was a purpose behind this invention, for Paracelsus was anxious to distinguish the real esoteric alchemy (spagiricus) from the venal art of the gold-seeker (alchemy).

marvellous powder, telling us only that it is made from the *Elixir*. This *Elixir* remains one of the most closely guarded of all alchemical secrets. It is our conclusion that the *Azoth* (which may or may not have been a real powder) is a symbol of initiation – a recognition that those men and women who were supposed to carry the powder with them were initiates, probably into what Nostradamus, in an enigmatic phrase, called '*la faculté Iatrice*', the faculty of healing.

A treatise would be required to account for the *Azoth*, or *Azoc* as Paracelsus often calls it. Azoth is the secret of secrets, the Mercury of the Philosophers (and not, as Paracelsus hastens to inform us, crude quicksilver). It is the powder which purifies impure bodies with the help of fire. It is, in a word, the secret power of initiation, which works from the spiritual into the three worlds of man – into the Intellect, the Emotional and the divine Physical. According to the more recent writings of the adept Fulcanelli, the making of this *Azoth*, which he calls 'animated mercury', may be studied in the stonework of that alchemical masterpiece, Notre Dame of Paris – a stone book which Nostradamus must have read, along with other occultists, during his visits to Paris.* In the English edition of Jacques Sadoul's book on alchemy, there is an arcane reference to this mysterious powder.[12] The frontispiece of the book is the title-page of a sixteenth-century version of Basil Valentine's *Azoth* (*fig. 6*), while, at the end of the book, an appendix reflects on the fact that early alchemists must have had access to some secret elixir. In this appendix, Sadoul lists nine of the greatest alchemists known to the West, and shows that they had an average age

---

* In Nostradamus' day, almost all the French cathedrals and major abbey churches (not to mention Italian duomi) were arcane stone books. The most impressive in Nostradamus' time would be Chartres, Amiens, Paris and Vezelay. Less impressive, but near to Salon, is St Trophime, at Arles.

of 82, during a period of history when average age was less than half that. Perhaps the *Azoth* was no mere phantastical?

By a curious coincidence, the first man to translate all the Nostradamus quatrains into English was also a medical man who faced problems with the plague. This was Theophilus Garencières, who had trained and qualified in both Caen and Oxford, and who (unbelievably) appears to have been forced to use the quatrains of Nostradamus as a primer in the French language. Faced with the horrors of the Great Plague of 1665, which ravaged London and many parts of England, he recommended a remedy called Venice treacle, to be taken internally.[13]

Returning to the few trustworthy facts about Nostradamus' life, we can be certain that during the later part of his life he authored a number of books. It is likely that his fame as an astrologer was derived in the first instance not from his *Prophéties*, but from his annual *Almanachs* of predictions and weather forecasts, with foreseen events for the months headed with four-line verses, as decasyllabic quatrains (*fig. 7*). A few of those linked with his name, even in early times, are forgeries, yet it is certain that the *Prognostication nouvelle . . .* of 1555 was from his hand, even though it was probably not the first. We shall have occasion to examine one of these almanacs later: meanwhile, we should note that it was probably the popularity of these annual publications which suggested to him the idea of a series of prophetic quatrains, dealing with the future of Europe.

In addition to preparing his annual almanacs, Nostradamus also published a translation of a paraphrase of Galen (the second-century Greek physician, whose writings on medicine formed the main corpus of knowledge in the medieval world),[14] a translation from Latin; a treatise on cosmetics;[15] and (perhaps) a translation into French of a hieroglyphics book based on Horopollo, a pseudo-Egyptian writer who was popular among the humanists of the first half of the sixteenth century.[16]

As we have noted, the tradition is that it was Nostradamus' grandfather who taught him astrology, along with the ancient classics and Hebrew. However, this savant died when Nostradamus was very young, and it is more likely that he learned these languages and the stellar arts by way of ordinary education, which then encouraged study in all these subjects. How Nostradamus received the tuition in astrology which led to his being the finest exponent of the art in the sixteenth century remains a mystery, and is part of the fascination we feel for this great man.

The friendship which Nostradamus established with Scaliger has been given too much emphasis in previous accounts of his life. Julius Scaliger did not travel from Italy merely to be with Nostradamus, as so many biographers have suggested – in 1525, he travelled to France to act as physician to the bishop of Agen, the city in which Nostradamus happened to be living. This is how the friendship with Nostradamus was established: however, the humanist's stay in the area was protracted when, at the age of 45, he married a 16-year-old beauty, Andiette de Roques-Lobejac, with whom he had 15 children. We may be sure that Scaliger was involved in some esoteric discipline, not merely from hints in his own writings, but through his friendships with Gauricus (who is supposed to have taught him astrology) and the German painter, Albrecht Dürer, who had once journeyed to Venice in search of certain arcane secrets linked with the Neoplatonic school of Florence. Whether these arcane interests were transmitted to Nostradamus is not known.

As the French commentator P. V. Piobb has pointed out, one tantalizing clue to a possible initiation school surfaced long after the death of Nostradamus.[17] In a colophon at the foot of the title-page of the 1668 Amsterdam edition of the

Prophéties is a well-disguised reference to the 'Son of the Widow'. The colophon reads:

A Amsterdam Chez Iean Iansson à Waesberge et la Vesve du Feu Elizée Weyerstraet. l'An 1668.

At Amsterdam, at the house of Iean Iansson at Waesberge and the Widow of the late Elizee Weyer- straet. The year 1668.

However one reads this, it remains curious (*fig. 8*). Under the rules of the arcane tongue, the repetition of *Iean Ian* is intended to point to the importance of Jean (*Jan*) and the *son* of *Iansson* as two separate words, leaving as an undertone meaning the idea of 'son Jean'. *Vesve*, which could also be read *Vefue*, is widow (*veuve*) in French. It is from verbal acrobatics around this secret argot of the colophon that we derive the only sensible interpretation — namely, that it was intended to indicate a connection with the Sons of the Widow.

'Son of the Widow' may sound an innocuous phrase, yet even today it is an important Masonic term, and was used in both alchemical and arcane circles even before the institution of masonry in Europe. The source for the phrase is Biblical. Hiram Abif, sometimes wrongly claimed as the architect of Solomon's Temple, is called a widow's son, of the tribe of Naphtali. According to the detailed account in *Kings*, Hiram was a skilled metallurgist and craftsman, who decorated the inside of the Temple.[18] Within an esoteric context, Hiram is the name given to one who undertakes to design, build and finish the inner temple, the operative work of the refinement of the inner man. Because of this, Hiram is sometimes given as a name to the one who has achieved this inner magistry, the 'decorating' of the inner temple which is the Self. The Widow's Son means

49

precisely the same as Hiram, and is used to denote an initiate of the highest order. In a survey of this allegory we reach into the mystery behind Madame Blavatsky's observation that the Temple of Solomon was 'a building which never had a real existence', meaning, of course, that it was a school of initiation.[19]

Contained within the name Hiram (which is masculine in Hebrew), is the feminine name Maria, obtained by the simple reversal permitted by occult usage called anastrophe (see Appendix Five). Thus, as in alchemy, the building of the inner temple is involved with bringing together in harmony the male and female, the eternal polarities of Sun and the Moon, King and Queen, *animus* and the *anima*. This was the original meaning in the arcane images of the *conjunctio*, or marriage of two souls, in the alchemical literature (*fig. 9*).

The mystery of the esoteric alchemical background to the Sons of the Widow is confirmed when we note that Maria (Maria Hebraea, Mary the Jew) is regarded as being the greatest of the early Hebrew initiates. Thus we have Hiram as a Hebrew initiate and his shadow-self anima, Maria, as a Hebrew initiate, both associated with Nostradamus through his racial background. The importance of Maria, as an arcane non-Christian name, may be grasped from the fact that the title-page of the remarkable *Symbola Aureae Mensae* of the alchemist Michael Maier portrays Maria at the top of his page, alongside the teacher of all arcane arts, Hermes Trismegistus (*fig. 10*).[20] This is no mere sixteenth-century invention: Maria is mentioned in the third century, both as Maria and as Miriam, the sister of Moses. The name survives in a semi-alchemical context even today, for a large kitchen pan, used for ordinary culinary purposes in France, and which was originally called in alchemical laboratories the *bain-marie*, is named after this same Maria Hebraea: the *bain* was originally a purification bath.

Perhaps this legitimate play with words may lead us to suppose that the initiation of Nostradamus was somehow connected with an arcane cabbalistic school. However – surprisingly in view of his background – there is little convincing evidence of distinctively cabbalistic methods in his quatrains, or in his other writings – unless, of course, this is so profound that it has evaded our gaze. It is evident from his own prose in the quatrains, and perhaps in a couple of verses themselves, that he had read some of the works of the astrologer-monk, Richard Roussat,[21] and we know that this latter had used the writings of the twelfth-century Jewish savant, Ibn Ezra, as the source for some of his chronological computations.

It is claimed – once again without documentary support – that round about 1532 Nostradamus married, and had two children. This reconciliation of opposites was not to last, for the plague, which he had successfully combated on behalf of others, paid him back by carrying away his small family. He seems to have spent the following seven or eight years travelling through various parts of France, and down into Italy. The Italian trip has been extended out of all proportion by some historians and commentators, but a few places do emerge from Nostradamus' own accounts in his *Traité des fardements et confitures*,* and may even be traced in one or two quatrains. He seems to have been in Savona

* Known briefly in the Nostradamian literature as *Fardemens et Confitures* (approximately, 'Cosmetics and Sweets'), the full title of the first 1555 edition is: *Excellent & moult utile Opuscule à tous nécessaires, qui désirent avoir cognoissance de plusieurs exquises Receptes, divisé en deux parties. La première traicte de diverses facons de Fardemens & Senteurs pour illustrer & embellir la face. La seconde nous monstre la facon & maniere, de faire confitures de plusieurs sorts, tant en miel, que succre & vin cuict, le tout mis pas chapîtres, comme est fait ample mention en la Table. Nouvellement composé par maistre Michel de Nostredame docteur en Medicine de la ville de Salon de Craux en Provence, & de nouveau mis en lumiere...*

and Milan, and some historians claim that he went as far east as Venice, which played such an important role in his future history of the Turkish Muslims. Of course, it is difficult to be sure whether he went further south, yet hints of the landscape in a couple of quatrains might suggest that he travelled as far as Naples, and saw the wonder of the new mountain (*Monte Nuovo*) which had been thrown up during a single night, in 1538, and experienced at first hand the disturbing sights of volcanic activity around that western coastline of Italy. It was local tradition which had these rare new islands grow out of the sea overnight, but eye-witness accounts suggest a slower, though equally dramatic growth.[22]

In the November of 1547, Nostradamus married a widow, Anne Ponsart Gemelle, or Anne Poussart, or Pons Jumel, or Genelle – commentators disagree about her name, though in the Latin epitaph she had engraved on the memorial to Nostradamus she is named Anna Pontia Gemella. The correct French name seems to have been Anne Ponsarde, and she appears to have been the widow of Jean Beaulme. While Leroy does not dispute the date of this marriage, he quite rightly wonders why Nostradamus should be portrayed as wandering through Italy within a few months of the nuptials.

The archives show that Nostradamus lived in the Ferreiroux quarter of Salon, and indicate that the town must have been very different in the sixteenth century. In fact, the shape of medieval Salon is revealed most clearly in its street plan, which still follows the outlines of the old defensive walls, punctuated by massive gates. Like many ancient French towns, Salon is a medieval centre besieged by modern traffic. A few medieval buildings have survived: the bell-tower of the church of St Michael still throws its sunrise shadow over the block in which Nostradamus' supposed house is located, and a few hundred yards to the south is the high escarpment which bears the massive château d'Emperi – now also a museum. The square to the south of the church, and below the château, is somewhat incongruously called La Place des Centuries, in homage to the seer. Beyond the ancient château and church – which in the days of Nostradamus saw the installation of the earliest *horlogium* in the south of France – little of medieval Salon remains. However, whatever time has destroyed, concern for tourism has attempted to remedy, with place-names, statues and a museum (*fig. 11 and fig. 12*). The house in the former Place de la Poissonnerie which, it is claimed, Nostradamus owned and died in, is now a sort of museum, of Tussaud-like effigies bathed in *son et lumière*. The narrow street itself has been renamed Rue de Nostradamus.

It was in this house that Nostradamus worked upon casting horoscopes for his many clients, upon his annual *Almanachs*, and upon the more mysterious *Prophéties*, for the remaining years of his life. It was here, as the archives reveal, that the children of the couple were born – Madeleine round about 1551, César perhaps in 1553, Charles in 1556, André in 1557, Anne round about 1558, and Diane in 1561. In fact, it is typical of the confusion surrounding the history of Nostradamus that there should be so much disagreement among writers as to just how many children he did have by his second wife. Jean-Aimé de Chavigny, who knew Nostradamus very well, made it six (three of them boys) while Garencières counted only three. In more recent times, Muraise lists the names of eight. All these accounts seem to be based on misunderstandings.*

---

* After examining the available literature, we must take as definitive the list of six children provided by Dr Edgar Leroy in his genealogical table 3, of *Nostradamus. Ses Origines. Sa Vie. Son Oeuvre,* 1993 edition. This list provides the names of their respective spouses, and reasonable estimates of their dates, along with page references to the textual studies relating to further details about their lives.

Leroy, writing in 1972, confessed with a sense of chagrin that all documents relating to the professional life of Nostradamus in Salon had disappeared. This was certainly true when Leroy's important book was published, but in 1983 Jean Dupèbe published a series of 51 letters (most of them in Latin) to and from Nostradamus, then resident in Salon. The correspondence, relating almost exclusively to his activities as an astrologer, throws a fascinating light upon his work and methods.[23]

In one of these letters, dated February 1556, Gabriel Symeoni – a writer and translator and well-known specialist in the history of the ancient Romans – expressed his hope that Nostradamus' recent visit to the court in Paris had been successful.[24] This passing reference was to one of the most important journeys which Nostradamus undertook in France: he had been commanded by Catherine de' Medici to visit the royal court, presumably to discuss the horoscopes of her children.

According to most commentators – including many respectable French scholars – Nostradamus began his long journey from Salon (the outward leg of which took just over one month) to Paris in 1556. However, it is clear from surviving documents that he arrived on 15 August 1555, which would suggest his journey was a consequence of his fame as an astrologer and almanac-maker, rather than as author of the *Prophéties*. According to César, on his arrival in Paris, Nostradamus was afflicted with gout for a few days, and could not quit his Parisian lodgings. Eventually, he was ordered to journey down to the château at Blois, on the Loire, where the Queen awaited him. The legends and pictorial anecdotes which have gathered around this visit to Paris and Blois have grown prodigiously through the years, and Leroy has made a convincing attempt to show the basis for some of the variations in misunderstandings arising from the subject matter of an engraving in a series of prints,

Theatrum Vitae humanae.[25] However, research has shown that the print in question has nothing to do with Nostradamus.

Equally important in the history of Nostradamus is the trip made by Catherine de' Medici to Salon. As with most tales attached to Nostradamus, this must be taken with a pinch of salt, for it has been so told as to suggest that Catherine went to Salon merely to seek out the savant. In fact, in 1564, the dynasty-builder Catherine determined to introduce her 14-year-old son Charles IX to France. She and her court gritted their teeth, and journeyed for over two years through her royal domain – an extraordinary journey extending over 3,600 kilometres.

It was a convoy which stupefied her subjects almost as much as Catherine. In the south, most of the cities and towns were being ravaged by the plague: huge fires burned openly, partly to dissolve the miasmas believed to encourage the plague, and partly to destroy dead bodies. Some of the towns were deserted: Montélimar was described by one of its inhabitants as nothing more than an open cemetery. Salon had been badly ravaged, as César recorded in his account of the period. Even so, the vast royal retinue arrived at the gates on 17 October 1564, finding a town totally unprepared to receive its unwelcome guests.

The Queen was lodged in the château de l'Emperi, a short walk from Nostradamus' house. Not only did she consult Nostradamus in the château, but she also deigned to visit him in Place de la Poissonnerie. The royal visit is memorialized in the waxen effigies which are supposed to lend a sense of history to each of the rooms of the Nostradamus museum, but the fact is there is little evidence to show what the Queen talked about with the magus. One might suppose that it was about the *Prophéties*, about the future of her children, about their horoscopes, even about the destiny of France and Europe – but the only two who were present at these conversations have held their silence.

Had Catherine the eyes to see futurity, she would have looked with some astonishment upon the destinies of her children – already revealed with such safe obscurity in the quatrains – and taken comfort from the prediction that her sons would all become kings. She is said to have given Nostradamus a purse of two hundred golden écus, and presented him with the patent as councillor and doctor in ordinary to the king. This invisible crowning of his life is almost bowdlerized in a crude portrait woodcut in the 1572 edition of *Prophéties par l'astrologue due tres chrestien Roy de France . . .* by Antoine Crespin, for the celestial globe which this pseudo–Nostradamus holds aloft bears a crown, and below the window are inscribed the words *Nostradamus Astrologue du Roy* (*fig. 13*).

It was in the house in Salon that Nostradamus passed away peacefully, in 1566. According to César, who found the body, Nostradamus had predicted the time of his own death: this legend (if it be legend) grew later into the idea, still given wide credence by the sub-cultural commentators, that Nostradamus predicted his own death in a quatrain. In fact, César was quite specific in his account: some time before, Nostradamus had taken up a copy of the Stadius *Ephemeris*[*] for 1566, and wrote in it *Hic prope mors est* (Here death is close). Later, long after the event, Chavigny recorded that Nostradamus told him, on 1 July, that he would not see him alive at the following sunrise. His body was found, almost cold, on the morning of 2 July, which has led most commentators to assume that he died on that day – especially since César adorned the death with

[*] An ephemeris (plural, ephemerides) is a tabular list, usually given in a sequence of consecutive days, of planetary positions. In the time when Nostradamus lived, all ephemerides gave the zodiacal positions of the planets in geocentric terms.

symbolism by pointing out that it was the festival of the Visitation, 'the true day of Notre Dame'.

What César did not know was that Nostradamus predicted the time of his death more accurately, but in a far more secret way. This prediction was not hidden in the Stadius *Ephemeris*, nor in a quatrain of the *Prophéties*. The prophecy (issued in the arcane manner we have learned to associate with Nostradamus) is found in his own *Almanach* for 1566, which was published by Volant and Brotor. A copy of this extremely rare book was reissued in facsimile by Chomarat in 1987, and is now available for general study.[26]

Following the established formula of these ephemerides, Nostradamus offered a monthly quatrain of predictions in far less obscure language than his more famous verses. The quatrain which heads the monthly predictions for July 1566 is only passably obscure. It contains the prediction, 'The great ones to die . . .' (*fig. 14*). For the brief weather prediction alongside the lunar position (the Moon being in Capricorn), the entry for 1 July notes that the Sun would be in opposition with the Moon, and that the weather would be extremely windy. Later in the same work, in a more extensive commentary for the same day (1 July), he notes once again the winds, the conjunction of Sun and Moon (this time, more specifically, in 7 degrees of Capricorn), but now he observes that the day will bring 'strange transmigrations' (*fig. 15*). Could we take it from these notes that Nostradamus expected to die on 1 July? The arcane references do lead us to suspect that he was under the impression that he would die on this day, rather than early in the morning of the following day, as those who found his body had surmised.

Research into the time of death leads in an interesting direction, and emerged only by accident when we were attempting to check and reconcile data according to the different time-systems used in late medieval Europe. The extraordinary fact is that the astrological data which Nostradamus gives in the entry in his *Almanach*, corresponding to his day of death, seems to be an occult blind!

Although the data is presented very precisely in his table (as one would expect in such a practical thing as an almanac) it is not even remotely accurate. The opposition between Sun and Moon which his *Almanach* predicted for 1 July did not take place until late into 2 July. In an almanac which is otherwise very accurate (given the knowledge of the day), we are led to the conclusion that Nostradamus intended it as an occult blind.

Because of the surprising nature of this information, we have treble-checked the data against a number of ephemerides. Data must allow for the fact that the *Almanach* is given in local time, according to a time system which is no longer in use, and, of course, is derived from the dating system which we now call Old Style – that is, according to the Julian calendar. According to the Julian calendar, the Sun would be in 19 degrees of Cancer on that day, which means that the opposition (*plein Lune*) could not take place for almost another day – certainly not until 2 July. According to the 1996 Winstar ephemeris, the opposition (full moon) would take place at 12.09 p.m., local time Salon, with the Moon in 19:21 Capricorn. However, Nostradamus had been quite specific in the tabulation that the Moon would be in 7 degrees of Capricorn at Full. This was quite impossible, for at full it would have to be diametrically opposite to the Sun, in 18 degrees of Capricorn. Of course, it would be reasonable to argue that the printers made an error – perhaps by inadvertently putting the sigil for the Sun opposite the first, instead of the second day of the month. However, such an argument holds no water, for in his *Prédictions de Juillet*, in the same *Almanach*, Nostradamus reaffirms that the full moon was to occur on the first day of the month, and reasserts that this will take place in 7 degrees and 25 minutes of Capricorn. This we know was quite impossible, so we can only assume that Nostradamus was presenting wrong information in order to make a special point.

The inaccuracy seems to centre only on the first and second days of July. The solar-lunar positions given for the next month, August, are presented accurately, within a few seconds or so: on 14 August the Sun and Moon would both be in 16 degrees Leo. Similarly, the opposition (full moon) for that month was also given accurately, as occurring on 30 August, in 13 degrees of Pisces.

We must assume from such data that the mistake must have been intentional. It is unlikely that Nostradamus would have allowed such an error to creep into his work unintentionally: indeed, he gives the later monthly conjunction (the nominal eclipse) accurately to within a minute or so, as occurring on 16 July, at 7.47 in the evening. What conclusion can we draw from this other than that Nostradamus was disguising, in not very opaque terms, a date (if not, indeed, the actual hour) when he would die? Anyone versed in sixteenth-century astrology would be able to read into this obscurantist play with figures precisely what Nostradamus was getting at, and it surprises us that the secret has lain undiscovered for so long.

The mention of a full moon on 19 degrees of the Cancer–Capricorn axis will have alerted the proficient astrologer to the possible (astrological) cause of death. It will be seen from the radical chart in *fig. 3* that the radical Mars was on 19 degrees of Cancer, and was in opposition to Neptune on 23 degrees of Capricorn. Here we have a basic configuration of a progressed death chart.* We may have

---

* In sixteenth-century predictive astrology, a progressed chart was one in which future expectations were explored by moving forward (that is, 'progressing') planetary and nodal positions by 24 hours (or Earth cycle),

little doubt that it was this configuration to which Nostradamus was pointing when he introduced an intentional error in his *Almanach* tabulations. We have dealt with the essential details of his progressed and transited death charts in the section on his horoscope, Appendix One.

After his passing, Nostradamus' wife, devoted to the last, left a lapidary inscription on his wall tomb in the chapel of the Convent of Les Cordeliers at Salon, in words which confirmed those of Paracelsus about his rare type of genius (*fig. 17*). The full text is given in Appendix Four.

As in the history of other famous men, his tomb was disturbed by later legends and historical events. From time to time, report was made of the discovery of his 'true' tomb, or of the secret opening of the one in Les Cordeliers. In every such legend, further pseudo-prophecies, preserved within the tomb, saw the light of day, with predictions allegedly of profound political importance for contemporaneous readers.[27]

Fact being stranger than fiction, the story of Nostradamus' tomb is more interesting than these pseudoprophecies could encompass. The Convent of the Cordeliers was attacked by soldiery during, or shortly after, the Revolution of 1789, and the tomb of Nostradamus was broken open.

against the natal, or radical, chart. This diurnal movement was taken as representing the passage of one year of life. The theory – in so far as it was expressed – seems to have been that a day in the life of the planets was equivalent to a year in the life of man. Thus, events at the age of 42 would be explored by considering a chart cast for 42 days after birth.

The transited chart was (and, indeed, still is) one in which the future is explored by considering the effects of the movements of planets on a given future day in relation to the planetary positions in the original (the natal, or radical) chart. The planets of the future positions could pass over (that is, 'transit') those of the natal chart, and thereby transmit influences which would be manifest in the life of the native around that time. Thus, in a chart cast for a birth in 1503, the effect of planetary and nodal movements as transits would be considered by examining a chart cast for 1545.

Legends around this pillage have added details which are not supported by the known facts – for example, one tale has a soldier drinking from the smashed cranium of the savant. Whatever happened during that Revolutionary period (which Nostradamus and other prophets had predicted with such accuracy, as will be shown later), the damage to the Convent of the Cordeliers was so extensive that his remains were moved to the church of Saint-Laurent, where they are still preserved. The original epitaph has long been lost – presumably it was destroyed during the pillage of the Convent. That now on the surface of the western wall of the Chapel of the Virgin is the reconstituted version of 1813. The Latin text for this is given in full in Appendix Four. It is recorded that a painting (perhaps, at one time, two paintings) by César used to hang near the tomb – some accounts place them on either side of the walled stone, others place them on the chapel wall opposite. These have disappeared – as the official handbook for Saint-Laurent informs us, 'stolen some years ago'.

A remarkable textual prevision of Nostradamus is contained in a last testament of 1566, which he dictated to the notary, Joseph Roche. In this he mentions quite clearly the wall-tomb of Saint Laurence, where his body was reburied after 1789. The text, scored out from the testament, but still legible, was recorded by Benazra:

> ... *en sépulture dans l'eglise colégié de Sainct Laurens dudict Sallon et dans la Chapelle de Nostre Dame à la muralhe de laquelle a voulu estre faict ung monument* ...

> In the sepulchre in the collegial church of Saint Laurence of the said Salon, and in the Chapel of Our Lady, in the wall of which it is desired to be made a monument ...

As Benazra points out, in his monumental bibliographic survey of Nostradamus, here is the 'ultimate proof' of the prevision of Nostradamus. It is a precisely worded accurate reference to the modern location of the tomb of Nostradamus which would not become a reality for over 220 years, until after the terrible mutations of 1789!

The Convent of the Cordeliers was destroyed shortly after the Revolution, and its memory survives only in the name of the street which skirts the southernmost edge of its former site. Near this spot, where the first tomb had been located, in the square now called Place de Gaulle, stands a fine statue of Nostradamus, sculpted in stone by Joseph Ré in 1867 (*fig. 12*). It is perhaps a fitting footnote that in a quatrain dealing with the Second World War, Nostradamus named the future general whose name is now enshrined in the square in which the seer's own statue would eventually stand.

Even during his lifetime, Nostradamus seems to have attracted many critics. However, there is no sign in any of these critical writings that the quatrains were understood correctly, or that Nostradamus' ability as an astrologer was being appreciated. In view of this, little of the criticism had any validity. Among these critics were those who saw the prediction of the future as being impious, those who could not accept the notion that it was possible to know about the future, and those who could not understand the specialist astrology with which Nostradamus worked. The earliest critique was the pseudonymous Latin tract of 1558, *La Première Invective du Seigneur Hercules le François, contre Monstradamus*, in which Hercules suggested that astrology is an attempt 'to pull God down from the sky by his beard', and put in His place a vain sense of fatality. The text degenerates to little more than uninformed personal abuse. The fact that Nostradamus uses astrology in the 'badinage' of his quatrains is explained as sorcery, designed to direct the ignorance of readers.[28] A pamphlet of the same year, presumably from the same source, is entitled *Le Monstre d'Abus*, which is a homophonic anagram of Nostradamus' name – a sort of contraflow of Green Language technique (which will be explained more fully in Appendix Five).[29]

Even those counted among his friends tended to misrepresent the ideas of Nostradamus. Among these was the disciple Jean-Aimé de Chavigny, who is said to have spent 28 years (too close to the lunar period for us to take this seriously) editing the *Prophéties* after the death of his mentor. The question is: how would it have been possible for even a disciple to have commented on the verses, as fewer than half a dozen had been fulfilled by the time the Master died and it is virtually impossible to read their meanings prior to the events they arcanely describe? As we shall have occasion to point out more than once, Chavigny's text proved notoriously inaccurate in its details of the history of Nostradamus.

So much of the history of Nostradamus is speculative – involving many dissensions as to dates, names and events among even his contemporaneous and early chroniclers – that we must have recourse to his horoscope to determine with any precision just what did and did not happen to him. A brief analysis of the figure is given in Appendix One. Meanwhile, we might ask how this powerful horoscope – a unique map of the skies – fits into the map of the earth.

Viewed with the clarity offered by retrospect, the map of sixteenth-century France revealed that tragic futurity which Nostradamus predicted in several quatrains. Behind almost the entire stretch of its eastern border, from the Mediterranean up to Calais, lurked the vast Germanic Empire. At the northernmost tip of this division was the enclave of Calais, which, as a relic of the battle of Crécy, belonged to the English and was still a thorn in the side of the French. By

1558, when Nostradamus probably published the second part of his *Prophéties*, the area would be captured by the duke of Guise, and returned to France. In one of his prophecies, Nostradamus foresaw that for a short interval during the century Calais would be taken once more by the Spanish, yet after the enterprise of Guise, it was rightly called the *Pays Reconquis*, the 'retaken territory'. To the south-west lay the Kingdom of Navarre, which separated France from the Kingdom of Spain.

Aloof to the north, protected by the Channel, was the Kingdom of England, which Nostradamus sometimes called the *Isles*, sometimes *Brittanique*, and which he foresaw would dominate the world with an Empire, or (as he called it in a famous quatrain) the *Pempotam*, or 'All-powerful'. If his contemporaries could have interpreted this quatrain correctly, they would have been surprised. In 1555, few Frenchmen rated England very highly: it was an error of judgement for which they would pay dearly over the next two and a half centuries. While they had no doubt that their belle France would lead the future, they were, in the mid-sixteenth century, a mite apprehensive about the threat from Spain, and a little uneasy about that long Germanic border to their east. The early commentators on this quatrain, being French, played down the lines about Britain, and saw in it a prediction that Germany would be subdued by a great French monarch, and the expanded French Empire would last without change into the future. All wishful thinking no doubt, but evidence of just how small was the part played by England in the French vision of their futurity.

As the prophecies of Nostradamus unfolded, they would reveal the dramatic interactions of these four countries, first in turn, then in concert. Mars – the god of war, rapine and carnage – would dominate: during the next four centuries there would scarcely be a decade when there was not some bloodlust of military action across one or other of these unstable and ever-changing borders.

France itself consisted of a medley of fiefdoms, where local traditions and loyalties ran more strongly than any sense of nationalism. When Nostradamus was called to Paris, and then to Blois, by Catherine de' Medici, he faced a difficult journey through at least seven different domains and duchies. The largest political unit in the country was the royal domain of France – large, but weakened by extensive borders, for it was something of a patchwork – including Normandy, the Ile-de-France (centred on Paris), Champagne, Berry, Poitou, Guyenne, Dauphine and Languedoc. The fiefdoms which had fallen to the French crown by 1527 included the huge terrains of the Duchy of Brittany, Picardy, and the Duchy of Burgundy, gathered in a triad-like protection – or threat – around Paris. To the south was Provence. Here, in tiny Salon, Nostradamus wrote his prophecies, and in modern times a gigantic acrylic fresco reminds one of his astrologic powers and of his connections with the royal court (*fig. 18*). To the north of Provence was the Dauphiné, which included Lyons, where his first books of *Prophéties* were published, from 1555 onwards. A tiny wedge of country between the Dauphiné and Provence, bordering to the west on Languedoc, was Venaissin (which embraced Orange and Avignon), a cartographic hangover which still belonged to the Italian Papacy, and was inhabited among considerable pomp by a Papal Legate. Other fiefdoms included Angoulême and the Duchy of Bourbon, added to the French crown in 1527, and the buffer fiefs along the border with Navarre.

If one seeks to understand the cryptic writings of Nostradamus, then one has to picture with some accuracy this maze of duchies, fiefdoms and domains, since the Master would sometimes use the name of a town or city – or even the name of a river – to denote an area. This

method, which belongs as much to exoteric literature as the
esoteric, was sometimes called synecdoche (see Appendix
Five). By means of this technique, Nostradamus might
write a verse threatening future warlike events for the cities
of Pau, Tarbes or Auch, which would in reality presage a
future conflict between the Kingdoms of France and
Navarre.* This event might occur so long in the future
that the map of France would have changed, leaving the old
divisions merely as memories, defunct keys useful only for
the unlocking of an antique quatrain. It is this which
explains why so many commentators have constructed
gazetteers – usually of questionable value – to help those
seeking meaning in the *Prophéties*.[30]

In this patchwork of domains, Paris was France.
Ensconced in the walled city was the reigning monarch,
King Henry II, to whom Nostradamus dedicated the
second book of his *Prophéties* which appeared in 1558 –
which explains why the stylized head of the monarch is
found in later editions (*fig. 19*). Married to the formidable
Catherine de' Medici, and enamoured of several pretty
mistresses, Henry was under the dominion of women all his
life. Although physically active, he was of mediocre
intelligence, and it was doubtful he would have understood
the secret history of future France which Nostradamus
dedicated to him in 1558. We suspect it unlikely that he
took up the offer of Nostradamus to explain the meaning of
these arcane predictions, and the future of his beloved
France: if he did, then he remained silent about the
outcome, and, like so many things connected with Nostradamus, the explanation is now shrouded in the past.[†]

---

* Of course, the old Kingdom of Navarre no longer exists: it was sliced
up first by Ferdinand, and then by Henri IV. Pau is now in the Basses-
Pyrénées, Tarbes in the Hautes-Pyrénées, and Auch is in Gers.
† We think that Nostradamus said that he could explain the meaning of
his quatrains to the king out of politeness, or respect (he was, after all,

In 1559, Henry's robust energies would prove his undoing, for he would die in a jousting tournament, knowing full well that clairvoyants had warned him not to indulge in such activities. His painful death would bring instant renown to Nostradamus, for in the 1555 printing of his *Prophéties* the savant had recorded this future event in a remarkably precise verse (see page 235 ff). The king's death had helped Nostradamus, for after 1559, his reputation as a seer was assured: it was probably a good thing for the *amour propre* of his contemporaries that they could not read the future he foresaw for their city and country.

The eternal city of Rome, the nominal centre of Catholicism, was a long way from Paris in the sixteenth century, yet its influence was so pervasive in France that it was almost as though its ancient walls footed on the Seine. This perhaps explains why Nostradamus so frequently dated the events of his quatrains by arcane reference to this or that reigning Pope, as though a pontiff might carry the Saturnine scythe as arbiter of time. The year 1555 was almost unique, for it saw three Popes in Rome. At the death of Julius III, Marcello Cervini was elected as Marcellus II in April, yet he died in the same month. He was succeeded by Giovanni Pietro Caraffa, who took the name of Paul IV. Paul was of noble birth, nepotistic and autocratic in attitude, with an unerring ability to upset almost every foreigner with whom he had dealings. Even before his elevation, he had lent limited support to the extermination of heresy through the instrument of the Inquisition, but,

currying royal favour). Nostradamus would have known that the king would not really be very interested – he was a royal bear of little brain. More to the point, Nostradamus knew that the king did not have much longer to live. The *Epistle*, like most medieval dedications, was probably intended to solicit royal patronage and royal attention – both of which he received.

once in power, he let this repressive streak have its head, much to the horror of the Italians around him.

In the year of his election, Paul IV entered into a pact with France to drive the Spanish from Italy, but the arms of Philip II soon proved too much for him. In spite of this setback, throughout the remainder of his life he never ceased in his attempts to foment a war between the two nations. It was largely his unfriendly attitude to Elizabeth I of England (whom he persisted in regarding as illegitimate, and, furthermore, a ruler of a country which really belonged to the Papacy) which deepened the Protestant schism in that country. When he died in 1559, Paul IV was so despised even by his fellow Italians that the populace of Rome took it upon themselves to demolish his statue and set free from his dungeons the prisoners incarcerated by the Inquisitors. It is not surprising that such a drama-filled life should be encapsulated into four prophetic lines by Nostradamus.

The major conflicts and fears of the century were born of religious differences. The internal differences in Europe were between the Catholics and the Protestants. The latter would shortly be called *Huguenots* by the French, supposedly a romance-softened version of the German word, *Eidgenossen.*

The external differences lay in the conflicts – seemingly perpetual – between Christian Europe and the Islamic Turks. Each of these internal and external religious conflicts figure in a large number of Nostradamus' quatrains, which noted the troubles between Catholics and Huguenots and the more disturbing rise and fall of the Ottoman Turks. Had his readers been able to tease meaning from the arcane verses, they would probably have looked forward to the future with more serenity. In a number of

---

* In German, *Eidegenosse* means confederate, and applies specifically to a Swiss subject. The root, *Eid*, is a solemn oath – the basis of confederacy.

quatrains, Nostradamus predicted that by the end of the sixteenth century the terrible threat from the Turks would recede (see page 131 ff). As it was, in their inability to understand the quatrains, his readers must have blanched each time they saw in the verses the word *Selin*, or one of its variants, as they would recognize in this either the name of the ruler of the Turks, or an arcane reference to the Muslims. Before this Islamic power waned, Nostradamus foresaw the terrible siege of Malta (which occurred the year before he died), and the later siege of Cyprus with its related sea battle of Lepanto.

In Geneva, Calvin's version of Protestantism was in the ascendancy. While the Genevois feared the *Selin* as a human monster, they feared Paul IV even more as the Antichrist incarnate. On the other hand, Marcellus, and Julius before him, had been Antichrists, for in the opinion of the Genevois, the Papacy itself was from the Inferno. In their break for papal domination, the Calvinists made from Geneva their own heaven, yet circumscribed it with hellish rules. When, in 1555, a Genevois goldsmith fashioned from gold a beautiful chalice for the Mass, he was punished for the crime, as this was rampant popery. Nostradamus was worried by Geneva, and left an admonitory, if somewhat ambiguous, quatrain about the dangers of the city (see page 254 ff). However, deeply felt as the quatrain is, Nostradamus must have been diffident about his verse. His great mentor, the Abbot Trithemius, had predicted that, after 1525, the religion of the Protestants would find itself in an ascendancy which would last until 1880, or 1881.

In spite of Calvin and his Antichrists, an even greater revolution was taking place. The earth was being tipped from its ancient sacred place at the centre of the cosmos, and into the vacuum was being levered the Sun. Copernicus had published his epoch-making *De Revolutionibus* in 1543, yet by 1555 those who accepted his views could be counted upon one hand. More usual was the attitude of Luther who observed tartly, and with a prevision he did not intend, 'The fool seeks to overturn the whole science of astronomy.'[31] The revolution might have begun in the sixteenth century, but it has rocked astrology scarcely at all since those days. While some modern astrologers do use heliocentric charts, the majority are just as happy with their geocentrics as those of the sixteenth century.

Who were these astrologers, and about what did they astrologize? Like all mathematicians (as Nostradamus was called reverently in letters from many parts of Europe), they cast personal horoscopes, and 'elections' relating to daily tragedies and joys – touching on robberies, losses, adultery, love-suits and so on. Those who served villages and towns seemed not always to have an easy time: in the eyes of the Church, astrology savoured of fortune-telling, which in turn smelled of demons, and such practitioners were frowned upon. In some cities and towns it was even proscribed.

It was a different story in the royal palaces and châteaux, however, for almost every power-possessor had his or her own astrologer. Probably the most enlightened patron was Philip II of Spain, who left his own monastic tomb, the Escorial, as a monument to astrology, but who was, in 1555, consulting his mathematicians regarding the outcome of his wars in Italy. Philip had required an astrologer to determine the orientation for his Escorial to the sunset of 10 August, the feast of St Lawrence: ironically, the battle of Saint-Quintin, fought in 1557 – and which the Escorial orientation nominally commemorates – had been predicted by Nostradamus in 1555. Philip numbered among his most illustrious horoscopists the great hermeticist, John Dee, who cast the King's chart on more than one occasion. In fact, different versions of Philip's horoscope appear in a large number of books on astrology published in the mid-sixteenth century: what is disturbing about them is that there seems to be little agreement as to precisely when Philip was born.[32]

In England, Elizabeth I employed the same John Dee as had cast the figures for the King of Spain. Dee was a Rosicrucian* and brilliant scholar, and the first man ever to write a whole book about a single occult sigil or sigillum. This was the famous 'Monad', of his *Monas Hieroglyphica* which appeared in 1583, and was eventually adopted as a secret symbolic device by other Rosicrucians. Astrology was still popular in Italy, even outside the courts, for certain forms of the art were studied in universities. As late as the first decade of the next century, it flourished even in the Vatican, for records show that Urban VIII (who helped in the condemnation of Galileo) studied the art under Campanella.

Catherine de' Medici's powerful position gave her licence to choose her astrologers, and, even though she consulted Nostradamus, she imported others from Italy. She was far too Italian ever to throw off her matriarchal

---

* In spite of many suggestions to the contrary, there is no evidence that Nostradamus was involved in the Rosicrucian movement. The name given to this initiate-led movement was first used in the fifteenth century, in reference to the followers of Christian Rosenkreuz. However, the movement did not come into the open until the publication of a text, the *Fama Fraternitatis*, in 1614. The essential idea behind the movement was to reform, by inner activities, meditation and political manipulation, the Christian religion. It was successful in so far as it preserved and promulgated certain tenets relating to esoteric Christianity, which are now an integral part of European culture. Its followers introduced into the stream of European culture a new awareness of alchemical symbolism, which led to the foundation of modern psychology, the beginnings of esoteric astrology, an esoteric approach to Christianity, and the principles of reincarnation. Altogether, it was the most important stream of medieval occultism to have permeated European life. However, as we shall indicate in Appendix Three, the indications are that Nostradamus belonged to a much older stream of initiation.

nature and aspirations. By all accounts, she used – or hired magicians to use – the forbidden necromancy to peer into the futurity of her sons. Perhaps it is this which explains why Jaubert should lament that the great Nostradamus was later tarred with the same brush of participating in looking into the future with the aid of demons.[33]

As we have seen, it is probably his reputation as an astrologer and almanac-maker that persuaded Catherine to order Nostradamus to Paris, where he might cast and read the horoscopes of her children. However, it can hardly have been his contact with these future kings and queens that induced him to include miniature future histories of their decline in his *Prophéties*. At least half a dozen of his quatrains relate to the sad history of the Valois dynasty,* and he recorded – fortunately in lines so cryptic that Catherine could not comprehend them – that she would outlive her beloved sons, who would be kings for only a very short time.

In spite of the Queen's interest, the art of astrology was at an all-time low in Paris. John Guido, working as a physician in Paris, published astronomical works in 1543 from which we learn something of his personal despair. In this year, he bemoaned the fact that few knew any longer how to predict by astrological rules. In his eyes, astrology had become the shield for the iniquities of the necro-mancers, and other pseudo-diviners.[34] His laments may

---

* The family of the Valois (which Nostradamus sometimes referred to as the Capet) came to the throne of France in 1328, with the accession of Philip VI. He was the first of what the French historians call the *Valois directs*, a line which came to an end with Charles VIII, in 1498. The second branch, the *Valois-Orléans*, was represented by Louis XII, who came to the throne on the death of Charles, and died in 1515. The third line, which was the main subject of Nostradamus' royal quatrains, was the *Valois-Angoulême*, which began with Francis I, and terminated with Henry III (the son of Catherine de' Medici and the unfortunate Henry II), who died in 1589.

have been valid for Paris, but astrology was alive and well in other parts of France, and one wonders what booksellers Guido frequented.

Many of the figures cast in these royal and aristocratic circles have survived into modern times, printed in the collections of such academic-occultists as the theologian and friar Junctinius, who devoted most of his working life to the study of astrology. In one such work, the German astrologer, John Garcaeus, furnished over four hundred figures, many of individuals who are still well known today. His main work, the *Brief Treatise*,[35] published in 1556, is an attempt to establish a proper method of determining and reading horoscopes in order to ensure accurate prediction.

A great many of the famous horoscopes of the mid-sixteenth century were cast by astrologers using the ephemerides, or planetary tabulations, of Regiomontanus. The beautifully printed Venetian *Almanach*, while not accurate by modern standards, offers a most useful record for assessing what sixteenth-century astrologers would have considered to be valid positions, in their own charting.

In the Paris of 1555, then, it was as though Copernicus, with his sun-centred planetary diagrams, had never existed, even though his *De Revolutionibus* had been published in an astrological spirit, and would soon provide a more reliable system for predicting the planetary positions. This system, the *Prutenic Tables* constructed by Erasmus Reinhold,* were ephemerides calculated according to the heliocentric systems of Copernicus; Stadius based his own *Ephemerides* for 1554 to 1570 on them. These were available to astrologers after 1551, and a new precision was possible,

---

* Erasmus Reinhold was professor of mathematics at Wittenburg university, a keen astrologer, and an early supporter of Copernicus. As early as 1542, in his *New Theory of Planets*, he recognized the need for a new set of more accurate ephemerides, derived from the Copernican model.

even if these were taken advantage of by few in Paris. In the sixteenth century, the tabular system of Regiomontanus, with its different approach to cusp interpretation, was favoured.

While there is no longer any mystery as to which tables and ephemerides Nostradamus used for his ordinary astrological purposes, whence he obtained his accurate data for the precise astrological predictions in the quatrains is one of the great mysteries of the age. One suspects that a seer who had the ability to perceive and predict stellar events – such as the Nova of 1572 (which, of course, occurred after his death – see page 247 ff) – and to date these, would seem to have no need of terrestrial ephemerides. The most intriguing mystery surrounding the astrology of Nostradamus is whence he derived his advance intelligence of precise planetary and stellar positions well beyond the twentieth century.

In the sixteenth century, the great Islamic schools of Baghdad still leaned over the shoulders of astrologers. The symbols of these Arabs had found their way on to the façades of Gothic churches* (the great receptacles of

---

* The ancient forms of astrology, as an esoteric science and practical art, were transmitted to Europe mainly by way of Islamic Spain, from the eleventh century onwards. Although the Church feared that the astrological symbols were essentially pagan, they recognized that there were some classical, and indeed early-Christian, justification for accepting and Christianizing them. The Arabic versions of the Graeco–Roman lore were of considerable importance, in view of the vast programme of building which the Church contemplated from the eleventh century onwards. The Church, having rejected in the early days the Gnostic cosmologies, which were astrologically based, really had no system of cosmological symbolism other than the Angelic Orders, or spiritual hierarchies, which the fourth-century Dionysius the Areopagite had linked with the planetary spheres. This meant that the Arabic symbols of planets, zodiac and stars was a blessing to the new Christian architects, and explains why the ecclesiastics permitted such pagan symbols into their church fabric, in the form of floor zodiacs and planetary images. The eleventh-century monastic building

arcane symbolism), and their lore was still whispered into the ears of astrologers. Even the symbols used by modern astrologers had been passed to medieval astrologers by the Arabs, engraved upon their astrolabes. Among the titles of three books which have turned up in recent times, bearing the *ex libris* signature of Nostradamus, is a work by Alcabitius (*fig. 20*) – a Latinized name for the tenth-century Arabic astrologer, Al-Kabisi, who was favoured by Chaucer for specific mention, alongside Ptolemy.[36] The Arab's astrological writings were so well known in six-teenth-century Europe that when a jurist sought to praise Turrel as a prodigy of learning, he called him 'another Alcabitius in Astrology'. Turrel would have been proud of the comparison, for he had a sufficient regard for Alcabitius to publish, in 1520, his work on judicial astrology, augmented with his own textual notes.

An important work by Oronce Finé,[*] relating to the use of almanacs, included a treatise on conjunctions (mainly the superior conjunctions, which were so important in Arabic predictive work) by Alcabitius. The *ex libris* edition seems to have come into the possession of Nostradamus too late to fall into our own rather specialist study of the

of Sagrada di San Michele, in the Val di Susa, Italy, is probably the earliest of the surviving buildings in which the Arabic cosmological symbolism is still evident. The prime arcane centre of this late-medieval astrology is the thirteenth-century San Miniato al Monte, in Florence, while the deepest esoteric stream of astrology still survives in the later cathedral at Chartres. For a deeper study, see F. Gettings, *The Secret Zodiac: the hidden art in mediaeval astrology,* 1979.

[*] Oronce Finé, usually Latinized in his works as Orontius Finaeus, was born in 1494, and was among the most influential French astrologers of the following century. In his youth, he had spent some years in prison because of his astrological predictions, but by the age of 36 had been made royal professor of mathematics. We shall mention several important astrological works by Finé, and comment on his connection with the school at Beauvais.

quatrains, but it does offer some evidence of the influence of Arabic astrology upon the master, as well as indicating his general interest in the superior conjunctions with which he peppers his own verses, and without an understanding of which the quatrains remain impenetrably obscure.

The literature of the sixteenth century was flooded with prophecy and prediction, much of which had little to do with astrology, but which had its roots in an ancient past. Among the early prophetical writings which mention Nostradamus by name is the *Pleiades* of Nostradamus' student Chavigny who, in 1603, offered an anthology of predictions relating to the downfall of the Turks, which he mingled liberally with stories of the future collapse of Christendom.[37]

Following the traditional lines of such books on predictions, Chavigny glances through a considerable number of prophecies relating to the supposed imminent triumph of France, and the decadence of the Turkish Empire. In his Preface, he announces that he is not merely attempting to explain these predictions, but seeking also to relate them to the prophecies made by Nostradamus. Unfortunately, he seems to make no serious attempt to keep this promise, though some of his one-liner descriptions of future events do appear to be lifted from the quatrains. One set of predictions he takes from François Liberati are based on the same astrological lore of trigon revolutions* that Nostradamus used in his verses.[38]

From his readings of Liberati, Chavigny concluded that from 1583 up to 1782 France would develop a sublime monarchy. Islamic law would last only up to the year 1980. In this same time, the monarchy of the Romans would also

---

* The theory of planetary revolutions derived from Arabic astrology, and applied by medieval astrologers to the study of historical events. The 'revolutions' of Jupiter and Saturn appear time and time again in the quatrains of Nostradamus.

burn up, and there would be great earthquakes (*tremblemens de terre*, he writes, in a style reminiscent of Nostradamus), apparitions and comets – along with the dissolution of kingdoms, laws and constitutions.

The popularity of such prophecies in the sixteenth century may puzzle the modern mind. In the twentieth century, while we may pay lip-service to the idea that there are certain cycles – fiscal cycles, economic cycles, life cycles, cycles of peace and war, perhaps even cycles determined by celestial events, such as the Takata effects and the Kolisko sap cycles – we have lost any feeling that the cosmos directs history, or that the cosmos is itself a living being.[39] Most of us cannot conceive of history as being the representation of Providence working out its own will. However, in the late-medieval period, it was believed that history was directed by spiritual beings – by angels, archangels and archai (approximately, 'the old ones'), the first of whom were concerned with individual destinies, the second of whom were concerned with the destinies of nations, and the third of whom were governors of historical periods. For the medieval mind, history was a meaningful process in which the Divine worked out the salvation of man. The Coming of the Antichrist, the renewal of the Church, the thousand years of peace, the manifestation of Christ – all such things were part of the Divine plan, prepared for by angelic beings. In the early part of the sixteenth century, the great Abbot Trithemius of Sponheim even named the planetary beings who governed history, and set out their periodicities with the precise dates when their reigns would begin and end (see pages 154–5).[40] On the strength of this knowledge (which seems to have been at least as old as Christianity), Trithemius even ventured a few prophecies himself, for in so doing, he recognized that he was serving God's purpose.

In the sixteenth century, almost all prophecy was rooted

in the notion that history was little more than the manifestation of God's purpose. Prophecy was one of several means of enabling men to work out the intention behind God's directing of history. This explains the preoccupation which Catholics and Protestants of the time had with the notion of the End of Things, the Last Judgement, the coming of the Antichrist, and their varied visions of the renewal (or *renovatio*, to use a term from the quatrains of Nostradamus, carried over from the traditional literature of prophecy) of a world sunken in iniquity, and the inevitable demonization of the leaders of the various religious or cult leaders, such as the Pope or Luther.

Biblical exegesis – especially of the 'prophets', and of Revelation – figures in most of the prophetical writings in the five centuries prior to the sixteenth. Perhaps the most important stream was that of the Joachimites,* around which a vast prophetic literature had developed. This persisted into the sixteenth century in the ideas of such revolutionary thinkers as Paracelsus, whose interpretation of the prophetic *Vaticinia* (an illustrated prophetic text, spuriously associated with Joachim di Fiore, dealing with the supposed future of the papacy, and, to a lesser extent, the history of Europe) was extremely popular, and in the more febrile writings of William Postel, perhaps the most learned arcanist of the sixteenth century and more of a visionary than was healthy for him.

Paracelsus seems to have published his collection of 32 woodcuts with Latin commentaries shortly after 1536, as

---

* The Joachimites were the followers of the twelfth-century monk-prophet, Joachim di Fiore. The prophetic stream in his thinking was derived from a play with the occult meanings of numbers, linked with somewhat imaginative Biblical exegesis. Some of his followers developed Joachim's theory of historical periods (on which his prophecies were based) beyond all recognition, and from these stemmed prophecies of the end of the world, for near the middle of the thirteenth century.

his *Prognosticatio*.[41] They were modelled on the Joachimite *Vaticinia*, yet remain enigmatic, for all they are 'explained' by the Paracelsian commentaries. The arcane imagery of the woodcuts convinces us that Nostradamus was familiar with the *Prognosticatio*. After all, his friend Scaliger knew them well enough to write a characteristic diatribe against them: at times we may even read the line of a quatrain as though it were a reference to one or other of these hieroglyphics. Depending upon how the images are translated, interesting parallels may be established with Nostradamus. For example, in 1536, the three *fleur de lys* on the dying branch (*fig. 21*) could refer to the future (more accurately, the lack of future) of the Valois dynasty. The last of the three scions would die out in France during that century. By the time Nostradamus wrote his quatrains, he was left only with the destiny of the Valois-Angoulême, a flower that would wither in 1589 with the assassination of Henry III, the son of his patron.

Postel was more overt than Paracelsus as to the purpose behind his prophecies. His call for a moral renewal, missionary zeal and military conquest was ostensibly directed towards allowing God's purpose in history to manifest into a New Order. This new dispensation was to be headed by a sovereign triplicity of Pope, King and Judge, benignly regnant over a world culture wherein the confused post-Babel tongues had been suppressed, along with other such evils as private property.

Almost up to the last year of his long life, in 1581, Postel was still proclaiming that the End was nigh, and attempting to persuade Henry III of France to institute reforms which would ensure the growth of his own Imperial triad. Postel had predicted that the Holy Land was to be the religious empire of the future, while his beloved France was to be the temporal centre of empire. We have to presume from this that even a man as proficient as Postel in occultism – and indeed in the Green Language – had not understood those quatrains in which Nostradamus apportioned the Empire of futurity to Britain (see page 427).

It is easy to dismiss Postel's dreams, in the light of what did happen in Europe after the sixteenth century. However, as Marjorie Reeves has observed, in her excellent book on the subject of medieval prophecy,[42] in seeking to place this 'fantastic dreamer' Postel in his setting, we should not forget that he had been a professor in the University of Paris, and had the ears of both the King of France and the Emperor Ferdinand.

The *Conseils et Predictions* of Jean de Blois, offered to King Charles VII of France in 1455, seems to have been a pot-pourri of all the usual prophets, including the dicta of those remarkable women the Sibyls and Hildegarde of Bingen, Joachim, the fourteenth-century hermit Telesphorus, and so on. Traces of most of these may be discerned in odd phrases and passing references in the verses of Nostradamus. Jean's predictions – borrowed from Telesphorus – proved to be universally wrong. Charles did not become the destroyer of Rome, and nor was he crowned emperor of the Western World by the mystic Angelic Pope. Nor did he retake the Holy Land from the Moors.

While it is evident that Nostradamus was influenced to some extent by such varied streams of prophecy, his interests are, on the whole, less generalized, less epic, yet more poignantly precise. He would not, like Jean de Blois, eulogize an emperor or king, though he would construct an arcane verse to say what that ruler might achieve, or how he would die. When Nostradamus dedicated the completed *Prophéties* to Henry II of France in 1558, he had already predicted, three years earlier, the precise and cruel nature of this king's death (see page 235 ff). Only the obscurity of his verse disbarred the king and his courtiers from being privy to the meaning of this quatrain.

There can be few more useful comparisons for reaching into the heart of Nostradamus than that which may be drawn between him and Wolfgang Lazius. Lazius was historian to the Emperor Ferdinand I, and the author of a number of erudite books. His compilation of prophecies, gathered from every available source, was more than the usual bland collection of ancient recipes for the future, for it attempted to draw from the ancient lines references which made sense in terms of history. Lazius was especially interested in sixteenth-century futurity, and in the significance of the Roman emperor, Charles V, who ruled during the greater part of Nostradamus' life. By 1547, he had compiled his definitive collection of predictions – incidentally, just in time to miss Nostradamus from his pages. Perhaps Lazius was right, and Charles V was a great emperor and courageous man, but unfortunately, he did not succeed in implementing a single one of the prophecies so carefully laid down for his future by the hapless historian-turned-prophet.

In contrast to the poor predictive record of Lazius, it is unlikely that a single quatrain of Nostradamus may be proved to have been incorrect. The historian had depended upon techniques of extrapolation and fervent hope, while, as we have emphasized, the Savant of Salon depended upon Divine Enlightenment, astrological learning, and the ability to read the Akashic Records. He depended, in a word, on his initiation into the secret lore (see Appendix Three), concerning which Lazius knew nothing.

Although a vast number of predictions and prophecies have survived from the sixteenth century, it is unlikely that the period was any more superstitious than any other. Probably, it was the influence of the new printing presses which lent so much weight to this popular genre, and earned for the century a reputation for an obsession with the future. Then, as now, the future was fed by present fears. The cheap prophetic pamphlets and broadsheets which poured from the presses in this period were mainly concerned with the bogeyman of sixteenth-century Europe – the Turk – but serviced on a much lower level (and perhaps with less accuracy) the need of peasant farmers to know about future weather conditions. Fear of Islamic expansionism was deep-seated, and understandably increased by the taking of Cyprus in 1571, dealt with by Nostradamus in another quatrain (see page 241 ff). The fear was only partly relieved by the battle of Lepanto in the same year. This latter event had been predicted and dated in the *Prophéties* in more than one quatrain (see page 129 ff), and his contemporaries must have been able to read the general meaning, if not the specific references, in these verses. In contrast to Nostradamus' accurate, and rather surprising, predictions that the Turks would be beaten by force of European arms, a dark prophecy by Johann Hilten (a Franciscan monk of Eisenbach, who died the year before Nostradamus was born), presumably based on mere extrapolation, maintained that by 1600 the Turks would have invaded and would be ruling both Italy and Germany.[43]

Along with the threat of Islam, the End of the World was a popular and highly saleable theme. In 1553 a noted German scholar, Gaspar Brusch, in a preface written to accompany an edition of the writings of the thirteenth-century abbot Engelbert, had proclaimed, in bland German doggerel, that the world would come to an end in 1588.[44] In fact, this was the German version of the verse which Gaspar Brusch found in the monastery of Noricum,[*] and which he supposed was written by the great astrologer Regiomontanus. Its banal style, devoid entirely of grace of inner content, or intelligent ambiguity, makes an interesting

---

[*] In ancient times, it was a province between the Danube and the Alps. Of course, archaizing medieval writers often kept these names alive, even after the countries themselves had disappeared.

comparison with the arcane verses of Nostradamus, and (incidentally) seems to release Regiomontanus of authorship. When Nostradamus came to 1588 in his visions, he presented a far less globular-threatening set of predictions – mentioning only the assassination of Henry of Guise at Blois and (some say) the great Armada of Philip II. The effect of the prediction (even in a period which was inundated by end-of-world prophecies) was very powerful, and must have contributed to the decision by Paul IV to put the entire corpus of Brusch on the Index,* in 1559.

As we shall see, when we examine a quatrain which contains a reference from the writings of Turrel, this astrologer's prophecy that the End of the World would come as a finale to the eighteenth century seems to have impressed several writers of the sixteenth century, including Nostradamus. (Turrel's prediction was not new, and was probably based on those made by the ninth-century Arabian astrologer, Albumasar, as a result of his study of planetary revolutions.) Turrel's version of the prophecy was made some time before 1531.[45] His method of reckoning was, even by the standards of sixteenth-century astrology, extremely arcane, but he came to the conclusion that the world would end about 1800 – which is 270 years

---

* The *Index Librorum Prohibitorum* (Index of Forbidden Books) is an official list kept by the Roman Catholic Church of books which are banned – banned in the sense that Catholics are prohibited from reading them, save under exceptional circumstances. The first Index appears to have been set up by the Inquisition in 1557, but long before that successful attempts were made to have specific books banned. At one time, the list was so extensive, so inclusive of quality literature, that a good Catholic would have found himself hard pressed to gain any culture outside the study of Church doctrine. It is certainly strange that a list which included the writings of Descartes, Montaigne, Pascal and Voltaire (to stay only with the French) never mentioned the far more revolutionary Nostradamus. No doubt, he was protected by his obscurity of expression.

after writing. Turrel seems to have died shortly after completing the French version of this Latin version, in 1531, which implies that the tradition that he predicted the end for 1789 or 1792 may not be far off the mark. In another passage Turrel predicts the Antichrist will appear some 25 years after a 'marvellous conjunction' expected in 1789. Did this prediction contribute to the idea that Napoleon was the Antichrist? It has been argued that Nostradamus was influenced by Turrel, but the issue is not that of influence so much as parallel visions. Nostradamus gave such precise details of what would happen in France in 1789, and subsequently, that we may be sure that he had some direct vision of these events. Turrel seems to have arrived at his date purely by consideration of astrology.

It is absolutely impossible to understand the astrology of the sixteenth century – and particularly the astrology of Nostradamus – without considering the many different forms of the art which were practised in those days. In so far as astrology played an important role in such historically motivated prophecy, it was through what is called Mundane Astrology. In this branch of the art, astrologers used what they called 'revolutions', 'ingresses', 'eclipse charts' and planetary conjunctions in the *trigoni elementali*. These trigoni seem to be fundamental to the astrological method of Nostradamus, and need some sort of explanation. The cycles of Saturn and Jupiter are such that they conjunct with a regular periodicity of approximately 20 years. A number of such conjunctions take place in zodiacal signs of the same elements. That is to say, for example, that for a specific number of years, Saturn and Jupiter will conjunct in the Earth signs of Taurus, Virgo and Capricorn (*fig. 22*).

Another astrological technique widely used in the sixteenth century was that of ingresses. An ingress is the movement of a planet (most usually, the Sun) into a new zodiacal sign. So far as the Sun is concerned, there are twelve ingresses each year. The predictive technique which revolved around ingresses consisted of casting a chart for the moment of ingress for a month (or, more usually, for the beginning of a season), to gain some insight into the events for that period. Several of the ingress charts cast by Nostradamus have survived. For example, in his *Almanach* for 1566, Nostradamus printed four figures erected for the seasonal solar ingresses (*fig. 23*): these seem to be the basis for his somewhat dire readings of futurity found in the almanac.[46] From such ingresses and conjunctions great floods, fires, and wars were predicted by astrologers anxious to make their mark, or a good living, by terrorizing their contemporaries.[47]

As in all ages, there was in the France of 1555 a plethora of astrological rubbish, cascading over and obscuring one or two gems. The rubbish is much like the popular astrology which abounds in our own day, and need not concern us here. What is of interest is that, while there seems to have been little astrological activity by native Frenchmen in Paris itself, there was a school of astrology in Beauvais, to the north of Paris.

The centre for this school – which seems to have had an esoteric base – was Oronce Finé, who had studied grammar and philosophy in Paris, yet somehow found himself teaching mathematics and astrology at Beauvais.[48] Finé appears to have been imprisoned for some years because of an astrological prediction which disturbed the political or religious status quo: among those who petitioned for his release was the influential occultist, Agrippa von Nettesheim. By 1530, Finé's misdemeanour seems to have been forgotten, for he was made royal professor of mathematics under Francis I. It has been argued that it is this royal appointment which shielded him when he elected to write and teach about astrology in a city generally unreceptive to such a subject. Whatever the reasons, he translated and published a number of works on astrology, and even on magic. As we have noted, a practical instructional guide to the use of ephemerides and almanacs, published as *Les Canons*, was reprinted in Paris in 1556, along with a work of the Arabic astrologer, Alcabitius, on the ever-popular superior conjunctions, but his most influential book was the *Mundi Sphaera* (*fig. 24*), which, along with the *Methodus* of Garcaeus was among the best of sixteenth-century texts on astrology.[49] Connected with this school was the German physician and astrologer Marstallerus of Breisgau, who acknowledged his debt to Finé, and in his valuable work on the art, published in 1549, concentrated on astrology as a tool for divination.[50]

The influence of an esoteric stream from Beauvais is perhaps also noticeable in Thomas Bodier's work on critical days – so important in medieval medicine – which combined medical work with astrology. Bodier dedicated it to Oronce Finé on its publication in 1554. Its case histories and horoscopes are still of interest even today.

We have already mentioned the name of the German astrologer, Garcaeus, and, indeed, it would be difficult to write of the art in the sixteenth century without reference to this remarkable man. Joannes Garcaeus combined an appreciation of the ancient forms – writing widely on Ptolemaic astrology (outlined in Appendix Six) – yet showed a lively interest in the developments in astronomy and astrology during the first half of the century, including in his works studies of the theories of Regiomontanus and Copernicus. Garcaeus did not become professor until 1561, yet his astrological works circulated in manuscript before this time. Nostradamus can scarcely have avoided his *Brief Treatise* of 1556.[51] The work is dedicated to an examination of the proper basis for drawing up a chart, in order to establish accurate prediction. Of interest in this work is the presentation of a wide range of available house-systems –

methods of dividing the diurnal and nocturnal time and space in a horoscope. Garcaeus seems to have favoured the thirteenth-century astrologer and geometrician Campanus, and the *Modus Rationalis* of Regiomontanus, which he recognized was based on the divisional method of the Arabic astrologer, Abraham Aven Ezra. It is remarkable that his collection of 400 horoscopes in the 1576 edition of *Astrologiae methodus*[52] did not include a horoscope of Nostradamus, though it did provide figures for such astrologers as Agrippa, Copernicus, Garcaeus himself, Peurbach, Regiomontanus and Trithemius. How Nostradamus could be excluded from such a gallery is a mystery for modern readers, and might suggest a conspiracy of silence.

In our examination of the quatrains of Nostradamus, we shall have occasion to look more deeply at the writings of some of these astrologers. However, having glanced at some of the contemporaneous astrological influences which were present in France when the master published his quatrains, we have to admit that Nostradamus seems to have developed his own form of astrology for these verses. Later, we offer an entire chapter to revealing the arcane astrology which permeates the *Prophéties* (see page 101): this serves to reveal Nostradamus as unique in the annals of astrology. Not only did he employ the techniques of astrology in a highly specialized way, using the traditional methods of revolutions and ingresses: he seems to have had access to tabulated material which was not published, or even available, in his own day. It was as though he could see not merely the events of future history unfolding in his visions, but even the planetary and stellar configurations which were to parallel or determine this futurity. The accuracy of his astrological predictions is unique in litera-ture, and is as much a mystery as the quatrains them-selves. No one has been able to explain how a sixteenth-century astrologer had access to planetary tabulations which would not be available for several hundreds of years. In our opinion, it is unlikely that the astrological secrets of Nostradamus will be found in books, but in some tradition derived from initiation schools.

Although sixteenth-century France seems to be swathed by streams of thought which nowadays we might classify as occult, the greatest occultists of the century were not from France. Certainly, they were not from Paris, where the academic circles in the university had stultified, and lacked that freedom of spirit which is a prerequisite for the study of arcane subjects. The brilliant Cardan was from Italy, Jean Taisnier from Hainault. Luca Gauricus, who was deeply interested in the predictions involving violent death, was Italian. The greatest occultist of the time, who dominated alchemical and creative medical thought for at least two centuries, was Paracelsus, who was from Switzerland.

Alchemy did not reach its literary Golden Age until the following century, yet alchemical manuscripts, and a certain number of influential books, were available, the majority written under the pervasive influence of Paracelsus. Not surprisingly, in one so dedicated to the arcane as Nostradamus, alchemical symbols appear in a number of the predictive quatrains. In the sixteenth century, the most popular transmission of arcane images was by way of the emblem books, or the *Horopollo* books, supposed translations of the Egyptian sacred writings, one of which, it has been claimed, was translated by Nostradamus.[53]

In 1556 a fine edition of Pierio Valeriano's *Hieroglyphica* had been published in Basle, while the *Emblematum liber* of Alciati appeared in several editions during the mid-century. The *Hypnerotomachia Poliphili* of Colonna, which had a profound influence on arcane art and literature, was published for the second time as a French version in 1553, by Kerver. There may be no doubt that this corpus of

arcane devices (*fig. 25*) had a similar influence upon
Nostradamus' literary symbolism as it did on certain arcane
woodcuts of Albrecht Dürer. Emblems and hieroglyphics
which, by their very nature, could conceal several meanings
at once were ideal for the transmission of esoteric lore. One
modern historian of alchemy, de Rola, traces this influence
into alchemical illustrations, yet it is just as easy to trace it
in literature. There may be no doubt that the arcane
predictive verses of Nostradamus were influenced by the
emblem books, the 'hieroglyphic' books, and alchemical
symbolism.[54] At least two quatrains seem to be rooted in
alchemical lore (for example, page 254 ff).

In mid-sixteenth-century France, beliefs abounded
which we might be tempted to regard as superstitious, were
these beliefs still not in fashion today. David Douglas, a
young Scot living in Paris, published his entertaining work
on the marvels of nature which was widely read until well
into the following century.[55] The book would sit comfort-
ably on any modern Fortean* bookshelf, with its concern
for rains of frogs and fishes. Among its unexplained tales of
mystery is that of the ship found buried in a mine near
Berne, still with sails raised and the bodies of its sailors
more or less intact. The sixteenth-century German Wolfgang Meurer was also a proto-Fortean who collected tales
of wonder, though a few of his references went back to
Aristotle. Among accounts of such natural phenomena as
freak lightning, he listed no fewer than 14 prodigies of rain,
which included rain of stones, iron and flesh, along with the
standard fishes, worms and frogs. He even turned hailstones into a wonder by noting that often they bore

---

*The term Fortean has been evolved in recent years to cover the interest
in, or study of, a wide range of 'unexplained' phenomena. The word has
been adopted in honour of the American, Charles Hoy Fort (1874–1932),
who spent his life collecting references to such things, and reflecting upon
their significance.

'marvellous images', such as a pig's head. In the spirit of the age, he interpreted these as a cosmic or God-given warning to mankind, to avoid living like swine. Meurer's interpretation of sky-born prodigies is medieval in its approach. While he recognized the rainbow as the outward sign of God's pact with man that the world will never again be destroyed by flood, he went one step further than Church orthodoxy by interpreting its strip of red colour as a promise of the final conflagration, and the end of the world by fire.

Two broadsheets which depict Fortean events contemporaneous with Nostradamus have been made famous by C. G. Jung, who, with considerable insight, treated them as the UFO phenomena they seem to have been.[56] A broadsheet from Nuremburg, dated 1561, shows a frightening spectacle of warring globes, crosses and curious plates around the Sun, on 14 April 1561. Samuel Coccius' broadsheet of 1566 shows an aerial warfare of globes, 'red and fiery', which occurred in the skies above Basle in August of that year (*fig. 26*). It is simply not possible to read through the popular proto-Fortean literature of the sixteenth century and not recognize that there were seen in the skies – with extraordinary frequency – what we would now call UFOs. The main difference between then and now was that few, if any, who saw such things were under the impression that they came from 'alien' sources: there would be no doubt that they were signs and symbols come (like all created things) from God.

A few of the images from popular sixteenth-century broadsheets have become popular in modern UFO lore, and may have contributed to the widespread modern sub-cultural notion that Nostradamus predicted the appearances of UFOs, alien invasions, and even a war of the worlds. Our own reading of the relevant quatrain removes such a cosmic bloodletting, however, and it is unlikely that

Nostradamus did see any space-aliens, unless angels might be classified in such terms (see, however, page 417 ff). More typical of Nostradamus – and indeed of sixteenth-century ufology – is the print which appeared in a German translation of one of his supposed works, published in 1554 (*fig. 27*). The woodcut on the broadsheet depicts a crescent moon spitting out an arrow of fire.[57]

The super-Fortean literature of the sixteenth century were the 'monster-books', in which strange births, fabulous animals and mythical creatures were recorded – not so much for the titillation of the readers' imaginations, but as signs of the way God would warn mankind from evil, or presage through such strange appearances dire events. Among the most outstanding monster books was the *Prodigiorum ac ostentorum chronicon*, of Conrad Lycosthenes – his strange surname being a scholarly Greek version of his real name, Wolffhart. This huge work, which contained over 1,500 images of strange monsters and aerial omens, 'appearing from the beginning of the World to the year 1557', was published in 1557, the year of his own death. *Fig. 28*, which depicts a 'monster of horrid aspect', is fairly typical of his gallery of rogues. Such pictures still enliven the Fortean books of our own age. Lycosthenes was more than merely a plagiarist and picture-collector: significantly, in this magnum opus, he requests his readers to get in touch with him if they witness, or know of, any other instances of such phenomena. Perhaps he was the first of a long line of genuine Fortean collectors to set up a central bureau of investigation? The passing mention which Nostradamus made to strange monsters in his quatrains is almost certainly linked with this literature of signs, symbols and portents.

In contrast to such continuity of interest, the horror of witchcraft has largely disappeared from our world, yet this terror dominated the mid-sixteenth century in France to an extent which we may scarcely visualize. Jean Bodin, one of the most notorious of the legalized murderers of witches, did not publish his *Demonomanie* until 1580, yet one of his most famous cruelties was recorded for 1556. When, in that year, a witch was burned alive in error near Laon, Bodin excused this mistake as a secret judgement of God against the victim. By 1555 he was deeply involved in his study of witchcraft and had become adept at interrogating, with an extraordinary personal brutality, unfortunate victims caught in a legal system which offered no chance of escape after arrest.

In fact, we should not be deflected from a study of Bodin by such stories, for there is no doubt that he is among the most interesting of all sixteenth-century figures. One has the uncomfortable feeling that there are three Bodins, all masquerading in the same body. There is the Bodin of the infamous witchcraft records (as accounted in the *Demono-manie* of 1580), Bodin the historiographer (as accounted in the *Methodus* of 1566), and the political theorist (as accounted in his *Republic* of 1576). It is almost impossible to research the sixteenth century without coming up against his immense genius, yet so divergent are these three strands of influence that one can follow the influence of one almost without being aware of the existence of the others.[58]

The first seven decades of the sixteenth century marked a growth of witchcraft trials in France. Prior to being executed in Paris, during 1571, the magician Trois-Echelles had claimed that there were a hundred thousand witches in the country. The story was probably nothing more than brain-damaged ranting as a result of torture, yet his account was widely reported and believed. It was perhaps witch-craft, associated in the popular mind (and even in the judicial mind) with the occult arts, that helped harden attitudes to astrology and prediction. In 1579, a Church

Council, held at Melun, decided that diviners, and those
who practised such predictive arts as necromancy, pyro-
mancy or chiromancy, should be put to death. It is this
reaction of legal institutions to divination which may
explain why every single quatrain from the pen of Nostradamus is opaque, and designed for the readership only of
those familiar with esoteric methods. Only one quatrain
seems to be concerned with the fate of a condemned witch,
and, as will be demonstrated, even this was a side-issue
arising from the related destiny of her more famous
husband (see page 293 ff).

Nostradamus is mentioned in many texts of the last half
of the century, usually in admiring terms, but sometimes in
ambiguous terms which suggest that his true prophetic
genius had not been recognized by his contemporaries. For
example, the poet Ronsard devoted over 20 lines to
Nostradamus in one of his poems, the ambiguity of which
suggests that he could sense the genius, but did not know
really how far it extended:

> *Que par les mots douteux de sa prophete voix,*
> *Comme un oracle anticque, il a des mainte annee*
> *Predit la plus grand part de nostre destinee.*

> That by the ambiguous words of his prophetic voice,
> Like an antique oracle, he has for many years
> Foreseen the greater part of our destiny.[59]

Modern interpretation of Ronsard's attack on 'l'histoire
monstrueuse' of his time has claimed that the poet was
attacking the writings of Nostradamus, and even the savant
in person, but this is not at all clear in the poem from which
we quote.[60] Indeed, it is from this same poem that Ward
elected to select a few lines in support of Nostradamus.[61] As
we have seen, Chavigny attempted to examine historical

prophecies in the light of Nostradamus – yet the first serious appraisal of his prophetic work did not come until 1656.

This was in the sympathetic study by Etienne Jaubert, some of whose misunderstandings persist even into modern potboilers about Nostradamus.[62] Even within a hundred years of the publication of the quatrains, Jaubert is already lamenting the enormous number of false prophecies which exist in the name of the master. Some of these falsities are due to misinterpretation of what Nostradamus wrote, but some are certainly a result of publishers climbing on the Nostradamus bandwagon, and selling newly writ empty promise behind the lure of a famous name. We also learn from Jaubert that Nostradamus was already tainted with that dark brush which touches the back of most genuine occultists at some time or another – he had been hounded with the reputation for being a necromancer, who communicated with the Angel of Darkness to obtain his visions. Above all, Jaubert records, with sadness and perplexity, the 'enormous faults of the first copyists of the quatrains, and of the poor, badly-corrected printings of his works'. Style aside, in most of his criticisms, Jaubert could almost be writing in the twentieth century.

Just over a century had elapsed between the publication of the first quatrains and Jaubert's own commentary. During that time, at least 50 of the Nostradamus verses had been fulfilled through striking historical events. It will be instructive for us to review some of these accurate predictions, if only to show how Jaubert missed them in his commentary. In reviewing Jaubert's view of the quatrains, we find ourselves asking just how Nostradamus' fame had spread so widely: few if any of the quatrains which Jaubert deals with seem to reflect the prophetic insight for which Nostradamus is now justly famous. In fact, Jaubert was far too concerned with showing the fulfilment of certain quatrains within a few years of their construction, and it is likely that he was too near to the historical events (indeed, perhaps too little of a historian, in the accepted sense of the word) to witness the confirmation of history in the quatrains. In some cases, Jaubert's approach was stymied by the fact that some of his commentaries dealt with prophecies which were not yet fulfilled, even though he assumed that they were. For example, he interpreted, in very general terms, a quatrain as a reference to a minor sea-fight in the English Channel, during 1555: later, however, that particular quatrain was fulfilled in every detail at the battle of Trafalgar (see page 369 ff).

The most satisfactory general account of the future history of Europe in the years following the death of Henry II, in 1559, is that given by Nostradamus in his *Epistle* to the King, written in the previous year. This text offers what is virtually a synoptic history of the future of France, up to and including the twentieth century. However, these prose prophecies have never been dealt with adequately, mainly because they were written in the same Green Language and crabbed arcane astrology as the verse quatrains, and therefore lay beyond the grasp of most commentators. For this reason, we shall concentrate only on the verses. The following is a selection of the most important of the fulfilled predictions relating to the century ending in 1655: it is illuminating that Jaubert either missed the significance of these predictions, or, for reasons which are obscure, elected not to write about them. We offer details of the relevant quatrains in the footnote at the end of the paragraph.

For 1556, Nostradamus predicted the Marian persecutions in London; for 1558, the marriage of Mary Queen of Scots to Francis II of France; for 1559, the tragic death of Henry II in a duel, and how his wife, Catherine, would mourn him for seven years, up to 1566. He foresaw the resignation of Coligny as Admiral of France, and how he would become commander of the Protestants, in 1569. For

1560, he foresaw the executions at Blois, the Huguenot plot at Lyons, and how Francis, King of France, would die shortly before reaching the age of 18 – noting how Mary Queen of Scots, his young wife, would return to the British Isles. For 1569, he foresaw how the Prince of Condé would be proclaimed leader of the Huguenot Assembly, and be shot after the battle of Jarnac. In several quatrains dealing with the Turks, he saw the 1570 siege of Cyprus, that of Famagusta in 1571, and the related victory at Lepanto. He predicted for the following year the massacre of St Bartholomew, after which Coligny was killed, and hanged by neck and feet from the Montfaucon gibbet just outside the walls of Paris. A further quatrain reveals how, in 1574, the same Montgomery who accidentally killed Henry II would be executed on the orders of Catherine; he foresaw the siege of Marmande for 1577, the assassination of Henry of Guise at Blois in 1588, and the death of Henry III, King of France. He foresaw how, in 1596, Philip II of Spain would send a fleet to take Marseilles, how Charles de Casau would attempt to betray the city, and be killed. Among his final predictions for the century, in 1596, was the English raid on Cadiz by Essex and Raleigh.

For the first part of the seventeenth century, he foresaw the accession of James VI of Scotland as James I of England, in 1603, and seven years later the stabbing to death of Henry IV of France by a young fanatic. He saw Louis XIII, as Dauphin, entering Nancy in 1632, and Duke Henry Montmorency, who had led a revolt in the south, beheaded in a prison courtyard. He foresaw the rise to power of Richelieu, and the debacle, in 1642, with Henri de Cinq-Mars beheaded for conspiring against Richelieu. For Britain, the death of Charles I of England, in 1649; the coming of Oliver Cromwell; the end of Civil War in England, with the second siege of Pontefract, in 1649; the battle of Dunbar in 1650, followed by the flight of the future Charles II after the Battle of Worcester, and his return to England seven years later.[63]

These prophecies amounted to heady stuff, and it was probably for the best that they were beyond the wit of commentators to unravel. So far as we can see, Nostradamus was not proscribed because of his quatrains during his own lifetime – probably, he was adequately protected by his royal connections. His methods – rather than his quatrains – were criticized, for example, by Videl and Couillard.[64] This, of course, is not to say that either his predictions or his methods were understood. A similar dissident voice was that of William Fulke of London, who published an *Antiprognosticon* against useless astrological predictions made by Nostradamus and others.[65] However, there are no indications in Fulke's fulminations that he had grasped the astrological techniques of the master, or could interpret any of the quatrains. We learn from Laurent Bouchel, writing in 1615, that later in the sixteenth century, prognostications of the kind issued by Nostradamus broke the law.[66] Such forms of astrology had been forbidden under the Ordinance of Orléans, and almanacs required an ecclesiastical imprimatur prior to publication. Although Nostradamus was dead by the time this Ordinance came into effect, Thorndike suggested that it was the spirit behind such a law which explained why the savant chose to purposely cultivate obscurity.[67]

Such a legally threatening environment, in which a single injudicious word could lead to arrest for witchcraft, may explain partly why Nostradamus was reluctant to make his own powers of clairvoyance too evident. Jaubert was certainly not the first to lament the strangeness of the verse, which appears to be constructed in such a way as to be beyond comprehension: in his opinion, Nostradamus 'all too often, disguises the prophecies by terms so obscure that, without a very special genius, one may understand nothing'. In fact, Nostradamus was frequently criticized for his obscurity even in the matter of the personal horoscopy he practised for hard cash (or suitable gifts). The correspondence edited by Dupèbe throws much light on the difficulties which Nostradamus and his clients had because of the heavy demand on his time, and because of his tendency to phrase even personal predictions in obscure forms. In this respect, although he concentrated on the quatrains, Jaubert found himself, like most other commentators on the quatrains, in total empathy with Nostradamus' own forthright commentary on the subject:

> *Hence, O most humane King, the greater part of the prophetical quatrains are so full of obstacles that one cannot find a way through them, let alone interpret any . . .* [68]

Curiously, even though over four centuries have passed since Nostradamus penned this illuminating confession, no one has yet offered a satisfactory explanation as to why he couched his prophecies in such an impenetrable fashion. The mission of Nostradamus remains a total mystery. Why did this remarkable man publish accurate predictive quatrains 'so full of obstacles' that no one would be able to find a way through the maze they constructed? We can only presume that while he wished to demonstrate that it was quite possible to predict the future, he felt impelled to relieve his readers of any horror at the futurity they might find within his verse. This then is the core of the Nostradamus mystery: the savant wished to illuminate his readers, yet, at the same time, leave them free from fear. His quatrains reveal their secrets only after the events prophesied have entered the stream of time we call history.

Who was this man? All too often, as we have pored over

these crabbed and obstacled quatrains, we have found ourselves wondering what Nostradamus was really like. After years of studying his work, and related literature, we still find ourselves knowing almost nothing at all about his inner world: he remains for us an enigma. Perhaps the only thing we may be certain of is that he wrote the most extraordinary prophecies known to the Western world. It is almost an irrelevance that the one thing we do know about him is what he looked like: his face, painted by his son César, has stared on in bemusement at the world he foresaw for over four hundred years.

A remarkably large number of portraits of Nostradamus have survived, most of them, however loosely, based on the paintings done by César. A roundel copy of one picture is in the central concentric of the horoscope (*fig. 3*), and its original has been the source for hundreds of poor imitations. In his careful bibliography of the master's writings, Robert Benazra reproduces over ninety images of Nostradamus – most of them fairly crude, yet all refreshingly different, ranging from the simple title-page cuts of the sixteenth century (*fig. 29*), through to the sophisticated amateur drawings used in the liberally illustrated works of Torné-Chavigny (*fig. 30*). We estimate that, with very little trouble, we could add at least an equal number of other portraits to that total. A study of the development of these images would almost make a history of its own – how the benign face of the César portrait was transformed into the pensive archetypal Jewish savant on the wall of a shop in Salon (*fig. 18*); how this giant image came into existence by way of a nineteenth century lithograph, which was, in its turn, partly derived from a sixteenth-century woodcut (*fig. 31*).

In view of his reputation as an arcane astrologer, it is puzzling that none of the graphic images known to us are arcane, in the sense that they contain hidden inner wisdom.

However, a great number wisely portray the savant in the role of astrologer, whether this be by means of the symbolism of a clutter of celestial spheres and measuring devices (*fig. 32*), or by the more formal surround of zodiacal images and sigils, which represent Nostradamus as an almanach-maker, rather than as a prophet (*fig. 33*). This astral trend degenerated in some published works almost to burlesque, with the savant entrapped in a stellatum cage, and weighed down by the almanachs he sought to sell (*fig. 34*).

It is unlikely that the soul of Nostradamus will be felt through such images. The soul may be seen in the face itself, but scarcely ever in a portrayal of that face. What is really important about a human being may not be fixed in pigment or printers' ink. Perhaps, if we wish to catch a feeling for the real Nostradamus, we should not attempt to approach him through his physical appearance, but through his script – through the signature with which he witnessed his final testament (*fig. 35*). The signature, faltering near death, is almost illegible. This scrawling choreographic word-play, *M. Nostradamus*, seems to sum up the impenetrable soul of Nostradamus with far more poignancy than any number of portrayals of his outer appearance. Not only is there a raw symbolism in so scabrous a signature, but, as we shall discover, there is even mystery in the name of Nostradamus itself.

Chapter 2

The Astrology of Nostradamus

Quantum ad genituram Ioannis filii, quam ... ad te mitto, in ipso frontispicio cernere licet duo themata, alterum quidem meo more confectum, alterum ad viam et trutinam Astrologorum, primum est horoscopi, ascendentis secundum; sed omnia significata ex calculo constant triplici. Nec miraberis, heros nobiliss., a me in ea repetita esse quaedam, quod ideo factum est potissimum, quia planisphaerium cum instrumento abavi mei materni Magistri Io. Sanremigii ad harmoniam Astronomicam coniunxi, ne videlicet descriptio geniturae turpiter exaresceret, et taedium tibi nauseamve adferret. Multa tamen a nobis sunt consulto omissa, qua si perscribere voluissem, Iliadem mehercule confecissem potius, quam iustum geniturae circulum.

As for the chart of your son John, which ... I send you. On the first page of this, it is possible to distinguish two genitures. One has been cast according to my own method, the other according to the via and trutina. The first is by means of the ascendant degree, the second by means of [adjustment of] the ascendant: however all the significators involve a triple calculation. Do not be surprised, most noble sir, [to find] from me a certain repetition, because in this way the thing is done most preferentially, since the astrolabe of my great, great maternal grandfather, Jean de Saint-Rémy, has united [the two charts] in an astrological harmony, in order that anything in the account of the horoscope which is unsightly might be extinguished, and [thus] remove anything that might be tedious and upsetting to you. However, many things have been omitted by us, concerning which I would have wished to write: by my oath, it is an *Iliad* I would rather put together here, rather than a correct circuit of a geniture.

(From a letter addressed by Nostradamus to Hans Rosenberger, regarding the horoscope of the latter's son, dated Salon, 9 September 1561. The Latin is from Letter XXX, in Jean Dupèbe, *Nostradamus. Lettres Inédites*, 1983, p. 96)

Most of the early portraits of Nostradamus emphasize his role as a star-gazing astrologer (*fig. 36*), a reminder for us that he came from a background wherein astrology was important. At birth, he might have had his horoscope cast by his maternal grandfather, while he predicted his own death in an astrological document prepared for popular consumption. His famous epitaph, written by his wife, was a fine enough testament to his involvement in the art of the stars: according to this inscription he had been the finest astrologer of his age. To some extent, therefore, the tradition of Nostradamus as a star-gazing astrologer is probably accurate. In some of the more ancient portraits of Nostradamus, one has the impression that he is taking dictation from the stars themselves, with the same 'divine influx' as his contemporary occultists claimed was necessary in true divination.

When commenting upon the personal horoscope of Nostradamus in 1684, the English astrologer John Gadbury reminded his readers of the very first of the aphorisms of the ancient Roman astrologer, Claudius Ptolemy. This translates, 'None indeed but such as are Divinely inspired can predict the particular kinds of things.' Gadbury was wise to remind his readers of what was special about Nostradamus – his divine inspiration – yet, even the fact that Nostradamus was an astrologer has been largely forgotten or ignored by his commentators. This is because, under most circumstances, the references to astrological lore which appear in his quatrains seem either too simple to warrant undue attention, or so complex as to baffle the mind.

The recent discovery of copies of astrological corre-spondence maintained by Nostradamus has thrown consid-erable light upon his strange astrological methods.[1] It is evident from these letters that Nostradamus was occupied in the day-to-day business of casting and interpreting horoscopes, as well as in constructing his annual almanacs. Some account of this fairly mundane activity has already been given above. We point to it here mainly because there is a profound contrast between the type of predictive astrology which Nostradamus practised in these daily activities and that which appears in the deeply arcane quatrains of the *Prophéties*. The one thing which his day-to-day astrology had in common with his quatrains is the tendency for them both to involve prolixity, or arcanity, of expression.

A fine example of this arcanity may be seen in the section of the letter to Rosenberger, quoted at the opening of this chapter. After reading this section, one cannot help concluding that Nostradamus was being self-indulgently obscurantist. If this is a fair sample of what he could write to a non-astrologer, then it is hardly surprising that we should find some of his clients (including Rosenberger) claiming that they could not fully understand his written accounts of the horoscopes they had commissioned of him. One sympathizes with them: at least four of the technical astrological terms in this short quotation are so obscure that even a modern translator into French has proved incapable of making sense of them.[2]

What Nostradamus is saying to Hans Rosenberger about the horoscope he has prepared for the birth of his son is that he has cast the figure in the normal way, and has then justified this chart in accordance with the rules of the Trutine of Hermes; the usual purpose of applying it was to establish from a birth chart the moment of conception, with a view to determining the exact moment of birth. Now, the interesting thing is that there seems to be no earthly reason why Nostradamus should spell out these technical matters for a client such as Rosenberger, who had, more than once, admitted that he had no specialist knowledge. It is not clear whether Nostradamus was having fun with his client, was being flippant, was pulling the wool over his eyes, or was merely indulging in that arcane obscurantism which seems to have been his second nature.

However, besides being a useful document, which reveals interesting details of the ancient method adopted by Nostradamus in the casting of personal charts, the letter is of especial relevance to our own study because it mentions the astrolabe which seems to have been given him by his great–great–grandfather, Jean de Saint-Rémy.[3]

In fact, this passing reference to Jean (whom we must assume from his bequest to have been an astrologer) is intriguing, for until this letter surfaced, Jean had been something of a mystery.[4]

Nostradamus seems to have been a natural obscurantist, but in his astrological methods he takes obscurantism almost to a point where it seems to be meaningless. However, once the key to his astrological method is applied to the verses, then his use of arcane astrology is revealed as being the most remarkable in Western history. Without the key, his astrology remains obscure, and it is precisely because of this that it has been misunderstood by virtually all commentators in the past.

It is assumed by many commentators that, in mentioning the names of planets, Nostradamus is merely evoking their symbolic powers. In this view, Mars is a symbol for war, Venus a symbol for love, or peace, and so on. This is a misunderstanding of the genius with which Nostradamus worked. A recent book addressing the astrology of Nostradamus fails to lift itself from this level of interpretation, and seriously misrepresents what Nostradamus said.[5] A claim that he discussed the Aquarian Age, and intimated that it would bring a new awareness of the devastation resulting from man's disregard for his environment, may sound politically correct enough to please modern readers, yet Nostradamus made no such prediction, and never even mentioned the Age of Aquarius. We think it is also misleading to claim – as does this recent book – that the prophecies of Nostradamus do *not* foretell an unalterable future: the fact which is revealed, time and time again, is precisely that this is the kind of future the quatrains *do* foretell. When Nostradamus quoted in his *Epistle* to Henry II the old Latin adage, *Quod de futuris non est determinata omnio veritas* ('For, in so far as it concerns the future, truth may not wholly be determined'), it is clear from the context that he is writing with tongue in cheek, and with his eye to the Inquisition.

A parallel – and even more erroneous tradition – has gathered around the Nostradamus corpus: namely, that he used ordinary astrology in his quatrains. Nostradamus did *not* use ordinary astrology in the quatrains, and said as much in his two letters which preface the volumes of *Prophéties*. He admits that he looked into the stars, in order to discover cosmic correspondences with the events he

105

foretold, but there was nothing ordinary about the way he consulted the stars, and there was nothing ordinary in the way he used his cosmic insights in the quatrains. Nostradamus employed an extremely arcane method of presenting astrological data, as clues to heavenly events. In a different age, and in a different clime, he may have written his quatrains in a less prolix style. However, as we observed earlier, in his day divination was frowned upon, and, especially in Paris, it was unwise to be too publicly enamoured of practical astrology, as opposed to considering zodiacal and planetary influences in terms of philosophical machines. Even the great Michael Servetus, who had come to Paris round about 1536, seems to have had trouble at the university there: it was believed that he had strayed from his legitimate role as lecturer in astronomy into discussing the suspicious realm of judicial astrology – a form of astrology used for answering questions according to a chart raised for the moment of questioning.[6] With rules like that, Servetus found himself travelling a dangerous route, as few of his contemporaries could define with any precision the difference between *astrologia* and *astronomia*. The trial of Servetus need not concern us in this context, but it is sufficiently close to the time when Nostradamus wrote for us to see why our savant should choose to write verse so full of obstacles – so *scabreux* as he put it in his *Epistle* of 1558.

The astrology used by Nostradamus in his quatrains was of the arcane kind – nowadays called esoteric astrology, for it is rooted in a view of the planets and the zodiac as being the work of living, creative beings. Nostradamus promulgated an astrological method which was more akin to the alchemical astrology of Paracelsus, and the Boehmian astrology which developed in the following century, than to the astrology which is favoured today. This alone explains why the modern astrologer invariably flounders when

106

attempting to read the quatrains as though they were concerned with ordinary astrology. It also explains why the numerous erroneous traditions, which have built up around Nostradamus, are contradicted by the evidence of the quatrains themselves.

The verses fairly bristle with astrological references – with planetary and zodiacal names, sometimes in cypher or symbols – yet the fact is that Nostradamus used astrology in a form which is so arcane as to be beyond the understanding of most modern astrologers. There is no evidence that, in the quatrains, at least, Nostradamus used astrology in a conventional way at all, either as a tool for prediction, or as a standard system of symbols for elucidation. In this sense, his quatrains are not astrological predictions. On the other hand, there is a vast body of evidence to show that Nostradamus made use of astrological references to construct occult blinds, and to designate specific time-periods in his quatrains.

When interpreted correctly, several of his quatrains yield up very precise dates relating to future events. Those of his contemporaries who assessed Nostradamus as being one of the leaders in the field (at a time when astrology was practised by the leading intellectuals of Europe, though frowned upon by the university of Paris) were quite correct. Nostradamus uses astrology with a subtlety which is absolutely amazing. His references to planetary placings and aspects, when taken in context, can lead us to extremely precise dates for his predictions.

Inevitably, Nostradamus was a child of his age. In his annual *Almanachs*, he made extensive use of astrological techniques – such as the seasonal ingresses. He also used eclipse charts, drawing conclusions from charts cast for the monthly nominal eclipse, and reading from these the tenor of events for the following month, along with a whole battery of techniques which are still used in modern astrology. However, the astrology of his *Almanachs* is very different from that which he used in the quatrains – indeed it is of a type very different in the quatrains from any other literature before or since.

In the sixteenth century, the chief practice underlying astrological historical prediction was called Mundane Astrology. This was the astrological method concerned with predicting political, regnal and religious events. This Mundane form was one of the two great divisions of predictive astrology – which in effect divided most astrological practices into either the personal genethliacal horoscopy (i.e. the branch of astrology involved with casting and interpreting birth charts) and the Mundane type. This was an important form then called Revolutions. Thus, Revolutions was the study and manipulation (for predictive purposes) of the conjunctions of planets, emphasis being placed on the 'superiors' – Mars, Jupiter and Saturn.

A sixteenth-century plate which appeared in several astrological works demonstrates the theory behind these conjunctions (*fig. 22*). Approximately every 20 years, Saturn and Jupiter conjunct (that is, meet together in the same degree of the zodiac). In approximately 60 years, they mark out three conjunctions in signs of the same element. Such triple elemental signs are called trigons. In *fig. 22* the trigons are marked with sufficient clarity for us to see how astrologers could determine dates, according to a very precise cosmic rhythm.

From *fig. 22*, we can see for example how the conjunction of Saturn and Jupiter in the fire sign Sagittarius took place in 1723; this was followed by a conjuction of the two in the fire sign Leo in 1743, which was in turn followed by a conjunction in the fire sign Aries in 1763. These were conjunctions in the trigon of Fire. This figure is not really accurate in terms of modern tabulations, yet it permits us to see how the conjunctions occur approximately every 20 years, and how a complete trigonic cycle occurs every 60 years.

The word 'revolutions' contains a history of its own. It was derived from the Arabic literature which had, from the eleventh century, been seminal to the growth of European astrology. The most important of the Arabic writers on Revolutions had been an astrologer whose name was Latinized into Albumasar: the theory of revolutions proposed by this savant was so deeply imbued in European astrological prediction that traces of it may still be seen in popular forms of modern astrology. That Nostradamus would have been familiar with the techniques of Albumasar we may have no doubt: however, the recent discovery of a work by the great Arabic astrologer, Alcabitius, bearing the *ex libris* of Nostradamus himself, confirms the savant's interest in that part of predictive astrology concerned with revolutions.[7]

The importance of astrology in the sixteenth-century vision of history has been reassessed in the past two or three decades, for it reaches well beyond the confines of astrology. For example, the significance of the ephemerides used by Nostradamus has been reviewed by the French scholar Yves Lenoble,[8] and certain of the astrological ideas behind the quatrains have been subjected to systematic (if not altogether convincing) scrutiny by the German scholars, Wöllner and Ludwig Dinzinger.[9] The consequences of such researches will be a recognition of the depth of Arabic theories of cycles and history upon the West from the eleventh century onwards.

As Nicholas Campion has shown in his study of Bodin, the astrological references of the latter have been misunderstood or ignored by modern historians, largely because they are unfamiliar with the astrology of the sixteenth century, to which Bodin refers copiously.[10] The interesting thing is that it was precisely the same theories of sacred geometric cycles and astrology which so deeply influenced Bodin that Nostradamus used in his *Prophéties*. Most of the astrology which we will study through the quatrains seems to relate to Mundane Astrology. In the Arabic astrology, and in the medieval European astrology which it influenced, the revolutions of the superior planets were ascribed the greatest importance, so that by the sixteenth century the word was often used as though it referred only to the superior planets. In particular, the conjunctions of these planets were regarded as being indicators of historical change in the mundane sphere – that is, the sphere of politics, national life, and even religion.

The fact that astrological revolutions claimed to interpret the future potential of both politics and religion probably explains why the art was so unpopular in government circles in France. This was particularly the case in the political and monarchic centre of Paris, where the central issues so frequently revolved around the conflict between politics and religion. The theory of Revolutions, the scope of which offered predictions relating to the rise and fall of religions, of religious sects and dissidents alike, was abhorrent to the Catholic church. It was also abhorrent to the majority of the Protestant leaders who saw astrology as part of the all-embracing superstition over which the Papacy presided. Few Protestants would have noticed, let alone understood, the arcane astrological symbols in the church of St Pierre, which dominated their city of Geneva.[11] This rejection of mundane astrology by both the main religions is one of the contributory reasons why Nostradamus elected to couch his astrological quatrains in a form so arcane as to evade interpretation.

It is tempting to conclude, as we analyse certain of the astrological factors in the quatrains, that Nostradamus, like the Arabic astrologers before him, believed that specific astrological moments (such as the conjunction of Jupiter and Saturn in a specific sign of the zodiac), had a particular effect on the mundane sphere – that is to say, on history. As we have seen, there is no doubt that Nostradamus used such cycles, or revolutions, along with specific astrological moments, to *date* events in the future. This, of course, is a very different use of astrology from that written about by Bodin or most of his contemporaries. It is still the astrology of the Revolutions, yet one used outside a determinist credo, with purely chronological intentions. In this respect, Nostradamus seems to be unique among sixteenth-century astrologers, which is why we are so reluctant to describe him in any way which represents him as being an ordinary astrologer.

One other astrological predictive technique which had been imported into Europe from the Arabic writings was the theory and practice of ingresses. In simple terms, the astrological theory of history relating to ingresses was based on casting annual charts for the entry of the sun into the four cardinal signs. Of these four, the most frequently consulted was the sign Aries, precisely because it marked the beginning of the astrological year. Nostradamus frequently used this ingress technique in his own prophetic *Almanachs*: *fig. 23* is an example ingress chart from the prognostication he wrote for the year of his own death, 1566. In the medieval calendar, the solar ingress of Aries had even marked the beginning of the calendrical year, and was therefore deeply enmeshed in chronology. It is quite possible that in one quatrain Nostradamus refers to this astrological technique (see page 323 ff).

Mundane astrology was extremely important in the sixteenth century. Indeed, it retained a popular interest, if only through the medium of the popular almanacs, which usually incorporated mundane predictions of the dire sort, until well into the nineteenth century. The temptation is for us to think of Nostradamus in the same way as many of his contemporaries, as yet another manipulator of revolutions and ingresses. This would be a pity, for such a view of Nostradamus misses his true genius. He was not merely an advanced astrologer who happened to have framed his mundane predictions in a curiously arcane form. He was a man who, according to his own account, had been given a divine insight into the future, and used sophisticated astrological techniques as pegs to identify and date the events he foresaw.

Before glancing at a few instructive examples of Nostradamus' use of astrology, we should observe one further problem in the approach to Nostradamus, from an astrological point of view. The simple fact is that the majority of astrological references which abound in his quatrains are rarely quite what they seem. There is nothing traditional about the way Nostradamus uses astrology in his quatrains, and if we seek to understand his secrets, we must look to another, deeper level of meaning than mere symbolism, or classical horoscopic interpretation.

Our purpose in presenting the analyses which follow in this chapter is not to reveal all the various astrological techniques practised by Nostradamus. The fact that over 100 of the quatrains contain references opaqued in astrological symbols and data indicates that a full study of his methods is beyond the compass of one book. Our purpose here is merely to reveal that his astrology is of a unique kind, and intimately bound into both the time-structures of the prophecies, and the secret language – the Green Language (which will be examined in detail in Chapter Four) – in which Nostradamus wrote the *Prophéties*.

One of the most outstanding ways in which Nostradamus makes use of the astrological data is through ephemerides, the tables of planetary positions. His phraseology often suggests that he is involved in Mundane Astrology, when this is not the case. A casual-seeming reference to two or three planetary co-ordinates in a quatrain is almost always an indication that we should scurry to a set of ephemerides (or, in modern times, to a sophisticated computer programme) and locate his reference in time, for these usually provide a clue to the subject of the quatrain, and even to a precise date of the event in question. We may demonstrate the sheer brilliance behind Nostradamus' use of this kind of astrology only by means of examples. For this reason, we shall examine one or two astrological quatrains in some depth, starting with a particularly simple example, touching upon Nostradamus' obsession – the history of the French Revolution.

THE DESTRUCTION OF LYONS

Quatrain VIII.46 is outstanding among those verses which depend on astrology for a precise dating. Unique in arcane literature is the economy with which Nostradamus has introduced the reference to the astrological factors at play.

> *Pol mensolée mourra à trois lieuës du rosne,*
> *Fuis les deux prochains tarasc destrois:*
> *Car Mars fera le plus horrible trosne,*
> *De coq & d'Aigle de France freres trois.*

Since the quatrain encapsulates a secret astrology, a 'translation', however literal, is both clumsy and virtually without meaning:

Pol mensolée will die three leagues from the Rhône,
Flee the two near Tarara destroyed:
For Mars will make the most horrible throne,
Of cock and Eagle of France three brothers.

De Fontbrune argues that the opening word *Pol* is the name of the Pope, John-Paul II, combined with the start of the word *Pol*and, which was this Pope's birthplace. Such a reading – selective as it is – firmly places the quatrain in the twentieth century. By much twisting of meanings, de Fontbrune further reads into the word *mensolée* a reference to the prophecy of Malachai, apportioned to Pope John-Paul II (see, however, our comments on *Pol mensolée*, on page 40).

The Malachai prophecies offer single-line descriptions of a list of future Popes to the (now-imminent) end of the Papacy. These prophecies may have been written in the sixteenth century, but are claimed to be much older. Nonetheless, the oldest edition we have examined was late sixteenth century. In these Malachai prophecies, the Latin tag for John-Paul II is *De labore solis*, which means approximately 'concerning the work of the sun'. De Fontbrune argues that the Latin word *manus* means 'work' and, hence, *manus-solée* points to the Malachai prophecy. The argument is specious, of course.

The three brothers (*freres trois*) of the last line are transmogrified by de Fontbrune into 'three allies' of the King of France and the United States. Whether a new monarchy for France, or for a putative kingdom of 'France and the United States', is on offer is anyone's guess. Erika Cheetham reads the Eagle (*l'Aigle*) as a reference to the United States, and specifically to the Kennedy family, even though there is no evidence for either reading. However, the quatrain does not bear such interpretations. As we shall show, the verse is astrologically based, and relates to events in France shortly after the French Revolution.

We may confidently read the quatrain as relating to some event in Lyons. This reading is suggested by the word *tarasc* (the name of a local mythological monster) which in some early editions was rendered *Tarara*. This is certainly Tarare, on the River Turdine, a few miles from Lyons. Lyons is 'near Tarare' (*prochains Tarara*), and on the Rhône (the *rosne* of the first line). Nostradamus frequently identifies a city by referring to some small town or village in its environs: in this case, we shall see that there is a most important reason why he should not give the name of Lyons itself.

A first in-depth reading of the quatrain may suggest to the alert historian several events in France. For example, it is possible to regard the 'two' (*les deux*) of line two as reference to Henri d'Effiat (Cinq-Mars), and François de Thou, who were beheaded in Lyons, for plotting against Richelieu in 1642 (see page 294 ff).

Now, the fact is that Nostradamus very rarely includes in a single quatrain two events which are not in some way historically related. Therefore, we must ask if there is some other 'pair' (*les deux*) who are connected with this place near Tarara (*prochains Tarara*), and who were destroyed (*destrois*). The answer to the questions is both in the affirmative and surprising.

Oddly enough, the city of Lyons itself is the pair which forms the subject of the quatrain. During a brief and violent interlude in French history, the city had two names, and during this period it was almost completely destroyed. As we shall see, it is the fact of Lyons having had a double name which enables us to date the events previsioned by Nostradamus. This dating is confirmed by astrological factors built into the quatrain.

In 1793, because Lyons had defied the Convention (the *Convention Nationale* being the revolutionary assembly which succeeded the legislative Assembly in 1792), General Kellerman, the hero of Valmy was ordered to reduce the city to rubble. According to Haydn, the siege lasted 70 days, and ended on 9 October,[12] following which the

115

Convention decreed the demolition of the city on 12 October 1793.

The siege and atrocities which followed the breach of its walls were indeed terrible. During that time, Mars did keep his most horrible rule (*le plus horrible trosne*) as god of war. Pertinent to our quatrain is the fact that not only was a great part of Lyons physically destroyed, but even its old name was eradicated. From 1793, the Convention – with no trace of irony in its ruling – changed its name to *Ville-affranchie* (the freed–city). The original name was returned to the city only after the fall of Robespierre.

The fourth line reads: *De coq & d'Aigle de France frères trois* – Mars sits on a horrible throne which governs the cock and the Eagle. We shall see eventually that these two birds are the cock – France of the Revolution (see *fig. 46*) – and the Eagle – Napoleon (see page 340): the double symbol of the Emperor himself and the dethroned monarchy.

The three brothers of France are the three divisions of the French Assembly (*France freres trois*) established on 20 September 1792, which, within 24 hours, abolished the monarchy in France. The three divisions, nominally bound together by an oath of fraternity (*freres*) were the *Girondins* (to the left), the *Plaine* (the centre) and the *Montagnards* (the right, and so called because they were ranged on the highest benches in the Assembly).

The third line states: *Car Mars fera le plus horrible trosne*. As is usually the case with Nostradamus, the phrase has a double level of meaning. The very mention of Mars may evoke a warlike theme for the uninitiated, but for those familiar with the method of Nostradamus it is an invitation to examine terminologies, before looking into the planetary positions in ephemerides for 1792–3.

The image of Mars, the pagan god of war, taking the throne of France is highly pertinent, for this is the very same year that the 1,000-year-old throne (*trosne*) of France had been dispensed with. Those who abolished the traditional monarch immediately installed in his place the pagan god of war. It has been rightly said that if America first instituted modern democracy, it was the French who turned it into a military creed.

In the verse there are esoteric double-entendres which should be pointed out because of their astrological implications. The word *Pol*, which opens the quatrain, is a Latin interjection – a kind of mark of astonishment, or oath. It is a short form of *Pollux*, the violent (pugilistic) and mortal one of the celestial twins Castor and Pollux, the Gemini of the constellations. This fact leads us to a most remarkable astrological symbolism in the quatrain relating to the position of the planet Mars, mentioned in line three.

As we have seen, in one sense, the 'horrible throne' (*horrible trosne*) is to be read as a metaphorical reference to the bloody events subsequent to the establishing of the Assembly and the destruction of Lyons (both themes of this quatrain). However, in sixteenth-century astrology, the word 'throne' also has a specialist meaning. It relates to the sign associated with a particular planet through traditional rulership: a planet is said to be in its 'throne' when posited in a sign over which it has rule. The term is derived from the Greek *thronois* used by Ptolemy in his *Tetrabiblos*.[13] By the sixteenth century, the term seems to have been limited to the idea expressed in the ubiquitous images of the pagan gods riding their throne-like chariots, the wheels of which contained the relevant zodiacal images. Mars was said to be in its throne when in Scorpio.

On 20 September 1792 (and indeed on the following day), when the three houses (*trois frères*) of the French Assembly were established, and subsequently abolished the monarchy, the planet Mars was in the sign Scorpio – in its own throne.

There is an even more remarkable astrological reference encapsulated in the quatrain. In the last days of July 1793, when General Kellerman began his siege of Lyons, Mars was in conjunction with the fixed star Pollux, the beta Geminorum of the star system of Johann Bayer (1572–1625), the German astronomer and lawyer. In 1793, Pollux was in 21 degrees of Cancer. This explains the otherwise inexplicable *Pol* which has given so much trouble to commentators. The word *mensolée* is from a combination of Spanish and French: *men* means small, while *solée* is a variant on *soleil*, which means Sun. If this reading is correct, then *Pol mensolée* may be translated as 'Pollux, the little sun'. Nowadays, the image does not appear to be far-fetched, but in the mid-sixteenth century, the nature of the stars was still a mystery. Francesco Patrizi, who studied at the astrological centre of Padua, and whose books were put on the Index because of his forthright astronomical views, recognized not only that the universe was infinite, but that each star was a separate world. The idea, though strictly speaking heretical, was very much in the air in the mid-sixteenth century.[14]

Patrizi's views seem to reflect an intelligent concern with the major changes which were sweeping through astrology in the sixteenth century, due to the discoveries of Copernicus, the collapse of the Ptolemaic cosmoconception, and the Nova of 1572. This latter phenomenon, which Nostradamus predicted, had a more profound effect on the collapse of the old model than any number of books (see p. 247).

The orange star, Pollux (*Pol*), set in the head of the Southern Twin, is presently in 23 degrees of Cancer. With the modern computing systems which are available, we have been able to confirm the remarkable data given by Nostradamus in this quatrain, relating to the near-conjunction of Mars with Pollux. This match has been made possible not merely by reference to ephemerides,[15] but also from computerized simulated replays of planetary movements during July and August 1793. For this, and simpler astronomical replays, we used the *Windows 3.1 Microsoft Astronomer for Windows*, 1993. We have considered this computerized approach advisable for, while it is possible to make an educated guess as to which ephemerides Nostradamus might have used for particular quatrains, there is little evidence that he did need to rely upon contemporaneous data in his predictions. Remarkably, he seems to have been able to attain a precision beyond the limits of the ephemeridic tabulation available to him.

This example of how Nostradamus can relate a future conjunction between a star and a planet leads almost naturally into a study of how he uses conjunctions to denote events in the future. In many of his verses, a list of planets (however arcanely presented) usually points to a specific future conjunction which is so defined by the quatrain as to point to a single date. Invariably, this date is linked with the meaning of the quatrain.

THE PROTESTANT WARS

Few of the astrological directives from Nostradamus are quite so simple as those in line three of quatrain VIII.2:

> *Condon & Aux & autour de Mirande*
> *Je voy du ciel feu qui les environne.*
> *Sol Mars conjoint au Lyon, puis Marmande*
> *Foudre, grand gresle, mur tombe dans Garonne.*

> Condom & Auch & around Mirande
> I see fire from the sky which surrounds them.
> Sun and Mars conjoined in the Lion, then Marmande
> Lightning, great hail, the wall falls into the Garonne.

119

There is sufficient imagery of destruction here to excite the millennarists; Roberts goes further than most, for he interprets the quatrain as predicting the landing of extra-terrestrials, amid a great war in heaven. He has been caged into this latter view by his own copyist error in printing *grand gresle* as *grand guerre*, which means 'great war'.

In this quatrain, it is astrological data which determine the event described. The astrological conditions are expressed almost without ambiguity. Nostradamus tells us that the Sun and Mars are conjunct in Leo (*Sol Mars conjoint au Lyon*). On 10 August 1577 the Sun and Mars were in exact conjunction in 28 degrees of Leo. Allowing an orb of 5 degrees (as is perfectly acceptable in astrology), the conjunction could be said to be operative from 5 August until 12 August, when the planets left Leo. Without the date afforded by this conjunction, we would probably not have been able to pull the towns named in the quatrain into a meaningful historical order. These are Condom (*Condon*), Auch (*Aux*) and Mirande, all in Gers, to the south-west of France. Marmande is to the north, in Lot et Garonne. We have checked the similar astrological conditions for major events relating to their histories, and find 1577 the only satisfactory year. It was in 1577 that Marmande was besieged by Henry of Navarre, who was to become the first of the French Protestant kings, as Henry IV.

Why does Nostradamus write '. . . then Marmande' (*puis Marmande*)? He does this to indicate that the conditions he sets out relating to Mirande were connected in some way with the towns mentioned in the first two lines. The siege of Marmande was part of the attempt to establish Protestantism in southern France. In 1569 Condom, and several surrounding towns, were sacked by Gabriel, the Count of Montgomery, who had joined Condé against the Catholics.

This same Gabriel of Montgomery figured in the most famous of all the Nostradamus quatrains (I.35): he was the unidentified assailant (*Le lyon jeune*) whose splintered lance carried into the face of Henry II and put out his eye, in 1559 (see page 235 ff). His joining with the Huguenots was probably connected with this accident, for as a result of the incident he was disgraced and left Paris: shortly afterwards he allied himself with Condé. In the same year as they took *Condon*, the pair occupied Bearn and Bigorre, all within the same region as the towns listed in the first couplet of the quatrain.

Nostradamus is particularly astute in describing the conflicts as 'fire from heaven', around Condom, Auch and Mirande (*Je voy du ciel feu qui les environne*). The destruction wrought upon them was a result of a religious war (a 'heavenly' war, so to speak, a fire which started in the skies). The last line is perhaps equally periphrastic, for lightning and rains of giant hail were standard medieval images representative of God's displeasure. Nostradamus, as a member of a Catholic-convert family and a royalist, would be anxious to see the displeasure of heaven at the activities of breakaway Protestants. On the other hand, the account of a wall falling into the River Garonne was a practical possibility, for Marmande is situated on the River Garonne, mentioned in the quatrain.

THE FRENCH REVOLUTION

Quatrain I.16 is probably the most complex example of Nostradamus' use of arcane astrology, so a clear analysis of its various arcane elements should provide us with an insight into how Nostradamus uses astrological data. The quatrain reads:

> *Faux à l'estang, joint vers le Sagittaire,*
> *En son haut auge de l'exaltation*

Peste, famine, mort de main militaire,
Le Siecle approcher de renovation.

Since this is a truly arcane verse, we shall not attempt a translation at this point: the interpretation will emerge as we unravel its astrological import.

The key to its meaning lies in the terminology in the first two lines. Here Nostradamus makes arcane reference to both planets and zodiacal signs, thus demanding a certain amount of detective work to unveil his meaning. As we shall see, once this is done, a very precise date is revealed.

Faux means scythe, and is a reference to Saturn, who (in astrological symbolism) carries a scythe. The implement is a throwback to the origins of this planetary god as an agricultural deity, and as a descendant of the Greek time-god, Chronos. (The scythe-bearing 'Father Time' of modern imagery is cognate with this Saturn.) The old French *l'estang* (in modern French, *l'étang*) means pond or pool. Since fish live in pools, it is a reference to the aquatic zodiacal sign, Pisces. If these two readings are correct, then the phrase *Faux à l'estang* means 'When Saturn is in Pisces'.

Joint means joined, united, and is a substitute for the astrological technical term, 'conjunct', which denotes a situation wherein two or more planets are in or near the same degree of the zodiac. This term is not particularly obscure, for even in late-nineteenth-century astrological literature, the idea of conjunction is sometimes expressed in phrases such as 'Saturn conjoined with Jupiter in Leo'.

In this case, whichever planets are in conjunction are not in Sagittarius, but near (*vers*) this sign. Now, on either side of Sagittarius lie Scorpio and Capricorn. We must examine the remainder of the line to see if there is a clue as to which of these signs is intended.

The clue lies in the use of the word *exaltation*, which is a specialist astrological term, denoting a system of little importance in modern practical astrology (though its importance to the history of astrology has been recognized by several leading specialists).[16] In brief, it is a system wherein planets were assigned zodiacal signs in which their inherent natures were supposedly reinforced, or strengthened.[17] However, in traditional medieval astrology, no planet was assigned an exaltation *in* Sagittarius. Fortunately for us, Nostradamus is clear about this, for he says merely that the planet is '*near*' Sagittarius.

He says the planet, with its conjuncting planet(s) is: *En son haut auge de l'exaltation. Haut auge* is problematic. *Auge* could be read as the German for 'eye', but it is probably the French for the humble bucket. This may not appear to fit the context of the planetary placings until one visualizes the movement of the planets up and around the great circle of the zodiac, measured in the procession of degrees. Nostradamus seems to visualize this circle as a great water-wheel, swinging around the earth in its Ptolemaic concentrics, with the buckets carrying planets rather than water.

In a horoscope chart, the highest point of exaltation is the sign Capricorn. Significantly, this is usually represented in horoscope charts at the very top of the figure, which is relevant to the 'bucket' imagery of Nostradamus. Capricorn has been carried to the top of the water-wheel. Does this help us determine which planet the wheel carries to this highest point of exaltation of Capricorn?

If we refer to the medieval lists of exaltations, we find that Scorpio has no exaltation. Capricorn, on the other hand, is the exaltation of Mars. This suggests that the enigmatic conjunction (*joint*) involves the planet Mars, in the sign Capricorn.

If this astrological interpretation is correct, then the first two lines of the quatrain should translate: 'When Saturn is in Pisces, and Mars is in a conjunction, near Sagittarius, yet in Capricorn, its place of exaltation . . .' This is a very

123

precise astrological indication. Such a placing of planets is sufficiently rare for us to begin to hunt through ephemerides to see if we can discover the date of such a configuration. The question is, can we find a point in time – after 1555, the date of the first publication of this quatrain – when this astrological condition applied?

Nostradamus, realizing that he will have sent us searching through ephemerides, does offer a clue. This is found in the last line, which seems to translate: 'The Century approaches its renewal'. Clearly, Nostradamus is suggesting that we look into our tables for those decades towards the end of a century – not at the very end, but at an undefined point where it *approaches* its end. The date he is obscuring with such conviction in this quatrain relates to an event which will take place towards the end of a century.

If we look at the years prior to the end of each century, between 1599 and 1999, we find only three possible references which come anywhere close to satisfying the astrological conditions set down by Nostradamus.

Between January 1582 and April 1584, Saturn was in Pisces. During these years, Mars was in Capricorn between January 1584 and February of the same year. On 22 December 1583, Saturn being in Pisces, Mars and the Sun were conjunct in Capricorn.[18]

In this case, both the Sun and Mars were 'towards Sagittarius' – indeed, on the morning of that same day, the Sun had actually been in that sign. As a matter of fact, Venus was on the very edge of Sagittarius, in 29.50 degrees at 7.30 a.m., but in retrograde motion. It is very likely that the tables available to Nostradamus would have shown Venus to have been in Capricorn.

This horoscopic condition satisfies precisely the scenario set down by Nostradamus. Of course, this arcane dating is designed to point to a time which presages 'plague, starvation and death by military means'. Is there any event in 1583 which may be linked with such a prediction?

Unfortunately, there are very few periods free of warfare (as Nostradamus himself admits in another quatrain), and it is quite easy to find examples of plague, starvation and military death for 1583, as for almost every other year. For example, in that year the French under the Duke of Anjou besieged the city of Antwerp, with terrible losses on both sides, while in the religious wars ravaging Germany, 30,000 people died of starvation in the city of Munster alone. However, these events do not appear to carry us beyond the normal condition of what the esotericist Gurdjieff called 'the periodic outbreaks of reciprocal destruction' that appear to be the main theme of world history.[19] One would imagine that when Nostradamus penned this quatrain, he had in mind something altogether more momentous than either Antwerp or Munster.

In spite of all that is currently anticipated about the horrors due for the end of the present century, Nostradamus does not seem to have this in mind. The ephemerides for the end of our own century do not produce anything to fit the astrological conditions Nostradamus laid down. Between 29 January 1994 and 7 April 1996, Saturn was in Pisces. During these years, Mars was in Capricorn from 1 December 1995 to 9 January 1996. On 1 December 1995 Saturn was in Pisces, and both Mars and Venus were in Capricorn. Although this configuration is very close to the astrological stipulation set out in the quatrain, Mars and Venus are not actually in conjunction, and the latter is not close to the Sagittarius cusp.

By contrast, the end of the eighteenth century produces a very different series of events, which do relate to the astrological data in the quatrain. This is perhaps not surprising, for, in his *Epistle to Henry II*, published in the

1558 edition of the *Centuries*, Nostradamus singles out the end of the eighteenth century as marking a particularly important time in the history of the West. Significantly, in this letter he called it 'the renovation of the age', which is very close to the last line of the quatrain we are examining.

At the beginning of January 1789, Saturn was in Pisces, Mars was in Capricorn in conjunction with the Sun. On the first day of that year, the Moon was exactly in conjunction with Saturn. A few days later, the 'Mars–Sun' conjunction would be augmented with Mercury in Capricorn. On 2 January 1789, Saturn was in Pisces, while Mars, the Sun and Mercury were in Capricorn, the first two in almost precise conjunction. These conditions, so precisely pertinent to the quatrain, continued until 19 January 1789.

There may be little doubt, from the last data, that it is the year 1789 which Nostradamus has in mind in this precisely dated quatrain. This is the date arcanely hidden within the quatrain, and the indicator of the time when the 'Century is to approach its renewal'. The historical changes marked by this year are well known, and it has been called by more than one historian 'the Year of Fear'. The events of that year certainly changed the whole face of European and American history. Very quickly, 'as the century approached its renewal', the year saw the very conditions which Nostradamus predicted: *Peste, famine, mort de main militaire* – Plague, famine, death by military activity.

It is typical of the method employed by Nostradamus that he resorted to this obscure use of astrology to point with such remarkable precision to what would be the most important date in the future history of France.

Dissecting quatrain I.16 has allowed us to examine something of the esoteric astrology in which Nostradamus excels, without the distraction of other arcane methods. As a further example of arcane astrology, we need to move on a few years to the next major escalation of world violence which Nostradamus foresaw and dated. This prediction is contained in quatrain VI.4.

DATE OF THE SECOND WORLD WAR

The quatrain is an interesting one, and we shall examine it in some depth at a later point (see page 396). For the moment, our focus is one line from it, which appears to be entirely astrological: *Saturne, Leo, Mars, Cancer en rapine.*

However, as with most of Nostradamus' lines, this is not what it appears to be, since from an astrological point of view, it is sheer nonsense. Cancer, a zodiacal sign, is listed as though it were a planet; furthermore, rapine is not a recognizable astrologic term.

To begin to make sense of the line, let us assume that by *rapine*, Nostradamus means Aries, the sign associated with soldiery and with warfare, through the fact that it is ruled by the planet Mars.[20] (Within the context of the quatrain, this is probably a reasonable assumption, since Aries has rule over Germany, which is the subject of this quatrain.)[21]

However, if *rapine* does mean Aries, the line still does not make sense, as it is quite impossible for one sign, such as Leo or Cancer, to be in another sign (in this case, in Aries). Leo and Cancer must, in this context, mean something else. We must assume that, since they are each ruled by planets which are unique to themselves, and do not share a rulership over any other sign (as do the other five planets), the signs are, in this context, occult blinds for the 'planets' Sun and Moon, respectively. If this argument is valid, then the line: *Saturne, Leo, Mars, Cancer en rapine* may be translated as: 'Saturn, Sun, Mars and Moon in Aries'.

We now must establish what relevance this meaning has

to the preceding three lines, which relate to the destruction of Cologne during the Second World War. It is at this point that we begin to catch a glimpse of the sheer genius through which Nostradamus worked his astrology.

The Second World War began when the British and French declared war on Germany, on 3 September 1939. The extraordinary thing is that on that day, the Moon was in Aries (*Cancer en rapine*).[22] Now, as it happens, from 23 September 1939 until 20 March 1940, Saturn was also in Aries. A most remarkable coincidence is that on the same day that Saturn left Aries, on 20 March 1939, the Sun entered that same sign (thus *Saturne, Leo en rapine*)[23] This passage occurs very, very rarely in any sign, let alone in Aries: it is as though Nostradamus, seeking for some clear way of identifying a particular time in the future, latched upon this strange cosmic coincidence, near the beginning of the War.

The Second World War ended in Europe when the Germans surrendered on 7 May 1945. On that very day, Mars had just entered the sign Aries (hence *Mars en rapine*). What is more remarkable is that on that very day, the planet Venus went direct into Aries, and Mercury was also in Aries.[24]

These Arietan coincidences are too remarkable for us to ignore. Given that he was anxious to give dates for the beginning and ending of the War, Nostradamus was extremely precise: the planets Saturn, Sun, Mars and Moon were involved in coincidences relating to the sign Aries. We have in this one-liner practically two horoscopes for the beginning and ending of the most awful conflict the world has seen. We are told, by statisticians more competent than ourselves, that the likelihood of such factors being involved in a prediction of this kind by chance are billions to one.

THE BATTLE OF LEPANTO

'The great weakness of many of the commentators of Nostradamus,' says Woolf, 'has been their overwhelming desire to prove their own theories.'[25] This is particularly true when writers have assumed that the astrology he practised was little different from that in favour at the turn of the twentieth century. We shall discover in the following pages that nothing could be further from the truth.

Modern commentators have a marked tendency to interpret these late-medieval prophecies as though they were designed for our own contemporaneous world. A good example of this may be traced to quatrain III.3, which opens with a simple astrological time-frame.

Mars & Mercure & l'argent joint ensemble
Vers le midy extréme siccité,
Au fond d'Asie on dira terre tremble,
Corinthe, Ephese lors en perplexité.

Mars, Mercury and Moon joined together,
Towards the midi extreme dryness,
From the depth of Asia they will speak of an earthquake,
Corinth and Ephesus then in perplexity.

Read superficially, the quatrain seems to indicate that at a certain astrological moment, there will be dryness in the south, and that in Asia there will be some earth-shattering event. The cities of Greece and Turkey (represented by the process of synecdoche as *Corinthe* and *Ephese* – see page 541) will be in difficulties. Some modern commentators have interpreted the word Asia in a very liberal manner. For example, de Fontbrune sees in it a reference to an earthquake in Japan, leading to troubles between Greece and Turkey.[26]

Before attempting to determine whether this prediction

relates to our past or future, we should look into the astrological meaning of the first line. The two named planets are Mars and Mercury. However, *l'argent* is literally silver, and since this metal is ruled by the Moon, it may be used poetically to denote the earth's satellite. Probably, Nostradamus has occluded the word because the quatrain deals with the people of the Crescent Moon – who are the Muslims.

Mars, Mercury and the Moon are in the same zodiacal sign (*joint ensemble*) fairly frequently. Accordingly, we cannot read too precise a dating into this astrological reference. Cheetham implied that this prophecy relates only to the year 1977, but in fact exact conjunctions of the three may be determined on very many occasions in the centuries between 1555 and 1977.[27]

Nostradamus was obviously aware of the frequency with which the three planets conjuncted, and that the reference to this would not provide a firm dating for a prophecy. Let us suppose, therefore, that he had in mind a triple conjunction shortly after completion of the quatrain, in 1555, or even shortly after his own death. We find that, for example, the three planets conjunct in the sign Gemini, on 20 July 1564. In this case, the triple conjunction is fairly exact, but there is no reason to assume from the savant's words that this was a precise requirement. Nostradamus said that they should be *joint ensemble* (joined together): he did not employ any of the technical astrological words which describe *conjunction* itself, and so it is likely that he was implying that the planets need only be joined, or posited, in the same sign. If a wide orb (to use the technical term) is permitted, then the triple union becomes a very frequent event. For example, the conjunction would have become operative on 7 May 1560. It would be tiresome to list all the subsequent conjunctions – weak or exact* – but

* An exact conjunction occurs when the two planets appear, from a

it is worth observing that it is certain that Nostradamus had in mind a dating much closer to his own period than the twentieth century.

If we look at sixteenth-century history, we see that the quatrain has considerable relevance to the period around 1564. In that period, the threat from the Turks was at its height, and Nostradamus' contemporaries would be avid for prophecies which (albeit open-ended) promised earth-trembling events in Asia. These quatrains would be especially welcome if they implied a victory for the West, as this one does.

Since the conquest of Greece by the Islamic Turks had been completed by 1466, Corinth was under Turkish domination throughout the whole of the lifetime of Nostradamus. In addition, during his lifetime Turkish pressure on Europe increased, and shortly after his death, between 1566 and 1570, they took the islands of Chios, Naxos and Cyprus. If such cities as Turkish Ephesus and Corinth could be said to be 'troubled' or 'perplexed' (*en perplexité*), then this would make a good read for Nostradamus' contemporaries, desperate for release from the Asiatic threat. The horror of the Muslim domination of the eastern edges of Europe in the sixteenth century is now lost to us, but in those days there was great consternation that countries so close to Europe were being cruelly mistreated and forced to pay enormous taxes to Muslims. Especial indignation was reserved for the fact that those under Turkish domination were compelled to make annual tributes of Christian children, who were used as slaves and

geocentric viewpoint, to occupy the same degree, minute and second of the zodiac. In astrology, each conjunction is permitted an orb (or latitude) of a few degrees – the width of this orb depending upon the identity of the planets involved. A weak conjunction is when the two planets are separated almost to the limits of the permitted orb – usually between 3 and 6 degrees.

soldiers by the Muslim Turks. Within such a context, the quatrain has considerable significance, even if the promised date for its fulfilment was not the first triple conjunction of 1564. Could the date of a decisive conflict be traced to another late-sixteenth-century triple conjunction?

The year 1571 saw the power of the Turks unexpectedly broken in the east at the naval battle of Lepanto. In that year, the three planets – Moon, Mercury and Mars – were in the same sign of Aquarius. In fact, not only were these three planets in the sign Aquarius, but so also were the Sun and Jupiter.[28] Nostradamus was understating – offering a sort of extended synecdoche: the planets he mentioned were only three of five.

This analysis of the astrology within the quatrain leads to the conclusion that Nostradamus foresaw that 1571 would be when the earth would tremble for the Turks, and when both Corinth (enslaved foreign city) and Ephesus (Turkish homeland) would be in great difficulties. Significantly, he seems even to have pinpointed the site of the battle, which was off the Gulf of Corinth.

Nostradamus even seems to have used a Green Language technique to hint at the importance of the zodiacal sign Aquarius. The first two words of the middle two lines combine to form *Versau* (*Verseau*), the French word for Aquarius:

> **Vers** *le midy extréme siccité,*
> **Au** *fond d'Asie on dira terre tremble*

While this may be regarded as being coincidence in ordinary versification, it is a perfectly acceptable Green Language usage. One wonders, indeed, if it is this verse to which Collot d'Herbois referred in his short humorous stage play about Nostradamus, first performed in 1777. In

132

the second scene of this one-acter, Dastrimon (Nostradamus) exults on how exciting is his intimate contact with the stars: . . . *je pousse Mercure en passant, ici je salve Jupiter, je dis deux mots a Verseau, je fais une petite politesse aux Gemeaux* . . . [29] The astrological nuances are excellent. To remain on the good side of the planetary gods one *should* behave in such a way: one should push one's fortunes through the god of commerce, Mercury, one should salute the beneficient Jupiter, head of the planetary pantheon, and one should be polite to the twins (who represent both life and death – immortality and mortality). The puzzle is why one should say two words to Aquarius (*Verseau*). Is it possible that Collot had recognized the hidden two words in quatrain III.3?

In the light of our reading of the quatrain, the second line begins to take on an interesting significance. In traditional astrology, derived from the Ptolemaic literature (see Appendix Six), Aquarius is said to be a 'southern' sign (*midy* means southern), and is said to be 'hot'. Although each of these terms has largely been dropped from modern astrology, in the sixteenth century anyone familiar with the art would have recognized the implication of the two words. The 'southern heat' of Aquarius would cause dryness (*siccité*). Here, the reference confirms that the conjunction of the three planets takes place in the southern, hot sign of Aquarius – as was the case in 1571. 'Southern', 'hot' and 'dry' are all specialist astrological terms, and all relate to Aquarius. This is a combination of astrology and Green Language usage at its best.

Certainly the battle of Lepanto was one of the most momentous events of the sixteenth century. The Turkish fleet was defeated by the Holy League (Spain, Venice, the Papacy, and one or two Italian states), and the Turks lost 117 ships and over 30,000 men. Although the Turks soon regrouped and rebuilt their ships, and went on to take

133

Cyprus, the effect of Lepanto on the psyche of Europe was almost incalculable: it showed that, with determination, and with the sort of coalition which the Holy League offered, the Turks (hitherto believed to be invincible) could be defeated. In fact, the Turkish pressure did not really relax during the remaining years of the century: in the same year as Lepanto, the Turks reached Moscow and destroyed much of it, bringing back for their slave-markets over 100,000 captives. In the following years, they took the north-western coasts of Africa, leaving the Crescent ensign along the littoral even to this day. Nonetheless, European despair over Turkish expansion was rarely quite the same after 1571.

Our survey of the use to which Nostradamus put astrology has revealed to us some interesting facts. The arcane astrology in quatrain IV.100 is fairly easy to grasp. To some extent, the astrology of quatrain III.3 is more complex, yet still within the understanding of the layman. However, in certain other quatrains, Nostradamus exploits to the full the esoteric potential of astrology, and constructs verses which are extremely difficult to decode, even by those intimately familiar with astrological terminologies.

THE SECOND WORLD WAR

Among such verses is the outstanding example of quatrain I.50. It is only after a full analysis that this astrological quatrain is revealed as a vehicle for a precision of dating which is rare in the annals of prophecy. In the French, this quatrain reads:

> *Chef d'Aries, Iupiter et Saturne,*
> *Dieu eternel quelles mutations!*

Puis apres long siecle son malin temps retourne,
Gaule & Italie, quelles esmotions.

Until we are able to discern its hidden meaning, let us take
it that the verse means approximately:

> Head of Aries, Jupiter and Saturn,
> God eternal, what mutations!
> Then, after a long century his evil time returns,
> France and Italy – what emotions.

We shall show through analysis that it is the arcane
meaning hidden in the first line which reveals the secret
theme of this remarkable quatrain. The line may be divided
into two sections. The first, which mentions the 'Head of
Aries', is a specialist astrological term, referring to a specific
point in the zodiacal band. We shall return to this in due
course. The second part of the line names two planets – the
so-called 'ponderables', Jupiter and Saturn, and refers to
their coming together – their *conjunction*. This was one of
the most important of all planetary conjunctions, and its
nature can be clarified by a brief examination of some early-
sixteenth-century predictive literature, which preceded the
publication of the *Centuries*.

The conjunctions of the 'ponderable planets', Jupiter and
Saturn (so called in the sixteenth century because of their
seeming slowness), are called Great Conjunctions, and have
always been regarded as marking important points in
history. They occupied the minds of all the great astrologers of the sixteenth century, some of whose writings on
the subject certainly influenced Nostradamus. Some of the
more important literature of this genre seems to have been
directed to tracing the upheavals to which the ponderable
conjunctions would give rise – especially towards the end of
the eighteenth century.

Now, if Nostradamus had an obsession (beyond the

futurity of the century in which he lived), then it was with what he regarded as the pivotal point in history – the French Revolution. Several of his quatrains deal with the Revolution, and with its consequences for France, as well as for certain of the individuals who played a central role in the drama. However, it has long been recognized by historians that Nostradamus was not alone in perceiving the last decades of the eighteenth century as being crucial in the development of Europe, and perhaps of the world. As we shall see, the influential early-fifteenth-century astrologer, Pierre Turrel, who died before Nostradamus wrote his *Prophéties*, had given the precise date of 1789 as the beginning of the troubles, and insisted that this period of anarchy and disorder would last for 25 years.

There is internal evidence that Nostradamus was aware of the tradition to which Turrel refers. Nostradamus quite openly discussed a near date to this event (along with its implications) in his *Epistle* to Henry II, and this date proves to be the focus of several of his quatrains. We showed earlier, using an arcane dating system which we have managed to decode, that Nostradamus determined the crucial year 1789 with extraordinary precision in cosmic terms.

It must be borne in mind that Nostradamus often consulted and used the predictive and occult literature of his day as a suitable ground for his own prophecies. Laver recognized just such a reference in quatrain I.51, from an important book by Richard Roussat: *Le Livre de l'estat et mutations des temps*, 1550. In this is the curious phrase *renovation du monde* (which might be translated loosely as 'renewal of the world'), that appears several times in the *Prophéties*.

This 'renewal of the world' was foreseen by Roussat in connection with the Great Conjunction of Saturn and

Jupiter in Aries, supposed to take place in 1792. Significantly, in Roussat, the conjunction is to take place in the '*Chef d'Aries*', and it would seem that *Chef d'Aries* was borrowed by Nostradamus from Roussat. The latter claimed that the Great Conjunction would take place near '*la teste d'Aries*' (the head of Aries) in 1703.

We shall locate the precise position of this *Chef d'Aries*, and trace its significance, later. For the moment, let us turn our attention to the second part of the first line of the quatrain, which points to the conjunction between Jupiter and Saturn.

Since the conjunction involves two powerful planets, and occurred fairly rarely, it was used by astrologers as an important sign of changes in historical events. The sixteenth-century astrologer John Plonisco had based his predictions for a 40-year period merely on the famous conjunction of 1524.[30] (The conjunction of Saturn and Jupiter was especially powerful in this year, as it was enmeshed with a conjunction of 'almost all the planets in the sign Pisces in February of the year 1524 of the Incarnation'.)[31] Many (though not Plonisco) feared that this particular conjunction would result in a terrible flood (a prediction which proved, in the longer term, groundless). For example, the Italian astrologer-monk Nicolaus Peranzonus set out in considerable detail all the astrological factors which he proposed would contribute to a flood in that year,[32] the strongest of which was the Great Conjunction; as a result, he wrote, Piscean rains would pour floods over the entire northern hemisphere. (In a later chapter, we shall observe the influence which Peranzonus had on Nostradamus in a different context to the astrological.)

The next Great Conjunction would be in Scorpio, in 1544, and this troubled some astrologers, even though they recognized that its effects were not to last for long. That which followed, in August 1563, was to have a more enduring consequence for astrology. It was Tycho Brahe's observation of this conjunction which led him (at the age of only 16) to realize that the famous tables of Stadius were significantly in error; in consequence, Tycho Brahe spent his life observing and calculating, in order to construct an accurate ephemeris.[33] This is a relevant point, for while Brahe was attempting with the rational faculties to establish the accuracy of the timing of such things as the Great Conjunction, Nostradamus was foreseeing and charting (with extraordinary accuracy) Great Conjunctions, and their effects, nearly 400 years into the future. The irony is that, when not immersed in the astral inspection of futurity, and engaged in casting contemporaneous horoscopes, Nostradamus would almost certainly have recourse to the Stadius tables, for 1554 to 1570 – the very same tables in which he was said to have predicted his own death.[34]

Stadius noted, in the edition of the *New Ephemerides* which Nostradamus would have consulted, that planets could lead to the fatal downfalls of kingdoms. Writing on a more personal level, Stadius remarked that the captivity of Francis I of France had been accurately predicted (to the very hour) by a Franciscan monk, who had also foreseen the death of the Prince of Orange at the age of 26. Stadius may have confused this 'Franciscan monk' with the great early-fifteenth-century astrologer, Pierre Turrel, who made precisely such a prediction about Francis I. We shall soon confirm that it was this Pierre Turrel who had a powerful influence on Nostradamus, and even shaped the quatrain we are investigating, through his writings on such astrological predictive techniques as the Great Conjunctions.

In terms of human lifetimes, Great Conjunctions are relatively rare events. As we have seen from the medieval trigons diagram of *fig. 22*, they step through the zodiac in arcs of about 117 degrees, marking in their progress great triangles, which, generally speaking, fall into patterns of

The Astrology of Nostradamus

elemental groups. This means that for a specific period, the planets are in signs of the Earth quadruplicity,* followed by a session in (say) the Air triplicity, and so on. The trigons of the 1532 sequence had been the Watery signs, which is why the conjunctions were linked in the popular mind with flooding.

In approximately 800 years, the sequences of trigonal conjunctions pass through all the signs of the zodiac. It is for this reason that they were adopted by medieval astrologers (as always, following the Arabian astrologers) as useful indices of social change. Tycho Brahe wrote of the relevance to European history of the Great Conjunction of the two planets in Sagittarius, on 18 December 1603, for he saw it as marking the beginning of an age of peace. It is clear that the professional prophets – such as Nostradamus – were not in sympathy with this view. In fact, in strictly astrological terms, it would be more likely that conjunctions in the Fire trigons would bring discord and war.

This warlike nature of the Fire trigons explains why the date given by Nostradamus in his *Epistle*, as marking one of the perturbations of the future ages, is 1782. On 5 November 1782 Jupiter and Saturn conjuncted in 29 degrees of the Fire sign, Sagittarius.

Having established something of the astrological implications behind Nostradamus' innocent-seeming reference to Jupiter and Saturn (*Iupiter et Saturne*) in quatrain I.50, we should remind ourselves that the pair are visualized by Nostradamus as conjuncting in a specific point in Aries, in the *Chef d'Aries*, lifted from Roussat.

The Aries of the tropical zodiac is not the same as the Aries of the sidereal zodiac. Many non-astrologers might

---

* In the traditional astrological system, the Earth quadruplicities are Taurus, Virgo and Capricorn. They are triple, yet called quadruplicities because the latter word refers to the fact that there are four elements, which repeat three times in the twelve signs.

139

find this statement perplexing, so, as it is important to our approach to the quatrain, we shall make some effort to clarify it. The tropical zodiac is a circle marked out in the skies by the seeming movement of the Sun around the Earth. It is divided into 12 equal segments, and is ultimately the definer of the progression of seasons on earth. This zodiacal belt, measured out by the Sun, is, properly speaking, the only zodiac. It is the zodiac used by almost all astrologers in their computations of charts.

However, due to historical reasons, there are several other systems of stellar measurement which have been called zodiacs. Among these is the constellational zodiac, or sidereal zodiac. As the latter name suggests, this zodiac is not measured out by the movement of the Sun, but by the positions of the stars. It is not divided into twelve equal arcs. The sidereal zodiac has been defined in different ways, but usually, each of the 12 areas (often called 'asterisms') is defined according to the arc covered by a particular group of stars. None of the groups has equal arcs. For example, the star-group called Aries has an arc of about 24 degrees, while the star-group of Virgo has 46 degrees. A modern definition of this sidereal zodiac – the International Astronomical Union definition of 1928 – has actually represented 13 star-groups, the interloper being the asterism* Ophiuchus (i.e. a constellation which straddles the celestial equator in an arc of approximately 40 degrees).

The problem is that the two zodiacs, however defined, do not correspond spatially. By definition, the Aries of the tropical zodiac begins in the first degree of Aries. The asterism of Aries in the sidereal zodiac has drifted (due to

---

* An asterism is a collection of stars, but in most astrological contexts the word refers to a distinctive, historically described configuration of stars – usually a constellation, or a group of stars in a constellation. In modern times, the word is often wrongly used to denote a sign of the zodiac.

a slow and complex solar movement called precession) so that it is now well into the Taurus of the tropical zodiac.

Properly speaking, the sidereal zodiac should not be called a zodiac at all. It is a constellation grid, imposed upon a band of the skies. However, in the Ptolemaic astrology which the medieval world inherited, mention of these two distinctive zodiacs is commonplace, and in some cases it is necessary to know which an astrologer is talking about to determine accurately the co-ordinates he or she has in mind.

Whatever Roussat had in mind, when Nostradamus uses the phrase, *Chef d'Aries*, he is not referring to the tropical zodiac, but to a fixed star (or group of fixed stars) in the head of sidereal Aries. This means that the conjunction of Jupiter and Saturn to which he refers in this quatrain must be in zodiacal Taurus.

In the constellations, the 'Head of Aries' is marked by three stars. In the modern classification, these are *alpha*, *beta* and *gamma*. In the days of Nostradamus, these were called *Hamal*, *Sharatan* and *Mesarthim* – each name derived from the Arabic transmission of Ptolemaic astrology.

As we shall see, the supposed influence of these stars, as well as their location, is important within the context of the Nostradamus quatrain. The great Ptolemy, to whom every astrologer (including the Prophet of Salon) is indebted, had insisted that the stars in the head of Aries had an influence similar to that transmitted by Mars and Saturn. This planetary duad promises only evil influence, involving violence and discord.

Indeed, viewed in terms of astrological influences, this is an extremely unpleasant triad of stars. Hamal (now in 6 degrees of Taurus) is supposed to cause violence, cruelty and premeditated crime. Being in Aries, which rules the head, it is linked with violence to the head. Being a ruler of both Germany and England, it is connected with violence between or within these two countries. Sharatan (now in 2 degrees of Taurus) causes physical injuries, defeat, destruction by fire, war or earthquake.[35]

The astrology which Nostradamus offered was forthright. In making this reference to Taurus, he was pointing to a very precise moment in history: a Great Conjunction can only repeat its approximate location in the right ascension once every 800 years. What is this precise moment in history? Is the date specified by Nostradamus in this quatrain the same date given by Roussat – namely, 1702?

This Great Conjunction would take place on 21 May 1702, in 7 degrees of Aries. This would appear to meet the conditions set out in the Nostradamus quatrain, for this meeting of planets is near the beginning of Aries. However, in 1550, Richard Roussat had mentioned specifically the conjunction of the two ponderable planets which was predicted for 1702. This date lies at the very beginning of the century. Nostradamus, however, refers to another conjunction, which occurs 'after a long century'. Does this mean that he is referring to a conjunction of Jupiter and Saturn which is expected towards the end of the eighteenth century?

This suspicion may be confirmed by the fact that while the conjunction falls near the beginning (head) of Aries in the tropical zodiac, it is not near the fixed stars which mark the Head of Aries in the constellational or sidereal zodiac.

Roussat lifted most of his ideas from previous prophets. In this case – in the predictions for the eighteenth century – he filched text from the writings of Pierre Turrel. Turrel, from Autun, had a prodigious reputation for learning and astrological competence. In a famous posthumous work which is now lost, he dated the French Revolution exactly to 1789. This book was ostensibly a translation of a Latin manuscript, written and composed in the monastery of the three Valleys (*trois Valées*). Almost certainly this is an occult blind, for Turrel wrote the book himself around 1530. Discretion was necessary, however, as he had already been in trouble with the authorities for his wayward approach to astrology: no doubt he would prefer to hide behind the name of a mere translator of such radical ideas as this book contained.

Turrel's book, which is so scarce now as to be regarded by bibliophiles as completely lost, had the eye-catching title, *Le Periode, c'est-a-dire la fin du monde* ... Ironically, what was probably among the last surviving copies of this extraordinary book, which predicted to the year the French Revolution, was destroyed during that same Revolution. However, at least one copy must have survived that holocaust, for it was seen by Eugène Bareste before 1840. Lynn Thorndike admits to not having seen the book, though offers a footnote to the effect that a full account of it is given in an anonymous note in Guyton's *Recherches historiques*, 1874.[36]

Strangely, parts of the book *have* survived, as sections were summarized and short passages were copied before the destructive powers of the Revolution were unleashed.[37] From these we are able to deduce something of the import of this influential work, which has considerable relevance to the astrological techniques and cosmic rhythms adopted by Nostradamus. We know, for example, that Turrel reveals some knowledge of the Secundadeians' literature (though he is apparently in disagreement with Trithemius about the actual periodicities involved), which just may have been introduced to him by his acquaintance, the celebrated occultist Cornelius Agrippa. There are one or two other ideas which would have appealed to the Master of Salon – especially those relating to the precession of the equinoxes, the revolutions of Saturn (which give a 300-year period), and his own view that the world would come to an end round about 270 years from the time of writing. Significantly, given our theme, Turrel is fearful of the conjunction of Jupiter and Saturn, 'in the venomous sign of the Scorpion in 1544'.

In fact, the date given by Turrel for the end of the world – 270 years after writing – offers a clue to the date on which Turrel wrote *Le Periode*, for it is clear that his *annus terribilis* was 1789. This suggests that *Le Periode* was written, though not actually published, in 1519, or thereabouts. Although Laver has said that *Le Periode* was published in 1531, the edition had neither date nor named printer, and was published posthumously. It was not unusual in the late fifteenth and early sixteenth centuries for manuscripts to circulate for years prior to publication.

Certain prophecies from Turrel's book have survived because passages were lifted (without acknowledgement) by Richard Roussat, in 1550. As James Laver has pointed out, we are fortunate that the predictive passage relating to 1789 was copied by Roussat in *Le Livre de l'estat et mutations des temps*, 1550, or we might be tempted to disbelieve that the book had ever existed. Laver was wrong to some extent, as other notice of the work is on record, but the original Turrel book has certainly disappeared.

In one surviving passage, Roussat reads: *En apres la tres fameuse approximation et union de Saturn et de Jupiter qui fera **pres de la teste d'Aries**, l'an de Nostre Seigneur mil sept cens et deux ... grandes alterations et mutations*. The bold italics are our own, for they point to the source used by Nostradamus.

In yet another part of his book – and still no doubt plagiarizing Turrel – Roussat wrote, 'We are approaching the future renewal of the world, round about two hundred and forty three years ... taking the date of the compilation of this present tract.' Laver was the first to observe that, while the publication date was 1550, the dedication to *Le*

Livre is dated 1449: this means that the reference is to 1792, the year of the inauguration of the revolutionary calendar. We shall see Turrel's ideas reappearing in several of Nostradamus' quatrains, but it is difficult to determine whether these came from Turrel, or from other sources.

Does it matter whether Nostradamus is quoting Roussat or Turrel? Yes, given the ignorance in which we remain regarding the details of the Turrel book, it does. The first two lines of the quatrain which we are examining are lifted straight from Roussat, who refers to the 'famous orb and conjunction of Saturn and Jupiter which will take place *near the head of Aries*, in the year of Our Lord, one thousand, seven hundred and two' which will bring 'great alterations and changes'. Without doubt, the Turrel prediction depends upon the May 1702 conjunction of the two planets, at the beginning of Aries.

Here, then, we have the identifying phrase, *Chef d'Aries* (Head of Aries), which Nostradamus' readers would immediately recognize as a reference to the Turrel/Roussat predictions, published only five years before the *Prophéties*.

The importance of the Turrel/Roussat predictions lies in that we have been able to trace in them a meaning in the first two lines of the Nostradamus quatrain. However, we rephrase our earlier question, and ask if Nostradamus also had in mind, like the enforced twins, the year 1789 when he penned quatrain I.50.

Curiously, the answer is no. We write, 'curiously', for under normal circumstances, Nostradamus was ever keen to publish arcane references to the French Revolution.

If Nostradamus did *not* have in mind the conjunction of 1789 when he wrote the quatrain, what did he have in mind? To answer this, we shall have to search through the available computer ephemerides, glancing at the relative positions of Saturn and Jupiter.

145

After the 1702 conjunction, the next time Jupiter and Saturn conjoin near the stars in the head of Aries is in our own century. To put this conjunction in context, it is worth recording that the trigons for our own century are mainly in Earth signs, with one interval in the Air sign of Libra. Between 1901 and 2000, there have been, or will be, eight conjunctions.

The Earth trigon Great Conjunctions for our own century are as follows:

1881	18 Apr	2 TA
1901	27 Nov	14 CP
1921	10 Sep	27 VI
1940	8 Aug	15 TA
1940	20 Oct	13 TA
1941	15 Feb	10 TA
1961	19 Feb	26 CA
1981	1 Jan	10 LI (repeats in Libra 5 Mar & 24 Jul)
2000	28 May	23 TA

Anyone checking these dates against an ephemeris will realize that for several days before the precise conjunction, and for several days – even weeks – afterwards, the planets stalk each other, and even at times repeat their meetings, or conjunctions, as one or other of them goes retrograde.

Only the 1940 conjunction is within a degree or so of the fixed star, Hamal, set in the head of Aries. It had not been near that position for over 800 years. One wonders if Nostradamus, with his usual remarkable perspicuity, had known that by the time this event took place Hamal would have been classified as alpha, the first star of Aries marked by the first letter of the ancient Greek alphabet – which is to say, the chief of Aries, *Chef d'Aries*?

In the middle of June 1940, the two planets had entered into the orb of the conjunction. On the 17th, Jupiter was in

7 degrees of Taurus, and Saturn was in 11 degrees. On that day, Jupiter was within a degree of the fixed star Hamal. It was on this day that the French asked the Germans for an armistice, and France was technically defeated. On the following day, the evacuation of the British forces from Cherbourg was completed. Nostradamus' beloved France had fallen to the Germans, and Britain was left to face the German might alone.

We now begin to see the significance of Nostradamus' last line. In 1940 the evil times had returned, and *Gaule* (France) was going through *quelles esmotions*. Almost *en passant*, one finds oneself asking if this use of the word *Gaule* is in any way intended to prevision the French genius, General de Gaulle, who participated in the reversal of the French defeat. Remarkable as this might seem, the notion is not too far-fetched. Such a use of personal names is entirely in accord with Nostradamus' method: there are several quatrains in which he identifies the names of participants in the future actions. Perhaps, if there is such a thing as coincidence, then this *Gaule* is merely coincidental. Even so, Nostradamus did have available a number of other words and symbols to denote France, yet chose in this context the term *Gaule*.

One final question remains: why did Nostradamus mention Italy (*Italie*) in this context? Once again, the answer lies in the stars – or more precisely in the Great Conjunction against the skies.

For two or three months after August 1940, Saturn and Jupiter remained close to each other. This is mainly because Saturn was retrograde for all those months, while Jupiter also went retrograde, on 5 September. The planets played a sort of cat-and-mouse game near the degrees close to the fixed star Hamal. On 20 October 1940, the two ponderable planets conjuncted again, this time in 13 degrees of Taurus. This was the month when Mussolini invaded Greece, and brought Italy actively into the war.

AN ASTROLOGICAL PUZZLE

It must be clear from the example we have just studied that not all the 'astrological' quatrains are easy to translate. Since Nostradamus used his planetary and zodiacal references either to date a particular event precisely, or to give a general date for it, it is usually possible to scan the astrology to derive some information of value. But even when we have managed to calculate a date from examination of a quatrain, it is not always possible to interpret its significance. A good example of this is quatrain VIII.91:

> *Parmy les champs de Rodanes entrées*
> *Où les croisez seront presques unis,*
> *Les deux brassieres en pisces rencontrées,*
> *Et un grand nombre par deluge punis.*

The verse contains linguistic puzzles in each line. For the moment, let us take the following as a 'translation' guide:

> Entries among the fields of Rhodes
> Where the crossed will be almost united,
> The two shining ones to meet in the fishes,
> And a great number punished by deluge.

The third line of this quatrain is entirely astrological, which means that, properly interpreted, it should offer us a very precise date, or dates. *Les deux brassieres* means 'the two glittering or shining things'. The word is from the verb *brassiller*, which means to 'glitter', or 'shine', as does the sea in sunlight. Since these shining things are to meet in the

148

zodiacal signs Pisces (*pisces rencontrées*), we must deduce that they are two planets.

The phrase *brassieres en Pisces* has been misread by all commentators known to us. Anatole le Pelletier, the nineteenth-century French scholar, interprets it as a reference to Mars and Venus, basing his argument on details of mythology, while Garencières thought that it was a reference to a constellation, the *Croziers*.* The latter was wrong in his opinion, yet his instinct had carried him in the right direction. These are the same stars which Dante – with knowledge derived from initiation sources – wrote of in his *Purgatorio*:

> *e vidi quatro stelle*
> *Non viste mai fuor che alla prima gente . . .*

> and I saw four stars
> Not seen before save by the first people . . .

The mystic four are the constellation now called *Crux*. It is likely that Nostradamus had Dante in mind when he constructed the quatrain, as the Italian poet (who symbolically ended the three great books of his *Commedia* with the word *stelle*, 'stars') had seen the constellation using an occult technique known only to few, when Venus was in Pisces (*en Pisces*). The Dantesque reference enables us to make sense of the word *croisez* in the second line, for in 1520, Pigafetta, who had sailed with Magellan and seen the stars for himself, called them El Crucero, mentioning *en passant* that Dante had first described the constellation.[38]

---

* This is a version of Crux, the Cross, which (with very many variant names) is one of the constellations, with the brightest stars roughly forming a cross. There is meaningful, yet secret, magic in the ancient name: as the historian of constellation law, Richard Allen, points out, it could last be seen on the horizon of Jerusalem (latitude 31° 46′ 45″) at about the time that Christ was crucified.

Since the stars were seen by the first people (the *prima gente*, as Dante put it, who may or may not have been Adam and Eve),[39] it also helps us understand the reference to the flood in the last line of the verse; while the quatrain is certainly a prediction about some future event, Nostradamus has chosen to couch it in a Biblical framework which adds unity to the imagery.

The Greek names for the planets Jupiter and Saturn are both from a root connected with light and with shining. In Greek, Jupiter is *Phaithon*, which, besides denoting the planet, means radiant. Because it is 'radiant', the word is sometimes applied to the Moon, and to the Sun. Sometimes, the brilliant constellation Auriga is also called *Phaethon*. However, in astrological contexts, the word almost always refers to Jupiter: both names were well known to sixteenth-century astrologers as they were used by Ptolemy in the standard classical astrological textbook of the time. In accordance with the ancient belief that the planets were living beings, their physical bodies merely the outer aspect of their inner work, Ptolemy would often refer to them as 'the Star of' such-and-such a planetary god.[40] The same propensity, to see the planets as governed by spiritual beings, survives in a less impaired form in the Trithemius *De Secundadeis*, 1522, which deeply influenced Nostradamus.

The Greek *Phainon* is one of the most mysterious and arcane terms to have survived from the past. In astrology, it denotes the planet Saturn. However, the word is derived from the verb *phaino* meaning 'bring to light': it is ultimately the same root which gives us the modern word phenomena, reminding us that the great Greek astronomer Eudoxos called his book on the stars *Phenomena*. Now, in astrology, Saturn is regarded as the marker of time: man cannot travel in spirit beyond the confines of Saturn – it is the limiter of human experience (just as the phenomenal world is). There is clearly a much deeper meaning in the original Greek name for Saturn than the translation 'The Shining One' suggests.

In the third line of this quatrain, Nostradamus is telling us, in a fairly arcane way, that the two planets, Jupiter and Saturn, are conjunct in Pisces. We have already discussed the nature of such a conjunction – the Great Conjunction, as it is called – and we recognize that the event is rare enough to facilitate fairly accurate dating. In fact, from the time this quatrain was written, up to the end of the millennium, Jupiter and Saturn have conjuncted in Pisces only twice: 3 May 1583 in 20 Pisces, and 24 February 1643 in 25 Pisces.

Having arrived at two possible dates to which the quatrain may conceivably refer, we find ourselves at a loss to comment usefully on the remaining lines of the quatrain. It is obvious that Nostradamus is intending to tell us that a large number (of people?) will be punished by a deluge at the time of one or other of these conjunctions. There appears to have been no significant flooding during the years in question, and we must leave it to a more competent historian to determine to what event this quatrain might refer. We would be delighted to hear from specialists who might have proposals for interpreting this quatrain, for either of the two dates we offer.

Our survey of Nostradamus' use of astrology in his quatrains has carried us into fairly arcane themes. However, our final survey takes us into a realm so arcane that it has never really been fully integrated into modern occultism. This is the realm of the planetary angels, which reached Nostradamus through two main sources – the translation of Trithemius, and the misunderstandings of Turrel. This important astrological material is assessed in detail in the next chapter.

Chapter 3

The Planetary Angels

Plaira à vostre plus qu'imperiale Majesté me pardonner, protestant devant Dieu & ses Saincts que je ne pretens de mettre riens quelconque par escrit en la presente Epistre qui soit contrè la vraye foy Catholique, conferant les calculations Astronomiques jouxte mon sçavoir:

May it please your more than imperial Majesty to pardon me, protesting (as I do) before God and his Saints that, while presenting Astronomical calculations according to my knowledge, I do not pretend to set down in writing in the present Letter anything which might be contrary to the true Catholic faith.

(From the text of Nostradamus' *Epistle to Henry II*, immediately prior to dealing with the chronology which is the basis for the Trithemian dating system. The French is from the 1668 Amsterdam edition of the *Prophéties*.)

In his *Epistle to Henry II*, Nostradamus claimed that he had calculated his prophecies according to 'astronomical rule'. As we have already seen in the previous chapter, this is absolutely true – provided, of course, one interprets 'astronomical rule' in the light of arcane astrology. However, the justification for this astrology, which Nostradamus gives in his *Epistle*, does not make sense in either an astronomical or an astrological context.

This *Epistle to Henry II* is sandwiched between Centuries VII and VIII. In it, Nostradamus develops two long and complex paragraphs dealing with the chronology of the world. More than once, he insists that the chronology he offers is in accordance with the sacred scriptures. In the first section of this chronology, he seems to come to the conclusion that the world was created in 4757 BC. In the second section, he seems to come to the conclusion that the world was created in 4173 BC, or 4182 BC. The passages really appear to have no significance within this letter, and they may only be understood in terms of a wish to refer to an arcane system of dating which Nostradamus has used in the quatrains. It is no accident that this *Epistle* has been placed immediately after the seventh Century, as this dating system is based on septenaries.

In one of the long sections which deal with this question of the date of Creation, Nostradamus states that he has 'calculated these present prophecies in accordance with the order of the chain which contains the *revolutions*'. This passage has been the undoing of many commentators, who have failed to recognize that these 'revolutions' are the occult planetary system of dating published by the great arcanist Trithemius in 1522.

A sixteenth-century astrologer might be forgiven for assuming that the word *revolutions* referred to the planetary conjunctions of the superior planets, for, as we have seen, this word was often used to denote such slow-moving aspects (*fig. 22*). In this case, however, such an astrologer would have been wrong, and we must conclude that Nostradamus wanted him – like everyone else – to misread the text, as part of the extensive programme of intentional obfuscation.

The chronology to which Nostradamus points appears to

be Biblical, whereas it is really entirely esoteric, being derived ultimately from ancient Gnosticism. As we shall see, the references to surmised dates of creation are sure indications that Nostradamus has adopted an occult system of dating, according to a system of planetary archangelic periodicities. These archangels were called the *Secundadeis* by Trithemius in 1522, and it is almost certainly from Trithemius that Nostradamus obtained his information about these planetary beings, and their influence upon past and future.[1]

The theory behind the Secundadeian periodicities was very ancient, and, in his own text, Trithemius admits that he was merely presenting material formerly gathered from old documents by the 'Conciliator' – the name given in medieval literature to Peter of Abano, an occultist and astrologer of the turn of the thirteenth century, after the short title of his most influential book. In turn, Abano had taken the material from sources which can be traced back to the Gnostics. To appreciate the implications of this system of dating, we must glance at the ideas contained in these texts, and especially in the one which Trithemius published, 20 years before Nostradamus began work on his first batch of quatrains.

According to Trithemius, the Secundadeis are seven planetary angels, who rule European history for specific periods of time, in a pre-ordained sequence of rulerships. Each period is 354 years and 4 months in length. The first periodicity, marked by the governorship of the angel of Saturn, Ophiel, began with the creation of Adam. The sequence of rulerships and their corresponding dates, in years and months, as provided by Trithemius, are given below.[2]

Ophiel	Saturn	354	4
Anael	Venus	708	8

Zachariel	Jupiter	1063	
Raphael	Mercury	1417	4
Samael	Mars	1771	8
Gabriel	Moon	2126	
Michael	Sun	2480	4
Ophiel	Saturn	2834	8
Anael	Venus	3189	
Zachariel	Jupiter	3543	4
Raphael	Mercury	3897	8
Samael	Mars	4252	
Gabriel	Moon	4606	4
Michael	Sun	4960	8
Ophiel	Saturn	5315	

Aber nact der geburt Chrsti 109.

Jar was und Orifiel ein geyst Saturni inngemeltem (?) seiner Regiment gewesen 245 und 8 monat is Jesus Chrstus der Suhn Gottes am 25 tage der Christmonats zum Bethlehem der Judischen Lands auss Maria der Junctfrauen geborn.

Anael	Venus	462	4
Zachariel	Jupiter	816	8
Raphael	Mercury	1171	
Samael	Mars	1525	4
Gabriel	Moon	1880	8
Michael	Sun	2235	
Ophiel	Saturn	2589	4
Anael	Venus	2943	8
Zachariel	Jupiter	3298	
Raphael	Mercury	3652	4 etc.

Although both the Latin and German editions of Trithemius' work would have been available to Nostradamus, it would appear from the 'Biblical' dating in his *Epistle* that Nostradamus was intent on constructing his own system of dating. The following dates may be abstracted from this arcanely written letter:

Adam to Noah	1242 years
Noah to Abraham	1080 years
Abraham to Moses	515 years or 516
Moses to David	570 years
David to Jesus	1350 years
	————
	4757

Since a different date of Creation is implied, this differs from the Trithemian system by 667 years. Later in the same letter, and as though to entirely obscure the matter, Nostradamus reverts to this question of chronology. On this occasion he is more specific, and (with typical obfuscation) arrives at a different date for Creation. There is absolutely no agreement between this second list and the one we have just examined. Here follows merely a digest of the basis for his reckoning.

Adam to Noah	1506
Noah to Flood	600
Flood	1 and 2 months
Flood to Abraham	295
Abraham to Isaac	100
Isaac to Jacob	60
Jacob to Exodus	430
Exodus to Temple	480
From Temple to Jesus	490

Although Nostradamus claims that these periods give a total of 4,173, he is wrong – no doubt he did this to obscure an arcane structure, which has evaded the commentators. The addition gives a total of 3,962 years.

Even were these lists not occult blinds, with them Nostradamus merely provided a new date for Creation, which meant that he redefined the entire sequence of dates. This is a noteworthy point, because it means that if we were to elect to follow his system, then the dates given by Trithemius as the key-dates in history would not be the same as those given by Nostradamus. However, our careful examination of the quatrains has led us to the conclusion that Nostradamus nevertheless used the Trithemian system.

Besides offering a calendrical system by which the historical periodicities of the planetary rulers could be dated, Trithemius also offered one or two short predictions. Among these was one made concerning the changes which would take place due to the ending of the lunar periodicity in 1880 (some scholars point to an error of two or three years in the Trithemian system) when the solar Michael would take over from lunar Gabriel.

According to Trithemius, the beginning of this solar period would mean that the Jews would find their homeland. Although he gave no specific date, the event would be some time after 1881. This dating may well be linked with a completion of the septenary series from Michael to Michael (from Sun to Sun), for the Temple of Solomon was built during the pre-Christian rule of Michael, and one would expect a reinstitution of such an edifice in the post-Christian solar era. However, the basis for the prediction need not concern us in the present context – what is important is that Trithemius left us with an example of how the septenaries left their mark on history, in terms of cycles. The precision of the prediction emphasizes the need for accuracy in determining the date of Creation.

The fact is that the entire system hinges on the date presumed for the creation of Adam. We should observe, however, that Gabriel de Mortillet tabulated no fewer than 32 different authorities which present various and diverging dates for this event, the most antique of which was 6,984 years and the most recent 3,784 years.[3] It is significant that de Mortillet, who is interested mainly in scriptural texts, did not include in his classification the speculations of either Trithemius or Nostradamus.

The beginnings of respective eras has always been a problem for historians. The Olympiad dating of the Greeks was from our year 776 BC (this system seems to have continued up to AD 440). For the Romans it was the putative foundation of Rome – 753 BC. The Babylonians reckoned according to the era of Nabonassar – 747 BC. These dates seem to have been astrologically determined, and did at least obviate the difficulties which arose with the new Christian system of chronology. Following Dionysius Exiguus, the Christian era was presumed to have begun on 25 March, at the Annunciation, rather than the birth of Christ. This was still held to be true in the time when Nostradamus wrote.

Most authorities are now of the opinion that the birth of Jesus took place about 6 or 4 BC, yet the debate about this precise year raged in early Christian times: Eusabius, Irenaeus and Epithanius gave different dates for the birth of Christ.[4] This is presumably what Nostradamus had in mind when he admits, in his *Epistle*, that his own calculations differ from those of Eusabius. He could have mentioned at least 12 early Christian authorities as alternatives, and he was clearly anticipating much ecclesiastical criticism in a time when such criticism could lead, if not to the stake, at least to the courts. These minor-seeming considerations do play a part in the dating of certain quatrains, and on more than one occasion Nostradamus is careful to point out which calendrical system he has in mind, in order to avoid confusion.

In fact, from the internal evidence of the prophecies themselves, it is evident that, on the whole, Nostradamus has adopted the Trithemian series, and it is difficult to understand why he went to the trouble of publishing his own date for Creation, other than to demonstrate his fidelity to the Catholic faith. As we have suggested, the entire passage dealing with the 'date of Creation', and its many references to Biblical dates, seems to be nothing more than an elaborate occult blind. It was imperative that Nostradamus should appear to be working within a Christian tradition. In fact, he was in no danger with his astrology, for this had a long tradition in prophetic literature, and he had established himself as an astrologer through the publication of his *Almanachs*.

After the mid-sixteenth century, the Church rarely attacked those who wrote about astrology in an intellectual vein, and authorities lectured on astrology in universities throughout Europe. Of course, in their astrology, they still had to stay on the right side of the Church. It was really the popular practice of astrology which seemed to worry the Church, on the grounds that it was God, and God alone, who knew about the future. Nostradamus paid lip-service to this concept in his *Epistle to Henry II*, no doubt to protect himself. However, as must be evident from our text to date, a very large number of churchmen were excellent astrologers. Generally, while the ecclesiastical law was traditionally anti-astrology, the law was rarely acted upon. Nostradamus was among the happy few in any case, for he was protected by his royal connections. In addition, we have no doubt that one purpose behind his obfuscations was to protect himself. The fact is – perhaps a surprising fact – that the more one looks into his reputation, the more one finds that, in the beginning, he was more famous for his obscurity, and for what he himself had called his 'scabrous tongue', than for his predictions. His almanachs aside, his

159

fame during his lifetime seems to have rested mainly upon
the single prediction of the death of Henry II (see page 235
ff), and on his puzzling obscurity.

When, in 1558, Laurens Videl, secretary to the dukes of
Lesdiguières, criticized Nostradamus trenchantly and personally (in the spirit of the time), it was for supposed errors
in his almanachs, and for the obscurity of the verse. The
personal abuse from Videl was considerable – Nostradamus
was 'scabby, mangy, a poor fool, an ignoramus', and so on.
However, there was little actual matter in the criticism.
There is no valid criticism of the quatrains, simply because
he could not understand them. At best, all he could do was
criticize their obscurity. In this, Nostradamus would be in
total agreement with him.

Much earlier, Francois Rabelais, more qualified than
Videl to comment on the Green Language, had satirized
the almanach quatrain method in his *Gargantua* I.2, but the
beauty of his own quatrain is that it predicts nothing.
Rabelais could fool around with prophecies which prophesied things which would happen in the ordinary course of
events: Nostradamus was in a different league, for he
prophesied events which would not occur for hundreds of
years. His contemporaries were not to know this, and many
critics sniffed around in disgust at the barbarity of his
tongue, totally unaware of the sophistication behind the
barbarous-seeming Green Language.

However, the mid-sixteenth century was no period for even
reputable writers to espouse occult systems openly, if they
wished to remain on the right side of respectability. In the
same year that Nostradamus was writing his *Epistle*, 40
witches were burned in nearby Toulouse. It was not a time
to publish an occult system of dating, and Nostradamus
was probably sensible to argue so forcefully for a Biblically
sound date of Creation, even if he did ignore this in his

actual prophecies. The occult blind has served him well, for not only were the Inquisitors misled, but so were all subsequent commentators on the *Prophéties*, who were unable to read into his *Epistle* a reference to Trithemius.

Armed with the knowledge that Nostradamus not only mentions the system in this short (if opaque) letter, but also offers variants to the Trithemian dates, we should not be surprised to find it being used, with suitably arcane cover, in a number of quatrains.

THE WAR OF THE THREE HENRYS

Nostradamus' use of the Secundadeian system is so directed that, without an understanding of its implications, we would not be able to translate accurately the quatrains in which it is used. In some cases, such misunderstanding of the Secundadeian method, and its related astrological terminologies, has led to translations which are almost dangerous in their implications. For example, one commentator, J. Anderson Black, who failed to understand the basis of Nostradamus' method, was led to reading into one 'Secundadeian' quatrain a massive conflict between East and West, which we must presume from the text is still laid up for our own future.[5] He translated the third line of quatrain I.56 as: 'As Islam is thus led by its angel'. Now, what Nostradamus wrote was: *Que si la Lune conduite par son ange*. This has no reference to Islam, and it is merely wilful to translate the word *Lune* as representing Islam. The full quatrain reads:

> *Vous verrez tost, & tard faire grand change*
> *Horreurs extresmes & vindications,*
> *Que si la Lune conduite par son ange,*
> *Le ciel s'approche des inclinations.*

161

The angel (*ange*) that directs (*conduite*) the Moon (*la Lune*) in line 3 is none other than Gabriel, the lunar representative of the Secundadeian seven. This intelligency is not a symbol of Islam, but one of the Christian archangels. It is this fact which explains the last line, which has nothing to do with 'the heavens drawing near to the balance', as Black puts it. Black's interpretation is not based on the Nostradamus original, and, from internal evidence, seems to have been borrowed from the inaccurate translation given by Cheetham.

It is not our purpose here to analyse this quatrain, but merely to demonstrate the danger inherent in translating a verse without a knowledge of the seven Secundadeians. However, an accurate literal translation of the quatrain is:

> You will soon see, and later make great changes
> Outrageous horrors and revenges,
> That if the Moon directed by her angel
> The heavens approach the inclinations.

As with most literal translations of Nostradamus, this English does not appear to make much sense. However, it makes a great deal of sense when viewed from the point of view of the Secundadeian literature, for the Moon (*la Lune*) is ruled by ('directed by', *conduite par*) the intelligency Gabriel.

Strictly speaking, even the first, simple-seeming line is full of difficulties, for Nostradamus separates the word soon (*tost*) from 'and later' (*& tard*) by a comma, indicating that it is simply not acceptable to translate the line (as did Cheetham and Black) with the words: 'Sooner or later you will see great changes made'. This is not what Nostradamus wrote. Nor did he complete the line with a full stop.

What the commentators have overlooked is that the quatrain contains specialist astrological terms which make sense only in terms of the Secundadeian literature. The term inclinations (properly, *inclinaison* in French) is a sixteenth-century astrological term, with two general applications. First, it refers to the angle at which the orbit of a planet crosses another orbit: in connection with the Moon, this is almost always to the solar orbit, which is the ecliptic. The point of such intersection is called after the cosmic dragon, whence we derive such terms as *Caput* and *Cauda*, for the head and tail of this bisecting dragon (*fig. 37*). Secondly, it refers to the motion of a body (in this case, we must presume, the Moon) towards a position other than the one it held in a radical chart. To avoid abstract theory, let us confirm that it is the latter use to which the word *inclination* applies. It is, of course, not to the Moon as a planetary body, but to the Moon as symbol of Gabriel, that Nostradamus refers. It is not the Moon of the ephemerides, but the Moon of the more vast periodicities of Trithemius.

Now, according to Trithemius, the Moon took over control of European history in 1525 and four months, and was being directed by Gabriel towards 1881. This 'direction' fulfils perfectly the requirements of the last two lines of the quatrain, intimating that whatever is being predicted must occur in this lunar period of 354 years and 4 months. But Nostradamus clearly indicates that this event will be seen 'soon' (*tost*). Is there anything implicit in the astrological conditions set out in the quatrain which makes sense of the enigmatic last two lines? The answer is yes.

In order to reveal this answer, which is derived from the arcane contents of the verse, we must determine what Nostradamus had himself made of the Latin or German editions of Trithemius to which he had access.

As the data given above reveals, the date of Creation according to Trithemius seems to be 5424 BC. In terms of this system, Christ was born during the rule of the 15th period, when Orphiel, the planet of Saturn, ruled.

Although there are one or two small errors in his Latin and German texts, Trithemius notes that the birth of Jesus would have taken place during the age of Ophiel, the Saturnine ruler. This rulership would have come to an end in AD 109, and the sequence in Nostradamus' day, and in the period covered by his prophecies, would have been:

Samael	Mars	1171		1525 4 mnth
Gabriel	Moon	1525 4 mnth		1879 8 mnth
Michael	Sun	1879 8 mnth		2233

The 16th Secundadeian period would have brought the rulership of that archangel who governed the period in which Nostradamus lived, beginning in 1525 and 4 months. This rule would end in 1879 and 8 months.

The really interesting thing is that in May 1525 (the month immediately following 1525 and 4 months) there was a *revolution* in the skies. On 1 May 1525, both superiors, Saturn and Jupiter, were briefly in the same sign of Aries: Saturn was just entering Aries, while Jupiter was just leaving the same sign. It was a rare window which Nostradamus seized to determine a fiducial* for his quatrain.

What the quatrain implies is that these conditions, which pertained at the beginning of the inclination of the Moon, would repeat at some time in the future, before the inclination came to its end, and the Moon's reign was over. This repetition would, in some way, be connected with the horror and revenge with which the quatrain deals.

---

* The word fiducial is used in astronomy and astrology to indicate a marker, 'a faithful point' – some body or hypothetical point in the skies which is, for the sake of measurement, regarded as being static. The concept of a cosmic body or point being static is nothing more than a convention, yet without it, no measurements would be possible.

Perhaps, for the benefit of non-astrologers, we should spell out the fact that the events during an inclination can be defined in any way: were we to define it in terms of the Moon alone, then we would be committing ourselves to an event which occurred only within one month after May 1525, as the rapidly moving Moon will return to its radical degree within a month. Since Nostradamus was concerned with the passage of years, he wisely adopted the slowest of all indicators – Saturn and Jupiter, which were the slowest-moving planetary bodies known to Nostradamus, and widely used as fiducials in prophecy.

This perfectly acceptable reading of the term *inclination* invites us to glance at a sixteenth-century ephemeris, to see when Saturn and Jupiter are next in the sign Aries together. In 1555, Saturn was in Aries, but Jupiter was not. However, the next time Saturn swept its way back to Aries, so did Jupiter. At the very end of 1584 and for a few days into 1585, both planets were once again in Aries, and the conditions implicit in the inclination of the Moon, under the rule of Gabriel, was fulfilled again.

We observe that 1584/5 was 'soon' (*tost*) in terms of the prophecies of Nostradamus. '*You* will see it soon' (*Vous verrez tost*) he said to his readers, yet he knew that he would not see it. He died about 19 years before the Saturn-Jupiter conjunction was repeated. Even so, he knew that the event would be witnessed by the generation for whom he wrote.

Having arrived at a fairly convincing date, we must ask if there was any event early in 1585 which would seem to measure up to the promise of the first two lines – Outrageous horrors and revenges.

Inevitably, the answer is yes. However, before we recount a relevant history of horrors and revenges, let us glance in detail at the planetary positions to which the quatrain had pointed. The fact that the 'data' offered by

Nostradamus straddles two years is an extraordinary indication of the precision in his quatrains.

	Saturn	Jupiter
31 Dec 1584	00 AR 01	25 AR 41
12 Feb 1585	03 AR 32	00 TA 05

The times above are given for 6.00 a.m. local time. We observe that there is a window of just over one month and a half during which the inclination of the Saturn-Jupiter to Aries is completed. We are therefore invited to study the history in the last month of 1584, and in 1585.

In December 1584 the Guises entered into an undertaking at Joinville, with the Spanish King Philip II and the Pope, to drive Henry of Navarre from the French throne, and put in his place the Cardinal of Bourbon. Almost immediately, this led to the outbreak of yet another bloody French civil war, called the War of the Three Henrys, in which Henry III, Henry of Navarre, and Henry of Guise fought with each other. We need not deal here with the outcome of these religious wars. The trouble he foresaw from these encounters of the three Henrys induced Nostradamus to leave posterity with precisely formulated verses dealing with the destinies of the triple.

In quatrain III.51 we learn how Henry of Guise was murdered by Henry III, in 1588. In *présage* 58,[*] we learn

---

[*] The word *présage* is used to denote certain quatrains of Nostradamus which do not appear to have been written for the *Prophéties* canon. Usually, they were intended for the almanachs. The word is used in Nostradamus' almanach for 1555, in the phrase 'Cette *Prognostication* commence par un quatrain intitulé *Présage en général*' ('This Prognostication begins with a quatrain entitled *Présage* in general'). After the death of the Master, Jean-Aimé de Chavigny published some of these *présages*, one or two of which are from sources unknown to modern scholars, but which may be from Nostradamus texts now lost. Unfortunately, later editions of the *Prophéties* sometimes incorporated

how Henry III was killed by Jacques Clement in the following year (Clement was *Doux la pernicie* – see page 531). In quatrain III.20 we learn how Henry of Navarre succeeded the murdered king as Henry IV, and two decades later was stabbed to death by the assassin Ravaillac in 1610. It would be difficult to deny that we have here stories of horror and revenge, all of which came to a head in 1585.

DECLINE OF THE BARBARIC EMPIRE

Whilst an arcane system – in that it is involved with a pre-Christian angelology – the Secundadeian periodicities were popular among occultists in the sixteenth century. Its popularity among arcanists rests to some extent on the fact that it offers a system of dating which is quite outside the familiar calendrical system of the West. Additionally, since the system is based on simple cycles, which appear to have nothing to do with cosmology, or planetary rhythms, it offers a useful index for indicating the beginnings and endings of comparatively large periods of time. Each of these reasons which endeared the system to his contemporaries would have been very acceptable to Nostradamus, who was quick to recognize the arcane potential in any idea.

To sum up what we have said, the Secundadeian system is, in essence, a theory of historical periodicities. It postulates that a group of seven archangels (the *Secundadeis*, sometimes called the Planetary Rulers) rule in a predetermined repeating sequence, in periods of 354 years' and 4 months' duration. During these rulerships the archangels are tutelary over the development of civilizations. Inevitably, during these periods, each archangel leaves the stamp of his own being on history.

présages into the main predictive series, thereby obscuring the fact that they were originally intended to relate to specific years.

*

Since each Archangel is directly linked with a planet, or a planetary sphere, the nature of the rule is inextricably bound up with the nature and influences surrounding a particular planet. The sequence of rule follows this order: Saturn, Venus, Jupiter, Mercury, Mars, Moon, Sun.

As we are concerned with the Trithemian system only in regard to its relevance to Nostradamus, it is sufficient for us to note that a change of angelic rulership took place in 1525, when the planetary ruler of Mars (Samael) gave way to the ruler of the Moon (Gabriel). According to Trithemius, Gabriel's rule of 354 years and 4 months lasted until 1879 and 8 months. At this point, the archangel of the Sun, Michael, took over the direction of unfolding history. The use to which Nostradamus puts this Trithemian sequence may be seen from analysis of quatrain III.97, which many modern commentators insist points to the establishment of the State of Israel in our own century. The quatrain reads:

> *Nouvelle loy terre neuve occuper,*
> *Vers la Syrie, Judée, & Palestine,*
> *Le grand Empire Barbare corruer,*
> *Avant que Phebes son siecle determine.*

Approximately, this may be rendered:

> New law to occupy a new land,
> Towards Syria, Judaea and Palestine,
> The great Barbarian Empire to fall,
> Before Phebes ends her century.

Roberts sees this quatrain as anticipating 'the origin of the state of Israel'. Cheetham seems to believe that the first two lines of the quatrain 'speak for themselves' in describing the creation of the state of Israel. More remarkably, de

Fontbrune sees the quatrain as a reference to the Six Day War of 1967, and the occupation by Israel of Gaza, Transjordan and the Golan Heights. Even more surprising, his reading of the last line is that it denotes the date of the summer solstice, 21 June 1967. These interpretations are almost classical examples of how cavalier the translators of Nostradamus may be.

Let us look at what the quatrain actually says, rather than what the translators imagine it says.

First, we must note that there is no specific mention of Israel by name – merely a mention of Palestine, where (we now know) the State of Israel was founded. When viewed in the light of sixteenth-century history, we see that the prophecy is related to one of the most abiding fears of that time, which was of the Muslim advance from the East, westwards.

By the early decades of the mid-sixteenth century, the Turks were threatening to take over the Mediterranean completely, and to advance upon Europe. The pressure on Europe was tremendous, for the Turks controlled central Hungary and Poland, and were constantly in skirmish with Europe – in 1575 they even invaded Austria. By the time of Nostradamus – after their immense defeat of Malta, in 1565 – the Turks had overrun Greece, and by 1566 they had taken Chios, followed by Naxos, and within a year or so, Cyprus. These events, which boded evil for Europe, were bound to influence the content of the savant's quatrains.

In the light of this contemporaneous situation, we can see that the great Barbarian Empire (*grand Empire Barbare*), of the third line, is the Turkish threat – what was later called the Ottoman Empire, after the Osman dynasty. It is absurd for interpreters to read 'great Barbarian Empire' as a prevision of Israel, or even of Israel's traditional enemies.

169

The quatrain has nothing to do with Israel, and everything to do with that sixteenth-century bogey-man, the Turk.

When Nostradamus penned this quatrain, he may not have had a specific Muslim leader in mind. However, the word *Barbare* calls to mind the name of the renegade Greek, Khaireddin Barbarossa. In 1537, less than 20 years before the quatrain was written, Barbarossa, who had joined with Turkish corsairs to terrorize Mediterranean shipping, was appointed High Admiral of the Turkish fleet. The notion of the 'barbary pirates' was widespread, and is no doubt part of the stratification of meaning in the phrase, *grand Empire Barbare*.

In interpreting this quatrain, we must consider the date of anticipated fulfilment, which is hinted at in the last line. The reference to *Phebes* is fudged by most of the interpreters to somehow mean the twentieth century – even, as we have seen, to a specific day in 1967. Carlo Patrian recognizes the classical reference for what it is, yet adds no explanation as to its meaning within the quatrain. In order to squeeze this meaning from the reference, Roberts and Cheetham read *Phebes* as meaning the Sun, no doubt confusing *Phoebe* with *Phoebus Apollo*. To make this reading (or misreading) fit, they then say that the twentieth century is 'the century of the Sun'. They do not explain their grounds for this claim, and there is no reference in any esoteric tradition whereby centuries are linked with individual planets.

This kind of fudge is not really necessary, however, for Nostradamus is quite clear in his meaning. *Phebes* is merely another name for *Phoebe*, the Moon. In terms of Trithemian the period of the Moon lasted from 1525 to 1879. This 'cycle' is precisely what Nostradamus means when he writes the homonymic *siecle*. He tells us that, before the century of Phoebus has come to its end, the Barbarian Empire will fall. Note that Nostradamus does not write of the period of the Moon, but of the century. This is the sixteenth century, in which the rule of the Moon begins.

Examined in the light of contemporaneous knowledge, this quatrain III.97 is revealed as having nothing to do with the modern period, and nothing to do with Israel. The quatrain, written for Nostradamus' own contemporaries, predicts the fall of the then–dominant Turkish Empire in those occupied eastern regions, before the end of the sixteenth century. In short, the fall of the great Barbarian Empire would be assured in what was for Nostradamus and his contemporaries the not–too–distant future. In the context of the sixteenth century, this is a really remarkable prediction, for few of his contemporaries would have dreamed that the threat from the empire they dreaded would all but disappear within their own century.

In spite of all expectation to the contrary, the prediction proved to be accurate. As we shall see, it is thematically linked with a number of other important quatrains which touch upon the Turkish threat. As we have seen in another quatrain, Nostradamus offers an arcane encoding to enable us to date the key battle of Lepanto, which marked – however tentatively – the first signs of the end of the expansionist aspirations of the Turkish empire (see page 129 ff).

What concerns us here, however, is not the accuracy of the quatrain, or its relationship with the contemporary fears of those who read Nostradamus. Our concern is with the example of the Trithemian periodicity which is found in the last line of this quatrain: *Avant que Phebes son siecle determine*. Without a knowledge of the Trithemian system, this final line could have no possible meaning. In no other calendrical or cyclical system does the Moon rule so vast a sequence of a century or more.

PASTEUR

That Nostradamus employed the Secundadeis system when offering arcanely disguised dates for events set in his future is evident from such quatrains as I.25.

> *Perdu, trouvé, caché de si long siecle,*
> *Sera pasteur demy Dieu honoré,*
> *Ains que la Lune acheve son grand cycle,*
> *Par autres vieux sera deshonoré.*

> Lost, found, hidden for so long a century,
> Will pasteur be honoured (as) demi-God,
> As the Moon completes its great cycle
> By others the old one will be dishonoured.

This quatrain appears to deal with an event over 300 years into Nostradamus' future: it is one of several quatrains wherein the terms clearly relate to the Secundadeis planetary angels, and wherein the date of the event may now be cross-checked against historical records. This quatrain mentions Pasteur by name. It tells us that 'before the Moon has achieved its great cycle' his name will be honoured (and later dishonoured).

The quatrain is almost a check-list against the Secundadeian tables, for Louis Pasteur made his discovery regarding what he called the 'active immunization' of fowls between 1880 and 1881. This is within four months of the date given by Trithemius for the finale of the Moon's great cycle, under the lunar archangel, Gabriel: *Ains que la Lune acheve son grand cycle*.

According to Trithemius, in 1879 Gabriel would give place to the leader of the planetary seven, Michael. The modern esotericist, Rudolf Steiner, who was familiar with the Trithemian writings, readjusted the Secundadeian periodicities, and maintained that the Michaelic Age would begin not in 1880, but in 1881.[6]

THE END OF THE *PROPHÉTIES*

Trithemius' manuscript on the Secundadeians had circulated privately for some years before it was published in 1522. The result was that many astrologers took an interest in the lore contained within his computations. In particular, the monk-astrologer, Nicolaus Peranzonus, incorporated the Trithemius findings into his own prophecies relating to the Great Conjunction of 1524, which he published in the year prior to the expected great inundation.[7] He predicts that the conjunction of the three superiors, on 4 February, at 1.38 p.m., will bring earthquakes, imprisonments and heavy floods. Renewed conjunctions in the following weeks will lead only to further floods.

The prediction that 1524 would see a world flood is usually traced back, by those who have not read it, to the *Ephemerides* of Johann Stoeffler, published in 1499. However, Stoeffler merely pointed out that there would be 20 conjunctions in the February of 1524, 16 of which would be in water signs. This, he said, would bring in many mutations such as have not been seen for centuries. He did not mention a flood at all. Later astrologers were not so circumspect: if the conjunction of all the planets was to be in Pisces, then it would lead to a flood. We cannot discuss here all the literature and altercations around this prediction, but the interested reader is referred to the excellent summary in the chapter on the conjunctions in Thorndike.* Meanwhile, we might ask why the conjunction of 1524 should have stirred the expectations of Europe so completely. We suspect that the answer to this does not lie in any new development in astrology – such conjunctions,

---

* Thorndike, op.cit., Vol. 5, Chapter XI, p. 178 ff.

and the related Saturn-Jupiter conjunctions, had occupied the minds of predictive astrologers since the art came to Europe. We suspect the answer lies in the new development of printing.

By 1500 there were printing presses in every major city in Europe, and it was easy for astrologers – even mediocre astrologers – to publish tracts and predictions which would sell cheaply and rapidly. The Great Conjunction of 1524 was really the first one to occur after the spread of printing. For the first time in the history of the West, the presses were poised to inundate Europe with a popular sub-cultural astrological literature. Other factors which keyed up the prophetic hunger of the time were the widely known predictions of change to come in religious quarters, through the Secundadeian literature, and a wide range of published predictions which saw 1520–25 as key years for change. There was great uncertainty, and at such times, masses of people resort to prediction.

The significance in this for our study of Nostradamus is that Peranzonus regarded one of the contributing forces which would bring about the Great Flood as the fact that the ruling intelligence of that day was the planetary ruler of Mars, Samael, or 'Sammael', as he put it. The main reason why Peranzonus linked Samael, the ruler of the fire-planet Mars, with a watery flood was because (according to the calculations offered by Trithemius) it was Samael who had been planetary overseer during Noah's flood.

Now, whatever the reasons for Peranzonus' mention of Samael, we do have here an unambiguous reference to the dating system of the Secundadeis, only months after Trithemius had published his book. This is a useful reference for us, since it reveals the same duality of interest which we note in the arcane versification of Nostradamus, only 30 or so years later – namely, an interest in relating the planetary Secundadeis to a wider astrology.[8]

So far as we can tell from Peranzonus' wide-ranging study of floods, his reference to the Samael of Trithemius was perhaps a sign of the up-to-date level of his scholarship, yet his argument seems to rest upon the notion that history repeats itself *because* planetary rulers repeated their cycles. Whether his view of historical cycles was correct or not we are scarcely in a position to determine, but he was right in his argument that, according to the theory of Secundadeian rule propounded by Trithemius, Samael had ruled over the time of the Flood.

Among the most remarkable of what we might call the Secundadeian quatrains is that which Nostradamus wrote to determine the outer limit of his prophecies. This is quatrain I.48, which reads:

> *Vingt ans du regne de la Lune passez,*
> *Sept mil ans autre tiendra sa Monarchie:*
> <u>*Quand de Soleil prendra ses jours lassez,*</u>
> *Lors accomplit & mine ma prophetie*

Although, at a glance, the quatrain suggests few pitfalls, the words **jours lassez** and **mine** have several possible meanings. The following is intended as a useful guide:

> Twenty years of the reign of the Moon to pass,
> Seven thousand years another will hold his Monarchy,
> When the Sun will take the remaining days,
> Then is accomplished and ended my prophecy

We have observed that Nostradamus rarely gives dates outright. What, then, are the possible ways of interpreting this verse? Without doubt, the phrase *regne de la Lune* is intended to indicate the Trithemian periodicities. Now, in the tables, the reign of the Moon ends in 1880 and 4 months. In the first line, Nostradamus tells us that the date he has in mind is 20 years after this lunar rule. Thus, if we add to this 20 years, we arrive at 1901 – the very beginning of the twentieth century. In the Christian view of things, the twentieth century was to be the last century, the final century of the septenary chain of millennia.

Sept mil ans autre tiendra sa Monarchie: within the historical view generally accepted by sixteenth-century thinkers, Nostradamus was correct in linking the *Sept mil* with the beginning of the twentieth century (20 + 1880), because, according to the medieval tradition, this century was to mark the coming of the Antichrist.

Let us presume that by the second line Nostradamus was referring to the well-known Christian apocalyptic view that the world would come to a catastrophic end at the final year of the Seventh Millennium. As Nostradamus and his contemporaries believed that the world was created about 5,000 years before the Birth of Christ, it was reasonable for them to believe that they were living in the last millennium. Nostradamus, along with Trithemius, offered alternative dates for the Creation of the World, however. In the Epistle, he offered both 4173 BC and 4757 BC. In contrast, Trithemius, who clearly did not subscribe to the Seventh Millennium ending theory, gave the Creation as being in 5315.

While Nostradamus and Trithemius differ in their view of the world's end, the question still remains, who is this 'other' (*autre*) who will hold his monarchy in 1,700 years? Is this period to be added to the 2,000 years of the first line? If so, we have a figure of 3,700 years. Consulting the Secundadeian sequence, we discover that the archangel Raphael, the ruler of Mercury, will begin his rule in AD 3652. Is this distant date the one which will see the end of Nostradamus' prophecies? This is very unlikely, as the savant is quite specific about the limits of his prophecies, which have just over 200 years still to run.

In fact, there is less confusion about the arcane reference which relates to this 'final date', in the third line of the quatrain:

> *Quand de Soleil prendra ses jours lassez,*
> *Lors accomplit & mine ma prophetie*

'When the Sun takes his last days . . .' This is clearly another reference to the Secundadeian periodicity which was introduced in the first line. According to Trithemius, since the last months of 1880, Europe has been governed by the archangel Michael, ruler of the Sun. His last days will be in AD 2235. This appears to be the term to which Nostradamus sets his prophecies: *Lors accomplit & mine ma prophetie.*

Note that he sets a term only to his prophecies, not to the world, or to history. This point must be made, as some commentators, even though they have failed to identify the actual date or its real meaning, interpret it as relating to the end of the world.

Chapter 4

The Nature of the
Green Language

*Mais l'injure du temps ô serenissime Roy, requiert que
tels evenemens ne soient manifestez que par enigmatique
sentence, n'ayant qu'un seul sens & unique intelligence,
sans y avoir rien mis d'ambique n'amphibologique
calculation:*

But, O most serene King, the exigencies of the times
demand that such events (as I predict) should not be
made public other than by enigmatic sentence, having
only one single sense and unique meaning, containing
neither ambiguous nor equivocating calculation.

(Nostradamus, from the *Epistle to Henry II* in the
1668 edition of *Prophéties*)

*Et pource ô tres-humanissme Roy la pluspart des
quatrains prophetiques sont tellement scabreux qu'on n'y
sçauroit donner voye, ny moins aucun interpreter...*

Hence, O most humane King, the greater part of the
prophetical quatrains are so full of obstacles that one
cannot find a way through them, let alone interpret
any...

(Nostradamus, *A L'Invictissime, Tres-Puissant, et
Tres-Chrestien, Henry Second, Roy de France*, 1558, in
the second volume of *Les Prophéties*)

Tantost il la deguise par les termes si obscurs, que sans un genie tres-particulier, l'on n'y peut rien comprendre . . .

Sometimes (Nostradamus) disguises the verse with terms so obscure that, lacking a very special genius, one is unable to understand anything of their meaning . . .

(Etienne Jaubert, *Éclaircissement des veritables Quatrains de Maistre Michel Nostradamus . . .*, 1656)

In one of his letters, Nostradamus admitted the obvious – that he had written his quatrains in a strange language, a *scabreux* language, as he called it. In the arcane vocabulary, this language has many names; in astro-alchemy it is now usually called the Green Language and we have adopted that term throughout this text, but is also known as the Language of the Birds, with reference to legends of its origins. Before we turn to detailed analysis of the quatrains, and examine how Nostradamus used this secret language, we must consider its background.

The Language of the Birds has its roots in ancient mythologies. In the esoteric Norse epic, the *Volsunga Saga*, Sigurd (the Scandinavian equivalent of Siegfried in the Teutonic *Niebelungenlied*) kills the treasure-guarding dragon. Immediately afterwards, at the behest of Regin, the hero begins to roast the heart of the dragon. In so doing, he burns his fingers. To ease the pain, he puts his fingers in his mouth to suck them. Thus he tastes the dragon's blood, and is instantly illumined with the vision of initiation. The moment he drinks of the blood, Sigurd begins to understand the Language of the Birds. What he learns from the birds enables him to change his destiny, and gain for himself the treasure of the dragon, as well as his heart's desire, in the form of his sleeping Brunhild.

In this legend, we can trace the connection between

179

initiation – the legitimate growth into the higher spiritual realm – and the Language of the Birds. This is a language which – rather like the Music of the Spheres – may be heard only by initiates, by those who have clothed themselves in the skin of the dragon.

Why was the Green Language also called the Language of the Birds? Perhaps the simple answer is because it belonged to the air realm, the realm associated in occult correspondences with intellect and communication. However, a more accurate answer rests in the Green Language itself. The Latin, *aviarius*, with its root *avia*, means 'pertaining to birds'. We still have the word in our term *aviary*, of course. Now, the Latin morning greeting *ave* and the evening greeting *vale* have undertones of both greeting and saying farewell to the dead – that is, to those who dwell in the spiritual world. It is interesting that in the epitaph to Nostradamus (see Appendix Four) his wife, Gemella, ends with a *V.* abbreviation for *Vale*. The Language of the Birds was that addressed to those who, while yet dwelling in physical bodies, had access to that hidden realm, and had cognition of the spirit. So far as the living were concerned, these men had commerce with the dead, which was really the realm of the truly living – the spirits divested of physical bodies. These were the initiates, 'those of the two worlds'.

Further, the Latin *Avitus* carries with it the idea of sanctity derived from things ancestral (the adverb *avite* means 'derived from ancient times', but is entirely respectful). The language of the birds was just such a respectful thing, inherited from the ancients, and preserved in certain arcane schools. In their Masonic opera, Mozart and Schikaneder understood very well the nature of the Language of the Birds. In *The Magic Flute* (the libretto of which is rich in Green Language), the bird-catcher, Papageno, tells lies because he does not know how to use the Masonic secret tongue. He pretends to have killed the giant snake, for which lie he is punished by having his tongue locked.

In the Nordic myths above, the hero who *has* actually killed the serpent tastes the blood of the dragon with his tongue, and immediately can understand the song of the birds. Papageno's propensity to lie prevents this discovery. He remains a bird-catcher, anxious always to sell his birds, rather than listen to them. He is, as he admits to Tamino at the outset, a man. That, in esoteric terms, means that he is not an initiate. He plays the panpipes, not the magic flute: he does not understand the language of the birds he sells. He is like every ordinary man and woman: we can enjoy the singing of the birds, yet it has no real meaning for us.

According to the alchemist Fulcanelli, the Language of the Birds 'is the language which teaches the mystery of things and unveils the most hidden truths'.[1] The Incas called it the Court Language, because it was used by diplomats: to them it was the key to the 'double science', sacred and profane. The worldly cynic might infer that, by means of this language, the diplomat was able to say one thing and mean another, or mean one thing and say another. However, diplomacy was originally connected literally with 'diplomas' – with official documents – and was therefore a specialist art concerned with constructing and interpreting these. In this sense, diplomacy was originally the art of speaking and writing a specialist, if privileged, language wherein those not within the inner sanctum might easily be deceived.

The prophetic gift of the Green Language is not restricted to the Nordic mythology. In the classical literature, the name Tiresias is widely used to denote soothsayers and prophets who know the secrets of this avian tongue, and use it in framing their predictions. In Greek myth, the goddess Athene repents of having blinded the mortal

Tiresias for having seen her naked. She orders her serpent to put its tongue into the ears of the man, to cleanse them. By virtue of this serpentine magic, Tiresias is afterwards able to hear and understand the language of the birds, hidden to all who have not had this portal of the senses cleansed. The deeper symbolism of this story will be evident to anyone who has studied esotericism.

What is the purpose of the speech of the dragon-men, if it is not to allow conversing between initiates in a form which will not be understood by the uninitiated? Nostradamus could write his 'scabrous' verse in the full knowledge that it could be read by only a handful of his contemporaries. Even after the unfolding of the events predicted, there was usually argument about what he meant, among those who could not read this secret tongue.

Why is this language of the true occultist – used by the last great arcane prophet in the West – linked with the birds? Even the general name given to this speech is wrapped in an arcane mythology which may easily be misunderstood. It is said that when spiritual beings finally decided to take physical bodies, some descended too quickly to the earth. They were unprepared for the hardness of the earth, and were not able to accept its challenges. However, since they had dipped themselves into the earth stream, they were compelled to remain in physical bodies, in incarnate form. Unable to dwell intimately with the earth, they found it more comfortable to live some way from its surface: they grew wings, and took to flying in the air, building their nests in the trees. These creatures – who eventually became the birds – remained highly spiritual-ized, however, and watched in astonishment as those who followed them took bodies which could manipulate the earth while they could relate to it only as thieves and beggars. The speech of the birds – which sounds like a nonsensical twitter to ordinary men – was never contaminated by the dark material plane, and it remained the most spiritual of languages.

Another name for this language is the Gay Speech, or the Gay Science. The knowledge of the secret language was perhaps so called because of the symbolic associations with the supposed joys of inebriation. Just as one might become drunk on wine, so one might become drunk on words. The true initiate was ever a man a little drunk – or, to use the medieval Latin term, *dilutior* – in the eyes of the earthbound. This is certainly what the great French master of the Green Language, Rabelais – who may have met Nostradamus at Montpellier University – had in mind when he used the phrase *La Dive-Bouteille*.[2] It is no accident that a famous image from Rabelais' *Pantagrueline Prognostication* of 1533 showed birds winging through the skies, above the heads of two talking men, one of whom was dressed in the garb of a fool. Literally *La Dive-Bouteille* means 'Divine-bottle'. However, *La Dive-Bouteille* is a figurative way of saying, 'the bottle of Bacchus', or 'good red wine'. We may see the deeper level of meaning in terms of the ribald humour of Rabelais: what goes into the physical body of man as red wine comes out yellow-*green*. Here, typical of Green Language usage, we chance upon an example of the use of the *double science*, of the inner and the outer, united in a single word.

Perhaps Rabelais, with his finely attuned sense for meanings within meanings, had in mind the homophony permitted by the Gay Science, which makes of La Dive-Bouteille *la dive but oeil*. This is 'the divine purpose eye', which appears to be very close to the Masonic image of 'Divine Providence', but also refers to the initiate himself who has constantly in mind, or in view, the Divine purpose. Thus, a term hidden in Rabelaisian promise of Bacchanalian carousal contains a secret term relating to the whole purpose of life. The former – the red liquid – pertains to the outer life of man, the latter – the green liquid – to his inner life.

In modern times this avian language is usually called the Green Language. The name seems to have come down to us in alchemical sources, yet no satisfactory account has been given for the term. One explanation is derived from the idea that the green of Spring expresses the pristine and vital quality of the language. However, this explanation is somehow flat – there must be a deeper symbolism in the choice of a word used to describe so esoteric a form of communication. Certainly, in alchemical symbolism, green is a very special colour, for it describes a stage in the process of the perfecting of the stone. In a thinly disguised reference to the Green Language, the alchemist Eirenaeus Philalethes writes of the Green Lion. Who, he asks rhetorically, has ever seen such a creature?

> In hunting of the Lyon Greene,
> Whose colour doubtless ys not soe
> As that your wisdom well doe know;
> For no man lives that ere hath seene
> Upon foure feet a lyon greene,
> But our lyon wanting maturitie
> Is called green for his unripenes trust me . . .[3]

We have here a 'lyon' which is not a lion of this world. It cannot be seen by ordinary eyes, though it can be seen by 'your wisdom' – which is, of course, the wisdom of the initiates. Even the distinctive colour of this lion is not what it seems: 'doubtless ys not soe'. Thus, in Philalethes' poem, the lion which is not of this world is called green because it is unique and lacking maturity – not completely of this material world. Even its colour is an unreal thing.

On the other hand, illuminating as such texts are, it is

probably not necessary to look into the specialist terminology of alchemy to find the roots of the term 'Green'. The original source for the term Green Language was the French *Langue Vert*. The *Vert* (Green) is almost certainly an example of arcane aphesis (see Appendix Five). In French, *ouvert* means 'open'. The *Langue Ouvert* was the open language, the tongue of ordinary men. When *ouvert* became *vert* by this aphetic change, it meant the opposite of open, i.e. closed; the *Langue Vert* was therefore the 'closed language', the 'occult language', the 'hidden tongue'. The double science of the two languages – the sacred and profane, the closed and the open – is contained in this one French word *ouvert*. As a result, in this strange language, a word which may appear quite ordinary is invested with another, deeper meaning comprehensible only to those who anticipate such a hidden meaning.

For example, the very word which Nostradamus used to describe his own versification is from the Green Language: *scabreux* (meaning scabrous) contains the adjective *cabré*, which means 'rearing upwards'. Although the word is often used nowadays of a plane when it has its tail down, in the sixteenth century it was always used to denote the prancing or rearing of a horse. Furthermore, in both ancient and modern times it denoted a living thing which is rearing towards the skies, to the proper realm of the birds. In the light of this, Nostradamus wrote in the sky-drawn language of birds.

In view of the meaning occulted in the word *vert*, we may legitimately ask if there is a link between the green of our language, and the enigmatic green 'leaf man' (*le feuillu*) of the French, the 'Green Man' (*der Grüner Mensch*) of the Germans. While the *term* 'Green Man' appears to have been introduced in its arcane context, in reference to the enigmatic floriated faces of cathedral art, into the English language only in 1939,[4] the *image* of the Green Man face,

185

with its floriated mouth, belongs to the same esoteric
cathedral art as so much of the alchemical and astrological
lore of the medieval period. There is probably no accident
in the fact that the Green Language, like the Green
Children and Green Man of Nordic mythology, emerged in
the eleventh or twelfth century with the beginnings of what
we now call Gothic Art. One of the many names for the
Green Language was *argot*, which, as Fulcanelli has pointed
out, is a version of *Art Gotique*. It was in the late Gothic
period, with the development of the arcane inner science of
alchemy, that the Green Language came into its own. The
most remarkable medieval exponent of Green Language –
who, incidentally, also used arcane astrology with the same
adroit insight as Nostradamus – was Dante, who summarized for future generations the medieval view of the
cosmos.

Whether termed the Green Language or the Language of
the Birds, this language has the same feeling for vitality, for
primordial and pristine strength, as the Green Man faces of
medieval cathedral sculpture, and it is quite possible that
the green foliage emerging from these mouths is meant to
symbolize the rich 'greening' of the opaque language. To
select but one example, there may be no doubt that the
greenery in the mouth of Botticelli's Chloris in his
Primavera, in the Uffizi, is a reference to esoteric speech.
The flowers are anemones, roses and centauries, each with
their individual arcane symbolism, yet the wonder is that
they are issuing from the mouth, as though the goddess was
a Green Woman, breathing vegetation. Modern scholarship
has shown that this picture – perhaps the most arcane of all
Renaissance works – was painted for an esoteric group who
had a deep interest in the arcane secret languages.[5] Perhaps
the Green Man of medieval imagery is the initiate, the one
who knows how to see correctly, and therefore knows how

to speak correctly, with passion and truth. He is not the open man, but the secret man.

Because it was a fundamental belief of alchemists that their deeper secrets should not be made available to everyone, it was in their arcane practices that the Green Language was developed with especial subtlety. The result is that few, if any, of the ancient alchemical texts can be understood by those who have not learned to read this language. This explains why so many modern scientists and historians, unlearned in this language, either ignore or misunderstand alchemical and other occult texts. It also explains why the proficient arcanist is pained to read accounts of astrological and alchemical texts by academics who represent themselves as 'specialists' in the history of these subjects. More often than not these authors have missed not only the spirit behind alchemy, but even the substance. Although the cult of Jung has built a wall of pseudo-alchemy around modern psychology, the truth is that Jung was very far from understanding what alchemy was about. This deficiency seems to have arisen from the fact that he had no knowledge of the Green Language.[6]

It is curious that the modern historians of science should have failed to recognize the arcane basis of alchemy, for there is no shortage of references to the secret language in the main alchemical texts themselves. For example, the fourth-century Alexandrian alchemist Zosimus refers to the arcane language called The Tongue of the Angels.[7] Unfortunately, this reference has been misunderstood by many commentators, because it is so easily confused with a 'secret' alphabet, published in the early sixteenth century by the occultist, Cornelius Agrippa.*[8] However, we are

---

* Among the secret alphabets were his *Scriptura Coelestis* (the heavenly script), and *Scriptura Malachim* (the script of the Malachim). Malachim is the Hebraic term for the Angels. For examples, see F. Gettings, *Dictionary of Occult, Hermetic and Alchemical Sigils*, 1981.

fortunate that Zosimus left us an example of the working of
the Tongue of the Angels, thereby revealing it as a form of
the Green Language.

Zosimus explains why the teacher of the arcane lore,
Thoth, should be called 'the first man'. According to
Zosimus, the ancient mystery centres (he names among
these only the Chaldeans, the Parthians, the Medes and the
Hebrews) called Thoth by the name 'Adam'. This latter
name, he says pointedly, 'is a word in the language of the
Angels'.

Zosimus is quite correct. The Hebrew word *Adam* is
from a root meaning 'red', and is almost certainly connected with the idea of 'red blood'. In esotericism, Adam
was the name given to the future humanity that first
descended into physical bodies. The name denotes the first
spiritual entities who clothed themselves in the red of flesh
and blood.

The Hebraic word, *Adam*, means 'Earthling' – a further
reference to the notion that prior to the creation of Adam,
man was a spirit being not of the earth. Like most esoteric
ideas, this has been thoroughly debased in modern times,
by the superficialities of such writers as Von Daniken, and
demoted to the notion of alien invaders. However, the
genuine esoteric teaching about the 'red earthling', the 'red
hermaphrodite', and so on, is not in conflict with the Bible.
The account in *Genesis* is quite clear that, long before God
created Adam, He created 'Man-woman'.* [9]

To return to Zosimus – why was Thoth called 'the first
man' in the language of the Angels? The name is almost
certainly connected with the notion that Adam was the one
who first gave names to created things. The Egyptian god
Thoth was the one who, in esoteric mythology, first gave

---

* *Genesis* I.7: *Et creavit Deus hominem ad imaginem suam; ad imagininem
Dei creavit illum, masculum et feminam creavit eos.* The creation of Eve did
not take place until *Genesis* II.22.

the secret names to all created things – Adam was, indeed, the inventor of the arcane language of the Angels, our Language of the Birds. It is in this sense that Thoth was the first man, and the explanation accounts for why another term for the arcane tongue is the Language of Thoth, the hermetic tongue.

Chapter 5

Green Language Techniques in Practice

It is not our purpose now to examine the full implications of the secret yet all-embracing Green Language used in the quatrains of Nostradamus: it plays such an important part in his obfuscations that a full treatment would demand thorough analysis of all the thousand or so verses in the *Prophéties*. We intend instead to provide a brief *indication* of what the Green Language is, and how it works, in preparation for an approach to the quatrains.

In essence, the Green Language is a linguistic method of inducing hidden meanings into various words and phrases according to a system of arcane rules. The rules are complex; in Appendix Five we set out a number of terms which relate to the techniques most frequently used by Nostradamus, in so far as they correspond to recognized literary methods. Other techniques which are used in the *Prophéties* are unique to Nostradamus and are revealed in this present work whenever they appear in quatrains under examination. In addition to using this arcane language, Nostradamus included in many of his quatrains words and quotations in a wide variety of languages. These included French, German, English, Latin, Greek and Provençal. The French commentator Clébert seems to have been alone in modern times in recognizing something of the arcane nature of the writings of Nostradamus, when he invites comparison with the *pouesio macarouncio*, the burlesque macaronique style – very much a language of the people – used in Provence in the early sixteenth century.[1] Macaronique is a term used for a peculiar form of French versification, a burlesque poetry, in which the words of the vulgar language take Latinate terminations, among other linguistic changes which are sometimes meaningful, sometimes meaningless, but always humorous. The word is from the Italian *maccheronico*, which besides meaning burlesque, is also used to mean dog-Latin. The familiar Italian *maccherone* (macaroni, or spaghetti) is still used figuratively for 'dolt', or 'blockhead'.

Many quatrains also contain linguistic puns, inversions, apheses, metatheses and syncopes (techniques examined in Appendix Five) – just a few from among the many linguistic and literary devices which are an integral part of the Green Language literature.

As we suggested when looking at the *Langue Vert*, the idea behind the Green Language is that it is possible to offer a word or a phrase that the reader imagines he or she has understood: in this way, the attention of the reader is deflected away from a hidden meaning. When used in this way, that word or phrase is called the 'occult blind'. This blind works on the principle that the untrained reader, satisfied with his or her 'interpretation' of the blind, will pass on to the next word or phrase, leaving the real, or secret, meaning hidden intact and unread behind the blind. Occult blinds are used not merely in prophetic verses, such as the *Centuries*, but in many forms of painting, literature and symbolism. However, occult blinds were widely used in certain late-medieval arcane disciplines, such as alchemy, Rosicrucianism, and even poetry related to esoteric subjects. The consequence of this is that within such esoteric traditions there has developed a recognized discipline directed towards identifying and interpreting occult blinds.

The trained occultist, alert to the rules of the Green

Language, will be prepared to read Nostradamus on several levels; we shall study a few examples of this in the following text. The arcanist has usually developed a sensitivity for the meanings hidden in words or phrases, according to clearly prescribed rules. Green Language is multi-layered, and is rooted in the fact that words consist of far more than denotations – they also contain complex connotations which can be manipulated by one conversant with the language, and with the interconnected structure of language derived from what is now called the Indo–European root language. The reading of a text constructed in Green Language requires an alert awareness of possible hidden meanings in sounds and verbal constructs.

THE SILENT FOX

The word *renard* (which means 'fox') is found in quatrain VIII.41. Eventually, we shall glance at the general meaning of the entire quatrain, but for the moment, we need only study the first line: *Esleu sera Renard ne sonnant mot* – 'The fox will be elected, not saying a word'. Etymologically, *renard* comes from Old High German, *reginhart*, meaning approximately 'strong in rule'. As the modern linguist Nigel Lewis reminds us, it was probably this etymology which lay behind the symbolism of the German epic, known in English under the title *Reynard the Fox*, in which the wily Reynard represented the Church. Through this symbolism – and no doubt through the observable characteristics of the fox itself – the word has since begun to denote a wily or cunning personality.[2] All these associations – strength in rule, cunning, wiliness, and so on – are connoted in the word *renard*, when it appears in a Green Language context.

In addition, according to the rule of homophony widely used in the Green Language, *renard* breaks down into two

French words, *reign* (kingdom, reign, or king) and (since the last letter of a French word is rarely sounded) *art* (skill, dexterity) – not very far from the original German etymology. This implies that, as a Green Language term, the word *renard* may also be read as meaning 'dexterous in kingship' or 'skilled as a king'. As we shall see from the analysis of the quatrain below, Nostradamus seems to be using this double-entendre sardonically, for one who is really dexterous in kingship can hardly be at the same time foxy.

To appreciate fully how this Green Language term works, we must study it in context. There are, of course, many famous historical individuals who may be considered to have been either 'foxy' or cunning. There are even many famous kings (those skilled in kingship, *reign-art*) who have a deserved reputation for being wily or cunning. For example, in 1740, the anonymous interpreter D.D. saw in this quatrain the 'Usurper Cromwell', who was 'an incomparable Fox, an arrant Knave, and arch hypocrite'. More recently, Roberts proposed Paul Reynaud, who was elected to the French premiership in 1940. The quatrain actually relates to the life of Napoleon III, and while it is not our purpose here to comment fully on its meaning, a brief survey demonstrates how applicable is the word 'fox' (*renard*) to Charles Louis Bonaparte, who became Napoleon III. Each line of the quatrain is brilliantly apposite to his vulpine career.

> *Esleu sera Renard ne sonnant mot,*
> *Faisant le saint public vivant pain d'orge*
> *Tyrannizer apres tant à un coup,*
> *Mettant à pied des plus grands sur la gorge.*

While **vivant pain d'orge** may be read in several ways, this is probably an adequate 'translation', for the moment:

The Fox will be elected without saying a word,
Playing the saint in public while feathering his nest,
To tyrannize after such a coup,
Putting his feet on the necks of the greatest ones.

Bonaparte was almost unique in being literally elected (*esleu*), and in a most unconventional way, making Nostradamus' choice of the word quite remarkable. First of all, in 1848, he was elected to the revolutionary Government by four Departments.* This election was ratified, but with an eye to the future, and with extraordinary cunning, Bonaparte resigned. Then in December 1848 he was elected President of the Republic by an astounding majority. His ambitions were greater even than this achievement, however: he wished to become an absolute monarch, like his uncle. He was foxy with the Assembly, and managed to institute repressive legislation while hiding his real aims.

Line two may appear obscure until one learns that Napoleon did, indeed, play the saint in public. For example, when elected to the Presidency, he swore an oath to remain faithful to the democratic Republic, even while working to overthrow this by having himself made Emperor. This aim he achieved by stealth, finally by *coup*. The curious phrase *vivant pain d'orgue* is probably linked with the French *faire ses orgues* which means to 'feather one's nest' corruptly. Basically, this is precisely what Napoleon did with the whole of the French Republic.

As the third line intimates, he achieved his aim by a *coup d'état* (*tant a un coup*). On 2 December 1851, after incredible exertions to ensure that his own conspirator-supporters were established in important positions of

---

* After the Revolution, the French Assembly replaced the local divisions of France with 83 *départements*, each administered by a prefect supporting a *conseil*, or council. This entirely sensible and cohesive plan completely changed the map of France.

194

power, he carried out his *coup*, and was declared Emperor a year later. In fact, the third and fourth lines must be considered together, for they deal with his outrageous tyranny, after he was raised to a position where he might exercise that absolute power by which he was corrupted even more. The word *tyrannizer* is a perfect description of what followed. Napoleon changed laws to weaken the positions of the republicans and resorted to wholesale deportations of his political enemies, while his cudgel-bearing secret police, the *ratapoils*, terrorized the republicans. When the Empire fell (partly due to Napoleon III's incompetence at Sedan in 1870), the Bordeaux Assembly recognized the extent of the crimes and tyranny of *renard* Napoleon III, declaring him responsible for the ruin, invasion and dismemberment of France.

LECTOYRE

Our second example is connected with a word which has puzzled many commentators, including Charles Ward. The word is *lectoyre*, which appears in line three of quatrain VIII.43: *Dedans lectoyre seront les coups de dards* – 'Within lectoyre will be blows of darts'.

Now, it was evident to thoughtful commentators that this quatrain predicted a famous battle would be fought at the place *Lectoyre*, but no one knew where this was, or when the battle would be. Lectoyre remained a mystery, but there was no shortage of ingenious suggestions as to its meaning from commentators. After examining some remarkably accurate maps printed by the Dutch publisher Willem Blaeu (1571–1638), Ward – writing in 1891 and aware that Nostradamus often used anagrams as part of his linguistic subterfuge – noted that the bank of the Meuse opposite Sedan was called Grand Torcy and Petit Torcy.

He recognized Le Torcey as an anagram of *Lectoyre*, and suggested that the site of the predicted battle was Sedan.

In 1870, two months after Napoleon III foolishly declared war on Prussia, the French were soundly defeated at Sedan, and after fruitless negotiations with Bismarck, Napoleon III was taken prisoner. He literally folded up the flag, the tricolour which had been adopted in July 1789 by the Revolutionaries. Two days after Sedan, France was once again declared a republic.

As a matter of fact, Ward's detective work with old maps was unnecessary. Even in modern times, there is a Place de Torcy and the Prairie de Torcy on either side of the Meuse canal to the west of Sedan. As we have seen, Nostradamus did not need to depend upon contemporaneous maps or books for place names, or the names of future historical personalities. He actually left a more simple clue to the site of the battle, by means of the Green Language, with which Ward was not familiar.

The third line opens with the curious word *Dedans*. Scansion aside, the word, which means 'within', is not really necessary. Strictly speaking, it would have been sufficient to say 'at', or 'in'. Perhaps Nostradamus used *Dedans* to improve the scan or metre of the line, yet one cannot help observing that *Dedans* is virtually an anagram of Sedan. Indeed, if we inquire why *lectoyre*, which is clearly a place name, has no capital letter, then we might see this as an indication that the capital letter of *Dedans* should be ignored, giving *edans*, a true anagram for Sedan.[3] This aphetic interpretation is well in accord with the practice of Green Language. Thus the curious construction of the first two words of the line gives the precise location of the site which was important to the formation and end of the Third Republic. The only problem, of course, is that while the construction certainly contains the name of the place of battle, it would have been virtually impossible to interpret it correctly prior to the battle. As we have seen, this is precisely the reason why Nostradamus used Green Language, for his avowed intent was to predict the future, yet in a way which would be impossible for people to understand the meaning prior to events.

THE GIANT OGMION

In the example of *Dedans lectoyre*, we see Nostradamus using an obscure term which may or may not have been an anagram. Very often, his use of single Green Language words was less complex. He was especially adept at introducing multi-layered Green Language symbolism into innocent-seeming personal names. A fine example of this may be seen in his term *ognion*. This, a version of *ogmion*, appears in quatrain IX.89, which deals with events during the reign of Louis-Philippe, the last King of France. The final line of the quatrain announces that his power will be weakened by the young *ogmion*. In order to approach the meaning of this single word, we shall have to consider briefly the entire quatrain, which reads:

Sept ans sera PHILIP. fortune prospere.
Rabaissera des BARBARES l'effort.
Puis son midy perplex, rebours affaire,
Jeune ognion abysmera son fort.

Seven years will fortune prosper Philip.
He will put down the Barbarians.
Then his middle period will perplex, a difficult matter,
Young ognion will overwhelm his strength.

This is one of those quatrains where Nostradamus names the future protagonist (Louis-Philippe) without any attempt to disguise. It is difficult for us to appreciate that this Philip was still in the future for Nostradamus.

As the first line intimates, Philip's first seven years of reign went reasonably well, considering the conditions in France at that time. During this period he successfully invaded Algiers, in both 1827 and (more notably) 1830, which explains the word *BARBARES*, which in Nostradamus usually refers to the Turks or Arabs, who threatened sixteenth-century Europe (see page 169). The difficulties faced by the King are set out in the second line:

> *Puis son midy perplex, rebours affaire,*
> *Jeune ognion abysmera son fort.*

By 1836, Philippe was having problems with various attempts to usurp his role. The later source of his problems was his conservative minister, François Guizot, who remained obstinate in refusing liberal reforms, as a result of which a revolution broke out in February 1848. Just as Philippe had fled in 1795, so he fled once more – this time not to America but to England, where he died two years later.

The Green Language creation in this quatrain is *ognion*, in the last line. *Ogmion*, sometimes *Ognion*, sometimes *Ogmius*, seems to have come from the Celtic mythological figure, *Ogma*, who is supposed to have invented the *Ogham* alphabet (which some scholars argue may not even be Celtic in origin), which was at times called the *Ogam*, *ogum*, and (in Gaelic) *oghum*. When first translated to Roman Gaul, he was known as Ogmios, but this may have been due to the misunderstanding of the poet Lucian, who believed that he was a Gaulish deity, the nordic equivalent of Mercury, and tutelary over language. The Ogmios figure probably grew physically by association with later variant names on the

Italian debased–Latin, *orco*, meaning demon, which eventually flowered as the French word *ogre* some considerable time before Perrault used the word in his fairy stories, at the end of the seventeenth century. The later French encyclopaedists tried to fix him as *Ogmius*, and made him one of the Gallic gods, a version of Hercules.

In French romance and fable, with which Nostradamus would have been familiar, there are two important individuals with names derived from that of Ogma. The most important, *Ogier* the Dane, who figures in the Charlemagne stories, is one of the great folk heroes of medieval romance. The other is of Biblical origin, in the figure of *Og*, the giant King of Bashan.[4] It was this name which seems to have suggested to Perrault the name *ogre* to denote the man-eating giants.

Although it is not strictly accurate, some modern commentators (including Laver, who popularized the notion) have insisted that Ogmios is really Hercules. This is an intriguing argument, for Hercules did appear on an 1848 Republican five-franc piece. A similar image had appeared on a 1796 piece. *Jeune ognion* means the new Republic (1848) in contrast with the old. The argument follows that if Ogmios is on the Revolutionary coinage, then Nostradamus must have seen these in his visions. Laver writes, 'It is as if Nostradamus had actually travelled into the future, mixed with the revolutionary crowd and had the pieces of money in his hand.' Although this is an interesting idea, nicely expressed, we are of the opinion that Nostradamus did not have this coinage in mind when he wrote, and had no need to think numismatically. In any case, the giant on the coin is not Ogmios.

Laver gave the date of the first coin wrongly – the reverse bears the date *L'an 5*, which corresponds to 1796. The coin clearly portrays on its obverse the image of Hercules as a giant. He is standing between personifications of Liberty and Equality. The legend reads *Union et Force* (Union and Strength). There is no doubt, from the lion-skin attribute, that this image represents Hercules, rather than Ogmios or Ogier. Seemingly out of context, the *Hercules Gallicus* appears in a hermetic context in the frescoes by Tibaldi and Carducci in the Escorial, which represents the highest stream of public arcane imagery in Spain. Streams of power are being emitted from his mouth, and perhaps subduing those in front of him. Whatever the nature of this logos-like stream, it puts Hercules in context: he forms a link with the *Caput Hercules* which dominated the rectified chart of Philip II of Spain (see page 487).

The numismatic symbolism aside, we can see why Nostradamus chose the word *ogmion* to represent the giant which faced Philippe. As required of a Green Language construction, the word weaves together several strands of meaning, all of which would have appealed to Nostradamus' arcane and erudite mind. Ognion is a man-eater, just like the Revolution. Ogmios is a giant which cannot be controlled by mere mortals. Ogmios invented a secret form of writing. Ogmios is a folk hero, and is therefore a convenient symbol of the popular feeling which swept through France after 1848.

This last strain of symbolism points to one very deep reason why Nostradamus should have adopted this name in respect of a Revolution. Ogmion's namesake, Ogier the Dane, has a recurrent role as saviour of France. Aided at one time by Morgan le Fay, he saved France from the invading Paynims. According to popular belief, after repelling this foe, Ogier did not die, but (like his counter-part, Arthur) remains in Avalon, awaiting the call to save France at the hour of her need. We are not dealing here with a classical allusion to Hercules, but to a prophetic reference to the Charlemagne mythos, to a tutelary spirit of France.

The name *Ognion* is not of profound importance in the study of Nostradamus, but it does offer us an opportunity to see the Green Language at work. The wors had evoked many strains of connotation, from the Bible to mythology, from early French history, even into millennarian expectations. It unites French popular imagery with the notion of giants – as with a superior force or strength which does not die, but waits in the wings of history, so to speak, awaiting a call to save France – and therefore pertinently describes the popular revolutionary force which lies skin-deep behind the French political system.

EYES OF THE SEA

Not all Green Language is expressed in single obscure words. Very often, entire phrases are used to evoke arcane or literary references which would be recognizable only to initiates or, at the very least, to those familiar with classical literature. In some cases, the purpose is the introduction of nuances of meaning which would evade ordinary language; in others the intention was to disguise a place-name, or a date, in order to render the quatrain opaque until after the event. A good example of this is *L'oeil de la mer* ('eye of the sea') found in quatrain IV.15, which has caused much misunderstanding among modern commentators. In 1942 James Laver claimed that it referred to the periscopes of Hitler's U-boats in the North Atlantic, the tip of the periscope above the waves being the 'eye'.

The quatrain reads:

> *D'où pensera faire venir famine,*
> *De là viendra le rassasiement:*
> *L'oeil de la mer par avare canine,*
> *Pour de l'un l'autre donra huille froment.*

201

Tentatively, this verse translates:

> Where he will think to bring famine
> From there will come satisfaction
> The eye of the sea by canine avariciousness
> For the one will give to the other wheat-oil.

Almost all those who have commented on it since 1942 have adopted Laver's interpretation, yet it is quite wrong. Roberts alone deviates from this view, seeing an anticipation of off-shore drilling and the recovery of huge oil reserves – though he does not explain what the 'eye of the sea' is. However, we have no doubt that the quatrain does not relate to submarines or off-shore drilling. The reference to the eye of the sea is pure Green Language, and is derived from the Greek phrase *mati tis thalassas*, which translates literally as 'the eye of the sea'. Quite simply, the phrase means 'whirlpool'.

Within the methodology of the Green Language, the phrase is a reference to Sicily. In classical mythology, it is maintained that there is a great whirlpool, off the coast of this island, named Charybdis. In Homer, Charybdis is so immense that it swallows the waters of the sea three times a day.[5] In Ovid's *Metamorphosis*, with which Nostradamus was familiar, the whirlpool was located in the Straits of Messina (in spite of the fact that no actual whirlpool is found in this place).

The Homeric reference has led to the famous phrase (which may be traced back to the Roman author, Horace)[6] designed to represent two equal dangers – in trying to avoid the whirlpool Charybdis, one falls into the maw of Scylla. In the Ovid telling of the tale, Scylla is the six-headed sea-monster, with twelve feet, created by Circe. She would eat the 'dogs of the sea', as dolphins were called, along with as many mariners as she could entrap from passing ships. As she paddled in the sea, she found around her loins a belt of 'dogs, ringed in a raging row', and round her feet she found 'gaping jaws like Hell's vile hound', reminding us of the tradition that she herself would bark like a dog. It is not too imaginative to associate her with an avaricious canine, guardian of one of the two rocks in the straits between Sicily and Italy.

Clearly, the Nostradamus line is reference to the whirl-pool and the monster, rather than to any modern invention such as the periscope. Stripped of its Green Language obscurity, we see that the line is designed to indicate that the event described in the quatrain takes place in Sicily – probably near the Straits of Messina.

In some cases, Nostradamus' Green Language constructs are so deeply enmeshed in their contexts that it is almost impossible to separate them, as we have succeeded in doing with the single word *ognion*, or the phrase *L'oeil de la mer*. It is for this reason that we shall examine three further examples of his Green Language usage to study more fully his method of working with contexts.

The first quatrain deals with the problems touching upon an eighteenth-century papacy: in this, Nostradamus appears to use the Green Language only once. However, in addition to this single use of the occult tongue, the master also incorporates into the quatrain a number of interesting linguistic usages which provide a useful insight into his method. As we shall see, this quatrain illustrates one of the perennial difficulties in the approach to Nostradamus. The second quatrain, dealing with the suffering of Marie Antoinette towards the end of the eighteenth century, offers several nuances of Green Language use. The third qua-train, which we reveal revolves around the Peace of Ryswick negotiated in 1697, is among the most complex examples of Green Language in the Nostradamus oeuvre.

The Nostradamus Code

POPES, BALLOONS AND MEMORIALS

The first quatrain, V.57, reads:

> *Istra du mont Gaulsier & Aventin,*
> *Qui par le trou advertira l'armée:*
> *Entre deux rocs sera prins le butin,*
> *De Sext. mansol faillir la renommée.*

An approximate rendering may be:

There shall go forth from Mont Gaulsier and Aventine,
(One) who through the hole will direct the attention of the army;
Between two rocks will be taken the plunder,
Of Sext. Mansol to bankrupt the reputation.

This fascinating verse can be interpreted with complete conviction in terms of Green Language to show a prediction of hot-air balloon flight, and (presumably in order to date this event) the death of a Pope. However, this quality of conviction has been questioned – though not completely squashed – by recent French research, which has proposed an entirely different approach to the quatrain. This is most instructive, for it calls one to question just how many more 'translated' quatrains may be retranslated in future to give entirely different meanings, and, indeed, whether Nostradamus intended the quatrains to have more than one meaning, entirely integral to their structures.

Let us consider the meaning which may be derived from the quatrain by reference to the Green Language. Like most of the quatrains, this appears initially to be written in sixteenth-century French. However, this is misleading, since we shall find words and compounds which are in English and Latin (Nostradamus, of course, uses at least

204

seven different languages), along with a couple of words which are meaningful distortions and other words which are constructs from the occult tongue itself. As we shall see, this quatrain contains only one arcane reference, one Green Language term (as a Latin-English compound), one syncope, and a couple of arcane-seeming uses of sixteenth-century French. Fortunately, by normal syntactical and linguistic standards, this quatrain is relatively easy to interpret – which is one reason why we have chosen to look at it here.

Nostradamus frequently gives specific names for individuals and places in his quatrains. Here, for example, he mentions the Roman hill, the Aventine (*Aventin*). More often than not, however, in accordance with Green Language usage, such names are blinds. There are a couple of seeming place-names in this quatrain, but our analysis will reveal that neither is quite what it seems. The following analysis should alert us to this system of arcane blinds, and to the fact that the map of Europe has changed so many times since Nostradamus wrote that it is foolish to assume his own place-names are intended to denote the extant places on the European map.

Nostradamus has the disarming ability to write about places and locations as they will be in the future, contemporaneous with the events he predicts. (Later we shall see startling examples of this in his treatment of the United States of America, which, of course, did not exist in the sixteenth century.) Quatrain V.57 contains a French example, since the districts to which he refers were born of the French Revolution, and became cartographic memories shortly after the restoration of the monarchy.

In quatrain V.57 Nostradamus weaves into the four lines two separate contemporaneous events, the first two lines predicting the hot-air balloon, and the last two the contemporaneous destiny of the then-reigning Pope. As we shall see, both prophecies came true in France at the end of the eighteenth century.

Bearing these points in mind, we shall look at the quatrain in detail, taking the four lines in sequence. The first line is *Istra du mont Gaulsier & Aventin*: two mounts or hills, one appearing to be named *Gaulsier*, the other the *Aventin*. The latter is one of the seven hills of Rome. It is typical of the inversions used by Nostradamus that he should describe the Aventine as a 'mountain' (*mont*) when it is little more than a hill. (In the third line, we shall see that he also describes what is surely a mountain as a hill or rock (*roc*).) The first reference to a mountain may be understood only in terms of the Green Language. When Nostradamus wrote, the minuscule s and f were often used as inter-changeable, the latter being called the long s. In this way, *Gaulsier* looks like *Gaulfier*. Taken in connection with the preceding word (*mont*) we have *montGaulfier*. It is perfectly acceptable in Green Language usage to use vowelic hono-nyms to encapsulate in a strange-seeming term a different word with the same sound value – thus, *montGaulfier* sounds the same as *Montgolfier*, a reference to *Montgolfiers*, the two brothers who 'mount' the air in a hot-air balloon.

The reference to a Roman 'mount' (the Aventine hill) is an integral part of the prophecy, and points to the second skein of prophecies in this quatrain, which, as we shall see, is to one of the Popes, who ruled initially from the Vatican in Rome, but who died in France. Even the simple word *mont* is used to connote a relevant ambiguity: as a noun (*mont*), it means mountain, and as a verb (*monter*) it means to climb up, lift up, or ascend.

Having understood this, we see that the first line of the quatrain refers to the event-filled final decades of the eighteenth century. On 19 September 1783, at Versailles, before Louis XVI and his court, the Montgolfier brothers mounted sheep, cock and duck in a hot-air balloon. Their aim was to demonstrate that flight was possible, and to determine whether the rarefied atmosphere would have an ill effect on the animals and birds. In the same year, on 21 November, J. F. Pilatre de Rozier and the Marquis d'Arlandes made the first human ascent by balloon, from the Château de la Muette. They were carried at a height of some 300 feet for about 6 miles over Paris, which distance they travelled in about 25 minutes. After that, the balloon craze swept the whole of Europe.

Now let us look at the second line: *Qui par le trou advertira l'armée*. The mongrel verb *advertira* is from the Latin *adverto*, to turn something – especially one's attention – towards a particular place. This implies that the line means 'Who, by means of the hole, directs the attention of the army'. Clearly, this hole has some connection with the Montgolfier balloon. Within a decade of its invention, the hot-air balloon was already being used for the purposes of warfare – though restricted at this early stage to aerial reconnaissance. It was first used by the new French Republic, in 1794, at the decisive battle of Fleurus in Belgium. The navigators could look down at the terrain, and at the opposing army (*armée*), not through a hole (*trou*) in the bottom of the air-borne carriage, as Cheetham claims, but through the 'holes' of telescopes.[7] Delightful enamelwork on a contemporaneous French snuff-box portrays this balloon, tethered on long ropes behind the French lines and hovering over the Belgian army. This could almost be a painting of the scene which Nostradamus had envisioned, over two centuries earlier.

The third line is *Entre deux rocs sera prins le butin*. The reference to *deux rocs* may be among the most perspicacious of all Nostradamus' named visions, for the two rocks, between which the plunder was taken, were in existence for only a few years, as French departments. After 1792 (a date of considerable importance to Nostradamus – see page

323), the first stirrings of Republican expansionism resulted in the creation of a new department, which was named *Mont Blanc*. In the following year, the canton of Basle (Switzerland), which had already seceded from the Helvetic Confederation, also became a French department. It was called the Department of *Mont Terrible*. These departments lasted as cartographic entities for only a few years, but during that time 'the plunder' (*butin*) which was taken to France (see below) was conducted from Italy, between these two 'mounts'. This would not have been a normal route for someone travelling from Rome to France, but records show that after Pope Pius VI refused to renounce his temporal authority, he was taken prisoner, and conducted to Certosa, near Florence. When the French declared war on Tuscany, he was removed by way of the northern roads via Turin and Grenoble.

It is entirely in accordance with Nostradamus' methods that he has established a single theme – the pairs of hills (*mont Gaulsier & Aventin*) in the first line, and this pair of mountains in the third line – in this quatrain, to give it a unity.

The relevant plunder (*butin* also means 'prize') is undoubtedly a Pope identified, as we shall see, in line four. This is assured by the use of the ambiguous verb/noun, *prins*. The Pope is a temporal prince (the correct form in French would be *prince*). He is also captured, or taken (*prins* – the correct form in French would be *prise*) 'between two rocks'. As we shall see, in 1798, a Pope (*prins*) *was* taken prisoner (*pris*-oner) to Valence, on the Rhône, in France.

In passing, we should note that the probable reason why Nostradamus used the word *butin* to represent the Pope is because of its Green Language connection with *butte* (cf. the English *but*) which is mount or small hill, and therefore linked with the 'mount' theme of the quatrain.

Now we arrive at line four: *De Sext. mansol faillir la renommée*. To understand the abbreviated *Sext.*, we must look first at the following word, *mansol*; it appears in several quatrains, and is alchemical Green Language for the Papacy. It consists of the yoking together of the English word *man* with the Latin word for Sun, *sol*. As with most Green Language words, there is an additional hidden meaning, for *mansol* will metathese into *Solman*, a play on Soloman, the king of the Jews, renowned for his wisdom. The Pope is the wise Man-Sun, the human representative, on the earth plane, of the solar being, the Christ.

De Sext. is an abbreviation of the Latin *Sextus* (sixth). In the same year that Nostradamus published his first quatrains, Giovanni Pietro Caraffa ascended to the Papal chair, with the name of Paul IV. From that date, the first Pope to have the number VI (sixth) after his name was Giovanni Angelo Braschi who took the name Pius VI, and who was Pope from 1775 to 1799. This appears to make the seemingly esoteric *Sext.* both unambiguous and very easy to interpret. The notion of 'sixth' or 'six' is also hinted at in the first line of the quatrain, for symbolically speaking, one of the seven hills of Rome (the *Aventin*) is moved, leaving behind only six.

It might be argued that *Sext.* could refer to Felice Peretti, who became Pope Sixtus V, in 1585, or even to Paul VI, who became Pope in 1963. However, not only is Pius VI the first in the line to carry the numeral *Sextus*, but there is no relationship between these two later Popes and the events revealed within the quatrain. We may take it, therefore, that this *Sext.* is a reference to Pius VI who was the Pope, in Rome, during the time the Montgolfier brothers began their experiments with balloons.

The main strength of the Green Language is that it works by meaningful asssociation. Its technique is not involved merely with constructing alternative words by a variety of metatheses, hyphaereses or syncopes. The aim of verbal adjustments is to produce a new word, or words, which have meaningful associations. This may be seen in a sub-level of meaning in *De Sext*. Here is a most curious construction, even in Green Language, for it ellides to the Latin homonym, *dissectus* (the participle from the verb *dissecare*), meaning 'to dissect'. The reign of Pius VI marked the literal dissection, or severing, of the Papacy, since he was 'dissected' from Rome against his will, and never returned.

The curious phrase *failliér la renommée* also fits Pius VI very well. The verb *faillir* means to fail, to bankrupt, to transgress and ruin, while the adjective *renommée* means fame, reputation, renown. Pius VI did indeed witness the loss of the reputation of the Papacy, for though a remarkable and able man, he was called upon to deal with ecclesiastical, social and political upheavals well beyond the control of any human. As a consequence of Napoleon's occupation of Bologna, Ravenna and Ferrara, and the revolution in Italy which led to the proclamation of the anti-ecclesiastical Roman Republic, Pius was deposed in 1798. He died, a prisoner (*prins*) of the French at Valence, in 1799.

So far, the analysis is fairly convincing, for the two different skeins of prediction are united in the communality of period, as well as in the communality of the 'mont' theme which dominates the quatrain. However, this reading of quatrain V.57 is almost an object lesson in just how narrow is the line one walks when attempting to interpret Nostradamus. The reading we have offered above is a fair summary of how the quatrain may be interpreted with complete conviction, provided one has no knowledge of a locality near Nostradamus' birth-place, Saint-Rémy. In fact, in the past few years, the reading of this quatrain has been utterly changed due to the insight of the remarkable modern French scholar, Jean-Paul Clébert. Clébert's investigations into the implications of the word *Mansol*,[8] have profoundly influenced the reading of quatrain V.57, and it would be folly for us not to recognize that *Sext. Mansol* may not refer to Pope Pius VI, but to someone completely different – a Roman named Sextius.

As Clébert points out, *Mansol* could be the medieval Manseolo, located about one mile south of Nostradamus' birthplace, Saint-Rémy. The spot is now called after the church built there, Saint-Paul-de-Mausole. The area was, and is, well known for its Roman antiquities. Clébert indicates that a funerary inscription on a Roman mausoleum alongside Mausol (as it is now called) reads *SEX. L.M.IVLIEI C.F. PARENTIBUS SUEIS . . .* ('Sextius Lucius Marcius, son of Caius, of the Julii, to his parents . . .'). The *Sext.* of the final line of quatrain V.57 could be this Sextius, and the *Mansol* which follows it, the locality of the mausoleum.

Given that this is the locality of Saint-Rémy, the identity of the first mountain is now perfectly clear: it is Mont Gaussier, which guards the entrance of the road to Alpilles. The mountain is pierced by a corridor, between two rocks. Because of the curious shape of the mountain in this locality, the locals see a resemblance to a lion. Nostradamus refers to this in one of his other five verses in which the word *Mansol* appears: it is in the last line of quatrain VIII.34 (*Lyon Ulme a Mausol mort et tombe*). The hole, or corridor, between the two mountains is referred to in the second line of the quatrain currently being examined, V.57: it is through *this* that the army shall be warned.

In several other quatrains, Nostradamus refers to a secret treasure which will be discovered in this area. Perhaps it is between these mountains that the find (*butin*) will be carried. Perhaps, as this quatrain specifies, it will be the treasure (*butin*) of Sextius Lucius Marcius himself. Now, the word *Sextrophea* probably means 'Monument to Sextius' (the Latin *trophaeum* means memorial, trophy, victory, etc.). It is a word used by Nostradamus to describe his origins, in the first edition of his *Excellent & moult utile Opuscule* . . . , published in Lyons, in 1555.[9] Could this 'trophy' be the treasure which is to be found in this locality? Almost certainly, this is exactly what Nostradamus had in mind: the 'trophy' is a discovery made after the publication of his verse.

We write about this prediction of a treasure-trove as though this event is yet to come, but it is quite possible that a treasure has already been found at the excavated site (*trou?*) of Glanum which Nostradamus did not even see in his ordinary waking vision. In his *Almanach* for 1563 he had predicted the discovery of great treasures for that year,[10] but certain of the quatrains were less specific as to time and place. Could some connection be made between these and the six quatrains which deal with *Mansol?*

In the sixteenth century, the huge cenotaph[11] and arch stood (and still stand) alongside the road towards Baux, and Nostradamus cannot fail to have been familiar with these. However, the existence of ancient Glanum was unknown, save perhaps as an almost-forgotten name among a few historians, as the *Glanon* of Greek literature, or as the later *Glanum Livii* of the Romans. In ancient times, the city had been large and important enough to mint its own coins. The Roman city seems to have been destroyed about AD 270, and when the later city, which became Saint-Rémy, was constructed to the north, the ancient site of Glanum was deserted and soon entirely lost, save for the huge cenotaph and arch alongside the modern road. On occasions Greek or Roman artefacts and coins would turn up in the locality, and for a long time it was suspected that some secret lay near Saint-Paul-de-Mausole. But it was not until

1921 that excavations began, and the vast remains of Glanum, with its Roman treasures, were discovered. Was *this* the secret treasure to which Nostradamus referred?

Treasure, or Pius VI? The two possible interpretations which may be placed on the word *Mansol* – as future papal name, or as a reference to an extant Roman memorial – indicate the complexity of the Green Language devices, and the care with which Nostradamus erects occult blinds to deflect the unwary from the meanings in his prophetic verses.

QUEEN IN PRISON

A further instructive example of the Green Language is found in quatrain X.17, which deals with the sufferings of Marie Antoinette in prison. It reads:

> *La Royne Ergaste voyant sa fille blesme,*
> *Par un regret dans l'estomach enclos,*
> *Cris lamentables seront lors d'Angolesme,*
> *Et aux germains mariage forclos.*

The imprisoned Queen seeing her pale daughter.
By a regret enclosed in the stomach,
Lamentable cries will come from Angoleme,
And to the cousins marriage foreclosed.

There could scarcely have been a more apposite description of Marie Antoinette in the last two years of her life than *La Royne Ergaste*. *Ergaste* can only be from the Latin *ergastulum*, meaning a workhouse or a penitentiary, and must refer here to the Temple prison wherein Marie and the royal family were incarcerated in 1792. In fact, the Temple was not a prison until after 1792. In that year, the Chevaliers de

Malte (formerly the Order of St John of Jerusalem) was abolished, and the Temple property which they had held for centuries was expropriated. Its vast area was served by only one gateway, formerly in rue du Temple (*fig. 38*), and it was therefore an easily guarded enclosure. The Temple was used by the Directory – the name given to the government of France after 27 October 1795 up to its disbandment by Napoleon on 9 November 1799 – as a state prison.

The demoting of a sacred building, which originally served the ancient mysteries, to a prison would seem to sum up perfectly the destructive phase of the French Revolution. Nostradamus reflects this demotion in the choice of his word. With the homonymous use sanctioned by the Green Language, the word *Ergaste* also connotes the English 'aghast', seized with horror. To judge from the conditions under which Marie lived at that time, Nostradamus did not use the word inappropriately. The historical facts are these. In 1792, the royal family was taken to the Temple and lodged separately in one of the small towers in the grounds. Marie Antoinette was imprisoned in a tiny basement cell, its walls damp, its grated window all but occluded. For most of her time, she did not even have the benefit of a candle. She and her daughter – and at times the heir to the throne, the Dauphin – remained there until she was taken to the Conciergerie (in Revolutionary Paris, the prison for the most dangerous political prisoners), to await trial.

The word *blesme* is a version of the modern French *bleme*, meaning pale or wan. The poor young girl (*sa fille blesme*), Marie Antoinette's daughter, was white with horror not merely because she had been imprisoned in intolerable conditions in this *ergastulum*, but also because she had been forced to give evidence against her mother, concerning Marie Antoinette's alleged sexual misconduct with her son, the eight-year-old Dauphin. We should record that in spite of the contrary evidence, Marie Antoinette was found guilty. She was executed on 16 October 1793.[12]

The second line reads, *Par un regret dans l'estomach enclos*: 'By a regret enclosed in the stomach'. One possible interpretion of this line has quite extraordinary implications – 'By a regretful act in a forbidden stomach'. It is usually argued that Marie Antoinette did *not* commit incest with her son, and that the charge – like the trial itself – was based on falsehoods. However, it is possible to interpret this line as suggesting that the daughter was pale, and the Queen herself 'aghast' because of 'a regrettable thing enclosed by her stomach' – a periphrastic way of speaking about an illegal sexual encounter.

Is it possible that Nostradamus could see into a futurity an event which was misunderstood by subsequent historians? It is more usual to interpret this 'incest' line as a reference to the childlessness of Madame Royale, the daughter of Louis XVI and Marie Antoinette. However, this is contained in the final line of the quatrain, and was scarcely relevant during the time in the Temple prison, as Madame Royale was not even married at that period.

Let us glance at this last line: *Et aux germains mariage forclos*. In French, the two words *cousin-germain* mean 'first cousin'. Louis-Antoine de Bourbon, the duke of Angoulême, was Madame Royale's first cousin. Nostradamus could scarcely have written a more accurate description of this unfortunate liaison, for it was indeed 'foreclosed', or prevented. They married in 1799, after the deaths of her parents: they had been engaged to be married all through the Terror, having being betrothed in 1787. She never had children. Could the curious phrase *estomach enclos*, which literally means 'stomach walled-in', refer to this barren state of Madame Royale, perhaps caused by the things she experienced in the Temple?

THE PEACE OF RYSWICK

The final quatrain we have chosen to represent the Green Language is far more complex than the other two. This is quatrain X.7, which deals with – among a number of related themes – the Peace of Ryswick. The 'translation' of this complex verse is best offered as a commentary.

> *Le grand conflit qu'on appreste à Nancy,*
> *L'Aemathien dira tout je soubmets,*
> *L'Isle Britanne par vin, sel en solcy,*
> *Hem.mi.deux Phi. long temps ne tiendra Mets.*

The curious *solcy* in line three may be related to the verb *salir*, but (as we shall see) has been much 'defiled' itself to serve the purpose of the Green Language.

> The great conflict in preparation at Nancy,
> The Aemathien will say I submit all,
> The British Isle by wine, salt defiled,
> Hem.mi.deux Phi. will not hold Metz for long.

This is one of the most splendid examples of Green Language literature, and in order that we might fully appreciate its profundity, we shall have to consider the history to which it relates. The central issue is the Peace of Ryswick of 1697, which is intimately linked with the Spanish succession.

The first line points to a city – *La grand conflit qu'on appreste a Nancy*. Charles III (the Duke of Lorraine, usually known as Charles the Great) refortified the city of Nancy in the sixteenth century, and built the *ville neuve*. These fortifications were dismantled in the seventeenth century. The city was taken by the French in 1633, but restored at the Peace of Ryswick (1697). It passed to France with the rest of Lorraine in 1766. The eighteenth-century history of the city need not concern us. This potted history of Nancy points to the larger issue of the border disputes between the Spanish (who held Holland) and the French. This means that it touches upon the question of the Spanish succession. As we shall see, this theme forms the core of the last two lines of the quatrain.

Now to the second line: *L'Aemathien dira tout je soubmets,*. The Aemathien, in a variety of spellings, is usually a reference in Nostradamus to Louis XIV. Louis participated in the flight of James to France. The third line runs: *L'Isle Britanne par vin, sel en solcy*. The mention of the British Isles may seem to be quite out of place, until one recalls that Britain was involved in the Treaty of Ryswick. Through this treaty Britain established recognition by the French monarchy of the accession of William III to the British throne. It will be recalled that William, who became King of Great Britain and Ireland in 1689, was born in Holland. To counteract the aggression of Louis XIV, William formed a grand alliance of a European federation (1686), seeking to bring England into the conflict. Invited to take over the throne, he landed at Torbay in 1688. (This operation is dealt with in another Nostradamus quatrain (see page 298 ff), so it need not detain us here.) He and his wife, Mary, were proclaimed King and Queen in February 1689.

William, for the first time in English history, introduced a tax on salt (*sel*), as well as upon a range of alcohols (*vin*), in order to help finance his expensive wars.[13] This historical fact is used as a blind to obscure the inner content of the line. In terms of the Green Language, the line may also be read as: *L'Isle Britanne parvin selen sol ci*, meaning 'Here to the British isle arrives Moon and Sun'.

The linguistics behind this extensive metathesis are:

parvin	from the French verb *parvenir*	– to come, or arrive
selen	from the Greek noun *Selene*	– the Moon
sol	from the Latin noun *Sol*	– the Sun
ci	from the French adverb	– there

However, the final word, which is used generally in compounds, could be regarded as an abbreviation of the French *ici* (here), which is how we have translated it above.

The Moon and Sun are the archetypes for Queen and King in both astrology and alchemy. William and Mary were the first pair to be acclaimed King and Queen in British history. The line is of considerable importance in the context of the quatrain, for William's unique 'allegiance' with Britain, whilst never especially popular with the British, helped establish that country as an important political power in the European history which followed on the bloodless revolution of 1688 and the peace consequent to Ryswick.

When we look at the last line – *Hem.mi.deux Phi. long temps ne tiendra Mets* – we begin to see the great profundity with which Nostradamus uses the Green Language. *Hem. mi.deux Phi.* is a play on three Greek words which have survived, in both English and French, in a variety of terminologies. *Hem.mi.* is Latin for 'the half of', and is derived from the two Greek letters *He mi*. This Graeco Latin origin partly explains the third Greek-seeming letter, *Phi.*, which appears to be another Greek word, though in reality it is an abbreviation. When abstracted from Green Language disguise, the three abbreviations translate 'Half of two Phi.', giving the meaning 'Half of two Philips'. The two Philips were kings of Spain in the seventeenth century: Philip IV, King of Spain and Portugal (1605–65), and Philip V of Spain (1683–1746).

What we learn about these two Philips is that they will

not long hold Metz (*Mets*). The prediction came true. The city of Metz was ceded to France in 1648, but was restored at the Treaty of Ryswick in 1697. Hence, during the period between the two Philips France held Metz for 49 years. The two Philips overlap respectively the beginning and end of the period during which France held Metz. Philip IV reigned for 17 years after the ceding of Metz to France. Philip V was born 14 years before Ryswick.

The reason why Metz was taken as a symbol is not merely because it rhymes with the *soubets* of the second line, but because it was a useful symbol of Lorraine, which throughout history has changed hands because of its importance as a boundary between what is now Germany and France. It also had another meaning for Nostradamus and his contemporaries. Henry II of France had occupied Metz in 1552, and the attempts of the Holy Roman Emperor Charles V to retake the imperial territories failed – his siege of Metz in that year was not successful. It would have seemed to the contemporaries of Nostradamus that this part of Lorraine was finally in French hands. Nostradamus is, however, predicting the opposite. The disputed area of Lorraine has left its mark on each of the centuries since the sixteenth century, and Nostradamus was able to foresee this pattern which reflected alternately the expansionism of France and Germany.

Under the terms of the Ryswick treaty, Louis XIV recognized William III as King of Great Britain and Ireland. Chief fortresses in the Spanish–controlled Netherlands were to be garrisoned by the Dutch, though to remain under Spanish control. France restored Lorraine, keeping only Strasbourg. The issues dealt with in this treaty are those which Nostradamus chose to reflect upon in this remarkable quatrain, for in the space of four lines he mentions the central issues of Nancy and Metz (the French question), the Spanish kings (the Spanish succession question) and the British invitation to William (the British succession problem). This is more akin to history than prediction.

The quatrains examined above were chosen because through an analysis of them, the reader unfamiliar with the subtleties of Green Language usage may be able to perceive a range of effects achieved by Nostradamus, thereby taking on board a number of techniques to be found in the quatrains. We close this chapter with an investigation into two more sophisticated and demanding examples of Green Language usage.

NAPOLEON IN EGYPT

Quatrain X.79 offers a fine example of the Green Language in its most esoteric form:

> *Les vieux chemins seront tous embellis,*
> *L'on passera à Memphis somentrées,*
> *Le grand Mercure d'Hercules fleur de lys*
> *Faisant trembler terre mer, & contrées.*

Approximately, we may translate this as:

> The old routes will all be embellished,
> On them he will pass to Memphis, though briefly,
> The great Mercury of Hercules fleur de lys
> Making earth, sea and countries shake.

The commentaries afforded this quatrain in the sub-cultural literature are remarkably brief, but off the point. In the eyes of de Fontbrune, the mystic *grand Mercury* is merely a 'handsome young man'. We feel that the verse has been well protected by its maker, as though it were an amuletic charm.

220

As is often the case with Nostradamus, if we wish to grasp the theme of the quatrain, we must look beyond the first line. In this instance, we must consider at the outset the arcane third line: *Le grand Mercure d'Hercules fleur de lys*. The phrase *Le Grand Mercure d'Hercules* (the great Mercury of Hercules) is probably the most obscure of all the Nostradamus references, and reveals his familiarity with the arcane Gnostic tradition. In occultism, the *grand Mercure* is the 'thrice-great' Hermes. Trismegistus, the 'Thrice Great', is a name given to a magus archetype (perhaps once an actual teacher) of the Egyptian mystery schools, who brought initiation practices to the ancient Greeks. The invocatory name probably refers to his triple rank as philosopher, priest and king, but it may also refer to him as initiate of the three worlds (the spiritual, the mundane, and the infernal). He is identified with the Egyptian god Thoth, and with Hermes, the supposed founder of Greek hermetic thought, and the bringer of alchemy to Europe. Hermes is the Greek name for Mercury (which is a Roman name), and explains why the early arcane literature contemporaneous with early Christianity was often called 'hermetic'. The arcane writer, Hippolytus, in a fragment of this hermetic literature, mentions specifically the symbolism of Hercules, as it pertains to this Mercurial tradition.

Few writers interested in the history of the world, as was Nostradamus, could ignore Hippolytus' *De Antichristo*: as we shall see, certain ideas in this work resurface in the quatrains of Nostradamus. The main corpus of the second-century Hippolytus was not discovered until 1851, when his *Philosophumena* surfaced. In the days of Nostradamus the material set out in this section was thought to have been written by Origen. This does not affect our argument, however.[14]

Hippolytus, whose text offers Christian glosses on early-

Graeco–Egyptian mystery wisdom, observes that the name of the archetypal man (who is Christ) is *Geryon*. This Christ-man is so called, because He is triple, being psychic, mental and physical. The explanation is based on the identity of the giant Geryon of classical literature, who is triple-headed, or triple-bodied. This Geryon figures in the myths of Hercules, for as one of his labours, the Hero carries off his oxen.

It is in this last morsel of mythology that we begin to unravel the meaning in the Nostradamus quatrain. We learn from Ovid (whom Nostradamus quotes or shadows on numerous occasions in the quatrains) that Geryones was the name of a mythic king in Spain, whose oxen were carried off by Hercules.[15] At first glance, then, we may assume from this account that Nostradamus is describing some event in Spain – possibly an event involved with theft – as a parallel to the Hercules myth.

However, there is one small complication: Geryon is also associated with another part of Europe. In ancient times there was an oracle of Geryon, the *Geryonis oraculum* at Patavium in Italy. Patavium is the Latin name for modern Padua. Now here is another interesting and relevant association, for Patavium is said to have been founded by the Trojan hero, Antenor. Antenor was the noble Trojan who proposed restoring Helen to the Greeks, to bring the siege of Troy to an end. In this story we have almost a reversal of the Hercules myth – stolen property (in this case, the beautiful Helen) is to be *restored* to a rightful husband or country.

If we read this level of mythology into the quatrain, then we are dealing with some event in Padua, possibly involving the restoration of something stolen.

It does seems that Padua is deeply involved in this quatrain, within the general theme of rapacious 'theft'. Up to 1797 Padua was part of the Venetia, but in that year the city was taken by Napoleon when the Republic fell to him during his Austrian campaign. It was a brief occupation, yet one remembered for a long time by the Paduans because of the excesses of the French. Nostradamus regarded it as sufficiently important to write another quatrain about the event. Napoleon restored the city to the Austrians, five months later, in the same year.

It was in 1797 that Napoleon decided to invade Egypt. This date accounts for the quatrain number, 79: this is a play on the interior 79 of the year, 1797, as on a reversal of the last two digits. Nostradamus often forces some arcane reference through the arbitrary-seeming number apportioned to his quatrains.

Is there any other clue in the quatrain which will enable us to orientate ourselves further? The third line is completed by the easily recognized symbol – the *fleur de lys*. The arcane significance of the fleur need not detain us here[*] but we must observe the integrity with which Nostradamus works his symbols. Every word in the third line of this quatrain pertains to the mystery lore, even though each one has become externalized into exoteric mythology. In this context the flower symbolizes France, for the *fleur de lys* is the ancient emblem of the French monarchy, and was, even in modern history, the symbol of the Bourbons. When Paracelsus used the same image in his own sixteenth-century pictorial *Prophecies*, he portrayed three flowers on a dead tree. The arcane text appended to this image deals with reincarnation, and the stunned soul who forgets what has gone before, yet it is quite possible to

---

[*] Originally it was not a flower at all, but a bee, as Napoleon himself seems to have recognized, through his Masonic instructions. Alistair Horne records that at the onset of the 'Hundred Days' – the period in French history after Napoleon's escape from Elba – the fleurs-de-lys had been unpicked from the carpets of the Tuileries, and replaced with the Napoleonic bees. This was little short of sympathetic magic.

read the image on a more simple level, in historical terms, as relating to the future withering of the French monarchy, perhaps in three scions (the Valois, the Bourbons and the Napoleonic triad).

Napoleon made a serious attempt to reintroduce the arcane bee into the French national symbolism. A fine example is the flag made for the last public ceremony attended by Napoleon, and now in Les Invalides, Paris. It is almost Masonic in its symbolism. Even the arrangement of four groups of eight bees is designed to reflect the Seal of Solomon, and to evoke the Greek word *Nike* (Victory) sigil which is, of course, echoed in the capital N in the wreath. The arcane bee is found on the sculptures of Diana of Ephesus, and appears frequently in alchemical imagery: its significance is beyond the remit of this present work.

The *fleur* seems to have become emblematic of the French monarchy in the twelfth century under an ordinance of Louis le Jeune. However, legend carries the symbol back even to Clovis in the fifth century – almost back to the flower of the Gnostic tradition to which Nostradamus refers. Some esotericists insist that this *fleur* was originally a bee.

Within the Nostradamus quatrain, the *fleur* is a particularly poignant symbol, for by 1797 the French king had been guillotined, and the ancient power in the withered flower was in the hands of Napoleon, in Italy. However, one feels that Nostradamus has introduced the phrase merely to indicate the French connection, and evoke that individuality of Napoleon, who figures so frequently in the quatrains.

One key word in the quatrain is *Memphis*, in line three: *L'on passera à Memphis somentrées,*. For thousands of years, Memphis had been the capital of Egypt, and, within this quatrain, it may be taken as a symbol of the whole country. Napoleon, a Mason by inclination and initiation, had always

224

had a fascination for Egypt.[16] His Egyptian campaign was partly an attempt to strike at England, as well as a general part of his grand plan for French world domination, yet he was also intrigued by the ancient mysteries which Egypt was reputed to guard, and which were the supposed basis of many Masonic rites. It was no accident that the great Masonic opera, *Die Zauberflöte*, written in literary and musical Green Language, was set in Egypt.

The importance of Napoleon's Masonic connections has been overlooked by exoteric historians. At some point between 1795 and 1798 – and probably before the destined Egyptian campaign – Napoleon was initiated into Masonry. The delay is probably explained by the fact that French Masonic activity was savagely curtailed by the Revolution, many Masons losing their heads to the guillotine. However, the depleted Grand Orient and Grand Lodge were amalgamated and strengthened by 1799, due mainly to the efforts of Montaleau. Napoleon's brother-in-law, Murat (another subject for a quatrain – see page 355 ff), was proclaimed Grand Master of the Grand Orient at Naples, in 1809. According to McCody, the Napoleonic Brotherhood was founded in 1816 by those close to Napoleon. The storeys in the temple were named in the catechism of degrees, in which the first letters of each word combined to spell the name Napoleon: Naamah, Adam, Phaleg, Obal, Lamech, Eve and Naamah. Numerologically accurate, the progression was from eight (sounds) to seven (letters). This symbolism, though fascinating, is beyond the compass of the present treatment.

We should observe that the great star associated with Napoleon is Masonic. The five-pointed star is, of course, the sacred Egyptian *sba* star, one of the Egyptian hieroglyphic determinatives to pass over into the early repertoire of Christian arcane symbols. The *Rite of Memphis*, which may appear to have some relevance to quatrain X.79, seems first to have been established openly by Marconis, in Paris, round about 1838.

In fact, quite specific to the quatrain, the thrice-blessed Trithemius (*Le grand Mercure*) was supposed to have been the Thoth – the initiate teacher – of ancient Egypt, his principal centre being at Memphis. In the sixteenth century, Hermes-Thoth was not the shadowy figure which he now appears to be. Indeed, a work attributed to Hermes Trismegistus (the 'thrice-blessed') was circulating in the sixteenth-century astrological circles. Bound into an iatro-mathematical work by Bodiers was the *De Decubitu Infirmorum* attributed to this ur-initiate. We may presume that this work was known to Nostradamus for it was published in a translation in the ephemerides of Stadius which Nostradamus possessed (see page 56).

The brilliance of the third line is now clear, and the disparate symbols begin to cohere. In Napoleon we have the combination of French (*fleur de lys*) and giant (*Hercules*). He, or his armies, are involved in wholesale theft (like the theft perpetrated by *Hercules*) relating to the arcane wisdom, or ancient ways (*les vieux chemins*). Like Hercules of old, Napoleon would stay rapaciously in Egypt (*Memphis*) only for a short while (*somentrées*). The results – the laying bare of the ancient wisdom and the influence of 'Egyptian design' on the later French Empire – were indeed profound. It is possible that the last line – *Fasiant trembler terre mer, & countrées* – relates to the Napoleonic wars which followed the Egyptian campaign, but it need not. The legalized thefts of antiquities – and the promulgation of supposed sacred lore – subsequent to the campaign had a profound influence on Western culture.

One further interesting example of Green Language is *Terre mer*, which is printed without a separating comma in the original. This suggests that it may also be read as *Earth mother (Terre mere)* – a direct reference to the Isis cult of

Egypt. Is it perhaps the influence of this goddess which was to 'cause to tremble' the West? Much of the esotericism in modern Masonry, in so-called modern paganism (such as wicca cults) and general theosophical lore of recent years may be traced back to the theories which have evolved around the nature of the arcane in ancient Egypt. In most cases, this interest in arcane Egypt was subsequent to the discovery of papyri and antiquities as a result of the Napoleonic sojourn in Egypt. However, the imagery of the Egyptian hermeticism was well established in the alchemical literature of the sixteenth century. An excellent graphic summary is found on the title page of Maier's *Arcana Arcanissima* (*fig. 39* and *fig. 40*) which displays arcane symbols used by Nostradamus over 50 years earlier, including the lunar Apis the bull and the solar Osiris separated from the lunar Isis by a demonic Typhon, the very type of the Three Principles of alchemy.[17]

Within the framework of such arcane symbolism, the meaning of the second line takes on a new depth: *L'on passera à Memphis somentrées* – 'They will pass Memphis only for a short while'. Napoleon's troops arrived in Alexandria in July 1798, and had the country under control within three weeks. His army evacuated Cairo towards the end of 1801. They had been in the country for just under three years, yet the 'excavations' they undertook disgorged numerous extraordinary monuments and records which they took with them to France. The subsequent 'discoveries' made by French scholars still grace the museums of France. Indeed, one of the most sacred of all arcane objects – the great ceiling planisphere zodiac stolen from the roof temple at Denderah – is still displayed, however badly, in the Louvre, Paris. Is this wholesale theft of antiquities the equivalent of the theft of Hercules from Geryon? After all, Hercules stole cattle – cows and bulls – and the vast underground Serapeum at *Memphis* is the greatest grave-yard of sacred bulls in the world. This was discovered by the French Egyptologist Auguste-Edouard Mariette, in 1861, but the cult of the Apis bull was well known even before Napoleon went to Egypt. The Egyptian hieroglyph-ics were still undeciphered in the days of Napoleon, yet it was a direct result of his own scholars' work that Champollion was able to make the first successful transla-tions in 1821. The Rosetta Stone, which enabled Jean-François Champollion to solve the ancient riddle of the hieroglyphs, was found near Fort St Julien by Napoleon's officer, Boussard, in 1799. It finished up (yet more legalized theft) in the British Museum only because it had been erected by Napoleon at Alexandria, which was ceded to the British in 1801.

The theme of restoration hinted in the Antenor symbol-ism (Patavium) is now seen as an essential part of the quatrain. As a result of Napoleon's journey to Egypt, the ancient wisdom of Egypt was not so much stolen as 'restored' – in the Masonic temples, in art, literature and the spiritual life of Europe.

The first line of this quatrain (*Les vieux chemins seront tous embellis*), which seemed to be so simple, is now revealed as being delightfully ambiguous. *Embellis* could mean embellished, as we have 'translated' it above. However, *bellis* is a Latin plural ablative for wars (meaning, for example, 'in war'). Thus the Nostradamian invention of the non-French word *enbellis* would mean in Latin 'made warlike'. This could apply both to the ancient routes (those from France into Italy, and beyond into Egypt), or to the ancient arcane paths, the secret hermetic ways, which were embellished by the scholarship which followed on Napo-leon's curious interlude in Egypt. We see, then, that the ambiguity is meaningful, for both readings are relevant to the theme of the quatrain.

With the above information, we begin to sense something of the meaning hidden in the quatrain. It relates to the one permanent thing which resulted from the Egyptian campaign of Napoleon – an arcane culture. The ancient ways were embellished again: as a result of the campaign, the sacred writings were to be interpreted and the ancient wisdom of the Egyptians would be made available to the world. Such a recognition – albeit in his futurity – would have appealed enormously to a man like Nostradamus, so conversant with the Green Language. The quatrain stands out from all the others by the sheer brilliance of economy and complexity of symbolism: one feels that he wrote this more for himself than for his future readers.

A FAMOUS BATTLE

We have seen enough examples of the Green Language in the quatrains to have caught a feeling of its purpose. Now, in order to read Nostradamus more deeply, we should prepare ourselves to examine more closely his Green Language linguistic rules – at least, in so far as they can be formulated.

The anonymous 'D.D.' – who might have been a Doctor of Divinity – noted during a study of quatrain VI.4 that Nostradamus used the word *Agripine* to mean *Colonia Agrippinae*: this was *Synedoche partis pro toto*: 'very usual with Orators and Poets'.[18] Although D.D. never used the term 'Green Language', he was sufficiently representative of the culture of his age to be aware that Nostradamus wrote in code. He took it for granted – as remarkably few modern commentators do – that Nostradamus was hiding the sense in his predictions from the common gaze. Furthermore, D.D. realized that Nostradamus was by no means unique – encoded predictions, arcanized alchemical or astrological writing, and even occultized commonplace

prose and verse were important and even popular
domains in sixteenth-century literature. The Green Language used by occultists was merely a particularly complex
and well-thought-out form of a popular literary genre.

The appreciation of the coding system of Nostradamus,
and even of the fact that he wrote in a secret language, is so
little recognized by modern commentators that, rather than
attempting to solve the riddle of the sage, most commentators blame him for being unintelligible. One might just as
well blame the Chinese for speaking and writing a language
one does not understand. When faced with quatrain IX.14,
Cheetham threw up her hands in despair, dismissing it as a
typical 'unintelligible Nostradamus quatrain at its worst'.
However, when this verse is examined in terms of Green
Language techniques – that is, when Nostradamus is
appreciated as speaking a secret tongue – its meaning
becomes crystal clear.

In this quatrain, the place wherein its action takes place
is hinted at in the Green Language structure of the last line.
The linear structure, which is probably unique, seems to
have no name: were the whole line a word, it would be (to
stretch language beyond its natural bounds) an aphetic
apocope. However, as a line, we can only describe the
mutation as being a triple rebus – which is an odd
description to apply to verse:

Sept. fum. extaint au canon des borneaux.

In effect, the meaning of the line may be grasped only when
it is represented in triple form:

Sept.   fum. extaint au canon des   borneaux.

Let us examine the line in the light of three separate units.
The *Sept.* means literally 'seven', but its truncation

suggests that it is some kind of abbreviation. Following a sort of extended epenthesis, we must look to the end of the line for its completion, to the word *borneaux*. A *borne* is a landmark, and *bornoyer* means 'to mark out', as in surveying. Thus, *born eaux*, would be a terrain marked out by water. When the words at the beginning and end of the line are conjoined, they give *Sept.borneaux*.

Now, *Sept-Born* is the ancient name for Waterloo, where the famous battle of 1815 was fought. That the union of the two words was intended is confirmed by the full stop after *Sept.*, which had signed that it was an abbreviation. The use of an ancient name by Nostradamus is a particularly instructive form of archaizing – a Green Language technique which he used frequently.[19]

In the structure offered here, *Sept.born eaux* could be read as 'the waters of *Sept-Born*'. Here we have the archaic name and the modern name combined, for *Sept-Born* is the old name, while *eaux* offers a French version of half the modern name, *Water*loo. These intelligible words are separated by a curious word-picture: *fum. extaint au canon.* The word *fum* is an apocope from *fumée*, smoke or steam. *Extaint* is probably from the Latin *extenuo*, 'to reduce or diminish', but it could be from the French *extenuer*, 'to be worn out', or even from *etendre*, 'to extend'. There are other possible readings. However, in any of the readings given above, the gist is clear – namely, that smoke or steam is issuing from cannons, or that cannons are themselves (by hypallage, a term discussed in Appendix Five) worn out with issuing so much smoke. The important thing is that this image of smoking cannon is sandwiched between two words which mean Waterloo.

This triple structure is no accident, and points to an almost incredible numerology.

In quatrain VIII.1 Nostradamus introduces an evident anagram for Napoleon in the triple: PAU NAU LORON.

This is intended to read NAPAULON ROY – a fair
sixteenth-century approximation of the name which
brought dread to Europe in the first decades of the
nineteenth century.

In quatrain X.14 Nostradamus points to the war which
saw an end to this terror, the defeat of that great Emperor.
The two quatrains which mark beginning and end are
numerologically related. If we add VIII to X, we obtain
XVIII, which is 18. If we add 1 to 14, we obtain 15. When
we unite the two, we obtain 1815, which is the year of the
Battle of Waterloo.

Not only is the arcane numerology in itself impressive,
but so also is its structural link with the last line of quatrain
X.14. In order to understand the Green Language of this
last line, we have to reject (by epenthesis) the middle
section, and consider only beginning and end. Just so, in
order to arrive at the meaningful numerology, we have to
take a beginning and end (in an historical context), while
rejecting the quatrains which separate them. The century
numbers lead us to the century, while the quatrain numbers
lead us to the decade within that century.

Of course, given that we have determined that the theme
of the quatrain is the Battle of Waterloo, several elements
within the remaining verse are immediately revealed, but
these need not concern us here. It is sufficient that we have
shown how an intelligent – almost systematic – approach,
by way of Green Language techniques, can determine the
meaning of even the most recalcitrant-seeming quatrains.

Part Two

Predictions From the Sixteenth Century to the Twentieth and Beyond

Chapter 6

The Sixteenth Century

Europe alone will suffice, having been the Theatre of such Mutations as are not the least miraculous. . . . The Great Gustavus of Sweden begun the fatal Dance, & Germany still wears the masks of those Desolations which were occasion'd by his Arms. Portugal revolts from Spain, France is overrun with Civil Broils, Great Britain & Ireland are all in flames and confusion.

Scarce had the World begun to breathe the gentle Air of Peace, when the aspiring Spirit of France, big with the ambitious hopes of Glory, and puft up with a vain desire of the Sole Monarchy of the Western World, raises fresh Commotions in Europe, and has set all Christendom in flames of War. . . . These great Changes & Revolutions which have happened in the Affairs of the World, have always been ushered in with some strange Presages and Predictions . . .

(The Fortunes of France from the Prophetical Predictions of Mr. Truswell, the Recorder of Lincoln, and Michel Nostradamus, 1678)

In 1639, Cardinal Richelieu had a statue of Louis XIII placed in the centre of the Place Royale in Paris. Richelieu could not fail to realize that he himself had been included in the gallery of the future famous penned by Nostradamus, and he would certainly have recognized that the site he chose to honour his hero had been important to Nostradamus. It was in this square, in 1559, that occurred the fatal tournament between Montgomery and Henry II of France, which cost the latter his life. Nostradamus had predicted the event in one of his quatrains, providing remarkably accurate details of the accident and death. As the tragedy occurred only four years after the publication of the prophecy, it was the first of his quatrains to be fulfilled famously. Its accuracy, as much as the cleverly arcane way in which it had been framed, contributed enormously to the reputation of Nostradamus among his contemporaries, and coloured the view of his writings for hundreds of years. 'This,' wrote Garencières in 1672, 'is one of the Prophecies that hath put our Author in Credit, as well as for the clearness as for the true event of it.'

The quatrain has been dealt with, as an example of Nostradamian accuracy, by commentators since 1559. Even so, we must be forgiven for going over this old material once again, however briefly. The prophecy was set out in quatrain I.35:

> *Le Lyon jeune le vieux surmontera,*
> *En champ bellique par singulier duelle,*
> *Dans cage d'or les yeux luy crevera.*
> *Deux playes une, pour mourir mort cruelle.*

> The young Lion will overcome the old,
> On a warlike field by single duel,
> He will split his eyes in the golden cage.
> Two wounds one, to die a cruel death.

In spite of the fact that several prophets of the period had predicted that Henry II would die in a tournament, the King organized a jousting session. This was held as part of a celebration of the marriages of his daughter Elizabeth with the King of Spain, and his sister Margaret with the Duke of Savoy. On 30 June 1559, he tilted lances with Gabriel, Comte de Montgomery, then the lieutenant son of the Captain of the King's Scottish guards. Montgomery's lance broke, and a splinter went through the King's protective visor. In some accounts, the sharp wood pierced his temple, in others, his left eye. At all events, after a few days of agony, the King died on 10 July.

How do the details of history marry with the prediction? Although not old (he was 40 at his death), the King was certainly older than Montgomery, who was about 28 at the time of the accident. Thus, the young did overcome the old (*Le . . . jeune le vieux surmontera*).

The death did take place on a warlike field (*En champ bellique*) as a result of single duel (*singulier duelle*). Even if we translate the French *singulier* as meaning 'strange' the line is still applicable, for Henry had been advised to avoid such duels. However, the translation we have given above is accurate, since the term *singulier* was used, even in the sixteenth century, in a specialist sense to denote single combat.

The early commentators were excited by the arcane exactness of the third line, which was so designed as to be impenetrable until after the event. The golden cage (*cage d'or*) was, of course, the grilled ventail over the occularum of the helm, which was probably like that which has survived on the helm of Henry VI of England. It was through the bars of this that the sharp wooden splinters of the broken lance passed. Having accustomed ourselves to the extraordinary accuracy of Nostradamus, we are inclined to claim that the wood did pierce his eye (*les yeux luy crevera*), rather than his temple, though even contemporaneous accounts vary. According to the medical historian,

Howard W. Haggard, the records of Ambroise Paré, the chief Surgeon to Henry II, show merely that the lance pierced his brain.[1]

The fourth line, which would appear to offer no mysteries, is something of a problem: *Deux playes une, pour mourir mort cruelle.* There is no doubt that of the two men, Henry was the only one wounded in the duel, and that he did die a cruel death (*mort cruelle*) as a result of the exchange. Unfortunately, there are variants of this last line in some of the editions of the *Prophéties*, and most modern commentators have adopted the variant published by Antoine du Rosne in 1557.* Perhaps it is too much to read into the ambiguity of this last line the later cruel death of Montgomery, which Nostradamus dealt with in a further quatrain. However, in strict historical terms (and in spite of what some commentators have claimed) the beheading of Montgomery in Paris in 1574 had nothing to do with his being the unwitting cause of the death of Henry II.

Nostradamus' prophecy was recognized by his contemporaries as being far superior to those issued by other astrologers and seers. According to Percopo,[2] the astrologer Luc Gauric had predicted that Henry II would have some difficulty with 'horses and tears flowing from the left eye'. Another source, Ranzovius,[3] writing in 1580, tells us that Gauric had warned Henry to avoid a duel in the 41st year of his age, as the stars threatened a wound to his head which would result in blindness or death. Within a few years of the accident, many writers were attesting to the powers of a large number of clairvoyants who had foreseen the death, yet most of the stories seem to go back no further than Nostradamus, or perhaps Gauric. Perhaps the earliest

* *Deux classes une puis mourir mort Cruele* was used in the 1557 du Rosne edition.

account of the fulfilment of the prophecy (in that she might have witnessed the event) was that given by the Princess of Cleves. As Lynn Thorndike pointed out, we have here examples of prophecies becoming more and more accurate as the event approaches and passes.[4]

The horoscope of Henry II had been drawn up by several astrologers, including the sixteenth-century friar Giuntini. This is not the place to examine this figure in detail, yet it is worth noting that his death took place under astrological conditions so precisely predictive of death by a head-wound that it is surprising so many of his contemporaries missed it.

Not content with predicting the death of Henry II, Nostradamus proceeded to construct a quatrain which predicted a few details from the fascinating life and death of the man who killed him. In his *Influence de Nostradamus dans le Gouvernement de la France*, Torné-Chavigny, one of the most enthusiastic of nineteenth-century Nostradamians, claimed that the savant constructed a further eight verses which dealt with the consequences of this accident, of which the first two lines of quatrain III.55 were the most explicit:

> *En l'an qu'un oeil en France regnera,*
> *La court sera en un bien fascheux trouble*

> In the year when one eye reigns in France,
> The court will be in deep vexatious trouble

It is in the year 1559 that Henry 'one-eye' reigns and dies, and the court of France was indeed thrown into deep trouble. The reference to the eye of Henry II went even beyond the quatrains, for Nostradamus made a veiled reference to the King's future predicament in his open letter of dedication to Henry.

239

Nostradamus was careful to date his letter to Henry II, to whom he dedicated the last batch of quatrains, as June 1558. This was exactly one year to the month before the accident, and in the letter he actually mentions the King's eye, in a phase which would have passed notice at the time, but which would become poignant after the event. In a few lines, Nostradamus visualizes himself as being transported from his own obscurity by the presence of the King:

> ... *transportée au devant de la face du souverain oeil et du premier monarque de l'univers.*

> ... transported before the face of the sovereign eye and the first monarch of the universe.

The outer eye of the king was sufficiently powerful to lift Nostradamus (the inner seer) from obscurity to renown. The double meaning within this short reference is given an even deeper esoteric content when we realize that, even as he penned this dedicatory letter, Nostradamus knew that, in exactly one year, the monarch would have lost this outer vision, and the court of France would be thrown into mourning. As a result of the prediction which he had penned prior to this dedicatory letter, Nostradamus knew he would be lifted into fame. The sovereign eye was more than merely a literary device for the 'Seer'.

Nostradamus refers specifically to the king's death in one of his *Présages*, the name given to those verses collected from his various almanacs. In *Présage* 40, which corresponded to June 1558 (the month of the King's accident), Nostradamus had predicted: *De maison sept par mort mortell suite* – 'The house of seven by mortal death follows'. The house of seven (*maison sept*) were the Valois, the seven children of Henry II, all of whom would die without continuing the line.

AN INVASION OF CYPRUS

Understandably, a majority of the quatrains concentrate on issues which were of interest to sixteenth-century readers. Primal among these issues was the struggle against the Ottoman Muslims, who were threatening Europe from the eastern Mediterranean, and were infamous for their savagery. An example of a fulfilled quatrain, which appealed to the early readers of Nostradamus, and touched on this fear of Turkish invasion, is XII.36. This verse, written before 1558, predicted an invasion of Cyprus which took place within 12 years of the publication of the prophecy, and which had profound repercussions throughout the Mediterranean.

> *Assault farouche en Cypre se prepare,*
> *La larme à l'oeil, de ta ruine proche:*
> *Byzance classe, Morisque si grand tare,*
> *Deux differents. le grand vast par la roche.*

> A ferocious attack is being prepared on Cyprus,
> The tear in the eye, at your near ruin:
> Turkish fleet, and the Moors so great damage,
> Two different ones. the great deep by the rock.

Nostradamus put no great strain on his contemporary readers and commentators by this verse: they would have recognized that it dealt with a future conflict in Cyprus, spearheaded by the Turks.

However, precise details are not revealed with such clarity. Even after the event prophesied had been fulfilled, most commentaries on the verse stopped short at indicating that this was the famous attack mounted by the Turks in 1570. All the commentators we are familiar with have grasped the significance of such words as *Cypre* (Cyprus)

The Nostradamus Code

and *Byzance* (Byzantium), but have failed to include in their scrutiny many, if not all, the other words and phrases in the quatrain. Roberts merely recorded that the quatrain indicated that Nostradamus foresaw many battles between Islam and Christians.

We feel that such generalized interpretations are of little value: if Nostradamus was a great oracular source, then each and every word within his quatrains should have a meaning and relevance. As commentators, we sense that it is our duty to examine every nuance of a quatrain, and attempt to wrest from it the intended meaning. This is our intention here, as in the remaining analyses within this present work.

From the first line, we learn that a savage assault will be launched on Cyprus (*Cypre*). From the second line, we note that this assault will be ruinous, and close to the time when Nostradamus wrote (*ta ruine proche*). From the third line, we note that it involves the Muslims of Turkey (*Byzance* is Byzantium, the old name for Istanbul) and the Moors (*Moris* plus *que*, which means 'and'), both of whom will bring great destruction (*tare*).

In 1570, Sultan Selim II ordered the invasion of the island, and landed on its coasts over 60,000 men. When Nicosia was taken after a siege of 45 days, 20,000 inhabitants were slaughtered, and the remainder sold into slavery. Famagusta, which capitulated in August 1571 after a terrible siege of almost a year, was treated with particular savagery by the Turks. The torture, followed by the flaying alive, of the Venetian governor, Marcantonio Bragadino, and the slaughter of the inhabitants of the city became infamous even in the annals of Ottoman cruelty. The invasion was no passing thing: subsequent Turkish rule in Cyprus – which soon degenerated into brute repression – lasted for just over two centuries. The ruination of Cyprus was complete.

242

Clearly, the general consensus is correct: one need look no further than this invasion (*assault*) and destruction (*tare*) of 1570 and 1571 to determine the subject of the prediction. However, what can we make of the other, more obscure, references within the quatrain? For instance, given that we know the date of this event, and even the names of those who participated in it, how are we to interpret the enigmatic fourth line – *Deux differents. le grand vast par la roche*? What are the two different ones, or things? What is the great space (*grand vast*) by (or compared with) the rock (*la roche*)? What, indeed, is the rock?

The two different places (*Deux differents*) seem to be Famagusta and Lepanto. Both were sites of conflicts between the Turks and the Christians in 1571. Both conflicts were waged on the orders of Ottoman ruler, Selim II. The taking of Famagusta – the outcome of which we have noted – was conducted under the command of Lala Mustafa Pasha. The second battle was fought by the Christian League, formed mainly by Pope Pius V in defence of Venice, against the Turks under the command of Ali Pasha.

Within the context of the quatrain, the notable difference (*differents*) between the two was that in Cyprus the Ottoman Muslims were victorious, whereas at Lepanto they were destroyed. At Lepanto, Ali Pasha was made prisoner, and the greater part of the Islamic fleet was sunk, burned or captured. The consequences of the two main conflicts were indeed very different.

Lepanto is justly famous in naval history, not merely because it was the last great battle which involved oar-propelled boats, but also because of the huge numbers of casualties. At Lepanto, over 25,000 Turks lost their lives, and 15,000 Christian slaves were rescued from the Turkish galleys. Nostradamus was so moved by his vision of Lepanto that he dedicated several quatrains to it (see, for example, page 129 ff).

If Famagusta and Lepanto are the two different places united in the single date of 1571, what is the meaning of the great emptiness, vast or deep, and the rock (*le grand vast par la roche*)? We imagine that Nostradamus is reflecting on the different natures of the sites: the vast is the sea of the Gulf of Corinth (as the Gulf of Lepanto is now called) between the Peloponnese and the Greek mainland. However, the name *Lepanto* connotes in the arcane language employed by Nostradamus the Greek *panto*, from *pan*, which means 'all'. The great vast (*le grand vast*) is *le panto*, Lepanto. In sum, then, we observe that the contrast to the vast *panto*, the island of Cyprus, becomes the rock, or stony mass (*la roche*) – the very opposite of water.

In fact, the word *panto* has a particular interest within the framework of sixteenth century secret languages. There is no doubt that Nostradamus was familiar with the writings of another specialist in arcane languages, whose own lifetime and university life overlapped with his own. This was Rabelais, whose epic of humour, *The History of Gargantua . . .*, was begun in 1532, but not finished until after the second volume of the *Prophéties* had been published. In this work, the main character is *Pantagruel*, whose name (Rabelais tells us) was derived from the Greek *Panta*, and the Arabic *Gruel*, meaning thirsty – because he was born during a great drought. Actually, for all its bland honesty, this account of the etymology of the name is far from correct – his explanation is itself a typical arcane blind. However, what is relevant to us is that Rabelais adopted the same Greek word (*panta*) in an arcane subterfuge as did Nostradamus. It is typical of the arcane knockabout humour of the time – the *macaronnique* of Provence – that Rabelais should use the word to denote the idea of an all-consuming thirst, while Nostradamus used it to denote the idea of endless water. An additional overtone – perceptible to his more alert readers – would be that the name Pantagruel was, supposedly, partly Arabic. This would reinforce the link between his own construct *Le panto* and the Islamic forces which were destroyed there.

The word *vast* may have an additional hidden meaning. It could be a play on the origin of the word Peloponnese, which is from *Pelops*, a mythological giant, whose descendants were cursed by the charioteer Myrtilus, whom he had thrown into the sea off the peninsula. These classical associations with such a drowning off the coast of the Peloponnese (reflected in Lepanto) are evoked in this single word *vast*, for the Latin *vastus* not only means empty, and wasted (in the sense of unproductive and desolate), but also monstrous and large. As we shall see, Nostradamus is fond of tagging on extra meanings to classical terms: his mention of the Moors (*Moris*que) in line three may even be a further play on the word Peloponnese, for the medieval name for the peninsula was *Morea*, derived from the general notion that it was shaped like a mulberry. This word is from the same Italian word *mora* (mulberry or blackberry) as gave us the name Othello the *Moor*.

There is one further nuance within this quatrain which we need deal with here. Why does Nostradamus use the strange singular construction in the second line? Why does he write 'The tear to the eye' in such uneasy French (*La larme à l'oeil*) instead of the usual plural, *Les larmes*, or, following a more normal Nostradamian construction, merely *Larmes*? Nostradamus is, of course, juggling with words and meanings according to the methods of the Green Language. From the construction *La larme*, it is possible to derive both the French for alarm (*L'alarme*) – which is a fitting term within the sequence of the events he describes – and Lala (*La la*rme). The name of the conqueror of Famagusta was *Lala* Mustafa Pasha. Without his self-inflicted bad-French structure, such readings would not have been possible, and we can only presume that the structure was established precisely in order to carry one or other of these additional references to futurity.

Of course, this construction could have been offered in a different way: was there any great need for Nostradamus to include it in the phrase relating to 'tear in the eye'? This question takes us to a historical footnote which seems to confirm beyond doubt the link with Famagusta, and hence with 1571. After the surrender of Famagusta, the Venetian commander was put to a cruel death, contrary to all established usage of war, and contrary to his surrender agreement with the Turks. During the mutilations preliminary to torture, the Turks cut off his right ear (this was done personally by Mustafa), then his left ear and his nose. Only his eyes remained intact (*La larme à l'oeil*) for the remaining twelve miserable days of torture, before he was skinned alive.

Of course, one unfamiliar with the genius of Nostradamus might find themselves uncomfortable with the proposal that the savant could weave into a quatrain the name of a future thug, such as *Lala*, or precise details of an inhuman torture. Such a person might argue that it is unlikely that a prophet could be so familiar with the names of famous future protagonists and places as to make them the subject of a word-play in predictions. However, the fact is that Nostradamus *did* know such names, and *did* incorporate them into his quatrains. For example, staying within the historical context of the present quatrain, we should observe that, in other quatrains, he actually gives the name of the Ottoman leader, Sultan Selim III, and the precise date (even the day) for the battle of Lepanto. In other quatrains, we find Nostradamus giving details of places, personal names and exact dates which stun the reader into the delusion that he or she is reading history rather than prediction.

Ward listed over 30 'proper names, that Nostradamus

has anticipated'. We think this is not at all excessive: while we would not agree with all the examples given by Ward, we could add far more to his list. Naturally, since Ward wrote, several hidden words within the quatrains have revealed themselves as scarcely disguised proper names. We have included in our present work about half a dozen prophecies in which names are used virtually without disguise: the use of *Selim* in quatrain V.78, *Achilles* in quatrain VII.1, and the more modern *Franco* in IX.16 are noteworthy, though by no means unique.

THE STAR AND THE POPE

Nostradamus frequently uses stellar imagery, and this has led to some of his quatrains being linked with UFOs, and with Fortean phenomena. It is far more likely (given his period and his astrological interests) that such imagery is derived from apocalyptic Biblical literature, where such fire imagery abounds. In his recent study of Nostradamus, David Pitt Francis has published some useful material dealing with this Biblical influence. From the 40 examples which he adduces, from as many quatrains, we find four which emphasize stellar fire.

Among the quatrains, there is one which is distinctly stellar, but which has nothing to do with apocalyptic literature. In many respects it is a quite extraordinary quatrain, for it deals with an event which, in Nostradamus' own lifetime, would have been considered quite impossible – quite contrary to the ordinance of God. Yet, we have a quatrain which deals with a celestial event that occurred a few years after his own death, represented in a way which demonstrates, beyond a shadow of doubt, that he saw it – and its date – in some inner vision. This vision is presented in quatrain II.41:

La grand, estoille par sept jours bruslera,
Nuë fera deux Soleils apparoir,
Le gros mastin toute nuict hurlera,
Quand grand pontife changera de terroir.

The great, a star will burn for seven days,
A cloud will make two Suns appear,
The huge mastiff will howl all night,
When the great pontiff changes territory.

Our analysis will show that the above is far from being an adequate translation, but it does reflect the initial literal meaning of the quatrain. So obviously does this quatrain deal with stellar phenomena, through the mention of a star (*estoille*) and Suns (*Soleils*), that it is disturbing to see it being interpreted by Cheetham as relating to a description of the Third World War which is supposed to begin towards the end of the twentieth century. At that time, Cheetham explains (with reference to the fourth line), the Pope might well have to leave the Vatican, or even Europe . . .

De Fontbrune had no hesitation in seeing the star as a comet, and the mastiff (*mastin*) of the third line as Winston Churchill, though he gave no convincing reason for these interpretations. A serious analysis of the quatrain reveals that it has nothing to do with World Wars or even with bulldogs – though it *is* connected with an important Pope, long dead.

The star (*estoille*) is certainly the Nova of 1572, which caused such consternation in Europe, and indeed changed completely the late-medieval view of the cosmos.[5] Until this Nova was seen (first reported by Schuler in Wittenberg in the August of that year), it had been believed that the realm beyond the sphere of the Moon was immutable, a pure part of the Created realm linked with the purity of God. In this realm, nothing was to be born or die – it was the finished work of God. After the formation of the New Star, in 1572, it was recognized that even this pure zone was subject to change. It seemed as though nothing was free of mutation and decay: there was, so to speak, nowhere to hide from mutability, for even the realm of Heaven was subject to change. While Nostradamus tells us that it will burn for seven days (*sept jours bruslera*), it was visible for 16 months, and was one of the cosmic wonders of the age.

It is reported that the star caught the attention of Tycho Brahe when he was walking to his alchemical laboratory. So impressed was he by this new wonder that he pushed aside all future thoughts of alchemy and turned his attention to astronomy – a decision which resulted in, among other things, his brilliant star catalogue.[6] Although he was by no means the first to see the Nova, it was felicitous that the star should carry his name for over two centuries.

This particular Nova, in Cassiopeia, is said to have been the first such star to be located outside the solar system, by scientific measurement. Even in full daylight, it was easily visible to the naked eye, for it was considerably brighter than Venus: indeed, the astronomer Cornelius Gemma, who saw it in November, christened it the 'New Venus', though later it was more popularly called 'Tycho's Star'. So bright was the Nova that it was imagined to be the reborn Star of Bethlehem, and its appearance persuaded the sixteenth–century Swiss theologian, Theodore de Bese, into making an influential prophecy of the second coming of Christ.[7] Almost certainly, this is what Nostradamus means when he writes of the two suns (*deux Soleils*) appearing in the sky.

The word *nuë* can be translated as either 'swarm' or 'cloud', and it would be possible to describe the Nova as a cloud of light against the dark night sky. However, our own conclusion is that *nuë* is to be translated as 'cloudy' in the sense of 'obscured', intended to indicate that the Sun is not in the sky. The quatrain refers to night-time, when the light of the Sun is shrouded by the earth itself, reminding us that at night-time we are looking into the lengthened shadow of the earth.

Nostradamus writes of two Suns. Did he picture this Nova of 1572 as a sun? As we shall see, the answer to this question is yes. The two Suns which appear (*deux Soleils apparoir*) are suns which shine in the night sky. The clue to the identity of the second sun is contained in the words we have translated as meaning 'the great mastiff', in line three.

What is this great mastiff (*gros mastin*) which will howl all night (*toute nuict hurlera*)? Nostradamus uses the word *mastin* in several quatrains, and its meaning is not always entirely clear. In French the phase means literally 'a large mastiff', but etymologically the word is linked with the idea of mongrels. The verb *matiner* describes precisely such selective breeding. The word *mastin* is very close to the Greek words, *mastigo*, meaning to scourge, and *mastigias*, 'a rogue', a Greek etymology which has survived in the popular French *matin* for 'a disagreeable or evil fellow'. As we shall see, all these meanings are pulled together in the sense intended by Nostradamus.

In a quatrain given over so clearly to stellar phenomena, we have been tempted to see *Mastin* as a reference to the dog-star, *Sirius*. In the star-maps, Sirius is located in the mouth of *Canis Majoris* (the Greater Dog), which explains why it should be a *gros Mastin* in contrast to the stars in *Canis Minor* (the Lesser Dog). In the words of Homer, Sirius is the Autumnal star which:

> Shines eminent amid the depth of night,
> Whom men the dog-star of Orion call.[8]

The star has been represented as a canine since Egyptian times, and the hieroglyphic for the star (*Sihor*, as it was

250

called) was the image of a dog. That Nostradamus' great dog should bark all night may be a felicitous literary reference, for in ancient times the Phoenicians called it *Hannabeah*, which meant 'the barker'. However, as we shall see, Nostradamus took the nocturnal barking from a later astrological source.

Given that the *Matin* of Nostradamus is Sirius, what is the star doing in this quatrain? In the astrological tradition, its influence is baleful. This might be a sufficient explanation of the words *toute nuict hurlera*. In the *Shepheard's Kalender* for the month of July, we find the words:
The rampant Lyon hunts he fast with dogge of noysome breath Whose balefull barking brings in hast pyne, plagues and dreerye death.[9]

We are hardly suggesting that Nostradamus was familiar with Spenser's fine arcane poem, for it was not published until 1579, well after the death of the seer, and even after the event prophesied in the quatrain. However, Spenser had borrowed his own lines about the plague-dispensing sky-dog from Virgil's *Aeneid*, and no self-respecting medieval scholar could have avoided reading this great poem.

Now, the interesting thing is that the Roman astrologer-poet Manilius – who wrote his poem *Astronomica* near the beginning of the Christian era, and with whom Nostradamus was certainly familiar – had claimed that Sirius was a distant Sun, serving another stellar world. Was Sirius one of the two Suns (*deux Soleils*) in the night sky, alongside the newly born Venus-Star? This explains the reference to night (*nuict*), for if we were considering the Nova only, there would be two suns in the sky only during the daytime, and the brilliance of the Sun would diminish even the Nova. Sirius would not be visible during the daytime.

At night, things would be different, for during the night-times of 1572–3, the two Suns of Sirius and the Nova would be clearly visible in November (when Sirius culminates), around the time when the Nova was first observed by Tycho Brahe.

By now, it must be evident that the first three lines do not relate to UFO sightings, or a future war, but are designed to offer a precise date of a year which would be in futurity when Nostradamus penned the verse.

The star first appeared in 1572. The fourth line confirms the importance of this year with the reference to a great Pope (*grand Pontife*). In 1572 Pius V died, and Ugo Buoncompagno was elected as Gregory XIII. While this Pope achieved many things, including the reform of the Calendar which goes under his name, Nostradamus points to the changes which operated in the year following his election. Gregory XIII, having failed in his attempts to persuade Spain and Venice to fight against the Turks (quatrain III.3 dealt with the battle of Lepanto in the previous year), turned his attention away from Turkey to Europe. He took measures to help the Catholic League in France, and supported Philip II of Spain in his wars against the Netherlands.

These massive policy changes, which affected the whole of Europe, are what Nostradamus points to in his last line (*changera de terroir*). It is, of course, possible to interpret the last line as 'change territory', as we have done, for this is an entirely acceptable description of what Gregory did in this matter of support for warring factions. Equally, it is possible to read the French as meaning 'will change the terror', which is again applicable, for he changed his power for terror away from Islam to Protestant Christians.

The parallels between Nova and Pope are striking. Just as the Nova changed man's vision of the cosmos, so the Pope changed his own domain, looking no longer at the threat of Islam, but at the threat of internal Christian schism.

Sometimes, the prophetic genius of Nostradamus is so far-reaching that it sends the head into a spin. This is just such a quatrain, for there is a most extraordinary reason why the seer should have linked the Nova of 1572 with Gregory XIII, beyond the mere convenience of the communal date. The fact is that the name Gregory is still enshrined in our own name for the reformed New Style calendar, the Gregorian. It was Gregory who completed the work of this complex reformation, and rightly gave its name to the system. What is really remarkable is that the area of the sky in which the Nova was first observed (the modern triple *beta* of Cassiopeia) is one of the fiducials which marks the equinoctial colure.* It is thus an ideal place for marking sidereal time, and was therefore used as a fiducial for calendrical reforms. Just as Nostradamus brought the Nova and Gregory together in his quatrain, so the heavens brought the Nova and Gregory together in 1572.

THE PROTESTANTS OF GENEVA

A woodcut by Lucas Cranach the Elder depicts Martin Luther preaching. On his left, the Catholic clergy mill around in the jaws of hell, from which stream upwards the flames and smokes of the infernal regions. To his right, the Protestants take the bread and wine of the sacrament. On this side the spiritual powers are not visible, but the image of the crucified Christ reminds us that the renewing energies pour downwards from heaven, to nourish those below. This exchange of energies – of the infernal rising and spiritual descending – is emphasized in the gesture of Luther himself, for his left hand points downwards, and his

---

* The colures are two great circles projected into the Celestial sphere. They cut the projected equator of the earth at right angles, and pass through the poles of the earth. The equinoctial colure cuts the two equinoctial points.

right hand points upwards, as though he were some prototype for a Tarot card figure.

The theme of this woodcut seems to be similar to that adopted by Nostradamus in one of his most puzzling quatrains, but he was no supporter of Luther or the Protestants. As a relatively new convert to Catholicism, he was generally careful to represent himself in politically correct guises: when he found himself compelled to break through into forbidden territories, he resorted to obfuscation techniques which he knew would protect him well beyond the limits of his lifetime. As an initiate (see Appendix Three), he would know what the truths behind the schisms were, and as a clairvoyant he would have sufficient knowledge of the future to shrug off opinions which might be misinterpreted by the powers that be. It was not his destiny in this lifetime to be a martyr. The result is that his carefully crafted quatrain IX.44 will remain impenetrable for those who do not study it against the religious conflicts of his time.

> *Migrés, migrés de Geneve trestous,*
> *Saturne d'or en fer se changera,*
> *Le contre RAYPOZ exterminera tous,*
> *Avant l'advent le Ciel signes fera.*

> Leave, leave Geneva everyone,
> Saturn of gold will change into iron,
> The contrary RAYPOZ will exterminate all,
> Before the coming the Heavens will make a sign.

Understandably, this quatrain has given a great deal of trouble to serious commentators, and has over-excited the millennarians. For example, Roberts sees the quatrain as predicting the advent of atomic power and offering a warning of the eventual destruction of our civilization by means of atomic energy.[10] By contrast, the quatrain actually seems to have nothing to do with our future, and everything to do with events in Geneva shortly after the quatrain was written.

The word *RAYPOZ*, in such distinctive upper-case, is clearly intended to attract our attention. Nostradamus uses upper-case words 22 times in his quatrains, and we may infer from this that such an emphasized word has special importance. Nonetheless, we must admit that *RAYPOZ* is an obscure term, and was intended by Nostradamus to be obscure. Fortunately, when we have examined the rest of the verse, we shall be in a position to offer an account of its meaning which makes perfect sense within the context of the quatrain. For the moment, we may take it that the *RAYPOZ* is the equivalent of the invisible spiritual energy which, in the Cranach print, streams down as nourishment from Christ to mankind.

The curious phrase, *Saturn d'or en fer se changera*, may superficially seem to be connected with changes in atomic structures. It may suggest that a time will come when gold (*or*) may be changed into iron (*fer*). However, we are accustomed to thinking in twentieth-century terms, and have almost forgotten about the alchemical view of metals with which Nostradamus was familiar. In the sixteenth century, it was taken for granted that metals could change one into the other. We need only glance at the extraordinary writings of the esoteric alchemist Paracelsus to see how deeply embedded was this notion. To give Paracelsus his due, he was not writing of ordinary metals – of what we would nowadays call the elements. 'Nothing of true value,' he tells us, 'is located in the body of a substance, but in its virtue.'[11]

The esoteric alchemy of Paracelsus – and presumably of Nostradamus – deals with virtues, in the realm of what modern occultists might call the etheric. This much has to be said, for otherwise the writings of the sixteenth-century alchemists appear as so much gibberish. In fact, it is the materialism of modern science, and in particular the materialism in the modern psychology of the Jungian school, which has led to such a fundamental misunderstanding of alchemy in modern times. When, for example, Paracelus tells us that a certain change in the calcination of a metal may be observed from the glow which may be perceived above the crucible, he is not talking in material terms – in terms of what Jakob Boehme called the vegetative eyes – but in terms of what may be perceived with the spiritual eyes.

The German mystic, Jakob Boehme (1575–1624), was an initiate who perhaps did more than any other man to put into writing the arcane tenets of Rosicrucianism. The poetic term 'vegetative eyes' – used by both Boehme and William Blake (who was deeply influenced by the former) – is an attempt to distinguish earthly vision (earth-bound 'vegetable' vision of ordinary men) from spiritual vision, which is not tied to the earth and to the material senses, and which is the vision of initiates. This higher vision can be obtained only through the 'cleansing' of the portal of vision.

In reading sixteenth-century alchemists, we must be patient, for *we* are the ignorant ones; *they* the enlightened masters, which is why they were called the *Sapientiae*. The issue is not a matter of education or outlook, but of differences in visions.

In terms of the three metals listed in line two there is, in sixteenth-century terms, no danger implicit in the idea of their changing from one into the other. The primary question is, what precisely does Nostradamus mean? The phrase is very ambiguous, even within the realm of alchemy. Let us assume that he means: Saturn of gold will change itself into iron. In alchemy, every one of the seven planetary metals – Sun is gold; Moon is silver; Mercury quicksilver; Venus copper; Mars iron; Jupiter tin; and Saturn lead – is found in every other. Paracelsus opens his remarkable study of the Seven Metals with the observation that 'All things are concealed in all.' It is not his thought, but one of great antiquity, and a fine opening to a fine book.[12] This explains why he repeats the old alchemical teaching that any metal can be generated from Mercury.

If we have understood the Latinized French correctly, then Nostradamus is describing a generation of iron from either Saturn or gold, or some amalgam of both. Technically, this is a degenerative process, for gold is the Sun, and therefore the inner and outer light, while iron is a lower metal as its link with the centre of the earth (*en-fers*) implies. Perhaps this demotion, or darkening, of light explains the structure of the line, for it is designed to contain within it the French for the lower realms of hell, *enfers*: *Saturne d'or* en fer se *changera,*. Paracelsus deals with this generation of iron (*fer*) in his Third Canon. It is, he tells us, very difficult for a prince or a king to be produced out of an unfit or common man. But if Mars (*fer*) acquires dominion with strong and pugnacious hand, and seizes on the position of king, then such a change may take place. In alchemy, the king is gold (*or*), and the light of the sun (*sol*) through its connection with the zodiacal sign Leo, over which the Sun has rule. Saturn is the principle of age. Now, while there is in alchemy such a metal as Solar Saturn, or Gold-lead (*Saturn d'or*), the terms are acceptable usage to denote an Old King, and by extension Christ. Taking this into consideration, we may begin to understand the line in a different light: Mars (*fer*) is seizing the power of the old king (*Saturn d'or*), in an act which is natural, yet both seditious and overweening.

In the sixteenth century, and even while Nostradamus wrote this quatrain, Geneva was the centre of Protestantism, and a thorn in the side of the Catholics. After some initial inner dissent and conflict, Geneva had declared for the Reformed faith in 1536. Almost by chance, Calvin happened to pass through the town in the same year, and decided to remain. Among his many enterprises was the establishing of a school for Protestant missionaries. This meant that Geneva became the Protestant equivalent of Catholic Rome, and a refuge for persecuted Protestants from all over Europe. It was, in Sully's happy phrase, 'the holy city of Jerusalem'. It was the 'City of Saints', a holy commonwealth, an earthly glorification of God. John Knox, a contemporary of Nostradamus, wrote at about the same time as Nostradamus constructed quatrain IX.44, that Geneva was 'the maist perfyt schoole of Chryst that ever was in the erth since the dayis of the Apostillis . . .'[13]

Among the unresolved issues of the Protestants in Geneva during the lifetime of Nostradamus was that of the Holy Communion. The three different views regarding the sacraments in the sixteenth century may be represented by those of the Catholics, Luther and Zwingli. The last two rejected the Catholic view as being little more than ceremonial magic. In the view of Luther, the actual flesh and blood were coterminous with the substance of bread and wine, which became operative through faith. Zwingli alone denied the real presence of Christ in the sacraments, and regarded Communion as being a symbolic memorial of Christ. Deeply argued, the issue gave rise to one of the important schisms within the Protestant body. As a result, there was the formation of the Lutherans, who held the body and blood of Christ to be substantial (that is, real), and the Reformed, who held the body and blood to be virtual (spiritually present, through faith). Could this divergence of doctrine (of considerable import within the Catholic faith) be what Nostradamus has in mind in his 'alchemical' line? In alchemy, the spiritual event of the Mass may be described as the generation from the real body of Christ (*Saturn d'or*) to the red flesh and blood of Mars (*fer*).

In the light of this suggestion, we may see that Nostradamus' argument is that the contrary direct of the *RAYPOZ* will exterminate all. Whatever this *RAYPOZ* is, since it seems to be contrary to the alchemical direction of the second line, it must lead to *enfers*, which is the death of the soul. We can now consider the precise meaning of the word *RAYPOZ*. An explanation is suggested by two different words, one Greek, the other Latin. In accordance with Green Language methods, each must be combined for the full meaning to be savoured.

RAYPOZ is probably from the Greek *raibos*, which means crooked, or bent, and is often used to denote bandy legs. In the Nostradamian French, the Greek word has *beta* in place of *phi*, but the former is often pronounced as a P. It is standard procedure in Green Language to allow Y and I to stand for each other: for example, Rabelais used the name *Doribus* to represent *Ory*, the inquisitor who imprisoned Michael Servetus.[14] What is the relevance of the word 'crooked' or 'bandy-legged' in the context of this quatrain? Within the alchemical context, the question presents no problem, for the cosmic smith, Vulcan, was bandy-legged. Vulcan, the Roman god of fire (sometimes called Mulciber, 'averter of fire'), was identified with the Greek Hephaestus. This god was fathered by Zeus on Hera, but because he was born lame he was thrown down from Heaven to Earth. This is how it happened that a god gained mastery over earthly things, yet retained his cosmic knowledge. With this dual knowledge, he became the teacher of initiates, those of the double way, and was adopted as the patron of alchemy.

Vulcan, says Paracelsus, is the master of the alchemists and spagyrists, and the art of Vulcan is the art of separating the good from the bad. As the bandy-legged smith, he figures in an enormous number of their symbols and images. For example, *fig. 41*, from the title page of the 1618 *Tripus Aureus*, the 'Golden Tripod', by Michael Maier, depicts the three alchemists, Basil Valentine, John Cremer and Thomas Norton (whose works appear in the book) standing by a furnace, the flames of which are being tended by their mentor, the lame Vulcan. The Vulcanite tradition persists: in the twentieth century, one great alchemist and master of the Green Language adopted the name for his own pseudonym, as *Fulcanelli*, the 'little Vulcan'.[15]

There is one Latin verb of which *RAYPOZ* may be an intentional distortion. The word is *reposco*, which is from the verb meaning 'to demand back, or exact'. Perhaps Nostradamus put this interesting word in upper case to link it with the upper case C of *Ciel* in the line below, for *Ciel* means 'heaven'. Could *RAYPOZ* be read as 'a demanding back from Heaven'? In view of the context of a divine influx of sacrificial flesh and blood, this is not unreasonable. The Mass is a sacrament by which humans request the Divine to return to them a spiritual food, brought down to the plane of carnality (*fer*) from the spiritual realms (*d'or*).

If our theory is correct, the *RAYPOZ* Vulcan is the spiritual energy or fire of the Mass itself, and the contrary *RAYPOZ* (*contre RAYPOZ*) of the Mass is the fire which burns, which is harmful: it is that which is the opposite of the descending fire, being more akin to the ascending fire of hell. In a word, it is that from which those of Geneva should flee.

The *RAYPOZ* Vulcan is the one who can operate successfully the alchemical transmutation of the second line: *Saturne d'or en fer se changera*. With his fire and hammer, Vulcan is a fearsome creature whom, it seems, only the alchemists can tame. In the quatrain, Nostradamus visualizes a sort of anti-Vulcan, for it is a *contre RAYPOZ* that one must flee.

What is this volcanic fire that seems to threaten Geneva?

The clue is in the hidden word *enfers* (*en fer s*) of the second line, which besides meaning 'hell' is also *en fer*, 'in the fire'. *RAYPOZ* seems to be the inner fire, the volcanic sulphuric flames of unredeemed will. Had Michael Servetus not died in the flames of Geneva a few years before this quatrain was written, we might have seen him as the subject of this prediction. Yet, it is quite possible that Nostradamus had that illegal pyre – lighted with the full connivance of Calvin – in mind when he wrote the prediction. All those who would wish to escape such a fate (that is, the ambiguous fate – a burning to death, and Protestantism in general) should flee Geneva in haste.

If this important argument about the validity of the Holy Communion is indeed the theme of this verse, then the meaning of the fourth line is clear. Indeed, this fourth line is almost an announcement of the theme of the quatrain, for, according to the Catholic teaching, prior to every Mass, the Heavens do show a sign: *Avant l'advent le Ciel signes fera.*

Certainly, it is significant that the second line should encode the word for Hell (*enfers*), while this fourth line manifests the word for Heaven (*Ciel*, with a capital letter). The line reminds us that at the birth of the lame Vulcan, his parents threw him down from the Heavens to Earth. Vulcan himself was just such a sign.

Chapter 7

The Seventeenth Century

As for Nostradamus' Predictions, I am satisfied from a thorough examination of the Principles of Astrology, that it is a very vain thing to build any thing upon that Art: But there are some of his Rhapsodies that are confined to such individuating circumstances as I would fain hear your thoughts about them. He has not mentioned England much above 20 times in his many thousand Verses; and yet there are near half that number of Predictions which have been fulfilled in our Age, to the greatest exactness.

('J.F.' The Predictions of Nostradamus, Before the Year 1558, 1691 – licensed 26 May of that year)

When, in 1668, a Dutch publisher brought out what is probably the finest edition of Nostradamus' *Prophéties*, he emblazoned the title page with two dramatic engravings.[1] One represented London in flames (*fig. 42*); the other depicted the beheading of King Charles I (*fig. 43*). The title page is evidence that, within two years of the devastating conflagration, it had been recognized that Nostradamus had predicted the Great Fire of London, and dated it to 1666. Equally, almost two decades earlier, it had been recognized that the savant had predicted the execution of Charles I of England at Whitehall.

In pride of place, at the top of the engraving, is the execution of the King. Conflagrations were frequent occurrences in late-medieval Europe, but regicide was uncommon, and therefore newsworthy. This regicide print is rather crude, yet it had been copied from a fine painting by Weesop, who had inserted the two oval inset portraits. One shows the King in life, the other the King in death, beheaded. Holding the head is the executioner, Brandon. Weesop shows him unmasked, though he was not seen in this way on the scaffold, for he had so craved anonymity that he had insisted on a wig and false beard to hide his identity (*fig. 43*).

In both painting and engraving, the façade of Whitehall is identifiable: each shows the kneeling king receiving the fatal stroke. In the foreground of the Weesop canvas, a lady is fainting at the sight of the blood. The copyist for the Nostradamus title page was careful to translate this incident to his print. He was respectful of this detail for very good reason: this minor event was recognized as an important part of the 'action' of the Nostradamus quatrain. As we shall see, in the quatrain which relates to this execution, Nostradamus specifically mentioned the fall of a lady. The image was to prove one of the most intriguing in the quatrain, for commentators.

The image of the Fire, at the foot of the page, had also been lifted from an earlier image – from a broadsheet engraving. This print marked the area to the left of the bridge which spanned the Thames with the river-borne word, *Southwark*. The Amsterdam printer copied this picture fairly closely, but removed the identifying word. However, the picture is still recognizably that of pre-conflagration London, with the old London Bridge and the multitude of pre-Wren churches which would later fall to the flames. In the foreground, and fortunately on the safe side of the river, is the tower of St Mary Overies, which later became Southwark Cathedral. Although the engraver and publishers of this Nostradamus edition did not know it, this church played an important part in the prediction, which the Master had published in 1555.

According to some commentators, Nostradamus had conceived of the murder of Charles I by Parliament in 1649 and the later Fire of London as being connected in a curious occult way, and had believed that the blood of the murdered Charles called, by an arcane sympathetic magic, for the blood of London.[2] The suggestion seems to have originated with the seventeenth-century commentator Garencières, who recognized that the first quatrain dealt with 'the impious and execrable murder, committed upon the person of our last most Sovereign King Charles I, of blessed memory, to whose expiation it seemeth our Author (that is, Nostradamus) attribute the conflagration of London'.

The prophecy caught the imagination of the seventeenth century, for several commentaries upon it have survived. One long poem, in doggerel imitation of Nostradamus, is in a manuscript dated January 1671:

The blood of the Just London's firm Doome shall fix
And cover it in flames in sixty six
Fire balls shall flye & but few seemly traine
As farr as from Whitehall to Pudden Lane.
. . .
When bare fac'd Villany shall not blush to cheat
And Checquer dores shall shut up Lombard street:
When Players shall use to act the pacts of Queens
Within the Curtains and behind the Scenes.
When Sodomy is the Premier minutes sport
And whoring shall be the least sin att Court
A Boy shall take his Sister for his Mate
And practise Incest between Seven & Eight . . .[3]

This 'blood of the just' link between regicide and the two London disasters has been regurgitated by very many commentators. In fact, there is little evidence that Nostradamus seeks to link the two events, save in so far as they have a proximity in century and place. Did the designer of the 1668 title page have a similar view of history, prompting him to bring the two engravings together on the single page? It is probably more likely that the two images were used as timely adverts – little more than newsworthy items pointing to a couple of recently fulfilled predictions. Perhaps, indeed, the book had been hurried out in 1668, precisely to meet the excitement engendered by the recognition that Nostradamus had once again predicted the future, spanning the centuries with uncanny accuracy.

From our point of view, the really interesting thing about this title page is that the Amsterdam publishers had no doubt whatsoever that Nostradamus predicted the execution of Charles I and the Great Fire. An analysis of the relevant quatrains leaves us with precisely the same conviction, even though the commentaries we offer on these quatrains are different from those offered before.

Quatrain II.51 is perhaps the most popular of all Nostradamus' verses, if only because its prophecy seems to be crystal clear. In one line of the verse, in what appear to be no uncertain terms, Nostradamus predicts and dates the Great Fire of London:

Le sang du juste à Londres fera faute,
Bruslez par foudres de vingt trois les six,
La dame antique cherra de place haute.
De mesme secte plusieurs seront occis.

The blood of the just at London will be a mistake,
Burned by thunderbolt the twenty three the sixes:

The antique lady will fall from a high place,
From among the same sect several will be killed.

From the first line, we know that the prophecy relates to London. From the second line we surmise that there is a fire, and that it takes place in a year containing 66 (20 × 3 + 6), or even 666. As the Great Fire of London took place in 1666, commentators argue that this is (for once) a transparently clear prediction of this event.

Under scrutiny, this transparency is rapidly obscured. The word *bruslez* is probably *bruler*, to burn – but the line actually says *Bruslez par foudres*, 'Burned by a thunderbolt'. However, the Fire of London was not started by a thunderbolt or lightning flash. Perhaps, to retain the prediction, we could argue that *bruslez par foudres* means a fire by calamity as though directed by Divine anger, as though by the thunderbolts cast by Zeus.

The dating is also strangely obscure. Some commentators have wisely pointed out that the phrase *vingt trois les six* could be interpreted in several different ways, only one of which gives 666. However, the phrase is an ingenious way of representing the triple six (*trois les six*) and hinting at its full meaning, without resorting to a direct mention of the occult-seeming 666. Nostradamus would have a vested interest in not being too outright with this figure which is the number of the Beast in *Revelation*. To introduce this number into his quatrain would obscure entirely his meaning, and carry the prophecy into prophetic Biblical realms foreign to the subject. At the same time, each of the other dates which may be construed from the line do not offer the same precision: 236 (that is, 1236), and 2366 respectively precede and postdate the supposed confines of the prophetic period, so as to make them unworthy of consideration. Therefore, since this is probably the most onomatopoeic date in English history, we must give credence to the idea that *les six* is represented as plural to connote several sixes, as in 1666. So it would seem the quatrain promises that in the London of 1666, a fire would break out. This much admitted, we are faced with the fact that neither of the other two lines of the quatrain appears to make much sense.

What, for example, can we make of the antique dame, *La dame antique*, who will fall from a high place? Some commentators have speculated that Nostradamus, in his 'prophetic vision', saw a sculpted image of the Virgin Mary fall from the top of St Paul's Cathedral. For example, Chodkiewicz writes that the dame was 'probably a figure falling down after the collapse of St Paul's steeple'.[4] However, this was not possible, since St Paul's had lost its steeple long before the days of the Fire. Garencières seems to have been the first to suggest that the *dame antique* was St Paul's Cathedral, 'which in the time of Paganism, was dedicated to Diana'. The idea has survived into the modern sub-cultural literature, even though it is almost certainly incorrect.

By a very strange coincidence, the 493-foot-high steeple had been struck by lightning during 1561, and the fabric of St Paul's had caught fire. As a result, the steeple and nave roof collapsed, and while the roof was eventually repaired, the steeple was never rebuilt. We are forced to note that had Nostradamus not taken care to insert the strangely constructed date of 1666 into the quatrain, then we might readily have assumed that his prediction related to an event in 1561, only five years after his prophecy was published.

Some commentators have suggested that the *dame antique* was St Paul's itself. Little is known about the pre-1285 structure, but the dedication seems never to have been to the Virgin. The argument that St Paul's was built on the site formerly dedicated to a pagan goddess[5] simply does not hold water: it is the notion of something falling which is of importance to the prediction, and, by the time of the fire, any pagan traces had been removed for centuries.

Perhaps we should look around for alternative fallen women. We might inquire, for example, if the phrase might be a prevision of the Bank of England, for, within a few years of its construction, in 1734, it was being called *The Old Lady*.[6] Her full title was 'the Old Lady of Thread-needle Street'. This is relevant, because this area, like that around St Paul's, was so badly damaged by the Great Fire that it had to be rebuilt. To accept that the quatrain refers to the Bank of England means that the prophecy is at least dual – one part refers to the Great Fire, and the other part refers to a collapse of the Bank of England. Such a view means that this part of the prophecy lies in our own future.

Unless we assume that the fall of this mysterious old lady has nothing to do with the predicted Fire, then we have to admit that her identity remains a mystery. Many churches were destroyed by the fire. Eighty-seven parish churches and 44 company houses – not to mention over 13,000 private houses – went up in flames. The most impressive building in seventeenth-century London – the great Royal Exchange which had been financed by Sir Thomas Gresham – was utterly destroyed. It is conceivable that among the collapsing fabric of so imposing a building some item of statuary – perhaps an image of the Virgin Mary still displayed in that 'reformed' country – did fall.

For the moment, then, we must admit that the antique lady remains a mystery. In turn, this means, of course, that the last line of the quatrain (*De mesme secte plusieurs seront occis*) also remains a mystery. Oddly enough, we shall discover that through establishing a rationale behind this final line, we shall be led to an understanding of the identity of the fallen woman. Meanwhile, what is the *mesme secte* (the same sect)? It is reasonable to suppose that Nostradamus is referring to Protestantism which, in sixteenth-century Catholic France, was regarded with some disdain and fear as an heretical sect. In fact, records indicate that only six people died in the Fire of London: by the standard blood and thunder of prophecy, this was scarcely *plusieurs*.

In the sixteenth century – and especially in Nostradamian usage – the word *secte* could be read as *secteur*. Such a reading offers far more explanation of the line, for we could interpret it as meaning: In the same sector several will be killed. Now, with such an interpretation, the religious affiliation of the old lady is rendered unimportant: whomsoever or whatever it was that fell, a number of people were killed in the same area. We ourselves would not accept this last suggestion, but it does indicate that analysis reveals the quatrain as being more of a mystery than commentators usually admit. All we can extract with any certainty from its obscure references is that there will be a fire in London – probably in 1666.

Now let us examine the quatrain from a different standpoint. Let us assume that Nostradamus is not making the fall of the old lady, and the killing of those of the same sect, contemporaneous with the fire. As we saw, the first line reads: *Le sang du juste à Londres fera faute*. The phrase *fera faute* has many meanings. *Faute* can mean lack, or scarcity, and it can also mean mistake and error. As an intransitive verb, it can mean 'to go wrong', or even 'to be led into error'. In view of this, the line is not easy to translate, even if its drift is clear. As we have noted, some commentators suggest that the line refers to the blood of Charles I which was spilt in 1649, when the 'just King' was beheaded, a view partly supported by the fact that Nostradamus refers to his execution in at least two other quatrains.[7] However, by no stretch of the imagination could Charles I be described as just: he seems to have been a very brave man with some noble qualities, but he was not especially distinguished by his feeling for justice. His 11 years of tyranny are still pointed out as the improper use of the law, and an abuse of English liberties.[8]

On the other hand, Nostradamus was definitely a royalist, and the fact that he refers to Charles I more than once does suggest that he regarded the execution of a king – in his view, an agent of Divine rule – as perfidious. However, there is no internal evidence within the quatrain that the events of 1649 are linked with the Fire of 1666. If we free ourselves of this notion, then we can approach the quatrain from a very different point of view.

In the year that Nostradamus published the first batch of his prophecies, the persecutions of Catholics began in London. On 28 January, in what was then called St Mary Overies church, were held the first of many trials of Catholic heretics. No doubt it is accidental, but the image of this church is still preserved in the 'Fire of London' engraving which decorates the title page of the 1668 edition of Nostradamus' *Prophéties* (see *fig. 42*). The trials took place in the old Lady Chapel. The first group of heretics – like many who followed – were sentenced to be burned to death.

In the eyes of the world – and of course, in the eyes of the Catholic Nostradamus – these men and women were innocents, and their condemnation was unjust. Here, then, we may trace the meaning of the first line of the quatrain: *Le sang du juste à Londres fera faute* can mean, 'The blood of the just will be a mistake in London'.

The heretic fires for these Catholic martyrs burned for a number of years. A sample from Machyn's diaries for 1556 gives a first-hand view:

> *The xxvij day of June rod from Newgate unto Stratford-a-bow, in ii cares xiij, xj men and ij women, and there bornyd to iiij postes, and there were a xx M pepull.*[9]

In other words, on 27 June 1556, eleven men and two women Catholics were tied to four posts and burned alive, in the full view of 20,000 onlookers. It is therefore reasonable to trace in such events the meaning of the first and last lines of the quatrain: 'The blood of the just will be a mistake in London . . . Of the same sect several will be killed.' Within the framework of this proposed interpretation, the full meaning of the words *juste* and *secte* become crystal clear, as does the identity of the antique dame.

The antique dame is St Mary Overies itself.* Founded in the twelfth century by Mary, the daughter of a ferryman,[10] it survived the suppression of Henry VIII to become a parish church, and in the nineteenth century was made the Cathedral Church of the Diocese of Southwark. The name of the founder, Mary, was projected into the symbolism and imagery of the church. Even the seals of St Mary Overies show the Virgin Mary, often with the child on her knee. Sometimes, the image of Mary is enclosed within the *vesica piscis*. Is this deliberate symbolism perhaps a play on the ambiguous word Ovaries? The Mary of the church seal is carrying the Christ child, and is an ironic reminder that on the banners of the Armada of Philip II, which set out to invade England to impose the Catholic faith, was an image of Mary and the crucified Christ. It is a further irony that a church with an ancient Marian tradition should become the site of the Marian purges and burnings in the mid-sixteenth century. Surely we may trace in this a hint of what Nostradamus meant when he saw the ancient

* 'Ofers', the early form of Overies, means 'of the shore', though some read 'of the far shore', a word which, in either reading, refers to its position at the side of the tidal river. The popular legend relating to the foundation of the church, by a ferryman's daughter named Mary, may have grown around a misunderstanding of this early name, reducing it to 'of the ferries'. The name St Mary Overies was the vulgar name, of course: the early seals of the church give the name as Sancta Maria de Suthewercha.

woman falling from her high place in the Chapel of our Lady.

Our proposal is that Nostradamus saw the Great Fire of 1666 as a deserved fiat from God, in retribution for the maltreatment of those of the just men and women of the Catholic sect who were burned and killed. In many respects, this notion, that Nostradamus was referring to the supposed consequence of the burnings, makes more sense of the entire quatrain than does an explanation dealing merely with the Fire of London.

THE LONDON PLAGUE

The intepretation offered above of quatrain II.51 has been constructed from the internal evidence of the verse itself. However, another quatrain related to it serves to confirm this reading. It is quatrain II.53, separated from II.51 by one single verse that has nothing to do with the theme of fire, or the blood of the just. Its position reminds us that Nostradamus sometimes places related quatrains in such pairs, contiguous to a linking third, like carefully crafted literary bookends. In this case, the numerological relationship is deliberate, as the events described are separated by one year.

That the two verses are related is beyond doubt. This second quatrain deals not with the Fire of London but with the Great Plague, which had preceded the Fire by just over a year.

> *La grand peste de cité maritime*
> *Ne cessera que morte ne soit vengée:*
> *Du juste sang par pris damné sans crime,*
> *De la grand' dame par fainte n'outragée.*

Approximately, this translates:

272

The great plague of the maritime city
Will not stop (until) death has been avenged:
The blood of the just of (those) taken and damned
without crime,
Of the great woman by pretended outrage.

That Nostradamus could foresee a plague around the time
of this dated quatrain is itself remarkable. Plague was a
fairly common thing in sixteenth-century Europe, yet the
plague which began in London in May 1665 was on a vast
scale. In that year, 68,000 people died in the city alone.
When the Fire broke out, in the September of the following
year, the city had not recovered. As historians now
recognize, the conjunction of plague and fire was a blessing
in disguise, for it allowed the authorities to build the city
afresh, with incredible consequences for its future growth
and public health. In some respects, we have to thank the
Great Fire for much of the later grandeur and commerce
which flooded to London. Because London was rebuilt with
a deep concern for social and health needs, it was described
(in 1707) as 'the most healthy city in the world'. Such
factors undoubtedly contributed to its commercial success,
and to the accuracy of at least one other remarkable
quatrain by Nostradamus (see page 427 ff). However,
writing in the 1550s, Nostradamus was concerned only with
the horror of the plague and fire which he foresaw would
destroy the city.

Although in quatrain II.53 London is no longer mentioned by name, Nostradamus gives it a descriptive title as
the 'maritime city' (*cité maritime*). In the quatrain we find
the same forthright mention of the blood of the just (*juste
sang*), blood shed without crime, and probably the same as
that which was a leading theme of the previous quatrain.
Once again, this blood-letting seems to be associated with a
woman – this time a *grand' dame*, rather than an ancient.

273

This has to be the same woman as we saw in quatrain II.51, for the parallels between the two verses are evident. The play on words between lines three and four, around the different meanings of *damné* and *dame*, attests to that. If our commentary for the Fire quatrain is correct, this *grand' dame* is the Virgin Mary.

The interpretation of this later verse is relatively easy, provided we stay within the framework of the reading proposed for quatrain II.51. It sees the plague and the Fire as related in the mind of Nostradamus – both being signs of Divine displeasure at the treatment of the Catholics.

Once again, we have to note that some commentators explain this verse as relating to the revenge for the murder of Charles I, even though there is no material evidence whatsoever to link the events of 1649 with those of 1665 and 1666.

THE EXECUTION OF CHARLES I

This mention of the 'execution' prediction leads us to consider quatrain VIII.37, which deals with details of the execution of Charles I. Nostradamus writes:

> *La forteresse aupres de la Tamise*
> *Cherra par lors, le Roy dedans serré,*
> *Aupres du pont sera veu en chemise*
> *Un devant mort, puis dans le fort barré.*

Before pursuing an exegesis of this difficult quatrain, let us offer the following translation:

> The fortress near to the Thames
> It will happen that the King will be kept inside,

> Near the bridge he will be seen in a shirt
> One before dead, then locked in the fort.

Records of the Civil War show that some time after his defeat at Naseby, Charles was captured in January 1647 and imprisoned in Windsor Castle. Literally, this was 'a fortress near the Thames'. Now, one possible reading for *Cherra par lors* could be something like 'will fall down', suggesting, perhaps, that the fortress near to the Thames would collapse. The line might even be interpreted as implying that the fortress would fall down with the king still inside it.

Of course, this fortress did not fall down during this period, as so many translators have suggested. The phrase *par lors* must be read as *pour lors*, which means 'at that time'. Thus, the second line means approximately, 'It will happen at that time the King is kept inside'. The emphasis is extraordinary, for Windsor was theoretically the royal dwelling of Charles I: he was imprisoned in his own home *at that time*. As we shall see, in the same quatrain, he returns to Windsor at a later point in the story.

In spite of the antique punctuation of the quatrain, after the second line the site of the action changes. We learn that near the bridge he will be seen in a shirt. As Laver remarks in another context, it is almost as though Nostradamus were witnessing certain events in person, so often does he alight on significant details.

The bridge in question is London Bridge, which was at that time the only one across the river, that was otherwise well served by ferrymen. Whitehall was near the bridge, and it was from the banqueting-hall windows of this great palace that Charles stepped on to the scaffold, drawn up to its walls.

The shirt which Nostradamus mentions in the quatrain has come down to us in history as one of the peculiarities of that peculiar day when the English, acting like reluctant sleepwalkers, murdered their king. On that 30 January, Charles was wearing a white shirt (tradition insists that he had chosen to wear two white shirts), open at the neck in preparation for the deed ahead. With incredible courage, he remarked to Bishop Juxon, who stood with him on that bitterly cold day, that he hoped the crowd would not think that he shivered from fear.[11]

What may we make of the last line, which deals with the event after his death? *Un devant mort, puis dans le fort barré.* This is perhaps the most remarkable insight of all, for the one who should have been in front (*devant*) in a social and spiritual sense is now merely in front (*devant*) the crowd, and dead (*mort*). After the execution, the dead body is taken back to the fort – the same fortress at Windsor mentioned in the first line. Here his body is buried. He is literally barred up in the fort (*dans le fort barré*). He has made the return journey to Windsor which was hinted at in the phrase, *par lors*, which makes no sense unless it is read as *pour lors*. In the second line, the King is alive; in the last line, he is dead.

It might be argued that, in spite of this wealth of circumstantial detail, the King in question may not be Charles I of England. While the reference to the Thames and the oblique reference to Windsor really should assuage all doubt, we might observe that Nostradamus does seem to have included a Green Language structure into the awkward second line. In fact, it is the encoding of this line which explains the strangeness of the French (strange, that is, even for Nostradamus), as well as the use of the irregular future tense of the verb 'Choir', *Cherra*, which does not quite convey the sense intended. Is it stretching the imagination of those unfamiliar with the working of the Green Language to point out that it is possible to construct a sequence in this line which almost spells out the name of

Charles? Here it is: CHerra pAR LorS, LE ROY = CHARLS LE ROY

The French *le Roy dedans serré*, which deals with the imprisonment of Charles, now has an additional meaning – that of pointing backward in the same line to the name of the buried king, which is hidden within the line.

FLIGHT OF JAMES II

In our opinion, one other quatrain, VIII.58, relates to the history of the Stuarts – even though the real significance of this has been overlooked by commentators – and deals with the short but significant reign of James II, whose ignominious departure from England in 1688 marked the end of the line of Stuarts. It reads:

> *Regne en querelle aux freres divisé,*
> *Prendre les armes & le nom Britannique*
> *Tiltre Anglican sera tard advisé,*
> *Surprins de nuict mener à l'air Gallique.*

> Kingdom of the two divided brothers in quarrel,
> Take the arms and the name Britannic
> The Anglican title will be late advised,
> Surprised by night, carried the Gallic air.

The brothers divided (*freres divisé*) are Charles II and James II, the two sons of the unfortunate Charles I, whose end Nostradamus prophesied in quatrain VIII.37.

The two were 'divided' for many reasons. 'No two brothers could be a greater contrast,' remarked the great historian Feiling.[12] That their personalities opposed was perhaps acceptable, but their different reactions to their communal religion were handled in a way which emphasized their differences. Charles wisely kept back his own secret religion to the lasting security of his death-bed, in 1685. James was open about his allegiance to Rome, and this openness was an embarrassment to his brother in an England where it was dangerous to admit such things. James, although a potential future King of England, even had the gall to make a Catholic marriage to Mary of Modena. Such Catholic publicity in a Protestant England was unwise.

The affair of the 'Popish Plot', which was supposed to have as its aim the murder of Charles and the crowning of James, made both brothers more unpopular. While largely the invention of Titus Oates, accounts of the plot divided all England in quarrel. After two years of anarchic infighting, James (then Duke of York) was exiled, his rightful succession under review. In some respects, it was remarkable that, on the death of his brother, James was invited to take the throne: it is extraordinary that his reign lasted three whole years.

However, the strange history of seventeenth-century England should not deflect us from the brilliance of Nostradamus. With one single line the savant spears through the uniqueness of these two different brothers of the Stuart dynasty – the very strain of history which had brought them together, and, in their separate ways, to the throne of England: *Prendre les armes & le nom Britannique* – Take the Britannic arms and name.

Both Charles and James took not the arms of England, as English kings of yore, but the arms and name of Britain. Their father, Charles I, had been the son of James I of England, who was also James VI of Scotland. The line of Stuarts, which ended with James II, was the first to be truly British, rather than English. This was reflected in the armorial bearings, for, in the arms of James I, the lion supporter was the English device, while the unicorn supporter was Scottish. James I was the first king of Britain to bear such an armorial device (*armes*). However, the name (*nom*) of the reigning monarchs had been *Britannique* since the mid-fourteenth century, for they were styled kings 'of Great Britain' – and, with less truth, 'of France and Ireland'.

With the third line, the vision of Nostradamus permits him to spear the very essence of things: *Tiltre Anglican sera tard advisé*. The real reason why James had to flee England, and to lose his throne, lay in his Catholic religion. The very word *Anglican* – which appears only in this one line of the four thousand which Nostradamus wrote – points to the issue of religion.[13] The official English religion, in both law and practice, was Protestant – schismatic of the Roman church, to which James lent allegiance. This Protestantism is now called *Anglican* – a word which was introduced into the English language with its specialist meaning of 'pertaining to the reformed church of England' as late as 1635.[14]

If we consider the Nostradamus line, we see that this *Tiltre Anglican* was indeed advice received too late. The full implication of this will be seen when we have examined the final line of the quatrain: *Surprins de nuict mener à l'air Gallique*. We all know that James fled England, and went to France, but was he *surprins de nuict* (surprised by night)? Remarkably, records show that he was both 'surprised' and went 'by night': however, these two events were not contemporaneous. Once again, Nostradamus seems to have put his finger precisely upon unique circumstances attending a future event which was of considerable historical importance.

James tried to flee England *twice* in 1688. The first time, he was intercepted (*surprins*) by Faversham fishermen. His second flight, on 23 December, was more successful: he was carried (*mener*) by boat from Rochester. After two days and one *night* of travel, he was in France (*l'air Gallique*) in sufficient time to attend – with a great sigh of relief – the Catholic Christmas Mass.

With his departure ended the reign of the Britannic Stuarts. On the specious argument that James had abdicated, William and Mary were invited from Holland to become joint sovereigns of Britain, with an oath of allegiance which imposed severe restrictions on Catholicism. Perhaps in this colophon to the history of the Stuarts, we may see a deeper and more poignant meaning in the line, *Tiltre Anglican sera tard advisé* . . .

Events surrounding the murder of Charles, and the 'consequent' plague and fire, dominate the *Prophéties* in respect of the seventeenth century. Even so, a considerable number of other quatrains deal with seventeenth-century England, and many of these are susceptible to translation by way of extensive commentary. Each quatrain seems to pick out with remarkable accuracy some facet of British history, as though Nostradamus had the power of Zeus to freeze a moment in time with a lightning flash. It is this remarkable vision which enables us to trace the important trends of English history through the four vignettes we have just discussed – the execution of Charles I, the Great Plague, the Great Fire of London, and the retreat of the Stuarts. The Civil War, the conflict between Parliament and the monarchy, the rebuilding of London, the Protestantization of the monarchy – all may be subsumed from these four verses. Other quatrains do deal with related aspects of the seventeenth century: while it is beyond our compass to deal with these here, a summary of the more important predictions for France follow. It would be foolish to emphasize too greatly Nostradamus' concern with England, for Nostradamus was always inclined to concentrate on developments in France.

A STRONG KING OF FRANCE

One important quatrain, which deals with the seventeenth century, has been interpreted in recent times by Emile Ruir as relating to a crucial event in the history of the modern France. Ruir is one of several French interpreters who seems to have been obsessed with the restoration of the Bourbons. In *Le Grand Carnage*, published on the eve of the Second World War, he attempted an astrological interpretation of Century IV.86. He saw in it a prediction of the restoration of the monarchy in France for June 1944.[15] The verse reads:

> *L'an que Saturne en eau sera conjoinct,*
> *Avecques Sol, le Roy fort & puissant,*
> *A Reims & Aix sera receu & oingt,*
> *Apres conquestes meurtrira innocent.*

Because of ambiguities in the French, this is a difficult quatrain to translate. However, for the moment, we could perhaps read it as:

> In the year when Saturn in water is conjunct with,
> The Sun, the strong and powerful King,
> Will be received and anointed at Reims and Aix,
> After conquests an innocent will be murdered.

From this, Rochetaillée predicted that the Third Republic would come to an end in 1944. To supplement his astrological commentary, he offered a curious horoscope, cast for late in the day of 25 January 1944 – which date, he averred, would see 'the end of the agony' of the Third Republic (*fig. 44*). At the end of this agony, yet in the same year, a great King would be established on the French throne. Not quite knowing how to relate the last line of the

281

quatrain to these events, Ruir decided that it predicted a preliminary military conquest of Italy by the French.

As a failed prediction, we might choose to reject it, along with all the thousands of other inaccurate prophecies which have been built out of the Nostradamus quatrains. However, in many ways it is an interesting prediction, if only because it indicates very clearly how the prejudices of the interpreter can so easily lead to total misinterpretations, even when so precise a method of astrology is used.

In this case, the prejudice sprang from Ruir's myopia regarding the end of the Third Republic and the re-establishment of the monarchy, for which he seems to have longed. As it happened, his approach to the astrology in the quatrain was quite sensible. He rightly assumed that the astrological reference was designed to alert the reader to a particular year, in which would unfold the event predicted in the quatrain. The event would involve the anointing of a strong and powerful king, and some kind of murder of an innocent – a deed presumably also involving that king.

As Ruir was correct in his general theory, let us follow the rationale behind it, to see where he went wrong in his practical approach. His astrological argument was that the first lines of the quatrain mean: 'In the year when Saturn will be in Cancer conjunct With the Sun . . .' Now, it is true that Saturn was conjunct with the Sun in Cancer in June 1944. The conjunction was exact on 22 June. Unfortunately, Ruir seems to have overlooked that Nostradamus did not say Cancer, but *eau* (water). In theory, this word could refer to any of four zodiacal signs – Cancer, Scorpio, Pisces (the three water triplicities) and Aquarius, the Water-carrier. It is an astrological reference which Nostradamus used several times in his quatrains to lend benign obscurity to his meaning.

Perhaps it was Ruir's myopia – or perhaps mere astrological ignorance – but what he did not say was that the conjunction, even in Cancer, had occurred several times since Nostradamus wrote the quatrain. Indeed, it had occurred before even in the twentieth century, as lately as 31 March 1916.

If the quatrain is read as Nostradamus intended it to be read – namely, as *eau* rather than Cancer – then a large number of possible dates are applicable between 1555 and the twentieth century. For example, if we take only the first three decades of the sixteenth century, immediately following the first publication of the *Prophéties*, we find that the conditions in the quatrain could be fulfilled no fewer than ten times. The following positions are given according to the Julian calendar, with which Nostradamus worked:

Jun 1562 *Cancer*
Jul 1563 *Cancer*

Oct 1571 *Scorpio*
Nov 1572 *Scorpio*
Nov 1573 *Scorpio*

Jan 1580 *Aquarius*
Jan 1581 *Aquarius*

Mar 1582 *Pisces*
Feb 1583 *Pisces*
Feb 1584 *Pisces*

We see, then, that on the evidence of the astrology alone, there is no basis whatsoever for linking this quatrain with events in 1944.

Of course, we could cut these possible years down considerably if we could determine which of the four signs Nostradamus intended by the word *eau*. In an earlier use of precisely the same phrase, Nostradamus had used the word *eau* to refer to Aquarius.[16] This is not merely an iconomatic use of Green Language: the French for Aquarius is *Verseau*, which means that one can truncate the word, by the rules of abridgement, to give *eau*. The humour behind this Green Language surgery is, of course, that the word *eau* is, so to speak, already in a *vers* (the French for a line of poetry), so no real truncation has been done.

If we limit our search through the ephemerides to Aquarius, and apply the meaning of quatrain IV.86 to the dates then on offer, we arrive at a most interesting conclusion. The second time that Saturn was in Aquarius, after Nostradamus wrote the quatrain, was in 1610. On 3 February 1610 (New Style), Saturn and Sun were conjunct in Aquarius.

Now, Nostradamus says that in the year that this celestial event took place,

> . . . *le Roy fort & puissant,*
> *A Reims & Aix sera receu & oingt,*
> *Apres conquestes meurtrira innocent.*

The quatrain seems to suggest that a strong and powerful King will be received and anointed at Reims and Aix. After conquests he will murder an innocent.

The fact is that Ruir may be forgiven for believing that the quatrain referred to the coronation of a king. From the time of Clovis, in the fifth century, most of the French kings had been consecrated in Notre Dame in Reims. Not only had Nostradamus used the name of this city, but he had also mentioned anointing (*oingt*, an apocope of *oignant*). The abbey of St Rémi in Reims possessed the sacred phial of oil which was believed to have been transported from heaven by a dove, and it was this which was used in royal consecrations and baptisms. The consecration was last celebrated at Reims in 1824, at the coronation of Charles X, so it was reasonable for Ruir to expect that his future king of 1944 would also be crowned and anointed in Reims, as the quatrain suggested.

The unfortunate Ruir had merely got the wrong king and the wrong century. What Ruir foresaw for 1944 had actually occurred almost 350 years earlier.

In 1610 Henry IV of France was assassinated by François Ravaillac. That Nostradamus had this King Henry in mind is almost confirmed by the words he chose for another Henry, in his *Epistle* to Henry II, for in the dedication, he lauded the King as the '*Tres Puissant*', the very powerful.

The second line, which tells how this strong and powerful king will be received and anointed (*receu & oingt*), is not quite what a reader might reasonably expect from the verse. As a matter of fact, Henry IV *was* crowned and anointed at Reims. Indeed, the city was doubly important to him; it had submitted to him after the battle of Ivry: he had therefore received (*receu*) the city, in a very real sense. The important thing, however, is that astrology of the quatrain does not point to an anointing and coronation: it points rather to the year of the death of the King. This is typical Nostradamian obfuscation, to leave us looking for an anointing, whereas, in fact, we should be looking for an embalming.

The enigmatic fourth line relates perfectly to the history of Henry IV in 1607. The phrase, 'after conquests' (*Apres conquestes*), sums up the situation at his death very well: indeed, just before he was murdered (*meutrira*), he had declared war on the Emperor Rudolf II.

Henry IV was himself the 'innocent' of the quatrain. Ravaillac had murdered him because he believed the rumours that Henry was intending to make war on the Pope. The rumours were unfounded, and Henry was literally *innocent*.[17]

A PURSUIT OF MURDERERS

Nostradamus seems to concentrate his quatrains upon the main events in French history – the deaths of kings and queens, traitors and heroes, the glorious victories and tragic defeats, the revolutions. However, there are among the quatrains a number which seem to touch upon seemingly trivial events in the history of the country.

Reading through such verses one has not only a sense of frustration at the obscure methods to which Nostradamus resorted, but also a sense of impatience at one's own lack of knowledge about the byways of the history of Europe. Some quatrains seem to beckon, as though their arcane forms are ready to dispel their ancient wisdom, while others remain obdurate, sealed perhaps for ever. Sometimes, a single word offers a tantalizing clue, sending the alert researcher rushing to the ancient books, in the hope of untangling the knots which Nostradamus tied.

Among these 'single word' quatrains is one which revealed a fascinating vignette – a future footnote in French history, which is now all but forgotten save by a few specialists. The power of this quatrain is derived from the fact that a proper name used by Nostradamus has survived in documents from the seventeenth century. Without that single name, the entire verse would probably remain obscure and untranslated.

Quatrain IX.68 reads:

> *Du mont Aymar sera noble obscurcie,*
> *Le mal viendra au joinct de Saone & Rosne,*
> *Dans bois cachez soldats jour de Lucie,*
> *Que ne fut onc un si horrible throsne.*

For the moment, let us translate this as:

From the mount, Aymar will be noble obscurity,
The evil will come at the junction of the Saone and
Rhone,
In the woods soldiers are hidden on St Lucy's day,
That never was such a horrible judgement.

The clue to the meaning of this quatrain is found in the
name *Aymar*. The historic facts are that, on 5 July 1692, a
wine-merchant and his wife were murdered at Lyons
(which city marks the confluence of the rivers Saône and
Rhône, *au joinct de Saone & Rosne*). Unable to trace the
murderer by normal means, the officials called in the
rhabdomancer,[*] Jacques Aymar, to help them hunt down
their quarry. This ritual might surprise us now, but in the
seventeenth and eighteenth centuries, it was a fairly
common procedure to employ such men: it was widely
believed that the blood had a sacred power which called
after murderers, and could cause a murderer to collapse in
the presence of the corpse. Aymar seems to be the best of
such French professionals, which is the reason why his
name has come down to us.

Not only his name has been preserved – an engraving of
what is almost certainly Jacques Aymar using his divining
rod has also survived in Le Lorrain de Vallemont's book on
occult science, published at the end of the century (*fig.
45*).[18] We learn from his contemporaries that Aymar would
attune this rod, or *baguette*, to the blood of the victims, in
order to begin to trace the murderer.

In this particular incident, which Nostradamus foretells,
Aymar, after attuning his baguette, determined that there

---

[*] Rhabdomancy is an almost obsolete word for 'divination with sticks',
derived from the Greek word *rhabdos*, meaning 'stick'. In the sixteenth
and seventeenth centuries it was used not merely in a magical sense, for
what we might call radiesthesia, but also to denote those specialists who
divined for ores, in mining, the rhabdomants.

had been three murderers. Taking to the road, he followed the scent of the murderers, as this was revealed by the rhabdomantic rod, over a circuitous route, to the right bank of the Rhône. The extraordinary journey continued for many leagues as far as a military encampment at Sablon, where Aymar deemed that his official authority for pursuit ran out. He promptly returned to Lyons, obtained further support, and took up pursuit once more. Arriving on the blood-trail as far as Beaucaire, the group were led to the local prison, where they discovered a man recently arrested for petty larceny. Eventually, this man confessed to having been one of the three murderers of the wine-merchant and his wife. Taking up the trail again, Aymar followed the other two as far as Nîmes, on to Toulon, and then to the boundaries of the kingdom, where their licence for pursuit ended. The man apprehended was tried, found guilty and broken on the wheel, on 30 August 1692.

Blood, the most *noble* of liquids, is in this case *obscure* – followed merely by its trace. The evil (*mal*) did indeed reach the junction of the Saône and the Rhône, at Lyons.

Most commentators have translated the quatrain as relating to a supposed *Mont Aymar*, which dislodges the orthography of the verse.[19] However, so far as we can determine, there is no such place as *Mont Aymar*. In fact, Nostradamus seems to be aware of this, for he writes *mont Aymar*, rather than Mont Aymar, suggesting that the opening of the quatrain should be: 'From the mount, Aymar . . .'

What about the remaining lines of the quatrain – how do they relate to Aymar, if at all? *Dans bois cachez soldats jour de Lucie, / Que ne fut onc un si horrible throsne.* We have pictures of soldiers hidden in the woods on the day of St Lucy. Now, St Lucy was remembered on 13 December: Nostradamus could hardly forget this, as the name Lucia was printed above his own birthday in the Ephemerides.[20]

Since Aymer's rhabdomantic trip began in early July 1692, there is no way in which the second two lines of the quatrain can relate directly to the first two lines. Where does this leave us? In terms of the Green Language, we may take the reference to St Lucy as a clever reflection on the rhabdomantic method itself. St Lucy is the patron saint of those afflicted of the eyes. The story is told that, in order to avoid the attentions of a nobleman who admired the beauty of her eyes, she tore these out, and presented them to him on a platter. For this reason, she is usually represented carrying a pair of eyes. The relevance to Nostradamus is that Aymar followed his quarry without eyes, like Lucy herself: the rod was his vision. The relationship between the virgin (*virgo*) Lucy and the rod (*virga*) will not have gone unnoticed by Nostradamus. Indeed, this is one of the most common of all word-plays in Christian symbolism, and has entered the punning beloved of the Green Language.

It was once believed that Aymar and his rhabdomantic peers followed not an invisible blood-trail, but a general *matière meutrière* (murderous matter)[21] exuded by all murderers, and connecting them to their victims, as an invisible thread. In view of this belief, Nostradamus' phrase *noble obscurcie* is pertinent, and takes on a particular significance when related to the Lucy symbolism. What is *obscure* to human eyes is quite *lucid* to the virga, or stick.

As we have already noted, it often is the case that Nostradamus deals with two related events in a single verse, usually drawing some interesting parallel between these events. In view of this, it is quite reasonable to assume that the last two lines deal with a further exploit of Aymar.

In fact, the second half of the verse seems to touch upon an incident that would have set Nostradamus' teeth on edge, as a member of a recently converted Jewish family who had converted to Catholicism in order to survive. It seems that almost a decade after his famous Lyons exploit, Aymar was hired by the Catholics of the Cevennes to hunt down, by rhabdoscopic means, groups of Protestants, who were believed to be guilty of murder. As a result of this pursuit, 12 Protestants were arrested and executed: *Que ne fut onc un si horrible throsne.* This may be something of a dramatic overstatement, but it does contain some useful comment. *Throsne* is translated by most commentators as 'throne', even though it has no significance within the context of the quatrain. In French, 'throne' is *trone*. As there is no such French term as *throsne*, is it a Green Language term?

In Greek, *Thronos* has several related meanings, such as chair, oracular seat (in the mysteries), and (in a legal context) judge's seat. The last two meanings do have an immediate relevance to the quatrain, where a technique derived from the mystery wisdom (in this case, rhabdo-mancy) and legal judgement are implied.

However, as we have seen, the word also has an astrological meaning. In the sixteenth century, a planet was said to be in its 'throne' when posited in the same sign as that over which it has rulership. Thus, Saturn is in its throne when in Capricorn: the Sun is in its throne when in Leo. It is possible to read the phrase *horrible throsne* as a play on this usage. In astrology, the 'throne' is a beneficial position, a placing of strength. When a planet is in a sign opposed to its own rulership, it is said to be in a weak position: in seventeenth-century astrology, this was called *Carcer* (prison) or *Cadutus* (fall).

Thus, in terms of astrology, the *terrible throsne* is prison, which here represents the demoting of the oracular and judicial seats of dignity. The tracing of Protestants by occult means was perceived by Nostradamus as being of this order – the misuse of an oracular power by which judgement could be obtained.

Could the reference point to a pertinent astrological situation on the day of Lucy in 1692? That day, Mars was in conjunction with Saturn, in Sagittarius, and both were in opposition with Jupiter in Gemini. In terms of electional astrology, this could be interpreted as the capture or imprisonment (Saturn) of a fleeing felon (Mars in Sagittarius). We do not wish to labour the point, but it does make perfect sense of the reference which Nostradamus made to Lucy's Day.

The *terrible throsne* is a cosmic conflict that is echoed on the material plane, as a conflict in religious views. Although the Aymar story is set in France, and the various Stuart prophecies are set in England, they are united by this single concern for religious intolerance.

THE DEATH OF A TREASURER

Quatrain VII.1 is one of the few quatrains dealing with the seventeenth century which contains the identifiable name of a recognizable historical figure. In addition, the quatrain encodes the name of an individual who was involved in the drama described by the verse. Both names appear in the first line:

L'arc du thresor par Achilles deceu,
Aux procrées sçeu la quadrangulaire:
Au faict Royal le comment sera sçeu,
Corps veu pendu au veu du populaire.

The arc of the treasure deceived by Achilles,
To the begetters show the quadrangle:
To the Royal command the why and wherefore will be seen,
The body seen hung in the full view of the people.

L'arc du thresor is a Green Language play on the name of an individual and his political role. After arriving at the French court in the train of Marie de' Medici, the Italian Concino Concini bought his way into the French aristocracy when he purchased the marquisate of Ancre (*arc*). The word *arc* is, of course, anagrammatically close to the name *Ancre*. Was Nostradamus playing an esoteric joke in removing from the word *ancre* one of the consonants – the letter *n* – which proliferates four times in the name Concino Concini?

D'Ancre was eventually made first minister of the crown in charge of the Treasury (*thresor*), which explains the first four words of the French quatrain. In his lax and morally deficient guardianship of the treasury, he drew upon himself the hatred of many individuals, including Condé and (it is maintained) Achille de Harlay (*Achilles*).

Achille de Harlay, Baron de Sancy and Bishop of St Malo, had a reputation for generosity in every field of endeavour. For example, while ambassador in Constantinople he rescued many cruelly abused slaves from the clutches of the Turks – on one occasion he used his own personal wealth to purchase over a thousand French Christians from the Turks, and liberated them. He was recalled to France after becoming involved in Turkish succession politics. Later, he was one of those who visited England in attempts to persuade the English monarchy to re-establish Catholicism. His name may well be mentioned by Nostradamus because his personal generosity provides such a total contrast with the public rapine associated with the 'hero' of the quatrain.

The most intriguing thing about this prediction is its almost grisly accuracy. Concini was shot dead by Vitry, du Hallier and Perray, on the orders of the King (*Au faict*

Royal) on 24 April 1617. On the day of his death, and after a considerable amount of incriminating evidence had been found on his person and in his home, his body was buried in St-Germain-l'Auxerrois. However, on the following day, a large group of angry Parisians exhumed the body, dragged it to the Pont-Neuf, and hanged it from a standard which the marechal himself had erected to accommodate those who spoke against him. After this public viewing (*Corps veu pendu*), the body was cut down, and slashed into a large number of pieces.

There is, however, one detail of the prediction which, on first analysis, does not appear to be accurate. The last line indicates that Concini would be either killed or hanged on view in a large square (*la quadrangulaire*). This did not happen: according to the nineteenth-century historian Mme de Bolly, he was shot outside the Louvre, on the drawbridge to the palace, and we know that he was hanged on one of the bridges of the Seine.[22] Our experience has been that Nostradamus rarely makes an error, and we conclude that the quatrain relates not merely to the grisly destiny of Concini, but also to the equally grisly death of his wife, who, as a direct consequence of his own death, did die in a huge square.

Concini's wife Leonora Dori, who had been Marie de' Medici's favourite lady-in-waiting, was charged with sorcery. By the early part of the seventeenth century, Parisian judges were reluctant to consider charges of alleged witchcraft.[23] However, the historian of witchcraft, Montague Summers (who claims to have examined 15 contemporaneous accounts dealing with her trial and death), records that the charges involved Satanism, and that a large number of amulets and stuck poppets were discovered in her rooms.[24] Summers had no doubt that Leonora had been a witch, and based his conclusions on the original trial records. However, the truth seems to be that she was

293

condemned mainly on the testimony of her frightened servants, one of whom came out with the standard *grimoirie* that she had sacrificed a cock in a church at midnight. When several Hebraic books were discovered in her cabinet her case was virtually lost, and she was condemned (albeit not without dissent among the judges at her trial). She appears to have met her unjust death with extraordinary courage. In the same year, a satirical play dealing very inexactly with her life was published, a tragedy in four acts, *La Magicienne étranger*.

Because of her rank, she was not burned to death, according to the normal method of dealing with witchcraft. She was beheaded, on 8 July, at the Place de Grève, and her body was then burned on a huge public bonfire. As Summers concludes, 'Political animus, no doubt, sealed her doom . . .'

After being beheaded, her body (*corps*) would have been tied to a stake, in full view of the public (*veu pendu au veu du populaire*), before being burned. She died in the Place de Grève, which was the site of all capital executions until 1832, though since 1806, the great square has been known as Place de l'Hôtel de Ville. Under whichever name, the square is, of course, a vast quadrangle (*la quadrangulaire*).

A RICHELIEU QUATRAIN

One other verse dealing with the seventeenth century uses a name which, while not a proper name, leaves us in no doubt as to whom is intended. The *Vieux Cardinal* of quatrain VIII.68 must be Cardinal Richelieu. In fact, while Nostradamus seems to have been deeply concerned with the history of the royal family in the century following his own, he paid court to Richelieu in a number of quatrains, seeing him for what he was – a prime mover in the destiny of France. So clearly do one or two of these verses relate to the Cardinal that it was evident even to his contemporaries that he had been chosen by Nostradamus to represent his vision of French futurity. This may explain why several forged quatrains, purporting to be from the pen of Nostradamus, circulated during the lifetime of Richelieu.

This Richelieu verse, quatrain VIII.68, opens in an uncompromising style with a direct reference to the Cardinal:

> *Vieux Cardinal par le jeune deceu,*
> *Hors de sa charge se verra desarmé,*
> *Arles ne monstres double soit aperceu,*
> *Et liqueduct & le Prince embaumé.*

For the moment, let us translate this as:

> Old Cardinal by the young deceived,
> Outside his charge will see himself disarmed,
> Arles does not show the double is perceived,
> And fountain and the Prince embalmed.

As we shall see, the quatrain is partly astrological, and analysis shows that the entire verse is a reflection on the planetary conditions surrounding the last year of Cardinal Richelieu's life.[25]

The first line is a masterly summary of a complex history attending an actual deception which affected Richelieu deeply. In 1642, Richelieu was truly the 'Old Cardinal' (*Vieux Cardinal*), for it was the last year of his life. It was in this year that the young Henri de Cinq-Mars, 22-year-old favourite (*le jeune*) of Louis XIII, was discovered to be conspiring against the life of the Cardinal. As a result of his conspiracy, and his deceptive (*deceu*) negotiations with Spain behind the back of the King and Richelieu, he was beheaded in 1642 – the same year in which Richelieu died.

The ambiguous second line seems to describe the fate of the young Cinq-Mars, and of Richelieu himself: *Hors de sa charge se verra desarmé*. It was outside the control (*Hors de sa charge*) of Richelieu that Cinq-Mars should be beheaded, for the Cardinal had established an inflexible principle whereby favourites should not be accorded special privileges: conspiracy to murder was a beheading affair. There is also another possible interpretation of *Hors de sa charge*, as Richelieu learned of the conspiracy through the work of his exceptionally efficient secret service. We should observe that *desarmé* is fascinating in its implications, for the last word of the name Cinq-*Mars* is the same as the planet which governs military arms. At the same time, this same planet rules the head of the human body, through its sign Aries. Therefore, *desarmé* is singularly appropriate, for, in reference to Cinq-Mars, it connotes the severing of a head, and the ending of a family name (or *arms*) by means of the sword.

The last two lines of the quatrain are best considered together, for they denote a peculiar astrological condition: *Arles ne monstres double soit aperceu, / Et liqueduct & le Prince embaume.*

The time of the death of Richelieu was marked in the heavens by a combination which always excited Nostradamus – a conjunction of the planets Jupiter and Saturn. These are surely the *double* which would be perceived (*soit aperceu*). On the day Richelieu died, 4 December, the two planets were within orb of conjunction in Pisces.[26] However, the two did not reach their exact conjunction until 24 February 1643, by which time, as the quatrain admits, the Cardinal (*le Prince*)[27] was embalmed (*embaumé*). On the day of his entombment in the Sorbonne sarcophagus, Jupiter and Saturn were *exactly* in conjunction in 25 degrees of Pisces. The relevance of this precise conjunction is found in a Green Language construct.

Liqueduct is a fascinating word. It has confused some commentators sufficiently to persuade them to amend it to *l'aqueduct* (which renders the quatrain meaningless).[28] It is a Nostradamian Green Language construct, for while it means 'water-carrier', it can also mean 'carried in water': the word thus refers to *Pisces*. This zodiacal sign is represented by the two fishes which are carried (*ductus*) in the liquid (*lique*, from the Latin *liquefacere*, to make liquid).

Now the interesting thing is that on 24 February 1643, not only were the two ponderable planets in Pisces (*liqueduct*), but so were the Sun and Mercury.[29] It was a rare cosmic moment in which watery Pisces was being emphasized in a most unusual way. It would be inevitable that the astrologer Nostradamus, once appraised of the future date of the entombment of the great Cardinal, would seek to emphasize a reference to this in terms of a Piscean satellitium (a satellitium is a conjunction, or near conjunction, of three or more planets).[30]

Arles ne monstres does not make much sense unless we accord it an astrological significance, and read it as a misprint for *Aries ne monstres*. This reading is then perfectly in accord with the astrological symbolism of the events.[31] For conspiring against Richelieu, Cinq-Mars was beheaded. Aries rules the head, and the planet Mars (besides ruling Aries) governs such things as decapitation. The two men – the young and the old – died in the same year, but it was only the death of the great Richelieu which was manifested in the stars. Quite literally, Aries was not shown (*Aries ne monstres*) in the skies at the death of the young man.

This Richelieu quatrain must take its place as one of the most brilliant in the Nostradamian repertoire. In a few short lines, Nostradamus tells a complex future history which describes perfectly the two main protagonists, comments on the natures of their deaths, and reflects upon the planetary conditions surrounding their end.[32]

THE ELECTED KING OF ENGLAND

Quatrain IV.89 is notable for the precision with which a complex and unexpected history is woven into four lines of verse. The quatrain deals with the way William, Prince of Orange, was invited to the throne of England.

> *Trente de Londres secret conjureront,*
> *Contre leur Roy sur le pont l'entreprinse,*
> *Luy, satellites la mort degousteront,*
> *Un Roy esleu blond, & natif de Frize.*

The following tentative translation will be amended in the course of analysis:

> Thirty of London conspire in secret,
> Against their King on the point of the undertaking,
> To him, the satellites will taste of death,
> A blond King elected, and native of Friesland.

The word London (*Londres*), in the first line, sets the scene, but it is the last line of the quatrain which points to the subject of this quatrain: *Un Roy esleu blond, & natif de Frize*. William III is the only monarch in European history to have been elected (*esleu*) to the role of kingship, and it is evident that this quatrain relates to his election to the British throne, in 1689, to replace the absconded James II.

The term *esleu* permits us to recognize immediately the identity of this king, but the word *blond* gives us problems. It has been misunderstood by most commentators.

Charles Ward, who wrote at some length about this quatrain, was wrong about several of its details: the colour of William's hair, and his insistence that he wore a wig. Prior to being made William III, he did not wear a wig – entirely in accordance with Dutch fashion. Wigs were popular in the French and English courts, but not among the Dutch. William's hair was dark brown as the portrait by Lely, painted at the time of William's marriage in 1677 to Mary (eldest daughter of the future James II), reveals.

In fact, we suspect that the Nostradamus reference was not intended to mean 'blond' in respect of hair colouring. For some time, we were under the impression that it was derived from the Latin *blandus*, meaning 'pleasant, agreeable', etc., for the election of William *was* an agreeable one, even a necessary one, for England at that time. However, a chance observation of C. T. Onions' notes on the medieval Latin etymology of the word *blond* changed our opinion. According to Onions, the word is probably of German origin, and in the form *blondus* meant 'yellow'.[33] In the sixteenth century, there could be fewer less arcane ways of suggesting the name of the future elected king, who was William of *Orange*.

One of the earliest English commentators on Nostradamus, known only by the initials D.D., observed that while some of the details in the quatrain point to William III, one serious objection is that he was not from Friesland (*Frize*) – he was born in the Hague. However, Nostradamus does appear to have his details right: by the middle of the seventeenth century, what we now call the Netherlands and Belgium consisted of three main divisions. To the south, bordering on France, were the old Spanish Netherlands, acquired by war and diplomacy by France between 1659 and 1679. To the north of this were the remains of the Spanish Netherlands, bordering to the east on the German Empire (Bishopric of Liège), with Luxembourg ringed by the Empire and France to the south-east. The third, much larger tract, consisted of the United Provinces, which had been independent of the Empire since 1648. These stretched from just north of Bruges and Antwerp up to the North Sea, and included Friesland and Groningen in the north. Nostradamus described very well this new United Provinces more precisely by describing that acquisition of 1648.

What do we make of the 'thirty of London' (*Trente de Londres*) of the first line – is this a reference to those who were involved in secret negotiations against their king? In his account of the secret attempts to install William in favour of James II, the eighteenth-century historian Tobias Smollett gives a very specific list of those who drew up the first invitations to William. The phrase *secret conjureront* is apposite, for the first official overtures were made to William, in cipher-letter, which was signed by some of the great men of England – Shrewsbury, Devonshire, Danby, Lumley, Compton, Russell and Sidney. Whether there were precisely 30 involved in this cabal is not clear, but the total must have approached that figure. Smollet lists 14 of the more illustrious by name.[34] An anonymous commentator on Nostradamus, writing in 1691, observes that 'The thirty of *London* agree well with the 29 Lords mentioned in the *Gazette*, Decemb. 11–88.'[35]

The interpretation of the second line – *Contre leur Roy sur le pont l'entreprinse* – is far from easy. The French *sur le pont l'entreprinse*, which should be translated 'on the bridge the undertaking', does not appear to make much sense within the context, and it is tempting to read *pont* as an error for *point*. However, the bridge (*pont*), or, more precisely, the 'bridging enterprise' (*le pont l'entreprinse*), could be seen as the bridging of the channel between England and Holland – a most famous expedition at the time, with all the outer trappings of invasion, however peaceful and bloodless. The commentator J.F., in his *The Predictions of Nostradamus, Before the Year 1558*, seems to have been the first to propose this imaginative reading, and it does offer a sensible interpretation of an otherwise knotty line.

The third line – *Luy, satellites la mort degousteront* – also offers problems. To whom does the word *Luy* refer, and who are the *satellites*? It is tempting to take the latter as referring to the satellites (supporters) around James II, some of whom did later taste of death (*la mort degousteront*) – especially those among the Scots who remained loyal to him. On the other hand, it is more likely that the *satellites* are countries, rather than individuals. That would explain the curious structure of the line, which begins with a personal pronoun for which there is no identifiable person or verb. This is the word *Luy*, for the verb *degousteront* is plural, and therefore relates to *satellites*. However, read as a Green Language homophone, *Luy* would be Louis XIV, who offered succour to James II. By the time James reached Paris, France was at war with Holland, Spain and the Empire – the image of there being satellites around Louis XIV is brilliant, for he was indeed surrounded by a quiltwork of enemies. Certainly there was no shortage of blood-tasting on the Continent.

There is usually some deeper meaning in even the most bland-seeming lines of Nostradamus, and we wonder if this reference to Continental bloodletting is intended as a wry contrast to what happened contemporaneously in England. Ever since the election of William of Orange to the throne of England, the event has been called by English historians the Peaceful or the Bloodless Revolution.

A piece of doggerel, written towards the end of the seventeenth century, seems to complete the quatrain, in its vision of how a strengthened Prince of Orange would be able to deal more adequately with France – as, at the time, so many Englishmen fervently hoped:

If a Fury Poetick,
Foreknows things to come,
I may dare be Prophetick,
And foretell his just doom.
Besides old Nostredame
Has Predicted the same,
That if once the brave Orange approaches too nigh,
The gay Flower-de-luces will wither and dye.[36]

Chapter 8

The Eighteenth Century

Dès le Xe siecle, Albumasar avait calculé que l'année mil sept cent quatre-ving-neuf serait feconde en revolutions sociales, à cause de l'une des grandes conjonctions de Saturne. L'astrologie est vanité, erreur, mensonge, tout ce que vous voudrez; mais enfin voilà une prédiction d'une authenticité irrecusable.

In the tenth century, Albumasar calculated that, because of one of the great conjunctions of Saturn, the year one thousand seven hundred and eighty nine would be fecund in social revolutions. Astrology is vanity, error, dream – anything you wish: yet, when all is said and done, here is a prediction of unimpeachable authenticity.

(Migne, *Dictionaire des Prophèties*, ii., 339, derived from Albumasar, *De Magnis Conjunctionibus*, Tract. ii., Diff.8, quoted by Charles Ward, *Oracles of Nostradamus*, 1891)

When Nostradamus leafed through the visions of futurity recorded in the Akashic Chronicles, and looked into the Paris of the 1790s – perhaps at the courageous death of Marie Antoinette – he would have seen a statue of Liberty, wearing the Roman tunic. The huge statue would be

303

looking down on to the terrible Place de la Revolution, renamed later, somewhat euphemistically, Place de la Concorde. The female Liberty was standing on the same pedestal as had once carried Louis XV, after whom this enormous square was originally named. She was seated, ironically wearing a Cap of Liberty, derived from the ancient Phrygian headgear, which had once been a symbol of high initiation in the ancient mystery centres. The statue has been described with poetic precision as 'an alien among human beings'[1] for her stoneless eyes could not see the carnage or the suffering or the petitions of those who suffered. We may be sure that Nostradamus had some such vision as this, for he mentions the statue in one of his arcane verses, wherein he described her as the *Castulon monarque*, because she wore the Roman *castula*, or tunic.

Now another sacred mystery stands in Concorde – the massive Obelisk of Luxor, with its hieroglyphics praising the honour and glory of Rameses II, the god-king. This huge stone was presented by Mahommed Ali Pasha to Louis Philippe in 1836 after an epic journey from Luxor. It is said that the obelisk marks the precise spot where Louis XVI was guillotined. Nostradamus had his finger on the pulse of French history, for his quatrains include mention of Louis Philippe, the guillotining of Louis, and the Egyptian influence which would pervade France as a result of Napoleon's conquests in Egypt.

There is a general belief – derived from inexpert commentaries – that Nostradamus predicted the French Revolution for 1792. This is simply not true: he predicted it quite accurately for 1789, and dated several of the events which followed, among them the institution of the Revolutionary Calendar in 1792. The series of quatrains which describe the Revolution are quite incredible in their explicit detail. In reading them, the commentator cannot help feeling that he is seeing history being written, rather than futurity. The terrible events which we now call the French Revolution appear to have obsessed the Master, for over 40 quatrains seem to deal with the final two decades of the eighteenth century. The following quatrains, touching only on the years around the regicide, are worth noting.

For the seminal year 1789, quatrains I.3, I.14, I.53, VII.14 and VI.23 seem to deal directly with the events surrounding the actual Revolution, in Paris. For 1791, quatrain IX.20 touches on the flight of Louis and Marie Antoinette. The year 1792 is rich in Revolution quatrains. For example, quatrain IX.34 identifies the Tuileries, and details how Sauce, the royalist mayor of Varennes, helped prevent the escape of the royals. Quatrain VIII.80 touches on the excesses of the Revolutionaries, while quatrain X.1 deals with the pathetic image of Marie Antoinette and her daughter in prison. Quatrain I.42 follows with an account of the Revolutionary Assembly, while the year 1792 is rounded off with quatrain I.82, which gives a vision of the Guillotine, and the Franco–Austrian war. The year 1793 leads off with quatrain VIII.46, and the siege of Lyons, which was a direct result of the Revolution, then, in quatrains X.43 and VIII.87, paints a picture of the regicide of Louis XVI, with a kind of side–glance (quatrain I.57) at the day of his decapitation, followed by quatrain VI.92 which gives details of his burial. The aftermath of the regicide is studied in quatrain X.9, with an image of the Dauphin in the Temple prison. This dreadful year for royals is summarized in quatrain IX.77, with a further account of the deaths of Louis XVI, Marie Antoinette, the Dauphin and Madam Dubarry. Precisely when the Revolution began and ended is still under dispute. If we were to add to this list the post-Revolutionary wars, and the story of Napoleon, it would be a long and tedious list indeed.

305

THE GUILLOTINE

One of the most memorable of all Nostradamian images is that of the guillotine in motion. The humane killer is first mentioned in the opening of quatrain I.82.

> *Quand les colomnes de bois grande tremblée,*
> *D'auster conduicte couverte de rubriche,*
> *Tant vuidera dehors une assemblée,*
> *Trembler Vienne & le pays d'Austriche.*

For the moment, we may translate this as:

> When the great columns of wood are shaken,
> Led from the south, covered by rubric,
> Then shall cast out an assembly,
> Vienna and the country of Austria to tremble.

The great columns of wood (*colomnes de bois grande*) trembling at the fall of the heavy blade is a striking description of the decapitation machine. The image offers us an opportunity to put a date to the events in the quatrain. The device, recommended to the Assembly in 1789 by Dr Guillotin (but not invented by him, as is so often supposed), was used for the first time to execute a criminal on 15 April 1792. We may take it from the rest of the quatrain that the following reference is to the events contemporaneous with the Great Terror, which lasted from August 1792 to May 1793.

The word, *auster*, in the second line, means 'south wind'. However, this is a play upon Austria (also mentioned in the final line). The Prussians and Austrians invaded France in 1792. More or less as Nostradamus indicates, the Duke of Brunswick carried with him a famous declaration or Manifesto, which is probably the rubric (*rubriche*) of the second line. The curious term may have been chosen because of its subsidiary meaning, which expresses very well the idea of the blood-threat to the French explicit in this Manifesto, the original rubric being in red, the colour of blood. Curiously, Brunswick did not march from the south, but from the south-east.

The third line contains that most remarkable of all words, *assemblée*, which acquired its modern meaning during the period covered by the quatrain. This name was used of the Assemblée Legislative on 1 October 1791, which voted for the war with Austria and suspended the power of Louis XVI.

In the fourth line, *Vienne* is almost certainly Vienna, capital of Austria, rather than Vienne, in the southern department of Isère. The Austrians who shake (*trembler*) are those with the Prussians, who were defeated first at Valmy, and later by Napoleon in the ensuing wars.

A brief background history to the events covered by the quatrain will throw more light upon its meaning. During 1791, Vienna and Berlin agreed that measures should be taken against Revolutionary France. The Duke of Brunswick was ordered to march on Paris, towards which purpose over 100,000 Austrians and a smaller number of Prussians were mustered. However, their march was delayed by the crowning of the Emperor, Francis II. Prior to marching on France, Brunswick issued a declaration (the Manifesto of 25 July 1792) which threatened all Frenchmen who defended themselves, and Paris with ruination if the royal family were harmed. The Revolutionaries saw this as an opportunity to claim that Louis XVI was in league with these invaders. The Royal family, fearing for their lives, sought safety in the Assembly. Later, the Assembly decided that the monarchy should be suspended, and a revised Constitution should be established. Shortly after, Danton proclaimed the commencement of the Terror.

The Prussians, supported by an Austrian corps, invaded Lorraine. Longwy fell, and in September, Verdun. The army was turned back at Valmy – certainly not by French military genius, so much as by dysentery.[2] It was on the day of Valmy that the Assembly met in the Tuileries, and on the second day abolished the Monarchy.

DEATH OF LOUIS XVI

According to Ward, one quatrain deals with the aftermath of the Guillotine – or, at least, with the posthumous history of its most famous victim. This is contained in quatrain VI.92, of which we need only consider the last two lines:

> *La cité au glaive de poudre face aduste,*
> *Par trop grand meurtre le chef du Roy hay.*

The city to the blade of powder burns the visage,
By too great a murder, the head of the King hated.

The city of the blade, or the city (given) to the blade (*la cité au glaive*) is a most felicitous description of the Paris of the guillotine, operating daily under the eyeless gaze of Liberty. 'To devise epithets of this simplicity and force,' writes Ward in praise of Nostradamus, 'constitutes an author at once master of utterance. . . . But, when you find these startling felicities perpetually recurring to illustrate facts historical, – facts that will not come into mortal ken for centuries after the death of the writer, – stiff, indeed, must be the reader's neck if he cannot bow it a little, as to a man of God passing by.'[3]

The burning powder (*poudre . . . aduste*) which merges with this steel sword (*glaive*) is quicklime. After Louis XVI had been decapitated, the head and body of the hated King (*Roy hay*) were placed in wicker-work baskets, and carried to the cemetery of the Madeleine.[4] The trench into which they were thrown was about 12 feet deep, and had been spread with quicklime. The grave was reopened 24 years after this regicide (or 'too great a murder', as the royalist Nostradamus put it) to permit a more decent burial, but there remained, in Ward's words, 'a few fragments of calcined bone'. The site is now marked by the Chapelle Expiatoire, raised by Louis XVIII in 1826, in memory of the King and Marie Antoinette.

The events of the Revolution – not merely that great event itself, but its descent into mindless bloodshed, into regicide and the murder of innocents, and its warlike spread into Europe – seem to have obsessed Nostradamus. Indeed, if we had only the Nostradamus quatrains as history of this extraordinary event, then we would be able to piece together the general drift of the story, along with a few lightning-flash dates and images, relating to the events which struck at the heart of Europe towards the end of that century.

THE KINGDOM OF SARDINIA

Few of the quatrains offer such an obvious indication of the European consequences of the Revolution than VIII.88, which, in the first line, announces that a king will come to Sardinia. This may be old news for the modern reader, as Sardinia was a monarchy for so long that we tend to forget that the line of kings, which came to an end only in the twentieth century, did not rule Sardinia until well over a century and a half after the days of Nostradamus. The quatrain reads:

> *Dans la Sardaigne un noble Roy viendra,*
> *Qui ne tiendra que trois ans le Royaume,*

Plusieurs couleurs avec soy conjoindra,
Luy mesme apres soin sommeil marrit scome.

A noble King will come to Sardinia,
A Kingdom that will last but three years,
Many colours will be joined with him,
He himself afterwards care, sleep, grief and banter.

The verse claims that the king who comes to Sardinia will keep the kingdom for only three years. Were this true, then it would have been a remarkable prediction. However, on the face of it, this does not appear to have happened – once a king did take Sardinia as his kingdom, the line of kingship persisted for almost 200 years. But as is usually the case with Nostradamus, the quatrain is not what it first appears to be. Curiously, Nostradamus seems to be more interested in the fall of Spain, and the destiny of an Italian, than in the future of Sardinia.

The historical facts are that, consequent to agreements made under the Treaty of London, in 1718, Victor Amadeus II of Savoy took the title of King of Sardinia, in exchange for Sicily. Sardinia remained under the royal house of Savoy until 1878, when, on the death of Victor-Emmanuel II, the kingdom was ruled by the kings of united Italy. There seems to have been no break for three years, once Victor Amadeus had come to the throne.

However, for the few years immediately before Victor Amadeus came to the throne, Sardinia had had a rather chequered history. For almost two centuries the island had languished under the brutal and despotic Spaniards, until, at the Treaty of Utrecht (1713), it was assigned to Austria. This was too much for the great Jules Alberoni, Italian minister and cardinal, who had put himself entirely at the disposal of Philip V of Spain and his wife, Isabella Farnese. In 1717 Alberoni seized Sardinia from Austria, in the name of Philip. Now, Alberoni was exiled in the following year (for matters totally unrelated to his seizure of Sardinia) and Philip succeeded in holding on to the island *for only three years*: *Qui ne tiendra que trois ans le Royaume*. In 1718 – the year Alberoni was exiled to Italy – the Treaty of London determined that Spain should not keep Sardinia. The Treaty handed it over, lock, stock and barrel, to the house of Savoy, in exchange for Sicily, which was to go to Austria. However, Victor Amadeus II of Savoy did not take possession until 1720, when he assumed the title of King of Sardinia. We see, then, that the three years predicted by Nostradamus refers not to the new line of kings, but to the last three years of the Spanish reign, which Alberoni had negotiated by force of arms for Philip V.

Nostradamus, having announced that Sardinia would become a kingdom, reflects on the destiny of the man who handed it over to Philip for three years: *Plusieurs couleurs avec soy conjoindra*. We do not doubt that these colours (*couleurs*) are military flags,[5] and that Nostradamus is writing of the unfortunate Alberoni, who joined with the flags of war. In his zeal to recover the lost duchies of Parma, Piacenza and Tuscany for Isabella Farnese, Alberoni planned a war in Italy. The United Provinces, England and France combined against these aspirations in the famous Triple Alliance of 1717.

The British Admiral Byng destroyed the Spanish fleet off Cape Passaro, and war was declared in 1718. This was almost immediately lost by Spain. As a result, Philip dismissed and exiled Alberoni, partly to save face. From the height of power, as the Chief Minister of the Spanish crown, Alberoni fell into great need, and spent some time in an Italian jail.

The fourth line is: *Luy mesme apres soin sommeil marrit scome*. *Soin* is 'care', and *marrit* is 'grief'. *Sommeil* (sleep) is hard to account for save in so far as he probably had nothing else to do other than sleep in the Italian prison:

even in modern French, the verb *sommeiller* is sometimes
used figuratively meaning 'to lie dormant'. *Scome* appears
to be an apocope for the sixteenth-century Provençal word
scomma, meaning 'subtle banter'. The gist of the line is
clear: Alberoni had a hard time. Even this is not quite true,
however, for life is a mutable affair: Alberoni was considered for election to the Papacy in 1724 (though he obtained
only a minority vote of the conclave that finally elected
Pietro Francesco Orsini as Benedict XIII).

MUTATIONS IN SICILY

The history of the recently formed *royaume* of Sardinia is
continued in VIII.81.

> *Le neuf empire en desolation,*
> *Sera changé du pole aquilonaire,*
> *De la Sicile viendra l'emotion,*
> *Troubler l'emprise à Philip. tributaire.*

The new empire in desolation,
Will be changed from the northern pole,
The commotion will come from Sicily,
To trouble the expropriation to Philip. tributary.

Because of the cruel treatment which had been meted out to
Sardinia under the callous Spanish succession, the new
kingdom was desolate (*Le neuf empire en desolation*). Until
1720, Sardinia must have been one of the poorest and most
wretched lands in the West – mainly because of the
obdurate cruelty and *laissez-faire* of the Spaniards, who had
no interest in the island, except as a source of tribute.

According to Nostradamus, welcome change would come
from the north (*du pole aquilonaire*). In fact, the change,
which necessitated the expulsion of the Spanish, came
ultimately from Utrecht and London. It had been the

Treaty of Utrecht (1713) that handed the island over to Austria, leading to the invasion by the Spanish, and it was the Treaty of the Triple Alliance, in London (1717), which handed Sardinia to the house of Savoy.

The third line reads *De la Sicile viendra l'emotion* – 'The commotion will come from Sicily'. In 1717 the Treaty of London ordained that in exchange for Sardinia, Amadeus would have to give Sicily to the Austrians. The commmotion, the stir, which led to the establishment of the new kingdom of Sardinia came from this more southerly island, precisely as Nostradamus predicted.

In the final line we have a brilliant summary of the reasons why Sardinia was taken away from Spain by those of the north: *Troubler l'emprise à Philip. tributaire*. It was inevitable that the accord between the northern nations of England, France and the Netherlands (the Triple Alliance) should disturb (*troubler*) the expropriation (*emprise*) of *Philip*, who received the tribute (he was *tributaire*) from Sardinia. In this line every word counts, and every word tells its story in relation to Sardinian history.

PERSIA AND THE DECLINE OF THE OTTOMANS

Few of the Nostradamus prophecies extend beyond the confines of Europe. As we shall see, a few touch upon the Americas, but hardly any deal with the East, save in terms of when there appears to be a danger from the East for Europe. However, one quatrain, wherein Nostradamus offers a precise date, seems to express a genuine concern for events as far away as Persia. As we study this quatrain we will realize that while it examines with extraordinary precision events in Persia, it also has implications for the whole development of European history. The quatrain is III.77:

Le tiers climat sous Aries comprins,
L'an mil sept cens vingt & sept en Octobre,
Le Roy de Perse par ceux d'Egypte prins,
Conflit, mort, perte, à la croix grand opprobre.

Prior to the analysis, we may translate this as:

The third climate comprised under Aries,
The year one thousand seven hundreds twenty and seven
  in October,
The King of Persia taken by those of Egypt,
Conflict, death, loss, to the cross great opprobrium.

Although the first line may appear to be obscure, the
second line is refreshingly direct. The events of the
quatrain relate precisely to the year 1727, and from the
following line we may presume that this date has a
connection with the history of Persia.

The history of the years leading up to 1727 in Persia is
complicated, being little more than a series of warlike
interludes punctuating bloodbaths, chicanery and rapacious
cruelty. The great Shah ᶜAbbas had attempted some
reforms in the previous century, and had recaptured from
the Turks the cities of Baghdad, Kerbala, Mosul and other
important places in what was then Persia, and had built the
splendid Isfahan as a new capital. He emerged into
European history when he took by force the Portuguese
settlement on the Persian Gulf, and on the island of
Ormuz.

After his death, Persia fell once again into a terminal
decline. By 1722, the Afghan Khilzais of Kandahar, under
Mir Mahmud, captured Isfahan, and soon the city lay in
ruins. Mahmud, always given to unrestrained orgies of
bloodletting, finally went insane, and was killed by his
cousin, Ashraf. It is this same Ashraf who figured in the

Nostradamus quatrain, as events in Persia began to affect Europe.

In the hope of soliciting aid against the Afghans, Ashraf gave vast tracts of land to Russia, including Astarbad and Gilan. In 1724, with a little help from France, Russia and Turkey signed a treaty intended to annex and divide north-western Persia. However, Ashraf defeated the Turks, yet, in the decisive year of 1727, elected to cede western Persia to the Ottomans, with the proviso that they recognized his kingship. In the following year he died.

It is this year which Nostradamus had the foresight to perceive as being of prime importance for Europe. He was prescient, for the decisions made then are still the foundations for many of the Middle-Eastern conflicts and tensions which we have seen during the past 200 years and which, in some respects, still reverberate in our own day.

We may trace the extraordinary accuracy of Nostradamus' prophecy (i.e. that the gift of Persia to the Ottomans would be a great disaster) against a brief potted history. But to do so we must examine one or two of the technical terms which the Seer of Salon uses.

It is very unlikely that even well-read contemporaries of Nostradamus would have understood the first line of this quatrain: *Le tiers climat sous Aries comprins* – 'The third climate comprised under Aries'. Each of the two main concepts it contains are from the astrological tradition that was no longer of great importance in the sixteenth century. The third climat (*Le tiers climat*) is a term ultimately derived from Babylonian astrology, and would have been available to Nostradamus either through Ptolemy, or through translations of Arabic astrologers. The coordinates to which he refers seem to be derived from the Arabian astrologer Alfraganus, who recognized seven 'climates'.[6] The original Greek term was *clima* in the singular, and *climata* in the plural. For Alfraganus, the *climata* are

315

approximate bands of latitude, but they do not have the same three-dimensional definition, being determined by time, rather than spatial considerations. Naturally, the time divisions give rise to *climata* widths, which are translated into geographic zones of inaccurate, and seemingly arbitrary, specification.

We do not have to examine this system in depth, but to understand the Nostradamus reference, we must note that the *climata* are measured from just under 13 degrees parallel to the equator, and are numbered outwards, towards the north pole, whence they fall short by 900 miles. According to Alfraganus, the third climata is a band 350 miles wide, which begins 840 miles from the commencement line. This means that the third clima (*tiers climat*) is approximately the equivalent of 28 to 34 degrees north in the modern system of measurement. The band stretches around the globe, but in relation to a quatrain which mentions the King of Persia (*Roy de Perse*) we should observe that it includes most of modern Persia, Afghanistan to the east, and Iraq and the northern parts of Arabia to the west.

The second half of the line is also derived from astrology: *sous Aries comprins*. In the astrological system which Ptolemy called chorography, each country and major city was assigned to a particular planet and zodiacal sign. In his *Tetrabiblos*,[7] Ptolemy tells us that Persia falls under the rule of Taurus. This is curious, for Nostradamus distinctly writes of an area within the third *climata* which is 'contained under Aries'. What is the mystery here? If we glance back at Ptolemy's chorography,* we will see that

---

* Chorography is the name taken from Ptolemaic astrology to denote the system of ascribing zodiacal and planetary rulerships to localities – to countries, cities, and towns. Chorographic lists vary enormously, but the one most widely accepted in sixteenth-century astrology was the extensive one given by Ptolemy, who set out the astrological rules for determining

Syria, Palestine, Idumaea and Judaea fall under the rule of Aries. This is precisely that area of the Ottoman empire which bordered the west of Persia, to which Ashraf ceded the western half of Persia.

Nostradamus has therefore tied an important and far-reaching historical decision down precisely in space and time.

After setting down this specialist view of the terms which appear in the first line of the quatrain, we are in a position to offer a more accurate translation of the quatrain, as follows:

> *Le tiers climat sous Aries comprins,*
> *L'an mil sept cens vingt & sept en Octobre*

The latitude 28 to 34 degrees north, to the west of Persia, in the October of 1727

Such precision of description in regard to an event nearly 200 years into the future almost beggars belief.

The quatrain continues: *Le Roy de Perse par ceux d'Egypte prins, / Conflit, mort, perte, à la croix grand opprobre.* Now it is evident that Ashraf, still the King of Persia in 1727, was not himself taken by Egyptians, as a superficial reading of the line would suggest. It was Persia which the 'Egyptians' took, when he ceded half his land to the Ottomans. The reference to *ceux d'Egypte* is typically precise: Nostradamus does not say 'Egyptians', but 'those of Egypt'. The Ottomans, as the inheritors of the Islamic tradition, had almost imperceptibly taken over Egypt from the Arabs, who had invaded this antique land in the eighth century. Thus, in 1727, the Ottoman Turks did control Egypt, and could be described as *ceux d'Egypte*. They kept it

---

such rulerships. Even in the sixteenth century, attempts were made to bring the rulerships of the newly discovered Americas up to date.

until 1789, when the Mamluk forces under Selim III were
routed by Napoleon.

The history of the consequences of this gift of Persia is
essentially one of war between the Turks and the East and
West, which in later times was transformed into war
between Iraq/Iran and the East and West. The consequences finally played themselves out during the Second World
War, when Greece – the western battleground between
Italy and the Ottomans – reverted to the Greeks.

In both phases of this history, the conflict was fired by
religious differences between Islam and Christianity, and an
ensuing difference of world views. Although there was
never any period of peace in the region, between these
warring religions, the following dates give some indication
of the major crises. In 1733, the Mamluk sultan joined with
the Russians to attack Persia, the latter occupying the
Caspian regions and the Turks taking Azerbaijan and
Hamadan. They were defeated at Kirkuk by Nadir Kuli
Khan, who was soon warring with the Turks again for the
13-year period up to 1747, in Kars and Iraq.

The later wars of Napoleon and Nelson, the Russian
frontier wars (Treaty of Bukarest, 1812), the Serbian revolt
(Convention of Akkerman, 1826, and Treaty of London,
1827) which led to the establishing of a Russian protector-
ate over Serbia; the Morea and Moldavian insurrections of
1821, the capture of Missolonghi (where Byron died) by the
Turks in 1825, the invasion of 1828 by Russians of the
Turkish Caucasus provinces (Treaty of Adrianople, 1829),
Mehemet Ali's invasion of the Sudan, in 1821, and then
Crete and Morea, followed by the invasion of Syria in 1832,
and his expulsion under the terms of the 1840 Convention
of London; the Crimean War, which drew a deal of Europe
into action; the rebellion of 1875 in Bosnia and Hercegovina
(then still under Ottoman control); the related Serbian war,

followed by the Russian war of 1876 with Russia (Treaty of Berlin, 1878), which led to the British occupation of Cyprus – these, and other crises attending the decline of the Ottoman power, led inexorably to the First World War, in the twentieth century, and still stretch their ghostly fingers into our modern times.

It is no accident that this first of the wars of the world – ostensibly designed to restrain German expansionism in Europe – involved fighting in the old Turkish Empire, in Mesopotamia, in Palestine and Syria and in Egypt. In the face of this incomplete history of the wars which may be traced back to that historic decision to cede territory to the Ottoman Turks, Nostradamus is parsimonious in his words. He merely records: *Conflit, mort, perte, à la croix grand opprobre.* Above all, as the last five words imply, cleared as they are of all political correctness, Nostradamus realized that the wars which would follow that historic decision of 1727 might appear to be territorial, but were, in essence, rooted in religious and aspirational differences between Crescent and Cross.

CATHERINE THE VEXATIOUS

Few quatrains contain so many predictions as VIII.15; this covers 27 years and 5 major conflicts in Russian history:

Vers Aquilon grands efforts par hommasse
Presque l'Europe & l'univers vexer,
Les deux eclypses mettra en telle chasse,
Et aux Pannons vie & mort renforcer.

Towards the north great efforts by a masculine woman
To agitate almost (all) Europe and the Universe,
The two eclipses (she) will put in such a chase,
And will enforce the life and death of the Poles.

Aquilon is a term used frequently by Nostradamus to mean the North. Under normal circumstances, this is scarcely an arcane use, for the word is from the Latin, *aquilonius*, meaning 'northerly'. In this particular quatrain, however, it does have an additional meaning, for the Latin *aquila* means 'eagle'. This secondary meaning, which connotes a 'northerly eagle' perhaps points to Russia, which was among the several northern countries to adopt the double-headed eagle as official emblem.

Hommasse, which looks like a typical Nostradamian invention, is a late-medieval French word still in use today: it means 'masculine woman'. Its origin is not hard to find, for it combines *homme* (man) with the feminizing suffix *esse*, to give 'maness'.[8] That this person is Catherine II has been recognized by commentators for some time, for there are very few such distinctive masculine women in Russian history. It is typical of Nostradamus that he should introduce her curious designation as man-woman alongside a mention of her great efforts (*grand efforts*), almost as though he knew that she would be called by her contemporaries Catherine the Great – in French, *la Grande*. Strangely enough, she is sometimes also called *la Semiramis du Nord*, which relates directly to the second word of this first line, *Aquilon* (northerly), and points, by association with the Assyrian princess, to her famous sexual appetite.

While there may be in the second line – *Presque l'Europe & l'univers vexer* – some hidden significance which has evaded us, there is no doubt that this great Empress of Russia did disturb and damage Europe and the rest of the world. It is possible that the reference to the *univers* is a play on the word *Pannons* (third line), for while this means Poland, the Greek *Pan* means 'all' (see below). At the same time *l'univers* can be broken down into *luni vers*, which is close to the Latin meaning 'towards the moon': the relevance of this will become evident when we have considered the Turkish symbolism in the last two lines below.

The term *univers* could be a reference to her popular title of Semiramis, for the husband of this princess, Ninus, was known as 'King of the World . . . of the Four Quarters of the World'.[9] After the death of Ninus, she ruled in his place, just as Catherine ruled in place of the far less impressive Peter III, after his death at the hands of the Orlovs in 1762. The final word, *vexer*, is from the Latin *vexo – vexarier*, to shake or move violently or damage.

The remaining two lines should be studied together, for they describe the most damaging wars in which Catherine involved herself: *Les deux eclypses mettra en telle chasse, / Et aux Pannons vie & mort renforcer.* The two eclipses (*deux eclypses*) are the two wars she fought with Turkey. Nostradamus is quite right to call them 'eclipses'. The type of eclipse which Nostradamus had in mind was the eclipse of the Moon, which is thrown into total darkness when the earth's shadow passes over it, as the globe of the earth passes before the sun. The two wars were conducted between the solar-oriented Christian religion (Russia was officially Orthodox, of course) and the lunar-oriented Muslims of Turkey, who had adopted a crescent moon as their symbol.[10]

The first war was fought from 1768 to 1774, against Mustafa III. The second was fought from 1787 to 1791, against Abdul-Hamid I. In both wars, the savagery and might of Russia almost blocked out the lunar light of the Turks. It has been said that the Treaty of Kuchuk Kainarji (1774) was the most humiliating treaty the Turks had ever signed. The slaughter by the Russians of every man, woman and child after the captures of Khotin, Jassy and Ochakov was so horrific that (it is claimed) Abdul-Hamid died of shock. It was pertinent of Nostradamus to view these two wars as images of the Turkish moon being occulted by the Russian sun.

There is no such 'war of religions' in the second group of conflicts. The fourth line refers to the Poles (*Pannons*), and introduces the influence which Catherine's policies and armies had on them. The word *Pannons* is partly Greek and partly Green Language. Pannonia is the ancient name for a country which lay between Dacia, Noricum and Illyria. In this sense, therefore, it refers to a territory which corresponded to part of former Poland. A further stratification of meaning is contained in the fact that the Latin *pannosus* means 'ragged' and 'tattered', and is therefore descriptive of the state in which Catherine finally left Poland.

In the first line, we had noted a connection between the opening phrase *Vers Aquilon* and Russia – if only because of the two-headed eagle, which is symbol of that country. Now, with Poland established as a place-name, we can reinterpret this opening. The arms of Poland also displayed an eagle, but in this case, a single-headed eagle. The phrase *Vers Aquilon*, which certainly means 'Towards the North', may also be read as meaning 'Towards Poland'. With such a reading, the significance of the first line changes considerably, for it can read: 'Great efforts by a masculine woman towards Poland'.

To reduce the Poles, and expand her own territory, Catherine progressively partitioned Poland, stamping out any resistance with extraordinary brutality. In the first partition, of 1772, Poland lost about a quarter of its territory, and almost as much of its population. In the second partition, of 1793, Poland was reduced to a third of its original area, and with a population of almost a quarter. The third so-called partition, of 1795, was total, for even the name of Poland was erased from the maps, and remained absent for over a century. This was, literally, a progressive enforcing (*renforcer*) from life to death (*vie & mort*) for the entire Polish nation (*Pannons*).

After considering this digest of Catherine's warlike exploits (Martian exploits, in astrological terms), we can well understand why Nostradamus, searching for some new word to pin down her personality, should use the term *hommasse*, so close in sound to *homicide*, 'murderer'.

A STRANGE CALENDAR

Few commentators have known what to make of quatrain I.42. The influential French scholar Anatole le Pelletier was reduced to suggesting that the Nostradamus text of the quatrain was corrupt in places, and several modern commentators have adopted his view. The quatrain runs:

Les dix Kalendes d'Avril de fait Gotique
Ressuscité encor par gens malins,
Le feu estaint, assemblée diabolique,
Cerchant les os du d'Amant & Pselin.

For the moment, we will translate this as:

The tenth Kalends of April according to the Gothic
  system
Resuscitated again by evil people . . .
The fire put out, diabolic assembly,
Seeking the bones of d'Amant and Pselin.

Le Pelletier claimed that the penultimate words, *d'Amant &*, should be read as *Demon de*.[11] Even after such emendation, his interpretation was, to say the least, cryptic. His thesis rested on the notion that the quatrain was based on a Byzantine text, the *De Daemonibus* of the eleventh-century scholar, Michael Psellus. Unfortunately, this thesis is very weak. In any case, the argument that Psellus is the source does not for one moment explain the *meaning* of the quatrain. Yet, in spite of this deficiency, le Pelletier's view has been embraced by virtually every single commentator since 1867, when the Frenchman first published his scholarly-seeming tome on Nostradamus.

We must inquire whether this quatrain is that rare animal in the Nostradamus oeuvre – one that is in no way prophetic. Is it really intended as a rather meaningless reference to a witchcraft rite, or some black magical ritual, as the Psellus thesis implies? Is it really a quatrain in which some of the key words are corrupt?

The following analysis of the quatrain will show that it *is* prophetic, that it has little or nothing to do with black magical rites, and that the original text was *not* corrupt. It exhibits Nostradamus' mastery of both astrological symbolism and the methods of the Green Language.

Let us consider the first line: *Les dix Kalendes d'Avril de fait Gotique* – 'The tenth Kalends of April according to the Gothic system'. Most interpreters have assumed that the reference to the 'Gothic system' (*fait Gotique*) is to the Roman calendar designed by Julius Caesar, and known as the Julian. This system was not reformed until after the death of Nostradamus, so, under normal circumstances, there would be no need for him to refer to this calendar at all, save in a prophetic sense. In fact, analysis will show that, in this line, Nostradamus is referring not to the calendrical system, but to a method of determining the sequence of dates.

The Roman system of ordering the days of the month was essentially different from the one in use during the sixteenth century, just as it is from the one in use in modern times. The Roman month was punctuated by three cardinal days, the *Kalendae*, the *Nonae* and the *Idus*. The Kalends of every month always fell on the first of that month. In April, the Nones fell on the 5th, and the Ides on the 13th of the month. The reckoning of the days was not in sequential progression. The days between the Kalends and the Nones were reckoned as days prior to the Nones. Those between the Nones and the Ides were reckoned as days prior to the Ides. The remaining days were designated by reference to their prior sequence to the day before the Kalends, which meant, of course, the Kalends of the following month.

According to this method of reckoning, the tenth Kalends of April would correspond to 21 March.

Does this 21 March have any significance for Nostradamus? After the Gregorian bull of calendrical reform, of 1582,[12] ten days were annulled so that 5 October 1582 was to be reckoned as 15 October. This meant that the vernal equinox was moved to 21 March. In this date, as in the fact that Nostradamus refers to a specific period of ten days, we may trace the subject-matter of the first two lines of his quatrain. Nostradamus seems to be dealing with the important calendrical reform which was not instituted until 11 years after his death, and which did not become effective in France for a further five years. Even in this limited sense, therefore, the verse is prophetic.

We must admit that there is no evidence to suggest that Nostradamus, officially a sincere Catholic, would view these future reforms as being in any way diabolic. Yet, the remaining three lines of the quatrain do appear to point to some sort of witchcraft rituals, or black magical rites, linked with this Roman calendar.

In view of this, we should inquire whether there is any other calendar in which the date 21 March is regarded as having a particular significance. Is there any other calendar which is either non-Catholic, or pagan, that might relate in a significant way to this quatrain?

The answer is yes. The Revolutionary Calendar of 1792

was essentially pagan. It was also intended to mark a separation from the calendar that had been proposed and used by the Catholic papacy. The Revolutionary Calendar was adopted as a 'logical' calendar, supposedly divorced from all superstitions.

Before examining this calendar, we must reflect upon the final word of the first line: *Gotique*. Originally, the Goths were the Germanic tribes who invaded Europe in the third to fifth centuries, and established kingdoms in Italy, France and Spain. Their barbarian behaviour led to the word 'Goth' being equated with rude or uncivilized behaviour. However, as Fulcanelli has pointed out, in the Green Language, Gothic has a specific meaning.

The term 'art Gothique' is said to be the arcane cover for the word *argot*, or cant. On the one hand, this is the language of the common people, whose private language is slang. At the same time, *Argotique* is also the language of the initiates, reminding us of the esoteric nature of those who sailed the *Argo* in search of the Golden Fleece. Thus, we may take it that Nostradamus is admitting (to the initiated) that the obscure dating pertains to Green Language usage.

The common people acted in wanton destruction during and after the French Revolution. These people behaved like the invading Goths, destroying all things Christian and Catholic. Their new calendrical system might well be termed the Gothic system (*fait Gotique*). In view of this, we may assume that the first line of the quatrain refers to the Revolutionary Calendar system proposed in 1792.

This calendar was to commence from the foundation of the Republic, on 22 September 1792. Calendrical adjustments aside, each year was to have 12 months of 30 days, with the remaining five days regarded as complementaries, celebrated as festivals. The five intercalaries which made up the year of the Revolutionary Calendar were called the

Sanculotides (in English), or Sans Culottides (in French), dedicated to the Republican extremists, usually from the working class, who were *sans culottes* (without knee breeches). The five days were given over to holidays, presumably as a sop to the working classes.

Each month was divided into three decades of ten days. This calendrical reform persisted only up to 31 December 1805, when the Gregorian system was restored by Napoleon I. The relevant fact is that the Revolutionary Calendar designated 21 March as the first day of Spring, the first of *Germinal*.

One side issue, which carries us beyond the confines of the quatrain, is that Nostradamus had mentioned this year specifically, in his *Epistle to Henry II*. One year, which he designates by an arcane astrological configuration,[13] will see profound changes for the world, and the great persecution of the Christian Church,

> *... and in this year will begin a most great persecution of the Christian Church, such as was never made in Africa, And this will last until the year one thousand, seven hundred and ninety two, which they will believe to be a renovation of the century ...*[14]

It is quite possible to regard this quatrain I.42 as a commentary on, or a footnote to, this remarkable prediction. It was in this year that the Revolutionary Calendar was adopted. This was literally 'a renovation of the century'. Nostradamus' precision of dating must be admired, for the actual establishment of the Calendar was not decreed until much later, on 24 November 1793 (officially, 4 Frimaire of the year II).

As we have observed, the phrase: *Ressuscité encor par gens malins* ('Resuscitated again by evil people ...') has been interpreted as reference to witchcraft or to black magicians.

Le Pelletier, eager to show a connection between this quatrain and the writings of Psellus (see below), translated '*gens malins*' as '*habiles sorciers*' (clever magicians). However, the line is really an extension of the first: there is no comma at the end of the opening line. The phrase is intended to acknowledge that the Revolutionary Calendar was established by evil people. Those who had elected to kill their king were, by the standards of Nostradamus, evil indeed.

We should observe that the word *Ressuscité* seems to be a parallel, drawn by Nostradamus, to the word *renovation* in the *Epistle*. By this reasoning, the first two lines mean: 'The twenty-first of March, according to Gothic calendar / Renovated again by evil people'.

What is the purpose of this reference to a future calendrical system? *Le feu estaint, assemblée diabolique, / Cerchant les os du d'Amant & Pselin.* As we have observed, the accepted theory is that the quatrain deals with some unspecified diabolical witchcraft rituals, such as are discussed in the writings on demons by Psellus. Le Pelletier gives three parallels between this quatrain and a short passage quoted from Psellus. However, two of these are completely invalid, for they involve radical misreadings of the Latin version of the Psellus text (Psellus wrote in Greek). A third parallel seems to be valid, however.

In his book *De Daemonibus*, Psellus tells how, after the sacred lights are extinguished, the company gives itself up to licentiousness.[15] While it is tempting to read this witchcraft or diabolerie context into the Nostradamus quatrain, such a reading does not appear to have much significance in relation to so specific a date as 21 March, the beginning of the zodiacal year. We have to assume that all past scholarship applied to this quatrain is in error – especially when it has attempted to impute serious errors to Nostradamus or his printers.

However, when the description of the extinction of the sacred lights, and the behaviour of a diabolic assembly, are linked with the Revolutionary Calendar, all becomes clear.

For Nostradamus, the most significant, and horrific, of future events seems to have been the French Revolution. Among its consequences was the new calendrical system. This 'logical' calendar of the revolutionaries reflected precisely the date given, however arcanely, by Nostradamus. In the Revolutionary Calendar, 21 March was the first day of Germinal, the first day of Spring.

The assembly may not have been diabolic, yet it was certainly revolutionary. The reference to Psellus' text is merely intended to point to a type of behaviour. The fire (*feu*) of the third line which is put out (*estaint*) was, in the Psellus text, a sacred light. This was the sacred light of the French royal succession, which the Revolutionaries extinguished. There is deep significance in this theme of sacred fire, for 21 March is the day of the Vernal Equinox, when the Sun (symbol of the Divine light) starts its annual round of the zodiac. On that day, the Sun enters Aries, the Fire-sign of the Ram. Thus, the sacred light of kingship is put out, instead of being renewed. In consequence, the Revolutionaries revert to a pagan zodiacal system by which to measure the months and years in terms of that great light, which is the Sun.

Now we must examine the last two lines in the light of the above observations, and see how these may be interpreted in relation to the events of 1792. Line three runs: *Le feu estaint, assemblée, diabolique* ('The fire dead, diabolique assembly'). What is the fire which is dead? Almost certainly, this is the fire or light of the French line of kingship. Nostradamus recognizes the date when this event will take place, and intimates as much in his *Epistle to Henry*. In this text, he claims that the terrible times (represented astrologically) will last until 1792. The French

Revolution may be said to have begun in June 1789 and ended in 1792, when the new calendar was adopted.

With the two words, *assemblée diabolique*, we have yet another example of Nostradamus' extraordinary prevision. The calendrical reforms he foresees were instituted by the French Assembly, the latter being the very word he uses in this line of the quatrain. The term *Assemblée Nationale* was adopted in June 1789, and the gathering it described was one of the contributing factors which led to the French Revolution. It was this *Assemblée* which proclaimed the Declaration of the Rights of Man, and voted in the Constitution of 1791, creating all citizens equal in the face of the law; moreover, it voted in the Revolutionary Calendar – the subject of this quatrain.

Nostradamus calling the assembly diabolic (*diabolique*) is quite in accord with his royalist sympathies. We must not forget that he had dedicated these quatrains to the reigning monarch, and first mooted the significance of the years 1789 to 1792 in a letter to the same King. There may be no doubt that Nostradamus, while foreseeing the French Revolution, lamented its consequences.

Now we come to the last line, which has intrigued and confused many commentators. *Cerchant les os du d'Amant & Pselin* – 'Seeking the bones of Amant and Pselin'. Clearly, its meaning hangs upon the significance of *d'Amant & Pselin*. As we shall see, there was really no reason for scholars to amend these last words, or even to suggest that they are misprints, or otherwise in error. As usual, Nostradamus meant precisely what he wrote, *albeit he was writing in the Green Language.*

Previous interpretations held that the line is somehow a quotation from the Byzantine writer, Psellus (*Pselin*). Psellus is mentioned, but he is only one of two individuals mentioned in the line; furthermore, there is nothing in Psellus' book on demons, *De Daemonibus*, which relates to this 'seeking of bones'. The correct interpretation is as follows. *Amant* is Amand, the great apostle saint of Flanders, and Bishop of Maastricht. In the sixth century Amand evangelized and converted the greater part of Flanders, and even attempted the conversion of the Slavs. He acted as a sort of go-between for the Pope and the various bishops of Gaul (in those days, not all of France had been converted to the Christian faith). He founded many monastic houses in France, some of which still survive. All in all, Amand was a useful symbol to Nostradamus of the missionary life of the early Church in the West.

Pselin is Psellus, the eleventh-century Byzantine historian, who is nowadays mainly remembered because he wrote *De Daemonibus*. However, this was a minor work, and he is far more important in history for his *Chronologia*, an account of his century.[16] Besides being an influential and Machiavellian statesman, he was one of the greatest Christian scholars of the Byzantine Church. His main contribution to Western thought was his view that Platonism could be reconciled with Christian belief. This idea found a fertile climate in early-fifteenth-century Florence, after the visit of the eastern Patriarch. All in all, Psellus was a useful symbol to Nostradamus of the intellectual life of the early Church in the East.

These short biographies indicate something of what Nostradamus could have had in mind when he brought together Amand and Psellus. 'Seeking the bones of Amand and Psellus' could be interpreted as seeking the Christian missionary zeal of the former, and scholastic humanism of the latter. At the same time, the two are, in their own ways, representatives of the Western and Eastern churches. This suggests that implicit in the line is an idea of a search for the roots of Christianity, prior to the separation of Constantinople and Rome.

In terms of the quatrain as a whole, the line may be seen as relating to a search for the Christian spirit lost to France as a consequence of the Revolution. History would never be the same again. East and West would never meet ecumenically. The missionary zeal and ecclesiastical scholarship would be gone, buried like the bones of the Saints.

There is one further deep reason – itself linked with the methods of the Green Language – why Nostradamus should choose these famous figureheads as symbols for his quatrain. When we reflect upon these two historical characters – important, influential and famous in their days, yet scarcely remembered in modern times – we realize that Nostradamus had the opportunity to choose other names. He had access to any number of missionaries and scholars from the two Christian churches that would satisfy the demands of this last line of the quatrain. Certainly, this would have been the case had Nostradamus not intended to introduce a deeper level of meaning in this line – if he were not dealing with the Green Language. In view of this, let us examine the words in the light of the Green Language.

Amant (Amand) means 'they love', in Latin. In French it denotes a male lover. The word *Amant* begins with the letter *A*. As we shall see, this is important.

Pselin is not merely a mindless variation on the name Psellus. This point must be made because it is possible to explain the use of the name Psellus in the quatrain purely in terms of the literary reference to his notion of the dying fire or light (*Le feu estaint*) of line three. However, the French for Psellus is *Psellos*, while Nostradamus wrote *Pselin*. This peculiar orthography performs two functions. On the one hand, it reminds us of the recurrent word *Selin* (Pselin), which is used time and time again by Nostradamus to denote either the Turks or the Muslims (see pages 535–6). With this Green Language meaning, the word not

332

only refers to the Byzantine version of Christianity, but also to Mohammadanism. Recognition of this fact leaves us with a spare *P*, so to speak. This should alert us to the fact that the *P* has some significance, as a capital letter.

Now, the word *os*, which means 'bones', also sounds like the 15th letter of the alphabet, *O*. In terms of the Green Language, words which sound the same may be interchanged, through the rule of homonym. What could this 'O' relate to, if not to the great circle of the zodiac, which is the measure of the calendar dealt with in the first two lines of the quatrain?

A circle has neither beginning nor end. However, in the convention of calendrical systems, as in astrology, the zodiacal circle commences at Aries. In calendrical terms, the sun 'begins' its journey through the circle of the zodiac on 21 March – the first day of Germinal in the Revolutionary Calendar, the *dix Kalendes d'Avril de fait Gotique* in the quatrain. In the same conventions, the zodiacal and calendrical cycle ends in Pisces. Thus, on 21 March, Pisces ends and Aries begins.

The zodiacal sign Aries is linked with the love-impulse of Spring, with the male sexual energies of its ruling planet, Mars. *Amant*, which means 'male lover', is therefore an excellent Green Language construct by which to describe Aries. The word *Amant* has the added distinction of beginning with the same capital letter as the zodiacal sign, Aries.

Zodiacal Pisces is a water sign, which is one reason why the sign is associated with a pair of fishes. The word *Selin* takes its Green Language significance from the fact that it also means *Selene*, the Greek name for the Moon. The Moon is the ruler of the waters, ruler of the seas. The first letter of Pisces is *P*. If we add to the Green Language construct *selin* the letter P, as the first letter of Pisces, we obtain the name *Pselin*, which Nostradamus uses in the quatrain.

Is it too imaginative to trace in the names Amant and Psellus the capital letters *A* and *P* which start and end both the zodiacal and the calendrical circle with *A*ries and *P*isces? It may be too imaginative in exoteric thought, but it falls well within the limits prescribed by adherents of the Green Language. Furthermore, it is only an interpretation of this kind that will enable us to make sense of the last lines of the quatrain, in relation to the preceding lines.

So, after all our analysis of its Green Language elements what does the quatrain actually *mean*? In it, Nostradamus deals with the new Calendar of the Revolutionaries which will, in 1792, sweep away the nominal control of the Catholic religion, even over the structure of the year. This change will be initiated by evil men. The old order of religion (albeit only three religions are mentioned) will be threatened by these changes and by these men. Men will no longer be able to look to the religious figureheads of the past for answers to their problems. The bones of the Saints, and the ancient learning, will be lost.

A more devastating image of the future could scarcely be imagined by men of the sixteenth century.

THE FATE OF THE FRENCH ROYALS

As we have already noted, the Revolution, along with the State murder of Louis XVI and his family, horrified Nostradamus. Several of his quatrains refer to the matter, yet few of these are quite so economically succinct as IX.77:

Le regne prins le Roy conviera,
La dame prinse à mort jurez à sort,
Le vie à Royne fils on desniera,
Et la pellix au fort de la consort.

The government takes the incited King,
The captive Queen will be condemned to death by lottery,
Life will be denied to the Queen's son,
And the courtesan to the strength of the consort.

While there is some doubt about the precise meaning of the
first line, tragic history – let alone prediction of a future
tragedy – could not have been written with more direct
economy. These four lines tell the fate of the four most
important individuals in the court of Louis XVI, line by
line.

Louis XVI was indeed taken by the government – incited
(or invited – both words are applicable) to remain king, but
later guillotined by the same body. The captive dame was
Marie Antoinette, who was judged by a revolutionary
tribunal of jurors drawn from all classes of people – an
ordinary jury raised by lot. The Dauphin – then a mere
child, and of course the Queen's son (*Royne fils*), died in the
Temple at an unspecified date. The *pellix*, who had relied
upon the strength of her consort (*fort de la consort*), Louis
XV, was Madame Dubarry. It is this fourth line which
provides an excellent example of how economically Nostradamus uses the Green Language. The word *pellix* is clearly
a metathesis from the Latin *pellax*, which is in turn from a
Greek word meaning deceitful and seductive. Although not
etymologically connected with *pelleatus* (clothed in skin) or
pellis (a garment made of skin), the word does carry an
association of skin-deep beauty, a covering for immorality.
From this association alone, one can see how *pellix* took on
the meaning of courtesan.

Given the context, Nostradamus leaves us in no doubt
that this particular *pellix* is Madame Dubarry, who had
worked in a brothel before becoming the favourite mistress
of Louis XV. As Nostradamus seems to have been aware,

335

the word *pellix* (with its association with clothing) is especially relevant to Dubarry, for when she was a prostitute in Paris she worked under the name of *Lange*, which in French means 'swaddling clothes'.

Is there, one wonders, some hint in this quatrain of a history which has been lost to historians? The destiny of the Dauphin – theoretically, the future Louis XVIII – has remained a mystery. It has been suggested that he was put to death in the Temple on 8 June 1795.[17] However, there is something of interest in the quatrain, for each line seems to deal with the death of the four major protagonists in a sequence. We know that Louis (the *Roy* of line one) was executed on 21 January 1793. We know also that Marie Antoinette (the *dame* of line two) was executed on 16 October of the same year. We know also that Madame Dubarry (the *pellix* of line four) was executed two months later, on 7 December 1793. Does Nostradamus put the death of the Dauphin (*Royne fils*) in the third line to indicate that he died between October and December 1793?

THE KING WHO NEVER WAS

Quatrain X.9 deals with the imprisonment of the 'king who never ruled', or, as Nostradamus put it in the last line of the verse, the 'Never King' (*Onc Roy*), Louis XVII.

De Castillon figujeres jour de brune,
De femme infame naistra souverain prince
Surnom de chausses perhume luy posthume,
Onc Roy ne fut si pire en sa province.

The allegorical castle on the day of fog,
From the infamous woman will be born a sovereign prince
The surname of shoes before and after his death,
Never King was so unfortunate in his province.

Castillon is the Temple, used during the Revolution to incarcerate the royal prisoners (see *fig. 38*). That it should be described as a 'castle' (*caste*) is supported by contemporaneous prints which reveal it to be far more a forbidding place of turrets than the place of worship suggested by its name. The phrase, *Castillon figujeres* (*Castel figure*, or more precise to the latter word, *Castel se figurer*), may be translated loosely as 'allegorical castle', or 'figurative castle', or 'imagined castle', which fits the meaning very well. The Temple was originally a castle of the Knights Templars, but was used by the Revolutionaries as a prison, mainly because it was so well fortified, and was served by only one gate, which made it very easy to guard.

What is this day of brown (*jour de brune*)? On 27 October, the boy was separated from his mother, and moved to a larger tower in the Temple. In the Revolutionary Calendar, to which Nostradamus refers several times, this is *Brumaire*. The word *Brumaire* means both 'wintery' and 'hazy' or 'misty'. The word *brune* is a sufficiently simple metathesis of the root word *brume* for our purposes, and the latter is clearly hinted at (in Green Language terms) in the invited rhyme with *posthume*, in the third line.

What of the second line – *De femme infame naistra souverain prince*? The *femme infame* is the Dauphin's mother, Marie Antoinette. She was infamous among the Revolutionaries for her profligate life, and, later, among the general populace as a result of the trial which involved charges of child abuse. However, there is also a play in the homophony of *femme* and *fame* – she is a woman who is 'not-a-woman' (*femme infame*, or *in-femme*). We have already mentioned the sexual abuse charges levelled against Marie Antoinette, and noted that Nostradamus seems to support the validity of these charges, in the face of official history (see page 213 ff).

Louis was born a sovereign prince (*naistre souverain prince*), because, as the first-born, he carried the title of Dauphin. Unofficially, he became king when his father was guillotined, yet he never reigned. Thus, a 'not-a-woman' or 'not-a-mother' (*infame*), gives birth to a king who is 'not-a-king' (the *Onc Roy* of the final line).

Surnom de chausses perhume luy posthume is the third line. *Surnom de chausses* might be translated as 'surname of shoes'. On 3 July 1793, the Committee of General Security, named as the Dauphin's guardian a cobbler called Simon. *Chausser*, among other things, means 'to make shoes for'. There is almost a linguistic pun on *surnom* and *Simon*: however, even if this was not intentional, the fact is that as a legal guardian, Simon had legal power over (*sur*) the name (*nom*) of his charge.

Anyone with a knowledge of the curious history of the Dauphin will prick up his or her ears at the final phrase of this line; *perhume luy posthume* should be translated approximately as 'prior to his death and after his death'. In fact, because of the rules of homonymy, the phrase *perhume luy* might even be read as 'prior to the death of Louis'.

So far as we know, there is no French word *hume*, or *perhume*, but the verb *humer* means to inhale or suck in. As we have here a Green Language construct, with *perhume* designed to contrast with *posthume*, we may take it that the thing being sucked in is life itself, which is given over in the posthumous stage. Recognizing the complexities of Nostradamus' vision, we must ask if this 'inhaling' has anything to do with the keeping back of the secret of the life (or death) of the Dauphin. This need not be directly linked with the cobbler *Simon*, but with the author *Simien* Despreaux, who seems to have been the authority on the survival of the boy: the two homophonous Simons relate to the pre-humous and posthumous life of the boy. The homophony is at least

338

striking, for one is concerned with his pre-mortem existence (so to speak), while the other is concerned with his putative post-mortem existence.

The strange phrase, which intimates a death and posthumous existence, is applicable to the Dauphin, for although official records suggest (albeit tenuously) that the boy died in the Temple fortress, many accounts circulated later claiming that he was still alive.

From this quatrain, we may assume that Nostradamus did not foresee the death of Louis in the Temple prison. This is no place to deal with the complicated history of the 'posthumous' survival of the Dauphin: it is sufficient to say that while the official report maintained that the ten-year-old boy had died, the autopsy (a somewhat clandestine affair) was widely believed to be a cover-up. It was maintained that the dead child was a substitution (a deaf mute), and Despreaux was notable among those who maintained, as late as 1814 (when Louis XVIII, a grandson of Louis XV, born in 1755, returned to Paris) that Louis XVII was still alive. However, by that time, the survival of the latter was of supreme indifference to the Revolutionaries and Royalists alike – the majority of the latter supported the claims of Louis XVIII.

It is the fourth line – *Onc Roy ne fut si pire en sa province* – which determines beyond a shadow of doubt that the quatrain deals with Louis XVII, whose reign was indeed uniquely unfortunate. The youthful Louis was *Onc Roy*, which means literally 'Never King' – a phrase which can be applied to very few historical rulers. By extension, he was a never-king who was unfortunate (*pire* means 'worse') in his province. In Green Language usage, we can read *province* as meaning France, the realm of kingship, and, of course, the Temple prison, where he spent his entire miserable 'reign'. Nostradamus is careful to point out that this Never King was unfortunate in his 'province', not in his kingdom.

339

Louis had been only seven when he became (in the eyes of the Royalists, though not in the eyes of France) the King of France, at the murder of his father. His reign was passed in the prison of the Temple, and even if he did survive the Temple, he never had official recognition of his kingship. No king could have been quite so circumscribed, so unfortunate (*si pire*).

Before leaving this remarkably precise prediction, we should note the felicity of the literary style, and the beauty of the meaningful homophonies of *femme infame* and *perhume*. The French word, *posthume*, points to a precision of thought which lifts the verse into a high class of literature. Marie Antoinette was both *femme* and *in-femme* (*infame*), in the eyes of history. Louis (*luy*) is both *perhume* and *posthume*, so far as history is concerned. One feels that if Nostradamus had not written the finest predictive verse the world has ever seen, then he would at the very least have written excellent poetry.

THE COMING OF NAPOLEON

If, in the view of Nostradamus, the penultimate decade of the eighteenth century was dominated by the French Revolution, the final decade was to be dominated by Napoleon. The mark of this great man is noted in an early verse, quatrain I.31, which announces the wars which will follow on the Revolution:

> *Tant d'ans les guerres, en Gaule dureront*
> *Outre la course du Castulon Monarque,*
> *Victorie incerte trois grands couronneront*
> *Aigle, Coq, Lune, Lyon, Soleil en marque.*

So many years will wars last in France
Beyond the course of the Castulon Monarch,

Uncertain victory three great ones will be crowned
Eagle, Cock, Moon, Lion, Sun in marque.

As we have seen (page 303), the Castulon Monarch was the
statue of Liberty which overlooked the Place de la
Revolution in Paris, where the guillotine plied its trade
during the French Revolution. It had replaced one of Louis
XV torn down in 1792, and was sculpted by Dr Lemot in
the classical style, the female wearing a tunic or *castula*,
favoured by Roman women. The statue was short-lived – as
are most things steeped in guilt – remaining on its pedestal
for only eight years.

Perhaps the quatrain is ambiguous. Are there to be so
many wars *after* the removal of the Castulon Monarch, or
will the wars last for the same period – namely, eight years?
If we believe that Nostradamus is always right, then we
must accept the former, for in the unerring hands of
Napoleon, the wars lasted for well over eight years. In fact,
Nostradamus *does* offer us a useful clue as to which wars he
is speaking about, for, in the final line of the quatrain, he
draws up some astrological data: *Aigle, Coq, Lune, Lyon,
Soleil en marque.*

The symbolism is overtly astrological. The eagle (*Aigle*)
is the avian attribute of Jupiter. The cock (*Coq*), being a
male bird, is a symbol of Mars. A most interesting plate,
dated 1789, has survived those terrible years (*fig. 46*). It
shows the cock, symbol of martial France, crowing on a
cannon, over the barrel of which lies a broken chain,
symbolic of Liberty. Above the cock are the words '*Je
chante pour la Liberté*' ('I crow for Liberty').

Lune is of course the French for moon. *Lyon* is the lion
of Leo. *Soleil* is the French for Sun. *Marque* is Gemini,
since the bow-man Sagittarius, on the opposite side of the
zodiac, aims his arrows at this sign, intending to leave upon
it his mark (*marque*). The twins of Gemini are literally the

target of Sagittarius, who feels himself to be half-beast, and longs to become entirely human, both godlike and mortal, like the celestial twins. Thus interpreted, the line indicates the following planetary schema:

Sun	*Gemini*
Moon	*Leo*
Mars	*Leo*
Jupiter	*Leo*

Is there a period, relevant to the quatrain, when these astrological conditions exist? In the three-day period around 16 June 1801, the following planetary arrangement is seen:

Sun	25	*Gemini*
Moon	24	*Leo*
Mars	08	*Leo*
Jupiter	05	*Leo*

These positions are given for midday on 16 June. The arrangement may therefore be said to have persisted for almost two and a half days, covering most of the 15th, and the first hours of the 17th.[18] Almost certainly it would have been possible for Nostradamus to choose some other unique astrological data to represent the middle of 1801 (and thus designate the year) – however, he was probably intent on choosing some data (the *Leo* of this horoscope) which would symbolize the *Lyon* in the name Napo*leon*, for, as we shall see, this name is of great importance to the meaning of the quatrain. This day is virtually the middle of the calendrical year – we may take it that Nostradamus had in mind that the entire year of 1801 would be special in regard to peace, or at least, the end of wars in France.

Amazingly, this year saw no fewer than four treaties

which proclaimed peace for France. The peace at Luneville (9 February) ended the war with Austria. The peace of Aranjuez (21 March) proclaimed peace between France and Spain. The Treaty of Florence (28 March) and the Treaty of Madrid (29 September) established peace between Spain and Portugal, thus confirming peace for France. That these treaties did not last for very long may be what Nostradamus had in mind when he wrote of *Victorie incerte* as a prelude to introducing the idea that three great men would be crowned.

Who were these three great men (*trois grands*)? We observe that Nostradamus did not write of 'great kings' – it was as though he could see that the events of 1789 would imply a temporary end of the ancient blood-line of kings in France. The three men were the three Napoleons, all of whom were crowned (*couronneront*) Emperor in the years after 1801.

Napoleon literally crowned himself in Notre Dame, Paris, in 1804. His son, Francis Charles Joseph, was proclaimed Emperor Napoleon II during the Hundred Days. Finally, in 1851, Louis Napoleon organized a coup which led to the re-establishment of the Empire, confirming himself as Napoleon III in the following year. His sad history is told in other quatrains – see pages 192–7.

Chapter 9

The Nineteenth Century

*When we come to enumerate some few of the opinions
that have been expressed on the writings and character of
Nostradamus, it will be seen that a vast number of them
condemn him for charlatanry and imposture, especially as
we approach our own day. For now what is denominated
science accepts nothing for true but what is deducible from
the reason; it takes for granted that nothing can be
known respecting the future, beyond what cultivated
prudence can gather from a politic acquaintance with the
past . . .*

*(Charles A. Ward, Oracles of Nostradamus, 1891,
p. 35)*

Modern Paris might appear to have forgotten Nostradamus: not even a street, a boulevard or a square bears his
name. Even so, hidden away in various corners of Babylon
– as Nostradamus occasionally called the city – we may still
trace one or two stray footnotes that remind us of the
Master of Salon. For example, in the Musée des Souver-
ains are the short and long coats of the Emperor Napoleon,
both of which were famous in their days. These are rightly
taken by one modern commentator[1] on Nostradamus as
evidence of the accuracy of Quatrain VIII.57, which
presaged: *De robe courte parviendra à la longue* – 'From a

short coat he will attain to a long one.'

For all its strangeness, there is little of the esoteric in this line. The short coat was Napoleon's personal dress, which was noted as being short even in his lifetime: the long one is the trailing ermined coronation robe.

It is very possible that the two coats are displayed in the museum more in celebration of Nostradamus than of Napoleon. Both these men of genius are rightly revered by their countrymen, and many learned French scholars were, and are, aware of the importance of the coats both to the Master of Salon and the Master of the Empire.

The survival of one other such Nostradamian footnote is perhaps less likely to be intentional, however, for it has suffered so many mutations that we must accord its survival to nothing more remarkable than pure chance. In the Place Vendôme, in Paris, is a memorial officially called the Colonne d'Austerlitz, and popularly dubbed the Colonne Vendôme. Near the base is the Roman date for 1805: its bas-reliefs illustrate the heroic events in the German campaign conducted by Napoleon Bonaparte. The inscription opens with a dedication to the Emperor: NEAPOLIO. IMP. AUG. The last two words relate to the Roman concept of the *Imperator Augustus*, a title of the Emperor, and a reminder that Napoleon elected to adopt the ancient Roman garlands in place of the corrupt kingship which had led to the French Revolution. The first word, *Neapolio*, is a Graeco-Latin version of Napoleon's personal name. It is very possible that the choice of this version of the name for the memorial of 1805 was suggested by a quatrain written by Nostradamus. The French scholar Le Pelletier seems to be the first to point out that the Vendôme column bears the Graeco-Latin inscription, yet he did not see the implications of this for quatrains I.76 and IV.54.[2] It is true that since Le Pelletier wrote, the column has suffered various mutations: it was toppled in 1871 during the Commune, but was set up again in 1875, apparently at the expense of Gustave Courbet. The bronze plating was recast from the original moulds, so the inscription which Le Pelletier recorded is still *in situ*.

Both Nostradamus and Napoleon were men of destiny. In a very real sense, the two men represent the polarity of French achievement. On the one side, there is the mystic who could see into the future, and on the other hand the military genius, who created the future. It is almost inevitable that the sage should deal with the soldier in such depth.

The best modern study on Nostradamus and Napoleon is by Stewart Robb, who has provided a series of convincing commentaries which show that at least 41 quatrains deal with the exploits of this great Frenchman.[3] Nostradamus must have rated Napoleon's destined influence as being supreme in the history of France, for the futurity of no other individual – not even the Valois succession – receives such extensive cover in the *Prophéties*.

ANAGRAM FOR NAPOLEON

In the very first quatrain of Century VIII, Nostradamus opens with a triple anagram which is a scarcely disguised name of Napoleon:

PAU, NAY, LORON plus feu qu'à sang sera

PAU, NAY, LORON will be more fire than of blood

This is probably the most famous anagram in the whole of the Nostradamus oeuvre, if only because it is so transparent. Almost from the day Napoleon's name was written on the slate of history, the significance of the anagram has been recognized, for the three words may be reduced to the two:

NAPAULON ROY. As a result, the first line of the quatrain translates: 'Napoleon the King will be more fire than blood' – an almost perfect description of an Emperor who fought and manipulated his way to the French throne by war and not by the lineage of the blood-line which normally determined the succession of French kings.

Garencières, while offering a botched translation and commentary on the quatrains in 1672,[4] admitted that he did not know what to make of the prophecies which we now recognize as relating to Napoleon. For example, quatrain I.60, which we might have little difficulty in relating to historic Napoleon, troubles Garencières:

Un Empereur naistra pres d'Italie,
Qui à l'Empire sera vendu bien cher,
Diront avec quels gens il se ralie
Qu'on trouvera moins Prince que boucher.

An Emperor shall be born near Italy,
Who shall cost dear to the Empire,
They shall say, with what people he keepeth company!
He shall be found less a Prince than a butcher.

For once, Garencières gets fairly close to the French original, yet he remains puzzled by the prophecy. Since 'such an Emperour was not heard of . . .', Garencières rightly decides that the quatrain must be designed for fulfilment in the future. One can understand Garencières' perplexity in the seventeenth century, for the key to understanding the 40 or so Napoleon prophecies rests on issues unique to this great man – on such things as the curiosity of Napoleon's name, on the fact of his becoming an Emperor at all, on his unique symbols, and on his place of origin – all of which would remain shrouded in mystery until the actual event itself.

THE WILD NAME

Nostradamus dwells several times on the meaning of Napoleon's name. In the first line of quatrain I.76, in what is surely the Master's most amusing use of the Green Language, Nostradamus refers to a name which can only be that of Napoleon. The verse reads:

D'un nom farouche tel proferé sera,
Que les trois soeurs auront fato le nom:
Puis grand peuple par langue & fait duira,
Plus que nul autre aura bruit & renom.

At this stage, let us assume that the verse translates as:

Of a wild name, such as will seem,
That the three sisters would have pronounced the name:
Then he will lead great people by (the power of) his tongue and deeds,
More than any other he will have fame and renown.

First we must ask, what is wild or bestial about the name Napoleon? It might be argued, tongue in cheek, that Bonaparte means 'good only in part' (*buona* is Italian for 'good', and *parte* is 'in part'). However, this has nothing to do with his personal name, which seems to be derived from the Latinized version of Novapolis, that became the modern Naples (Napoli), the original 'New City', in the Greek, *Nea Polis*.

In reflecting upon the sound of this original name, for what he later (in quatrain IV.54) describes as a 'new name', Nostradamus exploited the arcane implications in a Green Language construction involving the word *Apollyon*. Napoleon became the New Apollyon – the *Ne'apollyon*.[5]

In the grimoire literature, derived from Biblical demonology, *Apollyon* is explained as Greek for 'the destroyer'. The name is the Greek equivalent of *Abaddon*, the demon king of the Bottomless Pit, so named in the *Book of Revelation*. In this grimoire literature, with which Nostradamus would have been familiar, this 'terrible being is reputed to appear in guises so grotesque that even those who conjure him by legitimate means may under certain circumstances be (quite literally) scared to death'.[6] It has been argued that the construction intended by Nostradamus is the Latin primitive negative, *Ne*, giving *Ne-Apollyon* – '*not* the Destroyer'. However, even the construction on the Place Vendôme column, thoroughly Francophile as it is, rejects this construction.

Obfuscations aside, Napoleon remains the archetypal destroyer. There is contemporaneous confirmation of this in a more ephemeral art form than the famous column. A cartoon by James Gillray (1756–1815) shows the general as the archetypal demonic Frenchman, with sharp horns and that grotesquely large hat which Gillray loved to caricature, addressing his buffoonish troops. The caption reads: 'Apollyon, the devil's generalissimo, addressing his legions'.

It is the literary demonic tradition which explains why Nostradamus can call Napoleon *un nom farouche* (a wild-beast name), deriving the name from that given to one of the most terrible demons of Biblical lore. When Lord Byron wrote an epic on Napoleon, he was clearly influenced by what Nostradamus had written nearly 300 years previously:

Thy wild name
Was ne'er more bruited in men's minds than now.

It is more likely that Byron was influenced by the *nom*

farouche of the *Prophéties* than by any thought of Greek etymology, as some commentators appear to believe. There is more than one line in Byron's *Ode To Napoleon* and *Ode From The French* which suggests a confident reliance upon the verses of Nostradamus.

The 'wild name' is one thing, but the Three Sisters are something else. They feature in line two (*Que les trois soeurs auront fato le nom*). What has this dubious christening to do with these three sisters? On one level, they are the three Fates, which explains the double-entendre towards the end of the second line: the sisters who have *fato* the name. The Latin word which has come to mean Fate in several European versions was derived from the past participle (*fatere*) of the verb 'facere'.

The first two lines constitute a couplet of real genius. Nostradamus not only uses the Green Language to denote the name of the great man who almost destroyed Europe, but even reflects on the fact that his passage through life was decreed by Fate. He was, in a famous phrase, a Man of Destiny. In making his name, which would reveal his terrible destiny, the three weird sisters elected to weave into it the name of the demon-prince of the Bottomless Pit. One of the unwritten implications in the verse is that the great people he leads (namely, the French armies, who will ravish Europe) will be conducted by him to the Bottomless Pit – which is hell. For this achievement, his name will receive fame and renown. When the Green Language nuances of this quatrain are stripped bare, are we entitled to sense a touch of irony in the verse?

There is some evidence to suggest that Napoleon was aware of the possible interpretations in the quatrains relating to his achievements. It is likely that he wore his distinctive hair-style, *teste raze* (shaven head), to meet with those quatrains which presaged such a close cropping.* As we have already observed, it is also likely that the short coat for which he was remarked could have been adopted to point to the corresponding line in prophecy VIII.76. It is even possible that his choice of stellar symbolism, which later raised Byron to irony (see below), was also influenced by the exegesis of the Nostradamus quatrains, once they had been applied to Napoleon.

NAPOLEON KING OF THE GAULS

A later quatrain which deals with Napoleon seems to sum up his progress through Europe admirably, and even takes note of his love-life. As in the previous case, quatrain IV.54 opens with a reflection upon his name:

Du nom qui oncquez ne fut au Roy Gaulois,
Jamais ne fust un fouldre si craintif,
Tremblant l'Italie l'Espagne & les Anglois,
De femme estrange grandement attentif.

In comparison with the preceding quatrain, this translates with admirable simplicity, even though some of the terms are sixteenth-century:

Of a name which never before was (given) to a French
   King,
Never was a lightning flash so to be feared,
Italy, Spain and the English tremble,
Nobly attentive to a foreign woman.

---

* Nostradamus used *teste raze*, in various orthographies, to denote Napoleon. The words pertain not merely to the Emperor's famous haircut, but also to the fact that his own 'reign' was possible only because the previous king had been disposed of by having his 'head cut off' (*teste raze*).

The name Emperor had not been given to a French king for 1,000 years, no more than was the name Napoleon, prior to the coming of the Corsican to power. We might observe that *fouldre* (which we translate as 'lightning flash') is the modern *foudre*, which also means thunderbolt. The French *craintif* actually means fearful (literally 'full of fear'), so we construct the translation to indicate that the lightning flash is to be feared. Napoleon successfully invaded both Italy and Spain, and with his threat of invasion of England, he could be said to have made even the English tremble. However, if the English had known their Nostradamus writings more fully, they would have recognized that the sage promised safety for their country, and final victory.

The word *estrange* in the last line of the quatrain is the equivalent of the modern *étrange*, meaning 'strange', as well as 'foreign'. Napoleon had several foreign ladies, to all of whom he was very attentive. The only one of importance who was both foreign and strange was Josephine, who besides being a Martinique creole, was deeply interested in the occult. It was this lady whom he married, in 1796: her previous husband had been guillotined two years before.

We cannot pass this quatrain without reflecting upon the importance of the symbolism in the first line, which is extraordinary in view of the fact that it refers to something which occurred over 200 years after the writing.

The lightning-flash imagery entered readily into Napoleonic mythology, for the Emperor is frequently linked with the image of a falling star, a meteor, or even a comet. One of the most simple examples is a contemporaneous woodcut depicting Napoleon confronting the Turks, in 1798 – presumably before or after the battle of the Pyramids. Hovering in the sky, between the aggressive Napoleon and the cowering Turks, is a radiant star, symbol both of Napoleon as the nascent star of Europe, and of the notion of Destiny, as God-given duty. With far deeper feeling for aesthetics, the poet Byron returns to this notion of the star time and time again, though the poet's star usually has a more apocalyptic ring about it than the crude woodprint.

In his *Ode To Napoleon*, Byron falls easily into stellar imagery, for it combines the classical thunderbolt fire of Zeus with the falling imagery of Biblical Apollyon:

> Since he, miscall'd the Morning Star,
> Nor man nor fiend hath fallen so far.

In the same ode, written in a single day on receiving news of the Emperor's abdication, Byron reveals his grasp of the stellar symbolism. He develops the conceit that Napoleon himself was aware of his link with the star of destiny, with the falling Morning Star, the Wormwood Star which would fall to the bottom of the Pit, for he elected to wear it upon his breast:

> The gewgaws thou were fond to wear,
> The star, the string, the crest?

In his *Ode From The French*, the poet waxes apocalyptic about his military hero who disappointed him by his later actions:

> Like the Wormwood Star foretold
> By the sainted Seer of old,
> Showering down a fiery flood,
> Turning rivers into blood.

One might be tempted to assume that the *sainted Seer* is Nostradamus, who did describe Napoleon in stellar terms. However, there is no doubt that Byron had in mind St John, the supposed author of *Revelation*. It was from this

Biblical prophetic text that both Nostradamus and Byron derived their imagery of the star called Wormwood.[7] The implications of this Biblical source for other Nostradamian quatrains will become clear later (see page 419).

The first line sets out a thing of great importance (for a French royalist writing in the sixteenth century), which is that this 'lightning-flash man' will have a name that was never before used by a French king. Not only would Napoleon refuse to be a king (he would elect to inaugurate the French title of Emperor); with the coming of Napoleon, the French line of kingship effectively came to an end, petering out finally with the Third Republic. Furthermore, among the line of kings which followed the writing of this quatrain, no new name was adopted until the coming of Napoleon. This can only mean that, in order to construct this first line, Nostradamus must have been aware of the progression of royal names which were to grace the throne of France for well over two centuries.

Even the name which Nostradamus adopts in later quatrains that deal with Napoleon reflect on this 'end of the line of kings'. As we saw earlier, one of the nicknames which Nostradamus uses for Napoleon is *teste raze* (shaven head). It is commonplace for commentators to point out that this is a reference to the fact that Napoleon wore his hair cropped short, and that such a style marked a profoundly symbolic departure from the practice of the French kings, who had worn luxurious periwigs. However, as is so often the case with Nostradamus, we can perceive a second level of meaning in this curious name, 'shaven head', for, with the coming of Napoleon, the head of kingship was (quite literally) cut off when Louis XVI was guillotined on 21 January 1793.

In quatrain VII.13, we learn that *La teste raze prendra la satrapie*, which means: 'The shaven head will take the satrapy'. According to the quatrain, he will hold as a tyranny for 14 years (*Par quatorze ans tiendra la tyrannie*). The coup of the 18 Brumaire (9 November) 1799 surely marks the beginning of this tyranny. It is tempting to follow the arguments of James Laver,[8] and look to Napoleon's abdication at Fontainebleau on 11 April 1814 as marking its end. Unfortunately, this carries the period some five months beyond the predicted period, and (as we have seen) Nostradamus is usually a stickler for accuracy in such things as dates and periods.

In fact, it was the defeat at Leipzig on 18 October 1813 which proved to be the final straw for Napoleon. It was as a direct result of this battle that France was invaded by the Duke of Wellington, Blücher and Schwarzenberg. If we take this climacteric as the standard, then the Napoleonic 'satrapy' came to an end in just a few days short of 14 years.

NAPOLEON'S TRAITOR

The more glorious years of Napoleon's traitor really belong to the eighteenth century, but we shall deal with this period here. In quatrain X.34, Nostradamus writes:

Gaulois qu'empire par guerre occupera,
Par son beau frere mineur sera trahy,
Par cheval rude voltigeant trainera,
Du fait le frere long temps sera hay.

The Frenchman who occupies the empire through war,
Will be betrayed by his younger brother in law,
He will lead with a boisterous leaping horse,
For this deed, the brother will be hated for a long time.

For once, there is little obfuscation and all is clear after the event. First, we must observe that, in the days of Nostradamus, there was not even a dream of Empire in

France, yet here it is mentioned openly – along with the intimation that a Frenchman would occupy this same Empire in wars. With the advantage of hindsight vision, we have none of the problems which faced Garencières, as we recognize in the line the Emperor Napoleon. The brother-in-law who will betray the Emperor is somewhat less famous, yet he was no mere fabrication of a sixteenth-century poet – he did have an actual existence. Joachim Murat was one of the many of humble origins who rose in the ranks through the Revolution and the wars which the Revolution bred.

Murat was invaluable to Napoleon in the early years. It was Murat who had helped Bonaparte in the famous *coup d'état* of 1799. It was he who led the retreat from Moscow, after Napoleon returned to France. It was he who suppressed the rising in Madrid, and although he was defeated by the English in Sicily, he was with Napoleon at the victorious battle of the Pyramids.

Murat married Caroline Bonaparte, and thus became Napoleon's brother-in-law, fulfilling some of the requirements of the second line of the quatrain. Born in 1767, he was older than Napoleon by two years, but he was minor (*mineur*) to him in rank, even after Napoleon made him King of Naples in 1808. In order to save his own throne, when Napoleon's power seemed to be on the wane, Murat negotiated behind the Emperor's back with the Austrians. The idea of his being a peasant turncoat is perhaps one of the layers of meaning in the strange phrase, *rude voltigeant*, which can mean something like 'impetuous changeable one'. Napoleon was shocked by the treason, and perhaps even more shocked by the recognition of the precision of Nostradamus' prophecy, which must have been brought to his notice.

The curious reference, in the third line, to the boisterous

leaping horse (*cheval rude voltigeant*) is to Murat's future fame as a highly skilled cavalry officer. The phrase, *cheval ... voltigeant*, could be translated as 'flying horse', but *voltige* can also mean mounted gymnastics, and a *voltigeur* is a light-infantry soldier. It was this very characteristic (perhaps, again, spurred on by his reading of Nostradamus) that Byron dwelled upon in his *Ode From The French*:

> Then sold thyself to death and shame
> For a meanly royal name;
> Such as he of Naples wears,
> Who thy blood-bought title bears.
> Little didst thou deem, when dashing
>   On thy war-horse through the ranks,
>   Like a stream which burst its banks
> While helmets cleft, and sabres clashing,
> Shone and shiver'd fast around thee –
> Of the fate at last which found thee!

The fate which did at last find Murat was not one anticipated by a distinguished cavalry leader: in 1815 he was put against a wall and shot. This execution is hinted at in the curious finial to the quatrain. The orthography of *hay* suggests the sixteenth-century equivalent of the transitive verb *hair*, to hate – which is how we have translated it above. However, the French *haie* can also mean a line of rifles, or bayonets. Perhaps, with his usual verbal cunning, Nostradamus has both meanings in mind, for, without much dislocation, the line might read: *Du fait le frere long temps sera hay* ('Because of this, the brother will eventually be put before bayonets').

The interesting fact is that Murat, and his relationship with Napoleon, occupied Nostradamus in a different context. The complicated history of the first decade of the nineteenth century contained within what we might call the 'historical summary' of the *Epistle*, written in 1558, deals with this:

> ... *par le tiers qui estendra ses forces vers le circuit de l'Orient de l'Europe aux pannos l'a profligé & succombe & par voile marine fera ses extensions, à la Trinacrie Adriatique par Mirmido & Germaniques du tout succombe & sera la seste Barbarique de tout des Nations grandement affligée et dechassé.*

> ... by the third estate, which will extend its powers toward the edge of the East of Europe to the ragged peoples there profligated and conquered, and by maritime sails will make extensions, to Sicily, to the Ottoman Adriatic and Germany. All will be brought low, and the Barbarian gauntlet will be greatly afflicted and dispossessed by all the Nations.

This short excerpt from the prose of Nostradamus shows just how deeply committed he is to Green Language obscurity. We must read *le tiers* as a reference to the *Tiers*, the third estate which gave rise to the French Revolution, on the back of which Napoleon (and, of course, Murat) rose to greatness. While it is evident that *Tiers* must be translated as Third Estate, it has been taken by some French commentators as reference to the Third Republic.

Pannos is a curious word. While the Greek *Panos* means 'torch', we feel that the Latin *Pannosus* is probably more apposite, meaning 'ragged, tattered'. We hazard a guess that by *Mirmido*, Nostradamus meant Greece – connoting that the country would have been taken over by ruffians – that is, the *Turks*. The *Myrmidons* were a class of martial men who lived in Thessaly, northern Greece. They entered popular literature at the siege of Troy, which is part of the symbolic background to this Nostradamus text. By extension, the word can mean 'hired ruffian'. *La seste Barbarique* seems to be ambiguous. It is probably *la ceste Barbarique*, the barbaric gauntlet. The *cestus* is the *caestus* used in gladiatorial boxing displays – a kind of weighted glove made of leather thongs and metal strips. In this context it certainly refers to the notoriously cruel, heavy-handed Ottoman glove. It is quite typical of Nostradamus that he should combine, in one quatrain, two specialist terms from a similar historical context – in this case, from the Roman gladiatorial combats – the *caestus* and the *Myrmillo*, or net-fighter. The notion of an Ottoman empire in retreat would have been a great surprise to the contemporaries of Nostradamus.

Once Green Language obscurities in the French passage have been removed, we see that it contains a fair description of the extent of Napoleon's empire, along with his aspirations for consolidation of the Empire. At the point of its greatest power, Napoleon's domain stretched from the North Sea to Sicily (*Trinacie*), including much of what we now call Germany and Italy. There was a mafia-cabal of Napoleon's brothers acting as kings on the edges of the European empire – Louis in Holland, Jerome in Westphalia and Joseph (who figures in the quatrain) in Naples.

The circuit of the east of Europe (*le circuit de l'Orient de l'Europe*) is a very apt phrase in the Napoleonic context. Napoleon did attempt to establish a secure eastern edge to the Mediterranean, even going so far as to attack Syria.

We read *Mirmido* as relating to Greece, at that time in thrall to the Ottomans of Turkey. A French treaty with the Ottomans, signed in 1802, established freedom of navigation in the Black Sea. Sebastiani, a Corsican colonel, was entrusted in 1801 with taking the draft of the treaty to the Ottoman leader, Selim. Following orders, he spied out the land during his journey through the Ionian islands, in preparation for the invasion of Egypt, which was visualized as possibly being directed from Greece. This preparation led to Napoleon's winning the battle of the Pyramids and taking control of Cairo. The quatrain relating to this enterprise is discussed on page 220 ff.

THE ITALIAN EARTHQUAKE

Just as Nostradamus pinpointed the French Revolution of 1789 as pivotal for French history, so he pinpointed 1848–9 as pivotal for the history of Italy. While it is clear that IX.31 involves the Garibaldini exploits of 1849, it is also evident that quatrain X.64 relates to the destinies of the various cities in northern Italy, in what were then Savoy, Venetia and the Duchy of Florence. The centres for each of these regions are mentioned by name in X.64:

> *Pleure Milan, pleure Lucques, Florence,*
> *Que ton grand Duc sur le char montera,*
> *Changer le siege pres de Venise s'advance,*
> *Lors que Colonne à Rome changera.*

For the moment, we may translate the verse as:

> Cry Milan, cry Lucca, Florence,
> That your great Duke will mount the chariot,
> To change the siege he advances near Venice,
> When the Colonne will change in Rome.

The quatrain deals with the future history of these domains in 1848–9. To appreciate the significance of the quatrain, we must glance at events in these three cities during that period. In one way or another, these cities were involved in the terrible fight to expel the Austrians and to set up a constitutional democracy.

In the first line – *Pleure Milan, pleure Lucques, Florence* –
Milan and Lucca (*Lucques*) are the cities which weep. The
Austrians were forced to leave Milan, and by the beginning
of July all northern Italy was under the aegis of the House
of Savoy. However, after the armistice agreed by Charles
Albert, Lombardy and Venetia were ceded to the Austrians.

Lucca alone almost helps us date the quatrain, for in
1847 it fell under the control of the Duchy of Florence. In
the mid-nineteenth century the city of Florence was the
centre of a vast Duchy of Tuscany, ruled by the Grand
Duke. This explains *grand Duc* in line two. In 1849, the
Grand Duke of Tuscany was Leopold II. In this year, the
republic was proclaimed in Tuscany, and Leopold left for
Gaeta, ostensibly to confer with the Pope. Perhaps this is
what the second line means: *Que ton grand Duc sur le char
montera* – When your Grand Duke climbs 'into his
chariot.'

'Your', in this instance, means 'the Florentines'. In fact,
this line is typically ambiguous. The image of the Grand
Duke in his chariot may refer not merely to his final
departure (after his expulsion by his subjects) in 1859, but
also to his return from Rome in 1849. Both journeys were
of great significance in the history of northern Italy. When
the Grand Duke returned to Florence in July 1849, he did
so under the protection of an Austrian army, which lost
him his popularity, and marked the beginning of the end
for the Duchy. In 1852 Leopold rejected the demands for
both a constitutional Tuscany and a united Italy. In
1859, when another war between Piedmont and Austria
threatened, the Florentines rose. The grand Duke climbed
into his chariot for the last time and quit Tuscany, for
good, in April 1859. He abdicated after refusing to take part
in the war against Austria, and to grant a constitution.

Line three of the quatrain refers to the siege of Venice.
Blockaded by sea, and reduced to starvation, the city
capitulated on 24 May. The last line (*Lors que Colonee à*

Rome changera) seems to refer to the famous Colonna family of Rome, but its meaning remains obscure. The first French attacks on Rome were repulsed by Garibaldi, but in July 1848 a larger French force re-established the temporal power of the Pope. Victor Emmanuel II was the only hope for achieving national unity.

It is understandable that so many commentators have read quatrain IX.31 as relating to an earthquake, or a bombardment. The opening phrase, *Le tremblement de terre*, 'the trembling of earth', could easily be seen as a reference to such a cataclysm:

> *Le tremblement de terre à Mortara,*
> *Cassich sainct George à demy perfondrez,*
> *Paix assoupie, la guerre esveillera,*
> *Dans temple à Pasques abysmes enfondrez.*

Earth tremble at Mortara,
Cassich saint George half-founded,
Peace puts to sleep, war awakens,
In (the) temple at Easter abysses will be undermined.

Roberts sees the quatrain as predicting terrific artillery fire, the 'almost defeat' of England, and the bombing of Coventry in 1941. He gives no evidence for this choice of city or date. Cheetham sees the quatrain as referring to an earthquake, but cannot understand how this can involve England (like Roberts, she has tripped over the arcane reference to St George). However, careful analysis shows that the quatrain has nothing to do with an earthquake, save perhaps in a figurative sense.

Mortara, in the first line, sets the scene and date. Jean-Charles de Fontbrune seems to have been the first to note the historical context of the quatrain, which is revealed through the word Mortara.[9] Unfortunately, his translation of the quatrain is absurd: it is simply not true that half the Italian army was overthrown at Mortara.

The Austrians defeated the Piedmontese at Mortara in Lombardy in 1849 – a key date in Italian history. The theme of the quatrain is revealed as the watershed of the Austrian struggle to keep control over Italy. It also points to an important theme of the quatrain – the sense of unity which developed among Italians as a result of the struggle against the weakening Austrian dynasty.

In 1849, Charles Albert of Sardinia broke the armistice he had signed with the Austrians occupying northern Italy, and attacked them. While fighting took place at Mortara on 21 March, his disastrous five-day campaign ended at Novara. After his defeat, on 23 March 1849, he abdicated. The great Victor Emmanuel II entered the scene, negotiating strongly with the Austrians by steadfastly refusing to accept their terms. He was soon established as the champion of Italian freedom.

The date of the former conflict, in this first line, is linked with the fourth line, wherein Easter (*Pasques*) is mentioned. This affords a precise date to locate the quatrain. In modern times, Easter is a movable feast determined as the first Sunday after the full moon following the vernal equinox. However, Nostradamus was writing before the Gregorian reformation, and the church of Gaul (which included those cities and towns wherein Nostradamus lived – and, incidentally, those mentioned in this quatrain) observed Easter on 21 March. This, as we have seen, was the date of the battle of Mortara.

Typical of Nostradamus, we have been given one clear place-name and one encoded date, by which we might identify the theme of the quatrain. Beyond these two, the remaining references within the quatrain, though relatively arcane, are explicable. Outside the present context, the

place-name *Cassich* has no meaning, there being no town or
village of this name. There may be some connection with
Garibaldi, who was born at Nice: Cassis is 44 kilometres
from Toulon. With a stretch of imagination, it may be
argued that *Cassich* is Casale Monferrato in Piedmont,
which resisted the Austrians in 1849, the date (as we
shall see) to which this quatrain refers. In 1859, the
Cacciatori delle Alpi, under Garibaldi's command, combined with the *Carabinieri Genovesi* in Casale, at the
beginning of the second Lombardy campaign. However,
internal evidence does not suggest this as the subject of the
quatrain.

It is more likely that the word is Green Language, based
on the name *Via Cassia*, the ancient Roman roadway which
led from the north of Italy – from Modena in Lombardy –
to Rome. Its importance is that the Duke of Modena was
Francis V, who succeeded in 1846, and, as a result of local
agitation, invited to his support an Austrian garrison. This
is a theme dealt with in another quatrain. Perhaps the
Germanic ending to *Cassich* (*ich*) is a play on this notion of
Austrian dominance, even though this is not really an
essential part of the Green Language referent. Even so, the
fact is that Francis was driven from Modena by events in
Italy, and ended his life in Munich (Mun*ich*), under the
protection of the Austrians. The importance in the quatrain
is what lay at the other end of the *Via Cassia* – the city of
Rome.

The reference to *sainct George* is not to England, as so
many modern commentators assert. It is offered by Nostradamus as a clue to a *date*: the festive day of St George, 23
April. On 23 April 1849, the Garibaldini were called from
Rieti to Rome. To arrive at this city the soldiers would have
taken the road south, following the ancient *Via Cassia*. On
the next day (24 April) Garibaldi was made Brigadier
General of the Roman Republic. In the following week, he

had his first victory over the French at Rome, but was wounded. This short-lived Republic fell in less than two months, but it was a herald of things to come, which is possibly why Nostradamus refers to the event as half-founded (*demy perfondez*).

Why does Nostradamus, usually so economic with his words, expend a whole line on a fairly obvious 'Third Man cuckoo–clock' theme – namely, that peace puts to sleep, while war awakens? In fact, analysis shows that this innocent-seeming line is the key to the significance of the quatrain. In line three (*Paix assoupie, la guerre esveillera*), *assoupir* can mean 'to make drowsy, or sleepy'; but in a figurative sense it means to 'stifle, deaden or suppress'. Just as *assoupir* has to do with sleeping, so *esveillera* (*éveiller* in modern French) has to do with awakening. The Italian word *risorgimento* literally means 'awakening'. *Il Risorgimento* was the awakening to national greatness witnessed in the revolutionary impulse of the mid–nineteenth century. One readily forms the impression that Nostradamus knew the key word which historians would use later to denote the main stream of events in Italy during the nineteenth century. As Nostradamus recognized in this line, it was the wars to expel the Austrians which really awoke Italian desire for unification, and changed the future of Italy.

We now see what seems to be an 'earthquake' (*tremblement de terre*) for what it really is. It is a prediction of the spiritual trembling and awakening of the whole land (*terre*) of Italy. Although the word in Green Language has overtones of terror (the Latin *terra* is, by homophony, also *terror*), this line was no presage of catastrophe, but a recognition of the sundering which would be required to forge a united Italy.

The abyss which had swallowed up Italy – the Austrians – was removed. The phrase *abysmes enfondrez* in line four is a curious one, and the latter word does not exist in the

French language. The verb *fonder* is used in a typical Nostradamian duality of rhyme. Since the verb *fonder* means to lay a foundation, the phrase seems to mean, approximately, the abyss is undermined. What, then, is the abysm – the gulf or depth? Surely it was the abysm of Austria, which had swallowed up Italy, and which was itself weakened – soon to be removed by the Garibaldini. It is pertinent that the imagery continued in the line is that of laying a foundation stone of a temple. One wonders, indeed, if the fourth line relates to one of the most famous and typical of Garibaldi's unconventional acts. When in Palermo Cathedral (perhaps the *temple* of the line) he sat on the high throne of the altar during mass, dressed in his revolutionary red shirt, and unsheathed his sword during the reading of the gospel.

EARTHQUAKE IN NAPLES

'The French,' wrote Garencières trenchantly, 'have many Villeneufues, the Germans many Newstads, the Italians & Spaniards many villanovas.' He was writing of quatrain I.24, in which the words *Cité nefue* (new city) appeared for the first of many times in the *Prophéties*. Roberts translated this particular *Cité nefue* into a quasi-Americanese, and obtained *Nu-Rem-Burg*, which carried him far away from Nostradamus, and into his own dark hobby-horse, the Nazis. Le Pelletier, with more sense and more feeling for the French language, observed that *cité neuve* is a reference to the Paris reconstructed under Napoleon III. The two words seem to have been a problem for commentators from very early times. In 1656, Jaubert found them puzzling, for he admitted of verse X.49 (in which the same two words appear) that 'it is difficult to discover what this quatrain means . . . for in Europe are many towns called the New City'.[10] He came to the conclusion that Nostradamus was using a Provençal term, related to the *Cité Neuve de Malthe* (Malta), the Valetta which had been built after the great siege of 1565.

Nostradamus uses the pair of words frequently, and we have come to the conclusion that they are rarely intended to mean the same thing: a clue to the intended place-name must be derived from the sense within the relevant quatrain.

The prophecy runs:

> *Jardin du monde aupres de cité neufve.*
> *Dans le chemin des montagnes cavées,*
> *Sera saisi & plongé dans la cuve,*
> *Beuvant par force eaux soulphre envenimées.*

> Garden of the world near to the new city.
> In the route of the caved mountains,
> Will be seized and plunged in the vat,
> Forced to drink enpoisoned sulphurous waters.

The three words, *Jardin du monde* (Garden of the World), in this quatrain have given almost the same amount of trouble to interpreters as *cité neufve*. Jaubert's interpretation is unique, for he saw in it a reference to a particular person: he points out that *Cosme* in Greek means 'the world', and twists the phrase so that it relates to Cosme du Jardin.

Roberts, who saw this as a startling prophecy of catastrophe involving a tremendous tidal wave of poisoned waters, seems to have no problem identifying the Garden of the World. He suggests that Atlantic City, in the United States, fits this quatrain 'nicely', as the New City and Garden of the World. The poisoned waters will overwhelm the mountain-like skyscrapers (*montagnes cavées*) of such a modern city. In fact, we need not look beyond Europe for the site of the Garden of the World . . .

The British Library copy of Garencières' rare book on Nostradamus (1672) was owned in the seventeenth century by Daniel Thomas, who left some interesting manuscript notes in the margins.[11] The notes opposite quatrain X.49 would suggest that he had visited Naples as a tourist, for he seems to be ticking off each place he has seen, against the corresponding lines of the verse. He notes:

1. *Italy Is called the Garden of ye world.*
2. *new City is Naples (Neopolis).*
3. *Mount Posilip digged thro.*
4. *near wh Is ye burning [illegible] & ye sulphorous Grotto.*

Thomas seems to have had no doubt that Nostradamus intended the quatrain to refer to Naples in Italy, and we presume that he sees any threat in the verse as being linked with volcanic activity. He was quite right about the tunnelled mountain, which Nostradamus had described in the curious *Dans le chemin des montagnes cavées*. In AD 27, a tunnel, over 2,200 feet long, and in places over 70 feet high, had been cut through the promontory of Posilipo by Marcus Agrippa. It had been an extraordinary feat of engineering (though soundly beaten by the earlier double-tunnel of Eupalinus on Samos).

Is Nostradamus predicting an earthquake or a tidal wave for the land around Naples? The area is fissured, the telluric forces issue steam charged with hydrochloric acid, and boiling water lies only a few feet underground.

Since Nostradamus offered no internal clue by which we might date the event in the quatrain, we cannot be sure which earth disturbance the seer had in mind. The worst – the earthquake on the island of Ischia, in 1883 – did throw up terrible waters, and completely destroyed Casamicciola, as well as doing very great damage to Florio, Lacco Ameno and Serrara Fontana. The only comparable damage in more recent times was man-made, for much of Naples succumbed to allied US and British bombing during 1943.

Of course, as always with Nostradamus, the verse is not quite what it seems. The seer obviously intended an irony in the sweet-seeming phrase, Garden of the World (*Jardin du monde*), for while the area is one of intense natural beauty it was also feared in ancient times. The area between Puteoli and Naples (the modern Solfatara) was called the *Phlegreai Campi*, the Phlegrean Fields, the burning fields. The irony rests in the notion that *Phlegethon* (from the Greek word, meaning 'ablaze') is an underground river of fire in Hades. By association, the area mentioned in the verse becomes the Garden of the *Under*world.

Sadly, as we are unable to date the quatrain, we cannot determine whether the prophecy deals with the quake of 1883, or whether it is still laid up for our future. The one thing we may be sure of is that Nostradamus did not predict a sulphurous inundation of Atlantic City.

THE BATTLE OF TRAFALGAR

Three remarkable quatrains concentrate on the most important naval event during the Napoleonic wars – the Battle of Trafalgar, which marked the end of Napoleon's attempt to dominate the seas.

The most obvious of these quatrains is I.77:

> *Entre deux mers dressera promontoire*
> *Que puis mourra par le mords du cheval,*
> *Le sien Neptune pliera voille noire,*
> *Par Calpte & classe aupres de Rocheval.*

For the moment, we will translate this as:

Between two seas will rise a promontory
Who then will die by the bite of a horse,
Neptune's own will furl the black sail,
By Gibraltar and fleet near Rocheval.

The real problem for commentators is the second line, which is usually taken as referring to the unfortunate Villeneuve, who had commanded the allied Franco–Spanish fleet at Trafalgar. Some commentators have inaccurately claimed that the French Vice-Admiral's death was caused by the bite of a horse, precisely as the second line seems to indicate. However, he committed suicide by pushing a long pin into his heart.

In fact, one of the French words for a pin is *cheville*, sufficiently close to *cheval* to warrant attention. The *cheville* is the 'little key' or tenon which holds together pieces of wood, and can be made of either wood or metal. The French phrase *Avoir l'âme chevillé au corps* (to have the soul pinned to the body) may be relevant, for Villeneuve, in pushing a pin into his heart, was withdrawing his own soul, pinned as it was to his body.

However, in the sixteenth century, the word *cheval* was also used to denote a wooden trestle, used to punish disobedient or rebellious soldiers. This *cheval* is a flat piece of wood, laid upon its back and supported by a trestle, on which the condemned soldier is tied, with balls and chains attached to his feet.[12] We may have no doubt that Nostradamus was using the word in this sense, for although the unfortunate Vice-Admiral did not die strapped to such an apparatus, he had considered himself due for punishment as a rebel. That Nostradamus had in mind the death of Villeneuve in this line is almost beyond question because of the implications of the third line, which seems to refer to the death of his naval opponent, the great Nelson.

The black sail (*voille noire*) of the third line is a classical reference to the forgetfulness of the Greek hero Theseus,[13] who failed to keep his promise to change the black sails of his ship (required by tradition for those who sailed to the Minotaur of Crete). As a result of the error, his father Aegeus, thinking his son was dead, leapt to his death into the sea. It was Villeneuve's own imagination which led to his suicide.

One of the most extraordinary things about this prophecy is that there was, among the British ships at Trafalgar, a 72-gunner called *Theseus*. This had a direct link with Nelson, for it had been the ship in which he had first hoisted his flag as rear-admiral: it remains a poignant symbol of his own death at Trafalgar. In the tragic history of Villeneuve, the black sail was imagined, for Napoleon did not send a message of death, at all. Villeneuve committed suicide because he believed that he was to be disgraced by Napoleon. In the equally tragic history of Nelson, the black sail is both apposite to the history of Trafalgar and pertinent, in view of the name of his first flag-ship: '. . . the name of the *Theseus* shall be immortalized . . .' promised the ship's company, with Nelson over them.[14]

Le sien Neptune in line three is a curious phrase, yet it offers a construction sufficiently close to an anagram for Nelson to be worth noting: Le SiEN NEptune = NE L S EN.

The meaning of the fourth line seems something of a mystery, until one realizes that it pertains to the most important consequence of the battle of Trafalgar. *Calpte* is surely *Calpe*, one of the old names for Gibraltar: originally it was the ancient Greek for one of the pillars of Hercules which marked the entrance to the Atlantic Ocean. Cape Trafalgar, off which the famous battle is supposed to have been fought, is only a few miles off the western end of the Strait of Gibraltar. In fact, Trafalgar is merely a convenient name, since the battle was fought over a considerable distance in the seas between Cape Trafalgar and Cadiz. The battle ended with Gravina fleeing with his surviving French and Spanish ships, to Cadiz, only 25 miles to the north. Nostradamus is not merely pointing to the location of the famous sea-battle, but also indicating the British connection, for even in 1805, Gibraltar was firmly in the hands of the British.

We presume, from the context, that *Rocheval* must be so named to give a rhyme for *cheval*, and that Nostradamus was referring to a place-name beginning with Rock (*Roche*). This assumption is based on the recognition that there is no place in the area so named. Indeed, there is no important port in France, Spain or Portugal with the name Rocheval.

The only significant place-name on the relevant south-western littoral of Spain and Portugal is Roca (Cap da Roca). This is near Lisbon (*aupres de Rocheval*). Undoubtedly, this reading points to the history of Spain subsequent to the battle of Trafalgar.

VILLENEUVE

Napoleon, disappointed in his aims by Trafalgar, announced that he would conquer the sea by power of the land. He demanded that the various countries of Europe should close all their ports to the British, and refuse to supply Britain with goods. Portugal, being Britain's ally, refused to participate in this blockade and declined to close Lisbon. In support, the British Government sent an expeditionary force to Portugal, in August 1808. This was the thin edge of the British wedge which, under the guiding genius of Wellington, eventually drove Napoleon out of Spain. Nostradamus paints a picture of the consequences of the battle of Trafalgar that marked the downfall of the Napoleonic conquests to the west of France.

The earliest is quatrain I.24, which is, to say the very least, obscure:

> *A Cité neufue pensif pour condamner,*
> *L'oysel de proye au ciel, se vient offrir*
> *Apres victoire à captifs pardonner,*
> *Cremone & Mantoue grands maux aura à souffrir.*

> A new City thoughtful to condemn,
> The bird of prey in the sky, offers itself
> After victory captives to be pardoned,
> Cremona and Mantua will suffer great evil.

Cité neufue (new city) may be read as *Villeneuve* (new town). This was the name of the French Vice-Admiral who opposed Nelson on that fateful day in 1805. That he should have been *pensif pour condamner* is explained from the fact that, later, fearful that he was to be condemned and punished by Napoleon for a seeming failure to obey orders, he committed suicide. In a final letter he explained that, having been cursed by the Emperor, his life was 'a disgrace and death a duty'. By a strange twist of fortune, he was trapped in his own thoughts, and condemned himself, for Napoleon had planned not to punish him at all.[15]

L'oysel de proye is probably an equivalent of *oiseau de proie*, which means 'bird of prey'. One of the ships under the command of Villeneuve was the *Aigle*, or 'Eagle'. This ship, captured by the British, was driven ashore and wrecked during the storms which followed the battle. However, it is more likely that the bird of prey intended by Nostradamus is the ever-popular Napoleon, with his carefully adopted eagle symbolism, which he derived from that of the Roman Empire.

If *victoire* was intended by Nostradamus as a double-entendre for a proper name, then it corresponds to the

British flag-ship the *Victory*, which led the British fleet, and on the decks of which Nelson died. In fact, as the line indicates, the British treated the numerous French and Spanish captives with remarkable generosity after their victory – to a point, indeed, where some of the captured ships managed to escape. However, the reference could be restricted merely to Villeneuve, for the Vice-Admiral was taken prisoner, and repatriated in April 1806, in accord with a formal exchange of prisoners. His letters show that he was treated with infinite deference. If Villeneuve is intended, then the line may be construed to reflect the seeming injustice that while the British lost their own leader, Vice-Admiral Lord Nelson, the French leader survived as a prisoner, and was treated well.

One true and romantic story of a rescue of a French sailor has rightly been taken by the historian Geoffrey Bennett as a sign that Nelson did not pray in vain that 'humanity after victory' would predominate.[16] Among a number of French sailors rescued and taken on board the *Revenge* turned out to be a woman called Jeanette, who had stowed away with her husband. In one version of the story, she was naked, in another disguised as a man, but either way she was treated with extraordinary kindness by officers and men. The happy ending to this true story is that Jeanette was eventually reunited with her husband, who had survived the sinking of his ship, the *Achille*, which exploded during the conflict. Since Nostradamus is emphasizing names in this quatrain, it is probably not too far-fetched to propose (assuming that he foresaw the Jeanette incident) that he was showing that the *Revenge* chose not to live up to its name in deference to Nelson's wishes (*Apres victoire à captifs pardonner*).

The curious French word *maux*, in the final line, must surely be read as *maudit*, meaning 'cursed' or 'wretched'. This implies that the line should translate: 'Cremona and

Mantua will have great evils to suffer'. This line appears to be the only obstacle to affirming a link between this quatrain and Trafalgar. At first sight, neither Cremona nor Mantua (both in northern Italy) appears to have anything to do with the battle of Trafalgar, nor were there ships in the battle with names which make sense of either of these place – names. However, on analysis a meaning is revealed.

The collapse of Mantua to the French, on 2 February 1796, when the Austrians under the command of Wurmser surrendered, had marked the end of Austrians resistance in Italy. The city was assigned to the French under the Peace of Lunéville, but reverted to the Austrian again in 1814. It was in the same year that Cremona (like the rest of Lombardy) fell to the Austrians. We may therefore take each of these cities as symbols of the end of Napoleon's power to the east of Europe, just as Trafalgar was a symbol of his decline to the west of Europe. Both cities did indeed suffer greatly, when the French took over from the Austrians, and vice versa.

GRAVINA

Quatrain VII.26 has also been seen as relating to the battle of Trafalgar.[17] So far as we can determine, it deals with the aftermath of Trafalgar.

> *Fustes & galeres autour de sept navires,*
> *Sera livrée une mortelle guerre:*
> *Chef de Madric recevra coup' de vires,*
> *Deux eschapez & cinq menez à terre.*

> Gun-boats and war-galleys around seven ships,
> Will be given over to mortal war:
> The chief of Madrid will receive potent blows,
> Two escape and five are taken to land.

This quatrain clearly relates to a sea battle, yet Roberts sees in it the idea of flying boats, and a forecast of Howard Hughes' *Spruce Goose*. Along with this, he somehow sees in the quatrain references to multiple nuclear warheads being fired from underwater submarines! In the seventeenth century, Jaubert had been more restrained, for he interpreted it as relating to a horrible naval combat in November 1555. The fight had been between the French ships, out of Dieppe, and the Spanish. In this action, fought off Calais and Dover, the French captured five Spanish ships. Unfortunately, Jaubert overlooked the fact that this would scarcely have been a prediction, as quatrain VII.26 appeared only in the 1558 edition of the *Prophéties*, and was probably not even written until long after the event he described.

A more careful assessment of what Nostradamus actually wrote in the quatrain shows that it dealt with an important naval engagement which took place shortly after the battle of Trafalgar. The announcement of a naval battle theme is made brilliantly in the first line, by a unique use of language. *Fustes* is from the Italian *fusta*, and in the sixteenth century was used to denote the wooden carriage for the barrel of a gun. It is therefore a word ideally suited to denote wooden sailing cannon-vessels. The word *galeres* is defined as a ship of war designed for rowing, but with two masts, such as were used in the Mediterranean.[18] Later, we shall see why these different types of boats are represented as being among seven other ships.

Exceptionally with Nostradamus, if we seek to understand the meaning of this quatrain, we must turn first of all to the last line.

By 23 November 1805, two days after the battle of Trafalgar, and after a diminution of the full gales which followed, the senior French officer, Commodore Casmao-Kerjulien, decided to try and retake some of the allied ships which Nelson had captured. Commanding the *Pluton*, he led four other ships of the line, the *Rayo*, *Indomptable*, *Neptuno* and *San Francisco de Asisi*. The Commodore was not successful in his bid, for he was confronted by a line of British ships twice his number. Even so, his courageous attempt deflected the attention of the British long enough for the frigates accompanying them to retake the *Neptuno* and Alva's flagship, the *Santa Ana*, and see them safely into Cadiz. In this account we see a perfect explanation of the last line of the quatrain: in this incident, two ships escaped (*deux eschapez*), while the five that participated in their rescue also returned to port (*cinq menez à terre*). Quite typically of Francophile Nostradamus, the finale to the allied disaster of Trafalgar is represented in terms of French bravery.

What, then, are the seven ships (*sept navires*) of the first line? Clearly, this cannot refer to the full complement of ships that fought at Trafalgar. The allied fleet consisted of 33 warships and five frigates, which were confronted by 27 British battleships and six frigates. However, Nostradamus is being painfully specific. The largest ships in the battle were the three-deckers: the Franco-Spanish fleet had four of these, while the British had three. The Spanish three-deckers were the *Santissima Trinidad* of 140 guns, the *Santa Ana* and *Principe de Asturias* of 112 guns, and the *Rayo* of 100 guns. The British were the *Victory*, *Britannia* and *Royal Sovereign*, all of 100 guns. Could it be that these were the seven great ships, surrounded by the others, the *Fustes & galeres* of the first line?

The deadly war (*mortelle guerre*) of Trafalgar needs no retelling here. Suffice it to say that the British dead numbered 449, with 1,242 wounded. Details of the Franco-Spanish losses are not so precisely recorded, yet it is known that over 5,500 were killed or wounded. After the battle, the British held 17 ships of the line (some of which later escaped, or were wrecked during the following gales). All the British ships were intact, though many were badly damaged.

The third line is also pertinent to the post-Trafalgar episodes, for it refers to Frederico Carlos Gravina, formerly the Spanish ambassador in Paris, who was instrumental in influencing France to declare war on Britain. Shortly before the battle of Trafalgar, he was given command of Spain's principal fleet, based in Cadiz, and was subsequently a vice-admiral at Trafalgar. He was 'chief' of Madrid (*Chef de Madric*) in a double sense, therefore – at one time the ambassador, and then later the leader of the Spanish fleet at this historic battle. As Nostradamus implied would happen, he was badly wounded at Trafalgar, while serving on board the *Principe de Asturias*. He died a few months later.

THE TRAITOR

Nostradamus, admitted Charles Ward, 'is sometimes a pillar of fire, but oftener is he a pillar of cloud'.[19] There is probably no verse which would appear quite so cloudy as quatrain IV.65 before the event it prophesied, yet more like a pillar of translucent fire after its fulfilment in 1873.

The quatrain runs:

> *Au deserteur de la grand forteresse,*
> *Apres qu'aura son lieu abandonné:*
> *Son adversaire sera si grand proüesse,*
> *L'empereur tost mort sera condamné.*

To the deserter of the great fortress,
After having abandoned his place:
His adversary will be of such great valour,
The emperor already dead will be condemned.

The lucidity of the quatrain shines only after the fulfilment of the prophesied events, which unscrolled in France during 1873. After that date all ambiguity is removed, the great fortress is recognizably Paris, the deserter is seen as the unfortunate General Bazaine, and the Emperor is revealed as Napoleon III.

In 1870, when faced by the well-organized Prussian attack on France, Paris was reduced to turning itself into a fortress (*la grand forteresse*). The story of the siege is told admirably by Alistair Horne, and one line from this book sets the Nostradamian theme: 'As the Prussians drew closer, one thing was fairly apparent; there had seldom been a more powerfully armed fortress than Paris, or one apparently so strongly defended.'[20] We should add that the medieval-like walls enclosed Montparnasse, Belleville, Montmartre and Batignolles, and reached up to the Bois de Boulogne. A vast circle of 30-foot-high moated walls encircled Paris, supported by an inner circular railway which would supply troops to the defensive ramparts. Ninety-three bastions strengthened the walls, and beyond was a chain of powerful forts. The French general Louis-Jules Trochu, who was put in charge of the defence of Paris, strengthened these walls with additional forts, and the Parisians, enduring terrible conditions, held out against the Prussians for several months.

The French had been woefully unprepared when their Emperor declared war on Prussia. General Bazaine, who was at one point in charge of 200,000 men under war conditions, had never commanded more than 25,000 before, and then only during manoeuvres. At the outset of the conflict, his forces were cut off by the Prussians, and eventually he was penned in at Metz; here he endured a terrible siege of over two months, after which he surrendered and was taken captive. As soon as news of this defeat reached Leon Gambetta (then at Tours), Bazaine was proclaimed a traitor. Bazaine is still mentioned as a traitor in certain French history books, but this is an unfair judgement. He was merely a poor general, furnished with an inadequate and poorly equipped army and ordered to fight a war which he could not possibly win.

The important thing, however, is that the surrounded Parisians, and the one General still active beyond the walls (Gambetta) regarded Bazaine as a traitor, a deserter of their cause (*deserteur*). Nostradamus puts the emphasis on the fact that he is regarded as a deserter by others. The first line is delightfully ambiguous, for while it undoubtedly refers to Paris, it might also be read as relating to Metz, where Bazaine was also besieged behind fortress-like walls. The second line seems to confirm this, for Bazaine did not leave Paris, but Metz (*son lieu abandonné*). After this time, the enemy (*Son adversaire*) did show considerable valour (*si grand proüesse*), during both the siege of Paris and the many conflicts in the French countryside. They were such a formidable enemy that the French simply did not have a chance against them.

Nostradamus dealt with the career of Napoleon III (*L'empereur*) in several verses: we have encountered him already as the wily fox (*renard*) of quatrain VIII.41 (see page 192 ff). If it is possible to lay the blame for a war at the feet of one man, then we might claim that Emperor Napoleon III caused the ill-judged war with Prussia, and the resulting siege of Paris. As we have seen (page 196), after the battle of Sedan, he was taken prisoner. He was imprisoned in the castle of Wilhelmshohe in Prussia, and remained there for the duration of the war, during which time a Republic was declared in Paris. He was deposed by the Assembly (then at Bordeaux, as Paris was completely surrounded by the Prussians), which regarded him as responsible for the 'ruin, invasion and dismemberment of France'.

The last line of the quatrain is expressed perfectly, but it does not mean quite what one might imagine: it does not refer to an emperor-already-dead who will be condemned. Rather it refers to the destiny faced by two people, in the same year.

The year 1873 marked a watershed for France. On 9 January that year, Napoleon III died, bringing kingship to an end in France. The Emperor being dead (*L'empereur tost*), in that same year the unfortunate Bazaine was condemned to death (*mort sera condamné*). Happily, the sentence was later commuted, and he was imprisoned on the Ile Sainte-Marguerite. A year later, he escaped to Italy, and eventually went to live in Spain. He died in 1883.

Chapter 10

The Twentieth Century
and Beyond

*Like a Bible, like the Pyramids or a Sphinx, the
mysterious and enigmatic book of Nostradamus is a
fundamental pillar of human knowledge. Built according
to formulas on which were constructed these same
monuments, the work is nothing more than a modern
adaptation of geometric and cosmographic methods dating
back to the highest antiquity.*

(Translated from the *Preface* by P. V. Piobb, in the
Vigier and Brunissen *Texte Integral de Nostradamus*,
1936)

In 1966, to mark the 400th anniversary of the death of
Nostradamus, a modern statue was erected in Salon, at the
southern entrance to the city, near Place Gambetta (*fig.
47*). It was an impressive metal sculpture by François
Bouché, and depicted the great man in a scholarly late-
medieval gown, the vertical folds of which lent the figure
enormous dignity. His left arm was supported by an
armillary sphere, and at his feet was a celestial globe: the
sculptor was unambiguously certain that Nostradamus dealt
with the stars.

A few years after it had been erected, the statue was
badly damaged when a lorry accidentally crashed into it.
Bouché did not feel that he could repair the work, and, at

length, created another statue to replace it. The replacement was a huge concrete construction – perhaps more able to resist the impact of lorries, and the mutations of the world. This enigmatic figure, which has none of the clear symbolism of the destroyed metal predecessor, was erected in October 1979, and still greets the visitor to Salon, entering from the south (*fig. 48*).

The surprising thing about both these statues, however, is not so much their history as that they both represented Nostradamus as eyeless. The first statue had a head with no distinguishing facial features: its eyeless face was peering into an hour-glass. The later statue has a hollow where the face should be: if we seek the face, we look into the skies, and towards the stars. The Seer of Salon was portrayed as though his vision were directed inwards, or lacked humanity. Nostradamus, who could see the whole destiny of Europe, was represented as blind.

There is here true artistic insight into the subtle nature of Nostradamus, for he is portrayed as being more intimately linked with the stars than with humanity, to whom he scarcely belongs. As we saw earlier, for all he dealt with the future in a thousand or so verses, Nostradamus did not intend his readers to discern this future until it had become the past. He was truly the Janus-faced creature that the disciple Chavigny had incorporated into the title of the book dedicated to his master. Nostradamus, with the wisdom derived from his initiate knowledge, intended that mankind should look into the glass of futurity darkly.

We are tempted to interpret these statues in this way because, after years of researching the quatrains of the Master of Salon, we have been forced to the conclusion that he did not intend his prophecies to be understood prior to the unfolding of events they predicted. As Ward admits, after commenting on quatrain IX.34, which relates to the escape of Louis XVI, 'before the event forecast has happened, all the keys of interpretation are wanting, the prophecy looks like jargon, and is so for all practical purposes; but . . . once it has happened, or as we may say kissed sunlight, the keys appear with it, the light and the understanding awaken together'.[1]

The events of the twentieth century have troubled the whole globe, making Nostradamus' concern with Europe seem purblind. Even so, as we have already seen, the prophecies, written over 400 years ago, do deal in the most extraordinary detail with the two main events which have convulsed both Europe and the globe in modern times – the two World Wars.

Indeed, one of the great secrets of Nostradamus (hitherto unpublished) is that he constructed two quatrains in order to define and identify the particular crises to which the twentieth century would be heir. Thus, while it is common knowledge that Nostradamus predicted the date of the French Revolution, it should be recognized that, with even greater precision, he defined the century which would see the greatest perturbations of all.

Nostradamus 'defined' the twentieth century by means of arcane astrology, which probably explains why his secret has lain unnoticed for so long. In one quatrain, he tells us precisely when the twentieth century will begin, and in another, he tell us when it will end. The two quatrains both have something in common: they both refer to a specific point in Taurus, and they both use the word *tremblement* (which we might, for the moment, translate as 'earthquake') to describe the events of the century. Unless these two quatrains are seen as book-ends to the century, they make little or no sense.

The first quatrain is X.67: this refers to the beginning of the twentieth century. The second quatrain is IX.83: this refers to the end of the century. Between them, these verses constitute the most remarkable astrological predictions we have ever encountered.[2]

Quatrain X.67 reads:

> *Le tremblement si fort au mois de May,*
> *Saturne, Caper, Jupiter, Mercure au boeuf:*
> *Venus aussi, Cancer, Mars en Nonnay,*
> *Tombera gresle lors plus grosse qu'un oeuf.*

We shall attempt a translation once we have examined the arcane astrological content of the verse. In fact, the planetary positions are ambiguous, yet the following notes on Green Language specialist terms in the quatrain will help the reader come to his or her own conclusions.

Caper (which means 'goat', in Latin) is Capricorn. *Boeuf*, which means 'ox' in French, must be Taurus. As *Cancer* is a zodiacal sign, it cannot be posited in a zodiacal sign: we assume therefore that, in this context, *Cancer* means the Moon, which is the planetary ruler of the sign. *Nonnay* is Virgo, from the French word *nonne*, or *nonnain*, which means 'nun': in medieval iconography, the image of a nun, or female religious, is sometimes linked with Virgo, mainly because the sign was the Celestial Virgin, a cosmic prototype of the Virgin Maria, to whom nuns aspired spiritually. Finally, Nostradamus seems to have mentioned the *mois de May* to indicate that the Sun is in Taurus. This covert mention of the Sun means that we have that rare quatrain – one which mentions a position for each of the seven traditional planets. Nostradamus is taking no chances that the astute astrologer should misread the exact day that he intends for the quatrain. Given the meaning of these arcane terms, we may translate the primitive horoscope set out in the quatrain, obtaining the following data:

Sun in Taurus
Saturn and Jupiter in Capricorn
Mercury in Taurus
Venus also in Taurus, with the Moon
Mars in Virgo

The quatrain therefore translates:

The earthquake so strong in the month of May,
Saturn and Jupiter in Capricorn, Mercury in Taurus:
Venus and Moon in Taurus also, with Mars in Virgo,
There will fall hail as big as an egg.

So far as we can determine, since 1558 there has been only one day when *all* these astrological conditions pertain: 17 May 1901. For the sake of simplicity, we will give the positions posited by Nostradamus in the quatrain alongside the actual positions of the planets on that day. The sequence of planets follows the listing in the quatrain:

Sun in Taurus:	*SU 11*	*Taurus 08*
Saturn in Capricorn:	*SA 16*	*Capricorn 02 Ret.*[*]
Jupiter in Capricorn:	*JU 12*	*Capricorn 39 Ret.*
Mars in Virgo:	*MA 02*	*Virgo 06*
Mercury in Taurus:	*ME 28*	*Taurus 37*
Venus in Taurus:	*VE 29*	*Taurus 52*
Moon in Taurus:	*MO 25*	*Taurus 35*

Now we can see that it would be misleading to translate the first line as though it were intended to indicate that the threatened *tremblement* (earthquake) is in the month of May. It seems, rather, that the month of May (*mois de May*) is part of the astrological pattern which Nostradamus is seeking to describe. The month is important only in so far

---

[*] Retrograde.

as it indicates that the Sun will be in Taurus. We presume that the *tremblement* will be in the year in which all the six astrological conditions are met – namely, in 1901.

Now, curiously, there was an earthquake in the Scottish Grampians, in September 1901. However, in our opinion, it would be foolish to conclude that Nostradamus went to the trouble of constructing such an extraordinary quatrain as this merely in order to point to a minor earthquake in Scotland. We are convinced that the *tremblement* to which he refers is the hundred years of earthquake – the entire pattern of social, political and military upheavals which has occurred in the twentieth century. Using his arcane astrological technique, Nostradamus has indicated with extraordinary precision a unique configuration of planets which point to the first year of the twentieth century, the horrors of which he seems to have foreseen.

Quatrain X.67 marks the first year of the twentieth century. In a similar way, quatrain IX.83 marks the last year of the same century. Quatrain X.67 is one of the 'revolution' quatrains: it depends upon the pointers of Saturn–Jupiter conjunctions drawn in the cosmic clock of our skies (*fig. 22*). We have already noted several times that Nostradamus favours using Saturn and Jupiter conjunctions to denote important dates. Now, the interesting thing is that a similar great conjunction of Jupiter and Saturn as is seen at the beginning of the twentieth century also takes place in the year 2000. It is possible to construe one of the quatrains predicting a terrible 'earthquake' for that year. Remarkably, just as the first line of quatrain X.67 contained a reference to May-Taurus, so quatrain IX.83:

> *Sol vingt de Taurus si fort terre trembler,*
> *Le grand theatre remply ruinera,*
> *L'air, ciel & terre obscurcir & troubler,*
> *Lors l'infidele Dieu & saincts voquera.*

For the moment, we may translate this as meaning:

Sun in twenty Taurus, the earth shall tremble so strongly,
The great filled theatre will be ruined,
The air, sky and earth obscured and troubled,
So that the infidel will call upon God and saints.

The prediction seems to be a dire one, and it therefore behoves us to attempt to date the quatrain. First, we must ask, what does 'twenty Taurus' (*vingt de Taurus*) mean? It is possible to interpret it as indicating either 'twenty degrees of Taurus', or the 'twentieth day of the Sun in Taurus'. However, in view of the importance ascribed to the degrees occupied by the great conjunctions in medieval astrology, we should conclude that this first line of the quatrain relates to a period when an important conjunction is in twenty degrees of Taurus.

Taurus, Virgo and Capricorn were the Earth signs which (according to medieval astrology) would overlook the perturbations and troubles of the twentieth century. The last of these Earth trigons will take place on 28 May 2000, when the two ponderables meet in 23 degrees of Taurus. The Great Conjunctions in the Earth trigon for the twentieth century are represented in the following table:

1881	18 Apr	2	TA
1901	27 Nov	14	CP
1921	10 Sep	27	VI
1940	8 Aug	15	TA
1940	20 Oct	13	TA
1941	15 Feb	10	TA
1961	19 Feb	26	CP
2000	28 May	23	TA

While we obtain two close dates for this 'earthquake', or

mutation, there is no astrological data which will permit us to propose a year for this event. In fact, the closest date for which we can provide a correspondence with the quatrain falls in our own immediate future, in May 2000.

Now, since Nostradamus is quite specific about 20 degrees of Taurus, let us consider the implications of this for May 2000. On 7 May, Saturn enters 20 degrees of Taurus. However, while Jupiter is already technically conjunct with Saturn at this moment, it is actually only within 2 degrees of orb, in 18 degrees of Taurus. We must therefore ask if there is any other astrological moment in that month during which 20 degrees of Taurus is more emphatic. The answer is quite remarkable.

On 9 May 2000, precisely when the Sun is in 20 degrees of Taurus, there is a massive conjunction of six of the traditional planets in Taurus. The positions are:

Sun	*20*	*Taurus*
Mercury	*20*	*Taurus*
Venus	*11*	*Taurus*
Jupiter	*18*	*Taurus*
Saturn	*20*	*Taurus*

The two planets outside the satellitium are Mars, which is in Gemini, and the Moon, which is in Leo.[2] Needless to say, this configuration would repeat itself only over a period of several hundred years.

Although, at the time of writing, this planetary configuration lies in our own future, we can only presume that it relates to quatrain IX.83, for it is the only data in many hundreds of years which makes sense in terms of that verse. Nostradamus was too careful in his choice of words, and in his presentation of astrological data, not to have chosen a unique date. We presume that precisely what sort of mutation, earthquake or conflict is intended by the quatrain will, in accordance with the arcane blinds used by Nostradamus, become apparent only after the event.

Here, then, a precise and incontrovertible examination of planetary positions has given us two dates which mark the beginning and end of the twentieth century, between them predicting earthquakes, mutations and disasters. We have seen a sufficiency of the century to recognize just how accurate Nostradamus was. Nostradamus is always full of surprises, and it is just possible that he sees the AD 2000 prediction as relating to a vast earthquake or war, when the earth (the great filled theatre):

> The great filled theatre will be ruined,
> The air, sky and earth obscured and troubled,
> So that the infidel will call upon God and saints.

However, we are inclined to see it as a careful crafting of data to describe the end of a century which has probably seen more mutations than any other in the history of the world. The century begins peaceably enough, with hailstones as big as eggs, but finishes in ruin. This seems to us to be a fair summary.

In view of what Nostradamus envisioned for the twentieth century, it is scarcely surprising that the quatrains which he wrote for the years sandwiched between these two extremes of 1901 and 2000 are replete with verses dealing with war prophecies. One telling – even historically influential – example of this is the so-called Hitler quatrains.

THE HITLER QUATRAINS

The 'Hitler' verses prove to be good examples of this difficulty of prediction prior to an event. In quatrain II.24, Nostradamus uses the word *Hister*. Prior to the 1920s, this word was taken to be a reference to the river Hister, or less accurately, Ister – the Latin name for the lower part of the Danube. This was a reasonable assumption, in the general context of the verse, which dealt in the first line with the subject of rivers:

Bestes farouches de faim fleuves tranner,
Plus part du camp encontre Hister sera,
En cage de fer le grand sera trainner,
Quand Rin enfant Germain observera.

Beasts, wild with hunger, swim across rivers,
The greater part of the field will be against the Hister,
The great one will be dragged in an iron cage,
When the German child will see the Rhine.

In modern times, the quatrain has been subject to the most extraordinary translations, almost all of them based on a reading which takes Hister to denote Hitler.[3] Roberts insists that the quatrain is a prediction of the fate of Adolf Hitler, on the grounds that the iron cage (*cage de fer*) is a reference to the bunker in Berlin, where he died. De Fontbrune, aware that Hister refers to the Danube, still reads into the quatrain the fall of Hitler in April 1945. However, the iron cage has become the van in which Mussolini is dragged to his execution. The Italian commentator Patrian resists the temptation to link the quatrain with either Hitler or Mussolini, but he offers no explanation for the verse.

Our own translation is based on the assumption that the word *tranner*, at the end of the first line, is a version of the Latin infinitive, *tranare*, 'to swim through'. We recognize that the last line is ambiguous, for the subject of the final verb is not clear: it could mean, even, that the Rhine sees the German child.

Although the classically trained commentators on Nostradamus had no doubt that the word *Hister* referred to the Danube, once Adolf Hitler came to power, the word *Hister* took on a double meaning, and was immediately seized upon as a remarkable advance notice of the Fuhrer. Hitler himself was convinced that the word applied to him, even though he was aware of its original Latin meaning.

As Ellic Howe has pointed out, in 1967, both Hitler and Goebbels attempted to make capital out of this prophecy: it was probably this single word which spawned so many of the spurious 'Nostradamus' prophecies which were published by the Nazis and the Allies, during the Second World War.[4]

The Nostradamus prophecies had been quaintly translated by C. Loog, a German postal official living in Berlin, in his own highly personal interpretation of the *Prophéties*, published in 1921.[5] Loog was under the impression that he had discovered a numerological key to the quatrains, and came to many far-reaching interpretations based on the application of this key. Pertinent to our own research is the fact that Loog came to the conclusion, via his reading of III.57, that Britain would reach the end of its greatness, and slide into a decline after 1939. Somehow, this would be involved with its protection of Poland. Loog was wrong in his dating and in his identification of Poland: he wrongly translated certain important words used by Nostradamus, and fudged the dating system, remaining blithely unaware of the key to Nostradamus' calendrical system. Indeed, so far off the mark had been Loog's interpretations that, had it not been for a reference inserted in another book, his predictions might have been forgotten. However, a reference to the prediction, made by Dr H. H. Kritzinger in 1922, came to the notice of Frau Dr Goebbels.[6] Soon, the summary was regarded as being of great importance by Hitler and the Ministry of Propaganda.

David Pitt Francis is probably right to read into this late incident in the history of the *Prophéties* a degree of participation-fulfilment. It is very possible that the dating of the invasion of Poland by the Third Reich in 1939 was a consequence of the German hierarchies' belief in the accuracy of Loog's translation. As Francis observes, Loog's interpretation was 'a direct cause of one of the most devastating wars in the history of mankind'.

Pertinent to our own survey, however, is the undeniable fact that the different emphases which these two (the pre- and post-Hitlerian) translations of *Hister* lent to the verse inevitably gave rise to entirely different commentaries on the significance of the quatrain. That the word still makes more sense as a reference to the Roman river name has not deflected the majority of modern 'translators' from seeing it as a prefiguring of the Great Dictator. Almost certainly this is a consequence of the Loog blunder, which was carried into the sub-cultural Nostradamus literature by Cheetham.

Examples of the continuation of the error abound in modern literature. For example, in the somewhat super-ficial treatment of Arkel and Blake[7] we find the second line of the quatrain translated as meaning: 'Most of the battlefield will fall to Hitler', which is just about as far from the original Nostradamus as one can get.

THE RIVER QUATRAINS

The translators who insist upon reading *Hister* as Hitler tend to ignore the disconcerting fact that Nostradamus used the same river name in another verse, this time under the variant *Hyster*. This is quatrain IV.68, the third line of which reads: *De Rhin, & Hyster, qu'on dira sont venus.* There may be no doubt from the context that the line should be translated as: 'They will say they come from the Rhine and lower Danube'.

Strangely, another quatrain numbered 68 – quatrain V.68 – also refers to the Danube and Rhine, though this time with their modern names. These two verses might usefully be called the 'river quatrains'.

Was Nostradamus intending us to draw a link between these two quatrains, initially on the communality of their numbers? We need not attempt to answer this question, but since our thesis is that when Nostradamus mentions rivers by name, it is precisely the rivers he intends to denote, we should consider at least one of these verses in some depth. Let us glance at V.68:

Dans le Dannube & du Rin viendra boire,
Le grand Chameau, ne s'en repentira:
Trembler du Rosne & plus fort ceux de Loire,
Et pres des Alpes Coq les ruynera.

In the Danube and the Rhine will come to drink,
The great Camel, (of which) he will not repent:
The Rhône and even more those of the Loire to tremble,
And near the Alps he will ruin the Cock.

The quatrain is rich in associations, and we cannot guarantee that our proposed interpretation is correct. However, as we shall see, the main fact is that the quatrain does appear to relate to the life, times and achievements of Prince Eugene of Savoy, who was the subject of another quatrain. Before tracing these connections in detail, we must examine some of the Green Language in the quatrains.

The interpretation of the quatrain seems to hinge upon the meaning of the strange word *Chameau.* In French, this literally means camel, but the capital letter would suggest that it is Green Language. In fact, the *Chamaves* were a Germanic people who eventually formed the confederation known as the *Francs*, from whom the name France eventually derived. That the latter part of the word *aves* has been changed to *eau* is of the deepest Green Language significance. In Latin, *aves* means 'bees': as we mentioned earlier, it has been claimed by esotericists that the original designs for the fleur-de-lys of France were 'bees'. This is why Napoleon insisted that the bees should be adopted as symbols for the Empire, as symbols of France's greatness. In French, *eaux* means 'waters', which is perhaps not a surprising word to find in quatrains which deal so openly with the names of rivers. In the light of these hidden meanings, we must presume that *Chameaux* is France – combining the tribal name with the national symbol – specifically that part in which the two rivers of Rhône and Loire run.

Note that the reference is not merely to *Chameau*, but to *le grand Chameau*, or the great Frenchman. Now, Prince Eugene of Savoy was a great Frenchman – perhaps, indeed, the greatest of his century (*fig. 49*). He had been born in Paris, but was banished under a decree issued against all Frenchmen who served in foreign armies. This may partly explain a subsidiary meaning behind the choice of the name *Chameau*, for in French slang usage the name camel was used to denote an unpopular fellow. He may well have been unpopular with the French, but he was highly valued by the more appreciative Austrians. He served under Leopold I, and his remarkable success against the Turks in the relief of Vienna in 1683 won him the reward of a regiment of dragoons.

The opening line of V.68 mentions the Danube and the Rhine. Vienna is on the Danube, and it was at the siege of Vienna that Eugene first made his reputation. He partici-pated in the defeat of the Turks, who had besieged that city, in 1683. This date introduces the important 68 which binds together the two river quatrains, and settles for us the decade to which the two verses refer. As a result of the successes at Vienna, the decade saw two important treaties: the Treaty of Vienna (1686) and that of Blasendorf, where the suzerainity of Leopold I was recognized, also in 1686.

As a consequence of his exploits at Vienna, Eugene gained the unlimited support of Leopold, who sent him to Italy during the Wars of Spanish Succession. This is dealt with in the second two lines of V.68. In spite of incredible difficulties, Eugene crossed the mountains (*Alpes*) from Tirol into Italy, and drove back the French troops. The French were eventually forced to relinquish their hold on Mantuan territory. His massive victory against the French at Turin in September 1706 sealed the fate of France (*Coq les ruynera*) in Italy, until the coming of Napoleon.

The second-line phrase, *ne s'en repentira*, clearly relates to an incident in Eugene's life. Although he had been banished from France, once his astounding military prowess became evident, he was secretly offered the baton of the marshal of France by Louis XIV. Eugene, a man of principle throughout his life, refused the offer, never repenting (*ne s'en repentira*) of his decision to fight for Germany and Austria (*Dans le Dannube & du Rin*).

CHANGES AT COLOGNE

In spite of the above example, the fact is that a great deal of the difficulty in translating Nostradamus lies precisely in the extraordinary accuracy with which he is able to reveal names and locations – setting down a whole chain of events in a single word or compound.

In the context of rivers, we may glance at a quatrain which is directed to the twentieth century. In several quatrains, Nostradamus foresees terrible floods and the emergence of a new geography in many parts of the world. Among these is quatrain VI.4, which, on first analysis, appears to insist that the river Rhine will so change its flow that the city of Cologne will no longer be on its banks. This, of course, suggests extraordinary geological upheavals in our future, and almost without exception the modern commentators have viewed it as a commentary on the general destruction which is promised in the near future. The first two lines of the verse read:

> *Le Celtique fleuve changera de rivage,*
> *Plus ne tiendra la cité d'Agripine;*

> The Celtic river will change its banks,
> No more it will touch the city of Agripine . . .

Now, it is quite clear that *Celtic river* could apply to very many European rivers, including the Thames, the Meuse, the Danube, the Roer, the Seine, and so on. It is the clue in 'the city of Agripine' (*la cité d'Agripine*) which enables us to identify the river positively. What we now call Cologne was originally Colonia Agrippina, the Roman colony named after Agrippina, the unfortunate mother of the mad Roman emperor, Nero. In ancient times, the inhabitants of the colony were called *Agrippinenses*.

However, on reflection, we may see that, within the framework of this interpretation, the first two lines have an ambiguous meaning. It is quite possible to see the verse as relating to a time when the river will change the direction of its flow – a cataclysm of nature by which the ancient river-bed is moved. On the other hand, if we regard the *Plus* of the second line as meaning 'Again', then the line could mean not that the river itself is changed, but that the ancient city, as named after Agrippina (i.e. Cologne), will not be left on the banks. Could this, therefore, be taken as reference to the destruction of the city during the Second World War? To some extent, this suggestion is supported by the third line of the prophecy: *Tout transmué ormis le vieil langage* – 'All is changed, except the old language'. During the Second World War, Cologne was subject to severe bombing by the Allies and was massively destroyed. Even the cathedral, miraculously not destroyed, needed drastic repairs. All was changed, except the old language – of the name. The Roman name, Cologne, survived.

The point here is not so much that this verse relates to the Second World War destruction, but rather that it is quite possible to translate it in such a way. However, when we examine the astrological meaning of the fourth line of the quatrain (see page 127), we shall see that there is no doubt that the reference is to the Second World War – that, in fact, the quatrain refers to something in our past, rather than to events still in our future, as many commentators believe. As we shall see, in an interpretation which is adequately supported by arcane astrological lore, the city of Cologne has already been destroyed, and, by virtue of having been rebuilt, has retained only its ancient name.

Now, since we may be sure that the location is Germany, and the time the end of the Second World War, we should note, in passing, that during the last days of the war (before Cologne was captured by the Allies, on 7 March 1945), another German river played an important and relevant role. When, by 11 February, the 1st US Army had fought its way to the upper section of the river Roer, the Germans breached the great dams. As a result the area was entirely flooded for over ten days, impeding further attacks. Could Nostradamus have foreseen in his vision this waterlogged country – the river-banks breached and hidden in the great expanse of water – and should we therefore read the *Celtique fleuve* as being the Roer? There is no necessary connection between the first and second lines of the prophecy, so such a reading is entirely possible. The flooding of the Roer and the destruction of Cologne were two distinct events, though almost contemporaneous. If this is true, we have yet again an example of Nostradamus' tendency to combine two related prophecies into the one quatrain.

HANGED FROM THE ANTENNA

Quatrain IV.92 is worth examining within a twentieth-century context, if only because it has been explained by several recent commentators as referring to a modern invention – the radio or television aerial.

Teste trenchée du vaillant Capitaine,
Sera jetté devant son adversaire,
Son corps pendu de sa classe à l'antenne,
Confus fuira par rame à vent contraire.

The severed head of the courageous Captain,
Will be thrown in front of his adversary,
His body hanged from the yard-arm of his ship,
Confused he will fly by oar-ship against a contrary wind.

Roberts, who sees in the word *antenne* (third line) a reference to radio, finds the quatrain obscure, but it is difficult to understand why he should imagine that it caused confusion in the mind of Nostradamus. Cheetham suggests that Nostradamus is using the word to indicate complex equipment with which he was not familiar, such as radar.

However, there is no need to see the word *antenne*, or the quatrain in which it is found, relating to modern times, since the word had a perfectly clear nautical meaning in the sixteenth century, when the old Latin *antenna* was still used to denote the yard-arm of a ship. In his own translation of

1672, Garencières had called it 'the Sails Yard', but, in the rush to bring Nostradamus into modern times, this has been missed by many commentators.

The quatrain describes the hanging of a sailor. We have not been able to identify with absolute certainty the sailor referred to in this verse. However, our main point – that *antenne* has nothing to do with radios or television – is supported by the translation of the quatrain. It is probable that the verse refers to the death of Prince Francesco Caracciolo in 1799. The prince was a Neapolitan admiral and revolutionary, who fought with the British against America during the War of Independence. In 1799 he took command of the new Republic's naval forces and fought against the British and Neapolitan squadrons. He was captured near Naples while trying to escape in disguise. He was put in chains and transported to Nelson's flagship, where he was sentenced to death. He was immediately hanged from the yard-arm of the *Minerva* on 30 June 1799.

The argument for Caracciolo as the one hanged is found in the meanings of certain words in the quatrain. *Trenchée* is probably from the verb *trancher*, which means literally to cut off, or to slice. This has led some commentators to translate the line as describing a decapitation. However, this conflicts with the third line, wherein the body is said to be hanged. In fact, *trancher* has a subsidiary meaning of 'settling', in the sense of determining: the phrase *trancher le question* means 'to clinch the matter', or to cut the Gordian knot. The French phrase *trancher du grand seigneur* means 'to lord it', or to pretend to be a great man. Caracciolo was being hanged precisely because (in the eyes of Nelson) he had pretended to a power he did not have. He had claimed to be a head (*chef*) of the Neapolitan fleet.

Certainly, this is one of the overtones of meaning in the line. The hanging was something of a fast solution to a problem, for Nelson must have realized that the trial and execution were illegal: it is said to have been a result of the personal spite of Queen Maria Carolina, who influenced Lady Hamilton (then on board the *Minerva* with Nelson) to persuade Nelson to the deed. *Adversaire* is an apposite word, for Nelson was Commander-in-Chief of the Neapolitan fleet. While Caracciolo was a revolutionary, he had been a Neapolitan admiral, and in charge of the new Republic's naval forces: he was indeed the leader of the adversaries. Caracciolo was tried by a court martial convened from his own Neapolitan officers, which explains why Nostradamus should write *de sa classe*, even though he was tried on board the English *Minerva*. However, the specific interpretation of this quatrain need not detain us. It is sufficient that we have noted how an obscure-seeming word has been misunderstood, and become prey to the imagination of modern interpreters.

THE BATTLE FOR FRANCE

So far as we can determine, the French writer de Fontbrune was the first to interpret quatrain IV.80 as a reference to the Maginot Line.[8] He made this suggestion in 1939, only four years after the renewed Maginot Line became operative, and he was therefore too early to see the full implications in the quatrain, which dealt with the battle for France, in 1940. The verse begins by describing a great ditch of excavated earth:

Pres du grand fleuve grand fosse terre egeste
En quinze parts sera l'eau divisée:
La cité prinse, feu, sang, cris, conflit meste,
Et la plus part concerne au collisée.

Near the great river a great ditch of excavated earth
The water will be divided into fifteen parts:

The city taken, fire, blood, cries, and mixed conflict,
And the greatest part concern with collision.

The Maginot Line ran for several miles to parallel the
Rhine (*Pres du grand fleuve*). It was indeed a great ditch
(*grand fosse*) of excavated earth (*terre egeste*, the latter word
from the Latin *egestio*, a carrying away). It ran for over 310
kilometres, in a chain of underground corridors and forts
which were, in places, dug sufficiently deep to receive
massive constructions seven storeys deep, consisting of
hospitals, sleeping quarters, offices, ammunition rooms,
and so on. The pits excavated to receive each of these
required the removal of three-quarters of a million cubic
metres of earth. Between 1930 and 1934, a good length of
the Maginot Line was newly constructed, but some of the
older fortifications, built in anticipation of the First World
War – such as those at Thionville and Metz, as well as the
trench-caps at Verdun and Belfort – were modernized, to
provide a second line.

In the 1940 invasion, the Germans shrewdly ignored the
Maginot defences and came through Luxembourg and
Belgium to throw an entire corps at the lightly defended
area near Sedan. They captured only one of the great forts
of the Maginot Line, but the French wisely withdrew,
recognizing that they had been outflanked.

Ironically, Sedan is a city already made famous in
another Nostradamus quatrain (see page 195). It was this
latest capture of the city, and the brilliant German
enclosing movement up to Abbeville, a port on the Somme
in northern France, which cut off the Allied army in
Belgium, that determined the course of the war.

For a long time, we could not fully understand the
second line of the quatrain. Why should Nostradamus
insist that the water was divided into 15 parts (*En quinze
parts sera l'eau divisée*)? What was the water, and why was

it important in relation to the Maginot Line? However, when we attempted to read the line in relation to the events following the Germanic bypassing of the Maginot Line, it made perfect sense. The German plan involved the taking of Sedan, at the northern end of the Maginot Line, followed by a hinged movement up to Abbeville. By this stratagem they cut off the British forces, resulting in the near-disastrous withdrawal at Dunkirk. The German move from Sedan to Abbeville was extremely rapid, and was carried out by three distinct columns, two panzer divisions to the north, ten to the south, and one centrally. To reach Abbeville, each of these three columns crossed one canal and four rivers, making fifteen crossings in all. The waters were the Ardennes Canal (which joined Meuse and Aisne), the Meuse itself, the Serre, the Oise, and the Somme, to the north of St Quentin. In a reading of the quatrain, published in 1980, de Fontbrune claimed that the drainage system of the Maginot Line was divided into 15 parts, but this was not correct. The fact that they crossed a canal explains why Nostradamus should write of dividing 'water' (*l'eau*) rather than 'rivers' (*fleuves*). In all, there were 15 crossings between Sedan and Abbeville.

In the light of this, the city captured by the Germans (*La cité prinse*, line three) is almost certainly Abbeville.[9] We should observe that *conflit meste* (which terminates this third line) could be a specialist military term. Even in the sixteenth century, *mestre* could mean the first company of a regiment: this means that the two words could denote a conflict of such companies. However, we feel that the sense of the quatrain as a whole favours our own reading of the ambiguous terminology.

There is considerable irony in the final line: *Et la plus part concerne au collisée* ('And the greatest part concern with collision'). The French had been intent on constructing a fortified line which would hold back the Germans – who were expected merely to collide (*collisée*) with the structure. Quite sensibly, the Germans ignored the formidable barrier, and merely skirted it.

This German plan determined the outcome of the battle for France, and explains the reason why Nostradamus considered it important enough to mention. The final line of the quatrain sums up the ineptitude of the Maginot plan: as it was impregnable, the Germans really had no choice but to go around it. The French, perhaps in deference to the Belgians, had terminated the defences at the top of the Ardennes – it was here, of course, that the Germans concentrated their attack. The French had visualized a head-on collision, but the Germans refused to play the French game.

MAN HALF PIG

While touching on twentieth-century warfare it is appropriate to comment on a curious quatrain which has caught the attention of several modern commentators. This is quatrain I.64, with its extraordinary line: *Quand le pourceau demy homme on verra* . . . ('When they see the pig half man . . .').

As the context of this quatrain is clearly descriptive of a war, the line has been taken by some commentators as a reference to the tank. Chodkiewicz affirms that his direct experiences during the Second World War confirmed that the *porceau demy homme* was a good description of the tank. We do not find this convincing. We need not look very far, in the context of the World War, to trace this strange phrase to the gas-mask, the carbon-container of which certainly gave the wearer the appearance of being a pig. Bearing this in mind, the extraordinary vision of a terrible war contained in I.64 is outstanding.

De nuict soleil penseront avoir veu,
Quand le pourceau demy homme on verra,
Bruit, chant, bataille au Ciel battre apperceu,
Et bestes brutes à parler on orra.

By night they will think to have seen the sun,
When they see the pig half man,
Noise, singing, warfare in the Sky appears to strike,
And brutish beasts they will hear speak.

The night sun (*nuict soleil*) which would convince one that night is day could be a reference to either searchlights or incendiary bombs – perhaps to both. The battle in the sky (*bataille au Ciel*) could be one of the several references which Nostradamus appears to have written as prophetic of aerial combat. At first glance, however, the bestial brutes (*bestes brutes*) are something of a problem: what are these creatures which will be heard to speak?

Chodkiewicz (who was sufficiently taken by Nostradamus' visions of modern war to provide one or two drawings to illustrate his points) suggested that the speech of the bestial brutes is the sound of radio–amplifiers. However, it would seem to us that the simple gas–mask is once again a sufficient explanation for the line, as anyone who has heard the *porceau demy homme* speaking through one – muffled, and distinctly bestial – will confirm.

THE SECULARIZATION OF TURKEY

Only a handful of the quatrains deal with the borders of Europe, but when this theme is touched upon the results are usually hypnotic. A good example is quatrain III.95, which has been radically misunderstood by commentators.

La loy Moricque on verra deffaillir,
Apres une autre beaucoup plus seductive,

Boristhenes premier viendra faillir,
Par dons & langues une plus attractive,

They will see the Moorish law weaken,
After another much more seductive,
The river Dnieper at first will begin to fail,
By gifts and tongues one more attractive,

Roberts sees the quatrain as a brilliant prediction of the decline of Islam and the rise of Communism. This commentary is published in the 1947 edition of his book, and he may therefore be forgiven for not being aware of the future rise of Islam and the decline of Communism. De Fontbrune emphasizes the future collapse of the Muslim law, which will (he maintains) be followed by the more seductive law of Communism. He interprets the verse as predicting that Russia will collapse, and be drawn to the benefits of the French language. Curiously, Patrian seeks to interpret the word *Moricque* as a reference to Sir Thomas More, whom he sees as a sixteenth-century supporter of a doctrine similar to Marxism. One wonders what edition of More's satire *Utopia* Patrian had read to draw such a conclusion.

As we see the quatrain, it implies that a time will come in some part of Europe when the Islamic law will weaken in place of another more seductive. Before this happens, Boristhenes will have to fail. Linked with this change in law, or with the failure of the Boristhenes, gifts and languages will result in the emergence of one more attractive.

As Nostradamus offers no clue to a date in the quatrain, we shall have to determine from the inner evidence which period is intended. On the other hand, the savant does offer us an opportunity of identifying the place. The one specific reference to which we can pin a locality is a mention of a river in what is now Russia. Since there is also a mention of 'Muslim law', which is *Shariyra* law, the implication is that we have two different places to consider in our approach to the quatrain. All the evidence suggests that these two places are Russia and the old Ottoman Empire, which have bordered upon each other around the Black Sea, and which had been in a state of warfare or armed truce for centuries.

As we shall see, the quatrain deals with a period of a few years when both the Russian Imperium and the old Ottoman Empire came to an abrupt and perhaps unexpected end.

The weakened Ottoman Empire could be said to have fallen in October 1923, when the republic of Turkey was proclaimed in Ankara. The Sultanate, upon which the old Ottoman Empire had depended, had been abolished almost a year earlier, but the ratification by the national assembly seems to have been the final nail in the coffin of the Ottomans.

Bearing this general translation in mind, let us examine the implications of this, as revealed in each line of the quatrain: *La loy Moricque on verra deffaillir* – 'They will see the Moorish law weaken'. In 1928, a short while after the Ottoman Empire had become technically defunct, the Turkish state was declared secular. This move had required that the *Shariya* law, the *loi Moricque* (Muslim law), should be abandoned, in favour of one more attractive to the aspirations of the Turkish nation. This occurred in 1926, when Muslim religious law was put aside in favour of a civil code based on a number of European laws. This farsighted decision was the first stage in a progressive attempt to both secularize the state and establish firm communication with the Western world, at the expense of the old Ottoman ties to the Arabic East. This is probably why Nostradamus could visualize the replacement model (the Roman alphabet) as being more seductive, for it beckoned a new future for Turkey: *Apres une autre beaucoup plus seductive* – 'After another much more seductive'.

Now we must ask what this reform in Turkey has to do with the third line: *Boristhenes premier viendra faillir* – 'The river Dnieper at first will begin to fail'. However it is interpreted, *Boristhenes* is a curious archaism. The Abbé Rigaux read the word as *Boristen*, and took it to refer to the descendants of Boris, the name attached to a succession of Russian princes before the sixteenth century. In fact, as we saw in another context, the word *Boristhenes* was the old name for the river Dnieper, which arises in the hills of Valdai, to the west of Moscow, and flows through Smolensk and Kiev, to fall into the Black Sea near Nikolaev, at the top of the huge peninsula that is the Crimea. The river is a symbolic divisor of Russia from Europe. Indeed, before Communism expanded to the west, the river marked approximately the divisions of Estonia, Latvia, White Russia, and the Ukraine (which it cut in two). The name was, therefore, a convenient symbol for Nostradamus to indicate what had to fall before the decline in the Moorish law could take place. The thing which had to fall was the arch-enemy of the Ottomans – Imperial Russia.

In the matter of the age-old warfare between the Russians and the Ottomans, dates are deceptive, but we may suggest that the Russian Imperium fell in 1917, with the Revolution.

As we have remarked in connection with another quatrain (see pages 318–19), it was the carving up of this interface area between East and West which laid the foundations for the two World Wars, mainly because each of the European countries had tried to keep their fingers in the pie crust around the Black Sea. The past and future histories extending beyond the date 1923 need not concern us here: what is of importance is that we should trace in the Nostradamus quatrain a reference to these two related events – the fall of Imperial Russia, and the end of the Ottoman Empire.

After the secularization of the Turkish State, the next stage in the removal of the antique Ottoman furniture was a reform of the alphabet. In 1928, the Roman alphabet was adopted to replace the Arabic script, and attempts were made to revitalize old Turkish words to take the place of the Arabic and Persian which had crept into the Ottoman language. This reform is surely that foreseen in the fourth line of the quatrain: *Par dons & languages un plus attractive.* The 'one more attractive' is the Western alphabet, which enables Turkey to reaffirm its cultural connection with the West, rather than with the Eastern realms it had once dominated.

THE TREATY OF LAUSANNE

Several of the lesser-known quatrains of Nostradamus deal with the consequences of the collapse of the Ottoman Empire. This is not surprising, for as we saw earlier, the threat of Islam had been very powerful in the sixteenth century, and his readers would have scanned his verses carefully for any reference to what might happen in the future. However, as we have learned to our chagrin, most of the verses are couched so obscurely that they would be quite impenetrable prior to the event, no matter how clear afterwards. What, for example, would a sixteenth-century reader make of quatrain VIII.10?

> *Puanteur grande sortira de Lausanne,*
> *Qu'on ne sçaura l'origine du fait.*
> *L'on mettra hors toute la gent loingtaine*
> *Feu veu au ciel, peuple estranger deffait.*

> A great foul smell will come out of Lausanne,
> Concerning which they will not know the origin.
> They will move out all the distant people
> Fire seen in the sky, foreign people discomposed.

Analysis shows that the verse is a reference to events surrounding the final collapse of the Ottoman Empire, as recorded in the consequences of the Treaty of Lausanne. In drawing up this Treaty in 1923, diplomats engendered impulses which carried through history to the very beginnings of the Second World War, after which the power of the Ottomans was completely vitiated.

Anyone who is familiar with the ultra-clean and beautiful city of Lausanne, in the most Virgoan of all countries, must be puzzled by any prophecy which suggests that a foul smell may arise from it, or even be connected with it. We must assume that Nostradamus had in mind not the city itself, but the Treaty of 1923, which was negotiated there, and which formed the background to the ratification of the Empire which Nostradamus' contemporaries had so feared.

Why might Nostradamus describe the Treaty of Lausanne as causing an offensive smell (*Puanteur*)? Probably the explanation is connected with the fact that the 1923 Treaty was badly drawn up, and was in any case largely ignored by the Italians, who were already building a hegemony in the Eastern Mediterranean, as the Turkish power waned. The Treaty did little other than foment further troubles between Turkey and Greece – even though its ostensible purpose was to reconcile the two. In fact, the Treaty was negotiated partly under a continued force of arms, for the Greeks invaded the Ottoman territory of Asia Minor, and were mutilated. Subsequent to this defeat, the Turks were strong enough to dictate terms at Lausanne that were to prove prejudicial to the future stability of the eastern rim of Europe. Among the most important deficiencies in the Treaty was the fact that it made no provision for the autonomy of the Kurds, which the allies had regarded as being of the utmost importance. While renouncing her Arab conquests, Turkey was allowed to recover the frontiers she had established before the outbreak of the First World War. The Treaty might be said to 'stink' because it was so one-sided, and left unresolved extremely important issues, which would come to a head later in the century.

After a survey of the history of the period, we find it much easier to explain why Nostradamus could claim that no one would know the origin of the conditions which led to the formulation of the Treaty: *Qu'on ne sçaura l'origine du fait* – 'Concerning which they will not know the origin'.

Not only was the history attendant on the Greek-Turkish clashes complicated in itself, and probably beyond the grasp of the diplomats who drew up the Treaty, but the issues arising from the conflicts were rooted in the centuries-old struggle between Christianity and Islam, with which Nostradamus was all too familiar. The Treaty, while recognizing border disputes and the consequences of previous belligerent actions, failed to take into account the root conflict, which lay in the religious aspirations that form social attitudes. This failure may have been an early example of the political correctness which has so bedevilled the thinking of the later part of the twentieth century. Nostradamus would have been surprised by such a fudging of the issues, for in the sixteenth century religious issues were set out in stark blacks and whites: one paid allegiance to the Cross, and fought against the Crescent.

However, whatever the political correctness behind the Treaty, it did make a rigorous attempt to settle the post-war boundary disputes between Turkey and Greece, and marked the final – albeit nominal – renouncement of the territories gained by the Turks. In turn, the Greeks renounced claims to the lands in Asia Minor.

Virtually unique in modern times (and perhaps even in ancient times), as a consequence of the troubles foreseen within the implications of the Treaty, a vast programme of resettlement of refugees and displaced nationals was organized. By clear forward planning, a relatively harmonious exchange of populations between Turkey and Greece was completed, under the supervision of the League of Nations. It is this which Nostradamus foresaw, in 1558, in his strange line *L'on mettra hors toute la gent loingtaine* – 'They will move out all the distant people'. *Gent loingtaine* is a happy phrase in this context, for these were not foreigners (for which Nostradamus would have used a word such as *étrangers*, as in the final line). These were 'distant people' – people at a distance, or displaced, from their homelands. Many were what we would now call displaced refugees, who were moved back to their original lands. The uniqueness of this relatively successful operation is well expressed in the third line of the quatrain.

But, given the context, what can we make of the last line? *Feu veu au ciel, peuple estranger deffait* – 'Fire seen in the sky, foreign people discomposed'. We must observe that the word *deffait* has many possible interpretations in this context, ranging from 'discomposed' and 'undone', to 'defeated': as we shall see, all these meanings have a relevance in the history to which the quatrain seems to refer.

While admitting that this final line is susceptible to interpretation in a variety of war zones of the twentieth century, we should observe that it is precisely relevant to events following on the Treaty of Lausanne in 1923. In that same year, an Italian officer was murdered in Epirus, Greece. In response, the Italian airforce (already in the grip of Fascists, but perhaps also stirred by racial memories of what had happened when the Ottomans drove them from Epirus) bombed Corfu. This they did without any prior warning, causing considerable casualties and damage to property. Here, once again, we have a precise record from the pen of Nostradamus of this futurity, for the fire *was* seen in the skies, and foreign people *were* discomposed or undone – not merely because so many Greeks perished, but also because the bombing caused an international incident which was only settled through the arbitration of the League of Nations (*peuple estranger*).

During the last days of the Ottoman Empire, the Dodecanese islands had paid tribute directly to Turkey. During the Italian–Turkish war of 1912, the islands were captured by the Italians, who soon proved more oppressive to the Greeks than the Ottomans. Many Greeks left the islands, and after some political posturing, the Italians began to establish a strong presence, constructing a powerful naval base at Leros. Under this calculated oppression, the Greeks were compelled either to leave the islands, or to take Italian citizenship. This situation continued until the devastation of the Second World War, after which the islands reverted to the Greeks. Under the Treaty of Sèvres drawn up in 1920, the islands were given, on a temporary basis only, to Italy.

THE SPANISH CIVIL WAR

Among the most interesting verses dealing with Spain in the twentieth century is quatrain IX.16:

De castel Franco sortira l'assemblée,
L'ambassadeur non plaissant fera scisme:
Ceux de Ribiere seront en la meslée,
Et au grand goulphre desnier ont l'entrée.

From Castile Franco will go out of the assembly,
They do not please the ambassador who will make a schism:
Those of Ribiere will be in the mix-up,
And to the great final abyss they have entrance.

The reason for this 'translation' will become clear during the following analysis.

The quatrain is one of those rare verses wherein there is virtually no disguise of names. The words *Franco* and *Ribiere* undoubtedly point to General Franco and Primo de Rivera, the latter of whom ruled Spain during the terrible Civil War of 1936–9. Even the slight change made in the structure of the name *Ribiere* is meaningful. It is likely that Nostradamus, tongue in cheek, has changed the v in the name of Riviera to a b, because this is the first consonant in the alphabet. *Primo*, in Spanish, means first.

Even the single place name in the quatrain is transparent. The word *castel* is Castile, which, in the sixteenth century, was the vast Kingdom of Castile and León, stretching from the Bay of Biscay through central Spain, to the borders of the Kingdom of Granada.

In this quatrain, with his accustomed economy, Nostradamus lays bare the strategy of Franco and Mola during the Civil War. While Franco moved into Spain from Morocco, to form a bridgehead to the west of Gibraltar, followed by the taking of Seville, Mola moved in from the north. As the quatrain indicates, Franco's troops did descend from the north, through old Castile (*castel*) and across the Tagus, into what, in post-Nostradamian days, was called New Castile (*castel*). His aim was to divide the Republicans by cutting through to the Mediterranean. This he did by a double attack from Saragossa and Teruel, thus dividing the Republicans into enclaves in the Catalonian region around Barcelona, and the area around Madrid, stretching as far south as Almeria. It was this severance, the last part of which was effected via Teruel in June 1938, which really marked the collapse of the Republicans.

Who is the ambassador (*L'ambassadeur*) of line two? We might imagine that he is the one who decided to fight against Franco on the side of the Republicans. In fact, it is not easy to determine exactly what Nostradamus meant by the second line: *L'ambassadeur non plaissant fera scisme.* In Nostradamian terms, *non plaissant* is ambiguous: it can mean 'they are not pleased' or 'not pleasant'. As the subject is singular, we tend towards the latter reading.

The ambassador who would not be pleased by the schism in Spain could be either German or Italian, both of whom recognized the Spanish Nationalists under Franco early in the civil war – presumably with an eye to gains in Spain themselves. Both these countries poured men and arms into Spain to aid Franco, and both were disappointed that Franco, while thanking them, did not allow them access to his country afterwards. It has been argued that Franco's refusal to allow Hitler access to Gibraltar was a major contribution to the Allied success in the Second World War. Neither the Italian nor the German ambassadors (or their respective governments) ever seemed to have enough power over the wily Franco to bring about a schism in Spain. Additionally, viewed in terms of the Green Language, the names of both Italian and German ambassadors are not particularly pleasant, which means that we cannot determine for sure even which country is intended in the line.

Roberto Cantalupo was Italy's first ambassador to Franco's regime. His surname means approximately 'singing wolf'. Could this be what Nostradamus had in mind when he described the ambassador as being 'not pleasant'? Certainly, he was disappointed at the slow and methodical way in which Franco proceeded with the Nationalist campaign during the civil war. Mussolini, who, like Hitler, had provided troops and military equipment to Franco, was in a hurry to see the Nationalists established in Spain, but Franco insisted that they should not expect him to hurry.[10] Franco emphasized time and time again that his prosecution of the Civil War had to be slow, in order to save Spanish lives.

General von Faupel was the first German *chargé d'aff-aires* appointed in Franco's Spain. Von Faupel had been Colonel in the regiment in which Hitler had served as corporal during the First World War. In the Green Language, *Faupel* is also not a particularly pleasant name, for it means 'putrid skin'. It is from the German *faul* (rotten, shady, decayed, etc.) and *pell* (husk, skin, etc.). The modern German, *faulpelz*, means sluggard.

In view of this difficulty, we are tempted to read the ambassador as a reference to the fact that both factions in the Spanish Civil War was supported by foreign nations, and that the German and Italian ambassadors played an important role in the development of the conflict. It is to Franco's credit that he gave no ground to either Hitler or Mussolini in return for the help given.

In the third line there is mention of Primo de Rivera (*Ribiere*), who was the ruler of Spain. Franco was, initially at least, one of his generals. This may well account for the reason why the quatrain appears to distinguish between the two men. Nostradamus tells us that Franco had an assembly (*assemblée*) – which is quite true, for he built up his army, and assembled his troops, in the north and south of Spain. Rivera, on the other hand, had those who were his own (*Ceux*). A ruler has no need to assemble, for he already commands.

In the fourth line, *Goulphre* means abyss, pit or whirl-pool. Surely it is the abyss of the savage Spanish Civil War? In the last two lines of the verse, Nostradamus claims that the followers of Rivera (*Ribiere*) are in the fighting (*meslée*), and implies (quite rightly, as history proved) that it was this

northern group that made the breakthrough which determined the final course of the conflict.

In the final line, the meaning of the word *desnier* is
questionable. As we have observed, Nostradamus' practice
is often to leave in the letter s in a word where in later
French its absence is marked by an acute accent. This
would imply that the correct reading is *denier*. However,
denier is neither correct grammar, nor meaningful, in the
context. On the other hand, *dernier* (which, since it means
'last', contrasts delightfully with *Primo*) is full of meaning.
This explains why we have translated the line as: 'And to
the great final abyss they have entrance'. The final abyss
was the fighting after the breach made by Franco's north-
ward drive from Teruel, in June 1938, as a necessary military
sequence to the first breach (made two months earlier from
Saragossa, to cut off Tortosa, Tarragona and Barcelona).

UFOS AND SKY-FIRES

The contemporary craze for Unidentified Flying Objects
has led inexorably to the reworking and retranslating of
several quatrains in modern times. The notion may seem
far-fetched, yet when certain of Nostradamus' verses are
approached superficially, they do appear to point to an
event – or perhaps to several events – involving the descent
of spacecraft and contact with aliens. This superficial
approach is not substantiated by a deeper research, however. The one real problem is that certain commentators
have taken it upon themselves to reword some of the verses
to make this prediction of UFO contact more obvious. A
good example of this latter procedure is found in the notes
of Henry Roberts, in regard to quatrain I.83, which reads:

La gent estrange divisera butins
Saturne & Mars son regard furieux,

Horrible strage aux Toscans & Latins,
Grecs qui seront à frapper curieux.

A fair translation of the verse is probably:

The strange tribe will divide the plunder
Saturn and Mars his furious stare,
Hideous confusion to the Tuscans and the Latins,
(Are) the Greeks whom they will be careful to strike.

Roberts, who had not copied the French of Nostradamus
accurately, claimed this quatrain predicts that extraterrestrial aliens will land on earth and terrify southern Europe.
In spite of the general inaccuracy and banality of the
Roberts translations, their influence on modern 'commentators' has been considerable, and similar 'translations' have
been offered, almost word for word, in other books on
Nostradamus. For example, Arkel and Blake appear to copy
the mistakes of Roberts, who had in turn copied those of
Garencières, written in 1672. The problem is that the
quatrain predicts no such thing as a space invasion: nor
does Nostradamus even mention extraterrestrials.

One other interesting verse also finds its way into the
modern 'UFO' anthologies. This is quatrain I.46, which
reads:

Tout aupres d'Aux, de Lectore & Mirande,
Grande feu du Ciel en trois nuicts tombera,
Cause adviendra bien stupende & mirande,
Bien peu apres la terre tremblera.

Very close to Auche, Lectoure and Mirande,
For three nights a great fire will fall from the sky,
The thing shall occur most stupendous and wonderful,
A short while afterwards, the ground will tremble.

The three pleasant towns of Auche, Lestoure and Mirande lie to the south of Agen, on the RR21, to the west of Toulouse, in the south-west of France. Even during the World Wars there appear to have been no pyrotechnics or incendiary events corresponding to the one described in such uncharacteristically simple terms by Nostradamus. We may therefore be led to presume that this three-day celestial fire, and the subsequent earthquake (if that is what the earth-movement is) lie in our own future. However, there is something almost personalized in the quatrain – almost as though it relates to something which Nostradamus himself had found stupendous and wonderful. We know that Nostradamus witnessed the splendid Halley's Comet of 1531, and it is therefore reasonable to wonder whether he is referring to just such a phenomenon. Perhaps, indeed, he experienced this comet from near the three places he mentioned in his verse?

From a vision of a comet or falling star, it is an easy distance to the words in the apocalyptic *Revelation*. In 8.5 of this arcane Biblical text we are presented with the image of an angel hurling fire towards the earth, after which follows an earthquake. Five short verses further on, in 8.10, we are told of a greater star, burning as a lamp, as it fell from the heavens. The name of this star was called Wormwood. The apocalyptic literature, which was wildly popular in the sixteenth century, is no stranger to curious fires in the heavens, and large numbers of pamphlets have survived from the period portraying celestial events which are nowadays interpreted as relating to UFOs (see *fig. 27*).

Whatever the celestial fire and earth movement described by Nostradamus in quatrain I.46, one finds no mention of space visitors or aliens in the verse. It is therefore rank irresponsibility by those who interpret the quatrain as pertaining to the arrival of visitors in spacecraft. Henry Roberts is in error in reading this verse as a forecast of an

419

extraterrestrial sighting and landing, 'with subsequent benefits to earth people'. In their treatment of this quatrain, Arkel and Blake depend entirely upon the Roberts version, and come to the conclusion that 'visitors from space will be arriving in a contingent'.

Quatrain II.46

Au ciel veu feu, courant longue estincelle
In the sky a fire is seen, dragging a tail of sparks

Quatrain II.96

Flambeau ardant au ciel sera veu
A burning torch in the sky will be seen

While the fecund imagination might wish to grasp at these lines as predictions of UFOs, the far simplest explanation is that Nostradamus is referring to comets or meteors. We have already observed how another quatrain, which has been equated with ufology, has nothing to do with extraterrestrials, but with the Nova of 1572, and the fixed star Sirius (see page 247 ff). A superficial analysis of this quatrain, which seems to mention two suns in the sky, and howling dogs, could easily have invited Forteanism gone wild: as it was, the quatrain invited dark prophecies of terminal wars, which Nostradamus certainly did not have in mind.

For all he was unique as a prophet, Nostradamus did not work entirely in literary isolation. The apocalyptic literature favoured by Nostradamus – mainly the Biblical *Isaiah, Ezekiel, Daniel* and St John's Apocalypse – contains a wealth of references to stellar fires, comets, falling stars, and the like. There may be no doubt that in such dramatic-seeming references, Nostradamus is merely adhering to the well-worn style of the traditional prophet within the accepted imagery of prophecy. The floods and rivers of blood, which are the standard images of the ecclesiastical prophets, are also found in the quatrains.

Quatrain I.69

> *Apres paix, guerre, faim, inondation*
> After peace, war, hunger, floods

Quatrain II.57

> *Aupres du fleuve de sang la terre tainte*
> The earth is stained around the river of blood

Quatrain IV.94

> *Rougir mer, Rosne sang Leman d'Alemagne*
> To colour the sea red, rosy, the blood in
> lake Leman, from Germany

Useful as a sample of such lines may be, our main purpose here is not to analyse all the so-called 'UFO' quatrains, or the related verses of the 'fire-from-the-skies' variety. Our purpose is merely to indicate that those who translate these verses in terms of modern superstitions are certainly in error. Most of this cosmological and atmospheric imagery is derived from Biblical lore, which was one of the staple influences in prophetic literature. As we have seen in several analyses of quatrains, Nostradamus rarely means literally what he says: *terre tremblera* ('earth will tremble') does not always denote an earthquake, and his *feu du ciel* ('fire from the sky') does not have a supernatural origin, though it may refer to aerial bombardment of the kind which was quite possible in the sixteenth century.

THE END OF THE GREAT WAR

A fine example of such a verse is quatrain IV.100 which could easily be interpreted as a UFO prediction but which, on analysis, is revealed as an astrological quatrain, predicting events in the First World War.

De feu celeste au Royal edifice,
Quand la lumiere du Mars deffaillira,
Sept mois grand' guerre, mort gent de malefice,
Rouen, Evreux, au Roy ne faillira.

Celestial fire on the Royal edifice,
When the light of Mars fails,
Seven months the great war, people dead of evil-doing,
Rouen, Evreux, shall not fall to the King.

The quatrain's first three lines inform us that a 'celestial fire' will fall on the 'Royal edifice', and that when the light of Mars 'fails', there will be seven months of the Great War. The last half of the third, and the last line, which need not concern us in the present context, tells us that a person (*gent*) will die through evil, and that the cities of Rouen and Evreux will not fall to the King.

As the commentator Chodkiewicz has pointed out, this quatrain is a reference to the last years of the First World War.[11] Chodkiewicz bases this reasonable assumption on the fact that the 'celestial fire' was the near-vertical drop of shells on Paris (the *Royal edifice*) from the long-range German cannon which was named 'the Long Max'. According to Chodkiewicz, this bombardment of Paris lasted for several days, the cannons firing their shells every 20 minutes, from a distance of 70 miles. No similar savage bombardment of a civilian city had occurred before: even the bombardment by the Germans during the siege of Paris in 1870 was not of this intensity. In fact, the German armies reached within 35 miles of Paris, and had ample opportunity to rain their destructive 'celestial fire' upon the city.

Clearly, the most enigmatic line is the second, which seems to contain an opportunity to date the quatrain by reference to astrology: *Quand la lumiere du Mars deffaillira.* The term 'Mars failing' (strict, *Mars deffaillira*) has no specialist astrological meaning though it does suggest a situation in which Mars is not working at its normal strength. In astrological terms, Mars can be weak only under two circumstances: one, when it is in the sign or degree of its own detriment, and two, when it is retrograde. In the sixteenth century (as in modern times), astrologers tended to see the latter as the weakest manifestation of a planet.

The great sixteenth-century French astrologer Morin de Villefranche, who was born 17 years after Nostradamus died, continued the medieval tradition of astrology by insisting that retrograde planets had an action contrary to their direct effects. This is to say that the strong planet Mars would be weak (*defaillier*) when retrograde. Morin was merely summarizing the astrological beliefs with which Nostradamus was familiar.[12]

How does this tradition of a retrogradation apply to the astrological conditions surrounding the events of the First World War? The retrogradation of Mars occurred only twice during the long period of this War. In the first instance, Mars went retrograde on 1 January 1916, and returned to direct motion on 22 March 1916. It was in direct motion for just over two years, until 4 February 1918, when once again it went retrograde.

It was during the second period of retrograde motion, precisely as Nostradamus had foreseen, that the Long Max cannons began to project celestial fire on Paris. However, the fact of the retrogradation of Mars ties in with the *Sept mois grand' guerre* of line three. The extraordinary fact is that after the retrogradation of Mars there remains only a period of seven months to the end of the war. The period between the ending of the retrograde motion of Mars, on 26 April 1918, and the Armistice, on 11 November 1918, is actually 6 months and 15 days.

May we take it as a sign of the genius of Nostradamus that he should use the very same term to describe this human conflict (*grand' guerre*) as those who participated in it? Until a further period of reciprocal destruction reduced this conflict to the status of the First World War, it was always referred to as the Great War.

Such is the extraordinary power of Nostradamus' vision that he was able to perceive a cosmic event which would parallel (not cause, we venture to emphasize) a period in the first of the wars he predicts for this century.

In this quatrain, then, we see Nostradamus using his knowledge of astrology to construct an arcane reference which will hide an important date. Surprisingly, in comparison with certain other quatrains, in which he adopts a similar approach, this is a very simple example.

Nostradamus seems to have delighted in dating conflicts by reference to the stars. Whether irony was intended in this method is not clear, but the image of the stars looking down on human frailty is an old theme in literature and art. No doubt, it is the celestial and cosmo-astrological references, as much as the Biblical imagery, which led the modern Forteans to trace 'ufological' ideas into these quatrains. In following such impulses, they are merely grafting modern superstitions on the vision of a sixteenth-century visionary who had no prevision of aliens or alien crafts – possibly even no prevision of such modern realities as aeroplanes.

THE POPE AND FIVE

Quatrain V.92 gives a prophecy which some commentators have argued relates to a list of future popes, scheduled by the medieval prophet Malachai for somewhere near the turn of this century.[13]

Apres le siege tenu dix & sept ans,
Cinq changeront en tel revolu terme:
Puis sera l'un esleu de mesme temps,
Qui des Romains ne sera trop conforme.

After holding the seat for seventeen years,
Five will change in just such a period:
Then at the same period of time will be the one elected,
Who to the Romans will not be too agreeable.

Many interpreters see this as a reference to a pope who will reign for 17 years, followed by a succession of five popes who will, between them, reign for a similar term. Others have seen it as a reference to a king who rules for 17 years. For example, Henry Roberts, in the 1982 edition of his book, claims that the quatrain refers to Louis-Philippe of France, who had five sons. Roberts claims that Louis-Philippe's reign lasted for '17 years' (*dix sept ans*), from 1831 to 1848. Unfortunately, this is not true: Louis-Philippe became king of the French on 7 August 1830, and fled to England in February 1848. Erika Cheetham, in the 1973 edition of her book, goes so far as to suggest that Nostradamus is 'slightly out' by two years, and refers to Pius XII who reigned for 19 years. On this basis, she points to the prophecies of Malachai, whom, she had been led to understand, gave only five more popes before the 'Final Coming', or the end of the Papacy. In fact, the quatrain appears to relate to both a pope and a ruler. It is the 17 years which offers the secret clue to the meaning of the quatrain, for, since the sixteenth century, the only pope to have reigned for 17 years was Pius XI. He occupied the Papal chair from 1922 to 1939. However, from the point of the usual reading of this quatrain, the problem with Pius XI is that his papacy was not followed by a group of five popes who reigned for a total of 17 years. This should alert us to the fact that there is no real indication in the quatrain that Nostradamus was referring to a succession of popes at all.

In fact, the structure of the quatrain (with *ans* – years – at the end of the first line) means that the *Cinq* (five) could refer to years, rather than to the *siege* (seat). From a historical point of view, it is significant that Pius XI died on the eve of the Second World War. The five years of warfare which followed his papacy saw profound changes in Europe. It is this period of five years to which the quatrain refers – the Second World War is the *Cinq changeront en tel revolu terme*. The most important clue to the meaning of the quatrain is contained in the first two lines. These allow us to obtain two dates which locate the quatrain in history. The beginning of the 17-year period is in 1922, the ending 1939. As we presume that the five years after 1939 were occupied by the Second World War, we must assume that the import of the quatrain is somehow directed towards this event. Who, we might ask, was of importance to the Second World War, connected with Italy, and elected to an important office in 1922?

The year 1922 was critical for the career of Benito Mussolini. He had stood as a Fascist candidate for Milan during the elections of 1919, but obtained only a handful of votes. His attempt to gain power in 1920 through siding with rebellious metallurgical workers also failed. In 1921, however, Mussolini was elected by the Fascists, and by the end of that year, Fascism had been organized into a party. The general strike called in 1922 was broken up by the

Fascists, and in the same year, Mussolini renounced his republicanism. It was in this same year that the Italian King entrusted Mussolini with the task of forming a new cabinet. By October 1922, the first Fascist Government was in power (with seven portfolios in the hand of *Il Duce* himself!) in Italy.

In the light of this interpretation, the last two lines of the quatrain take on a new meaning: *Puis sera l'un esleu de mesme temps, / Qui des Romains ne sera trop conforme.* During the 17-year period would grow the power of the one elected (*l'un esleu*) at the same time (that is, in 1922), who would prove not to be agreeable to the Romans. In this quatrain, as in so many, Nostradamus is using the code of taking an important city (Rome) to represent the entire country (Italy). The fact is that the machinations of *Il Duce* during the 17 pre-war years led Italy into a totally inappropriate alliance with the Italian-German pact he signed with Hitler in 1939 (the end of the 17-year period). The five years of war which followed were an unmitigated disaster for Italy.

THE BRITISH EMPIRE

One of Nostradamus' less opaque prophecies, quatrain X.100, relates to the future greatness of England:

> *Le grand empire sera par Angleterre,*
> *Le Pempotan des ans plus de trois cens:*
> *Grandes copies passer par mer & terre,*
> *Les Lusitains n'en seront pas contens.*

For once, a translation seems to offer few problems:

> The great empire will be with England,
> The all-powerful of more than three hundred years.

Great armies to pass by sea and land,
The Portuguese will not be content by this.

Seen in retrospect, this is one of the most outstanding examples of Nostradamus' power of prophecy. In the mid-sixteenth century, there was absolutely nothing discernible which would proclaim the emergence of England as a world Empire. The evidence in front of the eyes of the contemporaries of Nostradamus might suggest that either Spain or Holland would carry the future palm, while the more hopeful might conclude that the future lay with France. However, in spite of the evidence around him, Nostradamus offers a quatrain – possibly the final quatrain in his original sequence – which makes the promise that what we have since called 'the British Empire' would hold sway for 'more than' 300 years.

What is this Empire, this *Pempotan*? We cannot understand the implications of this remarkable quatrain without reflecting upon the arcane mastery which Nostradamus exercises in his invention of the word *Pempotan*. Although the word is not found in any dictionary we know, it is clearly a Green Language term, working as a compound of Latin and Greek associate terms. It is a hybrid of the Greek *pan*, meaning 'all', and the Latin *potens*, meaning 'powerful': thus, the entire hybrid means 'all-powerful'. However, by euphony it evokes the Greek adverb, *pennipotens*, 'able to fly' (from the term *potanos*, 'winged'), as well as the Greek noun *Potamos*, 'river'. In this last association, Nostradamus is clearly drawing a connection between British Empire expansion and the river Thames, which he mentions by name several times in the *Prophéties* as approximately the equivalent of London. One further arcane element is the change from the *pan* to *pem*, which appears to be designed to offer an opportunity for us to read into P*emp*otan the beginning of *Emp*ire.

The Green Language term connotes something which is

all-powerful, capable of metaphoric flight, and which derives its power from a river, or from water. This *Pempotan* is the cloak of greatness which will be passed to England for a period of more than 300 years.

Naturally, any Anglophile will want to know when that period began, if only to confirm the well-founded suspicion that the *Pempotan* has passed on. While few would argue that Britain still lives in the midst of the full flush of Empire, it is evident that it still lives in the last afterglow. Perhaps, following the wily reasoning of Parkinson's Law, we should seek the demise of the British Empire in the year 1948, when India House was finished.[*] More realistically, however, it is likely that when twentieth-century history is recorded with the impartiality that hindsight offers, it will be recognized that most of the early decades of the twentieth century were involved in the gradual winding up of the Empire.

Actually, we do not have to speculate too widely on the beginning and end of this 300-year periodicity, for Nostradamus leaves us a valuable clue as to when it began. This clue is found in his curious reference to the *Lusitains*, or Portuguese, which is only explicable in terms of offering a hint at the date.

The word *Lusitains*, whilst probably a meaningful denotation for his contemporaries, is an extremely early example of the word. Although the *Oxford English Dictionary* dates the word Lusitanian to English usage in 1607, it was employed by Nostradamus, in his typically unorthodox

---

[*] In one of his laws, Parkinson suggested that the main building (such as a headquarters) intended to serve a particular enterprise would be finished, and ready for use, only when that enterprise had reached the end of its active life. The law was a reflection on the slowness, fatuity, shortsightedness and general inutility of bureaucracy. So it proved with the building of India House, which served merely to oversee the withdrawal of the British from India.

spelling of *Lusitains*, as early as 1558. Of course, he may have been encouraged to use this ancient name to denote the Portuguese because of the *Lusiad*, the title which Luis de Camoëns had used for his national epic of Portuguese exploits, published in 1572. There is probably no accident in this derivation, for the *Lusiad* celebrates the greatness of Portugal, through the exploits of the hero, Vasco da Gama, and his role in the expansion of Portuguese trade in such places as India.

In the early sixteenth century the Portuguese explorers had the world at their feet. 'And, had the world stretched even further, they would have gone there, too', was how de Camoëns summed up this period of expansion, during which Magellan had circumnavigated the globe, and wrily considered claiming the whole world for Portugal. The Portuguese had footholds in Macao, Goa, Malacca, Greenland, Labrador, Tibet and the West Indies.

Unfortunately, while these adventurous souls roamed the new-found globe, errors were being made at home. Portuguese business acumen had been weakened by the expulsion of the Moors and Jews at the end of the previous century, and for a variety of internal reasons Portugal was not able to benefit from the extensive trade in those far-flung parts of the world. Religious and social regression reached a high-spot in 1536, when the Inquisition were allowed a foothold in the country, and expanded with incredible rapidity. The child-king Sebastian (*reg.* 1557–78) deflected attention from poor conditions at home by electing to attack the infidels in Morocco. This disastrous campaign lost him an army and his life.

Subsequently a loose union enforced by Spain meant that money poured from the coffers of the once-rich Portugal to the more voracious economy, centralized in Madrid. Portugal was already a vassal state when the

English and Dutch began to challenge the Portuguese sea power.

The destruction of the great Armada in 1588 marked the end of all pretence of power by Portugal. Although the Armada was not Portuguese, the Spanish had used the magnificent port of Lisbon to set out on their ill-advised invasion of Britain. Portuguese soldiers and sailors had been among those who sailed in the huge flotilla of 129 vessels. This is one reason why, having successfully seen off the Armada, the English attacked and sacked so many Portuguese settlements, in Pernambuco, the Azores and India.

It is this history of Portuguese decline – to a point where the nation was punished for being allies of a Spain which, in any case, treated them abysmally – that Nostradamus appears to have foreseen, and hinted at when he used the word *Lusitains*.

Not only was 1588 a low-point in the history of Portugal – by which the Portuguese could well be displeased – it was the outer marking of the British expansion. It seems that after destroying the Armada in 1588, few things could go wrong for British expansionism. Nostradamus was quite right in seeing that after this period, the British armies would pass over land and sea (*Grandes copies passer par mer & terre*), forging a great empire (*grand empire*) which would last for over 300 years.

In effect, it is merely this reference to the Portuguese (*Lusitains*) which suggests a beginning for the period. Nostradamus wisely left the term to the period loosely formulated. Apparently, it was this loose formulation which encouraged Hitler in the early days of his conflict with Britain. The dictator seems to have confused the demise of the Empire with the notion of a weak, impotent and friendless Britain. The fact that, during the Second World

War, the Empire was still sufficiently intact to wage a successful war might suggest that we could date the end of the Empire to 1947, when home rule was granted to India – the jewel of the Empire. If this date is taken, then it is possible that we should look for a year a little earlier than 1647 when the Empire might be said to have begun.

If we are correct in our surmise, and the date 1588 is that which Nostradamus had in mind for the beginnings of the British Empire, then this means that the end of that Empire should be found round about 1888. Perhaps it is tempting to date the end of the Empire to the death of Queen Victoria, in 1901, before Britain and Europe were wracked by the obscene wars of the twentieth century?

Not all commentators have accepted the starting date of the Armada. The English author, H. I. Woolf, reflecting on quatrain X.100, observed that when the verse was written, the Portuguese owned an immense colonial empire in Africa, India and South America. Accordingly, he did not link the quatrain with the Armada, but with 1578 when Sebastian of Portugal was beaten at Alcazar Quivir by Mouley Abd-el-Melik. His interpretation of the prophecy was general, for he did not see the displeasure of the Portuguese as being connected with the rise of the British Empire. He saw the colonization of the Atlantic seaboard of North America in 1607 as the starting point of this Empire, and the ruin of the Portuguese almost a century later, with the Treaty of Methuen, in 1703.

If we are to accept the Armada theory for the dating of quatrain X.100 – that is, accept 1588 as the beginning of this power of Britain – we may ask if there is any quatrain which deals with this event.

We might even resolve the problem by means of a different question: is there any quatrain which deals in a distinctive way with the end of the period? If there is, then might we find in it some clue as to the beginning or ending of this period of 300 years? Quatrain II.68 has been linked with the Spanish Armada invasion of Britain in 1588, but our analysis cannot support this interpretation. The quatrain reads:

> *De l'Aquilon les efforts seront grands,*
> *Sur l'Ocean sera la porte ouverte,*
> *Le regne en l'isle sera reintegrand,*
> *Tremblera Londres par voille descouverte.*

> The efforts of the North will be great,
> On the Ocean will be an open door,
> The kingdom of the island will be established again,
> London will tremble because of discovered sail.

This quatrain has caught the imagination of many commentators, who have argued for such diverse predictive histories as the innovations of Peter the Great in Russia, the return of Charles II to England and the Van Tromp threat. However, analysis of the quatrain suggests that it has nothing to do with any of these, nor with Spain. Probably the quatrain does not even involve an invasion of ships. Rather than being applied to the Armada which threatened England, it should be considered as relating to the Second World War, when London did tremble (literally) under a peculiar form of *voille*. Serge Hutin seems to have been the first to trace in it the German bombardment of London, but his argument for this was not very convincing.[14]

The fourth-line *voille* is a Green Language reading of *vols*, and *voile*, the former meaning 'aerial flight', the latter meaning, among other things, 'sails' and 'veils'. So intimately linked is *vols* with *voile* that the French *vol à voiles* means 'gliding'. When the sky is clouded over, it is in

433

French 'veiled' (the verb is *se voiler*). Each of these associations can be seen as linking with the idea of aerial flights which make a city tremble, and veil the skies above the city in smoke.

The *regne* of the third line could mean both 'line of kingship' and 'government'. In fact, both apply within the context of the Second World War, for shortly before the war broke out, the abdication of Edward VIII led to a hiatus until George VI took over, and thus reintegrated the reign. At the same time, the reign of Britain itself was once more re-established when, for a few months the island stood alone against the might of Germany, which occupied a vanquished continent.

Even the enigmatic second line makes sense within this World War context, for without the Atlantic Ocean being kept sufficiently clear for communication with the States, there would have been no possibility of Britain being victorious.

The *Aquilon* of the first line is both dual in meaning and ambiguous. On the one hand, *aquilon* is the French word for the north-wind. In this Nostradamian context, therefore, it refers to the North, which could be Britain, Germany or, at a stretch, even the United States (all of which made incredible efforts during the war years). However, some of the ambiguity is removed when we observe that Nostradamus gives the word a capital letter.

Aquila is the Latin word for eagle. Whilst this bird has been the symbol of the USA since the Seal of State was adopted in 1782, the States cannot accurately be described as being in the north, as may Britain or Germany. However, it was the ocean between Britain and the States which made the successful prosecution of the war possible. Even so, there is a degree of ambiguity in the reference: the eagle which was used as a Nazi emblem was double-headed, and has a far more ancient ancestry than the eagle of Jupiter adopted by the States.

It is evident that quatrain II.68 does not relate to the Armada, but on the contrary deals with a period some time after the putative end of Empire. In a recent book on the Empire, Gerald Graham traced the beginnings of the British Empire to Humphrey Gilbert's formal gesture of the possession of the island of Newfoundland in 1583.[15] Graham also observes that in 1896 (nearly 300 years after Gilbert's personally disastrous exploit) Lord Rosebery informed an Edinburgh audience that, within the past 12 years, 2,600,000 square miles had been added to the Empire. Would it be more proper to see the final days of the Empire in Resolution IX, placed on record at the Imperial War Conference in 1917?

No matter how we amend and adjust the beginning and end of this 300-year perodicity, we are left with a sense of wonder that Nostradamus – in spite of all the contemporaneous odds – should have foreseen this strange destiny for Britain, and expressed it with such profound accuracy.

As we have seen, Nostradamus usually has an astrological basis for his dates and periodicities. Is there anything astrological in this loose period of 300 years?

Nostradamus insists on a period of 'over 300 years' for this *pempotan*. The figure may be an attempt to offer a round number for his versification. However, it is worth recording that no matter how omniscient one may be, the very nature of history makes it hard to date the beginning of so complex a series of events as the decline and emergence of nations. On the other hand, a relevant periodicity close to the 300-year cycle may be traced through astrological periodicities.

Nostradamus (like many other prophets who relied upon astrology) placed much emphasis on the Great Conjunctions of Jupiter and Saturn. Since he recognized that

England was ruled by Aries, he might have been inclined to see the great conjunction of 1702 as marking the beginning of the Empire. This would be reasonable, for the 1702 trigon was in 6 degrees of Aries. Now, by a strange quirk, 280 years later, the great conjunction of 1981 occurred in 5 degrees of Libra – almost diametrically opposite to the Arietan conjunction. An astrologer could link the growth of power in an Aries nation to the 6 degrees of Aries, and trace the decline of that same nation to the opposite degree, in Libra. Just as the power of one *pempotan* declines, so it is passed on to a more receptive nation. By extending the method of Nostradamus, can we trace any post-1981 *pempotan* in future Great Conjunctions? The great conjunctions of the next century will be in the Air trigons.

There is one other way to establish the parameters of the 300 years, and that is to work backwards, from a date furnished by Nostradamus. On page 386 ff we analysed quatrain X.67 to show how it pointed to 1901, as the start of the horror of the twentieth century. The related quatrain IX.83, employing a similar astrological figure, marked the end of that same century, with extraordinary precision. Now, if we can believe Nostradamus, the world was going to change radically after 1901 – that is, in the twentieth century. If we take this beginning of the end of Empire as being 1901, we must go back to 1601, or thereabouts, in search of a beginning to the *Pempotan*.

We would therefore propose the year 1901 (which is technically the end of the Victorian era) as the formal end of British Empire. Since quatrain X.100 is intimately connected with quatrain X.66, we are tempted to interpret the first line of this latter verse – *La chef de Londres par regne l'Americh* – as an indication that the former grandeur of Empire centring upon Great Britain will pass over to America, on completion of the cycle, in the year 2000.

436

THE ISLAND OF SCOTLAND

This is probably a convenient point to examine the 'American' verse, quatrain X.66, which runs:

> *Le chef de Londres par regne l'Americh,*
> *L'isle d'Ecosse t'empiera par gelée:*
> *Roy Rebauront un si faux Antechrist,*
> *Que les mettra trestous dans la meslée:*

Although this is a very difficult quatrain to translate, we shall offer the following, if only as a basis for discussion:

The chief of London by the American reign,
The isle will divide thee from Scotland by frost:
They will have again as King one who is so false an Antechrist,
That he will put them altogether in a conflict:

With quatrains which relate to the future, there is so little for the commentator to grasp hold of that those who attempt such interpretations feel as though they are drowning in words. Our only consolation in the midst of this drowning is that not a single commentator has so far managed to make sense of the quatrain. The general drift of opinion is towards the notion that British and American political leadership will lead to the establishing of a Dictator (or an Antechrist) who will bring great troubles to the world (*Le chef de Londres par regne l'Americh*). *Americh* is certainly *Amerique* (America). There may be little doubt of this, since the Rigaud 1566 edition gives *Americh*, while the 1568 edition gives *Amerique*. We have already noted that, in the sixteenth century, this name was by no means commonplace. The first line is far from easy to grasp, as we do not know who the chief of London (*chef de Londres*) is, or will be. Presumably, by the synecdoche which Nostradamus favours, this is a leader of England or the British Isles. Even were we able to identify this personage, we would find it difficult to interpret the line, which is ambiguous. Does it mean, approximately: 'The leader of England by American power . . . ,' or, 'The leader of England by the rule of America'? The *regne l'Americh* could mean the kingdom of America, or (given the want of such a word in the sixteenth century) even the leader of the America Nation – that is, the President. If this were the case, then the line might be read as meaning something like: 'The leader of England, by power vested through the President . . .'

No doubt, when the quatrain is fulfilled, and the names of the participants recognized, then the words of the verse will become very clear. For the moment, however, we have to confess ourselves as being foxed as to its precise meaning.

While touching upon futurity, we should observe that the quatrain does not end in a full stop. The last line has a colon (as we represent it above). This termination to a verse occurs only rarely in the *Prophéties*, and we wonder if it is a device to suggest a connection with the next numbered verse. As it happens, this next numbered verse (X.67) is one which we have described as a book-end to the twentieth century, and is intimately linked with another quatrain (IX.83) which also deals with our own futurity – with AD 2000, to be precise. We have dealt with both above, on pages 384–90. It may be worth while glancing at the implications for these quatrains in the light of this present analysis of X.66.

The second line reads: *L'isle d'Escosse t'empiera par gelée.* Almost all commentators have interpreted this line as though it referred to Scotland, even though the words refer distinctly to an 'island' of Scotland, which has been hardened by ice. Cheetham suggested that the 'cold thing' (the ice, or *gelée*) was the Polaris submarine, presumably not realizing that the name of the craft was not intended to evoke the poles, but the fixed star, the *alpha* of Ursa Minor.

It might be argued that the word *Escosse* may have a different meaning, however. The French slang, *escoffier* means 'to write off, or kill'. Thus *L'isle d'Escoffe* could be the isle of death, where those who are killed end up: in this quatrain, it is visualized as being hardened by ice. This vision is familiar enough to the readers of Dante's *Inferno*, as the lake of ice at the centre of Hell. The island in this sea of death is Lucifer.

The verb *empierrer* means approximately 'hardened to stone by frost'. We must ask, why did Nostradamus introduce the personal diminutive, *t'empiera*, in the second line? Were the line read as relating to Scotland, then it would go something like: 'The island of Scotland will harden thee with ice . . .'

However, it is possible that the 1668 version of the quatrain has introduced an error here, for the earlier versions of the verse give the variant *tempiera* and *temptera*: both these verbs involve a radical change in the meaning of the line.

Let us consider the possibilities in the word *tempiera*. The Latin *temperor* means to divide in due proportion, and it is not far-fetched to see the Nostradamian word as meaning 'will divide'. Such a reading makes perfect sense in the line, for the ice-sheet at the centre of Purgatory divides the upper hemisphere from the lower. Strictly speaking, the line could read: 'The island will be divided from Scotland by ice'.

Within such a Dantesque context of Hell, the appearance of the name Antechrist in the third line begins to makes some sense. This word alone would reveal this as an apocalyptic quatrain: this also explains the number of the verse – 66 – for it evokes 666, which in *Revelation* is the number of the Beast.

By a most curious coincidence, two reports in *The Times* for 7 October 1996 touch on subjects which seem to have pertinence to Nostradamus predictions. One, relating to the dangers of the European Union, we shall examine on page 452 ff. The other seems to throw some light on this quatrain X.66. A report by Ian Murray deals with a planned engineering scheme to create a western water highway between the North Sea, and the Solway Firth. This northern 'Panama Canal' would have the technical effect of making Scotland an island. Presumably, such a canal would, from time to time, freeze over, thus dividing the 'island' (which in Nostradamian terms is England) from Scotland by ice. The link which this prediction (if it ever is fulfilled in this way) makes with a supposed false Antichrist is beyond our comprehension at present. However, a knowledge of Nostradamus' methods does suggest that the canal-building would offer a date framework on which the other details of the prediction would emerge.

However, before we attempt to come to grips with the idea of the Antechrist, we should make some effort to unravel the first two less dramatic – though more infuriating – words of this line: *Roy Rebauront un si faux Antechrist*. First, we should note the impossible tense of *Roy Rebauront* if *Roy* is taken as being nominative, meaning 'the King' (or, of course, being the proper name Roy). In either case, we have a singular noun with plural verb (if *Rebauront* is a verb). This suggests that the *Roy* is an accusative. While the word Roy means 'king' in French, there is no such word as *Rebauront*. However, the prefix *re* appears in many French words (for example, *rebatir*, to build again), and we might therefore be inclined to read the word as *re*, with the letter b, and the plural future of the verb *avoir*, which is *auront*: *Roy re-b-auront* – 'The King they will have again'.

The Greek-derived Latin *reboatus* (a shouting back) might be applicable to the line. If this meaning were adopted, then the two words *Roy Rebauront* would mean 'The King they shout back', or perhaps, 'The King they acclaimed back'. Who is this king (*Roy*) who is shouted back – presumably, invited back with clamour? It is tempting, in view of the general meaning of the quatrain (which we shall examine below), to see this *Roy Rebauront* as a play on a name of an individual who will become, nominally, if not in actuality, a 'king' (*Roy*) in a republican country. Whether this is a country in the 'European States' of what is now called the Economic Union, which is already, by its undemocratic structure, inviting the emergence of a single dictatorial head, or whether it is a presidential king for the United States, is impossible to determine before the event. No doubt the next few years will unfold the meaning in the curious words. Whatever emerges will be a surprise within the framework of existing political trends.

The two words have caused many scholars to have headaches, and much ingenuity has gone into their glossing. De Fontbrune saw the prediction as relating to the year 1999, when Asian Communist countries would be brought into a war. To facilitate things, he changed Nostradamus' two words, *Roy Rebauront* to *Roy Reb auront* ('They will have Roy Reb . . .'), with an unconvincing note to the effect that *Reb* was from the Latin *robeus*, meaning red. Seemingly, it was on the strength of this vague suggestion that he interpreted the quatrain as pertaining to Communism (the Reds!). He does not explain who Roy Reb is, was, or will be. Some commentators – including the Italian, Patrian – have claimed that Reb is a French abbreviation for *rebelle* (rebel), but even if it is, this throws little or no light on the quatrain.

Our familiarity with the methods used by Nostradamus has inclined us to consider Roy Rebauront as a meaningful play on a proper name, and, if this is the case, then all attempts to understand the word in our present time are bound for failure. Who, for example, would have understood the relationship of the word Achilles to Achille de Harlay, before 1617, and who would have understood the significance of the word Franco before 1930?

Now we should consider the fourth line – *Que les mettra trestous dans la meslée*. Whoever this Reb Rebauront proves to be, he (or perhaps she) will bring all (*trestous*, by which we suspect Nostradamus meant those of London and those of America) into difficulties. The word *meslée* is *mêlée*, conflict, scramble or scrum. In the light of these considerations, the last couplet may mean: 'They will call back again as leader one who is so false an Antechrist that he will put them altogether in a conflict'.

What we appear to have here is a prediction of a king, or, more likely, an important political figure (even a President of the USA), who will somehow appear to be on the wrong side. The question is, on the wrong side of what? Of history? Of the United States?

This individual will have the appearance of being an Antechrist, and he will bring his country into a very difficult position. We almost regret having written these words, yet feel they should remain as evidence of an honest attempt to interpret a quatrain which yet remains obscure through being so deeply entangled in the future.

It is very interesting, in view of the references to Scotland in this quatrain, that Nostradamus uses the semi-arcane reference *Cancer* for the Moon, in the verse which follows – quatrain X.67. There must have been some ulterior motive for using a zodiacal sign to stand for a planet, and we suspect this arises from the fact that, in the arcane tradition, Scotland is ruled by Cancer. Nostradamus seems to have been eager to affirm the connection between quatrain X.66, with its reference to Scotland, and X.67, which affords such a precise date (see page 387).

PEACE AND WAR

There is much discussion about the zodiacal ruler of the United States, but we are convinced that the States carries with it the power of Aquarius.[16] On 21 December 2020, the two planets Saturn and Jupiter – so important in predictive astrology – will conjunct in the first degree of Aquarius.

This date appears to hold much promise for Nostradamus. In quatrain X.89, thrust between other verses which predict dire events, he forecasts a period of peace for 57 years:

> *De brique en marbre seront les murs reduicts,*
> *Sept & cinquante années pacifique,*
> *Joye aux humains, renoüé l'aqueduict,*
> *Santé, grands fruits, joye & temps mellifique.*

Rarely, indeed, does a quatrain of Nostradamus offer so much hope. Its very gentleness and promise hides the fact that it is a brilliant astrological quatrain:

> The walls will be reduced from brick to marble,
> Seven and fifty peaceful years,
> Joy to humans, renewed the aqueduct,
> Health, great fruit, joy and sweet times.

Some commentators have suggested that the period of peace began in 1945, with the end of the Second World War. However, it would be wallowing in illusion to pretend that the conflicts in Korea, Vietnam, Kuwait, former

Yugoslavia, or even Suez and the Falklands, never happened, and that we are presently living through a peaceful era. As Rodney Collin concluded, when he attempted to draw up an appendix of 15-year Cycles of War, 'In fact, war is continuous, and (the measured) peaks seem only to represent its moments of maximum tension.'[17]

It would seem that the period of 57 years' peace would make contemporary sense only if we take it that Nostradamus is referring merely to Europe. Of course, there is some good argument in support of this notion, for, as we have seen, the quatrains centre mainly upon the history of France, and tend to regard Britain, Holland, Italy, Germany, Spain, Turkey and Greece as so many side issues. Most of the countries he mentions outside this limited European framework are referred to only in connection with Europe. Even his references to America seem to be bound up with the destiny of Europe. If this view is accepted, then we can presume that Nostradamus sees hostilities involving Europe commencing some time after the millennium – 57 years after 1945.

Is there anything in the quatrains which will throw light upon this prediction, or is there some other way of looking at this intriguing quatrain? The fact is that to understand this 'peace' prophecy of quatrain X.89, we must consider a 'conflict' prophecy, contained in IX.83. The extraordinary truth is that Nostradamus probably offers, within the structure of this latter quatrain, an insight as to when this period of peace will come to an end.

Having glanced at the Earth trigons, we should return to the consideration of the *aqueduict* of quatrain X.89, which marks entry into the Air trigons.

The next conjuction of Jupiter and Saturn is on 21 December 2020. This will take place in the first degree of Aquarius. It is this placing which explains the arcane references of the third line: *renoüé l'aqueduict*. The aqueduct (*aqueduict*) which to be renewed is zodiacal Aquarius. The word aqueduct is from the Latin meaning 'water-conduit', or 'water-pourer': the sign Aquarius is the Water-bearer. Since the 2020 conjunction occurs in the first degree of the sign Aquarius (actually in 00.29 mins), we may understand why Nostradamus wrote of it as 'renewing the Aqueduct', for it is literally in the first degree of the sign, renewing its grip upon the aqueduct after hundreds of years of absence. We should observe that the word *renoüé* also means 'to resume', and connotes the idea of coming together again – as one might speak of the meeting of Jupiter and Saturn in this new Aquarius. The two ponderable planets had not conjuncted so for over 800 years.

Those unfamiliar with late-medieval astrology will not recognize that many of the references in the quatrain are derived from specialist terms from astrological textbooks. Indeed, several terms in the quatrain also relate to the nature of Aquarius. In the arcane classification of the zodiacal signs with which Nostradamus was familiar, Aquarius was called a *human* sign – hence *Joye aux humains*. Aquarius was a *sweet* sign, hence the *mellifique*. It was a *fruitful* sign, hence *grands fruits*.[18]

We must admit that it is notoriously difficult to interpret a Nostradamus quatrain which deals with futurity, yet we feel on secure ground in this interpretation of quatrain X.89 as referring to a period of peace, lasting 57 years, and starting in 2020.

THE SEVEN CHANGES OF BRITAIN

Very near to the 300 years promised for the *Pempotan* of the British Empire is the prediction in III.57 which touches on the 290-year period during which the British people will see seven major changes.

Sept fois changer verrez gent Britannique,
Taints en sang en deux cents nonante an:
France, non point par appuy Germanique,
Ariez doubt son pole Bastarnan.

Approximately, this translates:

Seven times you will see British people change,
Stained in blood in two hundred and ninety years:
France, not so through German help,
Ariez doubts his Bastarnian pole.

The Chevalier de Jant,* like several French interpreters
who followed him, saw this quatrain as a prediction of
French greatness rather than a particular reference to
Britain. He read in the last two lines 'the union of the
German Empire and France, not so far removed (in the
future)'. He hazarded a guess that it would be in 1700 (less
than 30 years into his own future) when this union would
be completed. By this time the new and powerful French
Empire would also control Palestine. The Chevalier was
merely following Jaubert in his own commentary on this
quatrain, for the latter had interpreted it as relating to the
glorious durability of the French Kingdom.

Neither Jant nor Jaubert had sufficient knowledge to
interpret Nostradamus. Otherwise, they would have seen
the future very differently – perhaps in terms of the horrors
he had predicted for France in the eighteenth century. We

---

* Seventeenth-century (and later) commentaries refer to the Chevalier de
Gant, who was actually the Chevalier de Jant. Jacques de Jant was an
author of a set of commentaries on Nostradamus, two parts of which
appeared in 1673. He was the official in charge of the Cabinet des Raretés
of Philippe d'Orléans, brother of Louis XIV, and was fond of describing
himself as 'Chevalier' because he was chevalier of the prestigious Order of
Malta.

are now better informed than the two seventeenth-century writers, for the general drift of the quatrain has become clearer with the passage of time.

In the hope of abstracting a meaning from this complex quatrain, we must divide it into two couplets. After a detailed analysis of these pairs of lines, we shall be in a position to see that what unites them is the nature of the British constitution.

The important question is, when does this period of 290 years begin and end? If we are to construct a septenary list, which reflects the spirit of this quatrain, then we must recognize such changes as have (1) taken place in Britain (*verrez gent Britannique*), and (2) consequent to such changes, have involved blood-letting on English soil (*taints en sang*).

It is fairly certain that Nostradamus views the judicial murder of Charles I as the first 'blood staining' in English history, after 1555. However, in the post-1555 period, some may feel entitled to see the year 1587 as a watershed for Britain, for it involved a major change, and was stained in blood. The judicial murder of Mary Queen of Scots changed the British succession. For some reason, Nostradamus appears to ignore this – perhaps on the grounds that Mary, through her involvement with the Babington plot, was guilty. The seven events, besides influencing monarchial succession, seem to involve the spilling of innocent English blood on English territory.

We may assume Nostradamus was announcing that the period of 290 years was to run from the regicide of Charles I, which occurred in 1649, and was the inevitable conclusion to the bloodletting of the Civil War. This would mean that the terminus for the 290-year period would be 1939. Just within that period, in the last month of 1936, was the abdication of Edward VIII. Is it possible to trace five other events involved with a change in the succession to the

British Crown in that specified period of 290 years? Not only is it possible to do this: we may also find in the *Prophéties* certain quatrains relevant to each of these seven historical events. In these quatrains, Nostradamus mentions either the name of Britain or the English, and/or the fact of bloodletting.

Each of these shifts in succession is reflected in civil wars, insurrections against the monarchy, or a consequential shedding of blood on English soil. The purpose of the seven appears to be to account for major constitutional changes in Britain. It would seem that Nostradamus was less interested in changes in the blood–line of the British monarchy than in the internal (not to say civil) damage which they involved, if not actually precipitated. It will be worth our while glancing at these seven internal conflicts, in order to see how clearly the septenaries are measured by Nostradamus.

1. Charles I and the Civil War; ended with the regicide of 1649. See quatrains IX.49, II.51 and II.53 (*juste sang*) discussed on page 265. Nostradamus mentioned the siege of Pontefract of 1649. In III.81 he gives *Le pont rompu*, and Pontefract comes from *pontus fractus* – broken bridge. If this last battle of the Civil War is taken as the first year of the septenary sequence, then the period of the septenary lasts *precisely* 290 years as Nostradamus predicted.

2. Oliver Cromwell as military dictator, after 1650. Much bloodshed, the worst of which was in Ireland. See quatrains III.81 and VIII.76 (*saignera terre*).

3. Charles II restored, 1660. Largely through fear, Charles did away with the standing army, and severely weakened the navy. In June 1667 a Dutch squadron entered the Thames, bombarded Sheerness, and broke through to

Chatham. Fireships destroyed half the fleet, and the flagship *Royal Charles* was towed away as prize. See quatrain X.4 for return of Charles (*sept ans apres*).

4. James II: the ill-starred Argyll and Monmouth rebellion in which both rebel leaders lost their heads, and many Whigs lost their lives – Sedgemoor, 1685. See quatrain VIII.58 for flight of James (*nom Britannique*).

5. William III and the so-called 'bloodless revolution'. Prior to the accession of William, John Graham of Claverhouse, who became Viscount Dundee, attempted to raise the Highlands against the British King. Partly successful, he died in the attempt. One consequence of the rising was that, by 1692, every clan chief was required to swear an oath of loyalty. Macdonald of Glencoe was delayed by bad weather and signed six days too late. This led to the entirely unwarranted massacre of the Macdonalds at Glencoe. See quatrain IV.89.

6. George I (Hanoverian succession). Derwentwater and the Jacobite rebellion; the Jacobites reached Preston, 1715. Derwentwater was beheaded on Tower Hill in the following year. See quatrain V.93 (*Ecosse . . . Anglois*).

7. Edward VIII: abdication, 1936. This change prefaces 1940 as opening the war with Nazi Germany, and ending the cycle of 290 years. It is now recognized that Edward VIII was to a very large extent a supporter of the aspirations of Nazi Germany, and a contributing cause of bloodshed in Britain. Nostradamus appears to have noted this, in quatrains X.22, VI.13 and X.40. That Nostradamus recognized the importance of the First World War is beyond doubt (see quatrain IV.100, for example). However, in quatrain III.57, he is not interested in the perturbations

of British history so much as in the major changes in the reigning monarchy, which give rise to bloodshed.

Several attempts have been made to give an account of these seven British perturbations, and among these the most humorous must be that made by D.D., who was writing in 1740, when the period of 290 years had almost 200 years to run. Bravely, in view of his historical position, he sets the bloody year of 1649 as the beginning of the sequence, but crowds the next five changes into less than a hundred years. His penultimate flourish of 1714 is for King George I, in the hope that through his reign, 'nothing further of Factions shall be heard hereafter'. His adulation of George I is hard to understand: he was a King of England who could speak no English, and who had no great love for Britain. However, D.D.'s book on Nostradamus was published in 1715, when George was newly on the throne, which may account for his hopes, if not for the inaccuracy of his predictions. How disappointed D.D. would have been to learn of the history of factions which followed his hero's reign.

What is really interesting about the D.D. sequence is that, having started the periodicity in 1649, he recognized that it would end in 1939. Inevitably, this led him to one of his few predictions. Typically, he expressed this in royalist terms, for he saw it as '290 Years after the Death of King Charles the Martyr, the seventh and last revolution shall happen, as Nostradamus says'. Wisely, he does not attempt to describe the nature of this final revolution. Even so, his vision was blinkered by quite human aspirations, for he predicts that from 1714 to 1939 there will be no interruption in the Hanoverian succession.

Charles Nicoullaud, writing in 1914, proposed a slightly different order of seven changes: 1. The year 1603 saw James I of Scotland made King of Great Britain; 2. In 1653

Oliver Cromwell was made protector; 3. In 1660 there was the restoration of Stuarts in the name of Charles II; 4. In 1689 William III took (usurped, as Nicoullaud insisted) the throne of England; 5. 1702 saw a brief return of Stuarts, with Queen Anne, who was the daughter of the deposed James II; 6. 1714 brought the Hanoverians to the throne, in the portly figure of George I. Nicoullaud realized that there was a gap of over 200 years from this auspicious year to the end of the period, to the seventh change. He acknowledged, presumably in some trepidation, that the end would be in 1939. 'What will it be?' he asks. 'It is the secret of the future.' Of course, in terms of his own system of reckoning, he was wrong, for the Hanoverian Dynasty came to an end in July 1917 when King George V judiciously shed his German titles, and embraced the name Windsor.

The French commentator Jaubert, writing in 1655, suggested that the period had already been in operation for a century: clearly, he considered that the period should begin at the time of the earliest publication of the quatrains. He insisted that, of the seven events, England had already seen four fulfilled. The first was Mary Queen of Scots, who brought back the Catholic faith, and whose brother Edward VI almost ruined England. The second was Elizabeth I, who re-established the heresy of Protestantism. The third was James I, who changed the country through introducing the Union of the three kingdoms of England, Scotland and Ireland. The fourth was the expulsion of the legitimate King, Charles I, and the insinuation of Cromwell. France, he pointed out (with a touch of that pride which usually comes before a fall), would not change at all, neither in religion nor in government. The phase *par appuy Germanique* he interpreted in true Francophile spirit, claiming that this was a sure prophecy that the King of France would take over the throne of the German Empire.

Now we must turn to the more difficult couplet in the

quatrain. For once, we have to admit to being stumped in attempts to interpret the remaining two lines in terms of history. Our suspicion is that it must continue the theme of the quatrain, and pertain to the constitutional future of Britain. If this is so, then, without the theme of the quatrain, it relates to a fundamental change in the monarchy and to future bloodshed.

> *France, non point par appuy Germanique,*
> *Ariez doubt son pole Bastarnan.*

Literally (if anything written by Nostradamus can be taken literally), the couplet means:

> France, not so through German help,
> Aries doubts his Bastarnan pole.

Unless we make a very daring interpretation of the quatrain, the couplet remains obscure. However, before hazarding such a reading, we should glance at the obscurities. The third line, touching on France and its support from the Germans, is puzzling within this context of monarchy and bloodshed. France seems to have had its own sequences of royalty-induced bloodshed, yet prior to 1939, Germany certainly gave scant support to either France or the French monarchy.

The *Bastarnan pole*, a Nostradamian arcanity which seems to have brought the Nazis to a study of Nostradamus (see page 390 ff), has caused incredible difficulties for commentators. Even the anonymous D.D. – normally quite restrained in his scholarship – found himself so lost in these two lines that he was reduced to claiming *Bastarion* as an Arabic word, meaning *humanus*. In fact, the curious word is an archaic name used to designate a vast tract of land to the east of Europe. The *Bastarnae* of Roman times

452

was that area marked from the lower Danube to its mouth at the Black Sea, and from the source of the Vistula to the Carpates, even into its mouth in the Baltic. In modern parlance, it seems to correspond to the river boundaries of Austria, Czechoslovakia and Hungary, and Poland, to the east of Germany.

Could the German commentator, Loog (who, as we have seen, indirectly influenced Hitler), have been right in his theory that these two lines of the quatrain indicated a weakness in Britain arising from her dealings with Poland? It certainly seems that he was correct in his general view that the quatrain marked some sort of diminishing of British power in eastern Europe.

So far in our study, we have only rarely pointed to slight differences in the early printings of the quatrains, but an early variant in this last line seems to demand some sort of explanation. In the earliest editions – for example, in that published by Pierre Rigaud in 1558 – the last line reads: *Aries doubte son pole Bastarnan.*[19]

The curious verbal construction which we have carried over from the Amsterdam edition of 1668 is therefore resolved as a misprint. While *Ariez* makes no sense, *Aries* makes a great deal of sense. The fact is that zodiacal Aries rules over Germany and England – this, indeed, could be the polarity implied in the word *pole*. The fact that Nostradamus referred to Aries was recognized by early commentators, such as Garencìeres, even though he (like D.D. after him) turned his subsequent 'astrological' commentary into fantastical nonsense.

Along with other commentators, the seventeenth-century commentator Jaubert read the two words as *Aries double* – an astrological phraseology, intimating that the sign Aries has two poles. Unfortunately, he displays complete astrological ignorance, and, while it is surprising that his commentary has fooled anyone, it is even more surprising to see it extended into modern literature. In a further astrological mistake, Jaubert supposed that the sign Aries rules over France, Palestine, '*la Bastarnie*', and so on. This is not true. Had he consulted any important astrological textbook contemporaneous with Nostradamus, he would have discovered his mistake. For example, Luca Gauricus in his chorographic list (derived mainly from Ptolemy) tells us that Aries rules England, Germany and 'Polonia minor'. France (Gallia), on the other hand, is ruled by Cancer.[20]

Is there any possible way of interpreting these two lines with any conviction? The answer is yes – provided we are prepared to see this couplet as dealing with the *aftermath* of the British septenary. That is to say, in order to make sense of the couplet, we must view the couplet as relating to the history of Britain *after* 1939, and to the polarity of the Arietan countries, England and Germany. The effect of this polarity is to establish animosity between these two countries, for it is the clash of Mars. The two countries have an enormous respect for each other, in terms of martial qualities, but the fact that the Mars of Germany is not defined by sea-borders restricts its martian desire to expand. This, in turn, offers perpetual threat to the non-Mars country, France. There is no polarity between Germany and France, and consequently no respect for martial prowess. This means that the zodiacally weaker France must attempt to subdue Germany by political means, and by appeasement. In a sense, it is the enacting of these zodiacal impulses which we see motivating the unwise attempt to turn Europe into a federal state. The zodiacal animosities within the European countries will certainly make it difficult to establish the pan-European state visualized by Brussels, and will prevent such a state (even if established) lasting for very long. Viewed from the stand-point of esoteric history, one can see the amities and discords of the European Union purely in terms of the interactions of the ruling zodiacal signs.

At the expense of introducing complications into the reading, we should point out that in the ancient tradition (which goes back at least to Ptolemy),[21] Aries rules only England, and not the British Isles, which in the ancient astrological texts were generally treated as four distinct units. Ireland was ruled by Taurus, Scotland by Cancer and Wales by Capricorn. While these three countries would benefit in some ways from the appeasement of Germany which lies behind the facade of the proposed federal state, it would not benefit England.

Even when viewing this line in terms of these living chorographies, we encounter difficulties in the interpretation of the quatrain. It would be possible, for instance, to see the *Bastarian pole* as relating purely to Germany – to Germanic border problems to the east, and even to the now-healed division of Germany that occurred after the Second World War. However, this is unlikely, as the quatrain is clearly intended to deal with the destiny of England.

It is, of course, of great interest that the quatrain should mention in these two lines France, Germany and the ancient Bastarniae – all major participants in the Second World War. However, in our opinion, the theme of the quatrain is not war, but constitutional changes. The quatrain seems to point to a terrible consequence for the English nation in presuming to give up the sovereignty which it has established and refined through the septenary steps set out by Nostradamus.

We have already mentioned the curious coincidence that two reports in the single edition of *The Times* of 7 October 1996 seem to relate (unconsciously) to two Nostradamus reports. The first was to the proposal to cut a canal which would effectively sever Scotland from England (see page

440), pertaining to quatrain X.66. The second is an article by George Brock, headed 'Fears about Germany threaten France's Napoleonic influence in EU'. The article reflects on the fact that the proposed monetary union is little more than a Franco–German racket, which is setting the EU agenda, regardless of Britain, and other European countries. This does seem to be the underlying theme of quatrain X.89 – with the added proviso that the incredible cost of German Unification (the Bastarnian, eastern pole) will eventually be carried by all those who enter into the Economic Union. If the last two lines of the quatrain are interpreted in this way (and the French text does appear to support such a reading) then it would seem that the proposed union will not work. Whether this relates to political or economic union is not clear.

The fundamental change – perhaps with implications more profound than any war – which has taken place since 1939 has been the ease with which the British Government has relinquished the democratic constitution of the English peoples that has been won at such enormous cost through the centuries. In the last few decades of the twentieth century the British Government has handed over virtually all the legal rights which have been so painfully obtained, by legislation, agitation, regicide and confrontation with dominant authority, since 1649. The power has been nominally given to the European Union, but, when the history of this gift is placed in historical context, we see that the power has been handed over to the other Arietan pole, Germany.

The various enactments from the innocent-seeming proposals of the original Common Market, through to the potentially sinister European Union, have changed more profoundly the nature of the British constitution than any other event since the time of Nostradamus. Indeed, if the legal implications of the EC directives are taken seriously, we have to question whether any substantiality remains in the British monarchic system or democratic system, which formed the nexus of this quatrain. The old prophecy which maintained that Prince Charles would not become King of Britain may be seen in a new light, in the view of changes which have taken place in Britain in the past few decades. His personal destiny aside, it is quite possible that there will be no legally defined 'kingdom' for him to reign over.[22]

Whether this is for the good, and whether such radical changes will lead to yet further *Taints en sang*, is for the future to reveal. Either way, the second couplet of this quatrain makes perfect sense in the light of the proposed European Union, for it was essentially an attempt (born of eighteenth- and nineteenth-century politics) to create a single block power from France and Germany, with the latter nervously aware of the constant threat to its eastern borders, so carefully defined in Roman times as *Bastarnae*.

ROYAL DIVORCE

No doubt the final years of the twentieth century will attract clairvoyants and astrologers to comment freely upon the divorce of Prince Charles and Princess Diana. Inevitably, attempts will be made to direct attention towards quatrain X.22 which does appear to mention a royal divorce.

Pour ne vouloir consentir au divorce,
Qui puis apres sera cogneu indigne,
Le Roy des Isles sera chassé par force,
Mis à son lieu qui de Roy n'aura signe.

For not wishing to consent to the divorce,
Which afterwards will be recognized as unworthy,

457

> The King of the Isles will be driven out by force,
> Put in his place one who has no sign of Kingship.

The translation obscures further one or two notable obscurities. For example, there is ambiguity in the French as to whether it is the *king* or the *divorce* that is unworthy. The verse is also ambiguous as to whether it is the king or someone else who does not wish to consent to the divorce. There are other ambiguities: some commentators have held that the quatrain does not pertain to a royal separation at all, and that the word divorce is symbolic of the separation between Court and Parliament in Britain. Indeed, after a perusal of the many accounts of this quatrain, we are left with the impression that the only thing about which there is any agreement is that it refers to a King of Britain (*Le Roy des Isles*), and that some sort of separation is involved. There does not appear to be any internal evidence by which the verse may be dated.

In fact, the quatrain has attracted commentators to the house of Windsor before. For example, Woolf, writing in 1944, saw the verse as relating to the abdication of King Edward VIII,[23] and his view has been adopted by almost every commentator since. Earlier commentators had seen in the reference to 'divorce' not one pertaining to marriage, but to the crown, thus justifying a reading which drew Charles I and Cromwell as uneasy bedfellows in the quatrain. As we have suggested, in 1996 it would probably be equally tempting to see the quatrain as prevision of Charles and Diana – especially if there is some way of construing a meaning from the third line. If it does refer to Charles and Diana, then it seems to suggest difficulties after the divorce. How is it possible for a divorce not to be seen as worthy – worthy of what? Furthermore, how may Charles be driven by events after the divorce?

After giving the quatrain a great deal of thought, we have concluded that it relates to the divorce of Edward VIII.

Each of the four predictions in the line seems to correspond perfectly to what happened. Parliament was unwilling for the King to marry the divorced Mrs Simpson. After the abdication (and, in a small coterie, even before) Edward was recognized as being unworthy (*cogneu indigne*) of his position as King of Britain: his subsequent history of liaison with the Nazis, and his extraordinary statement that the Germans should bomb England into submission, confirm the general tenor of the second line. In spite of all, and with the misgivings of his father, King George V, Edward did become King of Great Britain (*Roy des Isles*), and he was indeed driven out of the country (*sera chasse par force*) by Parliament, his abdication being merely a formal recognition that he could no longer keep the crown in the face of such opposition. Perhaps the most questionable line is the fourth, for George VI, who was put in his place (*Mis à son lieu*), was scarcely one who had no sign of kingship about him (*Mis à son lieu qui de Roy n'aura signe*).

Could it be, then, that this line refers not to his successor, as is so often supposed, but to Edward VIII again? This latter was certainly 'put in his place', where he could no longer display signs of kingship. After his abdication, Edward was no longer allowed to call himself King, nor to display any indication of kingship (*de Roy n'aura signe*). He wandered through France, Spain and the United States with a woman who, by protocol, could be called neither a queen nor a princess.

THE GREAT KING OF TERROR

Without doubt, quatrain X.72 is the most famous of all the verses of Nostradamus. The fame stems from the fact that it is generally translated as referring to the descent of some awesome being – a frightful entity – who will come to earth in July 1999.

L'an mil neuf cens nonante neuf sept mois
Du ciel viendra un grand Roy d'effrayeur
Resusciter le grand Roy d'Angoulmois.
Avant apres Mars regner par bon heur.

For the moment, we may translate this as:

The year one thousand nine hundreds ninety nine seven months
From the sky will come a great King of alarm
To bring back to life the great King of Angoulmois.
Before after Mars to reign by good fortune.

The more bloodthirsty commentators tend to interpret this coming in dire terms – as a prediction of a world revolution, or disastrous war: some even insist that it is a prediction of the End of the World – though Nostradamus specifically denies this in his Preface to the *Prophéties*. Aside from such interpretation, the fact remains that it is one of the few quatrains which appear to offer a precise date, without arcane obfuscation.

As with most of the quatrains, the clue to interpreting this verse rests upon the meaning of a key word within the quatrain. Here the key word is *Angoulmois*.

For all its obvious importance, this word has never been adequately explained by commentators. Indeed, contemporary 'translations' of this curious word reveal quite clearly how those unfamiliar with the Green Language swim in very murky waters when attempting to read Nostradamus. Roberts in 1949 translates the word as relating to 'Jacquerie', suggesting the line means: 'To raise again the great King of the Jacquerie.'*

---

* We cannot explain the term Jacquerie in this context – it is a nonsensical reading.

He offers a footnote to the effect that 'Roy d'Angoul-mois' is an anagram for 'Roi de Mongulois' (King of the Mongolians). From this he interprets that the 'threat of war will come from the east. Eastern Russia? Tibet? China? Mongolia?' His interpretation is sheer nonsense. Cheetham translates the word as relating to the 'Mongols', suggesting the line means: 'He will bring back to life the great king of the Mongols'. For reasons which are not clear, she sees in this quatrain a reference to the 'King of the Mongols' as 'the Asian antichrist'. There is no indication of this in anything Nostradamus wrote. In 1983 de Fontbrune translated the word as relating to the French city Angou-lême, suggesting the line means: 'Reviving or recalling the great conqueror of Angoulême'. Who the great conqueror (Roy?) of Angoulême might be remains anyone's guess.

As we might expect, *Angoulmois* is a word straight from the Green Language. A correct interpretation of its meaning will throw a special radiance over the entire quatrain. Indeed, without understanding the meaning of *Angoulmois*, we will be unable to appreciate the ambiguity of the date in the first line of the quatrain. In view of this, we shall examine the third line, in which this key-word is found, before commenting upon the quatrain as a whole: *Resusciter le grand Roy d'Angoulmois*.

At first glance, the line translates approximately: 'Bring back to life the great King of Angoulmois'. The question is, what or where is *Angoulmois*, and who is its great King?

We shall see that the word is a Green Language construct, which breaks into three units: ANG OUL MOIS. Firstly, *Ang* is apocope for *Ange* – the French for 'Angel'. Secondly, *Oul* is an arcane term which divides *Angoulmois* into a meaningful structure. *Ol*, written in several different orthographic versions, is the name of one of the archangels of the Zodiac (we shall return to this meaning later). These names and sigils appear in medieval astrology, magic spells and grimoires, such as the fifteenth-century magical calendars. It would have been familiar to Nostradamus, under its version as Verchiel, through the magical *scala* of Agrippa's widely read *De Occulta Philosophia*.[24] Finally, *mois* is French for 'month'. So, in its triple constituents, the word consists of three distinct words, two French and one Latin. The phrase *Ange Ol mois* may be translated into English as: 'the Angel Ol month'.

Now, in medieval grimoires, the Archangel *Ol* was the zodiacal ruler of the sign Leo.[25] He had two variant names, Verchiel and Voel, and a number of angelic sigils. In the days of Nostradamus, the calendrical reforms had not yet disturbed the relationship between the months and the zodiacal signs: the Gregorian Calendar did not come into general use in France until 1582, after the death of our savant. This is why it was possible for him to equate an angelic ruler of a zodiacal sign with a single month. In any case, such an equation was preserved in the magical calendars, as we shall see. Such an equation is no longer valid. However, since in his day it was possible to consider July as the Leo month, the arcane phrase, Angol-*mois*, would mean July.

Given these historical facts, the three words which make up Angoulmois have a specific meaning, in sequence. First, the angelic type, in the nine hierarchies, is the *Archangel*. Second, it is the Archangel *Ol*. Third, Ol is the ruler of the month *July*. Having seen the hidden meaning in the triadic structure *Angoulmois*, we are in a better position to read the arcane meaning of the line.

First, we must ask, who is the *Roy* (King) of the month of July, the zodiacal ruler of Leo? In the astrological tradition, Leo is ruled by the Sun. In esotericism, the Sun is ruled by the Archangel *Michael*. In the esoteric tradition of *Secundadeis* (see page 168) with which Nostradamus was familiar, and which he mentions in his *Epistle to Henry II* in the *Prophéties*, Michael is the chief of the seven planetary archangels: therefore, he may be called the *Roy* or King of the Seven.

It is also worth recalling that *Sol* is the Latin name for the Sun, and that this is obviously the source, by aphesis, of the ancient arcane name, *Ol*, while the version *Oel* is an anagram for *Leo*.

The importance of this rulership of Michael over the seven planetary beings is emphasized in a hidden numerology, the meaning of which rests upon the fact that Michael is ruler of seven archangels. This numerology may be traced in the structure of the word *Angoulmois*, which gives *Oul*, balanced by words with three and four letters, giving a total of seven: ANG (three); OUL; MOIS (four).

It is evident, therefore, that Nostradamus is disguising the name of the planetary archangel *Michael* in the pseudo-epigraphic *Roy d'Angoulmois*. This septenary has relevance to the fact that in the Hebraic imagery attached to the Secundadeians, Michael is visualized as being the centre of the seven planets. There is a far more subtle numerological arcanity in this quatrain, however, and that is contained in the quatrain number, 72. In many respects, the number 72 is the most arcane of all numbers. Cosmologically, it is linked with the movement of the Sun, for in 72 years, the sun precesses against the backdrop of stars precisely one degree. This is one reason why, in arcane literature, the length of human life is symbolically expressed as being 72 years, for the human being is conceived as being born with a degree, and dying when that degree has moved: this is one of the contributing factors which explain why 72 is the most sacred of numbers in esotericism.

For the moment, we should note that this 'great King' (*grand Roy*) becomes '*le* grand Roy . . .' in contrast to the '*un* grand Roy . . .' of the second line. There is a deep arcane significance in this contrast, for it indicates that the great King of the second line is not the same as the great King of the third line.

Having placed the arcane word *Angoulmois* in its true Green Language context, we are in a position to look at the quatrain as a whole: *L'an mil neuf cens nonante neuf sept mois* – 'The year one thousand nine hundreds ninety nine seven months'.

It is very tempting to take this verse as referring to July 1999. This is the year in which the event predicted in the following three lines of the quatrain will come into effect. The astrological depths which we have begun to expect of Nostradamus might lead us to expect that this date corresponds to some remarkable cosmic phenomenon. However, this is simply not the case: there is nothing of particular interest in a planetary sense in that month. However, we have already remarked on the quatrain which draws attention to the planetary configurations which distinguish September 1999, and the even more remarkable configuration in 2002 and 2020.

Much is being made of the year 1999 by commentators. One has even been prepared to turn the last three figures over, to obtain 666 – the arcane number of the Beast in the Apocalypse. While this number is undoubtedly of great occult significance, it is unlikely that Nostradamus would require such an aphesis (of the first numeral) and inversion of the remaining three, without hinting at the need for such manipulation in the text.

There is, however, one important reservation about reading the first line as referring to 1999, and this is connected with the fact that Nostradamus rarely, if ever, means literally what he says. Any reader who has persisted so far in considering our study of Nostradamus will agree that, no matter how simple a line from his pen may seem, there is usually some arcane depth hidden behind it. This is why we find ourselves wary of reading a line which gives so ingenuously a precise day and year for a particular event. One must ask if there is some other way of interpreting this bland-seeming line.

The answer is that we might read the line quite differently in relation to the Secundadeian system which Nostradamus himself insisted he was using in the quatrains, and which we looked at in Chapter 3. This is not the ordinary familiar calendar, but one in use in occult circles.

In his arcanely written preface to his *Prophéties*, Nostradamus quite clearly tells us that he is using in the quatrains the system of dating which was promulgated by the great occultist, Trithemius (see page 153). In his arcane references to this dating system, Nostradamus points out that 'presently we are ruled by the Moon'. This was quite true, for Nostradamus was writing in 1555. According to Trithemius, the lunar archangel, Gabriel, had begun his rule over the ages in 1525. This rule, Nostradamus tells us, will last until 'the Sun shall come'. Now, according to Trithemius, the rule of the Moon would end about 1881, when the rule of the *solar* archangel Michael would begin. 'And then Saturn,' will follow, says Nostradamus, again echoing Trithemius. The rule of the archangel of Saturn, Ophiel, would begin in AD 2235. If we extend these rulerships by the 354 years alloted to each age, we discover something of great interest. Nostradamus is actually writing about a full periodicity of seven archangelic rules. In theory, the rule of Moon will commence again in AD 4005.

When Nostradamus wrote (1 March 1555), the reign of Gabriel was already 28 years old. If we subtract 28 years from 4005, we obtain 3977. This is an numerological anagram for the 3797 which Nostradamus specifically states is the date of the ending of his prophecies. The occult blind (which is so frequently used in arcane literature) is the transposing of two internal numbers of a date. What Nostradamus is disguising in his exposition of dates is that

his prophecies are linked directly with the periodicities of
the Secundadeians.

A month (twelfth) of the Trithemian Secundadeian
period of 354 years and 4 months is about 29 and a half
years. According to the first line of our quatrain, the event
is due for the seventh month of *Ol*, which is to say 7 × 29
and a half years after the beginning of the rule of Michael.
This is 206 and a half years after the first year of Michael's
rule, of 1881. This in turn means that the prophecy in this
X.72 quatrain could well be related to AD 2087.

One thing is sure – whether we read the prophecy as
relating to 1999 or 2087, the quatrain is not a prediction of
the end of the world. Nostradamus admits as much when
he insists that his 'Astronomical Stanzas' relate to the
period extending up to the year 3797.

As Nostradamus published the first batch of prophecies
in 1555, this means that the predictions extended over a
futurity of 2,242 years. Now, this is a most interesting
figure, for it is very close to one of the great Ages – the
divisions of the so-called Great Year.* In modern times, it
is known that, due to precession, the Great Year lasts 2,160
years. This precision of dating was not available to
Nostradamus, who must have been familiar with at least
half a dozen theories relating to the length of this Great
Year. It was widely believed in the sixteenth century that a
period of precession was equal to one degree in every
century. This was the periodicity popularized by Dante,
who had followed the writings of the Arabic astrologer,
Alfraganus.

* In medieval astrology, the Great Year is that period of time taken by
all the planets to return to a given fiducial: there is no agreement as to
how long this period is, but William of Conches believed it was 49,000
years. The Platonic Year was sometimes called the Great Year – this was
the precessional period of 25,920 years.

Immediately after informing his readers that the prophecies extend for a period of 2,242 years (that is, up to 3797 BC) Nostradamus writes a very perplexing sentence, which may be translated as follows:

> *If you live to the natural age of man, then you shall see, in your proper place on the globe of the earth, and under the heaven of thy horoscope, the future things that have been foretold.*

The informed occultist will see in these words a reference to reincarnation. According to the arcane doctrine, a human being is born once as a man and once as a woman in each Age. This means that Nostradamus is saying that every human being must witness something from the period for which he has issued prophecy. Whatever is to happen in 1999 (if, indeed, that is the intended year) it is not the End of the World.

Let us consider line two again: *Du ciel viendra un grand Roy d'effrayeur.* – 'From the sky will come a great King of alarm'. As with many of Nostradamus' terms, things are not quite what they seem. While *effrayeur* certainly means alarmist or frightener, the elided *defrayer* means to amuse, or entertain. On the other hand, the noun *frayeur* means fright, or terror. Some translators have chosen to adopt this latter sense, and have called this entity 'a great King of terror'. There may be also a subsidiary meaning in the *effrayeur* as the French verb *rayer* means 'to erase or scratch out'. Within the Green Language, each of these meanings is valid, and it may be assumed that Nostradamus chose the curious term to connote each of them. We see, therefore, that there is a degree of ambiguity about the nature of this 'great King' who may both frighten, alarm and terrorize. For sure, this King will come from the sky. Inevitably, this in itself has stirred the hearts of many a modern ufologist, who believe that the future destiny of the earth will lie in the hands of aliens.

We must presume that one reason why Nostradamus has elected to describe this great King in such ambiguous (and even vague) terms is because he was anxious to assure us that this was not taken as a reference to the Second Coming. In the sixteenth century, a mention of the descent from the skies of a great King, without an alarmist description, might easily have been taken for a reference to Christ.

In fact, there seems to be little point in speculating about this great King – whatever he or it may be, it is clearly not something with which we are familiar in an ordinary sense. As we shall see, the identity of this being may be gleaned only from other references in occult literature. However, it is worth pointing out (because no commentator to date seems to have realized it) that this entity is not the same great King as is mentioned in the next line of the quatrain. Here is line three again: *Resusciter le grand Roy d'Angoul-mois* – 'To bring back to life the great King of Angoulmois'. As we have identified the great King of Angolmois as a Green Language form for the archangel Michael, we may see that this line does *not* carry the dire predictive power usually ascribed to it. We must observe that *le* grand Roy is obviously different from the earlier *un* grand Roy. The prophecy is therefore dealing with *two* great Kings: the latter (Angolmois), it seems, brings back to life the former.

But what of line four? It states: *Avant apres, Mars regner par bon heur* ('Before after Mars to reign by good fortune'). The two words *Avant apres* are very troublesome, for they appear to negate each other. One solution, suggested by some scholars, is to read it as *Avant et apres*, meaning before and after. Again, *a pres* as an adverb can mean 'almost' – as for example in the phrase *a peu pres*, 'nearly so'. Perhaps, therefore, we may read *Avant a pres* as 'Almost immediately before'.

Our own feeling is that the two words refer to the two different 'kings' – the one who comes *before*, and the one who comes *after*. It is as a result of the polarization to which they give rise that Mars will reign (i.e. that war will flourish). Will this war be between the protagonists of the two great kings?

Now comes the real difficulty – what does Nostradamus see as happening, either 'Before and after'? What does this enigmatic phrase mean, that has Mars reigning by good fortune? Mars, whose ruler is Samael in the Secundadeian literature, is not due to begin his earthly rule until well beyond the period covered by Nostradamus' prophecies. This suggests that another interpretation must be placed upon the word Mars in this present context. In French *par bonheur* means 'luckily'. Usually, the reference to Mars as a ruler denotes war, but one has to query how a war can be conducted 'by good fortune', or by luck.

Could we take this last line to mean that 'Before and after, Mars finds his own delight'? Certainly, *Faire le bonheur de quelqu'un* means 'to delight someone'. This is to interpret the line as meaning that Mars is in his own delight – i.e. wading through blood and strife.

Suppose, however, we go back to the Nostradamus text, and treat the two words *bon* and *heur* separately – which is how they were printed in the early editions. Good (*bon*) may be used of the archangel, Michael. *Heur* (taken as an obvious Green Language apocope for *heure*, the French for 'time') may well be taken as an epithet for the being who opposes Michael, for, in esoteric circles, he is known as *Ahriman* – the one who rules Time. Wars will be fought between the followers of these two great beings.

A further, and more hopeful, reading of the line is to see

in it a prediction that Mars will no longer be operative –
that it will be a period of 'good fortune' – that wars will
cease. Unfortunately, the quatrains we have already examined, and which clearly deal with the first decades of the
twenty-first century, suggest otherwise.

How best may we summarize these complex analyses of
sixteenth-century arcanities? Perhaps we should say that
Nostradamus seems to suggest that in the year 1999, or
2087, some great entity – possibly harmful to humanity,
and certainly a being of terror – will descend to the earth.
The effect of his evident evil will be to polarize our
civilization: while many will be persuaded to follow this
terrible being, others will find themselves charged with a
renewed spirituality – with a feeling for the work of
Michael, the archangelic governor of our times. As a result
of this, there will be warfare and great social upheavals. As
we have seen, however, there is sufficient ambiguity in the
verse to suggest that this great King may not be terrible at
all. Were we to take into account the fact that Nostradamus
was working within the esoteric tradition, then we might
see his prediction as a long-term confirmation of the event
which has been widely anticipated in modern esoteric
literature – the entry of the Christ into the spiritual realm
contiguous to the physical plane.

Our general feeling, based on a considerable familiarity
with the prophetic literature of the sixteenth century, is
that Nostradamus constructed this quatrain for his contemporaries, to satisfy their own expectations regarding the
'End of Things' in the seventh millennium. This form was,
so to speak, an occult blind. It was designed to make sense
to his contemporaries, yet point to the spiritual event which
will mark out the twentieth century as being so important
to the spiritual life of mankind.

FUTURE SPIRITUALITY

Almost all the quatrains deal with specific events in the future – which, after all, is what might be expected of prophetic verse. However, a mere handful of quatrains appear to be ruminations of profound philosophical import, quite timeless save in so far as they point to the future. Quatrain IV.25 is one of these verses, and the spiritual implications of its contents are such that we have reserved it for our final analysis.

Corps sublimes sans fin à l'oeil visibles,
Obnubiler viendra par ses raisons,
Corps, front comprins, sens, chef & invisibles,
Diminuant les sacrées oraisons.

Bodies sublime and infinite, visible to the eye,
Will become clouded over by their own reasons,
Body, including the forehead, senses, head and invisibles,
Will diminish the sacred prayers.

This quatrain, being more of a poem than a prediction, is at once among the most beautiful and curious of the quatrains. Yet we fear that if it is a prediction, then it points to a terrible future.

We presume that the sublime bodies (*corps sublimes*) are the cosmic bodies – the planets, and stars – which are visible to the eye (*à l'oeil visibles*). This description emphasizes the notion – well established in the sixteenth century, and quite explicit in the writings of Trithemius, as we saw earlier – that the planets were spiritual beings, guided by high intelligences. That these celestial bodies might be infinite would be taken for granted in our own age, but for the contemporaries of Nostradamus, the proposition was startling and new. The curious *par ses raisons* of the second line would make more sense translated as 'for their own reasons'.

Perhaps the only line which would need extensive commentary is the third: *Corps, front comprins, sens, chef & invisibles*. This is not merely a description of the human physical and spiritual body. It is a meaningful arcane description, designed to link with the cosmic nature of the first line. The references here only make sense in relation to the traditional image of the zodiacal man. The mention of the forehead (*front*) is surely intended to refer to the zodiacal sign Aries, the ruler over the head (*chef*) and forehead (*front*). This rulership is confirmed in the traditional images which portray the Ram of Aries resting upon the head of cosmic man (*fig. 50*). Aries had the outer rule over the physical body, and an inner rule over human thought. Within the late-medieval philosophical view, thought was an operation whereby human beings made contact with the higher spiritual realm. The physical gestures required of one praying, like the emotional praxes or mantras demanded of those involved in a religious discipline, were designed merely to help deepen the spiritual contact between the praying human and the spiritual realm which took place at the head. This partly explains the arcane significance of the connection between the Ram of Aries and the Lamb which is Christ. In true prayer, the Ram and the Lamb merge, the outer and the inner become one. While a feeling for this notion is expressed in the third line, Nostradamus emphasizes the link between the physical and the spiritual in the second line by beginning the line with the visible physical (*Corps*) and ending with the invisible spiritual (*invisibles*).

The last line points to the separation which will take place between human beings and the cosmos, or spiritual realm, for the effect of this clouding of the spiritual, the effect of this weakening of the bond between the cosmos and man, will weaken even prayer: *Diminuant les sacrées oraisons.*

The early-sixteenth-century Italian philosopher Pietro Pomponazzi had merely followed the ancient traditions when he announced that seers and sibyls are inspired by the stars. Nostradamus, being an initiate (see Appendix Three), would have known that all people are so inspired, that the lives of all subtend from the cosmic world. What Nostradamus seems to predict in this beautifully worded quatrain is that human beings are going to lose their connection with the spiritual realm, their own bodies (both the physical and the invisible spiritual organs) occluding more and more the life–giving power of the stellar world.

To what extent this has happened since the sixteenth century, through the black-magical operations of what is proudly called materialist thought, must be determined by individual readers.

There is the way of nature, and the way of spirit. The way of nature is subject to entropy, and to what is now called the second law of Thermodynamics. The law of spirit is subject to no such entropy or energy loss. This quatrain speaks of the separation between these two ways, a separation which is all too clear, even today, for those with eyes to see. In terms of humanity, this division is reflected in the arcane teaching which portrays the future of mankind as being involved with a split in humanity. A proportion of mankind will sink, with relative rapidity, into moral and physical decline, while a smaller proportion will begin to move towards a spiritual growth. This division (sometimes called a separation) cannot occur without considerable conflicts between the two divisions.

To what extent the dictats and wiles of the gross body – of what, as we saw earlier, Jakob Boehme called the vegetative world – still offer a sufficiently sensitive and willing recipient of soul and spirit, must become part of the

473

inner searching of all who wish to side with the evolving
portion of mankind in the years ahead. As Nostradamus
implies, only the individual may decide whether his or her
allegiance will be fixed on nature or on spirit.

Conclusion

. . . I look at what I have written with some alarm, for I have told more of the ancient secret than many among my fellow-students think it right to tell.

(W. B. Yeats. From 'Magic', quoted from *W. B. Yeats. Selected Criticism*, edited by A. Norman Jeffares, 1970 ed., p. 93.)

What conclusions can we draw from our study of Nostradamus? Perhaps the most exciting conclusion is that his *Prophéties* demonstrate, beyond a shadow of doubt, that it is possible to predict future events several centuries before they occur. Of course, in this respect, Nostradamus was far from unique: other genuine prophets have written about the future, and often with equal precision.

However, we must conclude that Nostradamus *was* a unique prophet. He was unique not only because of the immensity of his vision and the quality of his literature, but also because of the nature of the occult technique in which he framed his prophecies. More than once we have lamented, along with many other commentators of old, the obscurity of his quatrains. More than once, we have stumbled over Green Language terms and astrological references, which we cannot elucidate. However, this obscurity should not surprise us, for the very style of

475

Nostradamus is obfuscation: obscurity seems to be the canon of his uniqueness as a prophet. Perhaps, if our study has taught us anything, it is that we should be prepared to question our own expectations of the prophetic genre, rather than the self-assured methods of the genius himself.

The quatrains were designed by Nostradamus so that their meanings would evade us prior to the event predicted. It is remarkable that, in all our extensive reading of the many published commentaries, glosses and explications offered in the name of Nostradamus, we cannot think of a single case where a quatrain has been accurately interpreted in advance of the event it predicts. This in itself is a remarkable achievement for a man so famed as a prophet.

It would seem that Nostradamus had a vision of the future which he elected not to reveal to his readers. Undoubtedly this is frustrating for those who are anxious to peer into the future, yet in some ways it is a sign of just how extraordinary was the genius of the Savant of Salon.

We have savoured enough of the quatrains of Nostradamus to be aware that he positively delighted in word-games, in arcane references subtle enough to drive even the seasoned arcanist mad. This penchant for obscurity seems to have poured even into his non-arcane writings, such as the *Fardemens* (his treatise on cosmetics), and the *Almanachs*, all of which were supposedly aimed at a non-specialist readership. We know from surviving personal letters that Nostradamus was, by his intrinsic nature, given to circumlocution, and that it was second nature for him to express his thoughts in obscure ways. His whole creative activity seems to have been merged with a tendency to literary disguise. Even so, even after recognizing this fact, one cannot resist feeling impatient with his most famous work, the *Prophéties*. Perhaps it does represent the flowering of an ancient line of thought which occupied the greatest minds of the medieval period, perhaps it is a work of literary genius – but, we have to ask in all seriousness, is it worth all the effort it demands? Should a writer be allowed to get away with literature which virtually no one can understand? The questions are valid, for our whole cultural tradition has prepared us to expect that when an author publishes a book – when he 'brings it into the light of day', as they would say in the sixteenth century – then it is with the intention of making his ideas accessible. With growing impatience, we begin to ask if there is any real purpose behind this impenetrable obfuscation of the quatrains?

Due reflection reveals that this obfuscation has a purpose. Nostradamus *did* make his ideas accessible, *though his aims and achievements must be measured in his own terms, rather than in our own.* He brought into the light of day a type of literature with which we are uncomfortable and which is not of the kind that our familiar traditions and education have led us to expect. Once we have recognized this fact, we might perhaps stop lamenting the 'obscurity' of Nostradamus, and begin to savour the peculiar genius of his game. For the simple truth is that Nostradamus was a prophet who refused to prophecy, save in retrospect. This is the sophisticated game he plays with history, and with his readers.

When we look without prejudice into the *Prophéties*, we discover that, in some uncanny way, Nostradamus wrote to us not from the past, but from the future. In this lies the secret of Nostradamus. The fault is ours: our own blinkered vision cannot measure up to his. We are blinded by our own contemporaneity, unable to make that visionary leap which permits us to discern, in advance of unfolding history, the futurity hidden in his words. Unlike Nostradamus, we are pinned to the material realm of shadows, ignorant of the future until the predicted event emerges on the plane of our familiar experience. Not only do the events of history unfold, but so, also, do the meanings of the quatrains.

Nostradamus, then, is master of the Game. His is the game of Time, in which the thing prophesied unlocks the quatrain, rather than (as one might expect of a prophet) the predictive quatrain unlocking the future. If Nostradamus limited the game spatially to Europe, he seems not to have limited it in time at all, for each moment an event prophesied comes to fruition, a quatrain is newly brought to life.

We still participate in the game of futurity which Nostradamus invented in the middle of the sixteenth century, and which (if he is to be believed) will run for almost another three centuries. This is the real secret of Nostradamus – not that he speaks to us from the past, but that by the magic of his literary technique, he still plays with us from the far side of that veil which we call the future.

Of course, many questions remain unanswered about Nostradamus and his *Prophéties*. Not least among these questions is, why did he write this set of arcane verses? Not, why did he write them in such an obscure form, but why did he write them at all?

It is clear from his prophetic vision, and from the way he couched his vision in arcane literary and astrological terms, that he was an initiate (see Appendix Three). Perhaps he was one of the Sons of the Widow; however, the order of his initiation is no longer of any great importance. He was clearly one of the *sapientiae* – the 'men of knowledge', as initiates were often called in medieval literature – and therefore permitted unrestricted access to the two worlds of matter and spirit.

Initiation carries with it many responsibilities. Initiates, who by their very nature have a knowledge of the past and future not available to ordinary mankind, usually elect to remain silent about what they know. Indeed, in most initiate schools, a strict adherence to silence is the prime precondition of initiation. Why, then, did Nostradamus feel free to speak out, in howsoever obscure a manner? In speaking out, was he breaking some vow of silence? Was Nostradamus a rogue initiate, who divulged his secret knowledge? Did he, in the words of another initiate, Agrippa von Nettesheim, feed sugar to sparrows and freely cast pearls before the profane? Did he do the forbidden thing, and speak when he should have reserved intact the hermetic silence?

That Nostradamus cast pearls, there may be little doubt. The *Prophéties* is great literature in the genre of Green Language, and the wisdom within it was vouchsafed to few men. Yet it is a moot point whether he cast such pearls before the profane at all. He gave forth his wisdom in the full knowledge that it would be useless save to those who really knew.

Did Nostradamus believe that in speaking such riddles, he was not really breaking a taboo of silence? If this were so, then it would be the answer to the strange obscurity of the verses. It would explain why the magus went to such pains to ensure that the prophecies would be clear only after the event. By means of this approach, the hermetic silence would be observed until his words could do no damage. By such means, Nostradamus would not commit the usual error of clairvoyants, and participate in the fulfilment of the event prophesied.

What did Nostradamus achieve? On the one hand, he seems to have succeeded mainly in creating little more than a sub-culture in his own name. On the other hand, he did create an astounding hermetic document. The *Prophéties* is supreme as Green Language literature, revealing its secrets to those fortunate few who know how to apply the hermetic keys. As Nostradamus points out to Henry II, the stanzas are so difficult that there really is no way of interpreting them. What kind of literature is that, other than occultism for occultists?

Did Nostradamus set out to achieve this double standard – to erect this most sophisticated of occult blinds, with an outer form designed to fool and perplex, yet with an inner content which spoke to the *sapientiae*? Was this really his aim – to create the most sophisticated occult blind in Western literature?

Though we may not doubt that he had a purpose in committing his vision to verse, we may only guess as to what this was. Perhaps the secret of his gift lies in the fact that the *Prophéties* is a monument to an astrological Green Language which is no longer a living part of our literary tradition. Perhaps, with his divining eye, Nostradamus could foresee that in the coming centuries his art of astrology – the divine science of the *sapientiae* – would lose its spiritual roots, and become merely an instrument for the aggrandizement of the ego. Did he perhaps sense that it was his destiny to use this sacred art, and the secret language of the initiates, in the construction of one final colossal monument to occult thought? Did he perhaps, in the light of what he could foresee, feel impelled to set down in literary form a supreme example of a form of prophecy which went back beyond the Sibyls of the ancient world? Did he perhaps, with some justification, see himself as the last of an ancient line of initiate prophets, and elected to mark the end of his beloved tradition by composing one of the most remarkable documents of the late-medieval world, in which this tradition is used to the full?

This view would at least explain one strange reference in his letter to Henry II. When touching on the influences which allowed him to write such prophetic verses, he mentioned what he called 'the natural instinct given by my progenitors'. This is usually taken as referring to his Jewish background, perhaps even to the cabbalistic lore in which the Jews were so proficient. However, a far deeper meaning may be contained in his words – perhaps he saw his true progenitors as the prophets of old, whom he wished to emulate as their ancient tradition came to an end.

Appendix One

The Horoscope
of Nostradamus

. . . quapropter eas obsigno tenacissima cera, anulo meo
superinsculpto, cuius ad oram nomen est meum, Solis
figura supremum locum tenente, tribusque planetis infi-
mum.

. . . because of this I seal up these [letters] with the
most tenacious wax, impressed with my signet ring,
on the edge of which is my name, the figure of the
Sun holding the higher part, and with the three
planets in the lower part.

(The only known reference made by Nostradamus to
his own horoscope, in a letter from Nostradamus to
Lorenz Tubbe, dated 15 October 1561)

Perhaps one day a researching scholar will uncover the
natal chart of Nostradamus, drawn up in his own hand.
Given the importance of a recent discovery of batches of
the correspondence of Nostradamus, along with authentic
copies of a few of his charts, this is not too hopeless a wish.[1]
Unfortunately, at present no such chart is known, and
until one surfaces, all horoscopes for the savant must be
regarded as speculative. The fact is that the all-important
moment of his birth seems not to have been reliably
preserved. There appears almost to be a conspiracy of
silence about his chart, for it is quite inconceivable that one

should not have been cast to mark his birth, according to the custom of the time. Yet, if it were cast for the old-style date of 14 December 1503, then all trace of it – even contemporaneous references to it – have disappeared, and we are dependent upon the unreliable Chavigny for information.[2] Fortunately, as we shall discover shortly, Nostradamus did go to the trouble of leaving behind one or two clues to his chart, almost as though he realized that it would be lost.

The lack of a genuine horoscope is doubly strange, for his maternal grandfather was reputed (though this reputation has faded under the masterly research of Leroy) to have been a fine astrologer, while one of his forebears was also renowned in the art – though perhaps not with all the qualifications and pomp claimed for him by biographers.

The more one researches the chart of Nostradamus, the more of a mystery it becomes. In the sixteenth century, it was commonplace for the figures of famous individuals to be published – sometimes, even against their will. In those days, far more people were able to read horoscopes, and see the arcane implications in charts and progressions derived from them, than is the case in modern times. In view of this, it is curious that the figure of Nostradamus was not published during his lifetime. Indeed, it is remarkable that contemporaneous astrologers, such as Johann Garcaeus, who included in an extensive collection of 400 horoscopes the birth data of such famous sixteenth-century personalities as the occultists Trithemius, Agrippa and Lazius, arcane symbolizers such as Alciati and Dürer, astronomers such as Copernicus, medical men such as Hutten and Vesalius, and neoplatonists such as Bembo and Mirandola, ignored the horoscope of the equally famous Nostradamus.[3] This omission is perplexing, for we cannot doubt that Garcaeus would have been familiar with the chart of the leading prophet-astronomer of the period. In fact, Garcaeus actually published, by way of a sample chart, a horoscope which was only a few days removed from that of Nostradamus.[4] One wonders why he could not have used the seer's figure to illustrate the point he wished to make, for, in the example chart he did elect to use, Saturn had retrograded only one degree, and Jupiter just over two, from the positions in the chart of the great seer.

Luca Gauricus, in a work which included over 200 famous horoscopes, included the charts of Regiomontanus and Agrippa, as well as those of Henry II of France and his dominating wife, Catherine de' Medici, yet missed out Nostradamus, possibly because the seer's fame was not consolidated for another three or four years.[5] However, the chart was not added in later editions.

Even more disturbing is that Cardan, in his book on judgements of 1578, published the horoscope of the Duke of Farnese, born in Rome exactly one month prior to Nostradamus, and even mentioned the stars which had become operative due to the conjunction of the superiors.[6] The Jupiter of this chart was, as Cardan put it, 'on the second magnitude Apollo, of the nature of Mercury': this was the late-medieval designation for the fixed star Castor, the *alpha* of Gemini, which, as we shall see, was an important element in the chart of Nostradamus. The Moon was in 14 degrees of Sagittarius: as Cardan himself pointed out, the Moon was 'on the star in the Head of Serpentarius, of the third magnitude'. This was the sixteenth-century designation for the star Rasalhague, the *alpha* of Ophiuchi.[7] From such observations, we see the tremendous importance placed by sixteenth-century astrologers on fixed stars in interpretation. Nostradamus' chart was perhaps one of the most remarkable of the sixteenth century precisely because of its trigonal configurations, and the relationship the superiors had to significant fixed stars.

It has amused us to adjust this interesting oversight of

the sixteenth century astrologers by, somewhat belatedly, constructing a chart in the form it would have taken had it been published (*fig. 16*). The importance of the fixed stars would have been noted in the chart, and perhaps even remarked upon in a gloss integrated in the figure. The horoscope is based on the sigillic method used by the sixteenth-century astrologer, Garcaeus, and employs the house system of Regiomontanus favoured by Nostradamus.

When a birth-time is not known, the astrologer has recourse to a technique called 'rectification' in order to establish an accurate time which will give some account of the events (presuming the dates of these to be known) in the chart of that native – the one for whom the *natus* (an old term for the birth chart) is cast. As we shall reveal, our own examination of the progressions and transits relating to the few dated events in the life of Nostradamus has brought us to the conclusion that he was born at 12.14.20 p.m. local time. This time, while arrived at by a process of rectification which we shall examine shortly, offers a chart which confirms an intriguing reference that Nostradamus made in a recently discovered letter. It also gives a *Pars Fortunae* which is exactly upon the important Astrologer's Arc, which figures in the charts of so many astrologers. As we shall see, this rectified chart also offers clues to certain surprising events in the life of the great savant.

Whatever time of day Nostradamus was born, his chart is dominated by a most distinctive configuration. This is an aspect of a triple conjunction, opposed by the Sun. In fact it is this distinctive aspect which seems to afford the only known contemporaneous reference to Nostradamus' chart. In the letter to Lorenz Tubbe, dated 15 October 1561, quoted as header to this chapter, Nostradamus gives a description of the impression left by his personal signet ring, so that Tubbe may be sure that letters are really from him.

485

This description seems to offer a clue to his horoscope.[8] The Sun of his chart is in Capricorn, while the three planets (the superiors, Mars, Jupiter and Saturn) are on the opposite side of the zodiac, in Cancer. It is reasonable to suppose that, for the design of his personal ring, Nostradamus abstracted the essence of his horoscope, the aspect of an opposition involving the Sun and the triple conjunction of superiors. This passing reference to his seal would be precisely apposite if Nostradamus had been born near to midday, for the Sun would then be at its highest point, and the three planets at the lowest point in the skies, which astrologers called the *Imum Coeli* (*fig. 3*).

In her French translation of the Nostradamus correspondence, Bernadette Lecureux does note that the sentence is a reference to the horoscope. However, what Nostradamus has reduced to a simple figure is not the horoscope, but the aspect-diagram of triple conjunction and solar opposition. This relationship – the structure of the aspect – would not change, no matter where one placed the Sun in the signet ring. Fortunately, other astrological conditions support the previous interpretation, by pointing to a near-midday birth.

We have observed that the 12.14.20 birthtime gives a *Pars Fortunae* which is on the important Astrologer's Arc. Is there any other factor in the chart which would relate a chart for this birth-time to astrology? The answer is yes. There is at least one factor, linked with a fixed star, which accounts for a most surprising fact in the life of Nostradamus – that, with all his undoubted talents, he did not publish until relatively late in his life.

The MC of his chart is in the 6th degree of Capricorn, and was therefore (in the first decade of the sixteenth century) on the fixed star *Pelagus*. This small star, the *sigma* of Sagittarius, was said by Ptolemy to be of the nature of Jupiter and Mercury. Now, since Nostradamus' own radical Mercury was on his Midheaven, this star redoubles the Mercurial principle in his life, and helps explain the large number of books he wrote, and his deep interest in medicine (Mercury is the Roman name for Hermes, the great healer, as well as the great esotericist).

What is of great interest to our research is the fact that, to judge from the comprehensive bibliography of Robert Benazra,[9] Nostradamus did not begin to publish his books until after 1553 – which is to say, in, or shortly after, his 50th year. Now, one of the most interesting things about the influence of *Pelagus* is that, when linked with Saturn, it delays success until after the age of 50: it also brings wealth towards the end of life, and a favourable marriage also late in life. Since the MC (the *Medium Coeli*, or Midheaven – symbolic of the highest point reached by the Sun in any locality) was in Capricorn, ruled by Saturn, these astrological conditions applied in the life of Nostradamus, and were unfolded appropriately.

Among the most important astrological traditions which still influenced medieval astrologers was the theory of the influence of the fixed stars. Individual stars, the *stella inerranta*, are mentioned more than once in the quatrains. They were so called, in medieval astrology, to distinguish them from the planets which were (in terms of Greek etymology) the wandering stars. Medieval astrologers, following their Arabic mentors who had specialized in these influences, insisted that certain stars could be accorded an influence in charts when they formed close conjunctions with planets or nodal points. Thus, when the Danish astrologer Matthias Hacus Sumbergius rectified the horoscope of Philip II of Spain, cast for 21 May 1527 (using, as his notes reveal, the ancient animodar system),[*] his clear

---

[*] Animodar is a term used to denote a rectification principle designed to establish the accuracy of a given birth-time, by means of reference to the last opposition or conjunction of Sun and Moon previous to that birth.

aim was to introduce the influence of a fixed star into the horoscope. To achieve this, he adjusted the birth-time sufficiently to move the Ascendant from 1 degree Scorpio back into 28 degrees of Libra (*fig. 51*). While there was no powerful star on the original Scorpionic degree, the star *Caput Herculis* just happened to be on the Libran.[10] Just so, the rectified chart of Nostradamus reveals the influence of a fixed star on the *Medium Coeli*.

Animodar method or not, Sumbergius was more interested in the star than in the precise ascendant degree. He would have known that the image of that constellation was used by medieval talisman-makers to bring victory in war – a reminder, of course, that Philip's palace-tomb of the Escorial was oriented in such a way as to commemorate a victory over the French. Inevitably, Hercules was later given prominence in the arcane and astrological and hermetic frescoes which Philip had painted (naturally under his own careful supervision) on the ceiling and upper walls of his vast library in the Escorial.[11]

Virtually all the important medieval books on astrology incorporated lists of stars, with accurate positions for a stated year. More often than not, this material was incorporated into sample horoscope readings. Garcaeus, whose work on astrology was probably the most influential of the century, provided details of 54 stars in his own tables of 'stellarum inerrantum', and referred this table to several of the charts which he analysed in his book.[12]

In view of the importance of this tradition, those sixteenth-century astrologers who considered the horoscope of Nostradamus would have taken into account the powerful fixed stars which dominated his chart, even without recourse to rectification. They would have recognized that the remarkable gathering of the superior planets in Cancer

The term is derived from Egyptian astrology, by way of Ptolemy.

were conjunct with the fixed stars *Castor* and *Pollux*. Such factors in a personal chart would remind them of those important elements which they considered in Mundane Astrology – the astrology concerned with politics, history and religions. In the Arabic tradition, which served the fixed stars well, the star *Castor* (which we now recognize as a binary) was said to induce a keen intellect, success in publishing and sudden fame, often followed by great affliction involving family. When pulled into prominence by Jupiter – as in the case of Nostradamus' chart – the star would bring occult interests, yet great danger of an unfortunate judicial sentence. The star *Pollux*, the *beta* of Geminorum, would bring family losses, as Nostradamus was painfully aware. The Moon in his natal chart was on *Bungula*, said to be the star nearest to our own solar system, and a binary. In the Arabic astrology, it was believed to bring many close friendships yet render the native diplomatic and secretive. Clearly, it is to *Castor* that one must look for an explanation of Nostradamus' occult ability, to *Bungula* for his delight in the Green Language, and to his *Pars Fortunae* for his genius as an astrologer.

This type of stellar astrology is rarely practised in modern times, and even its underlying theses are misunderstood. One exception to this is the astrological readings of 'Raphael', published in the first decades of the twentieth century, which were based on similar fixed-star reading methods as those used in the sixteenth century. In 1927, after noting that Mussolini's Saturn was on the fixed star *Aldebaran* (Britain's star),* and that other planets were on the meridian of France, 'Raphael' recognized that they would 'bring war, disaster, and downfall to his country'. Almost as a rider, 'Raphael' predicted Mussolini 'will meet

---

* In the arcane astrological tradition, each country is said to be governed by a particular fixed star.

a violent death'.[13] According to some modern commentators, Nostradamus had foreseen much the same future for *Il Duce*, centuries before he was born (see, for example, quatrain V.92, page 426).

No reputable astrologer of the sixteenth century would have dreamed of reading a horoscope bereft of the fixed stars, or the so-called Arabic Pars, and it is to the detriment of the art that these are no longer considered important. However, the loss of the old wisdom has been made up by a new sort of wisdom, and the truth is that we can learn more about Nostradamus from a computerized chart than his contemporaries would have learned with all their tables, instruments and Arabic books. It is an extraordinary experience to watch on a computer screen the slow unfolding of Nostradamus' natal planetary configuration, during a computerized astronomy visual display.[14] The conjuncting triad of superiors is so close to the two stars that these are almost occulted on the screen by the planets. As simulated skies of pinprick stars revolve on the screen, the three superiors seem to dance around *Castor*, and so close is Mars to *Pollux* that at times the star is hidden behind the red disc. This slow dance of planets around stars which marked out the unique genius of Nostradamus is all that is needed to convince one of the majesty of the ancient form of divination, which embraced stellar lore into horoscopy.

One cannot consider the nature of sixteenth-century astrology without reflecting upon the nature of the two sets of tabulations used by astrologers of that period – the tables of houses and the ephemerides, in which the planetary tabulations were recorded. Of course, scholars have learned not to rely too heavily on the tabulations available in the late-medieval period. After all, it has been shown by Boffito that even the symbolically important Morning-Star Venus in Dante's *Commedia* was a result of an error in tabulation, rather than divine inspiration.[15] Given the state of planetary tables in his day, Nostradamus' own chart would not be as accurate as those established through modern tabulations, yet it would afford us a glimpse of what his contemporaries must have thought about Nostradamus, in astrological terms. According to the data given by Regiomontanus in 1489,[16] the planetary positions (computed for Ulm) for midday of the 14 December 1503 were:

> *SU 01CP52   MO 16SC14   ME 09CP43R*
> *VE 01AQ11 MA 16CN28R   JU 10CN58R*
> *SA 17CN17R   DH 28PI40*

The data makes a most interesting comparison with that derived from the Microsoft computer system, WinStar, in the chart in *fig. 3* (computed for St Rémy) for 12.14.20 p.m. of the same day. We have elected to present this horoscope in the sixteenth-century manner – in the Modus Rationalis – but the following is the data derived from the WinStar ephemeris:

> *SU 01CP38   MO 16SC04   ME 04CP12R*
> *VE 02AQ23 MA 18CN38R   JU 10CN57R*
> *SA 15CN24R   DH 28PI41*

> *UR 08PI39   NE 22CP40   PL 03SG40*
> *AS 10AR36   MC 05CP14   PF 25AQ02*

The Regiomontanus positions for the luminaries are very accurate, but those for the superior planets are out by several degrees – Saturn and Mars by almost 2 degrees. Mercury is the worst offender, being out (given the time lapse) by about 5 degrees. Our point is that almost any respectable astrologer of the sixteenth century would have cast a near-midday chart for the birth of Nostradamus along the lines of the Regiomontanus tabulations, which we now know to have been inaccurate to some extent.

In an essay on the ephemerides of Nostradamus, Yves Lenoble reminds us that Nostradamus certainly possessed the tables of Stadius, and probably those of Leowitz, but also points out that he could not have used these for the charts which appear in the Nostradamus correspondence published in Latin by Dupèbe, and in French by Lécureux.[17] This means that for the charts which have survived, Nostradamus could have had recourse to the ephemerides of Stoeffler, Regiomontanus or Plaum. The conclusion is that the tables of Stoeffler were used, even though this necessitated the introduction of errors. The significant thing, however, is that since the house-tables used by Stoeffler were those designed by Regiomontanus then a method of house-interpretation favoured by this great German astrologer was used by Nostradamus. This much is confirmed in the charts (albeit copies) known to have been cast by Nostradamus (*fig. 23*). This house-system is no longer favoured by modern astrologers, yet its wide use in the sixteenth century should be taken into account by all those who seek to interpret the charts drawn up by Nostradamus, in the light of how the master interpreted them. Regiomontanus had established a unique method of interpreting the house-cusps – a method which does not correspond to that widely used today.

As we might expect of an individual who has been under the occult spotlight for some many years, there is no shortage of later versions of the chart. Unfortunately, each of the horoscopes we are familiar with is inaccurate in one way or another. Most of them incorporate glaring inaccuracies, even for the chosen data, and all too frequently they are copied unthinkingly from earlier data and/or charts.

The oldest chart we know is that given in 1686 by the English astrologer, John Gadbury (*fig. 52*), who dubs him an 'Astroloster', and 'Author of those Stupendious *Prophe-cies . . .*' The chart is a noon-time speculative – possibly based on data from Garencière's unreliable book, to which Gadbury refers.[18] Fortunately for us, it is unlikely that Gadbury recognized the birth-time was dubious, for had he known this, then he would not have included it in his collection of ten specimen charts, since a speculative figure would undermine the astrological principle (relating to Cardinality)[*] with which his book dealt. 'A *Meridian Glory* is always the greatest, and the most dazling', he writes, for, with a noon-time birth, this is precisely what one has in a chart. The data for the chart is given in round figures, and the retrogradation of the superiors is not symbolized in the figure:

SU O2CP   MO 05SC   ME 10CPR   VE 01AQ
MA 16CN   JU 12CN   SA 17CN
DH 29PI   PF 14AQ

AS 11AR   II 01GE   III 21GE
MC 02CP   XI 18CP   XII 12AQ

There was considerable interest in Nostradamus in English occult circles during the last half of the seventeenth century. Derek Parker, after recording that several English printers had been fined in 1562 for selling the Prognostication almanacs of Nostradamus, is quite wrong to claim that Nostradamus was never in good repute in Britain.[19] Garencières' curious book – the first translation into English of all the quatrains – had appeared in 1672, and in 1689 the astrologer John Partridge had published his pamphlet of Nostradamus' quatrains. After that time, Nostradamus

---

[*] In traditional astrology, the Cardinal signs are Aries, Cancer, Libra and Capricorn. They are so named because, in the horoscope figure, they lie on the cardinal angles – Aries to the East, Libra to the West, and so on.

became almost as famous as a prophet in England as he had been in France. 'The Book,' remarked Gadbury of the English translation of the *Prophéties*, 'hath procured him both a *good*, and a *bad Fame*.'

The lack of an early chart did not mean that Nostradamus' birth data was unknown. In the amusing play by Collot d'Herbois, *Le Nouveau Nostradamus*, composed in honour of the passage of the King's brother to Marseilles in 1777, the knock-about humour relating to Aries and Capricorn between Canzonin and the astrologer, Dastrimon (a near anagram for Nostradamus), indicates that the Ascendant and sun-sign were known, which implies a knowledge of the chart. In passing, we should observe that one or two references in the short piece seem to suggest a recognition of some of the arcane word-play meanings in the quatrains.

Although the Gadbury chart was copied (in English works, at least) for a considerable time, a few attempts were made to establish what the birth-time really was. Given the paucity of known facts about the life of Nostradamus, the results of rectifications were not very edifying, and this situation has subsisted until well into the twentieth century. The following survey covers only those charts which have been used in literature pertaining to Nostradamus, and does not include all the natal charts of the savant known to us.

The chart given in *Coming Events*, 1907–8, is quite incorrect. The amended version of this, printed in *Occult Review*, is better, but still inaccurate: both are recorded, without comment, by Alan Leo.[*][20] We mention this pair, and the summary provided by Leo, merely because the attention of James Laver had been directed to them by Nelson Stewart, while the former was preparing his book,

---

[*] Alan Leo was the pseudonym of the English theosophist and astrologer, William Frederick Allan (1860–1918), who wrote a large number of introductory books on astrology, not all of which are of high quality.

Nostradamus, or the Future Foretold, 1942. Laver, who had no astrological learning, seems not to have realized that these horoscopes were inaccurate, and that they did not even conform to the birth data he published in his own book. Laver was of the opinion that Nostradamus was born at midnight.

As we might expect, all the charts offered in the sub-cultural literature are of dubious value. The figure which appears on page 35 of John Hogue's *Nostradamus & the Millennium*, 1987, and acknowledged to be derived from Jeff Green,[21] is a midday chart of fair accuracy, though ironically Pluto is 3 degrees out. The chart which prefaces Arkel and Blake's *Nostradamus*, based on a midday putative time, is incorrect, and is probably derived from Jeff Green.

Most of the charts of professional astrologers known to us are inaccurate in some respects, and all of them assume the noon-time birth to be acceptable. André Pelardy's chart, from *Les Cahiers astrologiques*, No. 97, of 1962, is based on the information given by Chavigny, which, as we have seen, hazards the birth time as being 'about midday'. The Pelardy chart has Mercury, Venus and Mars inaccurately placed. The data he gives for the death of Nostradamus is not progressional, and is, in any case, inaccurate in certain planetary positions, even though no time is specified. The horoscope proposed by Libow in 1963[22] is several days out, seemingly because of Libow's misunderstanding regarding sixteenth-century calendrical changes: it is cast for midday on 5 December 1503. The chart give by Eric Muraise in 1969 is difficult to read, as planetary positions are given against an ungraduated scale: however, Mercury could not be to the west of the Sun, in Sagittarius, nor could Mars be in Leo.[23] It is difficult to see whence Muraise derived his data. The figure cast by Hélène Kinauer-Saltarini, and published by Patrian in the 1981 edition of *Nostradamus: le Profezie*, is inaccurate, and worth

495

mentioning only because it shows the nativity with the speculative death data, the birth set for midday, the death for 'night-time'. Unfortunately, information in both charts is incorrect: almost all the planets are in the wrong degrees, while Mercury is 7 degrees out of position. One presumes that Patrian was not aware that the factors leading to death would be manifest in the progressed chart (see below), rather than in the transits. Max Duval's chart, published in 1992 by Robert Amadou, gives an Arietan ascendant, and places the Sun exactly on the MC, on the fixed star Vega, which is surely an astounding error.[24] In 1503 Vega would have been in 9 degrees of Capricorn, whereas Nostradamus' Sun was over 7 degrees away from this position.

Our own version (*fig. 3*) has been cast using the Matrix Software WinStar system, with the *Ephemeris Update* from 1996, along with fixed star readings from the Microsoft *Astronomer for Windows*. After rectification against known events (see below) we have decided upon a birth of 12.14.20 p.m. local time.

Rectification is difficult in the case of an individual with so few authentically dated events on record. However, Nostradamus was careful to leave records of four dates which were probably intended as a rectification guide: he dated the two letters in the two separately printed volumes of the *Prophéties*, and, in his work on facial creams, he offered the dates for the beginning and ending of his medical studies.[25] We have no doubt that Nostradamus left this data to afford a glimpse into his horoscope: when they are used as the basis for rectification, they confirm his birthdate with reasonable precision. This rectification has been checked against two other dates which have survived from the sixteenth century: the times of his marriage and death.

Before glancing at the data around these rectifications, we should observe that, in our opinion, the most certain confirmation of the accuracy of the proposed natal chart is that it places the *Pars Fortunae* firmly on the traditional Astrologer's Arc, in 26 degrees of the Leo–Aquarius axis. In 1503, this degree was occupied by the triple, *alpha Leonis*, probably called by Nostradamus *Cor Leonis*, though Copernicus had already renamed it *Regulus* – a new name taken up by Garcaeus in his influential treatise of 1576. We know of no Arabic reading for the *pars fortuna* on this star, but the thirteenth-century Florentine astrologer, Guido Bonatus, wrote that when the star is in the Ascendant (with which the pars is intimately related) this signifies a person of great note and power, 'too much exalted'.[26] As Allen records, William of Salysbury (writing in 1552), called it 'the Royall Starre, for they that are borne under it, are thought to have a royall nativitie'.[27] It is not curious that *Regulus* should be so intimately connected with the Astrologers' Arc, which in turn gave the calendrical setting for the Astrologer's Annual Feast, held in London during the seventeenth century.

The rectified birth date is 12.14.20 p.m. (local time), 14 December 1503, St Rémy, France. The rectification is from four sets of the six data, noted above. The first is the publication of the first part of *Prophéties* (signed by Nostradamus *De Salon, ce j. de mars 1555*), 12.00 (tem. spec.), 1 March 1555. Two, the publication date of the second part of the *Prophéties*, from the signed *Epistle* to Henry II, *Salonae Petrae Provincae*, 12.00 a.m. (tem. spec.), 27 June 1558. Three, the progressed chart for his marriage to Gemelle, which is said to have occurred on 11 November 1547; and four, the progression for his death, which probably took place very early on 2 July 1566 (see page 57 ff).

In our own house-charting, we have used the Regiomantanus tables, as we know these were the ones employed by Nostradamus. In medieval times, the method was called the Modus Rationalis, and was popular among such important astrologers as Cardan and Garcaeus. As we have already noted, Regiomontanus insists that his house system requires a different interpretation of the cusps, which he regarded as marking the central and most powerful areas of the houses. The useful thing about this approach is, of course, that it reconciles the Ascendant degree with the centre of the First House. Methods of rectification must take these issues into account, but modern astrologers who have attempted to reconcile the known Nostradamus charts with readings have failed to consider this important issue. We have taken this into account in our own progressions.

Both progressed charts for the two published letters show several planets in the 9th house, which, of course, governs publishing. In the 1555 chart, the progressed Sun has just entered 24 degrees of Aquarius and is therefore in opposition to the natal *Pars*, and, while thus being conjunct, the Astrologer's Arc is in opposition to the important *Cor Leonis*, then in 23.55 Leo. Mars, which is now direct, is applying to the retrograde Jupiter. The progressed Venus is in opposition to the radical Saturn. The Caput is on the eleventh cusp, ensuring popularity.

In the 1558 chart, the progressed, the general stellar aid to publishing is still evident, but now the progressed Moon is on the radical Moon (the second lunar return in the life of Nostradamus).

The progressed marriage chart, for November 1547, is an almost classical confirmation of the proposed natal chart. Having said that, we must point out that in the sixteenth century, marriages were often contracted for financial and social reasons, so that the planet Venus (and even Mars) tends not to figure in such charts quite so strongly as in modern synastry.* Given that Nostradamus benefited from the marriage in terms of the acquisition of property (if

* In astrology, synastry is the name given to the art of comparing horoscope charts, with a view to establishing antipathies and sympathies, as well as the general drift of combined destinies.

not actual wealth), the importance of the marriage progressed chart is the fact that the triple conjunction of
superiors is now centring on the second house cusp. In
addition, progressed Jupiter and Mars are on the radical
IC,* relating to home and family.

It is inevitable that the astrological factors relating to the
death of Nostradamus should be important. The contact of
the fixed star *Pelagus* traditionally offers a natural and
peaceful death, and it is this which Nostradamus experienced. The exact time of death is not on record: however,
for reasons which must be evident from the observations on
page 57 ff, we have progressed the death chart to a few
minutes before midnight on 1–2 July 1566.

One may see almost at a glance why Nostradamus was
going to die at this time. The anaretic,† which is Saturn,
has progressed (by retrogression) to 11.10 of Cancer, and is
therefore on the radical Jupiter. In addition, the progressed
Ascendant is in opposition to the radical Sun. The
progressed Sun is in conjunction with the radical Uranus,
while the progressed Mars is in opposition to the radical
Mercury.

The death chart supports the idea of death in the early
hours of the morning, corresponding to the 3.00 a.m. which
Nostradamus indicated in his wrongly tabulated *Almanach*
for 1566 (see page 58). The following data should support
this notion. At 3.00 a.m. on 2 July, the transiting Moon is
in opposition to the radical Saturn. The transiting Sun is
conjunction to the radical Mars. The transiting Pluto is in
conjunction with the radical Moon.

While considering his death chart, it dawned upon us
that there was one other possible chart for the birth of

---

* The IC is the *Imum Coeli*, or lowest point in the heavens – the
opposite of the MC, dealt with earlier.
† The anaretic is that power (usually a planet) in a natal horoscope which
brings about the death of the native.

Nostradamus – this being linked with data which Nostradamus left behind. Interestingly, the chart which is derived from this information amends the rectified horoscope we have already examined by only a few degrees.

On page 56 ff we dealt with the intentional error which Nostradamus introduced into his *Almanach* for 1566, in order, as we surmised, to reveal a prediction for the time of his own death. It was while considering the reason why he should give such precise data for the inaccurate lunar position that we realized his aim. The position he gave in his *Prédictions de Juillet* for the Moon placing was 7 degrees and 25 minutes of Capricorn:

> *Dans ce mois de Iuillet 1566. sera pleine Lune le premier iour a 23.h.o.m.apres midy, a 7.deg.25.m. de Capricornus . . .*

As we saw, this was a placing many degrees off true. While considering this problem, it dawned on us that the reason why Nostradamus specified this exact degree was to leave a further clue as to his horoscope: the 7 degrees 25 minutes in Capricorn could be taken as relating to the MC in his own chart. Given the latitude of his birth, this would amend his Ascendant to 14 degrees 58 minutes of Aries.

Once we had realized what Nostradamus may have been up to, we cast a chart in order to obtain this precise MC, and arrived at a natal chart as follows:

SU 01CP39   MO 16SC09   ME 04CP11R
VE 02AQ23   MA 18CN38R   JU 10CN57R
SA 15CN24R   DH 28PI41

UR 08PI39   NE 22CP40   PL 03SG40
AS 14AR58   MC 07CP25

Nostradamus died towards the end of his ninth septenary, which marked the 63rd year of his life. As an astrologer, he would have been aware in advance of the time of his death, and one wonders if quatrain 63 of Century I is an arcane commentary upon this, and upon his eventual reimbodiment:

> Les fleaux passez diminue le monde,
> Long-temps la paix, terres inhabitez.
> Seur marchera par le ciel, terre, mer, & onde,
> Puis de nouveau les guerres suscitez.

In view of its context – touching on the post-mortem experience, and reincarnation – we feel the verse is too arcane to translate here. We should note, however, that in Bodin's seminal *Republic*, the number 63 (precisely as the ninth septenary) was regarded as being fatal. This view is far more ancient than Bodin, however.[28]

We have examined most of the obvious astrological sources in the hope of tracing the horoscope of Nostradamus, and have been disappointed by the hiatus between his birth and the earliest known figure, that cast by Gadbury. Naturally, we would be pleased to enter into correspondence with anyone who can provide specialist information relating to a birth-chart published (or even in manuscript!) in the sixteenth or seventeenth centuries.

Appendix Two

Early Editions of the *Prophéties*

C'est une commune opinion dans la France, ... que Nostradame à estré non seulement le plus grand Astronome qui ayt paru, depuis plusieurs Siecles, mais aussi qu'il à esté particulierement favorisé du don de Prophetie. Cette verités'est encore mieux soustenüe, par les Escrits qu'il a laisée à la posterité, que par la grande reputation qu'il eut pendant le cours de sa vie.

It is a common opinion in France ... that Nostradamus was not only the greatest astrologer to have appeared during several centuries, but that he was particularly favored with the gift of prophecy. This truth is all the more sustained by the Writings which he has left to posterity, as much as by the great reputation which he had during the course of his life.

(Le Chevalier de Jant, *Predictions tire'es des Centuries de Nostradamus. Qui vray semblement ce peuvent appliquer au temps present, & à la guerre entre la France & l'Angleterre contre les Provinces unies,* 1673)

Modern scholars of Nostradamus are deeply indebted to the bibliography of Robert Benazra, who, in his *Répertoire Chronologique Nostradamique* of 1990, offers a survey of the literature pertaining to the Master, from 1545 to 1989.

According to Benazra, no fewer than nine separate editions of the *Prophéties* are on record as being published in France during the lifetime of Nostradamus. However, in four cases these are known only from later bibliographical notes, and (if they ever existed at all) have been totally lost. The nine recorded printings, which offer considerable variations in the titles, are:

1555 at Lyons, by Macé Bonhomme.
1555 at Avignon, by Pierre Roux.
1556 at Avignon, perhaps a version of the 1555 Lyons.
1556 at Lyons, by Sixte Denyse.
1557 at Lyons, by Antoine du Rosne.
1558 at Lyons.
1558 perhaps at Avignon.
1558 at Lyons, by Jean de Tournes.
1560 at Paris, for Barbe Regnault.

Much to the chagrin of scholars, very few copies of these early editions survive. Fortunately several reliable edited copies have been published, and, in some cases, useful facsimile editions have been printed. Among the facsimiles which we have consulted for our present work is the Lyons (Antoine du Rosne) 1557 edition, published by Benazra in 1993. A scholarly activity of editing and reprinting continued after the Master's death, as a result of which we have had access to such excellent works as the Benoist Regaud variations, printed at Lyons in 1568. This was the 12th edition of the *Prophéties*, and appeared in two parts.

Inevitably, after the death of Nostradamus, very many editions – of more or less dubious authenticity – were published. Within a short while, a general publishing formula of the type which we now recognize as the *Prophéties* form was established. The original two volumes

– which may indeed be a binding together of two separately printed works – were pulled together: the first was prefaced by the *Letter to César*, followed by seven centuries (not always complete – there being an enormous number of variations), a *Legis Cautio* between Centuries VI and VII, and the *Epistle to Henry II*, followed by the remaining quatrains.

Perhaps most impressive among the editions printed almost within a century of the death of Nostradamus is the single, well-edited version in the Amsterdam edition printed by Jean Jansson, issued in 1668. This was the *Les Vrayes Centuries et Prophéties de Maistre Michel Nostradamus*, and while it did not include the *Preface* letter to César, it did contain the 141 quatrains which are called *Présages*. It is unlikely that many of these were from the hand of the Master, and even if they were, it is unlikely that they were intended for anything other than his *Almanachs*. In addition, there appeared in this edition the 58 curious sixtains, or *Autres Prédictions*, one or two supplementary quatrains in Centuries VII and VIII, and the batch of quatrains known as Centuries XI and XII, most of dubious authenticity.

The material from this 1668 edition was reprinted in phototype, in 1936, and is known as the Adyar Edition. This reprinting added the letter to César, following the edited version made available by Eugene Bareste in 1840. The publication of this entire work has ensured a reliable edition of the original is available to modern scholars, and we have taken full advantage of this.

In 1650, Pierre Leffen printed a remarkable single-volume edition of the *Centuries*, based on the 1556 Avignon printing, and on the 1558 Lyons so-called *princeps*. This was *Les Vrayes Centuries et Prophéties de Maistre M. Nostradamus*. This is a rare edition, but a copy exists in the British Library: we have used this for making comparison and adjustments where difficult variations in texts were encountered during our studies of other editions.

A later edition from the house of Rigaud, printed by Benoist at Troyes in 1568, claims (with some good reason) to be a revised and corrected version of the Lyons edition. For modern scholars this has the advantage of being available in the National Library of Buenos Aires reprint. The quatrains in this edition vary only slightly from those in the 1668 Amsterdam edition, but in some instances the work has been useful as a suggestion for alternative readings.

To ensure that we had access to a reliably accurate version of individual quatrains for the present work, we consulted as many of the early works as were available to us. We found especially useful a comparison of the Pierre Leffen and Jean Jansson editions. A few minor deviations were found even between these excellent works, yet such deviations proved to be relatively unimportant, and seem to have little impact on the arcane method (or upon the astrology) used by Nostradamus.

We have listed these titles in some bibliographic detail because it was from these texts that we selected, and cross-checked, the French verses which we have used in our present study. In spite of all the efforts we have made to establish a version of these quatrains as we hoped Nostradamus penned them, we must admit that there is no surviving valid criterion of choice. Other than common sense, and a feeling for the exigencies of the Green Language, we have not been able to establish any valid rules to guide us as to which variations to accept or reject. Where serious doubt is raised by a word or phrase, we have tended to rely upon versions published during his lifetime, though we recognize that even this does not really offer a valid arbiter. In sum, we have to admit that even in his published quatrains Nostradamus still remains fundamentally a mystery –

unfortunately this is typical of an initiate who elects to work through published material.

Appendix Three

Nostradamus as an Initiate

Thou newly illumined one, a share in the resurrection has fallen to thee, through this initiation into the mysteries of grace ... May what though hast beheld in symbol now become thine in reality.

(Pseudo–Athanasius, *De Pascha*, quoted by Hugo Rahner in *The Christian Mystery and the Pagan Mysteries*, in *The Mysteries, Papers from the Eranos Yearbooks*, 1971 printing, p.398)

We have no doubt that Nostradamus was an initiate, working on behalf of a sixteenth-century arcane school. An initiate is one who, usually by dint of special exercises, has sufficiently refined part of his or her nature to permit untrammelled access to the spiritual world, which normally remains invisible to ordinary mankind.

The teachers who direct such initiations lead the neophyte literally by gradual (or graded) degrees towards their highest potential. The term *Master*, which is now used very loosely in our language, was once applied to the Magus, or one who has attained the magistry over the craft of initiation. As we shall see, Nostradamus, who seems to have been initiated to one of the highest possible degrees, had become a Master within a European school of initiation. Perhaps this accounts for the reason why so many of his contemporaries addressed him as Master, when officially his honorific was Doctor.

As the secret of Nostradamus is linked intimately with his initiate status, we should give some account of the background to this aspect of his life.

The arcane schools that direct the training of such would-be initiates usually work in secret, and leave little mark on history. This is the main reason why they are grievously ignored by modern historians, who depend so completely on documentation and visible records. It is also for this reason that it is virtually impossible to write intelligibly about the history and influence of initiation without appearing to be imaginative, or without giving the impression of being a poor historian, by modern standards. The poverty of documentation often requires that one must resort to mythology, or other methods of investigation, rather than to documentary evidence, in support of one's line of thought.

We preface the following notes on Nostradamus as an initiate with this warning, because what we have to say now will probably sound strange within an academic context. However, we recognize that the ethos of our times is changing and soon it will be possible for academics to write with confidence about such things as reincarnation without being sniggered at or condemned by those who have no knowledge of such mysteries.

The secret of Nostradamus seems to lie in the peculiar disciplines which he followed in a previous incarnation. These disciplines led to a particularly high grade of initiation. While we have mentioned several times that Nostradamus was an initiate, and have given some indication of the school of esoteric Christianity to which he probably belonged in the sixteenth century, we have not so far attempted to give any coherent account of the implications behind his considerable vision. There is little point in saying that a person is an initiate without giving some further account of what sort of initiate he or she is – that is, the degree, or *gradus*, attained, and to which stream of initiation that person belongs. It therefore behoves that we offer some account of the school of initiation which coloured the soul-life of Nostradamus to the extent that he could produce the unique literature of the *Prophéties*.

It is one of the characteristics of all great initiates who are called to prominence in world history that they help form the cultural or political life of their age, yet seem almost not to belong to that age. Just so with Nostradamus. What is of importance in the life impulses of Nostradamus do not really belong to sixteenth-century France: these impulses – indeed, his literary style – seem to well up from a distant past. The more one looks sympathetically into Nostradamus, the more one is forced to recognize that what was really important in his prophetic impulses and literary style, he brought over into the sixteenth century from a previous lifetime. All the writings of Nostradamus – and specifically the unique style of the *Prophéties* – are permeated with poetic qualities which have been carried into the sixteenth century from what we now call the Hibernian Mysteries. When we gaze on the formative initiate life of Nostradamus – at his mastery of the Green Language, at his use of gnomic prophetic utterance, at his grasp of the grand sweep of the history of north-west Europe – we are gazing into the mind of an initiate schooled in the ancient mystery wisdom centred in Ireland, and serving the life of the Celts.

When we seek for the roots of the *Prophéties*, then, we find ourselves in the rich poetic loam of sixth-century Ireland. For good esoteric reasons, during the first centuries of our era, Ireland had remained a backwater in European history. There is even some indication that the mystery schools of Imperial Rome had ordained that

509

Ireland should remain untouched as an un-Romanized periphery on the edge of the map of the Imperium. It was intended by the initiation schools that this map would correspond to the future Christian world. It had been part of the destiny of Rome to establish the ground for the development of the spiritual mysteries of the future – which was to be the new initiation schools of Christianity. Although the Roman soldiery did reach Ireland, they did not take over its cultural life, nor destroy its Druidic priestcraft, in the way they seem to have destroyed that in England, Scotland and (to a lesser extent) Wales. Thus, something of the great pre-Christian mystery wisdom survived in Ireland, and it was for this reason that it continued as the main esoteric centre of European cultural life. This is why Ireland became a refuge for esoteric Christianity – for what we might even term pre-Roman Christianity. What we now tend to see romantically, through the eyes of later poets, as the twilight of the Celts was really the dawn of esoteric Christianity, which has yet to speak in the future of Europe. The ancient Druidic wisdom which had served the soul-life of the North had already begun to give way to, or integrate with, the Christian Mysteries – to those mysteries which we would probably now call Celtic Christianity.

By the eighth century this impulse would, through the reforming zeal of the York-born Alcuin, re-enter the mainstream of European history. Following the ancient pathway of initiate knowledge, it would work back to its origins, its *fons*. It would move back from the periphery, which was Ireland, where it had gestated during a particularly chaotic period on the European mainland. From this periphery, it would move first to a mid-point, which was Charlemagne's Aachen, and thence back to Rome. The conflict between the esoteric Christianity and the Christianity of the Roman Empire would then begin to be formally settled at the synods, and informally unsettled through the proscription of opponents as heretics, until the final break with Rome occurred almost 800 years later, when Nostradamus was once again in embodiment, in Europe.

Time and time again, an echo of this conflict arises in the soul-life of Nostradamus. Within this powerful soul-life we find a tremendous urge to chain the Celtic initiate vision of the Hibernian poesy into the straitjacket of the official language of a culture steeped in Roman Christianity. Time and time again, we find him handling a language which is as strange to his contemporaries as early Christian Irish would be to us.

If our understanding of the importance of this previous lifetime is correct, then the ancestors Nostradamus acknowledged in the *Epistle to Henry II* are the Druidic-Christian priests of Ireland. In a previous lifetime he had lived among them as a great initiate, in an ambience far more in tune with his own prophetic insights and sense of poesy than was possible for him in sixteenth-century France.

To some extent the Welsh Myrddin, who is better known nowadays as Merlin, is a literary invention. He is a composite of various mythological strata, extending from folk legends, through romance literature into the inventive semi-histories of Geoffrey of Monmouth, in his own piratic version of 'The Prophecy of Merlin'.

Whether this accretion of legends were built around a historical personage or not is fairly irrelevant. The fact is that Myrddin, whether of Irish or Welsh ancestry, or whether merely a romantic fiction, is a *type* of the Celtic initiation figure. In so far as the Celtic magician Myrddin was founder of an initiate school and literature, then Nostradamus, in his sixth-century incarnation, was among its most proficient followers.

When the veils of language are pulled aside, the old myths and stories begin to reveal their deep wisdom. The legend that Myrddin, besides being a magician, was a great bard whose tongue could enchant animals, was merely another way of indicating that he was master of the Green Language. He was one who could speak with the tongues of angels, he was one who could play the magic flute. In one of the stories told in the Arthurian cycle, Myrddin is betrayed by Viviane (perhaps the Chwibmian of the Welsh legends) who is obsessed with obtaining his magic power. Once she has attained his knowledge, she incarcerates him in a prison of air, from which he can see and hear everything, yet not be seen himself. In this we see a classical initiation legend, for Viviane is his higher self, and his prison is nothing more than that separation from the material realm into the higher spiritual realm, with the wider vistas and range of perception, which initiation offers. The 'prison of air' is a nice touch, for it links with the element proper to the birds, over whose language he was an adept. His mastery over the air element is also emphasized in the *Gesta Regnum Britanniae*, where Myrddin causes the famous stone blocks of Stonehenge to fly through the air by the power of his song. The persistent legend that Myrddin built that astronomical and calendrical masterpiece of the ancient world, Stonehenge, is merely a periphrastic way of admitting his supreme knowledge of astrology.

The Irish proto-historical astrology is not a matter of romantic fiction. It may be studied working in man-made caves even to this day. Anyone who has had the privilege of watching the solstice light magic in the passages of Loughcrew, in Ireland, will recognize that the ancient designation 'Guardian of the Stones' was really intended to mark out the individual as a supreme 'astrologer'. The ancients arranged stones according to cosmic patterns, to reflect cosmic lighting, and for entirely cosmic purposes. To this day, the intriguing symbols carved on the back-stones of the surviving passages at Loughcrew still mark out even the minor deviances in the solar light over the four-year cycle at the winter solstice. This was astrological knowledge of the most refined kind, which has survived, through the guardianship of the secret schools, for 5,000 years. Myrddin was the guardian of such cosmic wisdom.

More important to our own theme of the initiation archetype is that Myrddin was a prophet, who saw and wrote of the future of Britain, especially of Wales. The legend that he was a prophet – a legend which, in any case, later materialized into a considerable literature – was an acknowledgement that Myrddin (by now widely known as Merlin) had second-sight, or the Vision. As with the prophecies of Nostradamus, these Welsh prophecies were obscure. Like those of Nostradamus, the main corpus of predictions – especially those in *The Black Book of Carmarthen* – became famous, even though few could interpret them, and most were assumed to have been restricted to the twelfth century. It is hardly surprising that the French writer Wace (who was canon of Bayeux in that century) decided to omit most of the prophecies of Merlin from his own work *because he could not understand them*!

In that same twelfth century the commentary on the prophecies of Merlin, which had been made by Alanus de Insulis, was very popular. It remained sufficiently popular to be published as late as 1603. Other versions, bereft of intelligent commentaries, had been published earlier, and were widely available in manuscript form. So well-entrenched was their popularity in both England and France that, in the mid-sixteenth century, a serious attempt was made to put them on the Index of forbidden books.

There has been some inclination among historians to draw an unconscious parallel between Nostradamus and this proscription of Merlin's prophetic writings. There is a tradition (seriously reported by many modern writers on Nostradamus) that he was called before the Inquisition at Toulouse to be judged as a heretic. According to this same tradition, Nostradamus elected not to appear. The story, which shows a profound ignorance of the working of the Inquisition, was retold in all seriousness by Torné-Chavigny as late as 1874, in his *Nouvelle Lettre du Grand Prophete Nostradamus Eclairci*. (See Appendix Seven for a brief résumé of Torné-Chavigny.)

It is, of course, of considerable importance that, in the same period that Nostradamus was writing his prophecies, those stemming from the initiation school to which he had previously belonged were being proscribed. This was, and is, the pattern of initiate involvement in history, that as one impulse dies out, another is designed to take its place. This situation should lead us to ask, why should the Church keep an eye on the past, yet miss, or elect to ignore, what was going on under their very noses? The answer to this question is perhaps obvious – Nostradamus was protected by his carefully cultivated royal patronage, by Catherine de' Medici, who was preparing herself and her progeny for a future which would never happen. It is also certain that, since he was working in an initiation stream, Nostradamus was also protected by other influential beings.

Now, in a very real sense, initiation works against nature. It is one of the tenets of initiation that ordinary history can be little more than an account of degeneration: if the world were left to itself, then it would rapidly fall into chaos. This is one reason why the great initiates are charged with giving regenerative impulses to the historical process. Historical events manipulated by the initiate schools seek to introduce a redemptive element, to counteract the degenerative force of ordinary history (one might even write, natural history). Our insights lead us to suspect that Nostradamus was the sixteenth-century guardian of that prophetic stream in which he participated in Ireland or Wales in the fifth or sixth centuries, and which was, by his day, in dire need of redemption.

We have dealt with the Merlin tradition at some length to establish the initiate background to the soul-life of Nostradamus, and to hint at the complex issues of his prophetic insights.

However, while Merlin was probably the most famous male prophet in the sixteenth century, his female counterpart was even more famous. The feminine tradition of prophecy was pagan, and served the prophetic needs of the ancient world. Known as the Sibylline books, this collection of oracles was originally preserved in ancient Rome. According to legend, it was partly destroyed by the Cumaean Sibyl in her attempt to sell the nine rolls of parchment and palm-leaves upon which they were preserved. The surviving three rolls were kept under guard in Rome by a specially formed college (a sign of the initiate background to their origin). For editorial reasons which are no longer clear, the emperor Augustus destroyed almost 2,000 of the verses, and placed the rest beneath the socle of a statue of Apollo, in his temple on the Palatine. It is claimed by exoteric historians that the entire collection was lost when the city burned during the reign of Nero, in 83 BC. The new compilation made to replace them survived until the fourth century.

No one educated in the classical manner of early Christian Rome, as many of the monks who fled to Ireland for refuge were, could have been unaware of the Sibylline tradition. However, the Sibylline cult was brought back into the light of day by Isidore of Seville in the seventh century, in a popular translation of what he fondly believed were the original prophecies. This found its way into both

Welsh and Irish manuscript literature. Indeed, it is hardly surprising to find some manuscript collections which contain the supposed prophecies of the Sibyls alongside the Myrddin prophecies.

Michelangelo finished his great ceiling of the Sistine Chapel when Nostradamus was nine years old. As anyone who has studied these frescoes will be aware, there had been several Sibyls, yet the one which had caught the attention and sympathy of Michelangelo was the Sibyl of Delphi. Usually, when a Sibyl was mentioned without her patronymic, the reference was to this Delphic prophetess. By a strange quirk of fortune – a sort of historical synchronicity – the name of that Sibyl surfaces in the family circle of our savant: his only sister was sometimes called Delphine.

It is sometimes claimed by art historians that this Sibyl – perhaps the finest figure in the Sistine cycle – was especially venerated because she was believed to have foreseen the coming of Christ. The truth is slightly different. Medieval monks had attempted to take over the pagan Sibylline tradition in order to Christianize it, and constructed prophetic verses which had each of the twelve (the Christian number, and certainly not the number of ancient times!) foretell the coming of the new Christian religion. The Delphic Sibyl was supposed to have prophesied the Virgin birth, and the crowning of thorns. It was this monkish Sibylline tradition, rather than the defunct classical one, that most sixteenth-century minds accepted. The Sibyls may have been pagan, but like Plato, they had such wisdom that they could foresee the need for the Incarnation of Christ to redeem the lost world of paganism.

Fortunately, we do not need to examine the extent of the genuine Sibylline tradition, or the authenticity of the later compilations and forgeries. Whatever sixteenth-century savants made of the surviving prophecies, one thing was clear, that it was widely believed that the Sibyl of Delphi had prophesied the coming of Christ to the pagan world. Almost universally, it is to this later tradition that medieval writers refer when they mention the Sibylline books. Although pagan, the Sibyl was proto-Christian, virtually a pagan goddess made whole through her vision of Christ.

In total contrast, the ancestry of the Merlin of the Arthurian legends was claimed to have been demonic. In some versions of the story, he was sired by a demon – an incubus possessed of human semen – who lay with his willing mother. In other versions, Merlin's birth was engineered by demons intent on bringing into the stream of history an Antichrist. The demons had hoped that by creating the Antichrist with a prophetic power, the Incarnation and Sacrifice of Our Lord would be rendered ineffective.

Clearly, there can scarcely be two more complete antitheses between the prophetess who was on the side of Christ, and the prophet who was against Him. Is any of this antithesis reflected in what we know of the life of Nostradamus?

It is well known that by the time he started publishing his books, perhaps in 1545, Michel de Nostradame had adopted a Latin version of his name. In spite of what is widely believed, this name is *not* a literal translation into Latin. Naturally, Nostradamus was aware of this. In his entry in the register of the Faculty of Medicine at Montpellier, dated 23 October 1529, he had admitted, as the rules of the University required, his correct Latinized name as 'Michaeletus de nostra domina'. Could his new name, the awkward Latinism, Nostradamus, be derived from the Green Language? In other words, has Nostradamus been misunderstood, even in this matter of his adopted name?

In the French language, the family name which Nostradamus inherited, *Nostredame*, means 'Our Lady', of which
the Latin would be *nostra domina*. We may not doubt that
the Lady in question was the Virgin Mary.[1] Yet, for reasons
he never explained, our prophet changed his name to
Nostradamus. What did he gain by this Latinization? In
terms of the Green Language, he gained a great deal. The
word *damus* (unlike *dame*) means 'we give', and indeed
became a part of anti-Nostradamian doggerel in his own
lifetime.[2] The word *nostra* (unlike *nostre*) is a feminization
of 'our', and still means precisely this in Italian. Thus, in
the arcane tongue, Nostradamus can be construed as
meaning 'our feminine we give'. On the one hand, it is
possible to interpret this as a reference to his own soul – his
own wisdom, which has always been expressed in the
feminine gender, whether it be *Sophia* or *Anima*.

There is, however, another way of looking at this esoteric
use of language. Is it possible that Michel de Nostredame
adopted the name Nostradamus to align himself with the
feminine of the two most important historical prophets of
his day – to the Sibyl who foresaw the coming of Christ?
Was the change of name, which would have been so
insignificant in one who was not learned in the magical
nuance of words, an attempt to associate himself with the
pagan female, and thus distance himself from the male who
was not only linked with the demons, but also proscribed in
the Council of Trent, held in the last years of his own
lifetime?

Nostradamus' connection with the past tradition – even
with the Sibylline tradition – was recognized even in his
lifetime. In his ode *A Michel de l'Hopital*, the French poet
Pierre Ronsard – himself a high initiate – recognized that
Nostradamus sprang from an ancient tradition of oracle
writing. As we have seen, in his longer poem, *Elegie à
Guillaume des Autels gentilhomme Charrolois*, he wrote:

Que par les mots douteux de sa prophete voix,
Comme un oracle anticque, il a des mainte annee
Predit la plus grand par de nostre destinee.

Through the doubtful words of his prophetic voice,
Like an oracle of ancient times, he has each year
Predicted the greater part of our destiny.

Ronsard is not being critical of Nostradamus with his *mots douteux*. This is nothing more than a reference to the arcane language, which contains words of doubtful meaning to the uninitiated. Equally, within the occult wisdom which poet shared with poet, the reference to *oracle anticque* is not merely poetic, but actually descriptive. Ronsard recognized the truth about Nostradamus, that he literally spoke as a voice from the past.

Nostradamus' single disciple, Chavigny, must have been something of a disappointment to the Savant, for he gave little sign of developing initiate wisdom, or even an understanding of the Green Language. However, in one telling phrase, written as part of a loving pen-portrait of his Master, Chavigny seems to reach into the mystery of this Savant.[3] After recalling that Nostradamus had the ability to learn and understand quickly anything he wished, he adds, in a delightful Latin which intentionally evokes a phrase from the famous epitaph, that he had *memoria pene divina* – 'an almost divine memory'. In this felicitous triad of words, he seems to reach, albeit unconsciously, into the deepest secret of Nostradamus. The pen almost divine of the epitaph (*pene divino calamo*) and the almost divine memory of the master (*memoria pene divina*) were one and the same thing, for the memory could reach back through his lifetimes to their rich and ancient prophetic source.

Appendix Four

The Two Versions of the Epitaphs of Nostradamus

En sepulture dans l'eglise colégié de Sainct Laurens dudict Sallon et dans la Chapelle de Nostre Dame à la muralhe de laquelle a voulu estre faict ung monument . . .

In the sepulchre in the collegial church of Saint Laurence of the said Salon, and in the Chapel of Our Lady, in the wall of which it is desired to be made a monument . . .

(A previsionary text in the form of a testament written to the dictation of Nostradamus before the notary Joseph Roche in 1566, but scored out. Quoted by Robert Benazra, *Répertoire Chronologique Nostradamique* (*1545–1989*), 1990, for the year 1566, p.73.)

1. The Epitaph composed by his son, César, and formerly in the Cordeliers, Salon, is often reproduced, usually with slight yet important variations. The example form, derived from that reproduced by Leroy, in 1993, follows. There are good reasons to suppose that it contains several copyist errors (not those of Leroy).

D.M.
OSSA CLARISSIMI MICHAELIS NOSTRADAMI
UNIUS OMNIUM MORTALIUM IUDICIO

DIGNI CUIUS PENE DIVINO CALAMO TOTIUS ORBIS ET ASTRORUM INFLEXU FUTURI EVENTUS CONSCRIBERENTUR. VIXIT ANNOS LXII MENSES VI DIES X OBIIT SALLONAE MDLXVI. QUIETEM POSTERI NE INVIDETE. ANNA PONTIA GEMELLA CON IUGI OPTIMO. V.F.

Errors in the Latin above make this inscription difficult to translate. See, therefore, the translation of the more reliable Latin version below. Meanwhile, we should note that *D.M.* is a standard classical abbreviation for the Latin, *Diis Manibus*, usually translated as 'Into the hands of the Gods', or 'We commend the Soul of . . .' It was Christianized into *Deo Manibus*, 'Into the hands of God (we commend the soul of . . .)' early in the history of the Church. The abbreviation, which may not have been copied accurately (see below) is of special interest, as César would have known, for Nostradamus uses it in one of his quatrains. The familiar phrase, HIC JACET (Here lies), or, in this epitaph, HIC JACENT (Here lie), is taken for granted. The *V.F.*, which seems to be another copyist error, may perhaps be taken as the abbreviation for *Verba Facit*, or 'Wrote these words', or for *Vale Felicit*, 'She wishes farewell'. Leroy seems to have adopted the former reading, even though he believed that César wrote the epitaph.

2. The Epitaph now in the church of Saint-Laurent, Salon, has slight variations, sufficient to mark it out as a more accurate copy of the writings of a good Latinist (which César certainly was).

RELIQIAE MICHAELIS NOSTRADAMI IN HOC SACELLUM TRANSLATAE FUERUNT POST

ANNUM MDCCLXXXIX. EPITAPHIUM RESTITUTUM MENSE JULIO MDCCCXIII.

D.O.M.

CLARISSIMI OSSA MICHAELIS NOSTRADAMI UNIUS OMNIUM MORTALIUM IUDICIO DIGNI CUIUS PENE DIVINO CALAMO TOTIUS ORBIS EX ASTRORUM INFLUXU FUTURI EVENTUS CONSCRIBERENTUR. VIXIT ANNOS LXII MENSES VI DIES XVII OBIIT SALONE ANNO MDLXVI. QUIETEM POSTERI NE INVID-ETE. ANNA PONTIA GEME [. . .] ALONIA CON-IUGI OPTAT V. FELICIT.

This may be translated as:

> *The remains of Michel Nostradamus were transferred to this chapel after the year 1789. The epitaph was remade in the month of July, 1813.*

[*D.O.M.* is usually taken as the abbreviation of the Latin triple blessing, *Deo Optimo Maximo*, meaning, 'To God the best, the greatest'. In pagan times, this was an invocation to Jupiter. However, it may also be taken as an abbreviation of *Datur Omnibus Mori*, meaning 'It is given to all to Die'.]

> *(Here lie) the bones of the most illustrious Michel Nostradamus, judged worthy among all mortals, with whose almost divine pen were put down in writing the future events of the whole world from the influence of the stars. He lived for 62 years, 6 months and 17 days (and) died at Salon in 1566. You who follow, be not jealous of his rest. His wife, Anna Pontia Gemella of Salon, wishes him farewell and happiness.*

The abbreviation *V.* is quite certainly intended for *Vale*, the classical end-of-day greeting – 'Fare thee well'.

Appendix Five

Green Language Techniques Used by Nostradamus

This is the language which teaches the mystery of things and unveils the most hidden truths ...

(Fulcanelli, *Fulcanelli: Master Alchemist. Le Mystère des Cathèdrales*, translated from the French by Mary Sworder, 1971 edition, p.44)

The Green Language has been used widely, in occult literature, but surprisingly there is no book dealing with its methods. As we have noted, some account of it has been given by Blavatsky and Fulcanelli, but the latter was interested mainly in its application to alchemy. Some of the codification methods used in the seventeenth century, and in an astrological and astronomical context, are dealt with in a most enlightened way by Ann Geneva in her useful study, *Astrology and the Seventeenth-Century Mind*, 1955, but (so far as we know) no similar work has been done on the codification methods and arcane astrological techniques of the sixteenth century. The Green Language used by such writers as Dante, Rabelais and Swift has been recognized by scholars, yet little attempt has been made to see these writers in the wider context of arcane literature.

Before going on to Green Language techniques themselves, it might be interesting to look at Swift in this context. He was no stranger to the occult tongue, or to

Nostradamus. He owned the Garencières translation of Nostradamus, and his library contained a large number of astrological and occult books, including the 1658 edition of the *Opera Omnia* of Paracelsus. Modern scholars recognize that Swift was deeply interested in etymologies, and word-play, but have never explored his connection with the arcane tongue. However, Swift's writings are so redolent of complex Green Language that it is difficult to do justice to the brilliance of his linguistic inventiveness.

In *Gulliver's Travels*, the ingenious Gulliver discusses the putative etymology of the word *Laputa*. This was the name given to the flying island he boarded and explored. Having told us that the word in Laputian means 'Floating Island', he confesses that he had never been able to learn the true etymology. On the other hand, he tells us, *Lap* in the obsolete language signifies high, and *untuh* a governor, 'from which they say by corruption was derived Laputa from Lapuntuh'.

Now, there may be no doubt that in its political strain of meaning, Swift intends the flying island (an island divorced from the land, so to speak) to symbolize the British Government, which Swift knew was rife with corruption. Laputa (whatever its origins), was derived 'they say by corruption'. The verbal display so far is typical of Swift in his humorous play with the English language. However, with Laputa, he offers a fine example of the Green Language, of which he is master. Taken in the context that the word represents the British Government, then *Lap* is revealed as a most brilliant word. In the seventeenth century, *Pal* (the reversal of Lap) was an accomplice in crime – from Swift's jaundiced point of view, an excellent word to describe the cabal which ran the country. However, although Swift hides his etymology behind a rigmarole of 'Laputian' etymology, the Green Language strain is essentially French. In the seventeenth century, the word *pute* was a variant of the modern word *putain*, which means 'whore'. *La pute* was 'The whore' – an epithet which Swift would have joyously applied to the British Government. Within this imagery of whoredom, the English word *Lap* begins to take on a different meaning, for it has sexual connotations. We must ask, why does Swift introduce the letter n in suggesting *untuh* as one of the roots of Laputa? Almost certainly it is to point to the construct *Lap untuh*. The first part of this construct sounds like *lapin*, which in French is 'rabbit'. Thus, in one clever word, Swift has succeeded in pointing to the organized corruption of the Government (that it is a cabal which will sell itself to all comers), and to its famous sexual immorality (the sexual mores of the rabbit had, in the eighteenth century, much the same meaning as now). The humour within the humour is the way Swift has used this Green Language construct, for he has corrupted the words *Lapuntuh* to give *Laputa*, reminding us of Laputian scholars who had said, 'by corruption was derived Laputa from Lapuntuh'. The three superfluous letters which make this corrupted etymology are *nuh*. In French, the word *nue* means uncovered, or naked. Thus is the British Government laid bare as a cabal of naked whores when the inner meaning of his word is revealed.

The following list of terms, used to describe some of the techniques of Green Language obfuscation, is derived mainly from the literary tradition: the definitions and examples are intended to act as a guide for those reading the following text.

There are other Green Language techniques which are not mentioned below: their omission is due to the complexity of the occult methodology, with which we need not trouble the general reader, even though we do make passing reference to one or two in the following text. In essence, these are numerologically based, and are linked with Hebraic Gematria, Notaricon and Temurah.

Gematria is a cabbalistic system based on the fact that the Hebrew alphabet has numerical equivalents. In Gematria, the numerical equivalents of a word, or phrase, are added together. These words and phrases are then regarded as having meaningful correspondences with words and phrases which have a similar numerical value.

Notaricon is a cabbalistic system of cryptographic word-play involved with the interpretation of each letter of a word as though it were an abbreviation for another word. The famous magical word, *Agla*, is notaricon of the Hebraic phrase which translates 'Thou art mighty for ever, O Lord'.

Temurah is a cabbalistic system of linguistic interchange wherein letters and words are substituted for one another by changing the orders of predetermined keywords. This substitution gives new words which, by analogic inferences, are seen as being linked with the original words. The same word is also used to denote methods of constructing alphabetic codes by means of fixed artificial keyletters or correspondences. For example, if the alphabetic sequence of A–Z were to be moved forward a letter, B–A, then the word BAD would read CBE.

The efforts of Valerie Hewitt in *Nostradamus. His Key to the Centuries*, 1994, to show numerological factors at work in Nostradamus, and reveal the great sage's concern with, for example, Margaret Thatcher and John Major, are nothing more than sub-cultural fun; however, they miss completely the point of sixteenth-century arcane techniques. The whole purpose of the Green Language is to obscure the intentions of the writer from a general reader, in favour of a specialist reader. In addition to achieving this aim, one proficient in the Green Languages can make use of terms which lend a second, or even a third, level of meaning to words and phrases. This, as we saw on pages 40 and 211, can even lead to a single verse giving rise to two (or even more) convincing readings. Curiously, then, the Green Language is expressedly used both to delude, elucidate and condense. Nostradamus practises this art with such consummate skill that Ward is right to observe, 'Nostradamus can hint in a phrase of three words what would require a long paragraph to make it explicit in an ordinary way. This is truly the language of prophecy.'[1]

Such word-puzzles will delude those who are not familiar with the art of the Green Language, yet elucidate for those who are familiar with such rules. This means, of course, that only an alchemist would be able to understand the Green Language used by alchemists, and only one learned in astrology would be able to understand the Green Language of astrology. The matter is further complicated in the case of Nostradamus, who was writing about the future in languages which, even were they not (in any case) intentionally obscured by Green Language, would have been obscured to some extent by the passage of time. We have already observed that Rabelais, who also used the Green Language, has actually been translated from his sixteenth-century French into modern French. This is an interesting reflection upon Nostradamus, for he wrote in a French – not to mention a style – which was far more obscure than that used by Rabelais. Among the letters from astrological clients which have surfaced in the recent discovery of the Nostradamus correspondence are several complaining that they do not understand what Nostradamus is saying, even in regard to personal horoscopy. Poor Hans Rosenberger, who seems to have had much trouble persuading Nostradamus to cast horoscopes, wrote to the savant asking him to remove the ambiguities from his recent chart-reading. 'To tell the truth,' he writes in 1561, 'I am not versed in the obscure language of the enigmatic arabians.'[2]

One must recall also that Nostradamus, while writing more or less in late-medieval French, was thinking in Latin – a point developed almost beyond sanity by Piobb and other French commentators. So obvious is this in the structure of his verses that some authorities have suggested that Nostradamus originally constructed the quatrains in Latin, and then translated them into a sort of vernacular. The implication in this is that the Green Language constructs are found not merely in linguistic changes to individual words, but also in grammatical structures. A large number of foreign and classical verbal injections play an important part in the Nostradamus technique, and since his use of such injections is unique there seems to be no way to link the technique with the literary tradition.

Finally, we have to stress that Nostradamus seems to have had at his command a wide range of European languages, and makes use of these frequently in his attempt to disguise or add connotations. We shall note such words from Greek, Latin, German, Spanish and English in the following analyses. In some instances Provençal is used – as for example in the words *bueire* (dissension), *monge* (nun) and *scomma* (subtle banter), the last of which becomes *scome* in quatrain VIII.88. Unfortunately for his future readers, Nostradamus had no compunction in subjecting words derived from these foreign languages to the same linguistic distortions to which he submitted the French language.

The following alphabetic list of Green Language techniques used by Nostradamus is probably not complete, but will certainly cover adequately the examples discussed in this present work. The names attached to the techniques, as denotations, are, with one exception, derived from the literary tradition. The single exception is the term 'occult blind', which is derived from the occult tradition. The fact that we can examine the techniques of Nostradamus in the light of the analytical tools of English literature should not disguise the fact that Nostradamus often made up his own linguistic rules. This, of course, means that in some cases his methods are beyond simple classification. We have attempted to give some insight into this complex use of words below.

ANAGRAM   A word, or phrase, in which the letters may be transported so as to form a new word or phrase. In Nostradamus, the word *Rapis* stands for Paris: in this case, as in most anagrams constructed by the master, the anagrammatic treatment is not merely intended to deceive or confuse, but also to produce a secondary meaning (raptor, rapist or raped) which would be relevant to the quatrain. The rape of Paris during the siege of 1870–71 would be a relevant example. *Mendosus*, which some have wrongly translated as meaning 'the liar', is directly from the Latin meaning 'full of faults', or 'deceptive'. The word is probably an aphetic anagram for *Vendosme*, or *Vendôme*, which may relate either to the department of that name or (more likely) to one or other of the Dukes of Vendôme. Nostradamus appears to have used few anagrammatic sentences, but perhaps the most famous was the triple PAU NAY LORON, which was not a bad approximation, in the sixteenth century, for NAPAULON ROY (see page 346). *Chien* is said to be a syncopic anagram (see SYNCOPE) for *Chiren*, which is in turn *Henric*, a sixteenth-century way of spelling the name of Henri II.

ANASTROPHE   A word used in Green Language to denote the reversing of a word, sometimes in terms only of letter forms, at other times only in terms of sound-values. An example of the latter, mentioned on page 38, is the anastrophe of *HIRAM* to *MARIA*, where the sound-value of the final A is regarded as being the equivalent of the Hebraic H. In exoteric literature the word is sometimes used to denote an unusual order of words, as well as incomplete inversions. If this ground rule were adopted in the study of Nostradamus, then virtually every line of the *Prophéties* must be considered anastrophic.

ANTONOMASIA The substitution of an epithet to stand for a proper name, or the use of a proper name to represent a general idea. A few of the antonomastic words coined by Nostradamus reflect his clairvoyance and his love for irony. For example, his word *doux*, the French for 'sweet, gentle and affable' stands for Jacques *Clement*, who assassinated Henry III in 1588: in Presage 58 – derived from a quatrain in one of his almanacs – Clement is *Doux la pernicie*. Nostradamus is being ironic, for the Latin *clemens* means just about the same as the French *doux*. Appearing frequently, *le grand*, or *la Dame*, are used to indicate important or famous people, whose identities must be determined from other clues within the context of the quatrain. We are reminded that in the entry for the month of his own death (see page 57 ff), Nostradamus predicted the deaths of *les grands*: the plural may be taken as a reference to the fact that Nostredame is a plural possessive. In at least three quatrains, *La Dame* is Catherine de' Medici, but the same word also represents Marie Antoinette in two verses. *La grande cité* is sometimes Paris. Le Pelletier notes that *la grande cité neuve* (the great new city), which some modern commentators have read as meaning New York, is a reference to the Paris reconstructed under Napoleon III. In quatrain X.49, on the other hand, the *cité neufve* is definitely Naples (the ancient Neapolis, 'new city' in Greek) – see page 366. In total contrast, the *Cité neufue* of quatrain I.24 is a reference to the name of the French Vice-Admiral, Villeneuve (*ville* means 'town'), who served under Napoleon – see page 369 ff. Precisely which new city

Nostradamus has in mind may only be determined from the context of the quatrain.

APHESIS Omission of a letter or syllable at the beginning of a word. For example, Nostradamus uses the word *bondance* for abondance: his aim is not merely to aid scansion, but to introduce the notion of the bondage to which abundance can give rise. The intriguing use to which Nostradamus put the simple word *eau* (water) is instructive, for in some cases it represented the water triplicities (Cancer, Scorpio and Pisces) by antonomasia. Just to add to the confusion, Nostradamus uses the same construction, in other cases, to represent Aquarius, by the aphesis of the French *Verseau* (as in quatrain IV.86 – see p. 283), and in others, it represented a river or a sea. A simple aphetic anagram used by Nostradamus is the innocent-seeming *Dedans* (within, or in) which is intended to read *Sedan*, the first important battle of which led to the fall of Paris, in 1871 (see p. 195). However, to make this reading viable as an anagram, the rule of aphesis must be applied.

APOCOPE The omission of a letter or syllable from the ending of a word. The apocope *Cap* stands for *Capet*. A more complicated example is *fum* for *fume*, or *fumée*: smoke, or steam. In this case, as the apocope is in a quatrain dealing with a battle (see p. 229 ff), the word may be intended to suggest onomatopoeically the distant sound of cannon – *fum*. In quatrain III.53, which deals partly with the treatment of the Jews under the Nazis, the two words *le pris* are probably abridged for *lepre* (leprosy), relating metaphorically to the Nuremburg laws. See also SYNCOPE.

ARCANE ASSOCIATION This literary technique lies at the very basis of the Green Language: it is the use of specialist words in such a way that they may be interpreted

as giving rise to further words with meanings evident only
to those familiar with the specialism. Thus, since one
zodiacal sign cannot be in another, the phrase *Cancer in
boeuf* is meaningless, in quatrain X.67. This will lead the
specialist to read Cancer as a reference to the Moon, as this
planet rules uniquely over the zodiacal sign Cancer. The
phrase would therefore read 'Moon in Taurus'. Nostradamus is particularly fond of this kind of Green Language.
Perhaps more subtle is the way in which Nostradamus
would refer arcanely to such things as horoscopes which
contained data that reflected significantly upon the quatrain: for example, in quatrain I.31 he evokes a horoscope
which emphasizes the sign *Leo* to point to the three letters
contained in Napo*leo*n's name.

Nostradamus is also fond of the arcane associations
offered by degrees of latitude. When using this method,
Nostradamus names a particular latitude (derived essentially from the astrological tradition) in order to designate a
city or town. The main problem is that without the further
coordinate of the longitude, such a reference is ambiguous.
Thus, when Nostradamus refers to 45 degrees (actually,
Cinq & quarante degrez) in quatrain VI.97, he could have in
mind such cities as Bordeaux – perhaps even Périgueux –
Turin, and perhaps Pavia, Cremona and Mantua, and,
given his clairvoyance, even Minneapolis, in the United
States. However, he would not have had in mind those
other cities of the USA which the irrepressible Roberts
proposed, such as New York (which is at latitude 41
degrees) and certainly not San Francisco (which is as low as
36 degrees) nor even Chicago (which is in 42 degrees).
Non-specialists have tended to misinterpret these degree
references: for example, the first line of quatrain V.98 (*A
quarante-huit degre climatterique* – 'At 48 degree climata')
has been translated as relating to Paris, and this degree –
technically inaccurate as it is – is given in the standard

astrological works of his day. However, this city is between 48 and 49 degrees, whereas Orléans, Le Mans and Freiburg are exactly upon 48 degrees, and this means that there is considerable ambiguity in the quatrains for the modern reader. Contemporaneous astrological texts, such as the Orontius Finé of 1544, list latitudes for the main cities of Europe, and however wrong they may be by modern standards, they were widely adopted by sixteenth-century astrologers. In the tables of houses published by Luca Gauricus in 1533, the following are given:

Sicily	37 degrees
Rome	42 degrees
Venice	45 degrees
Bologna	45 degrees
Paris	48 degrees
London	54 degrees
Berlin	54 degrees

Fig. 53, taken from Oronce Finé, shows the latitudes for the south of France, from 42 to 47 degrees – hence just short of Paris – which we presume Nostradamus used.[3] In the example, quatrain V.98, the word *climatterique* is an unnecessary repetition, perhaps intended to confuse the uninitiated. It is coined by Nostradamus to indicate that the degrees relate to the *climata*, the early-medieval equivalent of degrees of longitude, which were already almost defunct by the sixteenth century. In his *Mundi Sphaera* of 1542, Finé remarks that these latitudes are 'what the vulgar call the seven Climata'. When Nostradamus uses the degree system (or the word *climata*, in one form or another), then he is clearly inviting one to regard the quatrain in terms of arcane astrology.

ARCHAIZING The use of old terms to denote things

and places. Nostradamus is fond of disguising his place-names by using Greek and Roman names. One archaizing name of which he is fond is *Sextrophea*, with which he sometimes signs his almanacs: this refers to the monument which still stands a mile or so outside his native Saint-Rémy. As we see, on page 211 ff, this archaizing enters into the quatrains, though perhaps as a double occult blind. Nostradamus delights in the ambiguities which archaizing affords: for example, *Ausonne* is the old name for Bordeaux, but the Latin *Ausonia* meant the inhabitants of lower Italy. When he uses this term, Nostradamus more frequently intends the latter meaning. *Boristhenes*, the old term for the river Dnieper, is archaizing for Russia. *Lygustique* (as in quatrain III.23) is archaizing for Liguria, but it often means Italy, according to the law of SYNECDOCHE (see below). As though his astrology were not already complex enough, Nostradamus sometimes archaizes the planetary and zodiacal names, as for example in the *brassieres* of VII.91, derived from a Greek word which denoted Jupiter and Saturn. A most remarkable example of archaizing is in quatrain IX.14, which deals with the Battle of Waterloo, with the words *Sept.* and *borneaux*: see page 230 ff, above.

EPENTHESIS   The adding of a letter or syllable to the middle of a word. The *Calpre* of quatrain I.77 is epenthesis for Calpe, the cape near to Gibraltar.

HOMONYMS   Words having the same sound and/or spelling as another, but with a different meaning or origin. The word *Selin* was the name of a historical leader of the Turks (see page 242 ff), but it is also almost an homonym for Selene, a Greek name for the goddess of the Moon. The word *Gaule* is one of the names used by Nostradamus for France, yet it appears in a context wherein it may be taken as pointing to General Charles de *Gaulle*. In some cases,

Nostradamus creates his own homonyms, to give a double connotation to a word. Thus, *terroir* can mean both territory and terror, though properly speaking terror is *terreur*, while *terroir* means soil or ground, in the sense of 'territory'.

HYPALLAGE When, in a figure of speech, the epithet is transferred from the appropriate noun to modify another, to which it does not properly belong. The most cunning hypallage in Nostradamus is one that kept commentators in ignorance until after the event: this is the last line of quatrain IV.65: *L'empereur tost mort sera condamné*, from which one assumes (quite wrongly, as it happens) that the emperor lately dead will be condemned. The solution to the hypallage is given on page 378 ff.

HYPHAERESIS The omission of a letter to form a word. Sometimes, the omitted letter can be of considerable importance to the reading of the text. Nostradamus frequently omits the letter *s* from words, without inserting the traditional circumflex: an example which appears in several quatrains is the hyphaeresis *matim* for *mastim* (mastiff), as for example in quatrain X.59. In quatrain III.53, Gaul is represented as *Gale* (see however HOMO-NYMS, above). A typical hyphaeresis is *Aper* for Asper which is an anagram of *Aspre*. This is in turn an ellipsis for *Aspromonte* (a 'massif' in Italy), which Le Pelletier links with an incident from the life of Garibaldi.

ICONOMATIC This usage occurs when a word is intended to be read as a rebus, as though relating to a figure. Nostradamus, working only with words, uses the rebus technique suggested by the Horapollo or Icon books. The word *coq* is *Gallus* in Latin, which connotes France (the word *Gallus* in Latin meant both cock and that area of

Europe which corresponds approximately to modern France). However, the *Gallus* was also a priest of Cybele (the name said to be derived from the similarity between the delirious ravings of the priests and the crowing of cocks), and the connotation hinted at in the word *coq* is emasculation (a condition attributed to the priests of Cybele). In many instances, *loup* (wolf) is Italy, after the wolf which suckled Romulus and Remus. On the other hand, *Romulides* is also derived from the name of the 'founder of Rome', Romulus, and may denote either Rome, or Italy. In quatrain I.9, it seems to relate to the south of Italy, whence succour came for the great siege of Malta, in 1565. One iconomatic word has survived (like *coq*) into modern symbolism, for *l'ours* (the bear) is sometimes used of Russia.

INVENTION   The invention of a new word only peripherally connected with an existing word in a familiar language. In Nostradamus, the familiar language is usually Greek or Latin, but he occasionally invents from Hebrew, and such European languages as English, German, Italian and Provençal. The phrase *Mars en Nonnay* is invention, for there is no such planetary position: almost certainly, the *Nonnay* is Virgo, from the French *nonne*, or *nonnain*, as in quatrain X.67. Another example is the *sedifragues* of quatrain VI.94, which is from the Latin *sedem frangere*, 'to break a siege'. The phrase, *Le Port Phocen*, for Marseilles, seems to be a more complex invention, for the Greek *Phocis* was in ancient times a country of central Greece. The seaport town of *Massilia*, founded as a colony from Phocoea, was eventually known as Marseilles. Perhaps Nostradamus used the ancient Greek reference because the Phocens were warlike, being allied at times with the Spartans. The bellicose planet Mars, which begins the modern name *Mars*eilles, is connoted in the French word.

Phocus (with its undertones of homonymous 'focus') is not merely Marseilles, but a warlike Marseilles in a state of martial endeavour, or even revolution.

METATHESIS The interchanging of consonant sounds to produce different (though relevant) words. For example, *brune* is metathesed by Nostradamus in *brume*. In quatrain III.53, which deals with the Second World War, Nostradamus subjects the German place name Augsburg to metathesis by rendering it *Auspurg*. The new word is relevant because the quatrain seems to relate to the expulsion of the Jews, (literally, an *aus purgans*, to remain with the German) under the Nuremburg Laws.

METONYM A word used as a valid transference, in which an attribute of a thing or person is used to denote that thing or person. The word *bossu*, deformed, is used as a metonym for the prince of Condé, who was a small hunchback. A better example from Nostradamus is the word *boiteux* (lame) which could refer to the Duke of Bordeaux, who was lamed in a fall at Kirchberg in Austria in 1841. The application in this case is virtually double because of the close HOMONYM between *boiteux* and *Bordeaux*. In quatrain V.4, *le cerf* is probably a metaphor for Charles X, who was chased from France. Used in this sense, *cerf* is a metonym, yet it is something more than merely a metonym in its reference to Charles X as a hunted creature, driven from the fields of France. Charles, prior to being made king of France, was the Count of Artois: the *cerf* is, of course, the *hart* in English. After he was driven from France, he went to England. (By a strange coincidence, during his first stay in this country, he lived at Hartwell.)

PARAGOGE The adding of a letter or syllable to the end

of a word. *Selene* is a paragoge for *Selin*, but the former is intended to add an additional connotation to the latter, by virtue of its connection with the Moon (Selene was an ancient Moon goddess). The French word *Amerique*, which was used for the Americas in the sixteenth century, was subjected by Nostradamus to both SYNCOPE (Amerique to *Americ*), and paragoge when he offered the word *Americh*: whether this is paragoge or METATHESIS is anyone's guess. This version of the word appears in the first line of quatrain X.66. Whether he wanted to connote the fabulous riches (*rich*) of the place, which were in his day being exploited by the Spanish, or whether he had some other arcane design in mind is unclear. One thing is evident, however: in making this change, he elected for once not to make a rhyme with the third line (the normal rhyming structure is alternative in couplets). The word which would anticipate such a rhyme is *Antechrist*. The fact that the *H* of the Roman alphabet is the equivalent of the *E* of the Greek alphabet is probably significant here, for the difference between An*t*echrist and An*t*ichrist is of profound importance in the arcane and theological traditions. Perhaps Nostradamus is anxious to show that he is writing of the one who comes before Christ (An*t*echrist), rather than of the one who will oppose Christ (An*t*ichrist).

PROTOTHESIS   The adding or a letter or syllable to the beginning of a word.

REBUS   A riddle by which pictures, letters or sentences are read in terms of sound values. It is not surprising that Nostradamus should have used this device, since the rebus (for all it is a Latin word) was highly popular in France during the sixteenth century, when it was called '*style de Picardie*'. It has been argued by many that the dedication to Henry II, in the *Epistle*, was to some other king than the one who died in a golden cage (see page 236 ff). This argument (to which we do not subscribe) is supported by the reading of the words Henry II as *Henri secundus*, which means (in Latin), Fortunate Henry. Although the rebus is essentially a pictorially based art, Nostradamus uses it in clever literary ways. For example, he will refer to an heraldic coat of arms in order to distinguish (arcanely, of course) a ruler. The *lys* can be a French king, because the French coat of arms bears the fleur-de-lys (see page 223). The classical French rebus is *Ga*, which reads *G grand*, *a petit* (big G, small a). When pronounced in French, this reads: *J'ai grand appetit* (I have a big appetite). The word *rebus* is probably the only term used to denote a form of Green Language which is itself from that same strange tongue. Rebus, in its arcane sense, seems to be from alchemy, and is linked with *Rebis*, which means in ablative Latin, 'the thing twice'. The thing twice is the thing seen from two aspects, once in a material sense, a second time in a spiritual sense. The construction should remind us that the initiate is sometimes called 'the one of the two levels'. In some alchemical documents, the *rebis* is said to be an egg, or the contents of an egg, consisting of red and white, 'in the same proportion as in a bird's egg'. In this image, the red is the yolk, the white the glair. There are seven levels to every alchemical symbol, but this red and white is the blood and tissue of the human being who, as the Buddha said, lives in an eggshell, even though the shell of the philosophic alchemist is a far from auric thing, sheathing bodies quite invisible to ordinary vision. The Red (*rouge*) and the White (*blanc*) to which Nostradamus frequently refers in his quatrains, are at once alchemical, political and ecclesiastical symbols, according to the spiritual literacy of the reader. See also ICONOMATIC.

SYNCOPE   A Greek word meaning 'cutting short' – in

literature, an abbreviation. Technically, the word is virtually interchangeable with APOCOPE, but it seems to be accepted practice to denote massive cuts by syncope and the lesser abbreviations by apocope. For example, the *Ast* of quatrain II.15 is apocope for the place name, Asti. On the other hand, in quatrain II.83, the word *pille* (quatrain II.83) is syncope for *pillard* or *pillage* (pillage, or destruction). The syncope *Phi* means Philip. The word *Auge*, which could be taken as the German for 'eye', could also be a syncope of the verb *Augmenter*. As with the anagrams, one purpose (beyond mere disguise) is to add a further meaning to the word: thus, *Carcas* may mean Carcassonne, but the word also carries with it the idea of a dead body (*carcasse*), and hence a killing. Foreign syncopes are words or phrases derived from non-French sources, and in some way changed so as not to be immediately recognizable. *Cron* is an abridgement for the Greek *Cronon*, its significance in quatrain III.91 being that it is linked with a lame prince: not only is this prince in some way imperfect, but so is the word *Cron* an 'imperfect' form of a word. In this context, see *boiteux* under METONYM. The most remarkable sentence syncope we deal with in our text is the last line of quatrain IX.14, marked with the distinctive abridgment-sign *Sept.*, which we discuss on page 230. This is a curious apocope, for it is not completed until the last word of the same line.

SYNECDOCHE   A literary technique of 'part for the whole', by which a less comprehensive term (such as the name of a town) is used to represent a more comprehensive term (in this case, the country in which this town is located). The quatrains of Nostradamus abound in synecdoches. A good example is *Londres* (London) to represent England, or even the British Isles. In quatrain VII.26 *Madrid* stands for Spain, the *Chef de Madrid* being the

Spanish Admiral. The more obscure *Boristhenes* is the old name of the Dnieper, and therefore an example of archaizing, but Nostradamus uses it to denote the vast territories divided by this river – notably, the territory to the east, which is mainly Russia. *Blois* may stand for that city, but it may also stand for a particular ruler associated with Blois, such as Henry of Guise. The *Liguriens* should really mean those from Liguria, or the Genoese, but the word may also stand for the Italians as a whole. A remarkably prescient example of synecdoche by Nostradamus is his use of the word *Isles* to denote Britain, as the British Isles.

Appendix Six

Ptolemaic Astrology

It has long been recognized by the more thoughtful astrologers and historians of astrology that much of the philosophy underlying their science properly belongs to the ancient wisdom once taught in the Mystery centres of Egypt and Greece ...

(F. Gettings, *The Arkana Dictionary of Astrology*, 1990, revised edition, p. 180)

Ptolemaic astrology is a term applied to a complex corpus of astrological traditions gathered from Babylonian, Egyptian and Greek sources, by the Alexandrian, Claudius Ptolemaeus, in the second century AD, in his four books, *Tetrabiblos*. The system which came to late-medieval Europe had been refined by the Arab astrologers, who added invaluable material relating to the predictive side of the art. It is often claimed, by those who have not bothered to read the *Tetrabiblos*, that the Ptolemaic system of astrology is not very different from the late-medieval systems which the modern astrologers inherited. This is nonsense, for while some of the traditions recorded by Ptolemy have survived (notably, certain of the terms, the aspects, and the zodiacal and planetary rulerships), many have become obsolete. Perhaps more poignantly,

543

some of the Ptolemaic traditions which were of astrological value (and which certainly enriched the medieval astrology) have been dispensed with by modern astrologers. Among these lost valuables are the Arabized Ptolemaic theory of stellar influences, and the reliance upon interpretation of historical events (Mundane Astrology) by reference to the conjunctions of Saturn, Jupiter and Mars.

The Ptolemaic cosmic system – like most modern astrological systems – was geocentric. However, in his model, the planets were disposed in spheres (which were not the actual orbs of the planets themselves) in a sequence foreign to the one we are familar with today. Beyond the planetary spheres were a series of other spheres, constructed largely to explain diurnal and precessional movement. Ptolemy continued the Aristotelian dictum that the extralunar bodies moved in perfect circles, and tremendous effort was expended by later astronomers to establish a geometric system of epicycles which would reconcile this notion with the observable movements.

The astrology of the late-medieval world – that which Nostradamus inherited – was far more sophisticated than that proposed by Ptolemy. By the sixteenth century, something of the true nature of precessional motion was being understood, and the geocentric model of perfect circles was being made redundant, while the epicycle theory (*fig. 54*) had just about broken down under the weight of its own complexity, and there was a feeling of impatience with the inaccuracy of the planetary and stellar tables available. Even had Copernicus not come along and discarded the old cosmic model by displacing the central Earth, medieval astrology would have been compelled to change to rid itself of much that it had inherited from the Arabianized Ptolemaic model. It is quite remarkable that Nostradamus should have put his finger on the precise moment in the future when the Ptolemaic–Aristotelian model would collapse entirely, when the Nova proved that the Aristotelian theory of the incorruptibility of the heavens was invalid.

Appendix Seven

Torné-Chavigny

*The great weakness of many of the commentators of
Nostradamus has been their overwhelming desire to prove
their own theories.*

(H.I. Woolf, *Nostradamus*, 1944)

Torné-Chavigny was one of the most enthusiastic Nostradamians of the nineteenth century. He was originally the
abbé Torné, and one-time *curé* of La Clotte, in the diocese
of Bordeaux, but he changed his name out of respect for
Chavigny, the first disciple of Nostradamus. His highly
personal interpretation of the *Prophéties* was coloured by his
longing for a restoration of the monarchy, and by his
unshakeable belief in the coming of a French deliverer,
whom he identified as Henry V. His writings – especially
l'Histoire prédite et jugée of 1860 – worried the government,
and the first volume was seized. Torné, with some
dislodging of meanings, read one of the quatrains as
referring to this seizure. As James Laver has pointed out,
the plot has been thickened by later commentators, who
have claimed that the word Bleygnie (or perhaps Bleynie),
which was the name of the official Procureur who seized
the book, is hinted at in a verse in which Nostradamus
warns off certain critics. The word is in a line of Latin that
is sometimes wrongly taken as being a quatrain.[1] However,

the verse was printed in the early editions as a header for Century VII (*fig. 55*), and was not part of the predictive quatrains proper:

Omnesque Astrologi, Blenni, Barbari procul sunto

All Astrologers, Fools and Barbarians should keep away . . .

Blenni, which is the Latin for 'fool', is unlikely to be a reference to Bleynie, as there is no contextual reason for making such a link. In passing, we should record that Torné's book was examined and returned to him, with no restrictions on the printing, so the parallel loses any real relevance. Perhaps the official censor was as foxed by Torné's royalist interpretations as he was by the Nostradamian originals?

Among Torné-Chavigny's several obsessions was the belief that his own personal name had been mentioned in the *Prophéties*. The first line of quatrain VIII.5 reads:

Apparoistra temple luisant orné

There will appear (in the) temple star-bright (and) ornate

Groping, one feels, towards the Green Language Torné read the last two words as *luisan torné*, which he interpreted as 'shining Torné', or 'Torné throwing a light, like a lamp'. The word 'lamp' does appear at the beginning of the next line. Needless to say, Torné-Chavigny identifies himself with this lamp which, he claims, throws so much light on Nostradamus.

Although Torné-Chavigny did not know it, the quatrain is astrological in context, and has nothing to do with nineteenth-century France. Nostradamus often uses the word *apparoistra* ('will appear') when talking about heavenly phenomena, and this alone should have alerted Torné to the astrological nature of the verse. In the sixteenth century (in a tradition which survives into French astrology even to this day) *luisante* is the name given to the brightest star in a given constellation. In the second line of this verse, the constellation is identified in the first word, *La Lampe*. Nostradamus would be familiar with the fact that the most powerful (and extremely beautiful) stars in the Hyades were called *Lampadas*, which was the accusative plural of the Spanish word *lampada*, meaning torch, or lamp.[2] This word was applied to what Allen has rightly described as 'one of the most beautiful objects in the sky'. We need not examine this quatrain in more detail – our purpose is merely to show that there is an entirely different way of reading this quatrain which obsessed, in so personal a way, the abbé Torné-Chavigny.

Being an amateur artist, Torné illustrated some later versions of his writings on Nostradamus. In one large plate (of which a coloured version now hangs in the Nostradamus Museum, in Salon), he shows Nostradamus, with Torné himself gazing in admiration. Behind are the portraits of the great ones concerning whom the Master prophesied (*fig. 30*). The Comte de Chambord, whom Torné hoped would be the famed Henry V, is following Napoleon III. This prediction, given the history of the Third Repubic (formed in 1870, after Sedan), was a foolish editing of Nostradamus' predictive vision.

Appendix Eight

Bibliography

Seroit-il possible qu'un Medecin & Astrologue, qu'un faiseur d'Almanachs, & un du plus commun des Chrestiens, ait esté choisi de Dieu parmi tant milliers de se plus favoris, pour luy communiquer les grâce . . . d'un Sainct Jean l'Evangeliste.

Was it possible that a Doctor and Astrologer, a maker of Almanacs, and one of the most ordinary of Christians, was chosen by God from among the thousands of the more favoured, to bestow upon him the grace . . . fitting a Saint John the Evangelist.

(Etienne Jaubert, *Éclaircissement des veritables Quatains de Maistre Michel Nostradamus . . . Médecin ordinaire des Roys Henry II. François II et Charles IX. grand Astrologue de son temps, & specialement pour la connoissance des choses futures,* 1656)

The following alphabetic bibliography gives merely sources mentioned or quoted in the preceding text. The most satisfactory modern bibliography pertaining to Nostradamus (though weak on English titles) is BENAZRA, below.

AGRIPPA Cornelius Agrippa, *De Occulta Philosophia*, 1534. See also NOWOTNY, below.

ALCABITIUS *Preclarum Summi in Astrologia Scientia Principis Alchabitii Opus ad scrutanda Stellarum* . . . For an account, see *Cahiers Michel Nostradamus*, No. 4, Jul. 1986.

ALLEN R.H. Allen, *Star Names and their Meanings*, 1963 reprint of the 1899 *Star-Names and Their Meanings*, p.188.

ALVIN Louis Alvin, *Catalogue raisonné de l'oeuvre des trois frères, Jean, Jerome et Antoine Wierix*, 1866.

AMADOU Robert Amadou, *L'Astrologie de Nostradamus. Dossier*, 1992.

ANDERSON William Anderson, *Green Man. The Archetype of our Oneness with the Earth*, 1990.

ANONYMOUS 'J.F.', *The Predictions of Nostradamus, Before the Year 1558*, n.d.

ANONYMOUS (mss.) B.L. Add. mss. 34,362, *An ancient Prophecy written originally in French by Nostradamus, know (sic) done into English 6 Jan 1671*.

ANONYMOUS *A New Song of the French King's Fear of an Orange, circa* 1690.

ANONYMOUS (mss.) British Library, Sloane 3722: *New prediction said to be found at the opening of the Tomb of Michael Nostradamus, a famous prophet* . . . These spurious predictions deal with the period from 1713 to 1720.

ANONYMOUS British Library, Cat. No. 12316 e 30/ 5, *Nouvelles et curieuses Prédictions de Michel Nostradamus pour Sept Ans* . . . *Augmentee de l'ouverture du Tombeau de Nostradamus*. These are claimed to extend from 1818 to

1824, but are really edited versions of originals from the *Prophéties*.

APOLLINAIRE Guillaume Apollinaire, *Lettre à Lou*, 1915.

ARKEL Arkel and Blake, *Nostradamus. The Final Countdown*, 1993.

BALDWIN Richard Baldwin, *The Morinus System of Horoscope Interpretation*, 1974.

BARESTE Eugène Bareste, *Nostradamus*, 1840.

BARRETT William Barrett & Theodore Besterman, *The Divining-Rod. An Experimental and Psychological Investigation*, 1926.

BENAZRA Robert Benazra, *Répertoire Chronologique Nostradamique (1545–1989)*, 1990.

BENNETT Geoffrey Bennett, *The Battle of Trafalgar*, 1977.

BESANT Walter Besant, *South London*, 1889.

BLACK J. Anderson Black, *Nostradamus. The Prophecies*, 1995.

BLAVATSKY H.P. Blavatsky, *The Secret Doctrine*, 1888.

BODIN Jean Bodin, *Demonomanie*, 1580.

BOLLY Mme de Bolly, in the *Biographie Universelle Ancienne et Moderne*, 1857.

BOUCHEL Laurent Bouchel, *La bibliotheque ou thresor du droit françois*, 1615.

BRAHE Tycho Brahe, *Astronomia Instauratae Proegymnasmata*, 1602.

BREWER Ebenezer Cobham Brewer, *Dictionary of Phrase and Fable*, revised ed. 1963.

BRUSCH Gaspar Brusch. See *Engelberti abbatis Admontensis . . . de ortu et fine Romani imperii*, 1553.

BURLAND C.A. Burland, *The Arts of the Alchemists*, 1967.

BUSQUET Raoul Busquet, *Legends, Traditions et Récits de la Provence d'Autrefois*, 1932.

CAMPION Nicholas Campion, *The Work of Jean Bodin and Louis Le Roy*, in *History and Astrology. Clio and Urania confer*, edited by Annabella Kitson, 1989.

CAMPION Nicholas Campion, *Astrological Historiography in the Renaissance*, in *History and Astrology. Clio and Urania confer*, edited by Annabella Kitson, 1989.

CANNON Dolores Cannon, *Chronological List of Events Predicted by Nostradamus, Based on his Communications through Dolores Cannon's Hypnosis Subjects, between 1986 and 1989*, n.d.

CARDAN *Ephemerides Recognitae et ad Unguem Castigatae per Lucam Gauricum . . .*, 1533.

CARDAN *Hieronymis Cardani in CL. Ptolemei de Astrorum iudiciis . . .*, 1578.

CHAVIGNY Jean-Aimé de Chavigny, *La Première Face du Ianus François . . .*, Latin title *Jani Gallici Facies Prior . . .*, 1594.

CHAVIGNY Jean-Aimé de Chavigny, *Les Pléiades du S. de Chavigny Beau-Nois*, 1603.

CHEETHAM Erika Cheetham, *The Prophecies of Nostradamus*, 1973.

CHODKIEWICZ   K. Chodkiweicz, *Oracles of Nostradamus*, 1965.

CHOMARAT   Michael Chomarat, *Cahiers Michel Nostradamus*, various years. See NOSTRADAMUS, 1566, below.

CHOMARAT   Michel Chomarat, *Supplement à la Bibliographie Lyonnaise des Nostradamus suive d'un inventiare des estapes relative à la famille Nostradamus*, 1976.

CHOMARAT   Michel Chomarat, *Bibliographie Nostradamus XVIe–XVIIe–XVIIIe siecles*, 1989.

CLÉBERT   Jean-Paul Clébert, *Nostradamus*, 1993.

COLINES   Simon de Colines, *Les canons & documens tresamples, touchant luisaige & practique des communs Almanachz, que l'on nomme Ephemerides*, 1543.

COLLIN   Rodney Collin, *The Theory of Celestial Influence*, 1971 ed.

COLONNA   Francesco Colonna, *Hypnerotomachia Poliphili*, 1499.

COUILLARD.   Antoine Couillard, *Les Prophéties du Seigneur du Pavillon . . .*, 1556

DAVISON   Norman Davison, *Astronomy and the Imagination*, 1985.

D.D.   *The Prophecies of Nostradamus concerning . . . the Kings and Queens of Great Britain . . .*, 1715.

D'HERBOIS   Collot d'Herbois, *Le Nouveau Nostradamus, ou les Fêtes Provençales . . .*, 1777.

DINZINGER, Ludwig Dinzinger, *Nostradamus. Die Ordnung der Zeit*, two vols, 1991–2.

DOUGLAS   David Douglas, *De Naturae Mirabilibus . . .*, 1524.

DUPÈBE   Jean Dupèbe, *Nostradamus. Lettres Inédites*, 1983.

EDEN   Rycharde Eden, *Decades of the newe world or west India*, 1555.

EPHEMERIS   *Die Deutsche Ephemeride* (various years).

FABRICUS   Johannes Fabricus, *Alchemy. The Mediaeval Alchemists and their Royal Art*, 1989.

FAIRBAIRN   *The Imperial Bible-Dictionary*, 1887.

FEILING   Keigh Feiling, *A History of England. From the Coming of The English to 1918*, 1970 ed.

FINÉ   Oronce Finé, *Orontii Finei Delphinatis . . . De Mundi Sphaera sive Cosmographia . . .*, 1542.

FONTBRUNE   Jean-Charles de Fontebrune, *Nostradamus. Countdown to Apocalypse*, English translation of 1983.

FONTBRUNE   Jean-Charles de Fontbrune, *Nostradamus 2. Into the Twenty-First Century*, 1984 translation of the 1982 du Rocher edition, translated by Alexis Lykiard.

FRANCIS   David Pitt Francis, *Nostradamus. Prophecies of Present Times?*, 1984.

FRANÇOIS   Hercules le François, *La Première Invective du Seigneur Hercules le François, contre Monstradamus*, 1558, see the facsimile reprint in *Cahiers Michel Nostradamus*, Nos. 5–6, 1987–88.

FULCANELLI   *Fulcanelli: Master Alchemist. Le Mystère des Cathédrals*, 1971.

FULKE   William Fulke, *Antiprognosticon*, 1560.

GADBURY   John Gadbury, *Cardines Coeli*, 1686.

GARCAEUS   J. Garcaeus, *Johannis Garcaei, Astrologiae Methodus* . . . 1576.

GARCAEUS   J. Garcaeus, *Tractatus brevis* . . . *de erigendis figuris coeli*, 1556.

GARCAEUS   J. Garcaeus, *Astrologiae methodus in qua secundum doctrinam Ptolemaei genituras qualescunque iudicandi ratio traditur*, 1576.

GARENCIÈRES   Theophilius Garcencières, *The True Prophecies or Prognostications of Michael Nostradamus*, 1672.

GARENCIÈRES   Theophilius Garencières, *A Mite cast unto the Treasury of the Famous city of London, being a Brief* . . . *Discourse of the* . . . *Preservation from the Plague in this calamitous year 1665* . . ., 1665.

GAURICUS   *Ephemerides Recognitae et ad Unguem Castigatae per Lucam Gauricum* . . ., 1533.

GETTINGS   F. Gettings, *The Secret Zodiac. The Hidden Art in Mediaeval Astrology*, 1987.

GETTINGS   F. Gettings, *Arcana Dictionary of Astrology*, 1990 revised edition.

GIMON   Louis Gimon, *Chroniques de la ville de Salon, depuis son origine jusqu'en 1792* . . ., 1882.

GOETHE   W. Goethe, *The Green Snake and the Beautiful Lily*, quoted from Rudolf Steiner's *Goethe's Standard of the Soul*, 1925, p.87.

GOULD   R.F. Gould, *The History of Freemasonry*, n.d., but *c*. 1885.

GRAHAM   Gerald S. Graham, *A Concise History of the British Empire*, 1970.

GREEN Jeff Green, *Pluto, the evolutionary journey of the soul,* in *Astrology,* Vol. 37. No. 2, 1963.

GRUENPECK Joseph Gruenpeck, *De pestilentiali scorra, sive Mala de Franzos originem,* 1496.

GUIDO John Guido, *Ioannis Guidionis Villariensis medici Parisini de temporis astrorum . . .,* 1543.

GURDJIEFF G. I. Gurdjieff, *All and Everything,* 1958.

GUYNAUD M. Guynaud, *La Concordance des Prophéties de Nostradamus avec l'histoire, depuis Henry II. Jusqu'à Louis le Grand . . .,* 1712.

GUYTON L.M. Guyton, *Recherches historiques sur les médecins et la médecine à Autun,* 1874.

HAGGARD Howard W. Haggard, *Devils, Drugs, and Doctors,* 1929.

HATZFELD Hatzfeld and Darmesteter, *Dictionnaire General de la Langue Française,* 1888.

HAYDN Joseph Haydn, *Haydn's Dictionary of Dates and Universal Information . . .,* 1910, 25th edition under editorship of B. Vincent.

HAYWOOD H.L. Haywood, *Famous Masons and Masonic Presidents,* 1968 ed.

HELLER Joachim Heller, *Ein Erschrecklich und Wunderbarlich zeychen . . .,* 1554.

HEWITT Valerie Hewitt, *Nostradamus. His Key to the Centuries,* 1994.

HIEROZ J. Hieroz, *L'Astrologie selon Morin de Villefranche,* 1959.

HILTEN For the Johann Hilten prophecies, translated by Stoeffler, see THORNDIKE, below, Vol. V, p. 375.

HIPPOLYTUS   *Philosophumena*, 1851.

HIPPOLYTUS   *De Antichristo*.

HOBSON   B. Hobson and R. Obojski, *Illustrated Encyclopedia of World Coins*, 2nd edition, 1984.

HOGUE   John Hogue, *Nostradamus and the Millennium*, 1987.

HOMER   *Odysseus*.

HORACE   *Carmen*.

HORNE   Alistair Horne, *The Fall of Paris. The Siege and the Commune 1870–71*, 1967.

HOWE   Ellic Howe, *Urania's Children*, 1967.

HOWE   Ellic Howe, *Nostradamus and the Nazis. A Footnote to the History of The Third Reich* . . .

HUTIN   Serge Hutin, *Les Prophéties de Nostradamus; presentée et interprétés* . . ., 1966.

JAUBERT   Etienne Jaubert, *Eclaircissement des veritables Quatrains* . . ., 1656.

JANT   Le Chevalier de Jant, *Prédictions tire'es des Centuries de Nostradamus. Qui vray semblement ce peuvent appliquer au temps present, & à la guerre entre la France & l'Angleterrre contre les Provinces unies*, 1673.

JUNG   C.G. Jung, *Flying Saucers. A Modern Myth of Things Seen in the Skies*, translated from the German *Ein Moderner Mythus* . . ., 1958, by R.F.C. Hull, 1969.

KING   Francis X. King, *Nostradamus Prophecies Fulfilled and Predictions for the Millennium and Beyond*, 1995.

KRITZINGER   D. Kritzinger, *Mysterien von Sonne und Seele*, 1922.

LAING   David Laing, *The Works of John Knox*, 1864.

LAVER   James Laver, *Nostradamus, or the Future Foretold*, 1942.

LAZIUS   Wolfgang Lazius, *Fragmentum vaticinii cuiusdam Methodii . . .*, 1547.

LÉCUREUX   Bernadette Lécureux, *Nostradamus. Lettres Inédites. Édition Complémentaire*, in Adamou, *L'Astrologie de Nostradamus*, 1992.

LENOBLE   Yves Lenoble, *Les Éphémérides de Nostradamus*, 1992. See, AMADOU, above p. 301 ff.

LEO   Alan Leo, *Notable Nativities*, *c.* 1910.

LEROY   Edgar Leroy, *Nostradamus. Ses Origines. Sa Vie. Son Oeuvre*, 1972.

LEWIS   Nigel Lewis, *The Book of Babel: Words and the Way We See Things*, 1994.

LIBERATI   François Liberati, *Sur la fin de l'Empire Romain & Turc*, n.d., but quoted in CHAVIGNY, above.

LICHTENBERGER   Johann Lichtenberger, *Prognosticatio*, 1488.

LOISELEUR   J. Loiseleur, *Ravaillac et ses complices*, 1873.

LOOG   C. Loog, *Die Weissagungen des Nostradamus*, 1922.

LORIE   Peter Lorie, *Nostradamus. The Millennium & Beyond*, 1993, with Liz Greene as Astrological Consultant.

MACODY   Robert Macody, *A Dictionary of Freemasonry*, n.d., but *c.* 1890.

MAIER   Michael Maier's *Arcana Arcanissima hoc est Hieroglyphica Aegyptio-Graeca . . .*, 1614.

MALACHAI   *Malachiae de Pontificibus Romanis usque ad finem Mundi Prophetiae*, 1670.

MARSTALLERUS   Gervasius Marstallerus, *Artis Divinatricis quam astrologiam seu iudicariam vocant encomia et patrocinia*, 1549.

MCLEAN   Adam McLean, *The Magical Calendar*, 1980.

MEAD   G.S. Mead, *Thrice-Greatest Hermes: Studies in Hellenistic Theosophy and Gnosis*, 1906.

MILLER   John Miller, *The Life and Times of William and Mary*, 1974.

MONTEREY   Jean Monterey, *Nostradamus Prophéte du Vingtième Siècle*, 1963.

MONTGAILLARD   De Montgaillard, *Histoire de France*, 1793.

MOORE   Edward Moore, *Studies in Dante. Third Series*, 1903.

MORIN   Morin de Villefranche, *Astrologiae Gallicae*, 1661.

MORTILLET   Gabriel de Mortillet, *Dictionnaire des Sciences anthropologiques*, 1876.

MURAISE   Eric Muraise, *Saint-Rémy de Provence et les Secrets de Nostradamus*, 1969.

NICOULLAUD   Charles Nicoullaud, *Nostradamus, ses prophéties*, 1914.

NOSTRADAME   César de Nostradame, *Histoire et chronique de Provence*, 1614.

NOSTRADAME   Jehan Nostradame, *Les Vies des Plus Célèbres et Anciens Poètes Provensaux . . .*, 1575.

NOSTRADAMUS *Orus Apollo fils de Osiris Roy de Aegipte Niliacque des Notes Hieroglyphiques . . ., c.* 1545. See also ROLLET, below.

NOSTRADAMUS *Les Vrayes Centuries et Prophéties de Maistre Michel Nostradamus Où se void representé tout ce qui s'est passé, tant en France, Espagne, Italie, Alemagne, Angleterre, qu'autres parties du monde*, Pierre Leffen, 1650.

NOSTRADAMUS Michel Nostradamus, *Excellent & moult utile Opuscule à touts nécessaires, qui désirent avoir cocnoissance de plusieur exquies Receptes . . . Fardemens & Senteurs . . . de faire confitures*, 1556.

NOSTRADAMUS *Les Prophéties de M. Michel Nostradamus Dont il en y a trois cents qui n'ont encores iamais esté imprimées*, Antoine du Rosne, 1557.

NOSTRADAMUS *Almanach pour l'an M.D.LXVI. avec ses amples significations & explications, composé par Maistre Michel de Nostradame . . .*, 1566, facsimile in Michel Chomarat, *Cahiers Michel Nostradamus*, Nos. 5–6, 1987–88.

NOSTRADAMUS *Les Vrayes Centuries et Prophéties de Maistre Michel Nostradamus*, 1668.

NOSTRADAMUS *Paraphrase de C. Galen, sus L'exortation de Menodote . . .*, 1557.

NOWOTNY K.A. Nowotny, *De Occulta Philosophia*, 1967.

O'MALLEY C.D. O'Malley, *Michael Servetus*, 1953.

ONIONS C.T. Onions, *The Oxford Dictionary of English Etymology*, 1966 ed.

OVID   *Metamorphoses.*

OVID   *Heroides.*

PARACELSUS   *The Hermetic and Alchemical Writings . . . of Paracelsus the Great*, Vol. II, 1894, edited by A.E. Waite.

PARACELSUS   *De Origine Morborum Invisibilium*, first published *circa* 1530.

PARACELSUS   *Prognosticatio eximii doctoris Theophrasti Paracelsi . . .*, first published *circa* 1536.

PARKER   Derek Parker, *Familiar to All. William Lilly and Astrology in the Seventeenth Century*, 1975.

PELLETIER   Anatole le Pelletier, *Les Oracles de Michel de Nostredame*, 1867.

PERANZONUS   *Vaticanium de vera futuri diluvii . . .*, 1523.

PHILALETHES   Eirenaeus Philalethes, *Marrow of Alchemy*, 1650.

PIOBB   P.V. Piobb, *The Secret of Nostradamus*, 1927.

PIOBB   P.V. Piobb, *Le Sort de l'Europe*, 1939.

PLAYFAIR   G.L. Playfair and S. Hill, *The Cycles of Heaven. Cosmic Forces and What they are Doing to You*, 1978.

PSELLUS   *Chronographia*, ed. E. Renauld, 1926–28.

PTOLEMY   *Tetrabiblos*, F.E. Robbins trans., 1964.

RABELAIS   François Rabelais, *Pantagrueline Prognostication*, 1533, in the bilingual edition of Guy Demerson, 1994.

RABELAIS François Rabelais, *The History of Gargantua and Pantagruel*, 1564.

RAHNER Hugo Rahner, *The Christian Mystery and the Pagan Mysteries*, in *The Mysteries, Papers from the Eranos Yearbooks*, 1971 printing, p. 398.

RAPHAEL *Raphael's Astronomical Ephemeris of the Planets' Places for 1927.*

REGIOMONTANUS *Johannis de mont regio . . . Ephemerides (pro ano 1489–1506).*

REEVES Marjorie Reeves, *The Influence of Prophecy in the Later Middle Ages*, 1969.

RICE Eugene F. Rice, *The Foundations of Early Modern Europe 1460–1559*, 1970.

ROBB Stewart Robb, *Nostradamus on Napoleon*, 1961.

ROBBINS F.E. Robbins, *Ptolemy. Tetrabiblos*, edited and translated by F.E. Robbins, 1964.

ROBBINS R.H. Robbins, *The Encyclopaedia of Witchcraft and Demonology*, 1959.

ROBERTS Henry C. Roberts, *The Complete Prophecies of Nostradamus*, various editions, earliest consulted 1947.

ROBSON Vivian Robson, *Fixed Stars and Constellations in Astrology*, 1923.

ROCHETAILLÉE P. Rochetaillée, *Prophéties de Nostradamus. Clef des Centuries. Son application à l'histoire de la 3e République*, 1939.

ROLA Stansilas Klossowski de Rola, *The Golden Game: Alchemical Engravings of the Seventeenth Century*, 1988.

ROLLET Pierre Rollet, *Nostradamus Interpretation des*

Hieroglyphes de Horapollo. Texte inédit établi et commenté par Pierre Rollet, 1968.

RONSARD   Pierre Ronsard, *Les Poemes de P. de Ronsard . . .*, 1560.

ROUSSAT   Richard Roussat, *Le Livre de l'estat et mutations des temps*, 1550.

RUIR   Emile Ruir, *Le Grand Carnage d'après les prophéties de 'Nostradamus' de 1938 à 1947*, 1938.

SADOUL,   Jacques Sadoul, *Alchemist & Gold*, 1970, first published in 1970 as *Le Trésor des Alchimistes*.

SIBLY   Ebenezer Sibly, *The Science of Astrology, or Complete Illustrations of the Occult Sciences*, 1790.

SMOLLETT   Tobias Smollett, *A Complete History of England*, 1759.

SPENSER   Edmund Spenser, *Shepheard's Calendar*, 1579, etc.

SPORE   Palle Spore, *Les Noms Géographiques dans Nostradamus*, 1988. This appears in AMADOU, above, p. 457 ff.

STADIUS   Johann Stadius, *Ephemerides novae et exactae . . . ab anno 1554 ad annum 1570*, 1556.

STORY   Ronald Story, *The Space Gods Revealed*, 1976.

SUMMERS   Montague Summers, *The Geography of Witchcraft*, 1958 ed.

SWIFT   Jonathan Swift, *Gulliver's Travels*, 1726, etc.

TAYLOR   René Taylor, *Architecture and Magic*, in *Essays in the History of Architecture Presented to Rudolf Wittkower*, ed. by D. Fraser, H. Hibbard and M.J. Lewine, 1969 edition, p.86.

THORNDIKE Lynn Thorndike, *A History of Magic and Experimental Science*, 1941.

TORNÉ-CHAVIGNY H. Torné-Chavigny, *L'Histoire predite et jugee par Nostradamus*, 1860–62.

TORNÉ-CHAVIGNY H. Torné-Chavigny, *Influence de Nostradamus dans le Gouvernement de la France*, 1875.

TRITHEMIUS Trithemius of Sponheim, *De Septem Secundadeis*, 1522.

TRITHEMIUS Trithemius of Sponheim, *Von den Siben Geissten oder Engeln . . .*, 1534

TUCKERMAN *Planetary, Lunar and Solar Positions*, Vol. III, 1973 reprint.

TURREL Pierre Turrel, *Le Période, c'est-à-dire la fin du monde . . .*, 1531.

VALERIANO Pierio Valeriano, *Hieroglyphica*, 1556.

VALLEMONT P. de Le Lorrain de Vallemont, *La Physique Occulte*, 1693.

VIDEL Laurent Videl, *Declaration des Abus Ignorances et Seditions de Michel Nostradamus*, 1558.

VIOTTI Andrea Viotti, *Garibaldi. The Revolutionary and his Men*, 1979, p. 111.

WAITE A.E. Waite, *The Book of Ceremonial Magic*, 1911.

WARD Charles A. Ward, *Oracles of Nostradamus*, 1891, p. 28.

WEDEL T.O. Wedel, *The Mediaeval Attitude Towards Astrology, particularly in England*, 1969 reprint.

WILSON James Wilson, *A Complete Dictionary of Astrology*, 1880.

WIND   Edgar Wind, *Pagan Mysteries in the Renaissance*, 1958.

WÖLLNER   Christian Wöllner, *Das Mysterium des Nostradamus*, 1926. See AMADOU, above.

WOOLF   H.I. Woolf, *Nostradamus*, 1944.

YEATS   W.B. Yeats, 'Magic'. See *W.B. Yeats. Selected Criticism*, edited by A.N. Jeffares, 1970.

ZOSIMUS   See BURLAND, above.

ZWEIG   Stefan Zweig, *Marie Antoinette. The Portrait of an Average Woman*, translated by Eden and Cedar Paul, 1934 ed.

Bibliographic Notes

FOREWORD

1. In quatrain X.66, Nostradamus calls the Americas *l'Americh*. In the mid-sixteenth century, the Americas were still generally called the West Indies. Even as late as 1555, the Englishman, Rycharde Eden, ·in *Decades of the newe world or west India*, called the continents *Armenica*.

2. Apollinaire, *Lettre à Lou*, 1915.

3. P. Rochetaillée, *Prophéties de Nostradamus. Clef des Centuries. Son application a l'histoire de la 3e République*, 1939.

4. Rabelais, *Pantagrueline Prognostication* (1533), in the bilingual edition of Guy Demerson, 1994.

5. By far the best bibliographic study of Nostradamus is Robert Benazra, *Répertoire Chronologique Nostradamique (1545–1989)*, 1990.

INTRODUCTION

1. James Laver, *Nostradamus, or the Future Foretold*, 1942.

2. Charles Ward, *Oracles of Nostradamus*, 1891, p. 28.

3. H. C. Roberts, *The Complete Prophecies of Nostradamus*, 1947.

4. E. Cheetham, *The Prophecies of Nostradamus*, 1974 ed.

5. J. Anderson Black, *Nostradamus. The Prophecies*, 1995, p. 251. Cheetham gave as the opening line of quatrain V.8:

   Sera laisse le feu mort vif cache

   The Adyar version of Nostradamus gives:

Sera laisse feu vif, & mort cache

While the 1557 edition gives:

Sera laisse le feu vif mort cache

6. Jean Monterey, *Nostradamus Prophete du Vingtieme Siècle*, 1963, p. 181.

7. Jean-Charles de Fontebrune, *Nostradamus. Countdown to Apocalypse*, English translation of 1983.

8. David Pitt Francis, *Nostradamus. Prophecies of Present Times?*, 1984.

9. Robert Benazra, *Répertoire Chronologique Nostradamique (1545–1989)*, 1990.

10. 'D.D.', *The Prophecies of Nostradamus . . .*, 1715, p. 64.

11. Jaubert, *Éclaircissement des veritables Quatrains de Maistre Michel Nostradamus . . .*, 1656. For *Cheramongora*, see p. 91.

12. Anonymous, *Nouvelles et curieuses Predictions de Michel Nostradamus pour, Sept Ans Depuis l'annee 1818 . . . Augmentée de l'ouverture du Tombeau de Nostradamus.*

13. *Chronological List of Events Predicted by Nostradamus, Based on his Communications through Dolores Cannon's Hypnosis Subjects, between 1986 and 1989.*

14. 'D.D.', *The Prophecies of Nostradamus . . .*, 1715.

15. The anticipation of the restoration of the Bourbons is set out in the highly imaginative writings of H. Torné-Chavigny, *L'Histoire predite et jugée par Nostradamus*, 1860 ff. For other 'Third Republic' excesses, see P. Rochetaillée, *Prophéties de Nostradamus. Clef des Centuries, Son application a l'histoire de la 3e Republique*, 1939.

16. J. Laver, *Nostradamus, or the Future Foretold*, 1952 ed.

CHAPTER ONE

1. Edgar Leroy, *Nostradamus. Ses Origines. Sa Vie. Son Oeuvre*, 1972. We have used the 1993 impression. See also *Memoires de l'Institut Historique de Provence* article: *Origines de Nostradamus*, XVIII, 1941.

2. Jehan Nostradame, *Les Vies des Plus Celebres et Anciens Poetes Provensaux . . .*, 1575.

3. César de Nostredame, *Histoire et chronique de Provence*, 1614.

4. Jean-Aimé de Chavigny, *La Premier Face du Janus Francois* . . . , with Latin title, *Jani Gallici Facies Prior* . . . , 1594.

5. Jean-Paul Clébert, *Nostradamus*, 1993.

6. The quatrains are, in numerical order, VI.27, V.9, V.57, VIII.34, VIII.46, IX.85 and X.29.

7. The pyramid near Saint-Rémy (*où est debout encor la piramide*) in IV.27 is not a pyramid at all, but it still bears this name today. The goat-caves (*caverne caprine*) in X.29 certainly refer to the huge enclosures, partly excavated and partly natural, in the walls near the pyramid.

8. César, op. cit.

9. Michel Nostradamus, *Excellent & moult utile Opuscule à touts nécessaires, qui désirent avoir cocnoissance de plusieur exquises Receptes . . . Fardemens & Senteurs . . . de faire confitures* . . . , 1555, Ch. VIII.

10. Raoul Busquet, *Legends, Traditions et Recits de la Provence d'Autrefois*, 1932.

11. See, for example, Appendix III of *The Hermetic and Alchemical Writings . . . of Paracelsus the Great*, Vol. II, 1894, edited by A. E. Waite.

12. Jacques Sadoul, *Alchemist & Gold*, 1970, first published in 1970 as *Le Trésor des Alchimistes*. The Basil Valentine is his *Azoth, ou le Moyen de Fair l'Or caché des Philosophes*.

13. Théophile de Garencières, *A Mite cast unto the Treasury of the Famous City of London, being a Brief . . . Discourse of the . . . Preservation from the Plague in this calamitous year 1665* . . . , 1665.

14. Nostradamus, *Paraphrase de C. Galen, sus L'exortation de Menodote* . . . , 1557.

15. See note 9 above.

16. See the modern reprint, based on what is claimed to be an autograph manuscript, edited by Pierre Rollet, *Nostradamus. Interpretation des Hieroglyphes de Horapollo*, 1993.

17. P. V. Piobb, *Le Sort de l'Europe*, 1939.

18. *Holy Bible, I Kings*, 7:13 xiii ff.

19. H. P. Blavatsky, *The Secret Doctrine*, 1888, Vol. 1, p. 314.

The Nostradamus Code

20. See Stanislas Klossowski de Rola, *The Golden Game: Alchemical Engravings of the Seventeenth Century*, 1988, p. 114.

21. Richard Roussat, *Livre de l'Etat et Mutation des Temps*. For a brief survey, see Robert Benazra, *Les Prophéties. Lyons, 1557*, 1993.

22. The tradition is that these rare new islands grow out of the sea overnight, but eye-witness accounts suggest otherwise. Sailing the seas between Sicily and Tunisia, about 10 July 1831, the captain of a Sicilian vessel had reported seeing a waterspout, 60 feet high, and about 800 yards in circumference, followed by a rush of steam, which rose to 1,800 feet. Eighteen days later, on returning to the same place, the captain found a small island, 12 feet high, with a crater in its centre, from which was being discharged upwards a dense volcanic matter. By the end of the month, the island had grown to 90 feet in height, and was about three-quarters of a mile in circumference. It took almost three months for the action of the waves to reduce it to sea-level. Over 20 years later, there were still shoals where the mountain had been. Although it is unlikely that Nostradamus foresaw this particular new mountain, some of the future seismic disturbances in the Mediterranean intrigue him, as quatrain X.49 reveals.

23. Jean Dupèbe, *Nostradamus. Lettres Inédites*, 1983. The letters, which are copies of the last half of the sixteenth century, contain astrological diagrams and horoscopes which Dupèbe did not include. These lacunae have been filled by Bernadette Lecureux, with (poor-quality) facsimiles of the charts and specula, modern diagrammatic 'translations' of these, along with French translations of the Latin, in Robert Amadou, *L'Astrologie de Nostradamus*, 1789. We have used the 1992 edition as being the only one available to us. Regretfully, we must point out that the French translation contains many errors, mainly due to a misunderstanding of astrological technical terms.

24. Letter I, p. 63 of Amadou.

25. The engraving in question, which portrays the third Age of Man, is by Wierix. See Louis Alvin, *Catalogue raisonné de l'oeuvre des trois frères, Jean, Jerome et Antoine Wierix*, 1866. Leroy deals with the issue on p. 80 ff.

26. Only one copy is known to us – that in the British Library.

Fortunately, this rare work has been reissued in facsimile by Michael Chomarat, apparently from his own copy, in *Cahiers Michel Nostradamus*, Nos. 5–6, 1987–88.

27. Several versions of the 'posthumous' prophecies have survived. As an example of an unpublished manuscript version, we may take the 'translation' in the British Library, Sloane 3722: *New prediction said to be found at the opening of the Tomb of Michael Nostradamus, a famous prophet . . .* These spurious predictions deal with the period from 1713 to 1720. Among the published 'posthumous' series is *Nouvelles et curieuses, Predictions de Michel Nostradamus pour Sept Ans . . . Augmentée de l'ouverture du Tombeau de Nostradamus.* These are claimed to extend from 1818 to 1824, but are really edited versions of originals from the *Prophéties* (British Library Cat. No. 12316 e 30/5).

28. Laurent Videl, *Declaration des Abus Ignorances et Seditions de Michel Nostradamus . . .*, 1558.

29. For a biological note on the three related pamphlets, and a mention of the anagrammatic *Monstre d'Abus*, see Benazra, 1990, p. 31 ff.

30. See Palle Spore, *Les Noms Géographiques dans Nostradamus*, 1988. This appears in Amadou, 1992, p. 457 ff.

31. Eugene F. Rice, *The Foundations of Early Modern Europe 1460–1559*, 1970, p. 25. Rice, from whom the Luther quotation comes, actually says that those who accepted the view of Copernicus before 1560 can be counted on the fingers of one hand.

32. For example, in *Johannis Garcaei, Astrologiae Methodus . . .*, 1576, we are given four alternative ascendants from Gauricus, Stadius, a certain Spaniard, and a 'religious' individual. Garcaeus himself insists that Philip's ascendant is Scorpio.

33. Jaubert, *Éclaircissement des veritables Quatrains . . .* See note 11 in Introduction.

34. J. Guido, *Ioannis Guidonis Villariensis medici Parisini de temporis astrorum . . .*, 1543.

35. Garcaeus, *Brief Treatise on Erecting Figures of the Sky*, is discussed by Lynn Thorndike, Vol. VI, p. 102 ff.

36. The book, inscribed 'Ex Lib M. Nostradamis Et Amico Emptus . . .

1560' (Reserve 319834), is entitled *Preclarum Summi in Astrologia Scientia Principis Alchabitii Opus ad scrutanda Stellarum* ... It was discovered *circa* 1985 by Guy Parguez. For an account, see *Cahiers Michel Nostradamus*, No. 4, Jul. 1986. For the Chaucer reference, see T. O. Wedel, *The Mediaeval Attitude Towards Astrology, particularly in England*, 1920. We have consulted the 1969 reprint.

37. Jean-Aimé de Chavigny, *Les Pleiades du S. de Chavigny Beau-Nois*, 1603. We have had access only to the 1609 edition.

38. François Liberati, *Sur la fin de l'Empire Romain & Turc*, n.d., but quoted in Chavigny, above.

39. The literature attached to the cycles associated with the flocculation index of blood by the Japanese researcher, Takata, and the occultation cycles measured by the morphochromatograms of the anthroposophist Kolisko are considerable, and are now merely two series among many which have been observed and studied in the twentieth century. For a brief mention, and short bibliography, see Gettings, 1990 (bibliography) under 'Takata Effect' and 'Kolisko Effect'. For a fairly elementary study of cosmic cycles, see Rodney Collin, *The Theory of Celestial Influence*, 1971 ed. See also G. L. Playfair and S. Hill, *The Cycles of Heaven. Cosmic Forces and What They are Doing to You*, 1978.

40. Trithemius: see p. 114 ff, below. The information is from *De Septem Secundadeis*, 1522.

41. *Prognosticatio eximii doctoris Theophrasti Paracelsi* ..., written 1536.

42. Marjorie Reeves, *The Influence of Prophecy in the Later Middle Ages*, 1969.

43. For the Hilten prediction of papal decline after 1516, see Thorndike, Vol. 5, p. 375.

44. The prediction is found in the Latin poem, *Hodoeporicon Bavaricum*, and has been attributed (wrongly in our opinion) to the astrologer Regiomontanus. We have used the version given by Thorndike, *History of Magic and Experimental Science*, 'The Aftermath of Regiomontanus', Vol. V, p. 373. Of course, Regiomontanus was German, but capable of much better verse, in both Latin and Greek.

45. Unfortunately, the material in Turrel's *Le Periode, c'est-à-dire la fin*

du monde ... has survived only in the notes left by Guyton, *Récherches historiques*, 1874, pp. 70–74, though the astrological material has been reproduced by Thorndike (op. cit., Vol V, p. 310 ff). It is unlikely that the thorough Thorndike would have introduced the rather obvious astrological errors into the text, so we presume that these must have originated with Guyton, or his own source.

46. M. Nostradamus, *Almanach pour l'an M.D.LXVI*. For the modern reprint, see *Cahiers Michel Nostradamus*, ed. Michel Chomarat, Nos. 5–6, 1987–88.

47. See for example, what Simon de Colines calls 'Rigles particulieres' in *Les canons & documens tresamples, touchant luisaige & practique des communs Almanachz, que l'on nomme Ephemerides*, 1543, p. 32v. In fact, any of the standard astrological works of the period deal with the trigones: for example, the sixteenth-century Gauricus and Garcaeus texts (see Bibliography).

48. Oronce Finé, *Orontii Finei Delphinatis ... De Mundi Sphaera sive Cosmographia ...*, 1542.

49. Garcaeus, *Johannis Garcaei, Astrologiae Methodus*, 1576.

50. Gervasius Marstallerus, *Artis Divinatricis quam astrologiam seu iudiciariam vocant encomia et patrocinia*.

51. Garcaeus, *Tractatus brevis ... de erigendis figuris coeli*, 1556. Like Thorndike, we had access to the 1573 edition.

52. Garcaeus, *Astrologiae methodus in qua secondum doctrinam Ptoelmaei genituras qualescunque iudicandi ratio traditur*, 1576. A useful appendix providing names and data for 113 of the more famous (by modern standards) is given by Thorndike (op. cit.), in Vol. VI, Appendix 4, p. 595.

53. Nostradamus, *Orus Apollo fils de Osiris ... Notes Hieroglyphiques* (MSS B.N. 2594). See note 16 in Chapter 1.

54. See Stansilas Klossowski de Rola, *The Golden Game: Alchemical Engravings of the Seventeenth Century*, 1988.

55. David Douglas, *De Naturae Mirabilibus*, 1524.

56. C. G. Jung, *Flying Saucers. A Modern Myth of Things Seen in the Skies*, translated from the German *Ein Moderner Mythus ...*, 1958, by R. F. C. Hull, 1969, p. 102 ff.

57. Joachim Heller, *Ein Erschrecklich und Wunderbarlich zeychen . . .*, 1554. The sheet is reproduced by Michael Chomarat (with Jean-Paul Laroche) in *Bibliographie Nostradamus. XVIe–XVIIe–XVIIIe siecles*, 1989, p. 12.

58. We have spoken with students of his philosophical theory who would not believe what we told them of his connection with witchcraft. This we take as evidence of the dangers into which modern academic specialisms have plunged us. Anyone reading the brief modern histories of his life (in, say, Nicholas Campion or Rossell Hope Robbins) would be forgiven for believing that these are two different personages. See Nicholas Campion, *The Work of Jean Bodin and Louis Le Roy*, in *History and Astrology. Clio and Urania confer*, edited by Annabella Kitson, 1989, and R. H. Robbins, *The Encyclopaedia of Witchcraft and Demonology*, 1959. Campion gives the full titles of the Bodin literature to which we refer.

59. Pierre Ronsard, *Les Poemes de P. de Ronsard . . .*, 1560. The relevant lines of the poem, *Elegie à Guillaume des Autels gentilhomme Charrolois*, are reproduced by Benazra, 1990, p. 47.

60. See Clébert, pp. 83–5. Ronsard was a melancholic, and often wrote with cynical undertones: we are not convinced that Clébert was correctly assessing the style of Ronsard as being easy to read and clear of meaning.

61. Charles Ward, *Oracles of Nostradamus*, 1891. However, we should point out that Ward has modernized the sixteenth-century orthography, and has also given the wrong impression that the poem was entitled *To Nostradamus*. Our impression from the poem is that Ronsard is questioning the whole basis and legitimacy of the predictive method, yet recognizes that Nostradamus has the gift of divination through the power of God and astrology (*le ciel qui depart/ Bien & mal aux humains*).

62. An example of overspill from this work of 1656 into modern times is Jaubert's commentary on quatrain X.14, which describes it as being a horoscope of one Vrnel Vaucile. This is simply not true (Jaubert was no astrologer), yet we find the modern commentator, Roberts, describing the same quatrain as 'a reading of the horoscope of a

contemporary of Nostradamus, Urnel Vaucile'. Had Roberts looked at the original quatrain, he would have found that the two words were not intended as a name at all, and, indeed, had nothing to do with astrology. Not for one moment do I suggest that Roberts had read Jaubert – between 1656 and the twentieth century, other English commentators had protracted the error.

63.
1556 II.51	1558 X.39	1559 I.35, III.55
1566 VI.63	1559 VI.75	1560 X.59, X.39
1569 II.41	1571 XII.36, III.3	1572 IV.47
1574 III.30, III.39	1577 VIII.2	1588 III.51
1589 III.55	1596 III.88	1596 VIII.94
1603 III.70, VIII.58	1632 IX.18N	1642 VIII.68

1649 VIII.37, IX.49, X.40, III.81, VIII.76, III.81
1650 VII.56   1651 X.4

64. Antoine Couillard, *Les Prophéties du Seigneur du Pavillon . . .*, 1556.
65. William Fulke, *Antiprognosticon*, 1560. Although Nostradamus is named in this work, the criticism is not specific, and is directed against astrology as a whole.
66. Laurent Bouchel, *La bibliothèque ou thrésor du droit françis*, 1615. I am indebted to Lynn Thorndike for this reference (op. cit.), Vol. VI, p. 170.
67. Lynn Thorndike, *A History of Magic and Experimental Science*, 1941, Vol. VI, p. 170.
68. Nostradamus, *A L'Invictissime, Tres-Puissant, et Tres-Chrestien, Henry Second, Roy de France*, 1558, in the second volume of *Les Prophéties*.

CHAPTER TWO

1. See Jean Dupèbe, *Nostradamus. Lettres Inédites*, 1983. These letters are in Latin, and Dupèbe has elected not to include the horoscopes.
2. See Adamou, *L'Astrologie de Nostradamus*, 1992: Bernadette Lécureux, *Nostradamus. Lettres Inédites. Edition Complementaire*, p. 116. Lécureux seems to have misunderstood the general tenor of the paragraph, and clearly did not know what to make of the reference to

the Trutine of Hermes: nor did she appear to realize that (in the sixteenth century) the horoscope and the ascendant were identical. We should note, also, that Lécureux is incorrect in claiming that Nostradamus is referring to the fixed star Aldebaran, in respect of the horoscope of Rosenberger's second son, Karl. Unfortunately, this type of error is not unique in her translations.

3. It is typical that Nostradamus could simply have referred to the instrument as an astrolabe, but elected to describe it in far from technical terms. Again, this appears to be obscurantism. There is no doubt that he means to refer to the astrolabe. The planisphere was literally a projection of the celestial sphere (a schematic map of the heavens), and when half of such a projection was united with a complex series of instruments of Arabic design, they formed an astrolabe. This instrument was used for measuring ascendants, certain planetary positions, determining heights, directions, and so on. Why Nostradamus mentions it in this letter, and why he describes its ancestry, is not clear: perhaps it was merely part of his general tendency to obfuscation.

4. Leroy, op. cit., pp. 11–12.

5. Peter Lorie, *Nostradamus. The Millennium and Beyond*, 1993, with Liz Greene as Astrological Consultant.

6. See C. D. O'Malley, *Michael Servetus*, 1953, p. 158 ff.

7. See Michel Chomarat, *Cahiers Michel Nostradamus*, No. 4, Jul. 1986, p. 51.

8. See Yves Lenoble, *Les Éphemérides de Nostradamus*, p. 301 ff of Amadou, 1992.

9. For Wöllner, *Das Mysterium des Nostradamus* (1926), see p. 307 ff of Amadou, 1992. See also Ludwig Dinzinger, *Nostradamus. Die Ordnung der Zeit*, two vols., 1991–92.

10. Nicholas Campion, *Astrological Historiography in the Renaissance*, in *History and Astrology. Clio and Urania confer*, 1989, edited by Annabella Kitson.

11. F. Gettings, *The Hidden Art. A Study in Mediaeval Symbolism*, 1979.

12. Haydn (see Bibliography, above).

13. For a brief survey of the specialist term 'throne', see F. Gettings, *The*

Arkana Dictionary of Astrology, 1990 ed. See also Ptolemy, *Tetrabiblos*, I.19.

14. The astrological and astronomical views of Francesco Patrizi are dealt with by Lynn Thorndike, in Vol. VI of *The History of Magic and Experimental Science*, 1941.

15. Ephemerides such as Tuckerman, *Planetary, Lunar and Solar Positions*, Vol. III, 1973 reprint.

16. For the term 'exaltations', see F. Gettings, *The Arkana Dictionary of Astrology*, 1990 ed. For a rationale, see also Ptolemy, *Tetrabiblos*, I.19, in the Robbins parallel text translation, 1964 ed., p. 89.

17. Morin de Villefranche, *Astrologiae Gallicae*, 1661 ed. Some useful surveys in English and French have appeared. See for example, J. Hieroz, *L'Astrologie selon Morin de Villefranche*, 1959, and Richard Baldwin, *The Morinus System of Horoscope Interpretation*, 1974.

18. Information derived from the WinStar Ephemeris (1996) indicates:

SA 18 PI   SU con MA 7 CP

19. Gurdjieff, *All and Everything*, 1958, the English translation of *Recit de Beelzebub à son petit fils*.

20. Besides the associations drawn between Aries and martial 'rapine' and war, there is also the support of a rather obvious Green Language metathesis. By means of the syncope of P, RAPINE becomes an anagram for ARIEN.

21. For Aries as the ruler of Germany in sixteenth-century sources, see Gauricus, *Ephemerides Recognitae et ad Unguem Castigatae per Lucam Gauricum* . . ., 1533, and Garcaeus, *Johannis Garcaei, Astrologiae Methodus* . . ., 1576, p. 285.

22. On 3 September 1939 the data for the planetary positions of the bodies known to Nostradamus, given for civil midnight in the *Die Deutsche Ephemeride*, are:

SU 9VG35   M0 24AR30   ME 23LE01   VE 8VG49
MA 24CP35   JU 6AR50R   SA 00TA55R

23. On 23 September 1939, Saturn retrograded from Taurus into Aries, and on midnight was 29.57 in the latter sign.

24. On 7 May 1945 the data for the planetary positions of the bodies known to Nostradamus, given for civil midnight in the *Die Deutsche Ephemeride*, are:

    SU 16TA03   M0 08PI36   ME 20AR34   VE 17AR12D
    MA 03AR11   JU 17VG37R   SA 07CN07

25. H. I. Woolf, *Nostradamus*, 1944.

26. Jean-Charles de Fontbrune, *Nostradamus 2. Into the Twenty-First Century*, 1984 translation of the 1982 du Rocher edition, translated by Alexis Lykiard, p. 142.

27. Cheetham (op. cit.) was hard put to read any significance into her wrongly determined 1977.

28. The planetary positions for 4 February 1571 were:

    SO 15AQ   MO 10AQ   ME 10AQ   MA 29AQ   JU 26AQ

29. Collot d'Herbois, *Le Nouveau Nostradamus, ou les Fêtes Provencales . . .* , 1777.

30. John Plonisco: see Lynn Thorndike, *History of Magic and Experimental Science*, 1941, Vol. V, p. 218.

31. Quoted from the title of the book on the subject by Ludovicus Vitalis, then professor of astrology at Bologna. The book appeared in 1522.

32. So important is this Great Conjunction of 1524 in the history of astrology that the scholarly Lynn Thorndike devoted an entire chapter to the literature it spawned. We are grateful to this source for the leads which we were able to follow in our own assessment of the period – especially for the quotation relating to Peranzonus, *Vaticanium de vera futuri diluvii . . .*, 1523.

33. Norman Davidson, *Astronomy and the Imagination*, 1985, p. 135 ff.

34. Johann Stadius, *Ephemerides novae et exactae . . . ab anno 1554 ad annum 1570*, 1556. For mention of the Stadius predictions, see Thorndike, *History of Magic and Experimental Science*, 1941, Vol. VI, p. 15.

35. Vivian Robson, *Fixed Stars and Constellations in Astrology*, 1923.

36. Turrel's influential book, which is so scarce now as to be inaccessible,

was *Le Période, c'est-à-dire la fin du monde ...*, 1531. Lynn Thorndike, *History of Magic and Experimental Science*, 1941, records the survival of a manuscript by Turrel in Latin (*A Fatal Prognostication Revealing Marvellous Future Events regarding the Duration of the World and its Last Days*), and suggests that this is *Le Période* manuscript, which he translated into French. Uncharacteristically, Thorndike offers no information as to the whereabouts of this important manuscript.

37. Richard Roussat, *Le Livre de l'estat et mutations des temps*, 1550.
38. R. H. Allen, *Star Names and their Meanings*, 1963 reprint of the 1899 *Star-Names and Their Meanings*, p. 188.
39. Barlow, in his *Study of Dante*, tells us that the *prima gente* are not Adam and Eve, as Cary had suggested, but the early races of mankind, who according to the Ptolemaic model, would have been able to see the stars of Crux from latitudes higher than Italy. See R. H. Allen (op. cit.), pp. 196–7.
40. Ptolemy, *Tetrabiblos*, I.3–4. For a note on this with useful sources, see F. E. Robbins, *Ptolemy. Tetrabiblos*, edited and translated by F.E. Robbins, 1964, in the Loeb Classical Library, p. 35.

CHAPTER THREE

1. Trithemius, *De Septem Secundadeis*, 1522.
2. Trithemius, *Von den Siben Geissten oder Engeln ...*, 1534. Although the schema in the Latin *De Septem Secundadeis* of 1522 is presented in a different way from the later German edition, the dates correspond: however, the one or two insignificant errors in the original texts have been amended in our own tables.
3. Gabriel de Mortillet, *Dictionnaire des Sciences anthropologiques*. 1876
4. A brief but informative study and useful tabulation is included under 'Chronology' in Partrick Fairbairn, *The Imperial Bible-Dictionary*, 1887. It is interesting that the span suggested by Nostradamus corresponds more closely to the period set out in the Hebrew version of the Scriptures than in the Septuagint, which reckons the period at 6,000 years.

5. J. Anderson Black, *Nostradamus. The Prophecies*, 1995.

6. The only occultist to have dealt with the Secundadeians with any real insight in modern times is Rudolf Steiner. For a summary, see the entry under 'Secundadeian Beings', in F. Gettings, *The Arkana Dictionary of Astrology*, 1990.

7. Peranzonus, *Vaticinium de vera futuri diluvii declaratione . . .* , 1523.

8. The Secundadeians were not well understood by astrologers after the fifteenth century. The sixteenth-century astrologer, William Lilly, attempted to give a translation of the Trithemian text, but failed to understand its import. In the occult realm, the worst (but unfortunately, the most influential) attempt at transmitting the Secundadeian tradition was the pernicious version constructed by the soi-disant occultist Eliphas Levi, in the unreliable *Dogme et Rituel de la Haute Magie*, translated by A.E. Waite as *Transcendental Magic. Its Doctrine and Ritual*, 1896, p.353. Fortunately, shortly after Levi disseminated his nonsense, Rudolf Steiner began to mention in his lectures certain traditions relating to the Secundadeians: needless to say, Steiner's versions are entirely reliable.

CHAPTER FOUR

1. Fulcanelli, *Master Alchemist. Le Mystère des Cathédrales*, 1971 English edition.

2. Rabelais, *The History of Gargantua and Pantagruel*, 1564.

3. Eirenaeus Philalethes, *Marrow of Alchemy*, 1650.

4. See William Anderson, *Green Man. The Archetype of our Oneness with the Earth*, 1990.

5. See, for example, Edgar Wind, *Pagan Mysteries in the Renaissance*, 1958, and *Mercury of Angels*, in F. Gettings, *The Hidden Art. A Study of Occult Symbolism in Art*, 1978.

6. It is hard to know where to begin with Jung. The outrageous historical and academic errors in (for example) his *Transformation Symbolism in the Mass* (1941), republished in *The Mysteries. Papers from the Eranos Yearbooks* Series XXX.2, 1971 edition, indicate the specific errors (no doubt born out of an urgent enthusiasm for his

subject) to which he is prone. The pernicious influence on alchemy may be noted in Johannes Fabricus, *Alchemy. The Mediaeval Alchemists and their Royal Art*, 1989 edition, which tells us something about modern psychology, but little about alchemy.

7. Zosimus, quoted by C.A. Burland, *The Arts of the Alchemists*, 1967. See 'The Words of Power', p. 159.

8. By far the best available modern edition of Agrippa's famous book is K. A. Nowotny, *De Occulta Philosophia*, 1967.

9. The idea of gracing Erich von Daniken with bibliographic reference sticks in our throat. See, however, Ronald Story, *The Space Gods Revealed*, 1976. The pre-Adamic hermaphrodite is mentioned in *Genesis* I:27. The creation of Adam, the Earth-man who became a living soul, is not mentioned until *Genesis* II:7. The creation of the Earth-woman, Eve, is not mentioned until *Genesis* II:22. It is recorded that both Adam and Eve were creatures of the flesh.

CHAPTER FIVE

1. Jean-Paul Clébert, *Nostradamus*, 1993, pp. 25–7.

2. See Nigel Lewis, *The Book of Babel: Words and the Way We See Things*, 1994, p. 208. Although Lewis does not use the term Green Language, his fascination with the formation and influence of slang denotes an interest in those factors which lie behind the arcane tongue.

3. In proposing an altogether unacceptable reading in 1914, Charles Nicoullaud treated the word *dedans* as an anagram of Sedan, but missed the implications of the next word.

4. *Deuteronomy*, III:ii.

5. Homer, *Odyssey*, 12. For the later story, which is almost certainly the one Nostradamus was familiar with, see Ovid's *Metamorphoses*, 13.

6. Horace, *Carmen*, I.27.19.

7. Cheetham, op. cit, V.57.

8. Jean-Paul Clébert, *Nostradamus*, 1993, p. 175. Clébert is right to lament the mistranslation of *Mansol*. Erika Cheetham derived the word from the Latin *manens solus*, which she claims means 'the one

who remains alone', but we can see no relevance or import in this interpretation. For reasons which are just as unaccountable, Jean-Charles de Fontbrune interprets this quatrain as reference to John-Paul II. There is no support for this argument. In spite of Clébert's argument, we still believe the word is intended as Green Language.

9. Nostradamus, *Excellent & moult utile Opuscule . . . de plusieurs exquises Receptes*, 1555. On page 228 we find: *Michael Nostradamus Sextro-phoeanus faciebat Salone litoreae 1552.*

10. So far as we have been able to establish, there are three versions of *Almanachs* for 1563, one of which is clearly apocryphal, as Benazra points out. However, Muraise, in his *Saint-Rémy de Provence et les Secrets de Nostradamus*, 1969, devotes a chapter to the two treasures, and quotes from this almanac with some confidence.

11. The cenotaph, of the first century BC, may have been erected for Gaius and Lucius Caesar, sons of Agrippa and Julia.

12. The matter is dealt with admirably in Stefan Zweig's *Marie Antoinette. The Portrait of an Average Woman*, translated by Eden and Cedar Paul, 1934 ed.

13. See John Miller, *The Life and Times of William and Mary*, 1974 ed., p. 181.

14. Few writers interested in the history of the world, as was Nostradamus, could ignore Hippolytus' *De Antichristo*: as we shall see, certain ideas in this work resurface in the quatrains of Nostradamus. See also G. S. Mead, *Thrice-Greatest Hermes: Studies in Hellenistic Theosophy and Gnosis*, 1906.

15. Ovid, *Heroides*, 9.92. We shall see that usually Nostradamus is more inclined to quote from his *Metamorphoses*.

16. See R. F. Gould, *The History of Freemasonry*, n.d., but *c.* 1885. Many actions and events in the life of Napoleon may be recognized as being connected with this initiation, and we are surprised to find so knowledgeable a writer as H. L. Haywood, in *Famous Masons and Masonic Presidents*, deprecating Napoleon's Masonic connections. See also Robert Macody, *A Dictionary of Freemasonry*, n.d., but *c.*1890.

17. See Michael Maier's *Arcana Arcanissima hoc est Hieroglyphica*

Aegyptio-Graeca . . ., 1614. Michael Maier was born in the year that Nostradamus died. The *Arcana* was written in England, and (as the crude engraving suggests) published there.

18. 'D.D.', *The Prophecies of Michael Nostradamus Concerning the FATE of all the Kings & Queens of GREAT BRITAIN, since the Reformation . . .*, 1715.

19. Le Pelletier, who did not appear to see the full significance of this line, confirmed the archaic name *Sept. born* from the *Theatrum orbis terrarum (Brabantiae)*, 1570.

CHAPTER SIX

1. Howard W. Haggard, *Devils, Drugs and Doctors*, 1929.
2. Percopo, XVII ii, 39. This specific reference is said by Thorndike to be from a *Prognostic* for 30 July 1552, which we have been unable to trace. However, the prediction, in various guises, did circulate before the death of Henry, for we have come across it in several books published prior to the event.
3. Ranzovius, *Catalogus imperatorum . . .*, 1580.
4. Lynn Thorndike (op. cit.), Vol. VI, p. 101. It will be seen that the references to both Percopo and Ranzovius were suggested by this source, though we have come to different conclusions about the material.
5. For a full account, see Thorndike, Vol. VI, chapter xxxii, which deals with the New Star.
6. Tycho Brahe, *Astronomia Instauratae Proegymnasmata*, 1602.
7. See Allen, op. cit., p. 147.
8. Homer's *Iliad*, translated by Lord Derby, and quoted by Allen, p. 121.
9. Edmund Spenser, *Shepheard's Calendar*, for July. Quoted by Allen, p. 125.
10. With typical aplomb, Roberts mistranslates the French. We think he has relied too much upon the seventeenth-century English of Garencières.
11. Paracelsus, *De Origine Morborum Invisibilium*, Lib. IV.

12. Paracelsus, *Coelum Philosophorum*.

13. From *The Works of John Knox*, ed. David Laing, 1864, Vol. IV, p. 240. Quoted by Eugene F. Rice, *The Foundations of Early Modern Europe. 1460–1559*, 1970, p. 142.

14. This was the inquisitor-general at Lyons, Matthieu Ory, whose main fame now is that he interrogated and arrested Michael Servetus. Later in the same year Servetus was burned to death illegally in Geneva, with the connivance of Calvin.

15. Fulcanelli, *Fulcanelli: Master Alchemist. Le Mystere des Cathedrals*, 1971.

CHAPTER SEVEN

1. Amsterdam Edition of 1668 is *Les Vrayes Centuries et Prophéties de Maistre Michel Nostradamus . . .*, Chez Jean Jansson, 1668.

2. T. Garencières, (see Bibliography). As we shall see, the 'blood of the just' theme is taken up again in quatrain II.53.

3. *An ancient Prophecy written originally in French by Nostradamus, know* [sic] *done into English 6 Jan 1671*. This is in the British Library manuscript collection Add. 34, 362, f.50. With considerable variations it was published in Andrew Marvell's *Works*, 1872 edition, Vol. 1, p. 338 f. 50.

4. K. Chodkiewicz, *Oracles of Nostradamus*, 1965, p. 30.

5. The proposal that Nostradamus was referring to the pagan site of St Paul's seems to have originated with Garencières.

6. Brewer, in his *Dictionary of Phrase & Fable*, revised ed., 1963, p. 894, refers to the Gillray caricature of the Old Lady. This cartoon is dated 1797, but it is evident that the name was in use long before. The name Threadneedle, which is probably the Three Needles (perhaps from the coat of arms of the Needlemakers' Company), was in use in 1598.

7. Other quatrains dealing with Charles I include II.53.

8. One compelling argument in support of this epithet, *juste*, could be derived from the speech from the scaffold which Charles I made as he stood in open shirts – he is said to have put on an extra shirt

against the weather – on the bitterly cold day in January, 1649. While admitting some of his own errors, and expressing his belief that the freedom of people lay in the sanctity of law, he observed, 'God's judgements are just'. These were his last public words.

9. The quotation from Machyn's diary is from Walter Besant, *South London*, 1889.

10. In spite of the conflagration, St Mary Overies survived, and looked much the same in the 1790s. The name Overies is traced by Besant (see above) to the old word, *Ofers*, meaning 'of the shore', the reference being to the fact that it was built along the bank of the Thames. The original fabric of the foundation was destroyed in a fire in 1212, and the church was rebuilt in the fifteenth century. A pardon of 1,500 days is probably still operative for anyone who says a prayer for the soul of the poet, John Gower, a major benefactor of the church, who was buried there.

11. For the famous two shirts, see note 8 above.

12. Keith Feiling, *A History of England. From the Coming of the English to 1918*, 1970 ed., p. 569.

13. Nostradamus used other words or phrases to denote the English and the British. For example, he describes the British as 'gent Britannique'.

14. Our argument is not that Nostradamus used the word in its English sense before it was even in use in England, but rather that the word adduces his brilliance as a seer: Nostradamus, as always, was writing in French, but thinking in Latin. The word *Anglicus*, albeit in a Latin context, is firmly entrenched in non-pejorative pre-Protestant literature: for example, in the *Magna Carta*, we find the phrase *Anglicana Ecclesia*.

15. Emile Ruir, *Le Grand Carnage d'après les prophéties de 'Nostradamus' de 1938 à 1947*, 1938, p. 118.

16. Nostradamus is playing with the French word *Verseau*, meaning 'Aquarius'. It is a double entendre, as the word contains *eau* (water), and is also in the quatrain verse (*vers*).

17. J. Loiseleur, *Ravaillac et ses complices*, 1873.

18. Pierre de le Lorrain de Vallemont, *La Physique occulte ou traite de la baguette divinatoire*, 1696.

19. Cheetham corrects Nostradamus, and suggests (with no evidence) that *Mont Aymar* is actually Montelimart. Unaware of the deeper implications of the language used by Nostradamus, she elects to interpret this extraordinary quatrain as a reference to the sack of Lyons in 1793 by the revolutionary soldiers, clearly unaware that Nostradamus dealt with this siege in great detail in another quatrain (see page 113 ff). The main problem with the Cheetham suggestion is that Lyons was not sacked by the soldiers on 13 December 1793, as she claims. Also, Toulon and the Vendée suffered a similar fate, in December of the same year.

20. See for example the data for his own birthday in the *Johannis de mont regio . . . Ephemerides*, mentioned in Appendix One. The rubric *Lucia* appears on the day before his own birthday.

21. We learn from the Abbé de Vallemont (see note 18, above) that he personally investigated Aymar in Paris for two hours daily for a month, from 21 January 1698. He established that it was 'certain that the rod turns in his hands on the trail of fugitive thieves and murderers'. Quoted by William Barrett and Theodore Besterman, in *The Divining-Rod. An Experimental and Psychological Investigation*, 1926.

22. Mme de Bolly, in *Biographie Universelle Ancienne et Moderne*, 1857.

23. Needless to say, the Inquisition had a much freer dispensation in the outlying provinces. The Edict of 1682, promulgated by Louis XIV – and partly motivated by the *Chambre ardente* affair – virtually put an end to trials for witchcraft in France. This was done mainly by redefining witchcraft, and thus disabusing the Church of its hold on heresy. Probably the last burning for straight witchcraft was in Bordeaux, in 1718.

24. Montague Summers, *The Geography of Witchcraft*, 1958 ed., p. 421. We realize, of course, that Summers was a very biased historian, yet he did at least go to very great lengths to examine primary documents to support his prejudices.

25. To our mind, the astrological precision contained in *Et liqueduct & le Prince embaume* makes this line the most remarkable in the entire Nostradamian oeuvre. As we shall see, it is astrologically accurate to within a couple of minutes. How Nostradamus could prevision the embalming of Richelieu, a hundred years before it happened, is one question, but that he could tie this embalming to a precise cosmic event is almost beyond belief.

26. At noon, 4 December, Jupiter was in 9 degrees 50 minutes of Pisces, while Saturn was in 18 degrees 24 minutes of the same sign. They had *just* entered the orb allowed for this powerful conjunction.

27. Armand Jean du Plessis is called the *Prince* by Nostradamus because he stood next in power to the King. In any case, he was a Duke, his title being Duc de Richelieu.

28. The construct makes a fascinating comparison with the *l'Aqueduict* of quatrain X.89, which is a reference to the preceding sign Aquarius.

29. At noon, 24 February 1642, Saturn was 25PI04, Jupiter 25PI01. The relevant planetary positions were:

    SA 25PI   JU 25PI   SU 06PI and ME 13PI
    MA 01GE   VE 24AQ   MO 24GE

30. In the United States, the technical word for Satellitium is Stellium. However, this latter is etymologically incorrect.

31. We offer this amendment reluctantly, for it was *Arles* in the Pierre Rigaux printing of 1566 and in the Bonoist Rigaud printing of 1568. We prefer to offer this amendment to the alternative of adjusting history to fit the word, as other commentators have done.

32. We are aware that Pitt Francis comments on this quatrain, and recognizes that it deals with Richelieu. However, he draws from the commentary very different conclusions to our own, and introduces several errors. It would seem that his great error (not merely for this quatrain, we might observe) lay in relying on Cheetham for the translation and commentary. The serious historical errors in the Francis commentary are that Cinq Mars did *not* disposition Richelieu, the papers were *not* discovered at Arles, and Louis XIII did *not*

die in 1642. See David Pitt Francis, *Nostradamus. Prophecies of Present Times?*, 1984, p. 66. Neither Cheetham nor Francis realized that the quatrain is astrological.

33. C. T. Onions, *The Oxford Dictionary of English Etymology*, 1966 ed., p. 101.

34. Tobias Smollett, *A Complete History of England*, 1759, Vol. 8, p. 247. But see also *The History of England . . .*, by David Hume and W. C. Stafford (Vol. II, p. 295), which rests heavily upon Smollett yet extends the list of the cabal: Bishop of London, Earls of Danby, Nottingham, Devonshire, Dorset, the Marquis of Halifax, Duke of Norfolk, the Lords Lovelace, Delamere, Paulet, Eland, Messrs Hampden, Powle and Lester, besides 'many gentlemen of interest, and a great number of substantial citizens, joined in the application to the prince, intreating him to assist them in the recovery of their liberties'.

35. See the anonymous J.F., *Predictions of Nostradamus, before the Year 1558*, licensed 26 May 1691. (We had access to this rare work in the British Library: 718 g. 12.)

36. From *A New Song of the French King's Fear of an Orange*. An anonymous anti-Louis XIV scurrilous verse, undated, but printed towards the end of the seventeenth century.

CHAPTER EIGHT

1. Stefan Zweig, *Marie Antoinette*, 1934 (third ed.), p. 453.

2. The reasons why the Prussians and Austrians retreated at Valmy have never been explained adequately, though it is known that Brunswick was not at all keen on the entire incursion into France. The possibility is that the mud was too deep for the Prussian soldiers to cover the ground under fire. They did not retreat in disorder, however. Goethe famously said of Valmy, 'This field and this day mark the beginning of a new epoch in the history of the world.' It was by no means a great battle, being little more than a skirmish: one wonders, therefore, if Goethe – ever attuned to such things – sensed some supernatural cause behind the retreat.

3. Ward, op. cit., p. 263.

4. De Montgaillard, *Histoire de France*, 1793, iii, p. 415.

5. In the sixteenth century, the word 'colours' was already being used to represent military flags.

6. For a good description of the Alfraganus system, as it pertains to Dante (and thus potentially to Nostradamus), see Edward Moore, *Studies in Dante. Third Series. The Geography of Dante*, 1903. As Moore remarks, it is humiliating to see that the northern limit, which excludes the 'outer barbarians' who were scarcely worthy of notice, includes not much more than the southern part of Cornwall!

7. Ptolemy, *Tetrabiblos*, II.3.

8. It is so obvious that Catherine the Great is the subject of the quatrain that it is disturbing to find Cheetham translating this mannish-woman as a symbol of Germania.

9. So far as we can determine, this resounding title was found on a column in 1909. Semiramis was almost certainly a historical figure, but unlike Catherine, she was never investigated for her sexual prowess.

10. It is clear that Nostradamus was reserving his eclipse imagery for the Russo–Turkish wars, wherein the imagery had some cosmo–symbolic significance. However, it is worth noting that the second partition of Poland, which was signed at 3.00 a.m. on 23 September 1793, corresponded to an occultation of Saturn by the Moon.

11. Le Pelletier, p. 59. As a matter of fact, besides amending Nostradamus to suit his own interpretation, the French scholar also copies the original text wrongly:

    Le dix Calendes d'Avril de faict gotique
    Resusité encor par gens malins:
    Le feu estainct, assemblée diabolique
    Cherchant les os du Damant & Pselin.

    This offers no fewer than nine variations on the original Nostradamus text. The deviations may not be critical, in changing fundamentally the sense of the quatrain (as are so many of the deviations of modern commentators), yet, in a scholar, such an approach is unsupportable. To our mind, the 'scholarly' changes of seemingly obscure texts are just as unacceptable as those changes wrought in the sub-cultural works. Most modern interpreters follow this reading by Le Pelletier blindly, always misreading the *dix Calendes*, and ending up with a meaningless calendrical equivalent. Roberts settles for 23 April, while Cheetham sees it as 10 April. Patrian attempts no modern equivalent translation, while de Fontbrune does not attempt a translation in either of his two books on Nostradamus.

12. The Gregorian reforms of 1582, initiated by the Papacy, were not adopted in Protestant England until 1751.

13. Naturally, it relates to 1789, the year of the Revolution.

14. The original French of the 1668 edition runs: . . . *& commencement icelle annee sera faite plus grande persecucution* [sic] *à l'Eglise Chrestienne, qui n'a este faite en Afrique, & durera cette icy jusques à l'an mil sept cens nonante deux que l'on ciudera estre une renovation de siecle* . . .

15. Le Pelletier, *Post quaedam sacra extinctis luminibus, mistim coeunt, sive cum soror, sive cum filia, sive cum qualibet . . .*, p. 356.

16. Psellus, *Chronographia* (2 vols.), 1926–28, edited by E. Renauld.

17. For example, Stefan Zweig, *Marie Antoinette*, 1934 (third ed.), p. 465.

18. The dating is very precise, given the context. The slowest-moving planet of this quaternary is Jupiter. This planet was in Leo in 1789–90 and 1812–13, but the other planets did not repeat their corresponding positions during either of these periods.

CHAPTER NINE

1. Stewart Robb, *Nostradamus on Napoleon*, 1961.

2. Anatole Le Pelletier, *Les Oracles de Michel de Nostradamus*, 1867.

3. These are: I.27, I.32, I.60, I.76, I.88, II.67, II.30, II.44, II.66, II.69, II.91, II.99, III.35, III.37, III.93, IV.26, IV.37, IV.54, IV.82, V.30, V.39, V.60, V.79, V.99, VI.25, VI.79, VI.89, VII.13, VIII.8, VIII.17, VIII.46, VIII.53, VIII.57, VIII.60, VIII.61, VIII.76, VIII.88, IX.33, X.24, X.34, X.87.

Bibliographic Notes

4. Garencières, *The True Prophecies . . .*, 1672.

5. The Latin construction *Ne* is derived from the Greek meaning, 'really', so that we could just as well read *Ne Apollyon* as 'truly the destroyer'.

6. *Book of Revelation*, IX:11. The quotation from the grimoire is from F. Gettings, *Dictionary of Demons*, 1988, p. 35.

7. Note 6 above, Verse 2. 'And the name of the star is called Wormwood.'

8. James Laver, *Nostradamus, or the Future Foretold*, 1942. In the Penguin edition of 1952, p. 167.

9. In his *Nostradamus 2. Into the Twenty-First Century*, 1984.

10. Jaubert, op. cit.

11. Daniel Thomas, in the British Library copy of Garencières's work on Nostradamus (Cat: 718 i. 16), p. 423.

12. For *cheville* and *cheval*, in this specialist definition, see Hatzfeld and Darmesteter, *Dictionnaire Général de la Langue Française*, 1888.

13. For a mention of the black sails legend, see *Aegeus* in Hammond and Scullard, *The Oxford Classical Dictionary*, 1979 printing. Aegeus was, of course, the father of Theseus.

14. The quotation is from a note, signed by the Ships Company, and found by Captain Miller on the quarterdeck of the *Theseus*. The note begins, 'Success attend Admiral Nelson . . .' It is quoted in full in Geoffrey Bennett, *The Battle of Trafalgar*, 1977, p. 63.

15. See Geoffrey Bennett, *The Battle of Trafalgar*, 1977, p. 241. The irony was that the Emperor had decided not to punish Villeneuve: the Vice-Admiral was unaware that Napoleon had agreed he should be allowed to retire to his home in Provence, otherwise he would not have killed himself.

16. Geoffrey Bennett, op. cit., pp. 188–9. We are indebted to this excellent book for much of the factual documentation by which we have been able to construe the Nostradamus quatrains relating to the battle.

17. De Fontbrune has dealt with this prediction by the simple expedient of amending the historical facts (and the French of Nostradamus) to

591

fit the prophecy. Naturally, as a result, almost everything he says about the quatrain is as inaccurate as his view of what happened at Trafalgar.

18. For both *Fustes* and *galeres*, see Hatzfeld and Darmesteter, *Dictionnaire Général de la Langue Française*, 1888. Nostradamus' use of the former word is very clever, for he visualizes the fighting ship as being little more than a wooden support for cannon.

19. Ward, op. cit., p. 38.

20. Alistair Horne, *The Fall of Paris. The Siege and the Commune 1870–1*, 1967 reprint, p. 70.

CHAPTER TEN

1. Ward, op. cit., p. 254.

2. Were we required to carry a couple of portmanteau quatrains with which to prove the visionary power of Nostradamus, then we would choose X.67 and IX.83.

3. It may be the pernicious influence of the popular sub-cultural Nostradamus literature – or even the influence of the recent film, *Nostradamus*, which was rooted in the sub-cultural literature – yet, two of the most profound convictions one encountered among those who have never studied Nostradamus are that the Savant predicted the End of the World, and that he foresaw the role of Hitler in the last World War. Both convictions are ill-founded.

4. Ellic Howe, *Urania's Children*, 1967.

5. C. Loog, *Die Weissagungen des Nostradamus*, 1921.

6. Dr Kritzinger, *Mysterien von Sonne und Seele*, 1922.

7. Arkel and Blake, *Nostradamus. The Final Countdown . . .*, 1993

8. De Fontbrune was right about the theme of the Maginot Line, but wrong about everything else in the quatrain.

9. De Fontbrune insists that the captured city (*city prinse*) was Paris, when the evidence within the quatrain points to its being either Sedan or Abbeville: we have favoured the latter because it was at the end of the journey across the 15 lines of water.

10. Franco's neutrality during the World War certainly worried the Germans. Hitler had indeed planned an invasion of Spain.

11. K. Chodkiewicz, *Oracles of Nostradamus*, 1965.

12. J. Hieroz, *L'Astrologie selon Morin de Villefranche*, 1962. On p.120, Hieroz quotes Villefranche as follows:

    'les retrogrades ont une activité contrarie et presagent l'imperfection et l'interruption de leur effets.'

13. Malachai, *Q.B.V. S. Malachiae de Pontificibus Romanis usque ad finem Mundi Prophetia*, 1670.

14. Serge Hutin, *Les Prophéties de Nostradamus; présentées et interprétées . . .* , 1966. The William III theory was proffered by Cheetham. The Peter the Great theory is mentioned by Patrian. The Charles II/van Tromp theory has been put forward by Roberts.

15. Gerald S. Graham, *A Concise History of the British Empire*, 1970.

16. Our view of the Aquarian connection with the USA has been based on the horoscope cast by Ebenezer Sibly and published in arcane engraved plate on the Declaration of Independence in his *The Science of Astrology, or Complete Illustration of the Occult Sciences*, 1790. There are, of course, very many charts for the formation of the United States.

17. Rodney Collin, *The Theory of Celestial Influence*, 1954, Appendix Ten.

18. James Wilson, *A Complete Dictionary of Astrology*, 1880, says: 'Aquarius is a hot, moist, aerial, sanguine, masculine, diurnal, western, fixed, *human*, rational, speaking, whole, fortunate, *sweet*, strong, hyemal, southern, obeying sign . . . it is more *fruitful* than barren.' The italics are our own, intended to show how this list – which is entirely traditional – reflects the spirit of the quatrain.

19. We have in mind the text of Pierre Rigaud, published in Lyons (1558), which was made available by Le Pelletier. His version of the quatrain is very similar to the one we have taken from the 1668 Amsterdam edition, with the exception that in line three, he gives *Franche* instead of *France* – though the two have exactly the same meaning. In the fourth line, he gives *Aries* instead of *Ariez*. The later

edition of 1568, by Benoist Rigaux, corrects *Franche* to *France*, and confirms *Aries*.

20. Gauricus, *Ephemerides Recognitae et ad Unguem Castigatae per Lucam Gauricum . . . 1534–1554*, 1533.

21. C. Ptolemy, *Tetrabiblos* (op. cit.). The Ptolemaic method of determining such rulerships has little to do with modern methods. For a survey of this, see Gettings, *Dictionary of Astrology*.

22. We recall the prophecy circulating in the late 1950s.

23. H. I. Woolf, *Nostradamus*, 1944, p. 13 ff.

24. Agrippa, *De Occulta Philosophia*, 1533. The scalae begin on p. CIII, but the scala for the relevant duodenarii is on p. CXXXII. In the superb edition of *De Occulta* by K. A. Nowotny, 1967, the *Calendarium Naturale Magicum Perpetuum . . .* of Trithemius is given in Appendix V, p. 615. For a more readily available book, see Adam McLean, *The Magical Calendar* (of 1620), 1980 edition, the material of which is pre-Nostradamian. In these magical lists, the twelve Angels of the Signs are usually represented as sigils. Thus, in McLean, under Verchiel, p. 72; in Nowotny, p. 629.

25. The name *Ol*, which is sometimes given also as *Oel*, is found (for example) in the *Pauline Art*: see A. E. Waite, *The Book of Ceremonial Magic*, 1911, p. 70.

APPENDIX ONE

1. For an astrological appreciation of Jean Dupèbe's discoveries, made in 1983, see Robert Amadou, *L'Astrologie de Nostradamus*, 1987 and 1992. Dupèbe's work is entitled *Nostradamus. Lettres Inédites*, 1983.

2. Jean-Aimé Chavigny records that Nostradamus was born in the year of Grace, 1503, a Thursday, 14 December, round about 12 o'clock in the afternoon. Most horoscopes we know have been cast with this in mind, though the 'environs les 12 heures de midi' has been taken specifically to mean midday. Chavigny was frequently inaccurate in his data.

3. Garcaeus, *Johannis Garcaei, Astrologiae Methodus . . .* , 1576. Lynn Thorndike provided an Appendix with 113 of these charts, taken

from the above, and supplemented by a few from Sixtus ab Hemminga, *Astrologia ratione et experientia refutata*, 1583. See Thorndike, Vol. VI, p. 595 ff.

4. Garcaeus, op. cit., p. 115. He also offers a figure for January 1504, with Mars, Jupiter and Saturn in Cancer, within one degree orb of the elusive Nostradamus chart.

5. Gauricus, *Luca Gaurici Geophonensis . . . Tractatus Astrologicus*, 1552.

6. Cardanus, *Hieronymis Cardani in CL. Ptolemaei de Astrorum iudiciis . . .* , 1578.

7. Cardanus, op. cit., p. 694.

8. See Jean Dupèbe, *Nostradamus. Lettres Inédites*, 1983. Letter XXXI, p. 100. Dupèbe, who was not an astrologer, appears to miss the significance of this reference to the seal. See, however, Lécureux, p. 119. The relevant quotation is given as a header for this appendix.

9. Robert Benazra, *Répertoire Chronologique Nostradamique (1545–1989)*, 1990. The one exception to this 'fifty-year' rule is the Horus-Apollo (see Pierre Rollet), which has been attributed to Nostradamus, but may not be by him at all.

10. The two charts of Matthias Hacus Sumbergius, now in the Royal Library, Madrid, are reproduced by Taylor (see note 11, below), figures 15–16. The Ascendant for the *aestimata* is 1 Scorpio, while the Ascendant for the *rectificata*, which falls on *Captus Herculis*, is 28 Libra.

11. See René Taylor, *Architecture and Magic: Considerations on the Idea of the Escorial, in Essays in the History of Architecture, Presented to Rudolf Wittkower*, 1969 edition. The Hercules Galicus is reproduced in figure 6 of the article.

12. Garcaeus, *Astrologiae methodus in qua secundum doctrinam Ptoelmaei genituras qualescunque iudicandi ratio traditur*, 1576.

13. *Raphael's Astronomical Ephemeris . . . for 1927*, p. 41.

14. For such visual displays, we use the *Expert Astronomer for Windows*, 1993 edition, from Expert Software Inc.

15. See J. Boffito and C. Melzi d'Eril, *Almanach Dantis Algherii sive Prophacii Jadaei Montispessulani Almanach perpetuum ad annum 1300 inchoatum . . .* (the *Prophacius* is Jacob ben Machir ben Tibbon). The

matter is discussed in the *Modern Language Review* (July 1908), revised reprint, on p. 276ff of Edward Moore's *Studies in Dante. Fourth Series. Textual Criticism of the 'Convivio' and Miscellaneous Essays*, 1968 edition.

16. Regiomontanus, *Johanis de Monte regio ... Ephemerides (pro Anno 1489–1506)*.

17. Jean Dupèbe, op. cit. Since Dupèbe did not incorporate the astrological figures in the translation, we have used Lécureux's reading, given in Robert Amadou's *L'Astrologie de Nostradamus*, in the 1992 edition.

18. John Gadbury, *Cardines Coeli*, 1686, p. 60.

19. Derek Parker, *Familiar to All. William Lilly and Astrology in the Seventeenth Century*, 1975. p. 93.

20. Alan Leo, *Notable Nativites* (n.d., but *circa* 1910), as 795 and 932 respectively.

21. Jeff Green, *Pluto, the evolutionary journey of the soul*, Vol. 1, 1986.

22. *Astrology*, Vol. 37, No. 2, 1963, p. 69.

23. Eric Muraise. *Saint-Rémy de Provence et les Secrets de Nostradamus*, 1969. The chart is also reproduced on p. 27 of Amadou, op. cit., above.

24. Amadou, op. cit., above. Max Duval's chart for Nostradamus is on p. 13.

25. Michel Nostradamus, *Excellent & Moult Utile Opuscule à Touts Necessaire, qui desirent avoir cognoissance de plusieurs exquises Receptes . . .*, 1556. He wrote: '. . . depuis l'an 1521. iusques en l'an 1529. incessament courant pour entendre & savoir la source & origine des planetes & autre simples'. We suspect that he left these notes for astrological purposes, as an occult blind, for the word 'planets' is superflous in the context of 'simples'.

26. For the Guido Bonatus quotation, see Vivian E. Robson, *The Fixed Stars and Constellations*, 1923.

27. R. H. Allen, *Star Names. Their Lore and Meaning*, 1963 reprint of the 1899 *Star-Names and Their Meanings*, p. 256, wherein he quotes Wyllyam Salysbury, perhaps after Proclus.

28. For Bodin, see *Republic* VI, ii. We know of no academic study of the predictive numbers proposed by Bodin.

APPENDIX THREE

1. Actually, we might well doubt it. Pierre de Nostredame (*Petro de Nostra Domina*) of Avignon, who converted from Judaism some time before 1455, had been previously called Guy Gassonet as a Jew. After conversion, he seems also to have called himself Peyrot, or Pierre de Sainte-Marie. The question is, to which Mary was this reference? In 1464, he was still recording the name *Peyrotus de Nostradomina* with the local notaries of Avignon. For details of relevant documents, see Edgar Leroy, p.14 ff.

2. The verse, attributed by some to Jodelle, and by others to Théodore de Bèze, and by G. Patin to G. C. Utenhove, reads:

> *Nostra damus cum falsa damus, nam fallere nostrum est*
> *Et cum falsa damus, nil nisi nostra damus.*

What reads humorously in this Latin, falls flat in any translation:

> When we give falsely, we give our own, for it is ours to make mistakes
> And when we give falsely, then it is nothing but our own we give.

3. Jean-Aimé Chavigny, *Janus Gallicus*. More accessible is the French version of the portrait, given with a few Latin notes, by Leroy, p. 197.

APPENDIX FIVE

1. Charles Ward, *Oracles of Nostradamus*, 1891.

2. Jean Dupèbe, *Nostradamus. Lettres Inédites*, 1983. Hans Rosenberger's observation is from Letter XXII, dated 8 April 1561 (OS). Rosenberger was not alone: see, for example, letters XVIII and XX from Tubbe to Nostradamus.

3. Finé, *Orontii Finei Delphinatis . . . De Mundi Sphaera, sive Cosmographia*, 1542, p. 51.

APPENDIX SEVEN

1. Laver, for example, calls it Quatrain VI.100. The early texts make it quite clear that the Latin is intended to stand outside the main body of verses: the four lines of Latin are headed *Legis Cautio Contra Ineptos Criticos*. Of course, one could argue that Bleygnic was an inept critic.

2. The word *Lampadas* is used in the *Alfonsine Tables*, which Nostradamus must have consulted.

Pictures

It is unlikely that the soul of Nostradamus will be felt through such images.

[Page 100]

Portrait of Nostradamus (1503–1666) – roundel from a horoscope figure cast for the birth of the savant (*see fig. 3*), based on a portrait by César, the son of Nostradamus, in the Bibliotheque de la Mesjanes, Aix-en-Provence.

PROPHETIES
DE
M. NOSTRADAMVS

CENTVRIE SEPTIESME.

L'Ac du trefor par Achiles deceu,
Aux procrees fceu la quadrangulaire:
Au faict Royal le comment fera fceu,
Corps veu pendu au veu du populaire.

II

Par Mars ouuert Arles ne donra guerre,
De nuict feront les fouldarts eſtonnés:
Noir,blanc,à l'inde difſimulés en terre,
Soubs la faicte vmbre trai verez & ſônés.

Fig. 1 Woodcut from the title page of the 1557 edition of the *Prophéties*, portraying Nostradamus at his writing desk. This early version of the *Prophéties* has recently been reissued by Editions Michel Chomerat as a photo–litho copy. It does not include any quatrains beyond the first seven Centuries, which itself ends at quatrain 40.

Fig. 2 Sample page, from the opening page to Century Seven, in the 1557 edition of the *Prophéties*. The first quatrain of this plate is analysed on p. 291ff of our text.

Fig. 3 The horoscope of Nostradamus, cast for 12.14.20 on the Old Style date of 14 December 1503 at Salon. This modern horoscope for the savant is examined in Appendix One, p. 482ff.

Fig. 4 Bust of Nostradamus, in his birth town of St Rémy. The bust is above a working fountain on the corner of Rue Carnot and Rue de Nostradamus. The house claimed to be his birthplace is a short distance away, in Rue Hoche.

Fig. 5 Portrait of Paracelsus, used in a number of different titles of his books, including the complete *Works*: this print is from the 1894 A. E. Waite edition. On the pommel of Paracelsus' sword is the word 'zoth', which is Azoth – reputably the magical powder of the alchemist. In his *Aurora of the Philosophers*, Paracelsus says that the entire secret of the Art of Alchemy is to be found in Fire and Azoth.

Fig. 6 From Basil Valentine's *Azoth or the Way to Make the Secret Gold of the Philosophers*, 1650. The secret of the image lies in the combination of the two triangles. The upper triangle combines the seven planets, each of which is touched by a leaf of the Tree of Knowledge. The lower triangle is that of the Three Principles of Alchemy (Salt, Mercury and Sulphur). The union of the Seven and the Three will reveal Azoth – the secret of the spagyric Art.

A Amsterdam Chez Iean Ianßon à Waesberge et la Vefve du Feu Elizée Weyerstraet. l'An 1668.

Fig. 7 Woodcut from the title page of the almanach for 1566, by Nostradamus, in which he predicted (in arcane style) his own death. For details, see p .56ff of our text.

Fig. 8 The title page colophon of the 1668 edition of the *Prophéties*, which has been interpreted (with some justification) as revealing the initiate school to which Nostradamus belonged – the Sons of the Widow. For an analysis, see p. 48ff of our text.

Fig. 9 The alchemical conjunction, or union of the solar **Animus** (the King) with the lunar **Anima** (the Moon). The six rays of the flowers correspond to the meeting of the two triangles in the Azoth plate, in *fig. 6*. The archetypal star is brought to the earth plane by the Holy Spirit (dove), by which action alone the union of opposites (**conjunctio**) is made possible. Plate from the 'Rosarium Philosophorum', 1622.

604

Fig. 10 Details of two of the twelve roundel portraits from the title page of Michael Maier's *Symbola Aureae Mensae*, 1617. To the left is the fount of all alchemical lore, the Egyptian Hermes Trismegistus. To the right is Maria the Jewess (one of the alchemical 'Heroes' of the twelve nations, according to Maier), whose name is a reversal of Hiram. For a brief survey, see p. 50ff of our text.

Fig 11 The facade of the house in Rue Nostradamus, formerly Place de Poissonnerie, in Salon. It was here that Nostradamus is reputed to have written the *Prophéties*. The interior is now a museum and bookshop, dedicated to the study of the Master.

Fig. 12 Statue of Nostradamus, sculpted by Joseph Ré in 1866 (presumably to mark the third centenary of the savant's death). The statue is in Place de Gaulle, in Salon, very near to the place where the first tomb of Nostradamus was situated.

Fig. 13 Nostradamus as the Royal Astrologer, from an almanach by Antoine Crespin (who used the name Nostradamus spuriously in several books). *Prognostication, et Prediction des Quatre Temps…*, 1572. Crespin, who also used the name Archidamus, seemed to have no understanding of the arcane nature of Nostradamus' œuvre, yet appears to have profited by his use of the famous name.

IVILLET.

Par pestilence & feu, fruits d'arbres periront:
Signe d'huile abonder: pere Denis non gueres:
Des grands mourir mais peu estrangers sailliront:
Insult marin barbare: & dangers de frontieres.

1	g	Oct. s. Ioan.		à 3.h.o.m.ær turbidus..
2	a	Visitation.		
3	b	s. Tibault.		
4	c	s. Vldarich.		Feu du ciel en naues ardant.
5	d	P ier. de lucé.		

IVILLET.

Par pestilence & feu, fruits d'arbres periront:
Signe d'huile abonder: pere Denis non gueres:
Des grands mourir mais peu, estrangers saillèront:
Insult marin barbare: & dangers de frontieres.

Estrange transmigration.	1	g	D 7.	à 3.h.o.mi. Aër turbidus.
Les grades & grads differés.	g	a	D 19	Tout reduit par le magistrat
Par religions tout trouble.	3	b	⋙ 1	Promulgation nó obseruée.
Bóne fortune pour nauig.	4	c	⋙ 13	Feu du ciel en naues ardant.
Bons amis apparoistront,	5	d	⋙ 25	Deliurez de captiuité barb.
Se iettera au conflict.	6	e	H 7.	Caché dás l'eau gelée & sorti
Mandemét à Roine souspi.	7	f	H 20	Blessez en la teste, mourir.
Insipiétia delirans. (rer.	8	g	♈ 3	Par les chemins tout halé.
Merueilleuse inflamation.	9	a	♑ 6.	☾ à 17.h.20.mi.

Fig. 14 **Des grands mourir** (the great ones to die…). Detail of a calendrical column for the month of July, from Nostradamus' 'Almanach for 1566', showing the conditions pertaining to the date of his death. See also *fig. 15* (below), and the corresponding text on p. 57ff.

Fig. 15 **Estrange transmigration** (Strange transmigrations…). Detail of a calendrical column for the month of July, with a typical almanach quatrain (a so-called 'presage') and conditions pertaining to the date of his death. Compare with *fig. 14* (above), and the corresponding text on p. 57ff.

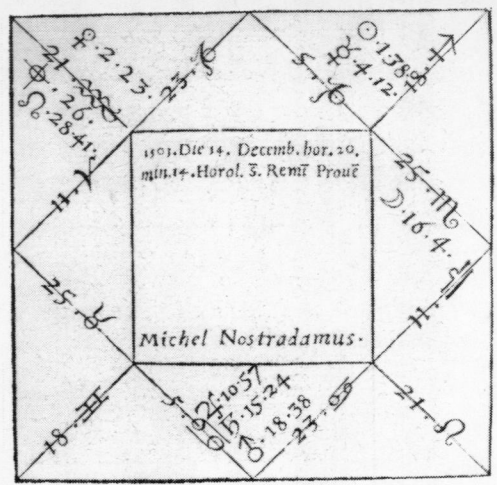

Inside the horoscope chart:

1503. Die 14. Decemb. hor. 20. min. 14. Horol. 3. Remũ Prouē

Michel Nostradamus.

D. M.

CLARISSIMI oſſa Michaëlis
Noſtradami unius omnium mortalium
judicio digni cujus penè divino calamo
totius orbis ex Aſtrorum influxu futuri eventus conſcriberentur. Vixit annos LXII. menſes VI. dies X. obiit
Salone IDLXVI. quietem poſteri
ne invidete Anna Pontia Gemella Salo-
nia conjugi optat veram felicitatem.

Fig. 16 The horoscope of Nostradamus, drawn up according to the method of
the sixteenth century.

Fig. 17 The epitaph of Nostradamus, as recorded *circa* 1798, in an edition of
Moult (*see fig. 34*). The Latin text of this epitaph corresponds fairly closely to
that now in the church of Saint-Laurent, Salon, whence the body of
Nostradamus was moved after the French Revolution (see Appendix Four).

Fig. 18 Modern giant portrait of Nostradamus on the wall over a shop contiguous with an alley leading to the church of St Michel, in Salon. The image is based on a nineteenth-century lithograph which emphasized the Jewish ancestry of Nostradamus.

Fig. 19 Henry II of France, portrayed after the title dedication of the open letter to this monarch in the 1558 edition of the *Prophéties*. It was Nostradamus' prediction of the painful death of Henry, in a duel in 1559, which first established the accuracy of the *Prophéties* for the majority of French people.

Fig. 20 Woodcut from the title page of the 'Alchabitius' text, a version of which was discovered round about 1985 by Guy Parguez bearing the names, in manuscript, of both Nostradamus and his son César. The French scholar, Michael Chomarat, has offered a brief but useful study of the Nostradamus copy, and of the Alchabitian literature, in the July 1986 edition of *Cahiers Michel Nostradamus*, p. 51 and 54 ff.

Fig. 21 Prophetic woodcut from Paracelsus' *Prognosticatio*, 1536. This is the second figure of the Paracelsian series of thirty-two arcane icons. The three **fleur-de-lys** hang upon a withered branch: some commentators have taken this image to predict the final demise of the Valois line, even though such an interpretation does not appear to have anything to do with the text which Paracelsus wrote to accompany the image. By the time Nostradamus wrote his quatrains, the only scion left was the Valois-Angoulême. See p. 79 of our text.

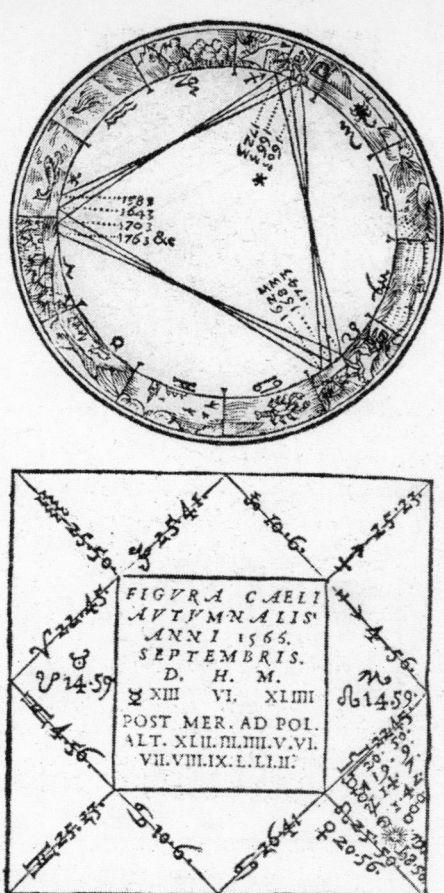

Fig. 22 The trigons, so important in medieval predictive astrology, shown here in the elements of Fire and Water, for 1583 to 1763. The figure is not accurate: the trigon for 1703 occurred in May 1700–2, and that given for 1763 in March 1762. However, in spite of such inaccuracies, the figure demonstrates clearly the basis for the 20-year and 60-year cycles underlying many of Nostradamus' predictions.

Fig. 23 Horoscope for the Autumnal ingress, cast by Nostradamus for his final annual prognostications, in 1566. See p. 85, and *fig. 14* and *15*.

Fig. 24 A late-medieval diagram of the elemental spheres around the Earth. The Earth itself, along with its seas, represents the elements of Earth and Water. Beyond is the clouded sphere which represents the element of air, while beyond is the flaming sphere of Fire, which surrounds and protects the mundane sphere. From Book I of Oronce Finé, *De Mundi Sphaera*, 1542.

Fig. 25 This woodcut, used in some seventeenth-century editions of Ripa's *Iconographia*, appeared in the Pierre Rollet version of Nostradamus' 'Horapollo', 1968. It is typical of the medieval 'hieroglyphic' imagery, which seems to have taken esoteric Egyptian images (perhaps this is a version of the uraeus serpent) and subjected them to highly personal, and entirely European interpretation.

612

Fig. 26 Disturbances in the skies, which we would now classify as UFOs, above the city of Basle, on August 1566, as recorded in a broadsheet by Samuel Coccius. See p. 90 of our text.

Fig. 27 UFO or comet – and, indeed, is there a difference? The crescent moon spitting out an arrow of fire. From the translated broadsheet of Joseph Heller, *Ein Erschrecklich and Wunderbarlich zeychen...Michael De Nostre Dame*, 1554. The sheet implies that the vision was seen in Salon on 19 March of that year.

Fig. 28 Woodcut of a humanoid monster child, which, according to
Lycosthenes, lived for only four hours, and announced, 'Beware, for the Lord
our God cometh'. Woodcut from the 1557 edition of Lycosthenes'
Prodigiorum ac ostentorum chronicon...

Fig. 29 Crude woodcut portrait of Nostradamus, from the title page of the
1644 edition of *Les Prophéties de M. Michel Nostradamus*, printed by
Huguetan. Even such a simple figure shows that the divine pen of
Nostradamus is guided by the stars. See p. 99.

Fig. 30 Nostradamus portrayed in front of the great men of history whom he allegedly refers to in his quatrains. The sycophantic figure to the right, gazing up in adoration at the savant, is Torné-Chavigny. See p. 546. Engraved drawing by Torné-Chavigny, published in his *Influence de Nostradamus*, 1878.

Fig. 31 Woodcut portrait of Nostradamus, said to have been drawn by Leonard Gaultier at the beginning of the seventeenth century. It appeared as portrait number 129 in a series of 144 portraits of famous individuals in *Le Theatre d'Honneur de plusieurs princes anciens et modernes*, 1618. In a useful study of the print, Michel Chomarat. in 'Cahiers Michel Nostradamus', March, 1983, has suggested that the portrait is among those considered the most authentic of that period, in terms of resemblance.

Fig. 32 Eighteenth–century portrait of Nostradamus in the guise of learned scholar. The evidence of stellar mediation, or of a cosmic prophetic source, which was so frequently symbolized in the old woodcuts, is drastically reduced in this engraving. The stars are merely symbolized by 'scientific' instruments, which lie on the floor, at his feet. The power now seems to rest with humans, rather than with the stars.

Fig. 33 Nostradamus in his studio at Salon, with a decorative border depicting the twelve images of the zodiacal signs. The five stars between Sun and Moon are the planets. The clouds, from which the inner image subtends from the zodiac, indicate that Nostradamus is writing to the dictate of the stars. From the (apocryphal) *Les Significations de l'Eclipse, qui sera le 16 Septembre, 1559...* by Nostradamus, 1558.

618

Fig. 34 Nostradamus in the guise of an almanac seller, enclosed (perhaps, indeed, entangled) in a celestial sphere. The banderolle issuing from the mouth announces 'Burlesque almanach', which might suggest that the cut was not intended for this title, Moult's *Prophéties de Thomas-Joseph Moult* (1789), compared (supposedly) with the predictions of Nostradamus.

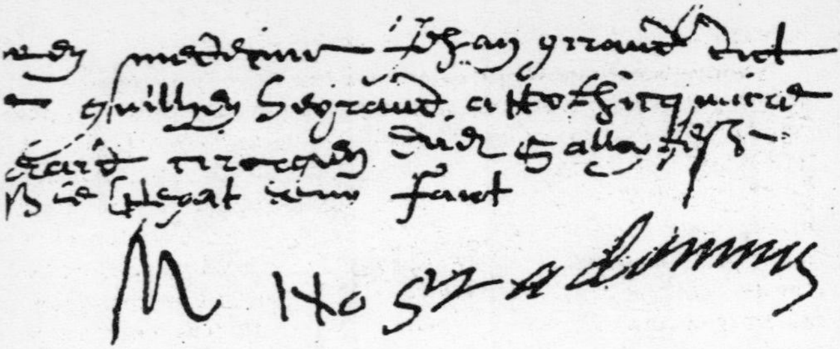

Fig. 35 Faltering last signature of Nostradamus, from a facsimile of his last will and testament. For notes on this form of signature, see p. 100 of our text.

Fig. 36 The cut, for all its crude quality, does show Nostradamus being influenced by both planets and stars – in keeping with sixteenth-century belief. The Sun, with six star-like planets, revolves in the skies to the left, while around the Moon are fourteen stars. The sphere symbolizes the stars brought to Earth, but the pointing Nostradamus (holding calipers, rather than the pen) seems to insist on the stellar source of his inspiration.

De imaginibus capitis & caudæ draconis Lunæ.   Cap. XLV.

Aciebant etiam imaginem capitis & caudæ draconis Lunæ, sci licet inter circulum aëreum & igneum serpentis effigiem, cum capite accipi tris illos circundantem, ad istar Græ ce literæ thita, faciebãtq; quando Iupiter eum capi te medium cœlum obti nebat, quam quidē imagi nem ad successus petitio num multum conferre af firmant, uolebantq; per eam imaginē bonum ac felicem dęmonem nota re: uolebãtq; eum per serpentis imaginem figurare: hūc enim Aegyptii atq; Phœnices super omnia animalia esse diuinum animal, atq; eius diuinam na turam celebrãt: quia in eo super cętera animalia spiritus acrior atq; amplior ignis existat: quę res cū ex illo celeri gressu ostenditur, sine ullis pedibus ma

Fig. 37 Image of the lunar dragon, from Cornelius Agrippa's *De Occulta Philosophia*, 1534. The two interlinked circles around the dragon represent the orbits of the Sun and Moon. Where they intersect – that is, where the path of the Moon crosses the ecliptic – are located the two nodes, called the dragon's head (Caput, in Latin) and the dragon's tail (Cauda, in Latin). In the text Agrippa deals with this powerful image – 'the divine dragon' – in terms of its amuletic power.

Fig. 38 The bridged entrance to the Temple, which the Government of France turned into a prison after the French Revolution, in 1789. The Temple is mentioned by Nostradamus in quatrain X.17 as the prison for the future Marie Antoinette: see p. 213 ff. Lithographic print by Pernot, from 'Le Vieux Paris', 1838–9.

Fig. 39 The bull of Apis with a lunar crescent, and the cynocephalus image of Thoth. Detail from the engraved titlepage of Michael Maier's *Arcana arcanissima*, 1614.

Fig. 40 The Egyptian god, Typhon, with axe and flame (this image later devolved into an image of a Sabbatic demon), flanked by the god Osiris and the goddess Isis. The three are a reflection of the secret Triplicity of the Alchemists. Detail from the engraved titlepage of Michael Maier's *Arcana arcanissima*, 1614.

622

Fig. 41 The lame Vulcan tending the flames of the alchemical fire. Vulcan is the 'bandy legged' (Greek *raipos*) expressed in the arcane word RAYPOZ of Nostradamus' quatrain IX.44. See p. 259 of our text. Engraving from the title page of Michael Maier's *Tripus Aureus*, 1677 edition.

Fig. 42 The Great Fire of London, 1666. The print deals with the fire as predicted by Nostradamus in 1555, in quatrain II.51 – see p. 262 ff of our text. Detail from the title page of the 1668 Amsterdam edition of the *Prophéties*.

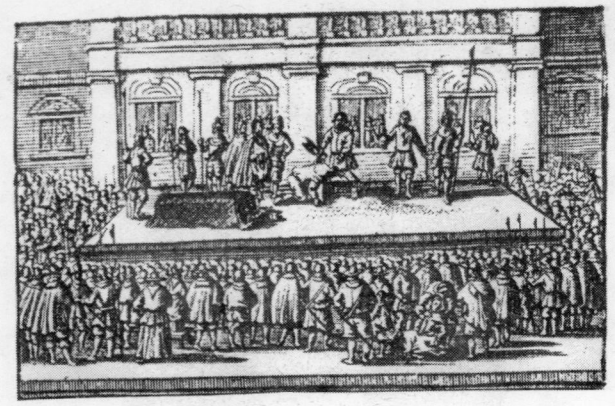

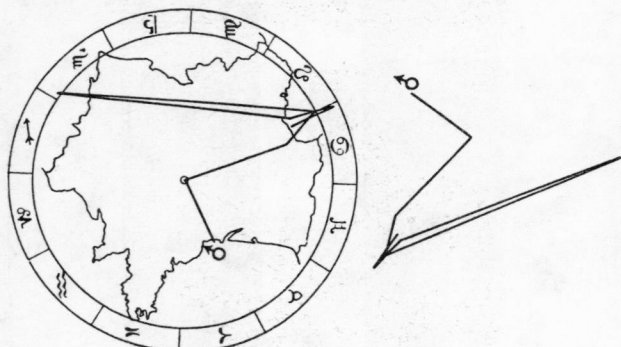

Fig. 43 The beheading of King Charles I, at Whitehall, in 1649. The print deals with the execution as predicted by Nostradamus in 1555 in quatrain VIII.37 – see p. 274 ff of our text. Note the falling woman in the foreground, which is mentioned in this quatrain: this interesting detail is portrayed also in the painting by Weesop (on which the engraving is based), though in this latter case it may symbolize the Queen, Henrietta Maria, who was in France at the time of the execution. Detail from the title page of the 1668 Amsterdam edition of the *Prophéties*.

Fig. 44 The curious 'horoscope' of France, with its imaginative splaying of Martian energy, which is supposed to resemble a machine-gun. The figure relates specifically to the interpretation of quatrain III.60, but confirms his interpretation of other quatrains. From P. Rochetaillée, *Prophéties de Nostradamus. Clef des Centuries. Son application à l' histoire de la 3e République*, 1939.

1789

Fig. 45 Aymar divining with the rhabdomantic rod. The secret and invisible energy seems to float like a cloud from the earth. Nostradamus' quatrain IX.68 deals with the story of two rhabdomantic exploits of Aymar in the seventeenth century. See p. 286 ff of our text. Woodcut from Le Lorrain de Vallemont's *La Physique Occulte*, 1693.

Fig. 46 Late-eighteenth-century device, revealing the cock as symbol of the newly awakened France. The crowing cock (here singing for liberty) which is France stands upon a cannon: the broken chains which lie over the barrel symbolize the recently attained freedom from repression: this imagery was adopted by artists during the early years following the American Declaration of Independence. Eighteenth-century painting.

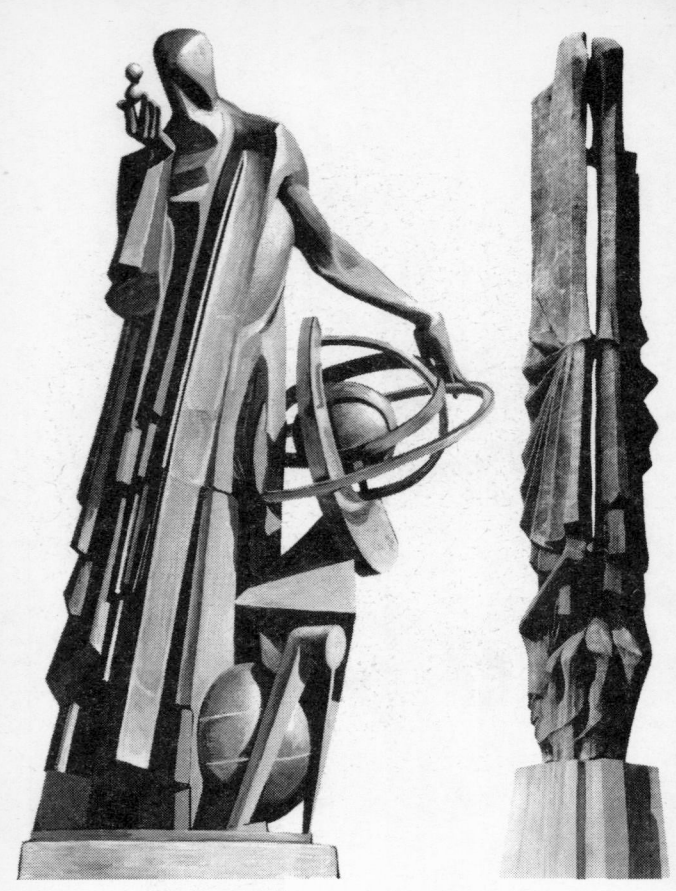

Fig. 47 (left) Metal statue of Nostradamus by François Bouché, sculpted for the 400th anniversary of the death of the savant, in 1966. Nostradamus is depicted resting upon a model of the spheres, staring down at an hour-glass. For an account of the statue (formerly in Salon, near Place Gambetta) and its curious fate, see p. 382ff of our text. Artwork by Pierre D'Esperance, 1994.

Fig. 48 (right) Giant concrete statue of Nostradamus, by François Bouché, erected in Salon in 1979. This impressive sculpture was designed to replace that reproduced in *fig. 47*, after a lorry had destroyed it. For a brief account, see p. 382ff of our text.

EUGENE Prince of SAVOY.

Fig. 49 Engraved portrait of Eugene, Prince of Savoy, by Ravenet. From Tobias Smollett's *A Complete History of England*, 1759. This remarkable Frenchman (named by Nostradamus 'chameau' – camel) is mentioned in Quatrain V.68. For details. see p. 395 of our text.

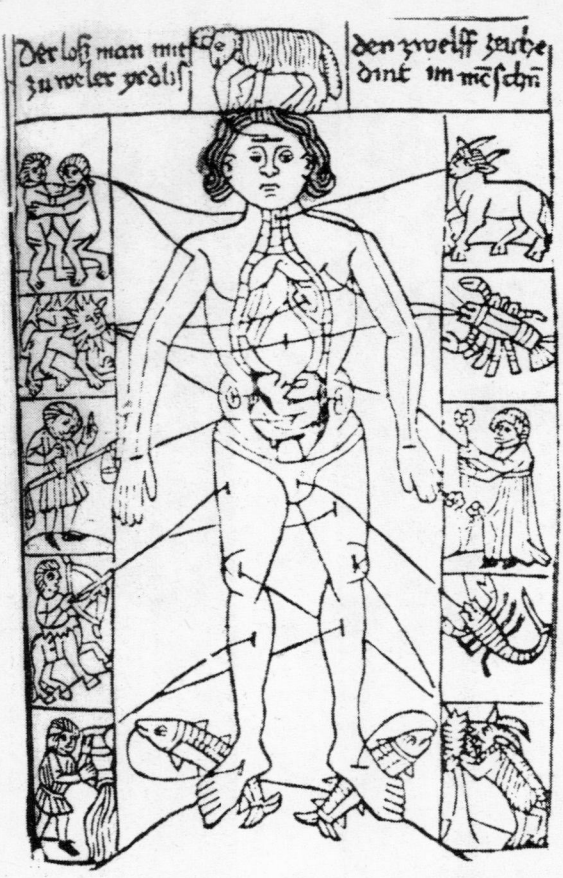

Fig. 50 Late–medieval German melothesic figure (zodiacal man), with each zodiacal image traced to the corresponding outer and inner parts of the human body. Line image made from hand–coloured loose print, loaned from the Charles Walker collection.

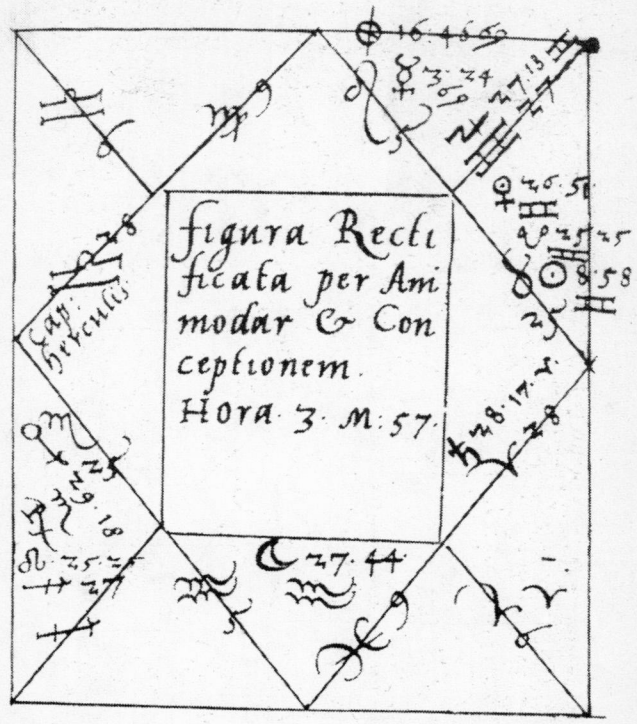

figura Recti
ficata per Ani
modar & Con
ceptionem.
Hora 3 M: 57

Fig. 51 The rectified horoscope of Philip II of Spain, made by the astrologer Hacus Sumbergius. The figure was cast for 21 May 1527, and was clearly rectified in order to bring Philip's ascendant into conjunction with the star Caput Herculis. According to the inscription within the figure, the rectification (adjustment made to ensure the chart was accurate) was by means of the animodar and the conception chart. For a brief account, see p. 487.

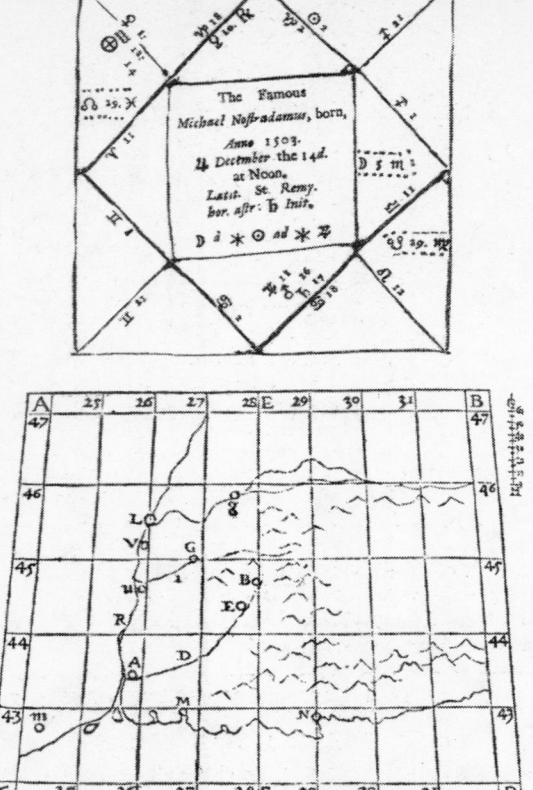

Fig. 52 The earliest known horoscope chart of Nostradamus. Woodcut from John Gadbury's *Cardines Coeli*, 1686. The figure, cast for noon on the Old Style date, 14 December 1503, is not accurate by modern standards. For a brief account, see p. 492 of our text.

Fig. 53 A sixteenth-century map of the territory familiar to Nostradamus, in the South of France, calibrated according to the contemporary notions of latitudes. The letter L represents Lyons, M Marseilles, N Nice, R the Rhone, and V Vienne. From Oronce Finé's *Delphinatis…De Mundi Sphaera, sive Cosmographia…*, 1542. Nostradamus used such latitudes (sometimes called *climata*) as arcane associations – even as occult blinds in his quatrains. See p. 534 in the present work.

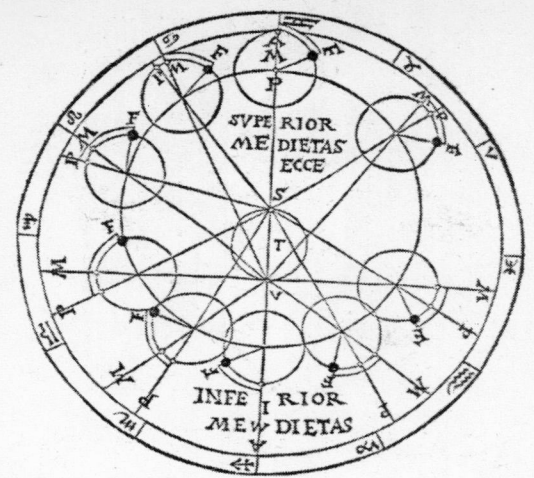

LEGIS CAUTIO CONTRA
INEPTOS CRITICOS.

Qui legent hosce versus, maturè censunto :
Prophanum vulgus & inscium ne attrestato :
Omnesque Astrologi, Blenni, Barbari procul sunto,
Qui aliter facit, is ritè sacer esto.

LES VRAYES CENTURIES
ET PROPHETIES
De Maistre MICHEL NOSTRADAMUS

Fig. 54 The late-medieval view, derived mainly from Ptolemy, of how the circular planetary movements are contained and directed within epicycles, which give the motions all the appearance of being erratic to the circular. From George Puerbach, *Theoreticae Novae Planetarum...*, 1543.

Fig. 55 Nostradamus' Latin 'Caution' against inept critics, from the 1668 edition of the *Prophéties*. For a brief account, see p. 546 ff.

Index